D0500047

ISSUES IN FEMINIST FILM CRITICISM

EDITED BY

PATRICIA ERENS

Indiana University Press

Bloomington and Indianapolis

© 1990 by Indiana University Press

All rights reserved

No part of this book may be reproduced or utilized in any form or by any means, electronic or mechanical, including photocopying and recording, or by any information storage and retrieval system, without permission in writing from the publisher. The Association of American University Presses' Resolution on Permissions constitutes the only exception to this prohibition.

The paper used in this publication meets the minimum requirements of American National Standard for Information Sciences—Permanence of Paper for Printed Library Materials, ANSI Z39.48-1984.

∞™

Manufactured in the United States of America

Library of Congress Cataloging-in-Publication Data

Issues in feminist film criticism / edited by Patricia Erens.
p. cm.
Includes bibliographical references.
ISBN 0-253-31964-1 (alk. paper). — ISBN 0-253-20610-3 (pbk. : alk. paper)
1. Women in motion pictures. 2. Feminism and motion pictures. 3. Film criticism. I. Erens, Patricia.
PN1995.9.W6I87 1990
791.43′652042—dc20 89-46336
CIP

6 7 8 9 00 99 98

For Jane, Meryl, Shom, Sondra, and Sue, who taught me what female friendship is all about. And in memory of my fiancé, Gerald Galler. For the sweetness of life we shared together. Alav Ha Shalom.

CONTENTS

IV. Assessing Films Directed by Women

ACKNOWLEDGMENTS

The following collection of essays represents the work of twenty-nine individuals. However, all of the writers have been influenced by many women and men who are not included in this text. In a way, therefore, *Issues in Feminist Film Criticism* reflects the thinking of a whole community of feminist scholars and is in turn dedicated to them.

There are a number of people who were especially helpful in bringing this project to fruition. In particular, I would like to thank my colleagues who were kind enough to give of their time and to share their expertise in the development of this anthology. This group includes Michelle Citron, Lucy Fischer, Claudia Gorbman, Barbara Klinger, Kaja Silverman, Ellen Seiter, Virginia Wright Wexman, and Linda Williams. A special thanks goes to Julia Lesage who gave the manuscript a close reading and who provided many invaluable suggestions.

In addition, I am indebted to several of my students at Rosary College who helped me with the necessary correspondence, typing, xeroxing, proofreading, and research. These students include Vincent Auriemma, Kristin Bartelli, Patricia McGuinness, Valerie Warner, and Lisa Winkelman, and one lifelong student who reviewed the introductions in the final stages of preparation, Sue Gray. Further appreciation goes to Lynn Hall, Babette Inglehart, and Lynn Weiner for their citations on non-filmic resources. I would also like to thank a young feminist, my daughter Pamela Erens, who worked on the manuscript, forcing me to tighten the wording and to clarify my thinking, while at the same time proving that women do fruitfully work together across generational boundaries.

At Rosary College there are many people who played a part in the progress of this book. First, I am indebted to the College which provided me the sabbatical leave to do the necessary research and writing. Second, a debt of gratitude goes to Inez Ringland and her library staff who processed my endless requests for books and articles. Third, I am continuingly grateful to my department chair, Ric Calabrese, who has not only encouraged and supported me throughout my professional career, but who has also been a cherished personal friend. Lastly, a special thanks goes to my students at Rosary College and at San Francisco State University who served as a testing ground for this collection, giving me a chance to "teach my next book." This book was strengthened by their suggestions.

And finally, love and thanks goes to my family, my son Bradley, my daughter Pamela, my mother Nettie Brett, Becky and Steve Galler, and Leslie and Adam Sharrin, for sympathetically listening to my frustrations and refusing to take me seriously.

Grateful acknowledgment is also made to the following sources for their permission to reprint the articles and excerpts in this anthology:

"Positive Images: Screening Women's Films," reprinted from *Jump Cut* 18 (1978), by permission of Linda Artel and Susan Wengraf and *Jump Cut*. Revised from their introduction to *Positive Images: Non-Sexist Films for Young People*. San Francisco: Bootlegger Press, 1976.

"There's More to a Positive Image Than Meets the Eye," reprinted from *Jump Cut* 18 (1978), by permission of Diane Waldman and *Jump Cut*.

"The Place of Woman in the Cinema of Raoul Walsh," from *Raoul Walsh*, ed. Philip Hardy (Colchester, England: Vineyard Press, 1974). Reprinted by permission of Pam Cook and Michael Hughes, executor of the estate for Claire Johnston.

"Visual Pleasure and Narrative Cinema," reprinted from *Screen* 16, no. 3 (Autumn 1975), by permission of Laura Mulvey and *Screen*. Reworked from a paper given to the French Department of the University of Wisconsin, Madison, Spring 1973.

"Film and the Masquerade—Theorizing the Female Spectator," reprinted from *Screen* 23, no. 3–4 (September-October 1982), by permission of Mary Ann Doane and *Screen*. Expanded from a paper presented at Yale University, February 1982.

"Hitchcock, Feminism, and the Patriarchal Unconscious," from *The Women Who Knew Too Much: Hitchcock and Feminist Theory* (New York: Methuen, 1988). Reprinted by permission of Tania Modleski and Routledge.

"Women and Representation: Can We Enjoy Alternative Pleasure?" from *Jump Cut* 29 (February 1984). Revised and reprinted in *American Media and Mass Culture: Left Perspectives*, ed. Donald Lazere (Berkeley: University of California Press, 1987). Reprinted by permission of Jane Gaines, *Jump Cut*, and the Regents of the University of California.

"Gentlemen Consume Blondes," reprinted from *Wide Angle* 1, no. 1 (1979). Revised and reprinted by permission of Maureen Turim and Johns Hopkins University Press.

"Pre-text and Text in *Gentlemen Prefer Blondes*," reprinted from *Film Reader* 5 (1982), by permission of Lucie Arbuthnot, Gail Seneca, and Northwestern University Department of Radio-TV-Film.

"The Case of the Missing Mother: Maternal Issues in Vidor's *Stella Dallas*," reprinted from *Heresies* 16 (1983), by permission of E. Ann Kaplan and *Heresies*.

" 'Something Else Besides a Mother': *Stella Dallas* and the Maternal Melodrama," *Cinema Journal* 24, no. 1 (Fall 1984), reprinted by permission of Linda Williams and the University of Illinois Press, copyright © 1984.

"Seduced and Abandoned: Recollection and Romance in *Letter From an Unknown Woman*," from *Shot/Counter Shot: Film Tradition and*

Women's Cinema (Princeton: Princeton University Press, 1989). Reprinted by permission of Lucy Fischer and Princeton University Press.

"Illicit Pleasures: Feminist Spectators and *Personal Best*," reprinted from *Wide Angle* 8, no. 2 (1986), by permission of Elizabeth Ellsworth and Johns Hopkins University Press. A revised version of this essay appears in *Becoming Feminine: The Politics of Popular Culture*, ed. Leslie G. Roman and Linda K. Christian-Smith (Philadelphia: Falmer Press, 1988).

"White Privilege and Looking Relations: Race and Gender in Feminist Film Theory," reprinted from *Cultural Critique* 4 (Fall 1986), by permission of Jane Gaines and *Cultural Critique*. An expanded version of this essay appears in *Screen* 29, no. 4 (Autumn 1988), pp. 12–27.

"The Political Aesthetics of the Feminist Documentary Film," reprinted from *Quarterly Review of Film Studies* 3, no. 4 (Fall 1978), by permission of Julia Lesage and *Quarterly Review of Film and Video*.

"Feminism, Film, and Public History," reprinted from *Radical History Review* 25 (1981), by permission of *Radical History Review*.

"Textual Politics," from *Women's Pictures: Feminism and Cinema* (London: Routledge & Kegan Paul, 1982). Reprinted by permission of Annette Kuhn and Unwin Hyman.

"In the Name of Feminist Film Criticism," reprinted from *Jump Cut* 19 (1978). Revised and reprinted in *Heresies* 3, no. 1, issue 9 (1980). Reprinted and expanded in *Movies and Methods*, Vol. II, ed. Bill Nichols (Berkeley: University of California Press, 1985). Reprinted by permission of B. Ruby Rich, *Jump Cut*, and the Regents of the University of California.

"Rethinking Women's Cinema: Aesthetics and Feminist Theory," reprinted from *New German Critique* 34 (Winter 1985). Revised and reprinted in *Technologies of Gender: Essays on Theory, Film, and Fiction* (Bloomington: Indiana University Press, 1987), by permission of Teresa de Lauretis, Telos Press Ltd., and Indiana University Press. Written initally for *Kunst mit Eigen-Sinn*, eds. Silvia Eiblmayr, Valie Export, and Monika Prischl-Meier (Vienna and Munich: Locker, 1985).

"Dis-Embodying the Female Voice," reprinted from *Re-Vision: Essays in Feminist Film Criticism*, ed. Mary Ann Doane, Patricia Mellencamp, and Linda Williams (Frederick, MD: University Publications of America, Inc., in association with The American Film Institute, 1984), by permission of Kaja Silverman and The American Film Institute.

"Images and Women," reprinted from *Hollywood from Vietnam to Reagan* (New York: Columbia University Press, 1986), by permission of Robin Wood and Columbia University Press, copyright © 1986.

"Unspoken and Unsolved: *Tell Me a Riddle*," reprinted from *CineAction!* 1 (Spring 1985), by permission of Florence Jacobowitz, Lori Spring, and *CineAction!*.

"Desperately Seeking Difference," reprinted from *Screen* 28, no. 1 (Winter 1987), by permission of Jackie Stacey and *Screen*.

"Feminist or Tendentious? Marleen Gorris's *A Question of Silence*," from *Film Feminisms: Theory and Practice, Women's Studies*, no. 56 (Westport, CT: Greenwood Press, 1985). Reprinted by permission of Mary C. Gentile and Greenwood Press, copyright © 1985.

"Female Narration, Women's Cinema: Helke Sander's *The All-Round Reduced Personality/Redupers*," reprinted from *New German Critique* 24–25 (Fall/Winter 1981–82), by permission of Judith Mayne and Telos Press Ltd.

"Anti-Porn: Soft Issue, Hard World," reprinted from *The Village Voice* (1983). Revised and reprinted in *Feminist Review*, no. 13 (February 1983). Reprinted by permission of B. Ruby Rich and *The Village Voice*.

"*Variety*: The Pleasure in Looking," reprinted from *Pleasure and Danger: Exploring Female Sexuality*, ed. Carole S. Vance (Boston: Routledge & Kegan Paul, 1984). Reprinted by permission of Bette Gordon and Unwin Hyman.

INTRODUCTION

Patricia Erens

It has been ten years since the publication of *Sexual Stratagems: The World of Women and Film,* a volume of essays that reflected the state of feminist film studies in the seventies. At that time scholars had just begun to write the history of women's contribution to filmmaking, to explore the changing images of women on the screen both here and abroad, and to develop theories related to female representation and reception.

Since 1979, an enormous amount of feminist film criticism has appeared, reflecting a growing sophistication about how film images are produced and received. The present volume shows the thinking and development that took place in the 1980s, although a few earlier essays have been included because of the influence of these pieces on later writings. Unlike the first volume of *Sexual Stratagems,* the present text does not include essays on the film careers of individual women; that work is currently being undertaken by several other scholars.[1]

In addition, I have not included filmographies. In the original *Sexual Stratagems* there were fifty-four pages listing films by any woman who had ever touched celluloid. This international filmography covering eighty-one years included narrative fiction, documentaries, animation, and shorts. As I updated this listing it immediately became clear to me that to cover the period from 1978 to 1988 would require a book in itself. Working solely with narrative fiction and feature-length documentaries on an international scale, I soon had sixty-eight pages. And this did not include the vast number of independent shorts, animation, and educational films produced by women. Surely these raw numbers alone attest to the creative vitality of women and the opening up of a field once totally dominated by men.

However, numbers do not tell the whole story. Women's access to the means of production does not ensure fundamental change or equality of opportunity. In the seventies women still talked optimistically of the day when they would enter film production in significant numbers and create their own screen images. To some degree that day has come and thus it seems an appropriate time to reevaluate many of the original tenets of feminist film criticism, to look at the writings of the last decade, and to assess current film production.

Issues in Feminist Film Criticism brings together a wide variety of writings by Anglo-American feminist film scholars, focusing on issues applicable to a large body of film or to filmmaking practice in general. Where analyses of individual works appear, they represent essays whose main concerns are theoretical. I have included as many approaches and methodologies as possible, because I believe that each has something to add to our understanding of the complex issues related to women and film and because I am suspicious of the orthodoxy of any one approach. In short, this text is structured as a series of debates. Each section includes articles that treat similar topics from opposing viewpoints. Where possible, I have tried to provide analyses of the same film using different methodologies so as to make apparent the virtues and limitations of each approach. It is my hope that this structure will meet the needs of a wide variety of users and will stimulate lively dialogue in the classroom.

The rise of feminist film criticism is an outgrowth of the women's movement, which began in the United States in the late 1960s, of feminist scholarship in a variety of disciplines, and of women's filmmaking.[2] The cross-fertilization cannot be overestimated, although it is not my intention to provide a detailed history of that development. Such a history would require a discussion of the critical debates, the film festivals, conferences, journals, and distribution companies, as well as of the articles written and the films produced. Further, one would want to include an account of what was occurring in women's studies inside the academy, as well as one of the political activism in the world at large. All of these realities had an impact upon feminist film criticism and are referred to in various ways in the articles. For a chronology of specific film events during the seventies, see B. Ruby Rich's "In the Name of Feminist Film Criticism."

The purpose of this Introduction is to provide a brief discussion of the key ideas that engaged feminist film scholars during the 70s and 80s. These topics include: images of women on the screen; questions of film realism; the notion of counter-cinema; the concept of "reading against the grain"; the use of pyschoanalytic theories; concerns over female spectatorship; women's place in specific genres, especially film melodrama; and issues related to race, class, and sexual preference as it intersects with feminism. Each of these topics will be taken up in depth in the essays.

On the heels of the first women's film festivals, two histories appeared: Marjorie Rosen's *Popcorn Venus: Women, Movies and the American Dream* (1973) and Molly Haskell's *From Reverence to Rape: The Treatment of Women in the Movies* (1974). Both works chronicled the changing image of women in Hollywood films and both used sociological approaches which highlighted how the female characters related to the history of the era, how these characters were stereotyped, how active or passive they were, how much screen time they were allotted, and whether they served as positive or negative models for women in the audience. The conclusions of both histories regarding female representation was summarized by Haskell, "You've come a long way baby . . . and it's all been downhill." These histories constituted image studies. The value of this approach is debated in articles by Susan Wengraf and Linda Artel and Diane Waldman in Section One.

Interest in image studies held sway for many years in the United States and can be found in the pages of *Women and Film,* the first feminist film journal (1972–1975), and the early issues of *Jump Cut,* which began in 1974 and remains a major vehicle for feminist criticism. However, beginning in the mid-seventies, image studies and the attempt to depict "real women," both in documentaries and in narrative fiction, came under attack by some critics as deriving from a naive understanding of the mechanisms of film production and reception. As the British film scholar Claire Johnston wrote, "If women's cinema is going to emerge, it should not only concern itself with substituting positive female protagonists, focusing on women's problems, etc.; it has to go much further than this if it is to impinge on consciousness. It requires a revolutionary strategy which can only be based on an analysis of how film operates as a medium within a specific cultural system."[3]

While feminist film critics in the United States continued to regard film as a vehicle for personal change and political activism, several women in England began to develop other theoretical models, influenced by Continental thinkers including Sigmund Freud, Jacques Lacan, Roland Barthes, Jacques Derrida, Christian Metz, Jean-Louis Baudry, and Louis Althusser. Their ideas were grounded in psychoanalysis, semiotics, and Marxist ideology. For this group, the major concerns centered around the production of meaning in a film text, the way a text constructs a viewing subject, and the ways in which the very mechanisms of cinematic production affect the representation of women and reenforce sexism. During the seventies, differences in approach and methodology between U.S. and British feminist film critics were very pronounced, although they have become less so during the eighties.

The results of these inquiries led to new forms of feminist film criticism. Claire Johnston edited a monograph entitled *Notes on Women's Cinema* (1973), in which she stated, "In rejecting a sociological analysis of woman in the cinema we reject any view in terms of realism, for this would involve an acceptance of the apparent natural denotation of the sign and would involve a denial of the reality of the myth in operation. Within a sexist ideology and a male-dominated cinema, woman is presented as what she represents for man."[4]

This monograph introduced semiotics to feminist film criticism, holding that women do not represent themselves on the screen, especially in Hollywood films, but are merely signs for all that is non-male. How this construction operates is discussed at length in the essay by Johnston and Pam Cook in Section One on the cinema of Raoul Walsh. At the same time, the monograph sounded a warning for those women who looked forward to the day when the movies would depict "real women."

As the seventies moved forward, women took up filmmaking in unprecedented numbers. The vast majority began in documentary film because costs were lower and production demanded less technical expertise. Furthermore, women urgently wanted to deal with issues that previously had been unaddressed on film, especially from a woman's perspective (abortion, rape, job discrimination, etc.); many felt this could be done most effectively with the documentary, a form that had long been associated with the concept of "truth" and "reality." For the first feminist filmmakers, the documentary also offered the possibility of replacing stereotypes with truer-to-life images.

The excitement of seeing ordinary women on the screen, speaking about their own lives and feelings, was enough to generate audiences in the first years, especially as a part of consciousness-raising groups and festival/educational programming. Most crucial at that time was actually hearing the voices of women, rather than those of the on- or off-screen males, who had once dominated documentaries. It is not surprising, therefore, that women's documentaries quickly became characterized by the use of "talking heads."

As women's documentary filmmaking developed, questions of realism arose here as they had with regard to fictional filmmaking. In "Documentary, Realism and Women's Cinema" (1975), Eileen McGarry cautioned viewers against taking images as direct reflections of reality. She pointed out that documentaries, like other forms of filmmaking, used coded language derived from the effects of a moving camera, composition, editing, lighting, and all varieties of sound, to create its illusions. In short, documentary images were no more "real" than images in fictional film.

Despite such reservations, the women's documentary was not without its advocates. Foremost was Julia Lesage, whose article "The Political Aesthetics of the Feminist Documentary" is reprinted in Section Three. Lesage felt that the traditional "realist" documentary structure could be appropriated by women in a subversive manner to challenge the status quo and to present women's bodies, women's voices, and women's domestic space in a new way. More recently, Barbara Halpern Martineau has defended the use of "talking heads" and *cinéma-vérité* techniques, stating, "Unlike the vérité films of Wiseman or King, [women's films] invite a questioning, critical stance towards the subjective attitudes they represent; unlike government or corporate propaganda, they represent a challenge to traditional authority."[5] Thus, whatever their limitations on achieving realism, there is little question that these early documentaries had enormous value for political organizing.

With regard to fictional filmmaking, feminist concerns about the shortcomings of Hollywood films led Johnston to propose a counter-cinema, one that rejected the Hollywood model. In Johnston's proposal, counter-cinema represented a "deconstructive" cinema in which sexist ideology was openly exposed and where works investigated the means of their own creation, especially from a feminist point of view. Similar concepts were also applied to the criticism of older Hollywood films, especially to the work of Dorothy Arzner, in which ruptures in the narrative allowed for a perspective to seep through that ran counter to the dominant ideology of the film. The problem with this type of subversive reading was that, ultimately, the number of films in which this occurred and the actual moments of rupture were insufficient to provide women with any sizable degree of satisfaction.

As filmmakers developed a woman's cinema, many took up Johnston's ideas, using alternative forms and experimental techniques, in the hope that they could encourage audiences to critique the seemingly transparent images on the screen and to question the manipulative techniques of filming and editing. The essay by Annette Kuhn included in Section Three discusses many of the films made in the name of a counter-cinema. The issue of realism, however, did not disappear. In "Recent Developments in Feminist Criticism" (1978), Christine Gledhill predicted, "Feminist film theory must inevitably encounter and do battle with the hybrid phenomenon of realism as a dominant expectation of the cultural production in the late 19th and 20th centuries which embraces both hegemonic and radical aspirations."[6] The use of realist aesthetics in women's cinema is treated by Florence Jacobowitz and Lori Spring in the essay on *Tell Me a Riddle* found in Section Four.

Not all feminist filmmakers and critics felt that counter-cinema was their only option; yet clearly everyone had given thought to how women's films would be like or different from those produced by men. Such discussions also occurred in other fields, especially in art history and literary studies.[7] One influential article on this subject was written by Silvia Bovenschen, who asked, "Is There a Feminine Aesthetic?" (1977). Challenging those women who supported art forms which deemphasized gender differences, Bovenschen said that as women's experience throughout history had been different from men's, therefore women's art would and should be different. Although she cautioned that no absolute criteria should be established for feminist art, she concluded, "feminine artistic production takes place by means of a complicated process involving conquering and reclaiming, appropriating and formulating, as well as forgetting and subverting."[8] Similar notions were also discussed by film scholars, most notably in "Women and Film: A Discussion of Feminist Aesthetics" (1978).[9]

Feminist reservations about Hollywood film were furthered by the publication of one of the most influential feminist essays, Laura Mulvey's "Visual Pleasure and Narrative Cinema," (*Screen* 16 [1975]), which is included in Section One of this book. In this article, Mulvey detailed the ways in which men consciously and unconsciously control the production and reception of film, creating images that satisfy their needs and unconscious desires. Drawing upon the work of Sigmund Freud and Jacques Lacan, Mulvey examined the ways in which cinema uses the image of woman to dissipate male castration fears (which come into play at the oedipal period) by forms of voyeurism, containing aspects of sadism and fetishism. Emphasizing the importance of "the gaze" in narrative cinema, she described how, on screen, men are the bearers of "the look," while women are the objects to be looked at, echoing John Berger's statement in *Ways of Seeing* (1972) that "Men look at women. Women watch themselves being looked at."[10]

Mulvey stated, "In a world ordered by sexual imbalance, pleasure in looking has been split between active/male and passive/female. . . . The determining male gaze projects its fantasy onto the female figure which is styled accordingly. In their traditional exhibitionist role women are simultaneously looked at and displayed, with their appearance coded for strong visual and erotic impact so that they can be said to connote *to-be-looked-at-ness*."[11] She went on to explain how the male viewer in the audience identifies with the male protagonist on the screen, the character who controls both events and "the look," concluding that Hollywood film set into play a text-spectator relationship from which women are excluded.

The implications of this essay were pessimistic indeed. Not only were women excluded, used, and abused in mainstream cinema, but Mulvey implied that by addressing the male viewer, Hollywood had nothing to offer women apart from images of their own objectification.

For a while, these theories were adopted as a means of explaining how sexual differences affected the dynamics of all dominant cinema. However, certain limitations gradually were noted by other scholars. Among the primary issues which Mulvey's essay raised, but did not answer, were questions of female spectatorship and pleasure in film viewing. The female spectator, both that constructed by the film and the real woman in the audience, became one of the most hotly debated subjects of the eighties. A few of the prominent articles are cited below.

B. Ruby Rich's "In the Name of Feminist Film Criticism" (1978), reprinted in this volume, asserted that despite Mulvey's essay, she (Rich) was a real woman sitting in the dark, interacting with the film with a "conspicuous absence of passivity." She argued that women's viewing experience under patriarchy is always dialectical, a process of absorbing and reprocessing (often resisting) what emanates from the screen. In this way Rich not only emphasized women's *active* participation in the creation of meaning, but also showed how works could be appropriated for other than their intended purposes by providing insights into patriarchal culture or by producing pleasure for women viewers. One application of this process came to be known as "reading against the grain," and is utilized to provide lesbian readings of *Gentlemen Prefer Blondes* and *Personal Best*, two essays included in Section Two.

Another challenge to Mulvey's ideas appeared in Janet Bergstrom's "Enunciation and Sexual Difference" (1979), published in *Camera Obscura*, a journal (founded in 1977) devoted to feminism and film theory.

Bergstrom rejected the notion that female viewers identify only with females on the screen and males only with males. She also challenged the dichotomy of active/male vs. passive/female, replacing it with the Freudian concepts of bisexual responses which would allow for multiple identificatory positions, which could occur either successively or simultaneously.

Mulvey published her own reconsideration on narrative pleasure in "Afterthoughts on 'Visual Pleasure and Narrative Cinema,' inspired by *Duel in the Sun*" (1981). Rather than holding, as before, that narrative cinema offered no place for female viewers, Mulvey now said that women could adopt either a masochistic female position by identifying with the female object of desire or a male position by becoming the active viewer of the text, thus assuming a degree of control through transsexual identification. Although these choices broadened the options available to female spectators, it did not solve the problem or please all feminists.

Another contribution to the theory of spectatorship was offered by Gaylyn Studlar in "Masochism and the Perverse Pleasures of the Cinema" (1984). Studlar asserted that film viewing relied on a regression to the preoedipal stage rather than the later oedipal stage discussed by Mulvey. As such, the image of woman, tied to the child's earliest view of the mother, had a significantly different symbolic value. Rather than representing the threat of castration, woman represented memories of plentitude. Most important, Studlar argued for a recognition of the masochistic pleasures of much film viewing which replicated the infant's earliest experiences.[12] These pleasures, found in certain Hollywood films she termed "the masochistic aesthetic," were available to both female and male viewers and thus challenged Mulvey's views that male viewing was always sadistic or fetishistic and that cinema offered no place for female viewers.

More recently Miriam Hansen, in "Pleasure, Ambivalence, Identification: Valentino and Female Spectatorship" (1986), demonstrated how spectators cross sexual boundaries, and how the male figure can serve as the erotic object of desire for a female viewer. Currently several other scholars are pursuing work on the representation of the male body in film, providing new insights on female representation as well.[13]

Drawing together several issues of the debates about female representation and sexual difference, especially the discrepancy between woman as the object of male desire and woman as historical subject, Teresa de Lauretis, in her 1984 work *Alice Doesn't: Feminism, Semiotics, Cinema*, asserted that the goal of feminist film criticism was *not* to bridge the gap, but rather to come to terms with the contradictions.

Along with theorizing on female spectatorship, feminist scholars have taken a closer look at several Hollywood genres, including film noir, the woman's picture, and the maternal melodrama, films which either depicted a strong, sexual heroine or seemed to address a female audience. This volume contains essays on three genre films: *Gentlemen Prefer*

Blondes, *Stella Dallas*, and *A Letter From an Unknown Woman*. In all of these works the central characters are female. Furthermore, in *A Letter From an Unknown Woman*, the story is narrated by the heroine. Such films intrigued feminist critics because they focused on women's issues (home, family, emotionality), presented subversive heroines who went against society's norms, and seemed to provide a feminine discourse. The critics were also prompted to write about these films because of the pleasure they provided for many female moviegoers. The results of such investigations have appeared in several book-length studies.[14]

The recent attention to film melodrama has not been accidental. In a comprehensive article on the subject entitled "Melodrama and the Women's Picture," Pam Cook asserts, "Melodrama has been more hotly debated than any other genre in cinema," adding that "recent feminist interest has focused on the way in which it deals with aspects of women's experience marginalised by other genres."[15] Cook points out that initially women regarded the woman's picture as conservative because of its tendency to punish women who acted on their own desires or who did not conform. However, closer scrutiny revealed that the films were more complex and more ambiguous than was at first apparent. Recent critics have revealed how these works not only foreground a female point of view, but also negotiate the "contradiction between female desire and its containment . . . often producing an excess which threatens to deviate from the intended route."[16] Thus, in its own way, the woman's film is capable of accomplishing much the same work as deconstructive cinema: revealing women's plight in a sexist society and subverting the traditional propaganda that reinforces this ideology. The three articles on melodrama in Section Two take up these issues.

Where, then, are we now? There has been a great deal of effort, in recent years, devoted to finding out more about actual viewers and individual interpretations. Janice Radway's book *Romancing the Reader: Women, Patriarchy and Popular Literature* (1984), based on interviews with women who read Harlequin romances, and Ien Ang's *Watching Dallas* (1985), based on viewers' responses to the evening soap opera, helped pioneer this approach in popular literature and television.[17] In film studies, similar work is being carried out, especially on the relationship between film exhibition, studio publicity, and female audiences.[18] The essay in this volume on *Personal Best* exemplifies, from a feminist point of view, the new attention to audiences, as well as to analyses of reviews and publicity campaigns.

"Star images" and the intersection between performance, biography, and studio publicity have been another developing area. The two important books in this field by Richard Dyer, *Stars* (1979) and *Heavenly Bodies: Film Stars and Society* (1986), have been complemented by similar approaches from a specifically feminist perspective.[19] These studies focus on how Hollywood molds female performers into familar stereotypes, then merchandises them as commodities, and how this process determines and is determined by pre-existing notions of femininity in the culture. Maureen Turim's article on *Gentlemen Prefer Blondes* in section two is an early discussion of some of these concerns.

Two areas not included in this anthology are women's contribution to production in capacities other then directing and studies of the early development of film aesthetics from a feminist perspective. However, both topics have been researched by other scholars.[20]

Finally, many feminist film critics are now investigating the differences between women, epecially how race and sexual preference, along with ethnicity and class, establish separate priorities.[21] Focusing on disparate social and cultural heritages and histories, this criticism not only speaks out for new representations, but also for a more diversified theory of female spectatorship. The two essays by Jane Gaines in this volume address these issues, as does the one by Teresa de Lauretis. It seems to me that it is in this area that much new work will be done. If the seventies and the eighties have been devoted to discovering the pervasive influence of sexual difference (male/female), then perhaps the nineties will be the decade when women will come to a better understanding of the differences between themselves.

NOTES

1. For information on early silent directors, see *The Memoirs of Alice Guy Blache*, ed. Anthony Slide, trans. Roberta and Simone Blache, Metuchen, NJ: Scarecrow (1986), and Nell Shipman, *The Silent Screen and My Talking Heart*, Boise, ID: Bosie State University Press (1987). For a current study of established women directors worldwide, see Barbara Koenig Quart, *Women Directors: The Emergence of a New Cinema*, New York: Praeger (1988). For information on Maya Deren, Shirley Clarke, and Joyce Weiland, see Lauren Rabinowitz, *Points of Resistance: Sex, Power and Politics in New York City Avant-Garde Cinema*, Urbana: University of Illinois Press (forthcoming). Also, *The Legend of Maya Deren*, by Veve A. Clark, Millicent Modson, and Catrina Neiman. New York: Anthology Film Archives, 1984 and 1988. For information on other independent filmmakers, see back issues of *Cineaste, Framework, The Independent, Jump Cut,* and *Millenium Film Journal.* Many of these are listed separately in the Bibliography. In addition, Indiana University Press is bringing out a series of books on individual filmmakers, entitled International Women Filmmakers, to be co-edited by Roswitha Mueller and Kaja Silverman.

2. For an overview of the history of the women's movement in the United States see Myra Marx Ferree and Beth B. Hess, *Controversy and Coalition: The New Feminist Movement*, Boston: Twayne (1985), and Sara Evans, *Born for Liberty: A History of Women in America*, New York: Free Press (1989). For a book on issues and publications related to the women's movement, see Hester Eisenstein, *Contemporary Feminist Thought*, Boston: G. K. Hall (1983). Several texts

have been especially influential on feminist film critics, namely Nancy Chodorow, *The Reproduction of Mothering: Psychoanalysis and the Sociology of Gender*, Berkeley: University of California Press (1978); Jane Gallop, *The Daughter's Seduction*, Ithaca: Cornell University Press (1982); and Carol Gilligan, *In A Different Voice: Psychological Theory and Women's Development*, Cambridge: Harvard University Press (1982). In addition, although this anthology does not treat the work of the French feminists, their writings have had an impact on Anglo-American film scholarship. For an introduction to the work of some of the French feminists, see the Special Issue on French Feminist Theory in *Signs* 7, no. 1 (Autumn 1984). For further information, readers should check individual texts by Hélène Cixous, Luce Irigaray, Sarah Kofman, and Monique Wittig.

3. Claire Johnston, "Women's Cinema as Counter-Cinema," *Notes on Women's Cinema*, ed. Claire Johnston, London: Society for Education in Film and Television (1972), p. 25.

4. Ibid., p. 25.

5. Barbara Halpern Martineau, "Talking about our Lives and Experiences: Some Thoughts about Feminism, Documentary, and 'Talking Heads,' " *Show Us Life: Toward a History and Aesthetics of the Committed Documentary*, ed. Thomas Waugh, Metuchen, NJ: Scarecrow (1984), p. 263.

6. Christine Gledhill, "Recent Developments in Feminist Criticism," *Quarterly Review of Film Studies* 3, no. 4 (Fall 1978), p. 461.

7. For works dealing with feminine aesthetics in art, see *Old Mistresses: Women, Art and Ideology*, ed. Rozika Parker and Griselda Pollack, London: Routledge and Kegan Paul (1981), and *Feminism and Art History: Questioning the Litany*, ed. Norma Broude and Mary D. Garrard, New York: Harper and Row (1982). For those works dealing with similar issues in literature, see *Gender and Reading: Essays on Readers, Texts and Context*, ed. Elizabeth A. Flynn and Patrocino P. Schweickart, Baltimore: Johns Hopkins University Press (1986); *The Poetics of Gender*, ed. Nancy K. Miller, New York: Columbia University Press (1987); and Sandra M. Gilbert and Susan Gubar, *No Man's Land: The Place of the Woman Writer in the Twentieth Century*. New Haven: Yale University Press (1988).

8. Silvia Bovenschen, "Is There a Feminine Aesthetic?" *New German Critique* 12 (1977), trans. Beth Weckmueller, pp. 111–37.

9. Michelle Citron, Julia Lesage, Judith Mayne, B. Ruby Rich, and Anna Marie Taylor. "Women and Film: A Discussion of Feminist Aesthetics," *New German Critique* 13 (Winter 1978), pp. 83–107.

10. John Berger, *Ways of Seeing*, London: British Broadcasting Corp. and Penquin Books (1972), p. 47.

11. Laura Mulvey, "Visual Pleasure and Narrative Cinema," *Screen* 16, no. 3 (Autumn 1975), p. 11.

12. Several articles on the relationship between masochism and film precede Studlar's work, most prominently Dennis Giles's "*Angel on Fire*: Three Texts of Desire," *The Velvet Light Trap*, no. 16 (Fall 1976), pp. 41–45, and "Pornographic Space: The Other Place," *Film Studies Annual II*, Pleasantville, NY: Redgrave, (1977), pp. 52–65; and Kaja Silverman, "Masochism and Subjectivity," *Framework*, no. 12 (1981), pp. 2–9.

13. For previous articles on the male body in film, see Richard Dyer, "Don't Look Now—The Male Pin-Up," *Screen* 23, nos. 3–4 (September/October 1982), pp. 61–73, Sandy Flitterman, "Thighs and Whiskers: The Fascination of Magnum, P.I.," *Screen* 26, no. 2 (November/December 1985), and Sarah Kent, "The Erotic Male Nude," in *Women's Images of Men*, ed. Sarah Kent and Jacqueline Morreau, London: Writers and Readers Publishing (1985). Steve Neale, "Masculinity as Spectacle," *Screen* 24, no. 6 (November/December 1983), pp. 2–16. For current work on the male body, see Peter Lehman, "*American Gigolo*: The Male Body Makes

an Appearance of Sorts," in *Gender: Literary and Cinematic Representations*, ed. Geanne Ruppert, Tallahassee: Florida State University Press (1989) and Gaylyn Studlar's "When A Man Loves: Male Spectacle and Female Pleasure in Films in the 1920s," presented at the Society of Cinema Studies in Iowa City (1989) and which is part of a larger work in progress.

14. *Women in Film Noir*, ed. E. Ann Kaplan, London: British Film Institute (1978); Andrea S. Walsh, *Women's Film and Female Experience 1940–1950*, New York: Praeger (1984); *Home Is Where the Heart Is: Studies in Melodrama and the Woman's Film*, ed. Christine Gledhill, London: British Film Institute (1987); and Mary Ann Doane, *The Desire To Desire: The Woman's Film of the 1940s*, Bloomington: Indiana University Press (1987).

15. Pam Cook, "Melodrama and the Woman's Picture," *Gainsborough Melodrama*, ed. Sue Aspinall and Bob Murphy, Dossier no. 18, London: British Film Institute (1983), p. 14.

16. Ibid., p. 21.

17. Janice Radway, *Romancing the Reader: Women, Patriarchy and Popular Literature*, Chapel Hill: University of North Carolina Press (1984) and Ien Ang, *Watching Dallas*, London: Methuen (1985), translated from the Dutch, which first appeared in 1982. For similar work on film viewers, see Angela McRobbie, "Dance and Social Fantasy," (on *Fame* and *Flashdance*), *Gender and Generation*, ed. Angela McRobbie and Mica Nava, London: Macmillan (1984) and Jacqueline Bobo, "Black Women's Responses: *The Color Purple*," *Jump Cut*, no. 33 (1988), pp. 43–51. And for a complete discussion of female spectatorship, see *Camera Obscura* 20–21 (1990) on "The Spectatrix."

18. Among several recent articles, see Diane Waldman, "From Midnight Shows to Marriage Vows: Women, Exploitation, and Exhibition," *Wide Angle* 6, n. 2 (1984), pp. 34–48; Charlotte Cornelia Herzog and Jane Gaines, "Puffed Sleeves Before Teatime: Joan Crawford, Adrian and Women Audiences," *Wide Angle* 6, n. 4 (1985), pp. 24–33; Special Issue on Female Representation and Consumer Culture, *Quarterly Review of Film and Video* 11, n. 4 (1989); Ben Singer, "Don't Overlook Mrs. Jones!: Female Spectatorship and Early Cinema, 1908–1918," paper delivered at Society of Cinema Studies, University of Iowa (1989); and *Fabrications: Costume and the Female Body*, ed. Jane M. Gaines and Charlotte Herzog, New York: Routledge (1990).

19. For some of the current work on star images, see Jane Clarke and Diana Simmonds, "Move Over Misconceptions: Doris Day Reappraised," London: British Film Institute, Dossier no. 4 (1980); Maria La Place, "Bette Davis and the Ideal of Consumption: A Look at *Now Voyager*," *Wide Angle* 6, no. 4 (1985), pp. 34–43; Andrew Britton, "Katharine Hepburn and the Cinema of Chastisement," *Screen* 26, no. 5 (September/October 1985), pp. 52–62; and Richard Lippe, "Kim Novak: A Resistance to Definition," and Florence Jacobowitz, "Joan Bennett: Images of Femininity in Conflict," both in *CineAction!*, no. 7 (December 1986), pp. 5–21 and 22–34, respectively.

20. For information on women in the industry, see Denise Hartsough, *Cutting Film: Women's Work*, Ph.D. diss., University of Wisconsin (1983); Katherine DiGuillio, "The Status of Women in the Animation Industry," paper delivered at the Society for Cinema Studies, Montana State University (1988); and Ann L. Warren, *Word Play: The Lives and Work of Four Women Writers in Hollywood's Golden Age*, Ph.D. diss., University of Southern California (1988). For work on early cinema history from a feminist perspective, see Lucy Fischer, "The Lady Vanishes: Women, Magic, and the Movies," *Film Quarterly* 33, no. 1 (Fall 1979), pp. 30–40 and Linda Williams, "Film Body: An Implantation of Perversions," *Cine-Tracts* 3, no. 1 (Winter 1981), pp. 19–35.

21. Among the materials available on issues of class, race, and sexual preference

as they intersect with issues of film and gender, see: Special Issue on Lesbians and Film in *Jump Cut*, nos. 24–25 (1981); Special Issue on Third World Film in *Jump Cut*, no. 27 (1982); Caroline Sheldon, "Lesbians and Film; Some Thoughts," in *Gays and Film*, ed. Richard Dyer, New York: Zoetrope (1984); Claudia Springer, "Black Women Filmmakers," *Jump Cut*, no. 29 (1984); *Gender and Generation*, ed. Angela McRobbie and Mica Nava, London: Macmillian (1984); Martina Attile, "Black Women and Representation," *Undercut*, no. 14–15 (Summer 1985), pp. 60–61; Coco Fusco, "*Las Madres de La Plaza de Mayo*: An Interview with Lourdes Portillo and Susana Munoz," *Cineaste* 15, no. 1 (1986), pp. 22–26; Gina Marchetti, "The Threat of Captivity: Hollywood and the Sexualization of Race Relations in *The Girls of the White Orchid* and *The Bitter Tea of General Yen*," *Journal of Communication Inquiry* 11, no. 1 (Winter 1987), pp. 29–42; Jacqueline Bobo, "Black Women's Responses: *The Color Purple*," *Jump Cut*, no. 33 (1988), pp. 43–51; Alile Sharon Larkin, "Black Women Filmmakers Defining Ourselves: Feminism in Our Own Voice," and Jacqueline Bobo, "*The Color Purple*: Black Women as Cultural Readers," both in *Female Spectators: Looking at Film and Television*, ed. Diedre Pribram, London: Verso (1988); Loretta Campbell, "Hurting Women" (on films by Christine Choy, Cynthia Maurizio, Camille Billops, and Marlene Damm), *Jump Cut*, no. 34 (1989); Mary Beth Haralovich, "Women, Class and Consumerism in the 1930's: The Accommodation of Contradiction" and Gloria J. Gibson-Hudons, "Only the Screen is White: Black Women Filmmakers COLOR Film History and a Contemporary Feminist Ideology," both papers delivered at the Society of Cinema Studies, University of Iowa (1989); Jacqui Roach and Petal Felix, "Black Looks," in *The Female Gaze: Women as Viewers of Popular Culture*, ed. Lorraine Gamman and Margaret Marshment, Seattle: Real Comet Press (1989); and Liz Kotz, "Unofficial Stories: Documentaries by Latinas and Latin American Women," *The Independent* 12, no. 4 (May 1989), pp. 21–27. For information on films by minority women filmmakers, contact: Third World Newsreel, 335 West 38th Street, New York, NY 10018 and Women Make Movies, Inc., 225 Lafayette Street, New York, NY 10012.

I.

Critical Methodology
Women and Representation

Emerging in the early seventies, feminist film theory and criticism sought not only to understand the stratagems of sexism, but also to encourage positive attitudes towards womanhood and an optimistic view about social change. If films that existed in the past did not serve women well, then the following questions arose: What kinds of images did women want? What was in their best interests? And what was possible within the system of film production as we know it?

Such questioning is apparent in the first two essays of this section which debate the pros and cons of producing positive images, images that show women as intelligent and autonomous, performing meaningful work, making reasonable choices, and living assertively. In "Positive Images: Screening Women's Films" (1978),[1] an essay which serves as the introduction to their book on non-sexist media for young people, Linda Artel and Susan Wengraf express their committment to creating an awareness of alternatives to sex-stereotyped behavior. Recognizing the powerful ability of film to encourage this awareness, they argue that positive images create important role models for females and undermine stereotypes that foster sexism in society.

Diane Waldman's response, "There's More to a Positive Image Than Meets the Eye" (1978), raises two objections: first, to the criteria used by the authors, and second, to the notion itself. Addressing the latter issue, she questions whether positive images are truthful ones. "Do they depict things as they really are, or as we think they should be?"[2] She is especially concerned that an emphasis on positive images fails to confront the reality of sexism. For Waldman, what is needed are methods for critiquing images, for understanding how viewers identify with film characters, and for analyzing how sexism functions in our society. She ends with a reminder that meaning is not located solely in the film, but also in the interaction between reader and text. As feminist film theory and criticism developed over the next ten years, these issues were to be addressed again, especially regarding the extent to which film can determine viewer responses and the variation of these responses to any given work.

"The Place of Woman in the Cinema of Raoul Walsh," by Pam Cook and Claire Johnston (1974), was one of the first essays to apply psychoanalytic theory (especially the work of Jacques Lacan) and semiotics to feminist film analysis. Cook and Johnston are vociferous in their rejection of a sociological approach, one which compares screen images of women with real women, past or present. For them, film is a coded artificial construct and the task of feminist criticism is to decode it.

The authors use Walsh for this project because his films often present strong women characters—positive images, if you will. However, Cook and Johnston set out to prove that these characters are not the independent agents they seem to be, but rather serve as signifiers encoded by a patriarchal culture. In Walsh's work, as they explain, women represent "at one and the same time the distant memory of maternal plentitude and the fetishized object of his fantasy of castration—a phallic replacement and thus a threat."[3] Furthermore, woman is "an object of exchange between men, . . . the means by which men express their relationships with each other."[4]

Cook and Johnston use their approach to address Walsh's *The Revolt of Mamie Stover* (1956). They explore the film's treatment of the relationship between money and phallic power and of how women are excluded from this relationship. They focus on the way Jane Russell's (Mamie Stover) "look" directed towards the men in the film and in the audience poses a threat to male privilege. They describe how "the central contradiction of her [Stover's] situation is that she can only attempt to assert herself as subject through the exploitation of a fetishized image of woman to be exchanged within the circulation of money: her independence and her desire for social and economic status all hinge on this objectification."[5] Finally they show how "By promising to marry and give it all up, she is reintegrated into an order where she no longer represents that threat."[6]

Despite the title of their essay, Cook and Johnston reject an auteur approach to film analysis, an approach which emphasizes the unity and personal vision of a director's oeuvre. In contrast, they read film as a text which contains the contradictory interplay of different codes. "A study of woman within Walsh's oeuvre, in particular, reveals 'woman' as the locus of a dilemma for the patriarchal human order, as a locus of contradictions."[7] Such as approach moves feminist film criticism beyond the study of positive and negative images.

The next selection, Laura Mulvey's "Visual Pleasure and Narrative Cinema (1975)," is the single most reprinted essay in the field of feminist film theory. In the essay, Mulvey uses psychoanalytic theory in a political way in order to demonstrate how Hollywood cinema is integrally bound up with aspects of patriarchy, particularly with unconscious mechanisms related to the construction of images, erotic ways of looking, audience identification, and the Hollywood editing style. According to Mulvey, woman stands in patriarchal culture as a signifier for the male Other, as a symbol of what woman represents to men, that is, as a symbol of their fantasies and obsessions. For Mulvey it is thus crucial to understand these mechanisms, as well as the pleasures offered by cinema viewing, before women can create alternatives more suited to their own desires.

Mulvey describes two sources of visual pleasure that were identified by Freud. "The first, scopophilic, arises from pleasure in using another person as an object of sexual stimulation through sight. The second, developed through narcissism and the constitution of the ego, comes from identification with the image seen. Thus, in film terms, one implies a separation of the erotic identity of the subject from the object on the screen (active scopophilia), the other demands identification of the ego with the object on the screen through the spectator's fascination with the recognition of his like."[8]

For Mulvey, visual pleasure as constructed in cinema is male pleasure. In line with patriarchal culture, pleasure in looking is split between active/male and passive/female: woman as image and man as the bearer of "the look," both on screen and in the audience.

Mulvey goes on to indicate how the active/passive heterosexual division affects narrative structure so that the image of woman as an erotic spectacle stops the flow of the narrative. As Mulvey explains, "the split between spectacle and narrative supports the man's role as the active one of forwarding the story. The man controls the film fantasy and also emerges as the representative of power in a further sense: as the bearer of the look of the spectator."[9] In short, men act and women appear.

Despite the fact that the male controls the gaze, the sight of a woman's body, due to its lack of a penis, produces in him the unpleasurable threat of castration, according to Mulvey. Castration, in its Freudian sense, is also the basis of sexual difference as represented in film. Like Cook and Johnston before her, Mulvey sees sexual difference in film representation as a question of male vs. non-male.

Castration fears are mitigated in two ways in film: a) by voyeurism (associated with sadism), which reenacts the trauma of separation from the mother and which finds pleasure in ascertaining guilt, asserting control, and subjecting the guilty person (woman) to punishment and/or forgiveness; and b) by fetishistic scopophilia, which disavows the threat by the substitution of a fetish object, and which builds up the physical beauty of the object (again woman) as something satisfying in itself. Finally, Mulvey demonstrates how these defense mechanisms operate in the films of Alfred Hitchcock and Joseph von Sternberg. She ends with an analysis of the cinematic codes which determine the ways of looking within cinema and with a call for the abandonment of traditional film conventions which have stolen and used woman's image.

Mulvey's essay had a profound effect on the course of feminist film writing. Dozens of writers applied Mulvey's ideas to their own critiques. Her essay constitutes part of the received wisdom that informs many of the selections included in Section Two. In addition, Mulvey was one of the first feminists to focus on the work of Alfred Hitchcock, which has since become a fruitful source for feminists film criticism.

Mary Ann Doane's "Film and the Masquerade—Theorizing the Female Spectator" (1982) builds on Mulvey's essay, also taking into account her revision, "Afterthoughts on 'Visual Pleasure and Narrative Cinema,' inspired by *Duel in the Sun*" (1981), which was discussed in the Introduction. For Doane, female spectatorship is not simply a question of "male/action" vs. "female/passive," or even one of women's ability to oscillate between these two forms of identification by temporarily becoming a "transvestite" (Mulvey's term). Rather, spectatorship revolves around questions of proximity and distance. This is especially problematic for the female spectator as she *is* the image, the object to be viewed. Thus, women are given two options: they can masochistically overidentify with female images on the screen (becoming overly involved—a frequent female response to melodrama), or they can narcissistically become their own image of desire.

Doane next takes up the notion of "the masquerade." She notes that it is clear why some women would want to emulate men, but questions why others choose instead to flaunt their femininity. Doane explains this in terms of the masquerade. As theorized by Joan Rivere in "Womanliness as a Masquerade" (1966), "Womanliness . . . could be assumed and worn as a mask, both to hide the possession of masculinity and to avert the reprisals expected if she was found to possess it. . . . The masquerade, in flaunting femininity, holds it at a distance."[10] The fact of this distance in part solves the problem of women's overidentification and transvestism. The masquerade, or excess of femininity, enables viewers to critique the socially constructed role of the feminine. In film, however, the masquerade often brings its own punishment—witness the fate of femme fatales in film noir or of any woman who attempts to take over the masculine activity of "looking."

Doane closes her essay with an analysis of Robert Doisneau's 1948 photograph '*Un Regard Oblique*,' using it as an example of how Hollywood cinema incorporates the male gaze into the narrative, while simultaneously denying the female one. She explains, "The object of the male gaze is fully present, *there* for the spectator. The fetishistic representation of the nude female body, fully in view, insures a masculinisation of the spectatorial position. . . . The photograph displays insistently, in microcosm, the structure of the cinematic inscription of a sexual differentiation in modes of looking."[11] For the present, Doane sees the position constructed for the female spectator as "ultimately untenable"; however, she also sees the masquerade, with its potential for drawing attention to the concept of femininity, as one way out of the dilemma. By producing a problematic image, the masquerade creates the necessary distance between the female spectator and the screen and generates an image readable by women.

"Hitchcock, Feminism, and the Patriarchal Unconscious" constitutes the introductory chapter to Tania Modleski's book *The Women Who Knew Too Much: Hitchcock and Feminist Theory* (1988). She observes how feminists have been "compelled, intrigued, infuriated, and inspired" by Hitchcock's works and how his films have played a central role in the formation of feminist film theory.[12] In reviewing this literature, she touches on many of the essays included in this anthology.

As interpreted by Modleski, despite the misogyny attributed to Hitchcock by many of his detractors, Hitchcock's films reveal a strong fascination and identification with femininity that undermine his so-called cinematic mastery. "What I want to argue is *neither* that Hitchcock is utterly misogynistic *nor* that he is largely sympathetic to women and their plight in patriarchy, but that his work is characterized by a thoroughgoing ambivalence about femininity—which explains why it has been possible for critics to argue with some plausibility on either side of the issue."[13] In order to understand this ambivalence, Modleski first addresses the ways in which masculine identity is bound up with feminine identity on both the individual and the social level. Next she turns to Hitchcock's films which "repeatedly reveal the way women are oppressed in patriarchy," and thus "allow the female spectator to feel anger that is very different from the masochistic response imputed to her by some feminist critics."[14] For Modleski, this is of crucial relevance for a theory of female spectatorship.

Modleski moves on to a discussion of recent writings which root female bisexuality in the daughter's early attachment to both the mother and the father. She shows how notions of bisexuality thus can help to explain women's viewing experiences in which they identify with contradictory points of view. For Modleski, Hitchcock's oeuvre, with its preoccupation with female bisexuality and its ability to draw viewers into a close identification with characters, proves to be a perfect vehicle to test this and other theories of female spectatorship, especially those posited by Mulvey and Doane.

The last article, by Jane Gaines, "Can We Enjoy Alternative Pleasure?" (1987)[15] stands in opposition to most of the articles included so far. Not only does Gaines attack the entire school of psychoanalytic feminism, but she also questions why a psychoanalytic approach has been preferred to a Marxist one, especially because Marxism was so vital to the theoretical underpinnings of the women's movement.

Gaines's objection to psychoanalysis is that the theory sidesteps issues of social class and history and also avoids the fact that gender differences are socially constructed. Gaines states that many Marxists feel that psychoanalysis, with its notion of "sexed identity," has generated pessimism among women about the possibility of creating political change. She also reiterates the objections of many towards the British film theorists whose use of pyschoanalysis and other specialized knowledge fosters an elitist position. In Gaines's view, feminist film theory is at a crisis point. Critics can continue to focus on women's silence, repression, and absence in the cinema, which is what has engaged the pyschoanalytic feminists, or they can begin to define a feminine specificity. For Gaines, the time has come to shift attention away from male pleasures and the male gaze to female pleasures.

Gaines discusses the construction of a women's cinema and of female pleasure. She sees counter-cinema as offering one possibility but is aware that the use of avant-garde techniques often alienates women viewers. "The subversion of sexual looking, although compelling as a concept, is not so riveting in its translation to the screen."[16] She questions why "a film that considers its own signification process necessarily require(s) its audience to know advanced film theory in order for them to enjoy, appreciate, and ideally, reflect upon what they see?"[17]

Most important, Gaines champions an array of works, many by black filmmakers, that use conventional forms and accessible techniques to challenge the political status quo. Gaines speaks forcefully for an active reading of the text. She points out how lesbian studies, which assign more power to the spectator than to the text, show how "the look" of female spectators can cancel out the male point of view and how they can find erotic pleasure in many mainstream films. For her, such work is as an important opening in the study of the double consciousness of oppressed groups. Her essay ends with a plea to take a second look at previously dismissed forms, such as soap opera and romance, which promise a model for an emerging feminist aesthetic. These concerns, as well as all of the issues raised by the essays in this section, become the basis for much of the criticism presented in Section Two.

NOTES

1. The book, entitled *Positive Images: Non-Sexist Films for Young People,* was published originally in 1976 by Bootlegger Press in San Francisco.
2. Diane Waldman, "There's More to a Positive Image Than Meets the Eye," *Jump Cut,* no. 18 (1978), p. 32.
3. Pam Cook and Claire Johnston, "The Place of Women in the Cinema of Raoul Walsh," in *Raoul Walsh,* ed. Phil Hardy, Colchester, England: Vineyard Press (1974), p. 95.
4. Ibid.
5. Ibid., p. 100.
6. Ibid., p. 103.
7. Ibid., p. 109.
8. Laura Mulvey, "Visual Pleasure and Narrative Cinema," *Screen* 16, no. 3 (Autumn 1975), p. 10.
9. Ibid, p. 12.
10. Quoted in Mary Ann Doane, "Film and the Masquerade—Theorising the Female Spectator," *Screen* 23, nos. 3–4 (September-October 1982), p. 81.
11. Ibid., p. 81.
12. These can be found on the pages of *Camera Obscura, Wide Angle,* and

Screen, anthologized in *A Hitchcock Reader*, ed. Marshall Deutelbaum and Leland Poague, Ames: Iowa State University Press (1986), Robin Wood's *Hitchcock Films Revisited*, New York: Columbia University Press, 1989, and *The Rereleased Hitchcock Films*, ed. Walter Raubicheck and Walter Srebnick, Detroit, MI: Wayne State University Press (forthcoming). Also see Jeanne Thomas Allen, "The Representation of Violence to Women: Hitchcock's *Frenzy*," *Film Quarterly* 38, no. 3 (Spring 1985), pp. 30–38.

13. Tania Modleski, "Hitchcock, Feminism, and the Patriarchal Unconscious." *The Women Who Knew Too Much: Hitchcock and Feminist Theory*, New York: Methuen (1988), p. 3

14. Ibid., p. 4.

15. An earlier version of this essay served as the introduction to a special section on Women and Representation, *Jump Cut*, no. 29 (February 1984).

16. Jane Gaines, "Women and Representation: Can We Enjoy Alternative Pleasure?" *American Media and Mass Culture: Left Perspectives*, ed. Donald Lazere, Berkeley: University of California Press (1987), p. 363.

17. Ibid.

POSITIVE IMAGES
SCREENING WOMEN'S FILMS

Linda Artel and Susan Wengraf

As feminist educators we are committed to facilitating young people's awareness of alternatives to sex-stereotyped behavior. As feminist *media* educators we recognize the powerful ability of film and video to present positive role models that encourage this awareness. In an effort to provide easy access to non-sexist media, we have compiled *Positive Images,* an annotated guide to over 400 short 16mm films, videotapes, slides, and filmstrips in educational distribution.

The primary aim of *Positive Images* was to evaluate media materials from a feminist perspective. We looked for materials that had at least one of the following characteristics:

- presents girls and women, boys and men with non-stereotyped behavior and attitudes: independent, intelligent women; adventurous, resourceful girls; men who are nurturing; boys who are not afraid to show their vulnerability.
- presents both sexes in non-traditional work or leisure activities: men doing housework, women flying planes, etc.
- questions values and behavior of traditional male/female role division.
- shows women's achievements and contributions throughout history.
- deals with a specific women's problem, such as pregnancy, abortion or rape, in a non-sexist way.
- contains images of sexist attitudes, behavior, and institutions that can be used for consciousness raising.

While many films contain important non-sexist elements, few fulfill an ideal standard. A number of films deal with feminist issues but are sexist in the way they treat the subject matter. For example, *Rape: A Preventative Inquiry* (1974) uses male police as experts but ignores knowledgeable female experts such as rape-crisis-center workers. Some films present women who talk about non-sexist ideas or do non-sexist work, but we see them acting in a way that limits their credibility, as with Mary Tyler

Moore in the women's history film, *American Parade: We the Women* (1974). On camera, Moore behaves in a coy manner that suggests she doesn't really want to be taken seriously.

Other films undermine women's credibility by using a male narrator who makes condescending remarks about the women in the film. Thus, *Persistent and Finagling* is a fascinating study of Montreal housewives who mount a successful grassroots campaign against air pollution. However, the value of what the women are doing is continually diluted by paternalistic comments from one of the husbands. Some dramatic shorts portray a strong and independent female protagonist until the final scene, when she is suddenly rescued by a man. For example, in the history drama *Mary Kate's War*, Kate, a newspaper publisher, develops as a courageous character with ethical integrity until the end when a male friend saves her from political harassment.

Some films are class biased: they present a viable alternative for upper-middle-class women and men but have little relevance for people in other economic situations. *Joyce at 34* (1972) shows a husband and wife—one a writer, the other a filmmaker—equally sharing childcare responsibilities. But this documentary shows no consciousness that this alternative serves only the few who have the luxury of flexible work schedules.

Some films cover women's subjects but lack a feminist perspective. We discovered several film biographies on women that failed to show the subject's strength. For example, a film on Louisa May Alcott depicts the author as a selfless, weepy woman. We also found films that were erroneously (and widely) publicized as non-sexist. In a prime example, *How to Say No to a Rapist—and Survive* (1974), Frederic Storaska, a self-appointed expert, lectures women on how to avoid physical harm from rape. He stereotypes women by dwelling on the use of feminine wiles as the best way to outsmart attackers and recommends several defense tactics that other rape experts have found to be ineffective and even dangerous.

Other films portray a strong female protagonist in a non-sexist way yet stereotype secondary characters. In *Madeline* (1950), the animation based on Ludwig Bemelmans's book, the title character is adventurous, but the other girls behave in a very conventional "good little girl" manner. A growing number of "career" films, especially those on vocational training, include a "token" girl or woman while the rest of the film presents the standard view of men in that field.

A number of excellent films—in content—have diminished effectiveness because of technical inferiority: poor sound, aimless visuals, slow pacing. In *Hey Doc* (1971), a film about a black woman doctor committed to healthcare for the poor, the camera does nothing more than trail after Dr. Allen, much as in a home movie.

Although we did find over 400 examples of what we call non-sexist films, we found that positive images still need to be created in the following areas:

• films for young children: only a handful of films present positive images at the preschool or primary grade levels. For example, adventure stories with exciting plots and strong female protagonists are rare.
• biographies of women: though there are three or four film biographies of Helen Keller and Eleanor Roosevelt, there are none of such women as Emma Goldman, George Eliot, Mother Jones, Rosa Bonheur, Sacagawea, Maria Mitchell, Simone de Beauvoir, and Elizabeth Blackwell.
• women's role in history: several films present a general survey of women's role in U.S. history, but very few deal with their role in specific historical movements and events (such as settling the west or the world wars). Even fewer deal with women's contributions to world history.
• women in non-traditional jobs: although a number of films survey women working in non-traditional occupations, new films focus on a particular occupation to give an in-depth view. Films about women scientists and mathematicians are notably absent.
• Third World women: while there are several films about black women, very few focus on women from other ethnic backgrounds. Furthermore, too many of the existing films treat their subjects as victims rather than as strong women who survive hardship.
• male liberation: few films offer meaningful alternatives to traditional masculine values. We did find several films in which boys express tender feelings, but those emotions are most often directed at pets, not people. Also, the sensitive male protagonists in these films are usually from minority ethnic groups—leaving the stereotype of the macho white male unchanged.
• changing definition of "family": although the number of single-parent families is steadily increasing, few films deal with divorce or show alternatives to the nuclear family, such as communal living or single parenthood, let alone explore the way these alternatives affect sex roles.

The school curriculum needs non-sexist visual media used in conjunction with books in every course. In addition, classroom visits from women and men working in non-stereotyped jobs can present effective and immediate role models. When students read texts and library books or watch films that perpetuate sex-role stereotypes, teachers should promote the kind of discussion essential to develop critical thinking. The curriculum should also include discussions about TV programs, commercials, and Hollywood films that students can watch in order to develop such an awareness.

A public film program of non-sexist films can effectively be presented at libraries, women's centers, or other community centers. We attracted enthusiastic audiences to a series in which the program each week focused on a particular aspect of sex-role liberation, such as new roles for work, sexuality, women's history, and childcare. Knowledgeable speakers from the feminist community led discussions after the films and helped make the programs an active experience for the audience.

We would like to see a time when films showing positive images of women will not require special notice but will be an integral part of our culture. As a means to that change, educators, librarians, and others involved with young people need to seek out and screen films that can educate them about non-sexist ways of thinking and behaving.

THERE'S MORE TO A POSITIVE IMAGE THAN MEETS THE EYE

Diane Waldman

Reviewing the book *Positive Images* is a deceptively simple task, for one would not expect much controversy to be generated by a catalogue, a resource for teachers and librarians, a book not designed to be read from cover to cover. The authors, Linda Artel, film consultant at the Pacific Film Archive, and Susan Wengraf, a filmmaker and educational media consultant, spent over two years in research previewing films and talking with teachers and librarians. The project culminated in this guide to over 400 films, videotapes, slide shows, filmstrips, and photographs, which in some manner deal with the problem of sex roles.

As such, *Positive Images* seems to be an extremely valuable resource. Not only do the authors cite films that have received attention in recent years, such as *Growing Up Female* (1971), *Union Maids* (1977), *The San Francisco Women's Film* (1971), they also unearth many unusual films that do not make the usual circuit of Women in Film courses and film festivals. (For example, I was unaware of the existence of *What Eighty Million Women Want*, 1913, an early suffrage film produced by Emmeline Pankhurst, much less of its rental cost or where it could be obtained.) The authors perform another service in that they have included a few films they do not recommend *because* "they are being widely and erroneously publicized as non-sexist."

Positive Images, then, performs the valuable function of helping teachers supplement and plan their courses. In addition, as the authors themselves note in their preface, they discovered:

> that some of the most exciting and effective non-sexist media are being distributed by independent filmmakers, feminist groups, and small, alternative companies. Providing information about these little known resources has become an important aspect of the guide, since such sources do not have the financial means for large-scale publicity campaigns.

Having stated what I find to be valuable and useful about the book, I now wish to state my reservations. My criticisms fall into two categories: first, the criteria involved in determining what is to be considered a "positive image," and second, the limits of the very notion of "positive image" itself.

In their foreword, the authors describe the "guidelines for selection and evaluation." This immediately introduces a problem on the theoretical level: what are "positive" characteristics, and what is the relationship of these images to the social reality? This problem can be articulated more explicitly if we look at the contradictions embodied in the pun that constitutes the title *Positive Images*.

When we speak of a "positive image" in film or photography, we mean that the lights and shades correspond to those of the original subject; indeed, by extension, one meaning of the word "positive" in a general sense is "concerned only with real things and experience; empirical." On the other hand, "positive" also means "affirmative," or "tending in the direction regarded as that of progress," or "constructive." Judging from the above criteria, both meanings are employed, but then we must ask, in ascribing "positive characteristics" to certain depictions are we claiming a truth value for them? Do they depict things as they really are, or as we think they should be? How do we deal with the reality of sexism as it currently exists? Because these questions are not raised by the authors, a tension between "things as they are" and "things as they should be" informs many of the film descriptions.

Let us see how the above criteria work in practice. At times they seem to be applied too narrowly, without regard for specific cultural situation or historical context. For example, the entry for *Boran Women* (1975):

> In a cattle raising community in Northern Kenya, the women perform the traditional tasks of child-rearing and food preparation while the men manage the herds. Although the women are also responsible for building the cowhide covered dwellings, this too is viewed as "women's work."

Does the term "traditional tasks" refer to a western tradition of sexual division of labor? Is the film included, then, because women are responsible for the "non-traditional" (in the western sense) task of building the dwellings, but then critiqued because even this is viewed as "women's work"? Is this a critique of the film, or a critique of the Boran culture?

In addition, this measuring of a film's worth against a checklist of "positive" characteristics can seem silly, as in the case of *Janie Sue and Tugaloo*:

> Eight year old Janie Sue lives on a farm and wants to become an accomplished rider. Her goal is respected by her grandfather who teaches her how to control her horse and how to herd cattle. Janie Sue handles her

> horse well and demonstrates perseverance in learning this skill. Unfortunately, the film shows her several times trying to corner a cow, but never gives us the satisfaction of seeing her succeed.

The authors seem to fault the film for leaving us with a sense of struggle or process instead of supplying the inevitable "happy ending."

The authors can also be humorless, as in the case of their description of *Free to Be You or Me* (1974).

> One animated sequence, "Ladies First," by humorist Shel Silverstein, is actually misogynist. A prissy little girl has always insisted that "ladies go first." When she and her friends are captured by hungry tigers, [the animals] say, "Ladies first," and eat her first. This story is an inappropriate way to convince little girls or boys that chivalry is ridiculous and even destructive.

Or they can be even cruelly absurd, as in *A Day in the Life of Bonnie Consolo*:

> Bonnie Consolo introduces herself and tells us that she was born without arms. We see Bonnie do an amazing array of tasks with her feet and legs. She cooks dinner, bakes bread, cans fruit, drives, shops, kills a fly, puts on a necklace, cuts her son's hair, and then hugs him. Although performing domestic duties that do not challenge the traditional female role, Bonnie does present the image of a woman who has overcome her particular obstacle with immense strength and courage.

One wonders whether Bonnie Consolo would have to operate a fork-lift before presenting a totally "positive image" in the authors' terms.

Similarly, we might question the authors' tendency to critique a film for presenting a woman in relation to history in lieu of concentrating on biographical information. Take, for example, *The Eleanor Roosevelt Story* (1965): "The film loses sight of Mrs. Roosevelt as it chronicles historic events." Or *Margaret Sanger* (1972):

> Unfortunately, this film spends very little time on the life of Margaret Sanger, the courageous, vital woman who defied societal taboos to create family planning clinics in America. Rather, the film documents the development of family planning and the problem of population explosion, using historic photographs along with early and contemporary motion picture footage.

Do we, as teachers, want to convey a history composed of the lives of "great women" merely to replace or supplement the dominant bourgeois histories of "great men"? Incidentally, by 1916 this "courageous, vital woman" was presenting birth control as the solution to working-class misery and as a means of controlling the birth rate of the "unfit."[1]

This brings me to another major point: the book employs a pluralistic conception of what constitutes a "positive image." The authors often lump together films that clearly represent different class interests, different types of role models, and discuss all with equal enthusiasm. I am reminded of the scene in *Adam's Rib* (1949) in which three women are brought into court by Katharine Hepburn to demonstrate women's equality and/or superiority over men: a forewoman in a factory, an incredibly strong acrobat, and a scientist with various degrees from prestigious universities and a specialty in biological warfare.

In *Positive Images*, for example, on p. 119 we find the *Are You Listening?* (1976) videotape series described as "a series of sincere and direct discussions among groups of people who are often talked about, but rarely listened to, in our society." Although these groups include "Black High School Girls" and "Welfare Mothers," they also include "Men Who Are Working with Women in Management," a group of male executives at AT&T, "Women in Management," and "Women in Middle Management." These latter two videotapes, ironically juxtaposed with an entry on *Women and Children in China* (1975), include a "discussion among women in management—a general in the army, a university president, corporation executives, and government officials. The wide-ranging discussion covers many important issues: the need to bring a new kind of humanism to management; to avoid playing by 'men's rules'."

On the following page we have *Women Workers* (1974), in which the director of trade union women's studies at the New York State School of Industrial and Labor Relations at Cornell talks with a union organizer for the Distributive Workers of America. "They believe that there is a new consciousness among office workers who are banding together for better wages and job conditions." How would this "new consciousness," one wonders, accord with the "new humanism" of the women in management?

In all fairness to the authors, both of these entries contain the "Not Previewed" designation. The authors in their introduction do note that "certain films present a viable alternative for women and men in the upper-middle class, but are of less relevance to people in other economic situations" and do include critical comments covering assumptions about class in films such as *Art of Age* (1971) and *Careers: Women in Careers* (1973). It is possible that a more critical analysis would have been included had they previewed a film such as *Women in Management* (1976).

However, something about the phrase "are of less relevance to people in other economic situations" seems to be slightly amiss: it accepts as a given the structure that permits those "other economic situations" to exist, and fails to distinguish those role models that serve to perpetuate it from those that actively challenge it. This failure to distinguish between types of "positive image" is, of course, not unique to this catalogue but has plagued the feminist movement from its inception, splitting those feminists who sought liberation and equality through solidarity with other oppressed groups and a radical transformation of society from those who wanted an equal share in the power structure as it existed, often at the expense of other oppressed groups. (For example, certain members of the suffrage movement consciously appealed to racist, nativist, and class sentiments in attempting to obtain the vote for women: "There is but one way to avert the danger [of the influence of 'undesirables']," argued Carrie Chapman Catt in 1894, "Cut off the vote of the slums and give it to women."[2])

Positive Images seems to be predicated upon a notion of a sexist society and media, but with little analysis of how this sexism functions in an advanced industrial capitalist society. In the authors' introduction, they describe the media as "controlled by men" and "notoriously sexist," but this is the extent of the analysis. It is little wonder, then, that the authors state, "The powerful effect of media can be refocused to question destructive patterns and demonstrate credible options," and that "Film and video can be highly effective tools for introducing new, non-sexist values and encouraging awareness of alternative possibilities for growth," without any indication of the magnitude of the problems involved: ownership of production, access to distribution networks, or transformation of society at large.

But this brings me to my second major criticism of this catalogue—the very notion of "positive image" as a critical concept and a pedagogical tool. The notion of "positive image" is predicated upon the assumption of *identification* of the spectator with a character depicted in a film. It has an historical precedent in the "positive hero" and "heroine" of socialist realism. It assumes that most of what children see are "negative images," distorted stereotypes, and that the corrective to this is exposure to "positive images" or non-sexist role models.

Yet the mechanism of identification goes unchallenged and unchanged, and introduces, I think, a kind of complacency associated with merely presenting an image of the "positive" hero(ine). That this attitude informs this catalogue can be demonstrated by quoting from the authors' instructions on "How to Use Visual Media for Greatest Effectiveness." We are told that "non-sexist visual media used in conjunction with books should be integrated into every part of the curriculum" and that "when students read texts and library books or watch films that do perpetuate sex-role stereotypes, discussion is essential to develop critical thinking." I would strongly emphasize this last sentence, but would extend the "necessary discussion" to those materials deemed "non-sexist" as well. For if the mechanism of identification goes unchallenged, how are students to distinguish between "positive" and "negative" images?

And more importantly, does this concept allow or does it mitigate against the development of those critical tools so necessary for dealing with the dominant media and society? If, as the authors say, "children spend more time watching TV than going to school," and, as a friend who teaches in a daycare center remarked, "Two minutes of the Six Million Dollar Man can counteract the effects of my teaching of non-sexist values for both boys and girls," then perhaps, as teachers, we should stress analysis, critical distance, and discussion of *any* material we use rather than rely upon the identification implied by the "positive image" concept.

Put another way, we should remember that meaning is to be located in the interaction between reader and image and not in the images themselves. This is stressed in an article by Elizabeth Cowie in *Screen Education*:

> Sexism in an image cannot be designated materially as a content in the way that denotative elements such as colours or objects in the image can be pointed to. Rather it is in the development of new or different definitions and understandings of what men and women are and in their roles in society which produces readings of images as sexist; the political perspective of feminism produces a further level of connotative reading.[3]

This latter point can be affirmed by anyone who has had the curious experience of re-reading or re-viewing a book or film and reacting in disgust and amazement not only at the representations but at one's former neutrality or even delight in those same representations.

We certainly should attack blatant sexual stereotypes and applaud "positive images" when they do appear: that these media images *do* serve to shape children's attitudes, behaviors, and expectations is undeniable. And I don't want to diminish the work which went into the compilation of this catalogue or the potential usefulness of *Positive Images*. My criticisms are intended to indicate the limits of the "positive image" concept and to demonstrate some of the important pedagogical issues that underlie such a compilation.

NOTES

1. From David Kennedy, *Birth Control in America: The Career of Margaret Sanger* (New Haven, Conn: 1970), p. 112, quoted in Eli Zaretsky, *Capitalism, the Family and Personal Life* (New York: Harper and Row, 1976), p. 123.

2. Cited in Ailen Kraditor, ed., *Up From the Pedestal* (Chicago, 1970), p. 125, quoted in William H. Chafe, *The American Woman: Her Changing Social, Economic and Political Roles, 1920–1970* (New York: Oxford University Press, 1972), pp. 14–15; see also Catharine Stimpson's " 'Thy Neighbor's Wife, Thy Neighbor's Servants': Women's Liberation and Black Civil Rights," in Vivian Gornick and Barbara K. Moran, eds., *Women in Sexist Society* (New York: Basic Books, 1971), pp. 622–57.

3. Elizabeth Cowie, "Women, Representation and the Image," *Screen Education* 23 (Summer 1977): 19.

THE PLACE OF WOMAN IN THE CINEMA OF RAOUL WALSH

Pam Cook and Claire Johnston

Between 1956 and 1957 Raoul Walsh made three films which center around the social, cultural, and sexual definition of women. At first sight, the role of woman within these films appears a "positive" one; they display a great independence of spirit, and contrast sharply with the apparent "weakness" of the male protagonists. The first film in this cycle depicts a woman occupying the central function in the narrative; the Jane Russell vehicle, *The Revolt of Mamie Stover*, tells the story of a bar-room hostess's attempts to buck the system and acquire wealth and social status within patriarchy. *The King and Four Queens*, made the same year, depicts five women who hide out in a burnt-out ghost town to guard hidden gold. *Band of Angels*, made the following year, tells the story of a Southern heiress who suddenly finds herself sold into slavery at the time of the American Civil War. Walsh prefigured the problematic of the independent woman before this period, most notably in a series of films he made in the 1940s, some of which starred the actress Ida Lupino, who later became one of the few women filmmakers to work in Hollywood: *They Drive by Night*, *High Sierra*, and *The Man I Love*. However, undoubtedly the most useful films for providing a reference point for this cycle are *Manpower* (1941) and *The Bowery* (1933); in these films, Walsh celebrates the ethic of the all-male group, and outlines the role which women are designated to play within it. Walsh depicts the male hero as being trapped and pinned down by some hidden event in his past. In order to become the Subject of Desire he must test the Law through transgression. To gain self-knowledge and to give meaning to memories of the past, he is impelled towards the primal scene and to the acceptance of a symbolic castration. For the male hero the female protagonist becomes an agent within the text of the film whereby his hidden secret can be brought to light, for it is in woman that his "lack" is located. She represents at one and the same time the distant memory of maternal plenitude and the fetishized object of his fantasy of castration—a phallic replacement and thus a threat. In *Manpower* Walsh depicts an all-male universe verging on infantilism—the camaraderie of the fire-fighters from the "Ministry of Power and Light." Sexual relationships and female sexuality are repressed within the film, and Marlene Dietrich is depicted as only having an existence within the discourse of men: she is "spoken," she does not speak. As an object of exchange between men, a sign oscillating between the images of prostitute and mother-figure, she represents the means by which men express their relationships with each other, the means through which they come to understand themselves and each other. *The Bowery* presents a similar all-male society, this time based totally on internal all-male rivalry; within this highly ritualized system the women ("the skirts") assume the function of symbols of this rivalry. Whatever the "positive" attributes assigned to them through characterization, woman as sign remains a function, a token of exchange in this patriarchal order. Paul Willemen in his article on *Pursued* describes the role of the female protagonist Theresa Wright/Thorley as the "specular image" of the male protagonist Robert Mitchum/Jeb: she is the place where he deposits his words in a desire to "know" himself through her.

In her book *Psychoanalysis and Feminism* Juliet Mitchell, citing Lévi-Strauss, characterizes a system where women are objects for exchange as essentially a communications system.

> The act of exchange holds a society together: the rules of kinship (like those of language to which they are near-allied) are the society. Whatever the nature of the society—patriarchal, matrilineal, patrilineal, etc.—it is always men who exchange women. Women thus become the equivalent of a sign which is being communicated.

In Walsh's oeuvre, woman is not only a sign in a system of exchange, but an empty sign. (The major exception in this respect is Mamie Stover, who seeks to transform her status as object for exchange precisely by compounding a highly articulated, fetishized image for herself.) The male protagonist's castration fears, his search for self-knowledge all converge on woman: it is in her that he is finally faced with the recognition of "lack." Woman is therefore the locus of emptiness: she is a sign which is defined negatively: something that is missing which must be located so that the narcissistic aim of the male protagonist can be achieved. The narrative structure of *Band of Angels* is particularly interesting in the light of this model. The first half of the story is concerned with events in Manty/Yvonne de Carlo's life which reduce her from the position of a lady to that of a slave to be auctioned in the slave market. Almost exactly half way through the story—at the "center" of the film—Clark Gable appears and takes possession of her: from that moment the unfolding of his "dark secret" takes precedence. It becomes clear that Manty/Yvonne de Carlo's story was merely a device to bring into play the background (the slave trade, crumbling Southern capitalism) against which the "real" drama is to take place. Manty/Yvonne de Carlo is created in Clark Gable's image: half black and half white, she signifies the lost secret which must be found in order to resolve the relationship between Clark Gable and Sidney Poitier—the "naturalization" of the slave trade.

One of the most interesting aspects of this mise-en-scène of exchange in which woman as sign is located is the way Walsh relates it directly and explicitly to the circulation of money within the text of the film. Marx states that under capitalism the exchange value of commodities is their inherent monetary property and that in turn money achieves a social existence quite apart from all commodities and their natural mode of existence. The circulation of money and its abstraction as a sign in a system of exchange serves as a mirror image for woman as sign in a system of exchange. However, in Walsh's universe, women do not have access to the circulation of money: Mamie Stover's attempt to gain access to it takes place at a time of national emergency, the bombing of Pearl Harbor, when all the men are away fighting—it is described as "theft." As a system, the circulation of money embodies phallic power and the right of possession; it is a system by which women are controlled. In *Band of Angels* Manty/Yvonne de Carlo is reduced to a chattel and exchanged for money on the slave market; she is exchanged for money because of her father's "dark secret" and because of his debt. In *The King and Four Queens* the women guard the gold but they cannot gain access to it directly. Its phallic power lies hidden in the grave of a dead husband, surrounded by sterility and devastation. Clark Gable gains access to it by asserting his right of possession by means of tossing a gold coin in the air and shooting a bullet through the middle of it, a trick which the absent males of the family all knew: the mark of the right of possession. The ticket system in *The Revolt of Mamie Stover* takes the analogy between money and women one stage further: men buy tickets at "The Bungalow" and at the same time they buy an image of woman. It is the symbolic expression of the right men have to control women within their imaginary system. This link between money and phallic power assumes its most striking image in Walsh's oeuvre when Jane Russell/Mamie, having accumulated considerable savings as a bar hostess in Pearl Harbor, declares her love for Richard Egan/Jimmy by asking him if she can place these savings in his safety deposit box at the bank: "there's nothing closer between friends than money." Recognizing the significance of such a proposition, he refuses.

The Revolt of Mamie Stover is the only one of these films in which the female protagonist represents the central organizing principle of the text. As the adventuress *par excellence* she is impelled to test and transgress the Law in the same way that all Walsh's heroes do: she would seem to function at first sight in a similar way to her male counterpart, the adventurer, within the narrative structure. But as the film reveals, her relationship to the Law is radically different. Her drive is not to test and transgress the Law as a means towards understanding a hidden secret within her past, but to transgress the forms of representation governing the classic cinema itself, which imprison her forever within an image. As the credits of the film appear on the screen, Jane Russell looks into the camera with defiance, before turning her back on America and walking off to a new life in Pearl Harbor. This look, itself a transgression of one of the classic rules of cinematography (i.e., "don't look into the camera") serves as a reference point for what is to follow. Asserting herself as the subject rather than the object of desire, this look into the camera represents a reaching out beyond the diegetic space of the film and the myths of representation which entrap her. The central contradiction of her situation is that she can only attempt to assert herself as subject through the exploitation of a fetishized image of woman to be exchanged within the circulation of money; her independence and her desire for social and economic status all hinge on this objectification. The forms of representation generated by the classic cinema—the myths of woman as pin-up, vamp, "Mississippi Cinderella"—are the only means by which she can achieve the objective of becoming the subject rather than the object of desire. The futility of this enterprise is highlighted at the end of the film when she returns once more to America in a similar sequence of shots; this time she no longer looks towards the camera, but remains trapped within the diegetic space which the film has allotted to her.

The film opens with a long-shot of a neon-lit city at night. Red letters appear on the screen telling us the time and place: SAN FRANCISCO 1941. *The Revolt of Mamie Stover* was made in 1956—the story is therefore set within the living memory/history of the spectator. This title is the first indication that the film will reactivate the memory of an anxiogenic situation: the traumatic moment of the attack on Pearl Harbor and the entry of the United States into the Second World War. Simultaneously, on the sound band, sleazy night-club music swells up (clip-joints, predatory prostitution, female sexuality exchanged for money at a time when the country, its male population, and its financial resources are about to be put at risk). A police car (one of the many representations of the Law in the film) its siren wailing insistently over the music (a further indication of imminent danger) drives fast onto a dockside where a ship is waiting. As it draws up alongside the ship, a female figure carrying a coat and a small suitcase gets out of the car and appears to turn back to look at the city from which she has obviously been expelled in a hurry. Jane Russell then looks straight into the camera (see above).

Up to this point the text has been multiply coded to signify danger/threat. The threat is closely associated with sexuality—besides the music, the red letters on the screen indicate red for danger and red for sex. Paul Willemen has pointed out that the "look" in *Pursued* is a threatening object: the *Cahiers du cinéma* analysis of *Young Mr. Lincoln* also delineates Henry Fonda/Lincoln's "castrating stare" as having the same threatening significance. Besides this threatening "look," Jane Russell has other dangerous connotations: qualities of aggression, of preying on the male to attain her own ends. Her "look"—repeated many times during the film, directed towards men, and explicitly described at one point as "come hither"—doubly marks her as signifier of threat. In the absence of the male, the female might "take his place": at the moment of Jane Russell's "look" at the camera, the spectator is directly confronted with the image of that threat. The fact that this image has been expelled from a previous situation is also important: Jane Russell actually represents the repudiated idea: she *is* that idea. Thus the threat is simultaneously recognized and recuperated: the female cannot "take the place" of the male; she can only be "in his place"—his mirror image—the "you" which is the "I" in another place.

This moment of dual fascination between the spectator and Jane Russell is broken by the intervention of a third organizing principle representing the narrative, as the titles in red letters "Jane Russell Richard Egan" appear over the female figure. The title has the effect of immediately distancing the spectator: it reminds him of the symbolic role of the narrative by locating Jane Russell as an imaginary figure. In psychoanalytic terms the concept "imaginary" is more complex than the word would immediately seem to imply. It is a concept central to the Lacanian formulation of the "mirror stage" in which the "other" is apprehended as the "other which is me," i.e., my mirror image. In the imaginary relationship the other is seen in terms of resemblance to oneself. As an imaginary figure in the text of the film Jane Russell's "masculine" attributes are emphasised: square jaw, broad shoulders, narrow hips, swinging, almost swashbuckling walk—"phallic" attributes which are echoed and re-echoed in the text; for example, in her aggressive language—she tells a wolf-whistling soldier to "go mend your rifle, soldier"; when Richard Egan/Jimmy fights Michael Pate/Atkins at the Country Club she shouts "give him one for me, Jimmy." The girls at "The Bungalow" hail her as "Abe Lincoln Stover." Jane Russell/Mamie is the imaginary *counterpart* of the absent spectator and the absent subject of the text: the mirror image they have mutually constructed and in whom both images converge and overlap.

Again, borrowing from Lacan, the function of the "Symbolic" is to intervene in the imaginary situation and to integrate the subject into the Symbolic Order (which is ultimately the Law, the Name of the Father). The narrative of *The Revolt of Mamie Stover,* in that it presents a particular model of the world historically, culturally, and ideologically overdetermined, could be said to perform a symbolic function for the absent spectator. The anxiety-generating displacement Jane Russell/Mamie appears to threaten the narrative at certain points. For example, after having promised to marry Richard Egan/Jimmy, give up her job at "The Bungalow," and become "exclusively his," and having taken his ring in a symbolic exchange which is "almost like the real thing" and "makes it legal," Jane Russell/Mamie leaves her man at the army camp and returns to "The Bungalow" to resign. However, she is persuaded by Agnes Moorhead/ Bertha Parchman to continue working there, now that Michael Pate/Atkins has gone (been expelled), for a bigger share of the profits and more power. Richard Egan/Jimmy is absent, so he won't know. His absence is important: it recalls another sequence earlier in the narrative which shows in a quick succession of shots Richard Egan/Jimmy and the army away at war while Jane Russell/Mamie is at the same moment buying up all the available property on the island, becoming "Sto-Mame Company Incorporated" with Uncle Sam as her biggest tenant. Jane Russell/Mamie makes her biggest strides in the absence of men: she threatens to take over the power of exchange. By promising to marry and give it all up, she is reintegrated into an order where she no longer represents that threat. Richard Egan/ Jimmy can be seen as the representative of the absent spectator and absent subject of the discourse in this structure: they are mutual constructors of the text—he is a writer who is constantly trying to write Jane Russell/ Mamie's story for her. When Jane Russell/Mamie goes back to work at "The Bungalow" she in effect negates his image of her in favor of an image which suggests destruction and purging—"Flaming Mamie"—and becomes again a threatening displacement, reproduced and enlarged 7 foot high. When Richard Egan/Jimmy is confronted with this threatening image at the army camp, when a soldier shows him a photograph of her, a bomb drops and he is wounded. In the face of this renewed threat he returns to "The Bungalow" and in his final speech to Jane Russell/Mamie repudiates her as his imaginary counterpart; the narcissistic fascination with her is ended; he realizes he can no longer control her image.

The symbolic level of the narrative in maintaining its order in the face of a threat is reasserted in the final sequence where the policeman at the dockside re-echoes Richard Egan/Jimmy's words of rejection: "Nothing's changed, Mamie. You aren't welcome here." Jane Russell/Mamie replies that she is going home to Leesburg, Mississippi (this is what Richard Egan/ Jimmy was always telling her she must do). When the policeman remarks that she does not seem to have done too well, she replies: "If I told you I had made a fortune and given it all away, would you believe me?" When he says "No," she replies "I thought so." This exchange contains a final assertion that the protagonist cannot write her own story: she is a signifier, an object of exchange in a play of desire between the absent subject and object of the discourse. She remains "spoken": she does not speak. The final rhetorical question seals her defeat.

On the plane of the image, the symbolic order is maintained by an incessant production, within the text, of images for and of Jane Russell/ Mamie from which she is unable to escape, and with which she complies through a mise-en-scène of exchange. In order to become the subject of desire, she is compelled to be the object of desire, and the images she "chooses" remain locked within the myths of representation governed by patriarchy. This mise-en-scène of exchange is initiated by her expulsion by the police at the dockside—the image of predatory whore is established. This image is elaborated during the next scene when the ship's steward tells Richard Egan/Jimmy about her reputation as sexual predator ("she ain't no lady"). Mamie interrupts the conversation, and realizing that Richard Egan/Jimmy as a scriptwriter in Hollywood is interested in her, she suggests he should write and buy her story—the hard-luck story of a "Mississippi Cinderella." Growing emotional involvement with him leads her to reject the idea of being "written" in favor of "writing" her own story, and to seek out an image more consistent with the wealthy "hilltop" milieu of which Richard Egan/Jimmy is part, epitomized by Jimmy's girlfriend ("Miss Hilltop"). Jane Russell/Mamie asks Richard Egan/Jimmy to "dress her up and teach her how to behave"; he refuses. Their relationship from then on is characterized as one of transgression: they "dance without tickets" at the country club, away from the "four don'ts" of "The Bungalow." For her image as a performer and hostess at "The Bungalow" Jane Russell/Mamie has dyed her hair red and has assumed the name of "Flaming Mamie" ("Mamie's not beer or whisky, she's champagne only"). The image of "Flaming Mamie" is at one and the same time an assertion and a negation of female sexuality; sexually arousing ("Fellas who try to resist should hire a psychiatrist" intones the song) but at the same time the locus of sexual taboo ("Keep the eyes on the hands" she says in another number—they tell the story). It is at "The Bungalow" that the ticket system formalizes this mise-en-scène of exchange; men literally buy an image for a predetermined period of time. (It is this concept of exchange of images which Jane Russell/Mamie finally discards when she throws the ticket away as she leaves the boat at the end of the film.) Reduced once again to the image of common prostitute when they go dancing at the country club and having decided to stay at "The Bungalow" in spite of Richard Egan/Jimmy, she finally assumes the iconography of the pin-up, with the "come hither" look; an image emptied of all personality or individuality; an image based on the effects of pure gesture. This image was prefigured in an extraordinary sequence at the beach when Jane Russell/Mamie jumps up from the sand where she has been sitting with Richard Egan/Jimmy in order to take a swim. As she does so, she turns back to look at him and her image becomes frozen into the vacant grin of a bathing suit advertisement. Talking about money, Jane Russell/Mamie describes herself at one point as a "have not"; this recurrent imbrication of images, the telling of story within a story which the film generates through a mise-en-scène of exchange, serves to repress the idea of female sexuality and to encase Jane Russell/Mamie within the symbolic order, the Law of the Father.

Walsh criticism to date has been dominated by the notion of "personality"; like the American adventurer *par excellence* he so often depicts, Walsh, as one of the oldest pioneers, has come to be regarded as of the essence of what is called "classic" Hollywood cinema—a cinema characterized traditionally by its linearity, its transparency: in short, the effect of "non-writing." Andrew Sarris has even gone so far as to say of him: "only the most virile director can effectively project a feminine vulnerability in his characters." This notion of authorship has been criticized by Stephen Heath in the following terms: "the function of the author (the effect of the idea of authorship) is a function of unity; the use of the notion of the author involves the organisation of the film . . . and in so doing, it avoids—this is indeed its function—the thinking of the articulation of the film text in relation to ideology." A view of Walsh as the originating consciousness of the Walsh oeuvre is, therefore, an ideological concept. To attribute such qualities as "virility" to Walsh is to foreclose the recognition of Walsh as subject within ideology. This feminist reading of the Walsh oeuvre rejects any approach which would attempt to delineate the role of women in terms of the influence of ideology or sociology, as such an approach is merely a strategy to supplement auteur analysis. We have attempted to provide a reading of the Walsh oeuvre which takes as its starting point Walsh as a subject within ideology and, ultimately, the laws of the human order. What concerns us specifically is the delineation of the ideology of patriarchy—by which we mean the Law of the Father—within the text of the film. As Lévi-Strauss has indicated: "The emergence of symbolic thought must have required that women, like works, should be things that were exchanged." The tasks for feminist criticism must therefore consist of a process of de-naturalization: a questioning of the unity of the text; of seeing it as a contradictory interplay of different codes; of tracing its "structuring absences" and its relationship to the universal problem of symbolic castration. It is in this sense that a feminist strategy for the cinema must be understood. Only when such work has been done can a foundation for a feminist counter-cinema be established. Woman as signifier of woman under patriarchy is totally absent in most image-producing systems, but particularly in Hollywood where image-making and the fetishistic position of the spectator are highly developed. This is indeed why a study of "woman" within the Hollywood system is of great interest. A study of woman within Walsh's oeuvre, in particular, reveals "woman" as the locus of a dilemma for the patriarchal human order, as a locus of contradictions. *Cahiers du cinéma* in an editorial described such texts in the following terms: "an internal criticism is taking place which cracks the film apart at the seams. If one reads the film obliquely, looking for symptoms, if one looks beyond its apparent coherence one can see that it is riddled with cracks; it is splitting under an internal tension which is simply not there in an ideologically innocuous film. The ideology thus becomes subordinate to the text. It no longer has an independent existence; it is presented by the film." The function of "woman" in Walsh as the locus of "lack," as an empty sign to be filled, the absent center of a phallocentric universe marks the first step towards the de-naturalization of woman in the Hollywood cinema. In a frenzied imbrication of images (*The Revolt of Mamie Stover*) the Phallus is restored; but in this distanciation the first notes of the "swan-song of the immortal nature of patriarchal culture" (*cf.* Juliet Mitchell) can be heard.

VISUAL PLEASURE AND NARRATIVE CINEMA

Laura Mulvey

Introduction

A Political Use of Psychoanalysis

This paper intends to use psychoanalysis to discover where and how the fascination of film is reinforced by pre-existing patterns of fascination already at work within the individual subject and the social formations that have molded him. It takes as a starting point the way film reflects, reveals, and even plays on the straight, socially established interpretation of sexual difference which controls images, erotic ways of looking, and spectacle. It is helpful to understand what the cinema has been, how its magic has worked in the past, while attempting a theory and a practice which will challenge this cinema of the past. Psychoanalytic theory is thus appropriated here as a political weapon, demonstrating the way the unconscious of patriarchal society has structured film form.

The paradox of phallocentrism in all its manifestations is that it depends on the image of the castrated woman to give order and meaning to its world. An idea of woman stands as lynch pin to the system: it is her lack that produces the phallus as a symbolic presence, it is her desire to make good the lack that the phallus signifies. Recent writing in *Screen* about psychoanalysis and the cinema has not sufficiently brought out the importance of the representation of the female form in a symbolic order in which, in the last resort, it speaks castration and nothing else. To summarize briefly: the function of woman in forming the patriarchal unconscious is twofold, she first symbolizes the castration threat by her real absence of a penis and second thereby raises her child into the symbolic. Once this has been achieved, her meaning in the process is at an end, it does not last into the world of law and language except as a memory, which oscillates between memory of maternal plenitude and memory of lack. Both are posited on nature (or on anatomy in Freud's famous phrase).

Woman's desire is subjected to her image as bearer of the bleeding wound, she can exist only in relation to castration and cannot transcend it. She turns her child into the signifier of her own desire to possess a penis (the condition, she imagines, of entry into the symbolic). Either she must gracefully give way to the word, the Name of the Father and the Law, or else struggle to keep her child down with her in the half-light of the imaginary. Woman then stands in patriarchal culture as signifier for the male other, bound by a symbolic order in which man can live out his fantasies and obsessions through linguistic command by imposing them on the silent image of woman still tied to her place as bearer of meaning, not maker of meaning.

There is an obvious interest in this analysis for feminists, a beauty in its exact rendering of the frustration experienced under the phallocentric order. It gets us nearer to the roots of our oppression, it brings an articulation of the problem closer, it faces us with the ultimate challenge: how to fight the unconscious structured like a language (formed critically at the moment of arrival of language) while still caught within the language of the patriarchy. There is no way in which we can produce an alternative out of the blue, but we can begin to make a break by examining patriarchy with the tools it provides, of which psychoanalysis is not the only but an important one. We are still separated by a great gap from important issues for the female unconscious which are scarcely relevant to phallocentric theory: the sexing of the female infant and her relationship to the symbolic, the sexually mature woman as non-mother, maternity outside the signification of the phallus, the vagina. But, at this point, psychoanalytic theory as it now stands can at least advance our understanding of the status quo, of the patriarchal order in which we are caught.

Destruction of Pleasure as a Radical Weapon

As an advanced representation system, the cinema poses questions of the ways the unconscious (formed by the dominant order) structures ways of seeing and pleasure in looking. Cinema has changed over the last few decades. It is no longer the monolithic system based on large capital investment exemplified at its best by Hollywood in the 1930s, 1940s, and 1950s. Technological advances (16mm, etc.) have changed the economic conditions of cinematic production, which can now be artisanal as well as capitalist. Thus it has been possible for an alternative cinema to develop. However self-conscious and ironic Hollywood managed to be, it always restricted itself to a formal mise-en-scène reflecting the dominant ideological concept of the cinema. The alternative cinema provides a space for a cinema to be born which is radical in both a political and an aesthetic sense and challenges the basic assumptions of the mainstream film. This is not to reject the latter moralistically, but to highlight the ways in which its formal preoccupations reflect the psychical obsessions of the society which produced it, and, further, to stress that the alternative cinema must start specifically by reacting against these obsessions and assumptions. A politically and aesthetically avant-garde cinema is now possible, but it can still only exist as a counterpoint.

The magic of the Hollywood style at its best (and of all the cinema which fell within its sphere of influence) arose, not exclusively, but in one important aspect, from its skilled and satisfying manipulation of visual pleasure. Unchallenged, mainstream film coded the erotic into the language of the dominant patriarchal order. In the highly developed Hollywood cinema it was only through these codes that the alienated subject, torn in his imaginary memory by a sense of loss, by the terror of potential lack in fantasy, came near to finding a glimpse of satisfaction: through its formal beauty and its play on his own formative obsessions. This essay will discuss the interweaving of that erotic pleasure in film, its meaning, and in particular the central place of the image of woman. It is said that analyzing pleasure, or beauty, destroys it. That is the intention of this essay. The satisfaction and reinforcement of the ego that represent the high point of film history hitherto must be attacked. Not in favor of a reconstructed new pleasure, which cannot exist in the abstract, nor of intellectualized unpleasure, but to make way for a total negation of the ease and plenitude of the narrative fiction film. The alternative is the thrill that comes from leaving the past behind without rejecting it, transcending outworn or oppressive forms, or daring to break with normal pleasurable expectations in order to conceive a new language of desire.

Pleasure in Looking/Fascination with the Human Form

A. The cinema offers a number of possible pleasures. One is scopophilia. There are circumstances in which looking itself is a source of pleasure, just as, in the reverse formation, there is pleasure in being looked at. Originally, in his *Three Essays on Sexuality*, Freud isolated scopophilia as one of the component instincts of sexuality which exist as drives quite independently of the erotogenic zones. At this point he associated scopophilia with taking other people as objects, subjecting them to a controlling and curious gaze. His particular examples center around the voyeuristic activities of children, their desire to see and make sure of the private and the forbidden (curiosity about other people's genital and bodily functions, about the presence or absence of the penis and, retrospectively, about the primal scene). In this analysis scopophilia is essentially active. (Later, in *Instincts and Their Vicissitudes*, Freud developed his theory of scopophilia further, attaching it initially to pre-genital autoeroticism, after which the pleasure of the look is transferred to others by analogy. There is a close working here of the relationship between the active instinct and its further development in a narcissistic form.) Although the instinct is modified by other factors, in particular the constitution of the ego, it continues to exist as the erotic basis for pleasure in looking at another person as object. At the extreme, it can become fixated into a perversion, producing obsessive voyeurs and Peeping Toms whose only sexual satisfaction can come from watching, in an active controlling sense, an objectified other.

At first glance, the cinema would seem to be remote from the undercover world of the surreptitious observation of an unknowing and unwilling victim. What is seen on the screen is so manifestly shown. But the mass of mainstream film, and the conventions within which it has consciously evolved, portray a hermetically sealed world which unwinds magically, indifferent to the presence of the audience, producing for them a sense of separation and playing on their voyeuristic fantasy. Moreover, the extreme contrast between the darkness in the auditorium (which also isolates the spectators from one another) and the brilliance of the shifting patterns of light and shade on the screen helps to promote the illusion of voyeuristic separation. Although the film is really being shown, is there to be seen, conditions of screening and narrative conventions give the spectator an illusion of looking in on a private world. Among other things, the position of the spectators in the cinema is blatantly one of repression of their exhibitionism and projection of the repressed desire onto the performer.

B. The cinema satisfies a primordial wish for pleasurable looking, but it also goes further, developing scopophilia in its narcissistic aspect. The conventions of mainstream film focus attention on the human form. Scale, space, stories are all anthropomorphic. Here, curiosity and the wish to look intermingle with a fascination with likeness and recognition: the human face, the human body, the relationship between the human form and its surroundings, the visible presence of the person in the world. Jacques Lacan has described how the moment when a child recognizes its own image in the mirror is crucial for the constitution of the ego. Several aspects of this analysis are relevant here. The mirror phase occurs at a time when the child's physical ambitions outstrip his motor capacity, with the result that his recognition of himself is joyous in that he imagines his mirror image to be more complete, more perfect than he experiences his own body. Recognition is thus overlaid with misrecognition: the image recognized is conceived as the reflected body of the self, but its misrecognition as superior projects this body outside itself as an ideal ego, the alienated subject, which, reintrojected as an ego ideal, gives rise to the future generation of identification with others. This mirror moment predates language for the child.

Important for this article is the fact that it is an image that constitutes the matrix of the imaginary, of recognition/misrecognition and identification, and hence of the first articulation of the I, of subjectivity. This is a moment when an older fascination with looking (at the mother's face, for an obvious example) collides with the initial inklings of self-awareness. Hence it is the birth of the long love affair/despair between image and self-image which has found such intensity of expression in film and such joyous recognition in the cinema audience. Quite apart from the extraneous similarities between screen and mirror (the framing of the human form in its surroundings, for instance), the cinema has structures of fascination strong enough to allow temporary loss of ego while simultaneously reinforcing the ego. The sense of forgetting the world as the ego has subsequently come to perceive it (I forgot who I am and where I was) is nostalgically reminiscent of the presubjective moment of image recognition. At the same time the cinema has distinguished itself in the production of ego ideals as expressed in particular in the star system, the stars centering both screen presence and screen story as they act out a complex process of likeness and difference (the glamorous impersonates the ordinary).

C. Sections II. A and B have set out two contradictory aspects of the pleasurable structures of looking in the conventional cinematic situation. The first, scopophilic, arises from pleasure in using another person as an object of sexual stimulation through sight. The second, developed through narcissism and the constitution of the ego, comes from identification with the image seen. Thus, in film terms, one implies a separation of the erotic identity of the subject from the object on the screen (active scopophilia), the other demands identification of the ego with the object on the screen through the spectator's fascination with and recognition of his like. The first is a function of the sexual instincts, the second of ego libido. This dichotomy was crucial for Freud. Although he saw the two as interacting and overlaying each other, the tension between instinctual drives and self-preservation continues to be a dramatic polarization in terms of pleasure. Both are formative structures, mechanisms not meaning. In themselves they have no signification, they have to be attached to an idealization. Both pursue aims in indifference to perceptual reality, creating the imagized, eroticized concept of the world that forms the perception of the subject and makes a mockery of empirical objectivity.

During its history, the cinema seems to have evolved a particular illusion of reality in which this contradiction between libido and ego has found a beautifully complementary fantasy world. In *reality* the fantasy world of the screen is subject to the law which produces it. Sexual instincts and identification processes have a meaning within the symbolic order which articulates desire. Desire, born with language, allows the possibility of transcending the instinctual and the imaginary, but its point of reference continually returns to the traumatic moment of its birth: the castration complex. Hence the look, pleasurable in form, can be threatening in content, and it is woman as representation/image that crystallizes this paradox.

Woman as Image, Man as Bearer of the Look

A. In a world ordered by sexual imbalance, pleasure in looking has been split between active/male and passive/female. The determining male gaze projects its fantasy onto the female figure, which is styled accordingly. In their traditional exhibitionist role women are simultaneously looked at and displayed, with their appearance coded for strong visual and erotic impact so that they can be said to connote *to-be-looked-at-ness.* Woman displayed as sexual object is the leitmotif of erotic spectacle: from pin-ups to stripe-tease, from Ziegfeld to Busby Berkeley, she holds the look, plays to and signifies male desire. Mainstream film neatly combined spectacle and narrative. (Note, however, how in the musical song-and-dance numbers break the flow of the diegesis.) The presence of woman is an indispensable element of spectacle in normal narrative film, yet her visual presence tends to work against the development of a story line, to freeze the flow of action in moments of erotic contemplation. This alien presence then has to be integrated into cohesion with the narrative. As Budd Boetticher has put it:

> What counts is what the heroine provokes, or rather what she represents. She is the one, or rather the love or fear she inspires in the hero, or else the concern he feels for her, who makes him act the way he does. In herself the woman has not the slightest importance.

(A recent tendency in narrative film has been to dispense with this problem altogether; hence the development of what Molly Haskell has called the "buddy movie," in which the active homosexual eroticism of the central male figures can carry the story without distraction.) Traditionally, the woman displayed has functioned on two levels: as erotic object for the characters within the screen story, and as erotic object for the spectator within the auditorium, with a shifting tension between the looks on either side of the screen. For instance, the device of the showgirl allows the two looks to be unified technically without any apparent break in the diegesis. A woman performs within the narrative, the gaze of the spectator and that of the male characters in the film are neatly combined without breaking narrative verisimilitude. For a moment the sexual impact of the performing woman takes the film into a no-man's-land outside its own time and space. Thus Marilyn Monroe's first appearance in *The River of No Return* and Lauren Bacall's songs in *To Have and Have Not.* Similarly, conventional close-ups of legs (Dietrich, for instance) or a face (Garbo) integrate into the narrative a different mode of eroticism. One part of a fragmented body destroys the Renaissance space, the illusion of depth demanded by the narrative, it gives flatness, the quality of a cut-out or icon rather than verisimilitude to the screen.

B. An active/passive heterosexual division of labor has similarly controlled narrative structure. According to the principles of the ruling ideology and the psychical structures that back it up, the male figure cannot bear the burden of sexual objectification. Man is reluctant to gaze at his exhibitionist like. Hence the split between spectacle and narrative supports the man's role as the active one of forwarding the story, making things happen. The man controls the film fantasy and also emerges as the representative of power in a further sense: as the bearer of the look of the spectator, transferring it behind the screen to neutralize the extra-diegetic tendencies represented by woman as spectacle. This is made possible through the processes set in motion by structuring the film around a main controlling figure with whom the spectator can identify. As the spectator identifies with the main male[1] protagonist, he projects his look onto that of his like, his screen surrogate, so that the power of the male protagonist as he controls events coincides with the active power of the erotic look, both giving a satisfying sense of omnipotence. A male movie star's glamorous characteristics are thus not those of the erotic object of the gaze, but those of the more perfect, more complete, more powerful ideal ego conceived in the original moment of recognition in front of the mirror. The character in the story can make things happen and control events better than the subject/spectator, just as the image in the mirror was more in control of motor coordination. In contrast to woman as icon, the active male figure (the ego ideal of the identification process) demands a three-dimensional space corresponding to that of the mirror recognition, in which the alienated subject internalized his own representation of this imaginary existence. He is a figure in a landscape. Here the function of film is to reproduce as accurately as possible the so-called natural conditions of human perception. Camera technology (as exemplified by deep focus in particular) and camera movements (determined by the action of the protagonist), combined with invisible editing (demanded by realism), all tend to blur the limits of screen space. The male protagonist is free to command the stage, a stage of spatial illusion in which he articulates the look and creates the action.

C.1 Sections III. A and B have set out a tension between a mode of representation of woman in film and conventions surrounding the diegesis. Each is associated with a look: that of the spectator in direct scopophilic contact with the female form displayed for his enjoyment (connoting male fantasy) and that of the spectator fascinated with the image of his like set in an illusion of natural space, and through him gaining control and possession of the woman within the diegesis. (This tension and the shift from one pole to the other can structure a single text. Thus both in *Only Angels Have Wings* and in *To Have and Have Not*, the film opens with the woman as object of the combined gaze of spectator and all the male protagonists in the film. She is isolated, glamorous, on display, sexualized. But as the narrative progresses she falls in love with the main male protagonist and becomes his property, losing her outward glamorous characteristics, her generalized sexuality, her showgirl connotations; her eroticism is subjected to the male star alone. By means of identification with him, through participation in his power, the spectator can indirectly possess her too.)

But in psychoanalytic terms, the female figure poses a deeper problem. She also connotes something that the look continually circles around but disavows: her lack of a penis, implying a threat of castration and hence unpleasure. Ultimately, the meaning of woman is sexual difference, the absence of the penis as visually ascertainable, the material evidence on which is based the castration complex essential for the organization of entrance to the symbolic order and the law of the father. Thus the woman as icon, displayed for the gaze and enjoyment of men, the active controllers of the look, always threatens to evoke the anxiety it originally signified. The male unconscious has two avenues of escape from this castration anxiety: preoccupation with the re-enactment of the original trauma (investigating the woman, demystifying her mystery), counterbalanced by the devaluation, punishment, or saving of the guilty object (an avenue typified by the concerns of the film noir); or else complete disavowal of castration by the substitution of a fetish object or turning the represented figure itself into a fetish so that it becomes reassuring rather than dangerous (hence over-valuation, the cult of the female star). This second avenue, fetishistic scopophilia, builds up the physical beauty of the object, transforming it into something satisfying in itself. The first avenue, voyeurism, on the contrary, has associations with sadism: pleasure lies in ascertaining guilt (immediately associated with castration), asserting control, and subjecting the guilty person through punishment or forgiveness. This sadistic side fits in well with narrative. Sadism demands a story, depends on making something happen, forcing a change in another person, a battle of will and strength, victory/defeat, all occurring in a linear time with a beginning and an end. Fetishistic scopophilia, on the other hand, can exist outside linear time as the erotic instinct is focused on the look alone. These contradictions and ambiguities can be illustrated more simply by using works by Hitchcock and Sternberg, both of whom take the look almost as the content or subject matter of many of their films. Hitchcock is the more complex, as he uses both mechanisms. Sternberg's work, on the other hand, provides many pure examples of fetishistic scopophilia.

C.2 It is well known that Sternberg once said he would welcome his films being projected upside down so that story and character involvement would not interfere with the spectator's undiluted appreciation of the screen image. This statement is revealing but ingenuous. Ingenuous in that his films do demand that the figure of the woman (Dietrich, in the cycle of films with her, as the ultimate example) should be identifiable. But revealing in that it emphasizes the fact that for him the pictorial space enclosed by the frame is paramount rather than the narrative or identification processes. While Hitchcock goes into the investigative side of voyeurism, Sternberg produces the ultimate fetish, taking it to the point where the powerful look of the male protagonist (characteristic of traditional narrative film) is broken in favor of the image in direct erotic rapport with the spectator. The beauty of the woman as object and the screen space coalesce; she is no longer the bearer of guilt but a perfect product, whose body, stylized and fragmented by close-ups, is the content of the film and the direct recipient of the spectator's look. Sternberg plays down the illusion of screen depth; his screen tends to be one-dimensional, as light and shade, lace, steam, foliage, net, streamers, etc, reduce the visual field. There is little or no mediation of the look through the eyes of the main male protagonist. On the contrary, shadowy presences like La Bessière in *Morocco* act as surrogates for the director, detached as they are from audience identification. Despite Sternberg's insistence that his stories are irrelevant, it is significant that they are concerned with situation, not suspense, and cyclical rather than linear time, while plot complications revolve around misunderstanding rather than conflict. The most important absence is that of the controlling male gaze within the screen scene. The high point of emotional drama in the most typical Dietrich films, her supreme moments of erotic meaning, take place in the absence of the man she loves in the fiction. There are other witnesses, other spectators watching her on the screen, their gaze is one with, not standing in for, that of the audience. At the end of *Morocco*, Tom Brown has already disappeared into the desert when Amy Jolly kicks off her gold sandals and walks after him. At the end of *Dishonoured*, Kranau is indifferent to the fate of Magda. In both cases, the erotic impact, sanctified by death, is displayed as a spectacle for the audience. The male hero misunderstands and, above all, does not see.

In Hitchcock, by contrast, the male hero does see precisely what the audience sees. However, in the films I shall discuss here, he takes fascination with an image through scopophilic eroticism as the subject of the film. Moreover, in these cases the hero portrays the contradictions and tensions experienced by the spectator. In *Vertigo* in particular, but also in *Marnie* and *Rear Window*, the look is central to the plot, oscillating between voyeurism and fetishistic fascination. As a twist, a further manipulation of the normal viewing process, which in some sense reveals it, Hitchcock uses the process of identification normally associated with ideological correctness and the recognition of established morality and shows up its perverted side. Hitchcock has never concealed his interest in voyeurism, cinematic and non-cinematic. His heroes are exemplary of the symbolic order and the law—a policeman (*Vertigo*), a dominant male possessing money and power (*Marnie*)—but their erotic drives lead them into compromised situations. The power to subject another person to the will sadistically or to the gaze voyeuristically is turned onto the woman as the object of both. Power is backed by a certainty of legal right and the established guilt of the woman (evoking castration, psychoanalytically speaking). True perversion is barely concealed under a shallow mask of ideological correctness—the man is on the right side of the law, the woman on the wrong. Hitchcock's skilful use of identification processes and liberal use of subjective camera from the point of view of the male protagonist draw the spectators deeply into his position, making them share his uneasy gaze. The audience is absorbed into a voyeuristic situation within the screen scene and diegesis which parodies his own in the cinema. In his analysis of *Rear Window*, Douchet takes the film as a metaphor for the cinema. Jeffries is the audience, the events in the apartment block opposite correspond to the screen. As he watches, an erotic dimension is added to his look, a central image to the drama. His girlfriend Lisa had been of little sexual interest to him, more or less a drag, so long as she remained on the spectator side. When she crosses the barrier between his room and the block opposite, their relationship is reborn erotically. He does not merely watch her through his lens, as a distant meaningful image, he also sees her as a guilty intruder exposed by a dangerous man threatening her with punishment, and thus finally saves her. Lisa's exhibitionism has already been established by her obsessive interest in dress and style, in being a passive image of visual perfection; Jeffries's voyeurism and activity have also been established through his work as a photojournalist, a maker of stories and captor of images. However, his enforced inactivity, binding him to his seat as a spectator, puts him squarely in the fantasy position of the cinema audience.

In *Vertigo*, subjective camera predominates. Apart from one flashback from Judy's point of view, the narrative is woven around what Scottie sees or fails to see. The audience follows the growth of his erotic obsession and subsequent despair precisely from his point of view. Scottie's voyeurism is blatant: he falls in love with a woman he follows and spies on without speaking to. Its sadistic side is equally blatant: he has chosen (and freely chosen, for he had been a successful lawyer) to be a policeman, with all the attendant possibilities of pursuit and investigation. As a result, he follows, watches, and falls in love with a perfect image of female beauty and mystery. Once he actually confronts her, his erotic drive is to break her down and force her to tell by persistent cross-questioning. Then, in the second part of the film, he re-enacts his obsessive involvement with the image he loved to watch secretly. He reconstructs Judy as Madeleine, forces her to conform in every detail to the actual physical appearance of his fetish. Her exhibitionism, her masochism, make her an ideal passive counterpart to Scottie's active sadistic voyeurism. She knows her part is to perform, and only by playing it through and then replaying it can she keep Scottie's erotic interest. But in the repetition he does break her down and succeeds in exposing her guilt. His curiosity wins through and she is punished. In *Vertigo*, erotic involvement with the look is disorientating: the spectator's fascination is turned against him as the narrative carries him through and entwines him with the processes that he is himself exercising. The Hitchcock hero here is firmly placed within the symbolic order, in narrative terms. He has all the attributes of the patriarchal superego. Hence the spectator, lulled into a false sense of security by the apparent legality of his surrogate, sees through his look and finds himself exposed as complicit, caught in the moral ambiguity of looking. Far from being simply an aside on the perversion of the police, *Vertigo* focuses on the implications of the active/looking, passive/looked-at split in terms of sexual difference and the power of the male symbolic encapsulated in the hero. Marnie, too, performs for Mark Rutland's gaze and masquerades as the perfect to-be-looked-at image. He, too, is on the side of the law until, drawn in by obsession with her guilt, her secret, he longs to see her in the act of committing a crime, make her confess, and thus save her. So he, too, becomes complicit as he acts out the implications of his power. He controls money and words, he can have his cake and eat it.

Summary

The psychoanalytic background that has been discussed in this essay is relevant to the pleasure and unpleasure offered by traditional narrative film. The scopophilic instinct (pleasure in looking at another person as an erotic object), and, in contradistinction, ego libido (forming identification processes) act as formations, mechanisms, which this cinema has played on. The image of woman as (passive) raw material for the (active) gaze of man takes the argument a step further into the structure of representation, adding a further layer demanded by the ideology of the patriarchal order as it is worked out in its favorite cinematic form—illusionistic narrative film. The argument returns again to the psychoanalytic background in that woman as representation signifies castration, inducing voyeuristic or fetishistic mechanisms to circumvent her threat. None of these interacting layers is intrinsic to film, but it is only in the film form that they can reach a perfect and beautiful contradiction, thanks to the possibility in the cinema of shifting the emphasis of the look. It is the place of the look that defines cinema, the possibility of varying it and exposing it. This is what makes cinema quite different in its voyeuristic potential from, say, strip-tease, theater, shows, etc. Going far beyond highlighting a woman's to-be-looked-at-ness, cinema builds the way she is to be looked at into the spectacle itself. Playing on the tension between film as controlling the dimension of time (editing, narrative) and film as controlling the dimension of space (changes in distance, editing), cinematic codes create a gaze, a world, and an object, thereby producing an illusion cut to the measure of desire. It is these cinematic codes and their relationship to formative external structures that must be broken down before mainstream film and the pleasure it provides can be challenged.

To begin with (as an ending), the voyeuristic-scopophilic look that is a crucial part of traditional filmic pleasure can itself be broken down. There are three different looks associated with cinema: that of the camera as it records the pro-filmic event, that of the audience as it watches the final product, and that of the characters at each other within the screen illusion. The conventions of narrative film deny the first two and subordinate them to the third, the conscious aim being always to eliminate intrusive camera presence and prevent a distancing awareness in the audience. Without these two absences (the material existence of the recording process, the critical reading of the spectator), fictional drama cannot achieve reality, obviousness, and truth. Nevertheless, as this article has argued, the structure of looking in narrative fiction film contains a contradiction in its own premises: the female image as a castration threat constantly endangers the unity of the diegesis and bursts through the world of illusion as an intrusive, static, one-dimensional fetish. Thus the two looks materially present in time and space are obsessively subordinated to the neurotic needs of the male ego. The camera becomes the mechanism for producing an illusion of Renaissance space, flowing movements compatible with the human eye, an ideology of representation that revolves around the perception of the subject; the camera's look is disavowed in order to create a convincing world in which the spectator's surrogate can perform with verisimilitude. Simultaneously, the look of the audience is denied an intrinsic force: as soon as fetishistic representation of the female image threatens to break the spell of illusion, and the erotic image on the screen appears directly (without mediation) to the spectator, the fact of fetishization, concealing as it does castration fear, freezes the look, fixates the spectator, and prevents him from achieving any distance from the image in front of him.

This complex interaction of looks is specific to film. The first blow against the monolithic accumulation of traditional film conventions (already undertaken by radical filmmakers) is to free the look of the camera into its materiality in time and space and the look of the audience into dialectics, passionate detachment. There is no doubt that this destroys the satisfaction, pleasure and privilege of the "invisible guest," and highlights how film has depended on voyeuristic active/passive mechanisms. Women, whose image has continually been stolen and used for this end, cannot view the decline of the traditional film form with anything much more than sentimental regret.

NOTE

1. There are films with a woman as main protagonist, of course. To analyze this phenomenon seriously here would take me too far afield. Pam Cook and Claire Johnston's study of *The Revolt of Mamie Stover*, originally published in Phil Hardy, ed., *Raoul Walsh*, Edinburgh, 1974, and reprinted in Section One of this anthology, shows in a striking case how the strength of this female protagonist is more apparent than real.

FILM AND THE MASQUERADE
THEORIZING THE FEMALE SPECTATOR

Mary Ann Doane

Heads in Hieroglyphic Bonnets

In his lecture on "Femininity," Freud forcefully inscribes the absence of the female spectator of theory in his notorious statement, " . . . to those of you who are women this will not apply—you are yourselves the problem. . . . "[1] Simultaneous with this exclusion operated upon the female members of his audience, he invokes, as a rather strange prop, a poem by Heine. Introduced by Freud's claim concerning the importance and elusiveness of his topic—"Throughout history people have knocked their heads against the riddle of the nature of femininity . . . "—are four lines of Heine's poem:

> Heads in hieroglyphic bonnets,
> Heads in turbans and black birettas,
> Heads in wigs and thousand other
> Wretched, sweating heads of humans . . . [2]

The effects of the appeal to this poem are subject to the work of overdetermination Freud isolated in the text of the dream. The sheer proliferation of heads and hats (and hence, through a metonymic slippage, minds), which are presumed to have confronted this intimidating riddle before Freud, confers on his discourse the weight of an intellectual history, of a tradition of interrogation. Furthermore, the image of hieroglyphics strengthens the association made between femininity and the enigmatic, the undecipherable, that which is "other." And yet Freud practices a slight deception here, concealing what is elided by removing the lines from their context, castrating, as it were, the stanza. For the question over which Heine's heads brood is not the same as Freud's—it is not "What is Woman?", but instead, " . . . what signifies Man?" The quote is taken from the seventh section (entitled "Questions") of the second cycle of *The North Sea*. The full stanza, presented as the words of "a young man, / His breast full of sorrow, his head full of doubt," reads as follows:

> O solve me the riddle of life,
> The teasingly time-old riddle,
> Over which many heads already have brooded,
> Heads in hats of hieroglyphics,
> Turbaned heads and heads in black skull-caps,
> Heads in perrukes and a thousand other
> Poor, perspiring human heads—
> Tell me, what signifies Man?
> Whence does he come? Whither does he go?
> Who lives up there upon golden stars?[3]

The question in Freud's text is thus a disguise and a displacement of that other question, which in the pre-text is both humanistic and theological. The claim to investigate an otherness is a pretense, haunted by the mirror-effect by means of which the question of the woman reflects only the man's own ontological doubts. Yet what interest me most in this intertextual misrepresentation is that the riddle of femininity is initiated from the beginning in Freud's text as a question in masquerade. But I will return to the issue of masquerade later.

More pertinently, as far as the cinema is concerned, it is not accidental that Freud's eviction of the female spectator/auditor is copresent with the invocation of a hieroglyphic language. The woman, the enigma, the hieroglyphic, the picture, the image—the metonymic chain connects with another: the cinema, the theater of pictures, a writing in images of the woman but not *for* her. For she *is* the problem. The semantic valence attributed to a hieroglyphic language is two-edged. In fact, there is a sense in which the term is inhabited by a contradiction. On the one hand, the hieroglyphic is summoned, particularly when it merges with a discourse on the woman, to connote an indecipherable language, a signifying system which denies its own function by failing to signify anything to the uninitiated, to those who do not hold the key. In this sense, the hieroglyphic, like the woman, harbors a mystery, an inaccessible though desirable otherness. On the other hand, the hieroglyphic is the most readable of languages. Its immediacy, its accessibility are functions of its status as a *pictorial* language, a writing in images. For the image is theorized in terms of a certain *closeness*, the lack of a distance or gap between sign and referent. Given its iconic characteristics, the relationship between signifier and signified is understood as less arbitrary in imagistic systems of representation than in language "proper." The intimacy of signifier and signified in the iconic sign negates the distance which defines phonetic language. And it is the absence of this crucial distance or gap which also, simultaneously, specifies both the hieroglyphic and the female. This is precisely why Freud evicted the woman from his lecture on femininity. Too close to herself, entangled in her own enigma, she could not step back, could not achieve the necessary distance of a second look.[4]

Thus, while the hieroglyphic is an indecipherable or at least enigmatic language, it is also and at the same time potentially the most universally understandable, comprehensible, appropriable of signs.[5] And the woman shares this contradictory status. But it is here that the analogy slips. For hieroglyphic languages are *not* perfectly iconic. They would not achieve the status of languages if they were—due to what Todorov and Ducrot refer to as a certain non-generalizability of the iconic sign:

> Now it is the impossibility of generalizing this principle of representation that has introduced even into fundamentally morphemographic writing systems such as Chinese, Egyptian, and Sumerian, the phonographic principle. We might almost conclude that every logography [the graphic system of language notation] grows out of *the impossibility of a generalized iconic representation*; proper nouns and abstract notions (including inflections) are then the ones that will be noted phonetically.[6]

The iconic system of representation is inherently deficient—it cannot disengage itself from the "real," from the concrete; it lacks the gap necessary for generalizability (for Saussure, this is the idea that, "Signs which are arbitrary realize better than others the ideal of the semiotic process"). The woman, too, is defined by such an insufficiency. My insistence upon the congruence between certain theories of the image and theories of femininity is an attempt to dissect the *episteme* which assigns to the woman a special place in cinematic representation while denying her access to that system.

The cinematic apparatus inherits a theory of the image which is not conceived outside of sexual specifications. And historically, there has always been a certain imbrication of the cinematic image and the representation of the woman. The woman's relation to the camera and the scopic regime is quite different from that of the male. As Noël Burch points out, the early silent cinema, through its insistent inscription of scenarios of voyeurism, conceives of its spectator's viewing pleasure in terms of that of the Peeping Tom, behind the screen, reduplicating the spectator's position in relation to the woman as screen.[7] Spectatorial desire, in contemporary film theory, is generally delineated as either voyeurism or fetishism, as precisely a pleasure in seeing what is prohibited in relation to the female body. The image orchestrates a gaze, a limit, and its pleasurable transgression. The woman's beauty, her very desirability, becomes a function of certain practices of imaging—framing, lighting, camera movement, angle. She is thus, as Laura Mulvey has pointed out, more closely associated with the surface of the image than its illusory depths, its constructed three-dimensional space which the man is destined to inhabit and hence control.[8] In *Now Voyager*, for instance, a single image signals the momentous transformation of the Bette Davis character from ugly spinster aunt to glamorous single woman. Charles Affron describes the specifically cinematic aspect of this operation as a "stroke of genius":

> The radical shadow bisecting the face in white/dark/white strata creates a visual phenomenon quite distinct from the makeup transformation of lipstick and plucked eyebrows. . . . This shot does not reveal what we commonly call acting, especially after the most recent exhibition of that activity, but the sense of face belongs to a plastique pertinent to the camera. The viewer is allowed a different perceptual referent, a chance to come down from the nerve-jarring, first sequence and to use his eyes anew.[9]

A "plastique pertinent to the camera" constitutes the woman not only as the image of desire but as the desirous image—one which the devoted cinéphile can cherish and embrace. To "have" the cinema is, in some sense, to "have" the woman. But *Now Voyager* is, in Affron's terms, a "tear-jerker," in others, a "woman's picture," i.e. a film purportedly produced for a female audience. What, then, of the female spectator? What can one say about her desire in relation to this process of imaging? It would seem that what the cinematic institution has in common with Freud's gesture is the eviction of the female spectator from a discourse purportedly about her (the cinema, psychoanalysis)—one which, in fact, narrativizes her again and again.

A Lass but Not a Lack

Theories of female spectatorship are thus rare, and when they are produced, seem inevitably to confront certain blockages in conceptualization. The difficulties in thinking female spectatorship demand consideration. After all, even if it is admitted that the woman is frequently the object of the voyeuristic or fetishistic gaze in the cinema, what is there to prevent her from reversing the relation and appropriating the gaze for her own pleasure? Precisely the fact that the reversal itself remains locked within the same logic. The male striptease, the gigolo—both inevitably signify the mechanism of reversal itself, constituting themselves as aberrations whose acknowledgment simply reinforces the dominant system of aligning sexual difference with a subject/object dichotomy. And an essential attribute of that dominant system is the matching of male subjectivity with the agency of the look.

The supportive binary opposition at work here is not only that utilized by Laura Mulvey—an opposition between passivity and activity, but perhaps more importantly, an opposition between proximity and distance in relation to the image.[10] It is in this sense that the very logic behind the structure of the gaze demands a sexual division. While the distance between image and signified (or even referent) is theorized as minimal, if not nonexistent, that between the film and the spectator must be maintained, even measure. One need only think of Noël Burch's mapping of spectatorship as a perfect distance from the screen (two times the width of the image)—a point in space from which the filmic discourse is most accessible.[11]

But the most explicit representation of this opposition between proximity and distance is contained in Christian Metz's analysis of voyeuristic desire in terms of a kind of social hierarchy of the senses: "It is no accident that the main socially acceptable arts are based on the senses at a distance, and that those which depend on the senses of contact are often regarded as 'minor' arts (= culinary arts, art of perfumes, etc.)."[12] The voyeur, according to Metz, must maintain a distance between himself and the image—the cinéphile *needs* the gap which represents for him the very distance between desire and its object. In this sense, voyeurism is theorized as a type of meta-desire:

> If it is true of all desire that it depends on the infinite pursuit of its absent object, voyeuristic desire, along with certain forms of sadism, is the only desire whose principle of distance symbolically and spatially evokes this fundamental rent.[13]

Yet even this status as meta-desire does not fully characterize the cinema for it is a feature shared by other arts as well (painting, theater, opera, etc.). Metz thus adds another reinscription of this necessary distance. What specifies the cinema is a further re-duplication of the lack which prompts desire. The cinema is characterized by an illusory sensory plenitude (there is "so much to see") and yet haunted by the absence of those very objects which are there to be seen. Absence is an absolute and irrecoverable distance. In other words, Noël Burch is quite right in aligning spectatorial desire with a certain spatial configuration. The viewer must not sit either too close or too far from the screen. The result of both would be the same—he would lose the image of his desire.

It is precisely this opposition between proximity and distance, control of the image and its loss, which locates the possibilities of spectatorship within the problematic of sexual difference. For the female spectator there is a certain over-presence of the image—she *is* the image. Given the closeness of this relationship, the female spectator's desire can be described only in terms of a kind of narcissism—the female look demands a becoming. It thus appears to negate the very distance or gap specified by Metz and Burch as the essential precondition for voyeurism. From this perspective, it is important to note the constant recurrence of the motif of proximity in feminist theories (especially those labeled "new French feminisms") which purport to describe a feminine specificity. For Luce Irigaray, female anatomy is readable as a constant relation of the self to itself, as an autoeroticism base on the embrace of the two lips which allow the woman to touch herself without mediation. Furthermore, the very notion of property, and hence possession of something which can be constituted as other, is antithetical to the woman: "*Nearness* however, is not foreign to woman, a nearness so close that any identification of one or the other, and therefore any form of property, is impossible. Woman enjoys a closeness with the other that is *so near she cannot possess it any more than she can possess herself.*"[14] Or, in the case of female madness or delirium, " . . . women do not manage to articulate their madness: they suffer it directly in their body. . . . "[15] The distance necessary to detach the signifiers of madness from the body in the construction of even a discourse which exceeds the boundaries of sense is lacking. In the words of Hélène Cixous, "More so than men who are coaxed toward social success, toward sublimation, women are body."[16]

This theme of the overwhelming presence-to-itself of the female body is elaborated by Sarah Kofman and Michèle Montrelay as well. Kofman describes how Freudian psychoanalysis outlines a scenario whereby the subject's passage from the mother to the father is simultaneous with a passage from the senses to reason, nostalgia for the mother henceforth signifying a longing for a different positioning in relation to the sensory or the somatic, and the degree of civilization measured by the very distance from the body.[17] Similarly, Montrelay argues that while the male has the possibility of displacing the first object of desire (the mother), the female must become that object of desire:

> Recovering herself as maternal body (and also as phallus), the woman can no longer repress, 'lose,' the first stake of representation. . . . From now on, anxiety, tied to the presence of this body, can only be insistent, continuous. This body, so close, which she has to occupy, is an object in excess which must be 'lost,' that is to say, repressed, in order to be symbolized.[18]

This body so close, so excessive, prevents the woman from assuming a position similar to the man's in relation to signifying systems. For she is haunted by the loss of a loss, the lack of that lack so essential for the realization of the ideals of semiotic systems.

Female specificity is thus theorized in terms of spatial proximity. In opposition to this "closeness" to the body, a spatial distance in the male's relation to his body rapidly becomes a temporal distance in the service of knowledge. This is presented quite explicitly in Freud's analysis of the construction of the "subject supposed to know". The knowledge involved here is a knowledge of sexual difference as it is organized in relation to the structure of the look, turning on the visibility of the penis. For the little girl in Freud's description seeing and knowing are simultaneous—

there is no temporal gap between them. In "Some Psychological Consequences of the Anatomical Distinction Between the Sexes," Freud claims that the girl, upon seeing the penis for the first time, "makes her judgement and her decision in a flash. She has seen it and knows that she is without it and wants to have it."[19] In the lecture on "Femininity" Freud repeats this gesture, merging perception and intellection: "They [girls] at once notice the difference and, it must be admitted, its significance too."[20]

The little boy, on the other hand, does not share this immediacy of understanding. When he first sees the woman's genitals he "begins by showing irresolution and lack of interest; he sees nothing or disowns what he has seen, he softens it down or looks about for expedients for bringing it into line with his expectations."[21] A second event, the threat of castration, is necessary to prompt a rereading of the image, endowing it with a meaning in relation to the boy's own subjectivity. It is in the distance between the look and the threat that the boy's relation to knowledge of sexual difference is formulated. The boy, unlike the girl in Freud's description, is capable of a re-vision of earlier events, a retrospective understanding which invests the events with a significance which is in no way linked to an immediacy of sight. This gap between the visible and the knowable, the very possibility of disowning what is seen, prepares the ground for fetishism. In a sense, the male spectator is destined to be a fetishist, balancing knowledge and belief.

The female, on the other hand, must find it extremely difficult, if not impossible, to assume the position of fetishist. That body which is so close continually reminds her of the castration which cannot be "fetishized away." The lack of a distance between seeing and understanding, the mode of judging "in a flash," is conducive to what might be termed as 'over-identification' with the image. The association of tears and 'wet wasted afternoons' (in Molly Haskell's words)[22] with genres specified as feminine (the soap opera, the 'woman's picture') points very precisely to this type of over-identification, this abolition of a distance, in short, this inability to fetishize. The woman is constructed differently in relation to processes of looking. For Irigaray, this dichotomy between distance and proximity is described as the fact that:

> The masculine can partly look at itself, speculate about itself, represent itself and describe itself for what it is, whilst the feminine can try to speak to itself through a new language, but cannot describe itself from outside or in formal terms, except by identifying itself with the masculine, thus by losing itself.[23]

Irigaray goes even further: the woman always has a problematic relation to the visible, to form, to structures of seeing. She is much more comfortable with, closer to, the sense of touch.

The pervasiveness, in theories of the feminine, of descriptions of such a claustrophobic closeness, a deficiency in relation to structures of seeing and the visible, must clearly have consequences for attempts to theorize female spectatorship. And, in fact, the result is a tendency to view the female spectator as the site of an oscillation between a feminine position and a masculine position, invoking the metaphor of the transvestite. Given the structures of cinematic narrative, the woman who identifies with a female character must adopt a passive or masochistic position, while identification with the active hero necessarily entails an acceptance of what Laura Mulvey refers to as a certain "masculinization" of spectatorship.

> . . . as desire is given cultural materiality in a text, for women (from childhood onwards) trans-sex identification is a *habit* that very easily becomes *second Nature*. However, this Nature does not sit easily and shifts restlessly in its borrowed transvestite clothes.[24]

The transvestite wears clothes which signify a different sexuality, a sexuality which, for the woman, allows a mastery over the image and the very possibility of attaching the gaze to desire. Clothes make the man, as they say. Perhaps this explains the ease with which women can slip into male clothing. As both Freud and Cixous point out, the woman seems to be *more* bisexual than the man. A scene from Cukor's *Adam's Rib* graphically demonstrates this ease of female transvestism. As Katherine Hepburn asks the jury to imagine the sex role reversal of the three major characters involved in the case, there are three dissolves linking each of the characters successively to shots in which they are dressed in the clothes of the opposite sex. What characterizes the sequence is the marked facility of the transformation of the two women into men in contradistinction to a certain resistance in the case of the man. The acceptability of the female reversal is quite distinctly opposed to the male reversal which seems capable of representation only in terms of farce. Male transvestism is an occasion for laughter; female transvestism only another occasion for desire.

Thus, while the male is locked into sexual identity, the female can at least pretend that she is other—in fact, sexual mobility would seem to be a distinguishing feature of femininity in its cultural construction. Hence, transvestism would be fully recuperable. The idea seems to be this: it is understandable that women would want to be men, for everyone wants to be elsewhere than in the feminine position. What is not understandable within the given terms is why a woman might flaunt her femininity, produce herself as an excess of femininity, in other words, foreground the masquerade. Masquerade is not as recuperable as transvestism precisely because it constitutes an acknowledgment that it is femininity itself which is constructed as mask—as the decorative layer which conceals a non-identity. For Joan Riviere, the first to theorize the concept, the masquerade of femininity is a kind of reaction-formation against the woman's trans-sex identification, her transvestism. After assuming the position of the subject of discourse rather than its object, the intellectual woman whom Riviere analyzes felt compelled to compensate for this theft of masculinity by over-doing the gestures of feminine flirtation.

> Womanliness therefore could be assumed and worn as a mask, both to hide the possession of masculinity and to avert the reprisals expected if she was found to posses it—much as a thief will turn out his pockets and ask to be searched to prove that he has not the stolen goods. The reader may now ask how I define womanliness or where I draw the line between genuine womanliness and the masquerade. My suggestion is not, however, that there is any such difference; whether radical or superficial, they are the same thing.[25]

The masquerade, in flaunting femininity, holds it at a distance. Womanliness is a mask which can be worn or removed. The masquerade's resistance to patriarchal positioning would therefore lie in its denial of the production of femininity as closeness, as presence-to-itself, as, precisely, imagistic. The transvestite adopts the sexuality of the other—the woman becomes a man in order to attain the necessary distance from the image. Masquerade, on the other hand, involves a realignment of femininity, the recovery, or more accurately, simulation, of the missing gap or distance. To masquerade is to manufacture a lack in the form of a certain distance between oneself and one's image. If, as Moustafa Safouan points out, " . . . to wish to include in oneself as an object the cause of the desire of the Other is a formula for the structure of hysteria,"[26] then masquerade is anti-hysterical for it works to effect a separation between the cause of desire and oneself. In Montrelay's words, "the woman uses her own body as a disguise."[27]

The very fact that we can speak of a woman "using" her sex or "using" her body for particular gains is highly significant—it is not that a man cannot use his body in this way but that he doesn't have to. The masquerade doubles representation; it is constituted by a hyperbolization of the accoutrements of femininity. *A propos* of a recent performance by Marlene Dietrich, Sylvia Bovenschen claims, " . . . we are watching a woman demonstrate the representation of a woman's body."[28] This type of masquerade, an excess of femininity, is aligned with the *femme fatale* and, as Montrelay explains, is necessarily regarded by men as evil incarnate: "It is this evil which scandalizes whenever woman plays out her sex in order to evade the word and the law. Each time she subverts a law or a word which relies on the predominantly masculine structure of the look."[29] By destabilizing the image, the masquerade confounds this masculine structure of the look. It effects a defamiliarization of female iconography. Nevertheless, the preceding account simply specifies masquerade as a type of representation which carries a threat, disarticulating male systems of viewing. Yet, it specifies nothing with respect to female spectatorship. What might it mean to masquerade as spectator? To assume the mask in order to see in a different way?

"Men Seldom Make Passes at Girls Who Wear Glasses"

The first scene in *Now Voyager* depicts the Bette Davis character as repressed, unattractive and undesirable or, in her own words, as the spinster aunt of the family. ("Every family has one.") She has heavy eyebrows, keeps her hair bound tightly in a bun, and wears glasses, a drab dress, and heavy shoes. By the time of the shot discussed earlier, signaling her transformation into beauty, the glasses have disappeared, along with the other signifiers of unattractiveness. Between these two moments there is a scene in which the doctor who cures her actually confiscates her glasses (as a part of the cure). The woman who wears glasses constitutes one of the most intense visual clichés of the cinema. The image is a heavily marked condensation of motifs concerned with repressed sexuality, knowledge, visability and vision, intellectuality, and desire. The woman with glasses signifies simultaneously intellectuality and undesirability; but the moment she removes her glasses (a moment which, it seems, must almost always be *shown* and which is itself linked with a certain sensual quality), she is transformed into spectacle, the very picture of desire. Now, it must be remembered that the cliché is a heavily loaded moment of signification, a social knot of meaning. It is characterized by an effect of ease and naturalness. Yet, the cliché has a binding power so strong that it indicates a precise moment of ideological danger or threat—in this case, the woman's appropriation of the gaze. Glasses worn by a woman in the cinema do not generally signify a deficiency in seeing but an active looking, or even simply the fact of seeing as opposed to being seen. The intellectual woman looks and analyzes, and in usurping the gaze she poses a threat to an entire system of representation. It is as if the woman had forcefully moved to the other side of the specular. The overdetermination of the image of the woman with glasses, its status as a cliché, is a crucial aspect of the cinematic alignment of structures of seeing and being seen with sexual difference. The cliché, in assuming an immediacy of understanding, acts as a mechanism for the naturalization of sexual difference.

But the figure of the woman with glasses is only an extreme moment of a more generalized logic. There is always a certain excessiveness, a difficulty associated with women who appropriate the gaze, who insist upon looking. Linda Williams has demonstrated how, in the genre of the horror film, the woman's active looking is ultimately punished. And what she sees, the monster, is only a mirror of herself—both woman and monster are freakish in their difference—defined by either "too much" or "too little."[30] Just as the dominant narrative cinema repetitively inscribes scenarios of voyeurism, internalizing or narrativizing the film-spectator relationship (in films like *Psycho, Rear Window, Peeping Tom*), taboos in seeing are insistently formulated in relation to the female spectator as well. The man with binoculars is countered by the woman with glasses. The gaze must be dissociated from mastery. In *Leave Her to Heaven* (John Stahl, 1945), the female protagonist's (Gene Tierney's) excessive desire and over-possessiveness are signaled from the very beginning of the film by her intense and sustained stare at the major male character, a stranger she first encounters on a train. The discomfort her look causes is graphically depicted. The Gene Tierney character is ultimately revealed to be the epitome of evil—killing her husband's crippled younger brother, her unborn child, and ultimately herself in an attempt to brand her cousin as a murderess in order to insure her husband's future fidelity. In *Humoresque* (Jean Negulesco, 1946), Joan Crawford's problematic status is a result of her continual attempts to assume the position of spectator—fixing John Garfield with her gaze. Her transformation from spectator to spectacle is signified repetitively by the gesture of removing her glasses. Rosa, the character played by Bette Davis in *Beyond the Forest* (King Vidor, 1949) walks to the station every day simply to *watch* the train departing for Chicago. Her fascination with the train is a fascination with its phallic power to transport her to "another place." This character is also specified as having a "good eye"—she can shoot, both pool and guns. In all three films the woman is constructed as the site of an excessive and dangerous desire. This desire mobilizes extreme efforts of containment and unveils the sadistic aspect of narrative. In all three films the woman dies. As Claire Johnston points out, death is the "location of all impossible signs,"[31] and the films demonstrate that the woman as subject of the gaze is clearly an impossible sign. There is a perverse rewriting of this logic of the gaze in *Dark Victory* (Edmund Goulding, 1939), where the woman's story achieves heroic and tragic proportions not only in blindness, but in a blindness which mimes sight—when the woman pretends to be able to see.

Out of the Cinema and into the Streets: The Censorship of the Female Gaze

This process of narrativizing the negation of the female gaze in the classical Hollywood cinema finds its perfect encapsulation in a still photograph taken in 1948 by Robert Doisneau, "*Un Regard Oblique*." Just as the Hollywood narratives discussed above purport to center a female protagonist, the photograph appears to give a certain prominence to a woman's look. Yet, both the title of the photograph and its organization of space indicate that the real site of scopophilic power is on the margins of the frame. The man is not centered; in fact, he occupies a very narrow space on the extreme right of the picture. Nevertheless, it is his gaze which

'*Un Regard Oblique*': a dirty joke at the expense of the woman's look.

defines the problematic of the photograph; it is his gaze which effectively erases that of the woman. Indeed, as subject of the gaze, the woman looks intently. But not only is the object of her look concealed from the spectator, her gaze is encased by the two poles defining the masculine axis of vision. Fascinated by nothing visible—a blankness or void for the spectator—unanchored by a "sight" (there is nothing 'proper' to her vision—save, perhaps, the mirror), the female gaze is left free-floating, vulnerable to subjection. The faint reflection in the shop window of only the frame of the picture at which she is looking serves merely to rearticulate, *en abŷme*, the emptiness of her gaze, the absence of her desire in representation.

On the other hand, the object of the male gaze is fully present, *there* for the spectator. The fetishistic representation of the nude female body, fully in view, insures a masculinization of the spectatorial position. The woman's look is literally outside the triangle which traces a complicity between the man, the nude, and the spectator. The feminine presence in the photograph, despite a diegetic centering of the female subject of the gaze, is taken over by the picture as object. And, as if to doubly "frame" her in the act of looking, the painting situates its female figure as a spectator (although it is not clear whether she is looking at herself in a mirror or peering through a door or window). While this drama of seeing is played out at the surface of the photograph, its deep space is activated by several young boys, out-of-focus, in front of a belt shop. The opposition out-of-focus/in-focus reinforces the supposed clarity accorded to the representation of the woman's "non-vision." Furthermore, since this out-of-focus area constitutes the precise literal center of the image, it also demonstrates how the photograph makes figurative the operation of centering—draining the actual center point of significance in order to deposit meaning on the margins. The male gaze is centered, in control—although it is exercised from the periphery.

The spectator's pleasure is thus produced through the framing/negation of the female gaze. The woman is there as the butt of a joke—a "dirty joke" which, as Freud has demonstrated, is always constructed at the expense of a woman. In order for a dirty joke to emerge in its specificity in Freud's description, the object of desire—the woman—must be absent and a third person (another man) must be present as witness to the joke—"so that gradually, in place of the woman, the onlooker, now the listener, becomes the person to whom the smut is addressed. . . . "[32] The terms of the photograph's address as joke once again insure a masculinization of the place of the spectator. The operation of the dirty joke is also inextricably linked by Freud to scopophilia and the exposure of the female body:

> Smut is like an exposure of the sexually different person to whom it is directed. By the utterance of the obscene words it compels the person who is assailed to imagine the part of the body or the procedure in question and shows her that the assailant is himself imagining it. It cannot be doubted that the desire to see what is sexual exposed is the original motive of smut.[33]

From this perspective, the photograph lays bare the very mechanics of the joke through its depiction of sexual exposure and a surreptitious act of seeing (and desiring). Freud's description of the joke-work appears to constitute a perfect analysis of the photograph's orchestration of the gaze. There is a "voice-off" of the photographic discourse, however—a component of the image which is beyond the frame of this little scenario of voyeurism. On the far left-hand side of the photograph, behind the wall holding the painting of the nude, is the barely detectable painting of a woman imaged differently, in darkness—*out of sight* for the male, blocked by his fetish. Yet, to point to this almost invisible alternative in imaging is also only to reveal once again the analyst's own perpetual desire to find a not-seen that might break the hold of representation. Or to laugh last.

There is a sense in which the photograph's delineation of a sexual politics of looking is almost uncanny. But, to counteract the very possibility of such a perception, the language of the art critic effects a naturalization of this joke on the woman. The art-critical reception of the picture emphasizes a natural but at the same time "imaginative" relation between photography and life, ultimately subordinating any formal relations to a referential ground: "Doisneau's lines move from right to left, directed by the man's glance; the woman's gaze creates a line of energy like a hole in space. . . . The creation of these relationships from life itself is imagination in photography."[34] "Life itself," then, presents the material for an "artistic" organization of vision along the lines of sexual difference. Furthermore, the critic would have us believe that chance events and arbitrary clicks of the shutter cannot be the agents of a generalized sexism because they are particular, unique—"Keitesz and Doisneau depend entirely upon our recognition that they were present at the instant of the unique intersection of events."[35] Realism seems always to reside in the streets and, indeed, the out-of-focus boy across the street, at the center of the photograph, appears to act as a guarantee of the "chance" nature of the event, its arbitrariness, in short—its realism. Thus, in the discourse of the art critic the photograph, in capturing a moment, does not construct it; the camera finds a naturally given series of subject and object positions. What the critic does not consider are the conditions of reception of photography as an art form, its situation within a much larger network of representation. What is it that makes the photograph not only readable but pleasurable—at the expense of the woman? The critic does not ask what makes the photograph a negotiable item in a market of signification.

The Missing Look

The photograph displays insistently, in microcosm, the structure of the cinematic inscription of a sexual differentiation in modes of looking. Its process of framing the female gaze repeats that of the cinematic narratives described above, from *Leave Her to Heaven* to *Dark Victory*. Films play out scenarios of looking in order to outline the terms of their own understanding. And given the divergence between masculine and feminine scenarios, those terms would seem to be explicitly negotiated as markers of sexual difference. Both the theory of the image and its apparatus, the cinema, produce a position for the female spectator—a position which is ultimately untenable because it lacks the attribute of distance so necessary for an adequate reading of the image. The entire elaboration of femininity as a closeness, a nearness, as present-to-itself is not the definition of an essence but the delineation of a *place* culturally assigned to the woman. Above and beyond a simple adoption of the masculine position in relation to the cinematic sign, the female spectator is given two options: the masochism of over-identification or the narcissism entailed in becoming one's own object of desire, in assuming the image in the most radical way. The effectivity of masquerade lies precisely in its potential to manufacture a distance from the image, to generate a problematic within which the image is manipulable, producible, and readable by the woman. Doisneau's photograph is not readable by the female spectator—it can give her pleasure only in masochism. In order to "get" the joke, she must once again assume the position of transvestite.

It is quite tempting to foreclose entirely the possibility of female spectatorship, to repeat at the level of theory the gesture of the photograph, given the history of a cinema which relies so heavily on voyeurism, fetishism, and identification with an ego ideal conceivable only in masculine terms. And, in fact, there has been a tendency to theorize femininity and hence the feminine gaze as repressed, and in its repression somehow irretrievable, the enigma constituted by Freud's question. Yet, as Michel Foucault has demonstrated, the repressive hypothesis on its own entails a very limited and simplistic notion of the working of power.[36] The "no" of the father, the prohibition, is its only technique. In theories of repression there is no sense of the productiveness and positivity of power. Femininity is produced very precisely as a position within a network of power relations. And the growing insistence upon the elaboration of a theory of female spectatorship is indicative of the crucial necessity of understanding that position in order to dislocate it.

NOTES

1. Sigmund Freud, "Femininity," *The Standard Edition of the Complete Psychological Works of Sigmund Freud*, ed. James Strachey, London: The Hogarth Press and the Institute of Psycho-analysis (1964), p. 113.

2. This is the translation given in a footnote in *The Standard Edition*, p. 113.

3. Heinrich Heine, *The North Sea*, trans. Vernon Watkins, New York: New Direction Books (1951), p. 77.

4. In other words, the woman can never ask her own ontological question. The absurdity of such a situation within traditional discursive conventions can be demonstrated by substituting a "young woman" for the "young man" of Heine's poem.

5. As Oswald Ducrot and Tzvetan Todorov point out in *Encyclopedic Dictionary of the Sciences of Language*, trans. Catherine Porter, Baltimore and London: Johns Hopkins University Press (1979), p. 195, the potentially universal understandability of the hieroglyphic is highly theoretical and can only be thought as the unattainable ideal of an imagistic system: "It is important of course not to exaggerate either the resemblance of the image with the object—the design is stylized very rapidly—or the "natural" and "universal" character of the signs: Sumerian, Chinese, Egyptian, and Hittite hieroglyphics for the same object have nothing in common."

6. Ibid., p. 194. Emphasis mine.

7. See Noël Burch's film, *Correction Please, or How We Got Into Pictures.*

8. Laura Mulvey, "Visual Pleasure and Narrative Cinema," *Screen* 16, no. 3 (Autumn 1975), pp. 12–13.

9. Charles Affron, *Star Acting: Gish, Garbo, Davis*, New York: E. P. Dutton (1977), pp. 281–82.

10. This argument focuses on the image to the exclusion of any consideration of the soundtrack, primarily because it is the process of imaging which seems to constitute the major difficulty in theorizing female spectatorship. The image is also popularly understood as a metonymic signifier for the cinema as a whole and with good reason: historically, sound has been subordinate to the image within the dominant classical system. For more on the image/sound distinction in relation to sexual difference see my article, "The Voice in the Cinema: The Articulation of Body and Space," *Yale French Studies*, no. 60 (1980), pp. 33–50.

11. Noël Burch, *Theory of Film Practice*, trans. Helen R. Lane, New York and Washington: Praeger Publishers (1973), p. 35.

12. Christian Metz, "The Imaginary Signifier," *Screen* 16, no. 2 (Summer 1975), p. 60.

13. Ibid., p. 61.

14. Luce Irigaray, "This Sex Which is Not One," *New French Feminisms*, ed. Elaine Marks and Isabelle de Courtivron, Amherst: The University of Massachusetts Press (1980), pp. 104–105.

15. Irigaray, "Women's Exile," *Ideology and Consciousness*, no. 1 (May 1977), p. 74.

16. Hélène Cixous, "The Laugh of the Medusa," *New French Feminisms*, p. 257.

17. Sarah Kofman, "Ex: The Woman's Enigma," *Enclitic* 4, no. 2 (Fall 1980), p. 20.

18. Michèle Montrelay, "Inquiry into Femininity," *m/f*, no. 1 (1978), pp. 91–92.

19. Freud, "Some Psychological Consequences of the Anatomical Distinction Between the Sexes," *Sexuality and the Psychology of Love*, ed. Philip Rieff, New York: Collier Books (1963), pp. 187–88.

20. Freud, "Femininity," op. cit., p. 125.

21. Freud, "Some Psychological Consequences . . . ," op. cit., p. 187.

22. Molly Haskell, *From Reverence to Rape*, Baltimore: Penguin Books (1974), p. 154.

23. Irigaray, "Women's Exile," op. cit., p. 65.

24. Mulvey, "Afterthoughts . . . inspired by *Duel in the Sun*," *Framework* (Summer 1981), p. 13.

25. Joan Riviere, "Womanliness as a Masquerade," *Psychoanalysis and Female Sexuality*, ed. Hendrik M. Ruitenbeek, New Haven: College and University Press (1966), p. 213. My analysis of the concept of masquerade differs markedly from that of Luce Irigaray. See *Ce sexe qui n'en est pas un*, Paris: Les Éditions de Minuit (1977), pp. 131–32. It also diverges to a great extent from the very important analysis of masquerade presented by Claire Johnston in "Femininity and the Masquerade: Anne of the Indies," *Jacques Tourneur*, London: British Film Institute (1975), pp. 36–44. I am indebted to her for the reference to Riviere's article.

26. Moustafa Safouan, "Is the Oedipus Complex Universal?" *m/f*, nos. 5–6 (1981), pp. 84–85.

27. Montrelay, op. cit., p. 93.

28. Silvia Bovenschen, "Is There a Feminine Aesthetic?" *New German Critique*, no. 10 (Winter 1977), p. 129.

29. Montrelay, op. cit., p. 93.

30. Linda Williams, "When the Woman Looks . . . ," in *Re-vision: Essays in Feminist Film Criticism*, ed. Mary Ann Doane, Pat Mellencamp, and Linda Williams, Frederick, MD: University Publications of America and the American Film Institute (1984).

31. Johnston, op. cit., p. 40.

32. Freud, *Jokes and Their Relation to the Unconscious*, trans. James Strachey, New York: Norton & Co., Inc. (1960), p. 99.

33. Ibid., p. 98.

34. Weston J. Naef, *Counterparts: Form and Emotion in Photographs*, New York: E. P. Dutton and the Metropolitan Museum of Art (1982), pp. 48–49.

35. Ibid.

36. Michael Foucault, *The History of Sexuality*, trans. Robert Hurley, New York: Pantheon Books (1978).

HITCHCOCK, FEMINISM, AND THE PATRIARCHAL UNCONSCIOUS

Tania Modleski

Hitchcock and Feminist Film Theory

In providing for a number of his films to be withheld from circulation for re-release many years later, Alfred Hitchcock has ensured that his popularity with a fickle filmgoing public remains as strong as ever. With this ploy, by which he has managed to continue wielding an unprecedented power over a mass audience, Hitchcock betrays a resemblance to one of his favorite character types—the person who exerts an influence from beyond the grave. That this person is often a woman—Rebecca in the film of the same name, Carlotta and Madeleine in *Vertigo*, Mrs. Bates in *Psycho*—is not without interest or relevance to the thesis of this book: Hitchcock's great need (exhibited throughout his life as well as in his death) to insist on and exert authorial control may be related to the fact that his films are always in danger of being subverted by females whose power is both fascinating and seemingly limitless.

Such ghostly manipulations on Hitchcock's part would be ineffective, however, were it not for the fact that the films themselves possess an extraordinary hold on the public's imagination. Of course, some critics have been inclined to dismiss the films' appeal by attributing it simply to the mass audience's desire for sensational violence—usually directed against women—and "cheap, erotic" thrills, to quote "Mrs. Bates." While these critics find themselves increasingly in the minority, it is nevertheless somewhat surprising to reflect on the extent to which *feminists* have found themselves compelled, intrigued, infuriated, and inspired by Hitchcock's works.

In fact, the films of Hitchcock have been central to the formulation of feminist film theory and to the practice of feminist film criticism. Laura Mulvey's essay, "Visual Pleasure and Narrative Cinema," which may be considered the founding document of psychoanalytic feminist film theory, focuses on Hitchcock's films in order to show how women in classic Hollywood cinema are inevitably made into passive objects of male voyeuristic and sadistic impulses; how they exist simply to fulfill the desires and express the anxieties of the men in the audience; and how, by implication, women filmgoers can only have a masochistic relation to this cinema.[1] Since the publication of Mulvey's essay in 1975, a number of feminist articles on Hitchcock films have tended to corroborate her insights.

Believing that the representation of women in film is more complicated than Mulvey's article allows, I published an article in 1982 on Hitchcock's first American film, *Rebecca*, which was based on the best selling "female Gothic" novel by Daphne du Maurier.[2] There I argued that some films do allow for the (limited) expression of a specifically female desire and that such films, instead of following the male oedipal journey, which film theorists like Raymond Bellour see as the trajectory of *all* Hollywood narrative, trace a female oedipal trajectory, and in the process reveal some of the difficulties for women in becoming socialized in patriarchy.[3] Subsequently, Teresa de Lauretis in *Alice Doesn't* referred to that essay and to Hitchcock's films *Rebecca* and *Vertigo* to develop a theory of the female spectator. According to de Lauretis, identification on the part of women at the cinema is much more complicated than feminist theory has understood: far from being simply masochistic, the female spectator is always caught up in a double desire, identifying at one and the same time not only with the passive (female) object, but with the active (usually male) subject.[4]

Mulvey herself has had occasion to rethink some of her essay's main points and has done so in part through a reading of Hitchcock's *Notorious* that qualifies the condemnation of narrative found in "Visual Pleasure."[5] Other feminists have returned, almost obsessively, to Hitchcock in order to take up other issues, fight other battles. In an extremely interesting essay on *The Birds*, for example, Susan Lurie analyzes a segment that has also been analyzed by Raymond Bellour: the ride out and back across Bodega Bay. Lurie is concerned to dispute the Lacanian theory relied on so heavily by Bellour and Mulvey—particularly in the latter's argument that women's body signifies lack and hence connotes castration for the male. In Lurie's view, women like Melanie Daniels in *The Birds* are threatening not because they automatically connote castration, but because they *don't*, and so the project of narrative cinema is precisely to "castrate" the woman whose strength and perceived wholeness arouses dread in the male.[6] Thus, if de Lauretis is primarily interested in complicating Mulvey's implied notion of femininity, Lurie is chiefly concerned with questioning certain aspects of Mulvey's theory of masculinity and masculine development. And both develop their arguments through important readings of Hitchcock's films.

Recently, Robin Wood, a male critic who has been a proponent of Hitchcock's films for many years, has become interested in these issues.[7] In the 1960s, Wood's book—the first in English on Hitchcock—set out to address the question, "Why should we take Hitchcock seriously?" In the 1980s, Wood declares, the question must be, "Can Hitchcock be saved for feminism?"—though his very language, implying the necessity of rescuing a favorite auteur from feminist obloquy, suggests that the question is fundamentally a rhetorical one. And indeed, although Wood claims in his essay not to be interested in locating "an uncontaminated feminist discourse in the films," he proceeds to minimize the misogyny in them and to analyze both *Rear Window* and *Vertigo* as exposés of the twisted logic of patriarchy, relatively untroubled by ambivalence or contradiction.

It may be symptomatic that in contrast to the female critics I have mentioned, the stated goal of the one male critic concerned with feminism is to reestablish the authority of the artist—to "save" Hitchcock. For Wood, political "progressiveness" has come to replace moral complexity as the criterion by which to judge Hitchcock's art, but the point remains the same—to justify the ways of the auteur to the filmgoing public. The feminist critics I have mentioned, by contrast, use Hitchcock's works as a means to elucidate issues and problems relevant to women in patriarchy. In so doing these critics implicitly challenge and decenter directorial authority by considering Hitchcock's work as the expression of cultural attitudes and practices existing to some extent outside the artist's control. My own work is in the irreverent spirit of this kind of feminist criticism and is, if anything, more explicitly "deconstructionist" than this criticism has generally tended to be. Thus, one of my book's main theses is that, time and again in Hitchcock films, the strong fascination and identification with femininity revealed in them subverts the claims to mastery and authority not only of the male characters but of the director himself.

This is not to say that I am entirely unsympathetic to Wood's position. Indeed, this critic's work seems to me an important corrective to studies which see in Hitchcock only the darkest misogynistic vision. But what I want to argue is *neither* that Hitchcock is utterly misogynistic *nor* that he is largely sympathetic to women and their plight in patriarchy, but that his work is characterized by a thoroughgoing ambivalence about femininity—which explains why it has been possible for critics to argue with some plausibility on either side of the issue. It also, of course, explains why the issue can never be resolved and why, when one is reading criticism defending or attacking Hitchcock's treatment of women, one continually experiences a feeling of "yes, but . . . " This book aims to account, often through psychoanalytic explanations, for the ambivalence in the work of Hitchcock. In the process, it continually demonstrates that despite the often considerable violence with which women are treated in Hitchcock's films, they remain resistant to patriarchal assimilation.

In order to explain the ambivalence in these films, I will be especially concerned with showing the ways in which masculine identity is bound up with feminine identity—both at the level of society as well as on the individual, psychological level. In this respect, the book will confirm that what Fredric Jameson says about ruling class literature is also true of patriarchal cultural production. According to Jameson in *The Political Unconscious*, consciousness on the part of the oppressed classes, expressed, "initially, in the unarticulated form of rage, helplessness, victimization, oppression by a common enemy," generates a "mirror image of class solidarity among the ruling groups. . . . This suggests . . . that the *truth* of ruling-class consciousness . . . is to be found in working-class consciousness."[8] Similarly, in Hitchcock, the "truth" of patriarchal consciousness lies in feminist consciousness and depends precisely on the depiction of victimized women found so often in his films. The paradox is such, then, that male solidarity (between characters, director, spectators, as the case may be) entails giving expression to women's feelings of "rage, helplessness, victimization, oppression." This point is of the greatest consequence for a theory of the female spectator. As I argue in the chapters on *Blackmail* and *Notorious*, insofar as Hitchcock films repeatedly reveal the way women are oppressed in patriarchy, they allow the female spectator to feel an anger that is very different from the masochistic response imputed to her by some feminist critics.

Not only is it possible to argue that feminist consciousness is the mirror of patriarchal consciousness, but one might argue as well that the patriarchal *un*conscious lies in femininity (which is not, however, to equate femininity with the unconscious). Psychoanalysis has shown that the process by which the male child comes to set the mother at a distance is of very uncertain outcome, which helps to explain why it is continually necessary for man to face the threat woman poses and to work to subdue that threat both in life and in art. The dynamics of identification and identity, I will argue, are fraught with difficulties and paradoxes that are continually reflected and explored in Hitchcock films.[9] To take an example suggestive of Jameson's mirror metaphor, when Scottie Ferguson in *Vertigo* begins investigating the mysterious Madeleine Elster, the first point of view shot shows him as a mirror image of the woman, and the rest of the film traces the vicissitudes of Scottie's attempts to reassert a masculinity lost when he failed in his performance of the law.

By focusing on the problematics of identity and identification, then, this study aims to insert itself in the debates circulating around Hitchcock's films and to examine some of the key theoretical issues developed in the various critiques. On the one hand, the book seeks to engage the problem of the female spectator, especially in the analysis of those films told from the woman's point of view (i.e., *Blackmail*, *Rebecca*, and *Notorious*). But even some of those films which seem exclusively to adopt the male point of view, like *Murder!*, *Rear Window*, or *Vertigo*, may be said either to have woman as the ultimate point of identification or to place the spectator—regardless of gender—in a classically "feminine" position. On the other hand, then, my intent is to problematize *male* spectatorship and masculine identity in general. The analysis will reveal that the question which continually—if sometimes implicitly—rages around Hitchcock's work as to whether he is sympathetic towards women or misogynistic is fundamentally unanswerable because he is both.[10] Indeed, as we shall see, the misogyny and the sympathy actually entail one another—just as Norman Bates's close relationship with his mother provokes his lethal aggression towards other women.

The Female Spectator

As the figure of Norman Bates suggests, what both male and female spectators are likely to see in the mirror of Hitchcock's films are images of ambiguous sexuality that threaten to destabilize the gender identity of protagonists and viewers alike. Although in *Psycho* the mother/son relationship is paramount, I will argue that in films from *Rebecca* on it is more often the mother/daughter relationship that evokes this threat to identity and constitutes the main "problem" of the films. In *Vertigo*, for example, Madeleine is the (great grand)daughter of Carlotta Valdez who seems to possess the heroine so thoroughly that the latter loses her individuality. *Rebecca*'s heroine experiences a similar difficulty in relation to the powerful Rebecca, first wife of the heroine's husband. Marnie's main "problem"—as far as patriarchy is concerned—is an excessive attachment to her mother that prevents her from achieving a "normal," properly "feminine," sexual relationship with a man. In other films, the mother figure is actually a mother-in-law, but one who so closely resembles the heroine, it is impossible to escape the suspicion that the mother/daughter relationship is actually what is being evoked. In *Notorious*, both Alicia and her mother-in-law have blonde hair and foreign accents; and in *The Birds*, there in an uncanny resemblance between Melanie Daniels and Mitch's mother, Lydia. In all these films, moreover, Hitchcock manipulates point of view in such a way that the spectator him/herself is made to share the strong sense of identification with the (m)other.

As feminists have recently stressed, the mother/daughter relationship is one of the chief factors contributing to the bisexuality of women—a notion that several critics have argued is crucial to any theory of the female spectator seeking to rescue women from "silence, marginality, and absence." Very soon after the publication of Mulvey's essay, feminist critics began to approach this idea of female bisexuality in order to begin to explain women's experience of film. A consideration of this experience, they felt, was lacking in Mulvey's work, which thereby seemed to collaborate unwittingly in patriarchy's plot to render women invisible. In a much quoted discussion among film critics and filmmakers Michelle Citron, Julia Lesage, Judith Mayne, B. Ruby Rich, and Anna Marie Taylor that appeared in *New German Critique* in 1978, one of the major topics was the bisexuality of the female spectator. In the course of the discussion, the participants, attempting to counter what might be called the "compulsory heterosexuality" of mainstream film, concluded that more attention needs to be paid to women's erotic attraction to other women—to, for example, Marlene Dietrich not only as a fetishized object of male desire, which is how Mulvey had seen her, but as a female star with an "underground reputation" among lesbians as "a kind of subcultural icon."[11] Several of the participants stressed that female eroticism is obviously going to differ from male eroticism; the experience of the female spectator is bound to be more complex than a simple passive identification with the female object of desire or a straightforward role reversal—a facile assumption of the transvestite's garb. Julia Lesage insisted, "Although women's sexuality has been shaped under a dominant patriarchal culture, clearly women do not respond to women in film and the erotic element in quite the same way that men do, given that patriarchal film has the structure of a male fantasy" (p. 89). In other words, there must be other options for the female spectator than the two pithily described by B. Ruby Rich: "to identify either with Marilyn Monroe or with the man behind me hitting the back of my seat with his knees" (p. 87).

Several of the women in this discussion were strenuously anti-Freudian, claiming that Freud's framework cannot account for the position of female spectators. Recent Freudian and neo-Freudian accounts of women's psychic development in patriarchy and applications of these accounts to issues in feminist film theory have, however, suggested otherwise. Thus Gertrud Koch, addressing the question of "why women go to men's movies," refers to Freud's theory of female bisexuality, which is rooted in woman's preoedipal attachment to her mother. This attachment, it will be remembered, came as a momentous discovery to Freud and resulted in his having to revise significantly his theories of childhood sexuality and to recognize the fundamental asymmetry in male and female development.[12] The female's attachment to the mother, Freud came to understand, often goes "unresolved" throughout woman's life and coexists with her later heterosexual relationships. Hence, Teresa de Lauretis's notion of a "double desire" on the part of the female spectator—a desire that is *both* passive and active, homosexual and heterosexual. Koch speculates that men's need to prohibit and punish female voyeurism is attributable to their concern about women's pleasure in looking at other women: "Man's fear of permitting female voyeurism stems not only from fear of women looking at other men and drawing (to him perhaps unfavorable) comparisons but is also connected to a fear that women's bisexuality could make them competitors for the male preserve."[13]

In her book, *Women and Film: Both Sides of the Camera*, feminist film critic E. Ann Kaplan draws on the neo-Freudian work of Julia Kristeva to make a similar point about men's repression of the "nonsymbolic" (preoedipal) aspects of motherhood. According to Kristeva/Kaplan, patriarchy must repress these nonsymbolic aspects of motherhood because of the "homosexual components" involved in the mother/daughter relationship.[14] Elsewhere, Kaplan analyzes *Stella Dallas*, a film about an intense mother/daughter relationship, in order to argue that the process of repression is enacted in classical cinema and that the female spectator herself comes to desire this repression and to endorse the heterosexual contract that seals the film at its end.[15] Another analysis of *Stella Dallas* by Linda Williams argues against this view and persuasively postulates a contradictory "double desire" on the part of the female spectator: on the one hand, we identify with the working class Stella and share her joy at having successfully sacrificed herself in giving away her daughter to the upper-class father and boyfriend and, on the other hand, because of the way point of view has been handled in the film, we are made to experience the full poignancy and *undesirability* of the loss of the close affective relationship with the daughter.[16] In other words, we could say that the spectator simultaneously experiences the symbolic *and* the nonsymbolic aspects of motherhood, despite patriarchy's attempts to repress and deny the latter.

In stressing the contradictory nature of female spectatorship, Williams's essay can be seen as a critique not only of the position that, given the structure of classic narrative film as male fantasy, the female spectator is forced to adopt the heterosexual view, but also of the opposite position, most forcefully articulated by Mary Anne Doane, which sees the preoedipal relationship with the mother as the source of insurmountable difficulties for the female spectator. Doane draws on the work of Christian Metz and his theories of spectatorship based on male fetishism and disavowal, in order to disqualify female voyeurism. According to Doane, woman's putative inability to achieve a distance from the *textual* body is related to her inability to separate decisively from the *maternal* body. Because women lack a penis, they lack the possibility of losing the "first stake of representation," the mother, and thus of symbolizing their difference from her (a "problem" that we shall see is at the heart of *Rebecca*): "this closeness to the body, this excess, prevents the woman from assuming a position similar to the man's in relation to signifying systems. For she is haunted by the loss of a loss, the lack of that lack so essential for the realization of the ideals of semiotic systems."[17] There are, I believe, several ways for feminists to challenge such a nihilistic position. One might, for example, point out the tortuous logic of these claims, as Hélène Cixous has done ("She lacks lack? Curious to put it in so contradictory, so extremely paradoxical a manner: she lacks lack. To say she lacks lack is also, after all, to say she doesn't miss lack . . . since she doesn't miss the lack of lack.")[18] Or, one might say with Linda Williams and B. Ruby Rich that the female spectator does indeed experience a "distance" from the image as an inevitable result of her being an exile "living the tension of two different cultures."[19] Or, one might question the very "ideals" of the "semiotic systems" invoked by Doane—and, in particular, the ideal of "distance," or what in Brechtian theory is called "distanciation."

According to Doane, woman's closeness to the (maternal) body means that she "over-identifies with the image": "The association of tears and 'wet wasted afternoons' (in Molly Haskell's words) with genres specified as feminine (the soap opera, the 'woman's picture') points very precisely to this type of over-identification, this abolition of a distance, in short this inability to fetishize."[20] Now, as I have mentioned, many of Hitchcock's films actually thematize the "problem" of "over-identification"—the daughter's "over-identification" with the mother and, in at least one film (*Rear Window*), the woman's "over-identification" with the "textual body." Given Hitchcock's preoccupation with female bisexuality and given his famed ability to draw us into close identifications with his characters—so many of them women—his work would seem to provide the perfect testing ground for theories of female spectatorship.

But the question immediately arises as to why a male director—and one so frequently accused of unmitigated misogyny—would be attracted to such subjects. I want to suggest that woman's bisexual nature, rooted in preoedipality, and her consequent alleged tendency to over-identify with other women and with texts, is less a problem for *women*, as Doane would have it, than it is for patriarchy. And this is so not only for the reason suggested by Gertrud Koch (that female bisexuality would make women into competitors for "the male preserve"), but far more fundamentally because it reminds man of his *own* bisexuality (and thus his resemblance to Norman Bates), a bisexuality that threatens to subvert his "proper" identity, which depends upon his ability to distance woman and make her his proper-ty. In my readings of Hitchcock, I will demonstrate how men's fascination and identification with the feminine continually undermine their efforts to achieve masculine strength and autonomy and is a primary cause of the violence towards women that abounds in Hitchcock's films. These readings are meant to implicate certain Marxist/psychoanalytical film theories as well, since by uncritically endorsing "distanciation" and detachment (however "passionate" this detachment is said to be) as the "proper"—i.e., politically correct—mode of spectatorship, they to some extent participate in the repression of the feminine typical of the "semiotic system" known as classic narrative cinema.[21]

Men at the Movies

The psychiatrist, the voice of institutional authority who "explains" Norman Bates to us at the end of the film, pronounces matricide to be an unbearable crime—"most unbearable to the son who commits it." In my opinion, though, the crime is "most unbearable" to the victim who suffers it, and despite the fact that a major emphasis of my book is on masculine subjectivity in crisis, its ultimate goals are a deeper understanding of women's victimization—of the sources of matrophobia and misogyny—and the development of female subjectivity, which is continually denied women by male critics, theorists, and artists (as well as by their female sympathizers). Some feminists, however, have recently argued that we should altogether dispense with analysis of masculinity and of patriarchal systems of thought in order to devote full time to exploring female subjectivity. Teresa de Lauretis, for example, has declared that the "project of women's cinema [by which she means also feminist film theory] is no longer that of destroying or disrupting man-centered vision by representing its blind spots, its gaps or its repressed"; rather, she argues, we should be attending to the creation of another—feminine or feminist—vision.[22] Although I fully share de Lauretis's primary concern, I do not agree that we should forego attempting to locate the gaps and blind spots in "man-centered vision." One of the problems with Mulvey's theory was that her picture of male cinema was so monolithic that she made it seem invincible, and so, from a political point of view, feminists were stymied. An analysis of patriarchy's weak points enables us to avoid the paralyzing nihilism of a position which accords such unassailable strength to an oppressive system and helps us more accurately to assess our *own* strengths relative to it. Moreover, I believe we *do* need to destroy "man-centered vision" by beginning to see with our own eyes—because for so long we have been not only fixed in its sights, but also forced to view the world through its lens.

While, as we have seen, some feminists have criticized Mulvey's "inadequate theorization of the female spectator," others have objected to her restriction of the *male* spectator to a single, dominant position, arguing that men at the movies—at least at *some* movies—may also be feminine, passive, and masochistic. Studies like D. N. Rodowick's "The Difficulty of Difference," Janet Bergstrom's "Sexuality at a Loss," and Gaylyn Studlar's "Masochism and the Perverse Pleasure of the Cinema" take issue with the view of sexual difference as organized according to strict binary oppositions (masculinity = activity; femininity = passivity, etc.) and emphasize the bisexuality of *all* human beings and "the mobility of multiple, fluid identifications" open to every spectator, including men.[23] These critics point to certain Freudian pronouncements to the effect that each individual "displays a mixture of the character traits belonging to his own and to the opposite sex."[24] In "Sexuality at a Loss: The Films of F. W. Murnau," for example, Janet Bergstrom refers to this aspect of Freudian theory in arguing that Murnau's films displace sexuality from the female body to the male body and thus carry "a shifting, unstable homoerotic charge" enabling viewers to "relax rigid demarcations of gender identification and sexual orientation."[25] Bergstrom concludes from this analysis that the issue of gender is not pertinent to a psychoanalytically oriented criticism, which ought to stress the bisexuality of all individuals, and should concern only those critics interested in "historical and sociological perspectives"—as if it were possible to divide up the human subject in this way.[26]

A passage from Bergstrom's earlier essay, "Enunciation and Sexual Difference," helps to illuminate the problem involved in considering the male spectator to be similar to the female spectator in his bisexual response. In that essay, Bergstrom had called for attention to be paid to "the movement of identifications, whether according to theories of bisexuality, power relations . . . or some other terms."[27] The weakness of this formulation, however, lies in its assumption that notions of bisexuality can be considered *apart* from power relations. On the contrary, in patriarchy the feminine position alone is devalued and despised, and those who occupy it are powerless and oppressed. The same Freud who spoke of bisexuality also, after all, spoke of the normal masculine "contempt" for femininity.[28] Freud showed very precisely how men tend to repress their bisexuality to avoid being subjected to this contempt and to accede to their "proper" place in the symbolic order. A discussion of bisexuality as it relates to spectatorship ought, then, to be informed by a knowledge of the way male and female responses are rendered asymmetrical by a patriarchal power structure. As Hitchcock films repeatedly demonstrate, the male subject is greatly threatened by bisexuality, though he is at the same time fascinated by it; and it is the woman who pays for this ambivalence—often with her life itself.

An interesting challenge to Mulvey's theorization of male spectatorship has been mounted by critics who have questioned its exclusive emphasis on the male spectator's sadism, man's need to gain mastery over the woman in the course of the narrative. A pioneering essay by Kaja Silverman entitled "Masochism and Subjectivity" and a later study by Gaylyn Studlar on the films of Josef Von Sternberg stress the male spectator's masochistic pleasures at the movies. In placing emphasis on this aspect of male subjectivity, both critics point to the importance of the preoedipal phase in masculine development. Hitherto, as I have said, many film theorists have insisted on the fact that narrative cinema closely follows the male oedipal trajectory outlined by Freud, and in doing so cements the male spectator into the male Symbolic order. In the Freudian scenario, the child renounces preoedipal bisexuality and the mother as "love object" for "the requirements of the Oedipus Complex," and in the process assumes his castration.[29] Arguing against this view, Gaylyn Studlar generalizes from an analysis of the films Josef Von Sternberg made with Marlene Dietrich to argue that at the cinema we all regress to the infantile, preoedipal phase, submitting ourselves to and identifying (fusing) with the overwhelming presence of the screen and the woman on it. "Castration fear and the perception of sexual difference," Studlar says, "have no importance" in her aesthetic, which aims to "replace" Mulvey's theory with a more benign version of spectatorship. Studlar's model "rejects" a position which emphasizes "the phallic phase and the pleasure of control or mastery" and thus, she maintains, can help deliver feminist psychoanalytic theory from the "dead end" in which it supposedly finds itself.[30]

While I believe that male masochism is indeed an important area for feminists to explore—is, in fact, one of the blind spots or "repressed" aspects of male-centered vision—the point surely is that this masochism, and the preoedipal relationship with the mother in which it is rooted, *are* in fact repressed by the male in adult life, as Studlar at one point acknowledges. For me the crucial question facing feminist theory is, "What are the sources and the consequences *for women* of this repression?" For that matter, what are the sources and consequences of the "dread of woman," of "ambivalence" towards the mother, of the equation of women with death, all of which are mentioned by Studlar as crucial components of the masochistic aesthetic? How do the answers to these questions illuminate the undeniable fact that Mulvey had sought to understand and that Studlar disregards: i.e., that women are objectified and brought under male domination in the vast majority of patriarchal films?

The fact that men are driven to repress their preoedipal attachment to their mothers in acceding to a patriarchal order would seem to invalidate any attempt simply to "replace" a political critique that focuses on the phallic, sadistic, oedipal nature of narrative cinema with an aesthetic that privileges its oral, masochistic, and preoedipal components. As Christian Metz noted some time ago, although cinema is situated in the realm of the Imaginary—of the preoedipal—the male spectator himself has already passed through the Symbolic,[31] has, then, internalized the "normal contempt" for femininity, repressed it in himself, and met—more or less—the "requirements of the Oedipus complex." Hence, the necessity of discussing the way sadistic and masochistic, oedipal and preoedipal, symbolic and nonsymbolic aspects of male spectatorship interrelate. In this complex undertaking Kaja Silverman's work on masochism seems to me to be of utmost importance.

In "Masochism and Subjectivity," Silverman examines Lacan's theory of the mirror stage and Freud's discussion of his grandson's "fort/da" game, on which Lacan's theory is based, and concludes that in decisive moments in the history of the subject, the individual learns to take pleasure in pain and loss. Cinematic activity, like many other forms of cultural activity, replays these moments of loss, which are as pleasurable for the male spectator as for the female spectator. Referring to theories of cinematic suture, for example, Silverman explains that in relating to films, we experience "a constant fluctuation between the imaginary plenitude of the shot, and the loss of that plenitude through the agency of the cut."[32] Yet, she admits, there is a significant contradiction here, since in films themselves it is most often women who are "placed in positions of passivity, and more generally men than women who occupy positions of aggressivity. On the other hand, the subject—whether male or female—

is passively positioned and is taught to take pleasure in his/her pain" (p. 5). Silverman "resolves" this contradiction by referring to Freud's theory of dreams, in which the dreamer, though perhaps absent "*in propria persona*" from the dream, may be represented by a variety of people, onto whom the dreamer displaces his/her own fears and desires. In films where the female character occupies a passive position, she enacts *on behalf of the male viewer* "the compulsory narrative of loss and recovery" (p. 5). Unfortunately, Silverman's essay, like Studlar's, ultimately refuses to cede any importance to sadism in the male viewer's response. Silverman writes, "Indeed, I would go so far as to say that the fascination of the sadistic point of view is *merely* that it provides the best vantage point from which to watch the masochistic story unfold" (p. 5, emphasis mine). Yet the reference to Freudian dream theory points to a way not of cancelling or "resolving" the contradiction she describes, but of understanding how it works *as* a contradiction. Just as Freud showed that the meaning of the dream resides neither in its latent content nor in its manifest content, but in the complex interaction of the two—in the dreamwork itself—so the male viewer's response might best be understood in the Freudian sense of a sadomasochistic dialectic rather than of pure sadism (as in Mulvey) or "mere" masochism.[33]

Thus, whereas Studlar's article places sole emphasis on the female as a possible figure of male identification—and mentions only in passing the fact that this identification is the " 'source of deepest dread,' "—Silverman's analysis helps to explain the workings of both the identification *and* the dread: the dream mechanism of displacement enables the male subject simultaneously to experience and deny an identification with passive, victimized female characters. By acknowledging the importance of denial in the male spectator's response, we can take into account a crucial fact ignored by the articles discussed—the fact that the male finds it necessary to repress certain "feminine" aspects of himself, and to project these exclusively onto the woman, who does the suffering for both of them.

It is part of my project here to explore this dialectic of identification and dread in the male spectator's response to femininity—the movement between the two poles Alice Jardine has said characterize contemporary culture: "hysteria" (confusion of sexual boundaries) and "paranoia" (their reinforcement).[34] The paranoia may be seen as a consequence of the hysteria but, as Jardine elsewhere observes, it is fundamentally a reaction against women who know not only too much, but anything at all: "Man's response in both private and public to a woman who *knows* (anything) has most consistently been one of paranoia."[35] "I know a secret about you, Uncle Charlie," says Charlie the niece to her uncle in *Shadow of a Doubt*, thereby arousing his murderous rage. Charlie is a typical Hitchcock female, both because her close relationship to her mother arouses in her a longing for a different kind of life than the one her father offers them and because she seems to possess special, incriminating knowledge about men. Charlie's attitude is representative of the two types of resistance to patriarchy I have been discussing here—that which seeks to know men's "secrets" (patriarchy's "blind spots, gaps, and repressed areas") and that which knows the kinds of pleasure unique to women's relationship with other women. This book is devoted to understanding how female spectators may be drawn into this special relationship and how men may react to women who are suspected of possessing such valuable secret knowledge.

A Frankly Inventive Approach

All of this is to suggest that Hitchcock films as I read them are anything but exemplary of Hollywood cinema. Rather, if the films do indeed invoke typical patterns of male and female socialization, as Raymond Bellour has repeatedly argued, they do so only to reveal the difficulties inherent in these processes—and to implicate the spectator in these difficulties as well. Interestingly, even Mulvey's essay, which uses Hitchcock films as the main evidence in her case against Hollywood cinema, actually ends up claiming that *Vertigo* is critical of the kinds of visual pleasure typically offered by mainstream cinema, a visual pleasure that is rooted in the scopic regime of the male psychic economy. In her reading of the film, Mulvey thus unwittingly undercuts her own indictment of narrative cinema as possessing no redeeming value for feminism.

Of course, Mulvey is not the first commentator to discover in Hitchcock films self-reflexive critiques of voyeurism and visual pleasure—a whole tradition of criticism celebrates the director's ability to manipulate spectators so as to make us uncomfortably aware of the perverse pleasures of cinema going. But for all the claims of traditional critics to have had their eyes opened to the moral ambiguities inherent in film viewing, most remain incredibly blind to the relation of voyeurism to questions of sexual difference. For example, male critics frequently point to *Psycho* as a film which punishes audiences for their illicit voyeuristic desires, but they ignore the fact that within the film not only are women objects of the male gaze, they are also recipients of most of the punishment. It is left to feminist criticism to point out that after Marion Crane is killed in the shower, the camera focuses on her sightless eye; that when Mother is finally revealed, it is Marion's sister who is forced to confront the horrible vision; that while she screams out in fright, the swinging lightbulb is reflected in the eye sockets of the female corpse; and that, finally, at the end of the film, "Mother" is agonizingly aware of being stared at and tries desperately to demonstrate her harmlessness to her unseen observers by refusing to swat a fly. In acknowledging such sexual asymmetry in desire and its punishment (where men possess the desire and women receive the punishment), we are forced to relinquish the more facile notions about Hitchcock's self-reflexivity and his critiques of voyeurism—at the very least we would need to invoke the notions discussed earlier of male masochism and its denial or displacement.

An analysis of voyeurism and sexual difference is only one of the ways in which a book taking a specifically feminist approach can provide a much needed perspective on Hitchcock's films. Indeed, there are many questions that I think begin to look very different when seen by a woman. What, for example, happens to the frequently noted theme of the "transference of guilt" when we insist against the grain of an entire history of Hitchcock criticism that a certain heroine is innocent because she was defending herself against rape? In patriarchy woman's sexual "guilt" is unique to her and is not "transferable" to men. Or, to take another example, how do the theatrical motifs so common in Hitchcock films change their meaning when considered in the light of Western culture's association of femininity with theater and spectacle? Or, again, how may we begin to rethink Hitchcock's "Catholicism" when we view it in the context of Julia Kristeva's work on religion and matrophobia—matrophobia being so strong an element in Hitchcock that it is acknowledged by even the most traditional of nonfeminist critics? While not the primary focus of this work, such concerns which have been central to Hitchcock studies will be given a new inflection in my readings. I am, however, by no means claiming to advance comprehensive, definitive interpretations of the films. Less ambitiously, I think of my book as a sustained meditation on a few of the issues that have been of paramount interest to feminist film theory.

In his recent work, *The World, the Text, and the Critic,* Edward Said has beautifully described the critic as one who "is responsible to a degree for articulating those voices dominated, displaced, or silenced by the textuality of texts. Texts are a system of forces institutionalized by the reigning culture at some human cost to its various components. . . . The critic's attitude . . . should . . . be frankly inventive, in the traditional sense of *inventio* so fruitfully employed by Vico, which means finding and exposing things that otherwise may be hidden beneath piety, heedlessness, or routine."[36] Feminism, too, has by now its pieties and routines. Insofar as it all too readily accepts the ideals of male semiotic systems, feminism also needs to be challenged by a "frankly inventive" approach, an approach that, if it seems alien at first, is so only because it is situated in the realm of the uncanny—speaking with a voice that inhabits us all, but that for some of us has been made strange through fear and repression.

If it did not sound more frivolous than I intend to be, then, I would say that part of my intention in these pages is to defend that much maligned women, Mrs. Bates, whose *male* child suffers such a severe case of "overidentification" with her that he is driven to matricide and to the rape/murder of various young women. At the end of the film, "Mrs. Bates" (who has the last word) speaks through her son's body to protest her innocence and place the blame for the crimes against women on her son.

I think she speaks the truth. As I will argue, the sons are indeed the guilty ones, and, moreover, it is my belief that the crime of matricide is destined to occur over and over again (on the psychic plane) until woman's voice allows itself to be heard—in women and men alike.

NOTES

1. Laura Mulvey, "Visual Pleasure and Narrative Cinema," *Screen* 16, no. 3 (1975): 6–18.
2. Tania Modleski, "Never to be Thirty-Six Years Old: *Rebecca* as Female Oedipal Drama," *Wide Angle* 5, no. 1 (1982): 34–41.
3. The most explicit statement of this may be found in an interview with Bellour conducted by Janet Bergstrom, "Alternation, Segmentation, Hypnosis: Interview with Raymond Bellour," *Camera Obscura*, nos. 3–4 (1979): 93.
4. Teresa de Lauretis, *Alice Doesn't: Feminism, Semiotics, Cinema*, Bloomington: Indiana University Press (1984), p. 153.
5. In an unpublished paper delivered at the conference "New Narrative Cinema," Simon Fraser University, September 1983.
6. Susan Lurie, "The Construction of the Castrated Woman in Psychoanalysis and Cinema," *Discourse*, no. 4 (Winter 1981–82): 52–74.
7. Robin Wood, "Fear of Spying," *American Film* (November 1982): 28–35.
8. Fredric Jameson, *The Political Unconscious: Narrative as a Socially Symbolic Act*, Ithaca: Cornell University Press (1981), pp. 289–90.
9. For one account of this process see Mary Ann Doane, "Misrecognition and Identity," *Ciné-Tracts* 3, no. 3 (Fall 1980): 25–32.
10. In *From Reverence to Rape: The Treatment of Women in the Movies*, New York: Penguin, (1974), Molly Haskell notes the "complex interplay of misogyny and sympathy in Hitchcock" (p. 32).
11. Michelle Citron, Julia Lesage, Judith Mayne, B. Ruby Rich, and Anna Maria Taylor, "Women and Film: A Discussion of Feminist Aesthetics," *New German Critique* 13 (Winter 1978): 87. Hereafter cited in the text.
12. Freud discussed differences between female and male sexual development in "Female Sexuality," *The Standard Edition of the Complete Psychological Works of Sigmund Freud*, trans. James Strachey, London: Hogarth (1974), Vol. 21, and "Femininity," *New Introductory Lectures on Psychoanalysis*, trans. James Strachey, New York: Norton, (1965), pp. 99–119.
13. Gertrud Koch, "Why Women Go to Men's Films," *Feminist Aesthetics*, ed. Gisela Ecker, Boston: Beacon (1985), p. 110.
14. E. Ann Kaplan, *Women and Film: Both Sides of the Camera*, New York and London: Methuen (1983), p. 6.
15. E. Ann Kaplan, "The Case of the Missing Mother: Maternal Issues in Vidor's *Stella Dallas*," *Heresies* 16 (1983): 81–85.
16. Linda Williams, "Something Else Besides a Mother: *Stella Dallas* and the Maternal Melodrama," *Cinema Journal* 24, no. 1 (Fall 1984): 2–27.
17. Mary Ann Doane, "Film and the Masquerade: Theorizing the Female Spectator," *Screen* 23, nos. 3–4 (September–October 1982): 79.
18. Hélène Cixous, "Castration or Decapitation?" trans. Annette Kuhn, *Signs* 7, no. 1 (Autumn 1981): 48.

19. Citron et. al., "Women and Film," p. 87. Quoted in Williams, "Something Else," pp. 19–20.

20. Doane, "Film and the Masquerade," p. 80.

21. The term "passionate detachment" is Mulvey's, but it has been picked up by Annette Kuhn, who uses it as the title for the opening chapter of her book, *Women's Pictures: Feminism and Cinema,* London: Routledge & Kegan Paul (1982), pp. 3–18.

22. Teresa de Lauretis, "Aesthetic and Feminist Theory: Rethinking Women's Cinema," *New German Critique,* no. 34 (Winter 1985): 163. Some of the reviews of the Kuhn and Kaplan books strongly criticized their tendency to focus on patriarchal cinema instead of concentrating on the female vision of women filmmakers. See in particular, Sarah Halprin, "Writing in the Margins: Review of E. Ann Kaplan's *Women and Film,*" *Jump Cut,* no. 29 (1984): 31–33.

23. Gaylyn Studlar, "Masochism and the Perverse Pleasure of the Cinema," *Movies and Methods,* Vol. 2, ed. Bill Nichols, Berkeley and Los Angeles: University of California Press (1985), p. 616. D. N. Rodowick challenges Mulvey's reliance on binary oppositions by pointing to Freud's essay, " 'A Child Is Being Beaten.' " See Rodowick, "The Difficulty of Difference," *Wide Angle* 5, no. 1 (1982): 4–15. This little essay of Freud's on a childhood masochistic fantasy has proved inspirational to several critics in thinking about spectatorship and identification. See, for example, Mary Ann Doane, "The 'Woman's Film': Possession and Address," in *Re-vision: Essays in Feminist Film Criticism,* ed. Mary Ann Doane, Patricia Mellencamp, and Linda Williams, The American Film Institute Monograph Series, Vol. 3, Frederick, MD: University Publications of America (1984), pp. 67–80; and Miriam Hansen, "Pleasure, Ambivalence, Identification: Valentino and Female Spectatorship," *Cinema Journal* 25, no. 4 (Summer 1986): 6–32. See also Gaylyn Studlar's response to Hansen's essay, *Cinema Journal* 26, no. 2 (Winter 1987): 51–53. The Freud essay, " 'A Child Is Being Beaten': A Contribution to the Study of the Origin of Sexual Perversions," may be found in the *Standard Edition,* Vol. 17.

24. Quoted in Rodowick, "The Difficulty of Difference," p. 15n. See Freud's *Three Essays on the History of Sexuality,* trans. James Strachey, New York: Basic Books (1962), pp. 7–14. Also relevant is Freud's paper, "Hysterical Phantasies and their Relation to Bisexuality" in the *Standard Edition,* Vol. 19.

25. Janet Bergstrom, "Sexuality at a Loss: The Films of F. W. Murnau," *Poetics Today* 6, nos. 1–2 (1985): 193n. For an excellent critique of this essay, see Patrice Petro, *Joyless Streets: Women and Melodramatic Representation in Weimar Germany,* forthcoming, Princeton University Press.

26. Bergstrom, "Sexuality at a Loss," p. 200.

27. Janet Bergstrom, "Enunciation and Sexual Difference," *Camera Obscura,* nos. 3–4 (1979): 58.

28. See Sigmund Freud, "Some Psychical Consequences of the Anatomical Distinction Between the Sexes," *Standard Edition,* Vol. 19.

29. See Claire Johnston's "Towards a Feminist Film Practice: Some Theses," in *Movies and Methods,* Vol. 2, p. 321.

30. Studlar, "Masochism and the Perverse Pleasures," p. 605.

31. Christian Metz, *The Imaginary Signifier,* trans. Celia Britton, Anwyl Williams, Ben Brewster, and Alfred Guzzetti, Bloomington: Indiana University Press (1982), p. 49.

32. Kaja Silverman, "Masochism and Subjectivity," *Framework* 12 (1980): 4. Hereafter cited in the text.

33. In other work, Silverman takes this dialectic more fully into account. See, for example, her relevant analysis of *Psycho,* which she considers in the light of theories of suture. In *The Subject of Semiotics,* New York: Oxford University Press (1983), pp. 203–13. For his discussion of the dreamwork, see Sigmund Freud, *The*

Interpretation of Dreams, trans. James Strachey, New York: Avon (1965), pp. 311–546. It should be noted that in his book on masochism, Gilles Deleuze insists that the process by which apparently masochistic urges of the tormentor are displaced onto the victim, thereby allowing an identification with the victim, is entirely compatible with sadism. Deleuze speaks of the "pseudo-masochism in sadism" and the "pseudo-sadism of masochism." See his *Masochism: An Interpretation of Coldness and Cruelty*, trans. Jean MacNeil, New York: George Braziller (1971), p. 109. Deleuze maintains that the two perversions ought to be kept entirely separate, and, indeed, such separation is preferable to the kind of confusion that reigns in the current theorizing of the problem. However, my own study does not follow Deleuze's line, but rather accords more closely with the Sartrean model of masochism and sadism as the two poles between which the subject oscillates in his attitude toward the other. In an excellent, as yet unpublished paper, "Masochism and Feminist Theory," Sonia Rein points out some of the more problematic aspects of film theory's adoption of the masochistic aesthetic and shows how masochism as it it theorized by Deleuze (upon whom Studlar heavily relies), is no more liberating for feminism than the sadistic model proposed by Mulvey.

34. Alice Jardine, *Gynesis: Configurations of Woman and Modernity*, Ithaca: Cornell University Press (1985), p. 48.

35. Jardine, *Gynesis*, p. 98.

36. Edward Said, *The World, the Text, and the Critic*, Cambridge: Harvard University Press (1983), p. 53.

WOMEN AND REPRESENTATION

CAN WE ENJOY ALTERNATIVE PLEASURE?

Jane Gaines

Feminist analysis of pornography's industry, image, and "effect," has overlapped at times with issues in contemporary film theory: the marketing of diversion and pleasure, the institutionalization of voyeurism, and the relationship between violent acts and representations of violence.[1] Debates around pornography in the first half of the 1980s have had a familiar resonance for those who follow feminist film criticism. At the time of the 1982 Conference on the Politics of Sexuality at Barnard College, the paradigm evoked in the discussions of pornography bore an uncanny resemblance to the dominant cinema/counter-cinema model introduced into feminist film theory in the mid-seventies. That paradigm is now, however, undergoing some change. In the struggle against the monoliths that serve male desire, feminist critics are asking if woman's pleasure as counter-pleasure can be a viable oppositional practice. The serious interest in women's sexuality—in fantasy and in practice—marked by the Barnard pro-sex conference and the publication of the proceedings, is a bold new tack for American feminism. *Pleasure and Danger*, the collection that contains the conference papers, suggests the way women's desire is inextricably linked with the prohibitions against it. In her introduction to the book, editor Carol Vance lines up those perils that historically have mitigated women's pleasure. "When unwanted pregnancy, street harassment, stigma, unemployment, queerbashing, rape, and arrest are arrayed on the side of caution and inaction," she says, "passion doesn't have a chance."[2] In Vance's analysis, women's passion is tentative and easily intimidated by antipornography rhetoric, which classifies all sexual expression as male.[3]

Until recently, the U.S. feminist stand on pornography appeared to be consistent with the toughest line of the most visible antipornography activist group, Women Against Pornography.[4] Some of the first signs of falling away from the hard line on pornography can be seen in the *Heresies* "Sex Issue." This issue, published in 1981, contains a variety of arguments for challenging the watchdog position on porn, among them that pornography is not a *cause* of violence against women but rather a symptom of patriarchal power relations, that concentration on the extreme and exotic can eclipse or even excuse the more common acts of degradation related to the requirements of heterosexuality, and even that pornography may have a subversive potential in a sexually repressive society.[5] One of the articles in the issue turns a critique of the antipornography movement into a statement of feminist strategy based on shifting our emphasis from men's pleasure to women's. "In placing the gratification of men above our own," says Paula Webster, "we pose absolutely no danger to male-dominated society"; the "active pursuit of our own gratification," then, is a political act. Webster acknowledges, however, that this pursuit will finally need to address the more difficult sexuality and power issue: What if women are aroused by the imagery designed exclusively for male satisfaction?[6]

This development finds its parallel in feminist film criticism, which has reached the point of exasperation with the cataloging and analysis of male pleasure. The use of the extreme to condemn the ordinary, as seen in the comparison between male voyeurism and cinema viewing (which has its equivalent in the comparison between pornography and sexual images of women), seems to have lost its original potency. Also, new work on popular fiction and film directs interest away from forms now established as "male" to forms marketed for female audiences. Since the mid-seventies, it has been the critical vogue to study the cinematic construction of male pleasure in the classic realist text—the ways in which the masculine "gaze" controls viewing within the film, sets up the spectator's "looking position," and coincides with the "look" of the camera. Analysis in this tradition has considered "sexual difference" to be the eroticizing hinge on which classical Hollywood cinema turns. For the female, there are two places in this construct—either as overvalued "fetishized" star image (Mae West or Marlene Dietrich), exhibited and displayed, no more than a sign in a "patriarchal exchange," or as audience, but occupying the point of view reserved for the male.[7]

The source of this method and the inspiration for so much of the current work on woman as spectacle is Laura Mulvey's 1975 essay "Visual Pleasure and Narrative Cinema," which marks the first attempt to use Lacanian psychoanalysis to develop a coherent feminist theory of narrative film as signifying system.[8] Claire Johnston's "Women's Cinema as Counter-Cinema,"[9] published two years before, had already analyzed the fetishized female image as substitute for phallic sexuality, following Freud's theory of symbolic displacement and male narcissism. Both articles extend the combination of Freud and Lacan suggestively used in *Cahiers du Cinéma*'s collective analysis of *Morocco*, originally published in 1970, but not translated into English until 1980.[10] With the publication of "Visual Pleasure and Narrative Cinema" in the issue following the translation of Christian Metz's "The Imaginary Signifier," the British journal *Screen* had thoroughly committed itself to an integration of Lacanian psychoanalysis into film theory.[11] For roughly ten years, terms such as "mirror phase," the "imaginary," "desire," and the "look," introduced in these two issues, seemed to be the favored critical currency of the exchange on women and cinema.

The connection between the Freudian notions of fetishism and voyeurism and the distinctly male spectator was not made immediately. In the United States, one of the earliest attempts to theorize the eroticized female image, Maureen Turim's "Gentlemen Consume Blondes," analyzes *Gentlemen Prefer Blondes* in Marxist terms of commodity exchange. Although men are implicated in the title, Turim makes no gender distinctions in her discussion of the way cinema makes voyeurs and fetishists of us while at the same time excusing our tendencies.[12] Soon after, Lucy Fisher, in her examination of Busby Berkeley's decorative uses of the showgirl, made a tentative connection between fetishism and male, as opposed to female, eroticism.[13] The *Cahiers du Cinéma* analysis of Marlene Dietrich in *Morocco,* which clearly influenced both Mulvey and Johnston, assumes a phallocentric society and is interested in both the economic and the erotic functions of the fetish.

Feminist analysis, however, has not pursued the Marxist notion of fetishism (that is, the attribution of magical qualities) to the commodity in capitalist economic relations or to the converse, commodification of noncommodities, for instance, the reification of the female body. I will suggest some of the reasons why the Freudian notion of the fetish has been preferred.[14] First, we have to consider the immediate appeal of the feminist argument, which links social practices with perversion. This argument often starts with a study of the exotic; through analogy, the more common practice is then implicated. Mulvey's theory of the female image as a phallic replacement that eases male fear of phallic loss was developed in an analysis of explicitly fetishist imagery. Just before the publication of "Visual Pleasure and Narrative Cinema," she undertook an attack on one of the most notorious exploiters of the female form in the British art world in an encyclopedic review of Allan Jones's visions of female body contortion and torture.[15] Fettered in the classic imagery of the private fetishist—belts, spike heels, rubber corsets, brassieres, and garters—Jones's models confirm feminists' worst fears about male fantasies. As the basis for an analysis of the onscreen image of woman, fetishism makes a stunning connection between aberrant eroticism and "normal" male sexual behavior.

However, this potent metaphor for cinema spectatorship has too quickly become a comprehensive explanation for all representation of the female form. Joanna Russ criticizes rhetorical use of the exotic to damn the ordinary as characteristic of feminist debates. Once the commonplace is likened to the extraordinary—as corset-wearing is compared with the fetishist's tight-lacing—or heterosexuality is equated with rape, we still have not explained the more routine acts, says Russ.[16] Feminists should be careful not to confuse the specialized sexual eroticism or the brutal crime with widespread practice, particularly since, she concludes, "nobody has decided what relation exists between rape, rape fantasies, clinical masochism, and ordinary behavior. And what are we to understand by 'ordinary behavior'?"[17]

Recent psychoanalytic theory hypothesizes that all conventional language and pictorial representation is male-biased, for reasons rooted in the psychology of infantile sexuality. To understand the dominant cinema as thoroughly voyeuristic and to identify all sexual representation of women within it as phallic substitution implies a definite political analysis. If even everyday viewing is organized along these lines, with patriarchal power relations being reproduced in every depiction of woman on a magazine page or billboard, then we are all ideological captives. Moreover, if we are ideologically "surrounded," if all language and every image produced in bourgeois society is steeped in patriarchal ideology—the female body always being a vehicle for something other than itself—then there is a definite advantage for feminists in borrowing a Freudian analysis that theorizes femininity as silence. Always discussing the image of woman in its negation, we are constantly qualifying representational practices and reminding ourselves of the impossibility of female expression in male-dominated culture. In their introduction to the most recent collection of feminist film criticism, Mary Ann Doane, Patricia Mellencamp, and Linda Williams defend this theoretical stance for its tactical avoidance of essentialism.[18] By shifting emphasis to the negative spaces—or, following the French feminists, to the linguistic in-between—the feminist critic sidesteps the assertion that any imagery could be naturally or essentially female.[19] But these authors find neither critical option satisfactory as a theoretical basis; hence the kind of crisis we find in feminist film criticism:

> The feminist theoretist [*sic*] is . . . confronted with something of a double bind: she can continue to analyze and interpret various instances of the repression of woman, of her radical absence in the discourses of men—a pose which necessitates remaining within that very problematic herself, always repeating its terms; or she can attempt to delineate a feminine specificity, always risking a recapitulation of patriarchal constructions and a naturalization of "woman."[20]

A theory based on the exclusion of women poses a special challenge to the feminist filmmaker who would create alternative representations or political commentary on the photographic uses of the female body. How can the feminist artist speak out or act to shape culture from a position of absence?

On this basis, some feminists have opposed all uses of Freud in criticism. Why borrow a method based on describing woman's repressed place in language and society? they argue. What new understanding of oppression can it yield? To be fair, the British feminist use of psychoanalysis follows Juliet Mitchell's rereading of Freudian theory, which she takes as a kind of description of the ideological, or an illumination of the site of gender construction.[21] In this analysis, Freudian theory is not taken to be anything more than social diagnosis. Jacqueline Rose further defends the feminist use of Freud: "The description of feminine sexuality is . . . an exposure of the terms of its definition, the very opposite of a demand as to what that sexuality should be."[22] Yet although it offers a social explanation of oppression, Freudian theory concentrates causality in a depository of its own invention that is characterized by its detachment from social conditions.[23]

For Marxists, the use of psychoanalysis is especially problematic both because it privileges an autonomous realm and because it poses a subject that is undifferentiated by either social class or history.[24] Although Marxist feminists have been able to compensate with Freud for what was missing in Marx—gender distinctions—the theoretical advantage of gender specificity is outweighed by the political disadvantage of expecting an already completely constituted subject to come to class consciousness. Terry Lovell sees the psychoanalytic notion of subject as having "deeply pessimistic" implications for women, because "an account of sexed identity which locates the constitution of women in processes so massively concentrated in the first few years of life more or less completed with the resolution of the Oedipus complex, is to place women . . . under a crippling burden of determination in an epoch of their lives in which they have the least possibility of control and change."[25] Following Althusser's introduction of Lacan into the Marxist theory of ideology, the apparent shift of emphasis from class struggle to ideological struggle seemed to concentrate effectivity in cultural products and to forgo political movement in favor of critical activity. Christine Gledhill, another British feminist who, like Lovell, has been critical of the incorporation of Lacan via Althusser into Marxist cultural studies, asks how this theory translates into political strategy. In her critique of feminist film criticism, Gledhill argues that if feminists are up against the "ideologically positioned" subject, political change begins to look like an impossible task. As she puts it, "We are clearly in a very weak political position if rupturing the place of the subject in representation is our chief point of entry." With no clear means of connecting gender construction to historically shifting economic conditions, she says, feminists may have difficulty formulating and implementing programs for social change.[26]

One of the related dangers of using Freudian theory is the ease with which it can be recuperated for a totally reactionary position. Since Freud strikes a mean between the biological and the social, and can often be interpreted both ways, a feminist case for understanding sexuality as a social construct may sound like a case for biological determinism. E. Ann Kaplan's definition of cinematic voyeurism, based on that of Mulvey, for instance, could lend itself to the analysis that viewers, especially biological males, are hopelessly doomed by instinct and cannot help their proclivity to look in a sexual context. "Pleasure in the cinema," she says, "is created through the inherently voyeuristic mechanism that comes into play here more strongly than in the other arts."[27] Implying that pleasure in looking is innate rather than learned, feminists back down from their best argument: that gender differences are socially constructed. But Freud is slippery, and an extra step makes this theory seem to serve a materialist position. Kaplan is thus able to justify her use of psychoanalysis because she will force it to "unlock the secrets of our socialization within (capitalist) patriarchy."[28] A similar stance may have been taken by other film theorists who depend heavily on psychoanalysis, but this would be difficult to tell from their work. Until recently, those feminist film theorists who recruited psychoanalysis into a Marxist analysis did not feel the need to answer the charge that Freudian concepts are ahistorical.[29]

Certainly the historical coincidence of the invention of a storytelling machine on the one hand and Freud's discovery of the unconscious within the bourgeois epoch on the other is remarkable, but this one fortuitous connection has too easily satisfied the need for historic specificity in Marxist-psychoanalytic film criticism. Although some of the post-1968 French film theory, which introduced Lacanian psychoanalytic concepts into cinema studies, was also interested in locating the historical moment of the construction of ideology in the invention of cinema technology, these historical reference points have dropped out in psychoanalytic discussions of the way the text positions its subject.[30] Early theorizations of the cinema subject began by citing the historical continuity between the perspective rendered by the camera lens and the Renaissance code of pictorial space. What had been considered a "scientific" instrument, the camera, reproduced ideology in its model of the idealist worldview, which organized vision around the human eye, flattering it with a godlike vantage point. This spectator eye, implied in the convergence of light rays and referred to by the vanishing lines, also defined a particular conception of the self.[31] Freud's analogy between photographic instrument and psychic process, each described as an *apparatus* in *The Interpretation of Dreams*, inspired and encouraged comparisons between the two.[32] Finally, in the notion of "the apparatus" and its operations, motion picture technology (a culmination of nineteenth-century invention) and the human psyche have become interchangeable. Here, then, the provocative play with metaphor, which in psychoanalytic theory teases out correspondences, seems to have provided a shortcut for theorists. Certainly there *are* connections among Freud's "dream economy," narrative economy, and the economy characterized by commodity production, just as there is a relationship between the projection mechanism and the mechanism of the unconscious, but in the way Marxist theory has borrowed Freud, it has still only suggested these links.[33]

Finally, other Marxist feminists have been critical of British feminist film theory because its specialized knowledge fosters an elite position. On this point, Kaplan was originally one of the clearest and strongest critics of the British. In an early review of "Women's Cinema as Counter-Cinema" and Pam Cook and Claire Johnston's work on Raoul Walsh and Dorothy Arzner, she noted that not only was a background in psychoanalytic theory a prerequisite to these discussions, but in order to follow the arguments the reader had to accept the Freudian premises without question. At the time, Kaplan asked what might be valuable about the Freudian interpretations already established in literary criticism, since "the predictable nature of such interpretations takes away from their interest . . . ; given the premises, everything else follows like clockwork."[34] Kaplan's remark describes much of the criticism that followed in this tradition, and here I refer to the bulk of the academic work extending feminist film theory in the United States from the mid-1970s into the present. To the insider, the appeal of this criticism explicating the "look" and unraveling the oedipal is that it *does* come off "like clockwork." To the outsider, this analysis is often as impenetrable as the patriarchal unconscious it hopes to unlock.

Analyzing patriarchal forms has only been half of the feminist project outlined by the dominant cinema/counter-cinema paradigm. "Breaking down" mainstream film has also meant constructing new forms that directly oppose classical conventions in order to withhold its two indulgent pleasures: voyeuristic "looking" and narrative closure. Again, echoing a strategy in women's movement politics, the creation of a new language of desire was made contingent on the destruction of male pleasure. Women's cinematic forms were not imaginable as long as illusionistic narrative cinema (the patriarchal favorite) retained its fascination for us. In theory, the feminist counter-cinema proposed by Mulvey and Johnston is a continuation of Godard's goals for a revolutionary cinema—to combat form with form. The disruptive fragmentation of continuity editing and point-of-view construction and the frustration of narrative unity pioneered a new aesthetic based on refusal. Theoretically, the inventive interruption of classical narrative is meant to destroy the codes of mainstream entertainment and ultimately replace them with a cinema that provokes thought and encourages analysis. Counter-cinema here borrows from Brecht the idea that critical distance, and ultimately consciousness-change, can be effected in the theatrical audience by annihilating the pleasure of identification. It also has in common with Brecht a bias against ease and satisfaction, which cannot be expected to serve the goals of political education. Recent reevaluation of these issues from a Marxist mass-culture perspective, however, reminds us that Brecht may not have intended such austerity.[35] People's pleasures (popular music, television, cinema, and other amusements) might serve politics after all if the fantasies they inspire help to feed an undernourished utopian imagination.[36]

Leftists have raised strong objections to a cinema that snubs popular appeal and that would spurn the more accessible pleasures for the "passionate detachment" of an intellectual experience. *Riddles of the Sphinx*, Laura Mulvey's high-theory film, for instance, austerely avoids continuity editing and withholds narrative resolution to such an extreme that women viewers have found it disorienting. The subversion of sexual looking, although compelling as a concept, is not so riveting in its translation to the screen. Finally, the "test" of counter-cinema implies a very difficult standard: the work must show that what we are seeing is shaped by cinematic form; at the same time, it must not give the impression (usually encouraged by conventions of cinematic realism) that there is any final reality that can be known outside the linguistic forms that access it. Does this political aesthetic make impossible demands on audiences—and on film texts? Those of us who eat, sleep, and breathe political theories of representation, who have made the politics of meaning our life's work, are not always aware of the ways our own consciousness is shaped by words, images, or other signifying material. Are we, in expecting a film text to effect change on its own, asking too much of it, especially if it is screened out of the context of political organizing and education efforts? Why should a film that considers its own signification process necessarily require its audience to know advanced film theory in order for them to enjoy, appreciate, and, ideally, reflect upon what they see? The futility of sharing this new cinema with a theoretically uninitiated audience is dramatized by this admission from a scholar in an adjacent field:

> An innovatory piece of work may be experienced as such, or as startling, shocking, disturbing, if the audience is sufficiently familiar with the conventions it seeks to challenge and subvert. . . . I am aware, for example, that, while I can see for myself a departure from tradition in a contemporary novel, I have to be told by others that such and such a camera angle or style of shot constitutes a rejection of bourgeois practice in film-making.[37]

The feminist case for counter-cinema is an argument for modernism, which undeniably offers rarefied pleasures and is a taste acquired through educational and cultural privilege.[38] Black women filmmakers, sensitive to the class bias of aesthetic preference, have as a whole chosen not to produce any media work that diverges from standard formats and calls attention to its own formal devices. Interviews with this new group of film and video makers—whose work is still unevenly available in the United

States even through alternative distribution channels—suggest agreement on the question of aesthetic style: It is more important to make comprehensible and accessible films than it is to experiment with subverting classical Hollywood narrative.[39] The films these women have produced deal with black body language and image, skin color consciousness, child custody, childbirth, single parenting, prostitution as survival, rape, and women's retaliation against sexual abuse, and their messages are an intentional affront to white male society. Do these films, then, constitute any less of a political challenge because they use conventional forms?

For all the interest in counter-cinema as theory, feminist film and video making in the United States seems to have been influenced relatively little by the original British models such as *Nightcleaners* (Berwick St. Collective, 1975) and *Riddles of the Sphinx* (Laura Mulvey and Peter Wollen, 1977). The small number of U.S. and British feminist works following in this tradition have received a disproportionate amount of critical attention. This response is evidence of the symbiotic relationship between these "avant-garde theory films," as E. Ann Kaplan calls them, and an evolving feminist criticism, which certainly has its significance; but the attention has also created an instant canon in a very new field of inquiry. Too quickly, a hierarchy of works has been organized, which has meant that many women's productions have been relegated to the periphery, and many others remain undiscovered. Those feminist works that may have been overlooked by theorists have been found by women's groups, however, particularly in the United States, where several traditions of radical filmmaking coexist. Documentaries in the style of *Union Maids* (Julia Reichert and Jim Klein, 1976) have been strong with unions and community groups. These documentaries use the rhetoric of archival footage or testimonial interview and thus employ realist conventions without question; but they are also effective as organizing tools, and in this sense they pose a challenge to the counter-cinema corollary that change cannot be effected by "revealing" the photographic "truth" of woman's oppression.[40] Third World film and video makers have consistently made their more radical statements in the documentary mode, a choice that indicates the power of politics to determine representational priorities. Leftist media workers cannot afford to undertake an abstract analysis or make an educational statement *about* representation if it is politically imperative that they make a representational reference to a "brutal actuality" in order to counteract its ideological version.[41]

For feminists, investigating women's pleasure as counter-pleasure has become politically imperative. We have already produced a potent analysis of patriarchal culture as oppressive monolith, but we are still determining the relation of woman's culture to the dominant. Is this culture excluded or "muted"? Does it modify or resist?[42] Annette Kolodny recently remarked that while sexual difference absorbed in the first two decades of the Second Wave of Feminism, the issue of the next decade will have to be how difference "interacts with the dominant."[43] The equation between mainstream cinema and male privilege set up by "Visual Pleasure and Narrative Cinema" may have diverted the attention of feminist scholars, but it seems also to have provided an "out" for them—by introducing interest in the gendered spectator into contemporary film theory.[44] The very questions that Mulvey did *not* address have become the most compelling: Is the spectator restricted to viewing the female body on the screen from the male point of view? Is narrative pleasure always male pleasure? Theoretical solutions to the enigma of female spectatorship range from the more pessimistic and dubious psychoanalytic analyses to the spirited reversal of the lesbian readings and the renewed expectations of the soap opera studies. Psychoanalytic analyses of the horror film show agreement on one point—that the female vision, whether perception or discernment, is jeopardized in this genre.[45] Punishments inflicted on female characters, as Marcia Landy and Lucy Fisher show in their analysis of *The Eyes of Laura Mars* (Irvin Kershner, 1978), may serve as a warning against female occupation of male points of view.[46]

Mary Ann Doane has theorized female spectatorship as a psychoanalytic and semiotic impossibility. For one thing, the female cannot assume a voyeuristic position in regard to the cinema spectacle, because she is semiotically too close to that image which is ultimately her own. Neither does she transform her own castrated figure in the same way the male spectator is thought to use his ability to "fetishize."[47] Following this line of thought, with sexual difference determining the construction and operation of classical narrative cinema *in all genres*, even those films centered on a female protagonist and directed toward a woman's audience will renounce female looking. Doane's study of the Hollywood woman's picture shows that the prohibition against female sight is so strong that some films must integrate this renunciation into the narrative. For example, one could understand Joan Crawford's dilemma, as patron and lover to concert violinist John Garfield in *Humoresque* (Jean Negulesco, 1946), as the denial of her control over him, worked out in terms of her surveillance of his performances and emphasized by the habitual removal of her glasses. Following Doane's suggestion, Crawford's tragic suicide (she walks into the surf to the strains of her lover's violin, broadcast from the concert hall) could be seen as resolving the tension between the desire to be viewed as a love object and the need to scrutinize an investment.[48] If even women's forms frustrate the spectator, what are we to make of women's attraction to melodrama? Do these entertainments offer a privileged point of view and the possibility of female desire—and then withhold the enjoyment of them?[49] Is the viewer tricked into a masochistic pleasure?

In contrast to psychoanalytic film theory, lesbian studies assign more power to the spectator than to the text. These analyses show that the female "look" cancels the male point of view and that active reading resists the flow of classical narrative. In one of the most convincing challenges to work on male pleasure, Lucie Arbuthnot and Gail Seneca argue that in *Gentlemen Prefer Blondes* (Howard Hawks, 1953), Jane Russell and Marilyn Monroe "resist objectification" and project an intimacy with each other that invites both identification and a kind of female voyeurism.[50] In this tradition, Chris Straayer and Liz Ellsworth have considered the feminist and lesbian reception of *Personal Best* (Robert Towne, 1982), demonstrating in two different studies that the power and force of the female "look" has been underestimated. Based on her observations that oppositional communities build their own interpretations and construct social pleasures to complement their fantasies, Ellsworth recommends that feminists work out strategies to maximize their "illicit" viewing pleasure.[51] Straayer's discovery of lesbian respondents' ingenious viewing strategies, which allow for the "clever co-existence of pleasure and displeasure," is an important opening in the study of the double consciousness of oppressed groups.[52] In contrast with formal analysis, these more sociological studies may seem relatively "messy," in the way they deal with "gut" feelings, inarticulate responses, and ordinary opinions; they are significant, however, because they remind us that meaning is always social and that hothouse studies of film language alone cannot construct a semiotics of the cinema.

An approach that considers the lesbian as spectator causes all the premises of feminist film theory centered on male voyeurism to shift. In the introduction to the *Jump Cut* "Lesbian Special Section," Edith Becker, Michelle Citron, Julia Lesage, and B. Ruby Rich describe how the exclusion of a lesbian perspective has seriously "warped" contemporary film theory:

> A true recognition of lesbianism would seriously challenge the concept of women as inevitable objects of exchange between men, or as fixed in an eternal trap of "sexual difference" based on heterosexuality. Feminist theory that sees all women on the screen only as objects of male desire—including by implication, lesbians—is inadequate.[53]

To consider the exquisitely fit female-fantasy bodies in *Flashdance* (Adrian Lyne, 1983) only in terms of male desire, one has to ignore women's responses to the film.

Likewise, to analyze the lesbian sexual awakening in *Lianna* (John Sayles, 1983) in terms of the male "look" negates the film's premises. Visually, *Lianna* is not the film that either a straight woman or a lesbian would have made in celebration of women loving women.[54] *Lianna* is not just cautious, it is apologetic about photographing women. The tentative representation of lesbian love-making, for instance, is an attempt not to intrude voyeuristically or shape salaciously, and clichés of sexual gazing are reversed in a female-body montage Lianna sees just after she has first made love with Ruth. Showing wholesome lesbian bodies with restraint neither withdraws the image entirely from male view nor subtracts the "to-be-looked-at" connotations from the female body. But finally, as a film about female desire *Lianna* is incredibly pallid. *Flashdance*, in contrast, is an alluring inducement to give oneself over to watching gorgeous women dance. Judging from the film's reception, women audiences have enthusiastically taken up the invitation to look. My informal poll of friends shows that both lesbians and straight women have claimed this film. Some women said that *Flashdance* was the first film in years that they had gone back to see a second time. Does its "fantasy of control" explain why women, after seeing the film, are dancing along with *Flashdance* videocassettes in their living rooms and signing up for classes in jazz dance?[55]

Do responses to *Personal Best* and *Flashdance* suggest that women are suddenly "ready" for an eroticized imagery of their own? Will they no longer have to steal their glancing pleasure in the cinema or reroute their own plots? It is not as though women's sexual fantasies have never been served. Feminist work on women's traditional fiction such as Harlequin and gothic novels, melodrama and soap operas, shows that women have historically turned to these forms, which direct their readers through familiar conflicts with loved ones and provide releases and gratifications women probably won't find in conventional marriage.[56] Ann Barr Snitow's consideration of mass market romance as women's pornography suggests that feminists should take a second look at forms so often dismissed as reactionary if we would define the rhythms and emphases of women's sexual imagination. "The romantic intensity of Harlequins—the waiting, fearing, speculating—is as much a part of their functioning as pornography for women as are the more overtly sexual scenes," she says.[57] Similarly, Tania Modleski identifies distinctive narrative forms in women's television programming and suggests that these forms derive from those experiences that are thought to be woman's "lot in life"—waiting, anticipating, and the state of being constantly distracted and interrupted. Modleski concludes her analysis of soap operas with the assertion that new forms of women's pleasure won't necessarily be "made from scratch."[58] These traditional female forms promise a model for an emerging feminist aesthetic, and ideally, this aesthetic would even be compelling to those Harlequin readers who finish reading a novel every other day.[59] The political countermove here is in the reclamation of narrative gratifications for ourselves, for, as Modleski says, "this pleasure is currently placed at the service of the patriarchy."[60]

What could be new or liberating about an aesthetic based on woman's plight? Again, one of the crucial concerns of feminist film theory intersects with a burning issue in women's movement politics—correct pleasure. To replicate the dominant/subordinate power relation in either sexual practice or fantasy life has been considered a political taboo for feminists.

In the turnabout in feminist discussions of sexuality I have described, women are daring to say that politically correct practices and proper fantasies do not necessarily fuel their passion. The alternative imagery of a radical pornography for women may leave us cold. "If pornography is to arouse," says Ellen Willis, "it must appeal to the feelings we have, not those that by some utopian standard we ought to have."[61] Of course, erotic tastes, just as preferences for romantic narrative resolutions, may be understood as the residue of oppression, but what if reactionary tastes are ingenious compensations? The woman's fiction studies to which I have referred point out that romance fantasies are a means of symbolic conflict management. Also, we have yet to understand the connection between fantasy and erotic acts. As Chuck Kleinhans and Julia Lesage remind us, "Fantasy is precisely what people desire but do not necessarily want to act on. It is an imaginative substitution and not necessarily a model for overt behavior."[62] Pointing out the discrepancies between feminist egalitarian ideals of desire and what women report they like is not an argument for indifference to the imagery of power imbalance or the industries that profit from reproducing this imagery. Women's erotic daydreams are clues to structures of sustenance and release, and are due for the same serious consideration that women's diversions have begun to receive from feminists.

Finally, for academics, I suggest that in our critical studies of the next wave of feminist media—women's video productions, the heirs of the countercinema tradition—we be clearer about the source of our own fascination with aesthetic "play," off and against the dominant structures of prime-time television and mainstream cinema. The "correct" formula for alternative feminist film practice, the rearrangement of the "relations of looking," and the rejection of closure offer feminists a rather tight-lipped satisfaction. Restrained intellectual pursuits have a specialized recompense that bears little resemblance to the absorbing delight that means "pleasure" to so many women. Correct pleasure is a very privileged pleasure.

NOTES

1. For further discussion of these similarities, see Julia Lesage, "Women and Pornography," *Jump Cut*, no. 26 (December 1981): 46–47; also see, in the same issue, Gina Marchetti's bibliography "Readings on Women and Pornography," pp. 56–60.

2. Carol Vance, "Pleasure and Danger: Towards a Politics of Sexuality," in *Pleasure and Danger*, ed. Carol Vance, Boston: Routledge & Kegan Paul (1984), p. 4.

3. Vance, "Pleasure and Danger," p. 6.

4. For more of this history, see the introduction to Ann Snitow, Christine

Stansell, and Sharon Thompson, eds., *Powers of Desire*, New York: Monthly Review Press (1983).

5. Ellen Willis has argued that women's enjoyment of pornography could be seen as a "form of resistance in a culture that would allow [them] no sexual pleasure at all" ("Who is a Feminist?: A Letter to Robin Morgan," *Village Voice*, 21 December 1981, p. 17).

6. Paula Webster, "Pornography and Pleasure," *Heresies* 3, no. 4 (1981): 50.

7. The majority of books published as feminist film theory would suggest the psychoanalytic vogue, if nothing else. After the first two collections of articles published in the United States—Karyn Kay and Gerald Peary's *Women and Cinema*, New York: Dutton (1977), and Patricia Erens's *Sexual Stratagems*, New York: Horizon (1979)—the basic texts have privileged the earliest work of the British feminist film theorists, which has been so solidly grounded in Freud. Here I refer to Annette Kuhn, *Women's Pictures*, London: Routledge & Kegan Paul (1982), and E. Ann Kaplan, *Women and Film*, New York: Methuen (1983), as well as E. Ann Kaplan, ed., *Women in Film Noir*, London: British Film Institute (1978). More recent attempts to creatively extend this theory can be found in Mary Ann Doane, Patricia Mellencamp, and Linda Williams, eds., *Re-Vision*, Frederick, Md.: University Publications of America (1984), and Teresa de Lauretis, *Alice Doesn't*, Bloomington: Indiana University Press (1984), which proposes a bridge between psychoanalytic semiotics and cultural semiotics.

8. Laura Mulvey, "Visual Pleasure and Narrative Cinema," *Screen* 16, no. 3 (1975): 6–18 (reprinted in Kay and Peary, *Women and Cinema*, pp. 412–428); and Gerald Mast and Marshall Cohen, eds., *Film Theory and Criticism*, 3d ed., New York: Oxford University Press (1985). Also see Laura Mulvey and Colin MacCabe's "Images of Woman, Images of Sexuality," chap. 4 in Colin MacCabe, *Godard: Images, Sounds, Politics*, Bloomington: Indiana University Press (1980); Dee Dee Glass, Laura Mulvey, Griselda Pollock, and Judith Williamson, "Feminist Film Practice and Pleasure: A Discussion," in Fredric Jameson et al., *Formations of Pleasure*, London: Routledge & Kegan Paul (1983), pp. 156–60.

9. Claire Johnston, "Women's Cinema as Counter-Cinema," in *Notes on Women's Cinema*, ed. Claire Johnston, London: Society for Education in Film and Television (1973) (reprinted in Erens, *Sexual Stratagems*, pp. 133–43); Bill Nichols, ed., *Movies and Methods*, Berkeley and Los Angeles: University of California Press (1976), pp. 208–17.

10. "*Morocco*," *Cahiers du Cinéma*, no. 225 (November-December 1970) (reprinted in Peter Baxter, ed., *Sternberg*, trans. Diana Matias, London: British Film Institute [1980], pp. 81–93). I am indebted to Chuck Kleinhans for pointing out this correspondence to me.

11. Christian Metz, "The Imaginary Signifier," *Screen* 16, no. 2 (1975): 14–76; Julia Lesage's "The Human Subject—You, He, or Me?" which challenged the editors of *Screen* on their incorporation of psychoanalytic terms into film theory, appeared in this same issue.

12. Maureen Turim, "Gentlemen Consume Blondes," *Wide Angle* (Spring 1976): 71.

13. Lucy Fisher, "The Image of Woman as Image: The Optical Politics of *Dames*," *Film Quarterly* 30 (Fall 1976): 8 (reprinted in Erens, *Sexual Stratagems*, pp. 41–61); and Rick Altman, ed., *Genre: The Musical*, London: Routledge & Kegan Paul (1981), pp. 70–84.

14. I refer here to Karl Marx's theory of commodity fetishism, in *Capital*, vol. 1.

15. Laura Mulvey, "You Don't Know What Is Happening, Do You, Mr. Jones?" *Spare Rib* 8 (February 1973) (reprinted in *Spare Rib Reader*, ed. Marsha Rowe, London: Penguin Books [1982], pp. 48–57).

16. Joanna Russ, "Comment on Helene E. Roberts's 'The Exquisite Slave: The Role of Clothes in the Making of the Victorian Woman' and David Kunzle's 'Dress Reform as Antifeminism,' " *Signs* 2, no. 3 (1977): 521. Gayle Rubin ("Thinking Sex: Notes for a Radical Theory of the Politics of Sexuality," in Vance, *Pleasure and Danger*, p. 306) is critical of the way the anti-pornography movement focuses on "non-routine acts of love rather than routine acts of oppression, exploitation, or violence."

17. Russ, p. 521.

18. Mary Ann Doane, Patricia Mellencamp, and Linda Williams, "Feminist Film Criticism: An Introduction," in Doane, Mellencamp, and Williams, *Re-Vision*, p. 8.

19. Hélène Cixous ("The Laugh of the Medusa," in *The Signs Reader*, trans. Keith Cohen and Paula Cohen, ed. Elizabeth Abel and Emily K. Abel, Chicago: University of Chicago Press [1983], p. 291) describes the way creativity might take place from the cultural "in-between":

> If woman has always functioned "within" the discourse of man, a signifier that has always referred back to the opposite signifier which annihilates its specific energy and diminishes or stifles its very different sounds, it is time for her to dislocate this "within," to explode it, turn it around, and seize it; to make it hers, containing it, taking it in her own mouth, biting that tongue with her very own teeth to invent for herself a language to get inside of.

20. Doane, Mellencamp, and Williams, "Feminist Film Criticism," p. 9.

21. Juliet Mitchell, *Psychoanalysis and Feminism*, London: Lane (1974).

22. Jacqueline Rose, quoted in de Lauretis, *Alice Doesn't*, p. 165.

23. Griselda Pollock ("Report on the Weekend School," *Screen* 18, no. 2[1977]: 112) cautions feminists about the use of Freud:

> Furthermore, in so far as Freudian theory correctly describes the laws by which we are placed as subjects within a particular social formation, it also posits an inevitable resistance outside clinical or quite specific situations to the very knowledge that psychoanalysis offers. Thus, even within a film theory that uses the concerns of psychoanalysis, these resistances operate to counter the radical possibilities offered by the use of the theory. There is therefore every likelihood that the repression of the feminine is doubly ensured even at the point of potential exposure in theoretical analysis of film.

24. I refer here to larger debates within Marxist cultural studies, focused around the British journal *Screen*'s introduction of Lacanian psychoanalysis into film theory. See, for instance, Anthony Easthope, "The Trajectory of *Screen*, 1971–79," in *The Politics of Theory*, ed. Francis Barker et al., Colchester, Eng.: University of Essex (1983), pp. 121–33; Kevin Robins, "Althusserian Marxism and Media Studies: The Case of *Screen*," *Media, Culture and Society* 1, no. 4 (1979): 355–70; Iain Chambers et al., "Marxism and Culture," and Rosalind Coward, "Response," *Screen* 18, no. 4 (1977): 109–22.

25. Terry Lovell, "The Social Relations of Cultural Production: Absent Centre of a New Discourse," in *One-Dimensional Marxism*, ed. Simon Clarke, Victor Jeleniewski Seidler, Kevin McDonnell, Kevin Robins, and Terry Lovell, London: Allison & Busby (1980), p. 243.

26. Christine Gledhill, "Recent Developments in Feminist Criticism," *Quarterly Review of Film Studies* 3, no. 4 (1978): 483 (reprinted in Doane, Mellencamp, and Williams, *Re-Vision*, pp. 18–45).

27. Kaplan, *Women and Film*, p. 14.

28. Ibid., p. 24.

29. For examples of the Marxist feminist reconsideration of psychoanalytic theory in response to this criticism, see Annette Kuhn, "Women's Genres," *Screen* 25, no. 1 (1984): 19–27; and Claire Johnston, "The Subject of Feminist Film Theory/ Practice," *Screen* 23, no. 1 (1982): 27–34.

30. Jean-Louis Baudry ("Ideological Effects of the Basic Cinematographic Apparatus," *Film Quarterly* 28, no. 2 [1974–1975]: 46n) gives the reader some help with the concept of "subject," at a time when the term was used more tentatively than it is now: "We understand the term 'subject' here in its function as vehicle and place of intersection of ideological implications which we are attempting progressively to make clear, and not as the structural function which analytic discourse attempts to locate. It would rather take partially the place of the ego, of whose deviations little is known in the analytic field." The editors also thought it necessary to make it clear to readers that "the term 'subject' is used by Baudry and others not to mean the topic of discourse, but rather the perceiving and ordering self, as in our term 'subjective' " (p. 40).

31. One of the most comprehensive discussions of this "spectator eye" appears in another post-1968 French work on technology and ideology, Jean-Louis Comolli, "Technique and Ideology: Camera, Perspective, Depth of Field," *Film Reader*, no. 2 (February 1977): 128–140; reprinted in Bill Nichols, ed., *Movies and Methods*, vol. 2, Berkeley and Los Angeles: University of California Press (1985), pp. 40–57.

32. This analogy is fully explored in Jean-Louis Baudry, "The Apparatus," *Camera Obscura* 1 (Fall 1976): 104–23.

33. My complaint here is that concepts which originally were forged within the terms of a materialist analysis have gradually become removed from the Marxist theoretical structures that first defined them. Another example of this is the way *signifying practice* has come to stand for nothing more than the construction of meaning. Originally, as theorized by Julia Kristeva (see her "Signifying Practice and Mode of Production," *Edinburgh '76 Magazine*, no. 1, pp. 64–76), *signifying practice* included both the social maintenance function and the subversive possibilities of linguistic practices, with meaning-making activities always relative to the mode of production in a society.

34. E. Ann Kaplan, "Aspects of British Feminist Film Theory: A Critical Evaluation of Texts by Claire Johnston and Pam Cook," *Jump Cut*, nos. 12–13 (December 1976): 54.

35. See Terry Lovell, *Pictures of Reality*, London: British Film Institute (1980), p. 94, for more on Brecht and pleasure.

36. For example, see Fredric Jameson, "Pleasure: A Political Issue," in Jameson et al., *Formations of Pleasure*, London: Routledge & Kegan Paul (1983); and Richard Dyer, "Entertainment and Utopia," *Movie*, no. 24 (Spring 1977): 2–13 (reprinted in Altman, *Genre*, pp. 175–189).

37. Michèle Barrett, "Feminism and the Definition of Cultural Politics," in *Feminism, Culture, and Politics*, ed. Rosalind Brunt and Caroline Rowan, London: Lawrence & Wishart (1982), p. 54.

38. See Terry Lovell, *Pictures of Reality*, pp. 87 and 95.

39. Claudia Springer, "Black Women Filmmakers," *Jump Cut*, no. 29 (February 1984): 34–38.

40. Claire Johnston, in "Women's Cinema as Counter-Cinema," p. 28, first articulated this in relation to feminist film theory: "The sign is always a product. What the camera in fact grasps is the 'natural' world of the dominant ideology. Women's cinema cannot afford such idealism; the 'truth' of our oppression cannot

be 'captured' on celluloid with the 'innocence' of the camera: it has to be constructed/manufactured."

41. Kimberly Safford, in "*La Operación:* Forced Sterilization" (her review of the film, in *Jump Cut,* no. 29 [February 1984]: 37–38), says that for the filmmakers, the most direct way to demystify sterilization for Puerto Rican women is to demonstrate using documentary realism that since women's tubes are always severed in surgery, the sterilization operation is not as easily reversible as many women continue to believe. *La Operación* makes this argument with a conventional journalistic technique—graphic detailing of the surgery itself, the theory being that photographic "reality" that directly contradicts viewers' conceptions has the power to reverse those conceptions.

42. The idea of women's culture as "muted" is Elaine Showalter's; see, for instance, "Feminist Criticism in the Wilderness," in *Writing and Sexual Difference,* ed. Elizabeth Abel, Chicago: University of Chicago Press (1982), pp. 9–35.

43. Annette Kolodny, informal talk at Duke University, 1 March 1985.

44. Mulvey has since modified her provocative position that spectator point of view in the cinema is consistently the male point of view. In "Afterthoughts on 'Visual Pleasure and Narrative Cinema' Inspired by *Duel in the Sun*" (*Framework,* nos. 15–17 [1981]), she admits that her "masculinized" spectator-screen image relation was a calculated irony and that the actual gender of the viewer was not a consideration here.

45. See, for instance, Linda Williams, "When the Woman Looks," in Doane, Mellencamp, and Williams, *Re-Vision,* pp. 83–99.

46. Marcia Landy and Lucy Fisher, "*The Eyes of Laura Mars:* A Binocular Critique," *Screen* 23, nos. 3–4 (1982): 4–19.

47. Mary Ann Doane, "Film and the Masquerade—Theorizing the Female Spectator," *Screen* 23, nos. 3–4 (1982): 74–87.

48. Ibid., p. 83; see also Mary Ann Doane, "The 'Woman's Film': Possession and Address," in Doane, Mellencamp, and Williams, *Re-Vision,* pp. 67–82.

49. Pam Cook ("Melodrama and the Women's Picture," in *Gainsborough Melodrama,* ed. Sue Aspinall and Robert Murphy, London: British Film Institute [1983], pp. 14–28) takes the position that female desire is conceivable in these genres but that the films themselves register this possibility as contradiction.

50. Lucie Arbuthnot and Gail Seneca, "Pre-Text and Text in *Gentlemen Prefer Blondes,*" *Film Reader* 5 (Winter 1981–1982): 14.

51. Elizabeth Ellsworth, "The Power of Interpretative Communities: Feminist Appropriations of *Personal Best*" (paper delivered at Society for Cinema Studies Conference, University of Wisconsin-Madison, March 1984).

52. Chris Straayer, "*Personal Best:* Lesbian/Feminist Audience," *Jump Cut,* no. 29 (February 1984): 40–44; for another viewpoint, see Linda Williams, "*Personal Best:* Women in Love," *Jump Cut,* no. 27 (July 1982): 11–12.

53. Edith Becker, Michelle Citron, Julia Lesage, and B. Ruby Rich, "Lesbians and Film: Introduction to Special Section," *Jump Cut,* nos. 24–25 (March 1981): 17.

54. See Lisa DiCaprio, "*Lianna:* Liberal Lesbianism," *Jump Cut,* no. 29 (February 1984): 45–47.

55. See Kathryn Kalinak, "*Flashdance:* The Dead-End Kid," *Jump Cut,* no. 29 (February 1984): 3–5.

56. See, for instance, Janice Radway, *Reading the Romance,* Chapel Hill: University of North Carolina Press (1984).

57. Ann Barr Snitow, "Mass Market Romance: Pornography for Women is Different," *Radical History Review* 20 (Spring-Summer 1979): 157 (reprinted in Snitow, Stansell, and Thompson, *Powers of Desire,* pp. 245–263).

58. Tania Modleski, *Loving with a Vengeance*, New York: Methuen (1984), p. 103.

59. Pat Aufderheide, "What Are Romances Telling Us?" *In These Times*, 6–12 February 1985, p. 20.

60. Modleski, *Loving with a Vengeance*, p. 104.

61. Ellen Willis, "Feminism, Moralism, and Pornography," in Snitow, Stansell, and Thompson, *Powers of Desire*, p. 463.

62. Chuck Kleinhans and Julia Lesage, "The Politics of Sexual Representation" (introduction to special section on Pornography and Sexual Images), *Jump Cut*, no. 30 (March 1986): 24–26.

II.

Rereading Hollywood Films

A wealth of feminist film criticism has been produced in the last ten years. The following selections are representative of the richness and variety of those pieces addressing mainstream cinema. This section could easily have filled a book on its own and hence the selection was very difficult. Final choices were based on a decision to include a variety of approaches—particularly those using theories covered in the previous section of this book and, where possible, to provide a debate by using two essays on the same film as a case study.

The first piece, by Maureen Turim, "Gentlemen Consume Blondes" (1979), focuses on the Hawks film *Gentlemen Prefer Blondes*. Here, Turim applies a Marxist approach to the work, demonstrating how capitalist values lie at the base of this Hollywood movie. As Turim shows, the film is split between the "sexual display made of these women (their exploitation as objects within the film's narrative and for the film's appeal) and the women's expressed cynicism and cleverness (the satire in which the objects take on the role of critical subjects)."[1] The article demonstrates the ways these contradictions alternate throughout the film.

Turim analyzes how the film's oppositions—"come ons" vs. "put downs"; musical numbers vs. narrative segments; blonde Monroe looking for money vs. brunette Russell looking for love—are ultimately reconciled. For instance, she shows how the stars' seductive performances are embedded in the narrative so that viewers need not consider themselves voyeurs. The prurient interests of the movie audience are disguised by the fact that the women's performances seem directed at the on-screen nightclub audience. Similarly, the superficial differences between the two women mask the ways in which both are sexually displayed and both finally tamed (through marriage) to form the film's closure.

Turim returns to the question of the film's satire and to whether indeed it serves as a critique of the movie's ideology. In answer, she points to Hawks's use of the female body, which is not merely displayed as a sex object but also serves as an object of exchange, one that is incorporated into another commodity (the film) and sold. For Turim this is part of the 1950s consumer society. And it is for this reason that Lorelei's (Monroe) gold digging is not condemned within the film, but rather viewed as a form of female enterprise and thus justified by the film's unquestioned acceptance of capitalism. In the final analysis, the satire never seriously undermines this assumption.

Another analysis of *Gentlemen Prefer Blondes*, "Pre-text and Text in *Gentlemen Prefer Blondes*" (1982) by Lucie Arbuthnot and Gail Seneca, provides an example of "reading against the grain," a type of subversive reading made possible when there are internal contradictions within the narrative.

Arbuthnot and Seneca begin by investigating why watching Marilyn Monroe and Jane Russell as showgirls in *Gentlemen Prefer Blondes* produces pleasure for them as women viewers. They isolate several factors including the energy of the two actresses, their ability to resist male objectification, and the film's depiction of a friendship between two strong women. Reading beneath the story of heterosexual romance, they discover another story which celebrates women's pleasure in each other.

The two authors then provide a subversive reading of the film, showing how the romantic narratives (the pre-text) is disrupted and undermined by the women's resistance to male objectification and by their bonding with one another (the text, which contains both narrative and non-narrative elements).

In analyzing the ways in which the stars resist objectification, the authors focus on many of the film's visual elements, especially its examples of body language (the women's refusal to avert their eyes in submission, their active looking at men, their assertive body stances, their encroachment into male space, and their control over their own space), costume, and Hawks's directorial choices (lighting and medium close-ups which emphasize the actresses' zest and personality).

Arbuthnot and Seneca also look at the relationship between the women. Here they find that pre-text and text collude to offer a positive image of the Monroe/Russell friendship. They note that the narrative constantly reinforces their commitment to one another and their lack of competition. Again on the visual level, body language (the interchange of loving glances, their affectionate touching), directorial choices (Hawks's use of point-of-view shots to show the women looking at one another and of framing which highlights their connectedness), and genre expectations (normally we expect to see musical numbers featuring a heterosexual couple—not two women—who perform the musical numbers and who represent the film's love interest) play a central role in creating a sense of female bonding. The authors further assert that the female characters' connection with each other facilitates the female viewer's connection and identification with them.

Although Arbuthnot and Seneca recognize that elements of heterosexual romance and of objectification of women are always present, they feel that the actions of Monroe and Russell work to subvert the film's intended meaning, thus producing tensions that open the way for a feminist reading. They conclude that feminist film criticism needs to focus more centrally on these types of readings, and on female experience, rather than on theories by male authors.

The next three essays analyze works which have been assigned to the genre of "the woman's film." The first piece, "The Case of the Missing

Mother: Maternal Issues in Vidor's *Stella Dallas*" (1983), by E. Ann Kaplan begins by charting the ways in which the Mother is repressed in patriarchal society. Utilizing the work of recent feminist writers who offer psychoanalytic and socio-economic insights, she discusses how mother figures are mythologized and how Hollywood perpetuates these myths, dichotomizing Mothers into "Good" (all-nuturing and self-abnegating) or "Bad" (sadistic, neglectful, or ineffectual).

Kaplan views *Stella Dallas* as a perfect example of how films "reinscribe the Mother in the position patriarchy desires for her and, in so doing, teach the female audience the dangers of stepping out of the given position."[2] In her reading of the film, Kaplan describes how Stella initially resists her role as Mother and establishes her own mores and manner of dressing. For this she is punished. More serious, she later refuses to give up her close relationship with her grown daughter Laurel. This not only violates the myth of the self-abnegating Mother, but it also threatens patriarchy in that female bonding excludes men. This transgression must also be punished.

Kaplan points out the ways in which the film is structured through editing and point of view to guide our judgments of Stella. The film wrenches us away from Stella's perspective, replacing it with that of other characters, so that we, like they, view her disapprovingly as a spectacle. She is further denigrated by being adversely compared with Helen Morrison, the film's ideal mother figure. From Mother-as-spectacle it is a small step to Mother-as-spectator, a marginalized figure who passively observes life from the sidelines. Focusing on the film's final scene, Kaplan draws a comparison between Stella, standing outside in the rain watching her daughter's wedding inside the Morrison mansion through the lighted window frame, and the spectators in the audience who, watching the screen, "learn what it is to be a Mother in patriarchy." She feels the time has come for a new treatment of the Mother as a participant in the action and a person in her own right.

Linda Williams's " 'Something Else Besides a Mother': *Stella Dallas* and the Maternal Melodrama" (1984) was written in direct response to Kaplan's ideas. Williams sees *Stella Dallas* as an interesting test case for recent theories of female subject formation and female spectatorship. She feels strongly that the rejection of realist narratives and the substitution of a counter-cinema does not solve the problem of creating a feminine subjectivity. What is needed, according to Williams, is an understanding of how women do speak to one another, especially in discourses where women express the contradictions they encounter in patriarchy. Melodrama is one such place.

For Williams, *Stella Dallas* is of special importance because it is a film containing a reading position for female viewers that is based on how women take on a female identity and function as the primary nurturers. Williams treats the work of several feminists addressing these topics, especially that of Nancy Chodorow, who sees the life-long closeness between mother and daughter as a positive model for connectedness to others rather than as a weakness or deviation from the male norm as many psychologists have previously thought. Williams addresses some of the same issues as Kaplan: Stella's transgression of proper behavior, the ways in which she is viewed by other characters within the film, the mother-daughter bond, the fetishization of Barbara Stanwyck's Stella, the establishment of Helen Morrison as the ideal mother, and finally Stella's role as a sacrificing mother. However, unlike Kaplan who sees the film as a lesson for female viewers in regard to their proper place as mothers, Williams, drawing on Tania Modleski's writings on multiple subject positions in soap opera,[3] feels that the film's ending is too complex for such a response. Instead of identifying with one viewpoint (which contains the "lesson"), we, like empathetic good mothers, identify with *all* of the conflicting points of view and characters.

Furthermore, Williams observes that we do not see and believe in the same way that Stella does. "We see instead the contradictions between what the patriarchal resolution of the film asks us to see—the mother 'in her place' as spectator, abdicating her former position *in* the scene—and what we as empathetic, identifying female spectators can't help but feel—the loss of mother to daughter and daughter to mother."[4] In this regard, Williams also argues against Mary Ann Doane who calls for women viewers to distance themselves from an over-identification with female images on the screen (see "Film and the Masquerade" in Section One). For Williams, women viewers need not give up their identification with the female image (anymore than they need give up their first love object—the Mother). She sees female spectatorship as a constant juggling of the non-exclusive positions of closeness and distance. "The divided female spectator identifies with the woman whose very triumph is often in her own victimization, but she also criticizes the price of a transcendent 'eradication' which the victim-hero must pay."[5] Thus, for all its masochism, the maternal melodrama offers an important source of realistic reflection on women's lives and demonstrates the possibilities of Hollywood films to generate feminist readings.

In addition to motherhood, the woman-in-love constitutes a recurrent theme in the woman's film. In "Seduced and Abandoned: Recollection and Romance in *Letter From an Unknown Woman*" (1989), Lucy Fischer draws upon the work of Simone De Beauvoir and other feminists writers in order to focus on the psychological dimensions of women in love. Fischer shows how the film dramatizes such common characteristics as women's efforts to find self-worth in their lovers' eyes, to live through and sacrifice for these men, to idealize them, to be swept away by sexual passion and delusional fantasies, and finally to indulge in long periods of waiting. Fischer notes however that, unlike many woman's films, *Letter From an Unknown Woman* elides over those periods in the heroine's life characterized by hardship and suffering and thereby avoids an emphasis on female masochism.

Fischer observes that despite certain heroic aspects, Lisa, the film's central character and seeming narrator, is ultimately denied a position of authority through restrictions on her point of view. Through the crucial shift from Lisa writing her letter, to Stephan, her lover, reading it (and thus taking over control of the voice), and finally through Stephan's chronic inability to remember her, Lisa as a person is diminished. Fischer concludes that in the end Lisa is an "unknown" woman, not simply to Stephan, but to herself. By living her life through him, she has accepted a traditional view of love and negated her own existence.

Elizabeth Ellsworth's essay, "Illicit Pleasures: Feminist Spectators and *Personal Best*" (1982), like Arbuthnot and Seneca's, argues for a negotiated reading. In addition, like these two authors (and others in this volume), Ellsworth is interested in coming to terms with historical (i.e., actual) female spectators. "I will discuss how feminist reviewers used their interpretations of *Personal Best* as attempts to build alignments and pleasurable identifications with particular feminist communities as oppositional groups."[6] For Ellsworth, interpretation is not just a rejection of dominant meanings, but also a process whereby a group defines itself collectively and politically.

Borrowing methods from cultural studies, Ellsworth analyzed reviews of *Personal Best* as an indication of the film's reception in different types of communities and what that revealed about their priorities and perceptions. Of primary interest was a comparison of feminist reviews with those in the dominant press. For feminists, three issues emerged as central: (1) the representation of women's bodies, (2) the status of women in sports, and (3) lesbianism. Most feminist reviewers were sensitive to how the film's style and narrative structure worked to undermine or celebrate feminist attitudes. *Personal Best* also became the occasion for women within the feminist community, both lesbians and non-lesbians, to engage in ongoing debates around issues such as pornography and female sexuality. In contrast to the feminist reviews, those in the dominant media gave only tacit acknowledgment to feminist issues, then submerged them beneath other themes such as "competition," "coming of age," or "goal seeking." The study of pressbooks revealed that Warner Bros. was most interested in selling *Personal Best* as a "sports film" about women athletes.

Finally, Ellsworth discusses the oppositional interpretations of the lesbian feminist reviewers. For Ellsworth the importance of *Personal Best* rests with lesbians' use of oppositional readings to produce illicit pleasures (personal) and more important, social pleasures (public), which are collectively constructed through a group's shared experiences as an audience. Such experiences create a sense of solidarity and validation and in itself constitute an oppositional act. Ellsworth sees *Personal Best* as a limit case for what is currently possible within a community maneuvering for pleasure.

The section ends with Jane Gaines's "White Privilege and Looking Relations: Race and Gender in Feminist Film Theory" (1986), an attack on much current feminist film criticism, especially on its insistent use of the psychoanalytic concept of sexual difference as the sole explanation of women's oppression. She points out that women of color often realize their oppression first as blacks rather than as women. Similarly, she voices her concern about the banishment of sociological and historical reference points in film criticism, especially in works about racial difference and sexuality. To bring these issues into focus, she offers an analysis of a Diana Ross star vehicle, *Mahogany* (1975), a film about a black fashion model.

Gaines chooses *Mahogany* because the film's connection of sadism, voyeurism, and photographic acts seems to invite a psychoanalytic reading along the lines offered by Mulvey and others. However, Gaines demonstrates that an analysis based on male/female opposition "locks us into modes of analysis which will continually misunderstand the position of many women" (women of color, working-class women, lesbians) and reinforce white middle-class values "to the extent that it works to keep women from seeing other structures of oppression."[7]

Gaines discusses *Mahogany* in terms of how race complicates the issues of female sexuality, pointing out the need to develop a theory of black female representation that accounts for black women's history. Most revealing is her analysis of how the black male protagonist's "look" is either repudiated or frustrated, proving that not *all* male characters are free to engage in sexual looking. She also points out the ways in which the film obscures the connections between race, class, and gender. Finally, Gaines concludes that there are issues relevant to *Mahogany* (issues of race, class, and gender as they occur *in history*) that override psychoanalytic interpretations, and that feminist film theory, and by extension all film theory, must find ways of incorporating the crucial role of history into its criticism.

NOTES

1. Maureen Turim, "Gentlemen Consume Blondes," *Wide Angle* 1, no. 1 (1979). Revised and reprinted in *Movies and Methods* Vol. II, ed. Bill Nichols, Berkeley: University of California Press (1985), p. 371 and the present volume.
2. E. Ann Kaplan, "The Case of the Missing Mother: Maternal Issues in Vidor's *Stella Dallas*," *Heresies*, no. 16 (1983), p. 82.
3. Tania Modleski, "The Search for Tomorrow in Today's Soap Opera: Notes on Feminine Narrative Form," *Film Quarterly* 33, no. 1 (Fall 1979), pp. 12–21.
4. Linda Williams, " 'Something Else Besides a Mother': *Stella Dallas* and the Maternal Melodrama," *Cinema Journal* 24, no. 1 (Fall 1984), p. 18.

5. Ibid., pp. 22–23.

6. Elizabeth Ellsworth, "Illicit Pleasures: Feminist Spectators and *Personal Best*," *Wide Angle* 8, no. 2 (1986), p. 46.

7. Jane Gaines, "White Privilege and Looking Relations: Race and Gender in Feminist Film Theory," *Cultural Critique*, no. 4 (Fall 1986), p. 65.

GENTLEMEN CONSUME BLONDES

Maureen Turim

I. Satire/Seduction—The Film as Entertainment Machine

The line which separates celebration from satire in American culture is perniciously thin; no place is that lack of differentiation more evident than in Howard Hawks's *Gentlemen Prefer Blondes*, in which the excesses of the representation create a terrain of ambiguity fertile enough to support the perfect mass entertainment—a film whose ideological foundations are at once so evident and so hidden as to escape analysis.

Gentlemen, an elaborate Technicolor production of 1953, is in this light a totally different cultural artifact from the short volume Anita Loos wrote in 1925 which served as the source for the Broadway musical from which the film was derived. Loos's original work, first run as a serial in *Harper's Bazaar*, was more clearly a satire. The narrative takes the form of diary entries made by a flapper whose malapropisms, misspellings and childlike reasoning have the same force as Tom Sawyer's observations, ridiculing the surrounding society.

The transformation of diary into spectacle affects the possibility of a primarily satiric mode; in Hawks's film, the flapper and her best friend become two showgirls, objects continually on display for us, the viewing audience. Before examining the significance of this transformation, it is useful to trace the development of *Gentlemen* through the versions which lie between the magazine serial and the Fifties movie.

> Edgar Selwyn persuaded Miss Loos to write a straight dramatic play based on her story, but after she signed the contract she discovered to her dismay that Florenz Ziegfeld, Jr. wanted to produce a musical version. . . . In collaboration with her husband, John Emerson, she wrote a comic play which starred brunette June Walker wearing a blonde wig to play Lorelei. . . . The show was successful both in New York and on the road, where at least three companies toured simultaneously.
>
> Paramount Pictures bought the film rights. The studio officials, deciding

> to cast an unknown actress in the role of Lorelei, selected Ruth Taylor, a wide-eyed blonde. . . . Miss Loos said that John C. Wilson had repeatedly asked her to adapt her story as a stage musical comedy, but that she had been too busy writing movie scripts. . . . Miss Loos went to work on the book and co-authored the adaptation with Joseph Fields. . . . [They] kept the spirit of the original book and the atmosphere of the 20s but gave the story a somewhat different treatment. . . .
>
> The plot was certainly farfetched, but the book was not the primary reason for the musical's phenomenal success. The dances, the music, the sumptuous sets, the costumes, the cast, and above all, Carol Channing as Lorelei made the production a fast-moving extravaganza with an emphasis on entertainment. Disregarding integrated score or songs that developed the action, *Gentlemen Prefer Blondes* followed the pattern of the old-fashioned musicals, which shunted plot aside to make way for elaborate musical production numbers.[1]

While the 1949 Broadway version contained many elements of the new brashness and sexual appeal infused into the original story by the addition of the musical performances, it remained deeply rooted in the Twenties, including an opening song about Prohibition and a closing number entitled "Keeping Cool with Coolidge." The Hawks film, then, was the first version to update the story, moving it to a Fifties setting, amplifying the sexual play/exchange against a backdrop of the increasing reification of consumerist values. The musical numbers are treated differently—there are fewer songs in the film and they are more integrated.

Marilyn Monroe and Jane Russell

Gentlemen opens with a dance number which is both invitation and threat as the "two little girls from Little Rock" maneuver their bodies in a perfectly matched and coordinated assault which begins with them tossing their ermines at the audience/camera. The channels of signification are flooded: ermines tossed away, the fantastic power of being able to discard a commodity of so great an exchange value in order to expose a more precious commodity, the sexually cultivated self-aware female body. The number stresses the cooperative effort of the two, as lyrics are either delivered in unison, or, as when Lorelei delivers her verse on her retribution of the boy who once broke her heart and Dorothy, left off-screen for the moment, comes back in to reunify the ranks for the chorus:

> I was young and determined
> To be wined and dined and ermined
> Every night opportunity would knock.
>
> For a kid from a small street,
> I did very well on Wall Street

Although I never owned a share of stock.

Men are the same way everywhere.

The lyrics enhance the provocation, opening a paradigm which informs the structure of the narrative—an opposition between the sexual display made of these women (their exploitation as objects within the film's narrative and for the film's appeal) and the women's expressed cynicism and cleverness (the satire in which the objects take on the role of critical subjects). This opposition between "come on" and "put down" provides the ambiguity which is essential to the ambience of the sophisticated tease.

This opposition is also evidenced in a larger structural alternation between segments of musical performances and segments of other kinds of narrative development. The songs function as structural high points, intense, privileged moments of the film's expressivity. Among the five songs, two can be distinguished as differing from the others: "Little Rock" and "Diamonds" stand apart since they are stage performances, therefore having double audiences (one represented in the film and the film's real audience) and both play on the codes of nightclub extravaganzas. These two performance numbers almost frame the narrative—"Little Rock" at the beginning and "Diamonds" close to the end. This framing function can be seen as extending to the songs in general since they are grouped towards the beginning and end of the film with a large narrative block uninterrupted by song comprising the film's center (from the cocktail party aboard ship to the hotel in Paris). Also, the songs are alternated with non-musical narrative sequences in the sections of the film in which they do occur:

OPENING SEGMENTS

STAGE	BACKSTAGE	BOAT	DECK	POOL
"Little Rock"		"Bye, Bye, Baby"		"Anyone Here For Love?"

CLOSING SEGMENTS

CAFE	BACKSTAGE	STAGE	BACKSTAGE	COURT	WEDDING
"When Love Goes Wrong"	CHEZ LOUIS	"Diamonds"		reprise "Diamonds"	reprise "Little Rock"

This alternation is important to the system of embedding, of narrative motivation operative in the film's use of songs. We are never given spectacle for its own sake—each instance of performance/seduction is grounded in a logical purpose, hardly "naturalistic," but not freestanding either. This embedding acts as a justifying force, tempering the eroticism—the film's audience is not watching an enticing performance directly exhibited for them, but rather the film's audience is witness to a nightclub performance directed at an audience within the film. So even though camera angles and distance increase and highlight the film audience's voyeurism and fetishism over what is attainable at the local establishment, this vision is made innocent. We need not consider ourselves voyeurs and fetishists, habitués of cheap strip shows—we prefer "sophisticated musical comedy."

A corollary function of the alternation of song and narrative segments is to structurally disperse and alternate moments of more intense titillation and provocation. The film as machine to entertain needs this pattern of dispersion; it is dependent on recurrent stimulation, not only on the sways, rhythms, and beats, but also on the very fact of creating moments when the spectator is encouraged to partake of the forbidden vision, to watch with prurient pleasure. The success of the entertainment derives from this indulgence of an erotic vision, but not continually. Intermittence—privilege—must be associated with this vision if it is to retain its power within the spectator's imagination.

II. Woman Object

Marilyn Monroe/Lorelei Lee—star persona and character—are flattened into a single myth. It is ironic that in a film about performances, acting is denied in favor of "matching." Even the Twenties locutions which remain ("Thank you ever so") become simply another of Marilyn's idiosyncrasies, part of her essence as instantaneous artifact and pop art sex goddess, part of the arsenal along with quivering lips and dresses drawn tight across her hips.

A major force developed in the film is the contrast/complement relationship between Lorelei and Dorothy, between Monroe and Russell. For beneath an initial opposition, Blonde/Money versus Brunette/Love, is an overriding similarity which ideologically anchors certain traits and powers as inherently female. This shared quality is the skillful manipulation of men (in the attempt to regain an incriminating photo: "If we aren't able to empty his pockets between us, we aren't worthy of the name Woman."). The courtroom impersonation of Lorelei by Dorothy emphasizes this sameness beneath the superficial difference—the difference is marked ironically by the disguise, the affected manners, while the sameness is marked by the willingness and ability to so deceive.

Hawks himself has interpreted this united front as a joke, a "reversal" of the sexual structures of his other films' narratives:

> *Gentlemen Prefer Blondes* was only a joke. In the other films, you have two men who go out and try to find some pretty girls in order to have a good time. We thought of the opposite and took two girls who go out and find some men to have a good time: a perfectly modern story. It pleased

> me, it was funny. The two girls, Jane Russell and Marilyn Monroe, were so good together that each time I didn't know what scene to invent, I just had them walk back and forth and everyone adored it; they never tired of watching these two pretty girls walk. I built a staircase so that they could go up and down and as the girls were well-built . . . [2]

Somehow Hawks's words are more revealing than informative. They disclose that beneath the "joke" of depicting women in an active sexual role is their exploitation as objects being trotted back and forth, up and down the screen like ducks in a shooting gallery.

Dorothy/Male Object/Love

The characterization of Dorothy as connoisseur of the male body and yet fall-girl for old-fashioned romantic love blends the modern (sexual) woman with the Victorian. Her number, "Ain't There Anyone Here for Love?" has her satirizing the athletic cult as sexual sublimation while she actively displays a body in training for sexual activity. "Love" here clearly equals sex, as Dorothy flings herself at the oblivious musclemen saying, "I need a shoulder to lean on and a couple of arms to hold me," and calls out such teasers as, "Doubles, anyone?" Ideological transformation: Dorothy's "excessive" sexuality, her freely expressed lust, disappears behind "true love" for Malone. Desire is tamed before the film's end.

Lorelei/Diamonds

Lorelei's desire to marry for money, unlike Dorothy's sexual drive, undergoes no transformation. It is merely explained in practical terms as good business sense, the female parallel to any male commercial transaction. Like "Little Rock," "Diamonds" puts golddigging into a social context which makes it highly rational:

> A kiss may be grand
> But it won't pay the rental
> On your humble flat
> Or help you at the Automat.
>
> Men grow cold as girls grow old
> And we all lose our charms in the end.
> But square-cut or pear-shape
> These rocks don't lose their shape.

Over and over the lyrics say men are undependable and women have one commodity to exchange, and that for a limited time (youth). At one point Lorelei is choreographed as the center of a cluster of women, her song offered to them as advice: Get diamonds, a commodity of ever-rising exchange value; get diamonds, security. It is the clever logic of a deeply alienated woman. A dramatic lighting change punctuates the number, coming in the middle of the line, "Stiff-backed or stiff-kneed, you stand straight at Tiff'ny's." Later Lorelei explains to Gus's father, "A girl being pretty is like a man being rich. . . . If you had a daughter, you'd want her to marry a rich man." The Fifties capitalist must agree, for what is being embodied in Lorelei is the understanding of the exchange value of sex, although not uniquely, not even primarily as concerns the golddigger. Rather, Lorelei must be seen as just an exaggerated form of the role assigned all middle-class women in Fifties culture, while Dorothy complements this role by being transformed by romantic love. The amalgam of the two is the ideological prescription of the film.

In the reprise of "Little Rock" for the marriage ceremony at the film's end, the women boast, "At last we won the big crusade." About to attain the ultimate victory, marriage, the two women stand as equally successful. For love or money, with blondes or brunettes, marriage provides the closure for this film as it does for so many in which happiness/success of women is sustained as the hermeneutic question, the question which informs the narrative. Considering this closure, considering the film's function as machine to entertain through intermittent stimulation, considering the cloaking of this stimulation in a narrative framework of "good cultural object" which justifies and excuses the inclusion of the erotic, what is left to be said of the satire? Is the satire gutless, only a variant on bourgeois entertainment with no power to challenge? Is it just a frill, an embellishment, or perhaps even part of the cloaking of the exploitation? Is it not perhaps the satire which provides a pleasing and necessary ambiguity which disguises the seduction and diverts our attention from the ideological functioning of the film?

What must be remembered in arriving at the answer to these questions is the manner in which this film uses the female body. It is the hourglass figure, the lush, full body of Fifties fashion which sells the film. The female body is not only a sex object, but also an object of exchange; its value can be sold (prostitution) or it can be incorporated into another commodity which then can be sold (the film).

> In the universe of consumerism, there is an object more beautiful, more precious, more striking than any other—heavier with connotations than even the automobile; it is the body. Its rediscovery after the era of puritanism under the sign of physical and sexual liberation; its omnipresence (and specifically the feminine body) in advertising, fashion, mass culture; the hygienic, dietetic, and therapeutic cults which surround it; the obsession with youth, elegance, virility/femininity, treatments, diets, and sacrificial practices attached to it; the Myth of Pleasure which envelops it—all are evidence that today the body has become a sacred object. It has literally been substituted for the soul in its moral and ideological function. . . .

> The status of the body is culturally determined. In each culture the mode of organization of the relationship to the body reflects the mode of organization of the relationship to objects and the social relations. In a capitalist society the general laws of private property apply to the body, to the social practice and the mental representation of it.[3]

These comments by Baudrillard on the status of the body invite speculation on the specific treatment of the female body in *Gentlemen* in relationship to American culture of 1953. There is the same combination of gaudiness and elegance evidenced in the finned Cadillacs. There is a fullness which can be associated with fertility and prosperity. This film is the product of an age when a fortune can be made on the skillful marketing of air-brushed pin-ups, an age which no longer exists in its pure form (styles change), but which was influential in establishing the social relations and mental representations which have lingered on over more than twenty years to find a new form today.

III. The Reference and the Symbolic: Ideological Functions

Is it by chance that "Piggy" Beekman, the object of Lorelei Lee's quest throughout the central portion of the film, is the owner of a South African diamond mine? Is it by chance that Lorelei Lee is a blonde? Is it by chance that the narrative centers on a voyage to France?

The referential code—the discrete references the text makes to social and historical phenomena—how do these references mobilize, reproduce, and generate cultural mythologies, in Barthes's sense of this term? Capitalist values are at the base of *Gentlemen*; they are the assumption, the context. Racist, sexist, and imperialist assumptions intriguingly surround the core depiction of consumerist values inherent in capitalism.

Piggy/South Africa/Diamonds

The text, even within its satire, treats this subject frivolously. The name "Piggy" is mildly satirical, but endearing. Piggy is ridiculous but not dangerous or evil. South Africa and diamond mines are part of a caricature, an idiosyncrasy, and are fundamentally depoliticized. When Piggy is first introduced to Lorelei, there is a shot of him, taken as her subjective vision, which has a diamond superimposed where his head should be. To Lorelei, Piggy has only one signification, wealth, which she intends to exploit, "to mine." If golddigging is justified within the film as the female form of capitalist enterprise, what underlies this "justification" is the assumption that capitalism and thus imperialism are unquestioned, natural. The satire does not touch this assumption.

Gentlemen Prefer Blondes

Blondness as a criterion for sexual preference is racist. Consider a publicity still for silent screen star Colleen Moore: a photo of her in blackface, wearing an Afro wig, bore this caption—"What will I do if it's true that gentlemen prefer blondes?" Blondness is also easily appropriated for commercial reasons—consider the years of Clairol ads, followed by a more recent series lauding Hanes stockings as blonde models are placed in the fetishist glance of males with the slogan, "Gentlemen prefer Hanes." Blondness is a cultural fetish, the sexual ideal of a racist society.

France/The Crossing on the Ile de France/ Les chanteuses américaines

Why does the theme of a voyage to France recur in the Fifties musicals—*An American in Paris* (1950), *April in Paris* and *On the Riviera* (1951), *The French Line* and *Gentlemen Prefer Blondes* (1953), *Silk Stockings* (1956), *Funny Face* (1957), *Gigi* (1958)? The luxury liner has its own mystique. It is a limited, intense time when anything goes, perfect for the portion of the narrative which necessitates complications, intrigues. The film can make use of this setting in innumerable imaginative ways: Lorelei surveying the passenger list or trapping herself in the porthole. France fits into the imaginary of musicals as a fantasy land of culture combined with risqué morality and sexual excitement, the blend which is the goal of the musical's structure.

Finally we come to the instance at which the reference and the symbolic become totally enmeshed. It is most helpful to this argument that Barthes, outside the context of this film, has already remarked on the relationship between women and diamonds which is so central to this film. He suggests that not only are diamonds considered a girl's best friend, but also that a girl is considered a diamond:

> The classical props of the music-hall. . . . Feathers, furs and gloves go on pervading the woman with their magical virtue even once removed, and give her something like the enveloping memory of a luxurious shell, for it is a self-evident law that the whole of striptease is given in the very nature of the initial garment: if the latter is improbable, as is the case with the woman in furs, the nakedness which follows remains itself unreal, smooth and enclosed like a beautiful slippery object, withdrawn by its very extravagance from human use: this is the underlying significance of the G-string covered with diamonds or sequins which is the end of the striptease. This ultimate triangle, by its pure and geometrical shape, by its hard and shiny material, bars the way to the sexual parts like a sword of purity, and definitively drives the woman back into a mineral world, the [precious] stone being here the irrefutable symbol of the absolute object, that which serves no purpose.[4]

NOTES

1. Abe Laufe, *Broadway's Greatest Musicals*, New York: Funk & Wagnalls (1969), pp. 133–34.
2. Jacques Becker, Jacques Rivette, François Truffaut, "Entretien avec Howard Hawks," *Cashiers du cinéma*, no. 56 (February 1956).
3. Jean Baudrillard, *La Société de consommation*, Paris: S. G. P. P. (1970), p. 196.
4. Roland Barthes, *Mythologies*, New York: Hill and Wang (1972), p. 85.

ADDENDUM (1979)

Looking back over this article, I realize I might now pose some of the questions it raises more forcefully. The question of adaptation and revision of the Loos book into a stage musical, into a film, with which the article begins could do more than raise the question of the difference in dominance between the satiric mode and the entertainment mode of celebration. It seems that these artifacts could be looked at from a perspective I have called elsewhere[1] "semiotic layering," that is, the accrual and transformations of meanings associated with an artifact as it passes through history, or as it is presented in different versions. In the case of *Gentlemen*, there is a curious shift of the Twenties heritage into the Fifties context which is then affected by our vantage point as analysts of the film in the late Seventies. The Twenties golddigger arose from the working class and the recesses of rural America alongside the other immigrant aspirants in America's rush for gold. It follows, then, that she should become a heroic figure of so many Thirties films as a reincarnation of a true-heart Susie, a working-class heroine who only *seems* to be lusting after money, but in fact seeks love, security, community, aspirations precariously mixed in the growth of sisterhood amongst the chorus and a final marriage which appears to doom that vital, creative group activity. She is a golddigger in ironic appelation only; actually, she is the "good wife," as exemplified by Joan Blondell in *Footlight Parade* kicking her rival, the pretentious floozy, out the door. When the Fifties *Gentlemen* returns to this golddigger myth, it is not just as renewal and updating into Fifties values, but it also holds on to the layers of meanings circulating in American popular culture for thirty years.

This explains the Pop Art, prefabricated texture of the Hawks film and of its "star," Marilyn Monroe (the quotations serve to remind us that she was still fighting for that status at the time of the film's production). Consider the availability of such curious manuals as the *Bonomo "Original" Hollywood "Success Course,"* published in 1945 (the quotes are in the "original" title).[2] Young Norma Jeans all over the country could study such texts, learning the correct answers to the questions provided in "Personality Tests" (pp. 81–82), such as "Do you laugh charmingly? Can you talk for half an hour without mentioning yourself? Have you looked at yourself in a triple mirror in the past two weeks?"

Obviously golddigging is to be taken very seriously in the Fifties as the entrance into the culture itself. I indicated this in the article by asserting that the amalgam of Lorelei and Dorothy was the ideological proscription of the film, telling us to temper an acceptance of the female position with both an understanding of the exchange value of sex and the channeling of the power of that sexuality into a romantic love; thus we again see the culture reifying contradictory values, that signal for the participants' suicidal deaths and bra advertisements.

It is interesting that, in the three years since the article first appeared, American culture has danced its way back to the high-heeled steps of the Fifties in which bustiers, cinched waists and tight skirts splash feminine charms in the face of the movement for feminist consciousness. Danskin brought out a leotard this year which resembles the "Playboy bunny" costumes used in the "Little Rock" opening number. Here we come to an analysis that overlaps with a topic on which I have continued to work, the role definition of fashion as transmitted through Hollywood films. These images have literally designed our lives for us, as we look in three-way mirrors before buying.

Another point that I find deserves some amplification is the analysis in the article of the psychoanalytic operation of the film as it manipulates the spectator through a network characterized by the body as source of spectacle by using such devices as doubling, repetition, alternation of denial and access, and the focusing on fragments as symbolic replacement which typifies fetishism. I want to make it clear that, in evoking these basic operations of fascination and pleasure, it is the specific ideological functions of their inscription in the film which is to be examined critically. The point is not to negatively critique all spectacle, as some film theorists have tended to do recently, but rather to show how the cultural references and ideological determinants of the commercial spectacle have in fact created a very restricted access to pleasure, to eroticism, to the viewing experience. This is what I tried to do in this article and continue to do elsewhere.[3]

To add, then, one point on this topic that is specific to *Gentlemen* which is not brought out in the article is the appeal of the two women performing movements in rhythmic coordination. How do we understand the fascination of what I called the "perfectly matched and coordinated assault" of this dancing team? Here I think we need to blend some very abstract psycho-perceptual concepts about the appeal of symmetry, rhyming, and patterning within a visual field with an historical analysis of how lesbianism has served in male-oriented pornography to increase visual stimulation and to ultimately give twice as much power to the eye, which can penetrate even the liaisons which would appear to deny male entry.[4] Lesbians exist in pornography and advertising as a trope; they are not really women given to each other erotically rather than to men, but pseudo-lesbians given over to the gaze which truly possesses them. In *Gentlemen* the narrative assures us that, despite the bonds between Dorothy and Lorelei, their relationship is not self-sufficient; it seeks males for completion, so that when (heterosexual) love goes wrong, nothing goes right.

NOTES

1. This was developed in a paper given at the Purdue Film Conference, 1979, called "Layers of Meaning: Enoch Arden and an Historically Wrought Semiotics."
2. Joe Bonomo, *Bonomo "Original" Hollywood "Success Course,"* New York: Bonomo Culture Institute (1945).
3. Here I refer to a paper I gave at the International Film Conference V: "Cinema and Language," Milwaukee, 1979, entitled, "Lifting the Veil: Women, Image and Desire."
4. *Ibid.*

PRE-TEXT AND TEXT IN *GENTLEMEN PREFER BLONDES*

Lucie Arbuthnot and Gail Seneca

I. Overview

As feminists, we experience a constant and wearying alienation from the dominant culture. The misogyny of popular art, music, theatrical arts, and film interferes with our pleasure in them. This essay discusses a departure from this familiar alienation. Howard Hawks's *Gentlemen Prefer Blondes*, a 1953 film starring Marilyn Monroe and Jane Russell as showgirls, is clearly a product of the dominant culture. Yet, we enjoy the film immensely. In this essay, we chronicle our search to understand our pleasure in this film.[1] We argue that *Gentlemen Prefer Blondes* can be read as a feminist text. We believe that it is important to recoup from male culture some of the pleasure which it has always denied us; we hope that our analysis of *Gentlemen Prefer Blondes* will suggest ways to discover feminist pleasures within films of the dominant culture, and indicate the kinds of films which might be most conducive to a feminist reading.

The logic of our argument about *Gentlemen Prefer Blondes* parallels the process we followed in trying to understand our pleasure in the film. We will briefly mention the key analytic stages of that process in this introduction, before describing each of them in some detail in the text of this essay.

First, we simply watched the film over and over to isolate what we most enjoyed about it. We realized we loved the energy that Monroe and Russell exude. Their zest and sheer presence overwhelm the film. Perhaps, we thought, we were seeing in Monroe and Russell what others have seen in such actresses as Dietrich, Garbo, and Hepburn: strong, independent women, who seem to resist to some extent objectification by men. But, our pleasure in *Gentlemen Prefer Blondes* seemed to far surpass that which we found in films starring Garbo, Dietrich, or Hepburn. We had found something more than the presentation of positive women who were strong enough to sometimes resist men and act for themselves.

We turned then to some recent feminist films, thinking they might suggest something about the source of women's pleasure in film, which could apply to our experience with *Gentlemen Prefer Blondes*. These films were helpful, however, only insofar as our consideration of them clarified our dissatisfaction with them. For example, feminist films in the French psychoanalytically inspired tradition (such as *Deux Fois* and *Thriller*) often present women in a manner which makes them inaccessible to male objectification. But such films focus more on denying men their cathexis with women as erotic objects than in connecting women with each other. Films such as *The Turning Point, Girlfriends,* and *Julia* showed friendships between women, but less openly and convincingly than *Gentlemen Prefer Blondes*. For *Gentlemen Prefer Blondes* presents women who not only resist male objectification, but who also cherish deeply their connections with each other. The friendship between two strong women, Monroe and Russell, invites the female viewer to join them, through identification, in valuing other women and ourselves.[2]

We read, then, beneath the superficial story of heterosexual romance in *Gentlemen Prefer Blondes,* a feminist text which both denies men pleasure to some degree, and more importantly, celebrates women's pleasure in each other.

II. Dietrich, Garbo, Hepburn

In *Gentlemen Prefer Blondes* Monroe and Russell portray strong, independent, and likable women. In attempting to understand our response to these portrayals, we reconsidered other positive Hollywood portraits of strong women. We concentrated on Greta Garbo, Marlene Dietrich, and Katherine Hepburn, because directors most consistently cast them in such roles.

We enjoy the presence of a positive woman, who acts in response to her own desires rather than in response to the desires of men, on screen. In many of the films starring Marlene Dietrich, for example, and particularly those directed by Josef von Sternberg, we are delighted with her open disdain for men. Even as she entertains men in *Morocco,* she is haughty and distant from them. When she wears a tux, and kisses a female patron of the club, in *Blonde Venus,* we can fantasize that behind the tux there might be a lesbian.[3] But almost always her anti-male posture and her power are eventually crushed by the male plot. There is no sign of her initial independence in the closing scene of *Morocco,* as she struggles abjectly through the sand following Gary Cooper into the desert. The kiss in the nightclub in *Blonde Venus* is the only sign that she might be more centrally connected to women than to men. The suggestion of her independence from men and affiliation with women raises our feminist expectations. Her inability to sustain these qualities deepens our disappointment.

Unlike most Dietrich films, those starring Garbo almost never center convincingly around the gratification of male desire and pleasure. She rarely seems emotionally vulnerable to men, and her appeal to feminist viewers may reside in this apparent aloofness. In *Anna Christie*, for example, she no sooner marries than she packs her husband off for an extended sea voyage, opting for a life of solitude. But that aloofness extends not only to men. It encompasses women as well, and more centrally her own emotions and desires. Garbo's face is a mask, a mask that hides her from men, from women, and from herself. We cannot know her strengths and vulnerabilities, her desires, because she seems untouched and untouchable.

It is the enigmatic quality of the characters played by both Dietrich and Garbo that allows us to project our own fantasies onto them; because they express no desires of their own, we can confer ours on them. But ultimately our desires, as women, are never reinforced. The film plots are constructed to excite and elude male desire. The enigma of Dietrich and Garbo, their passivity, is cultivated for the male viewer in order to entice and titillate him.

Turning to Hepburn—here we are thinking particularly of her films with Spencer Tracy—we find more possibilities of pleasure, pleasure in identification with a successful woman. Hepburn is undeniably active. She resists objectification or enthronement as the erotic object of the male viewer's fantasy. She is too powerfully present. She clearly has desires, believes in causes, and her desires are never convincingly annihilated. Even when she gives up her cause to please Tracy at the conclusion of a film, we see more rote obeisance to the dictates of a genre and a society, than consistency with her characterization in the rest of the film.

But even as we enjoy and identify with Hepburn's professional successes, we are aware of a fundamental absence in the character she portrays. Her interpersonal relationships seem to lack emotional depth. It is as if there were insufficient space to explore both a woman's professional life and her emotional life in a film. Because professional success is not expected of women, the filmmakers spend most of their time convincing us that Katharine Hepburn is an exception. Consequently, very little space can be devoted to an explanation of her emotional life.

Even in a film like *Adam's Rib*, in which Hepburn and Tracy have a caring relationship, and the film spends time showing that caring (for example, Tracy dropping the pencil in the courtroom scene in order to establish friendly contact with Hepburn under the table; the back-rubs they give each other), we still experience an emotional shallowness. This is perhaps most evident, for us, in Hepburn's lack of female friendships. The one relationship with a woman that we are shown (Judy Holliday) is marred by Hepburn's condescension and distance. The crux of our dissatisfaction with Hepburn is her lack of connection with other women, and therefore with us and other feminist viewers.

Even though Hepburn, Garbo, and Dietrich afford us considerable pleasure as feminist viewers, our pleasure in watching them did not rival the pleasure we experienced in watching *Gentlemen Prefer Blondes*. Perhaps an overtly feminist film would provide better clues to our emotional response to *Gentlemen Prefer Blondes*, we thought. We turned therefore to the emerging body of avowedly feminist films which consciously seek to destroy male voyeuristic pleasure and male identification, such as *Deux Fois* and *Thriller*.

We suspect that these films do successfully destroy male pleasure. Women are not shot for eroticism. No strong male characters are created with whom men might identify in objectifying women. Classic narrative structures are subverted to destroy "the ease and plentitude of narrative fiction film" for the male viewer.[4] In destroying male pleasure, however, these films also destroy our pleasure. They deny us voyeuristic pleasure, the pleasure of losing ourselves in a narrative, and most centrally the pleasure of identification with a positive female image.

We understand the impulse to destroy the male objectification of women. But the ways in which some feminist filmmakers do so—by destroying the narrative and the possibility of viewer identification with characters—destroy both the male viewer's pleasure and our pleasure. We believe that identification with positive female characters in a narrative should be encouraged rather than destroyed. It should be encouraged because human development requires identification with positive adult figures; and women's opportunities for such identification are consistently thwarted.[5] As women, we live what Adrienne Rich has called a "double life": a life in which we depend on men; a life in which we recall, but must suppress, our initial primary involvement with other women.[6] As difficult as it is in real life for women to live without positive identification with other women, most films—even such avowedly feminist films—make this identification virtually impossible.

Thus, in our search to understand our enjoyment of *Gentlemen Prefer Blondes*, feminist films in the European psychoanalytic tradition were helpful mainly in suggesting the importance of positive identification for the female viewer, which they ignore. Some Hollywood films provide a measure of that positive identification, particularly those portraying strong, independent women. But even in these, the primary focus is on women's allegiance to men, rather than women's connection with other women. In those rare films which focus on women's connection to each other, the possibilities for the female viewer's positive identification with characters are greatly enhanced. The female characters' connection with each other facilitates the female viewer's connection and identification with them. This is precisely what we find compelling in *Gentlemen Prefer Blondes*. Beneath their surface attentions to men, Monroe and Russell are undeniably and enduringly there for each other.

III. The Feminist Text

Gentlemen Prefer Blondes tells the story of two voluptuous showgirls, Marilyn Monroe and Jane Russell. It chronicles their adventures on a transatlantic sea voyage, during which they seek husbands and capture the attention of every male on board. Their quest finally culminates in a double wedding ceremony.

In our study of the film, however, we have found that this narrative of romantic adventure between the sexes is continually disrupted and undermined by other narrative and non-narrative elements in the film. This disruption is so severe and continual that we have come to regard the romantic narrative as a mere pre-text, a story which coexists with, contradicts, and disguises another, more central, text. This text consists of two major themes, neither of which fits comfortably with the pre-text of romance. The themes are the women's resistance to objectification by men, and the women's connection with each other. The following pages discuss the film's articulation of these themes, which comprise the text we read in *Gentlemen Prefer Blondes*.

(1) Resistance to Male Objectification

The theme of resistance to male objectification is most clearly articulated on a gestural level. Even where the narrative situation seems to code Monroe and Russell for objectification by men, they resist this objectification. We read this resistance in their gestural cues or body language. Specifically, we find this resistance in their look, stance, use of space, and activity. Their costuming and Hawks's use of camera and lighting also limit their objectification.

Look

Socially it is the prerogative of men to gaze at women and the requirement of women to avert our eyes in submission. The initiation of the gaze signals superiority over the subordinate.[7] Clearly, in *Gentlemen Prefer Blondes*, men do gaze at women; Monroe and Russell are spectacles for male attention. However, Monroe and Russell refuse to signal submission by averting their eyes; rather, they return the look. As Monroe and Russell walk through a sea of admiring spectators, they also actively search the crowd. Through their active and searching look, they appropriate the space around them, refusing to yield it to the male gaze. There are several particularly striking examples of this returned look, in which Monroe and Russell walk through a throng of gaping men but refuse to accept objectification by averting their own eyes, for example, during their initial walk through the ranks of the Olympic team on the dock, when they first enter the dining-room on board ship, and during their final walk down the aisle to the altar where they are to be married.

Stance

From the moment Russell strides onto stage in the opening number, we are cued to her resistance to male objectification. She virtually never moves in the constrained fashion of the "lady"; she strides, arms swinging at her sides, shoulders erect and head thrown back. Even when she is standing still, Russell's legs are often apart, her hands are on her hips and posture erect. Her stance speaks her strength and authority.[8]

Use of Space

It is a male prerogative to encroach on women's space not only through look, but bodily as well. Women are to be looked at, moved in on, and touched by men, rather than to look, to move, and to initiate touch themselves. Female space is violable by men. In a social situation, for example, men assume the right of entry into a female conversation; women typically do not assume the same rights with men.[9] In *Gentlemen Prefer Blondes,* however, Monroe and Russell clearly control access to their own space and also freely enter men's spaces. For example, when Monroe's fiancé, Mr. Esmond, wants to enter her dressing room in the Paris nightclub, he can do so only after Monroe and Russell consult each other:

> Mr. Esmond (running after Lorelei): Lorelei! Lorelei! Wait! Look Lorelei! I've flown the entire Atlantic Ocean just to talk to you.
> And now you . . .
> Lorelei: Well, you might come in for a minute, [turning to Dorothy], that's if *you* don't mind.
> Dorothy: I don't mind if *you* don't mind. [They open the door to their dressing room, making him precede them.]

Similarly, when the male Olympic team is working out, Russell strides through their ranks uninvited, looking the men over, squeezing their muscles, pulling one man down into her lap by his hair. In the courtroom scene, Russell not only confidently enters male space, but transforms it into a showcase for her dancing and singing.

Activity

In all these instances—through look, stance, and use of space—Monroe and Russell subvert male objectification. By becoming active themselves, they make it impossible for men to act upon them. They are actors and the initiators in their relations with men. When Russell and the detective (with whom she is allegedly in love) embrace on the moonlit deck, it is Russell who initiates the kiss. In order to retrieve an incriminating piece of film, Monroe and Russell deftly pin the detective down and pull off his pants. His helplessness is underscored when they ultimately send him off dressed only in his underwear and a frilly pink bathrobe.

It is interesting that Monroe and Russell's tight-fitting and stereotypically feminine dress does not diminish the power of their stance, their look, or their activity. Body language appears to be a more accurate index of power than clothing. Perhaps this is why, in film and in society, women can wear men's clothing without abandoning their "femininity." When Dietrich wears men's clothes, for example, she remains an object to be overpowered, because her body language signals passivity and invites seduction. Clothing cannot confer power. This is one of the reasons we find *Gentlemen Prefer Blondes* more conducive to a feminist reading than films in which Dietrich wears a tuxedo and top hat.

Costume

Costume could easily have been used in *Gentlemen Prefer Blondes* to reduce Monroe and Russell to mere objects of male sexual desire. In fact, their costuming partakes of the tension between objectification and resistance to objectification that we have described above. Their tight-fitting dresses are sometimes constraining, but they are rarely revealing. Given the mammary madness of the fifties,[10] it is striking that Hawks chose to dress Monroe and Russell in high-necked sweaters and dresses, jackets, and subdued colors. Even their most revealing costumes are cocktail dresses which neither expose nor reveal their breasts.

Camera and Lighting

Hawks's use of camera and lighting add to the effects of costume in resisting male objectification. Other directors frequently photographed Monroe and Russell in profile to emphasize their body contours. Hawks rarely does this in *Gentlemen Prefer Blondes*.

Similarly, overhead lighting could have been used to emphasize their bodies, but Hawks rarely chooses this effect. Their frequent costuming in black prevents any revelatory shadow play on their bodies. Hawks often shoots them in medium close-up, showing only their shoulders and faces. The use of medium close-ups in which Monroe's and Russell's zest and personality shine through is crucial in inviting us to identify with, rather than objectify, the two women.

Our discussion of body language, costume, and directorial choices illustrates our reading a feminist text in *Gentlemen Prefer Blondes*. This is not to suggest, however, that the text completely erases the pre-text. In fact, the pre-text constantly intrudes upon our reading of the film, threatening to obliterate it. A particularly blatant visual example of the pre-text is the stage set for Monroe's "Diamonds Are a Girl's Best Friend" number. Sadistic fantasy is personified in chandeliers and lamps elaborately decorated with women, all rigidly held in position with black leather halters and chains. Woman literally becomes an object. This stark explication of the pre-text, in which patriarchal relations of power between the sexes reign, ironically forms the backdrop for a song in which Monroe clarifies her preference for money over men. For us, this scene exemplifies the tension between the pre-text of male-defined heterosexuality and the text of female resistance to men and connection with each other.

Another example occurs in the moonlit love scene between Russell and the detective on the deck, in which Russell sustains her strong and active body language by moving toward the detective to initiate a kiss. Before she can reach his lips, however, Hawks interrupts Russell's movement toward the detective, cutting to a shot of the detective moving to kiss Russell. What we tend to remember is the detective's successful completion of the action; the text—Russell's activity—is suppressed. Nevertheless, each time the pre-text is reimposed, new possibilities are created for fissures through which the text may emerge again. In the last scene Monroe and Russell marry, threatening to finally destroy their independence; but even here the text emerges as they turn away from their husbands at the altar to gaze lovingly at each other.

(2) The Women's Connection to Each Other

Initially, we suggested that Monroe and Russell's resistance to male objectification was the primary source of our pleasure in viewing *Gentlemen Prefer Blondes.* We could think of no other film in which women so consistently subverted the objectifying male gaze. On subsequent viewings of the film, however, we realized that while we were delighted by Monroe and Russell's resistance to men, we were also deeply moved by their connection with each other. The destruction of opportunities for male objectification in this film gave us less pleasure than the construction of opportunities for our own positive identification with women in this film. As we suggested earlier, positive identification with other women is precious both because it is crucial to our own positive self-image as women,[11] and because it is suppressed both in life and in art. It is the expression and celebration of women's strength and connection with each other which so moves and pleases us in *Gentlemen Prefer Blondes.* Russell and Monroe neither accept the social powerlessness of women nor the imperative of a primary allegiance to men. Instead, they emanate strength and power, and celebrate their primary allegiance to each other. The friends' feeling for each other supersedes their more superficial connections with men, which fill the narrative core of the film's pre-text. At one point, Russell threatens to sever her romantic tie with the male detective if he interferes with the perjury she is committing on Monroe's behalf. While Monroe never so explicitly chooses between her male lover and her female friend, the narrative makes such a choice unnecessary. Monroe's fiancé is drawn as a ludicrous sap whose entire worth to Monroe can be measured by his bank account. Her emotional relationship with him is sheer pretense. With Russell, in contrast, Monroe is shown to care sufficiently to give her time and energy with no hope of financial recompense.

Unlike the resistance of objectification by men, which is conveyed primarily through the text of the film, both pre-text and text collude to present a positive image of Monroe and Russell's friendship. The friendship is celebrated in the film's narrative and through its visual codes.

On the narrative level, no one can miss the centrality of the women's connection to each other as Monroe spends her time on the transatlantic voyage looking for a suitable male escort for Russell, or when Russell perjures herself in court to protect Monroe. Their lives are inextricably and lovingly intertwined. They work together, sing and dance together, travel together, and get married together. We are rarely shown one on screen without the other. They also defend each other in the face of outside critics. When the detective disparages Monroe, Russell retorts vehemently: "No one talks about Lorelei but me." Monroe is equally strident in her defense of Russell: "Dorothy's the best friend a girl ever had." And the two women continually address each other with terms of endearment: "lovey," "honey," "sister," "dear."

One of the most extraordinary and positive aspects of *Gentlemen Prefer Blondes'* depiction of the friendship between the two women is the absence of competitiveness, envy, and pettiness. Commercial films rarely depict important friendships between women; when they do, the friendships are marred or rendered incredible by the film's polarization of the two women into opposite and competing camps. Consider, for example, *All About Eve, The Turning Point,* or *Girlfriends.* It is clear that such films portray female friends only with the specter of competition firmly implanted between them. It is also clear that this competition revolves almost exclusively around women's alliances with men. Either the friends compete for the same man or for the attentions of men in general. In a modern twist of the same theme, one friend may resent the other's freedom from men instead of seizing that freedom for herself. Or the single friend may feel herself abandoned by her married friend's frantic absorption in husband and children. In *Gentlemen Prefer Blondes,* the two friends work to form allegiances with men, but never compete for them; rather than dividing them, their search for men unites them in a common purpose. But their friendship is not limited to that search. It includes a joyful working and leisure relationship that endures through all the disruptions on their volatile relations with men. And ultimately, even as Monroe and Russell end their search with marriage, their friendship survives. As we will describe later, their double wedding scene underscores the depth of their friendship, and the superficiality of the commitments they are making to their husbands. The power of female bonds and the threat they pose to patriarchally defined heterosexual love is clarified, not eliminated, by this wedding scene.

These narrative elements in *Gentlemen Prefer Blondes* point openly to the centrality of the women's connection to each other. But the more subtle, non-narrative clues, are at least as important. These include body language (look, touch, use of space), and directorial choices, as well as audience expectations of the musical as a genre.

Look

Both on-stage, during their song and dance numbers, and off-stage, Monroe and Russell frequently gaze lovingly at each other. In "When Love Goes Wrong," they sit together at a Paris cafe and sing the initial portion of the song directly to each other. Even when they are with men, their gaze reflects their affection for each other. For example, when Mr. Esmond and Monroe are saying goodbye in the ship stateroom, Russell looks on tenderly; as Russell and the detective strike up a romance, Monroe beams warm approval at her friend. In all the songs which they sing together their look signals their focus on each other.

Touch

Both on-stage and off, Monroe and Russell freely and affectionately touch one another. In the opening "Little Rock" number, Russell dances with her hands on Monroe's shoulders. Off-stage, their comfort with each other's bodies is unmistakable. Russell frequently punctuates their conversation with affectionate caresses, or with more forceful gestures such as shaking Monroe or pulling her by the hand; they walk, stand, and sit in close proximity, frequently shoulder to shoulder.

Use of Space

We have already suggested that Monroe and Russell effectively resist male objectification by controlling access to their own space and by freely intruding on men's spaces. Their use of space also underscores their connection with each other. They frequently interrupt the other's private interactions with men, as if to say that a connection with men could never rival their connection to each other. For example, when Monroe is saying goodbye to her fiancé, Russell pushes him toward the gangplank, saying "You'd better go now." Similarly, when Monroe and Piggy are having their tête-à-tête in the ship stateroom, Russell barges in and virtually throws Piggy out.

Hawks's Directorial Choices

Hawks has also underscored Monroe and Russell's connectedness to each other through filmic means. The frequent use of over-the-shoulder shots or subjective shots, in which we are shown one woman from the other's point of view, visually emphasizes their involvement with each other. They are very often shown in close two-shots, with their faces filling the frame; their connection is enhanced by the absence of others in the frame, making them our exclusive focus. One of the most striking examples of this occurs in the last frames of the film where we are watching their double wedding ceremony: after briefly showing the brides and grooms together, the camera tracks in to a two-shot of Monroe and Russell smiling at each other.

Musical as Genre

One further way in which the primacy of Monroe and Russell's relationship is emphasized for the audience is its position within the movie musical genre. A typical characteristic of movie musical genre is that there are two leads, a man and a woman, who sing and dance together, and eventually become romantically involved; that they sing and dance so fluidly together is a metaphor for the perfection of their relationship. In *Gentlemen Prefer Blondes*, it is Monroe and Russell who sing—they even harmonize, adding another layer to the metaphor—and dance as a team. The men they supposedly love are never given a musical role, and therefore never convincingly share in the emotional energy between Monroe and Russell. All of that energy is reserved for the relationship between the two women. In one instance Russell even sings the part which was clearly written for a man. In "Bye Bye Baby," which is sung during the bon voyage party on board ship, Russell sings:

> "Although I know that you care
> Won't you write and declare
> That though on the loose
> You are still on the square."

Monroe answers her with the following lines:

> "And just to show that I care
> I will write and declare
> That I'm on the loose
> But I'm still on the square."

Although, as we have suggested, the pre-text and the text frequently collude to affirm the primacy of the two women's connection in *Gentlemen Prefer Blondes*, there are still moments, akin to the tension we described between objectification and resistance to it, when they are in contradiction. The narrative line does purport to show Monroe in love with her millionaire fiancé and Russell in love with her detective friend; and the women do get married in the end, despite their strong friendship. But while the strong tension between the pre-text of objectification and the text of resistance to objectification never permits either to fully obscure the other, the conflict between the pre-text of heterosexual romance is so thin that it scarcely threatens the text of female friendship. Even as they sing lyrics which suggest that heterosexual love is crucial for women, Monroe and Russell subvert the words through their more powerful actions. Here are the melancholic words to the song "When Love Goes Wrong," sung at the Paris sidewalk cafe:

"When love goes wrong
Nothing goes right . . .
The blues all gather 'round you
And day is dark as night
A man ain't fit to live with
And woman's a sorry sight."

They sing these words, not with melancholy, but with deep serenity, gazing at each other lovingly. Later they make a mockery of the song's sad theme by shimmying cheerfully to a jazzed up version of the same song in front of an admiring crowd. Men never convincingly appear as more important to Monroe and Russell than they are to each other.

It is the tension between male objectification of women, and women's resistance to that objectification, that opens *Gentlemen Prefer Blondes* to a feminist reading. It is the clear and celebrated connection between Marilyn Monroe and Jane Russell which, for us, transforms *Gentlemen Prefer Blondes* into a profoundly feminist text.

IV. The Role of Theory

We have argued here that feminist film criticism should begin to focus more centrally on our own experience as female viewers than on the male viewer's experience. Our analysis of *Gentlemen Prefer Blondes* centers on our own pleasure in the film, not on the ways in which the film affords pleasure, or denies pleasure, to men. For us, it is insufficient simply to expose and destroy male voyeuristic pleasure in film; the task, as we see it, is rather to use film to revision our connections with women. We suggest that it is time to move beyond the analysis of male pleasure in viewing classical narrative films, in order to destroy it, to an exploration of female pleasure, in order to enhance it. Our analysis owes no allegiance to male-defined paradigms since work with such paradigms tends to obscure our own female vision.

The question of the place of male paradigms within feminist scholarship, which surfaced in our work on *Gentlemen Prefer Blondes,* is a familiar yet disquieting issue. In our teaching of women's studies, we have endlessly struggled with this question. One of us, the sociologist, has always given male thought and action a central place in her courses. Students read Marx and Freud, and deal with male activity such as violence and sexual harassment. The other of us, trained in the humanities, has placed women at the center. Students read the works of women, and deal with such women's activities as artistic creation. A constant debate between us has been the extent to which male thought and experience must be analyzed in order to understand our own experience as women, the debate which remains unresolved for us. In developing our analysis of

Gentlemen Prefer Blondes, however, where our disagreements surfaced again, we arrived at a new understanding of the source of our differences.

Our differences stem, we believe, from our training in different fields, which have granted differential degrees of legitimacy to the development of feminist discourse. In sociology, the demonstration of competence in Marxism, structuralism, semiotics, or psychoanalysis, is a feminist's best chance of gaining legitimacy from male colleagues, as well as from feminist sociologists. Competence in feminist thought is not a sufficient academic credential because feminist thought is viewed as particularistic and productive of only partial truths. And sociology, in trying to present itself as a true science, is interested in universal truth. The humanities, in contrast, have granted more legitimacy to the production of a uniquely feminist discourse. Because there is no pretense of a search for the universal truth about a work of literature, the search for one's own particular and partial truth is legitimate. Thus, it is possible in the humanities to teach courses such as Women and Literature and to develop a feminist literary criticism. In sociology, in contrast, we teach the Sociology of Sex Roles, and we develop Marxist feminism.

Current film criticism stands midway between these two poles. On the one hand, some feminists are reading films from our own developing perspective, and seeking to define and name that perspective. On the other hand, some feminists are reworking and refining male paradigms and seeking to understand male experience with film. Our work with *Gentlemen Prefer Blondes* suggests to us that the concentration on male paradigms and male pleasure, even if only to challenge them, may simply miss the mark if our goal is to understand and affirm our own pleasure.

Feminist discourse within the social sciences has been muffled by the din of male paradigms. Feminist discourse in the humanities can be heard because no controlling male paradigms exist to silence it. If feminist film criticism is to escape the fate of feminist social science, it must also take the freedom to depart from male definitions and center upon its own.

NOTES

1. We are using the term "pleasure" here to refer to enjoyment and delight. We are not using the word to connote a psychoanalytic framework for our analysis.

2. In this paper we assume that film viewers identify with characters on screen, and that film viewers derive pleasure from seeing characters on screen who possess traits they admire and whom they can use as positive role models. We realize that this positive identification is influenced not only by narrative elements (how a person is characterized in the film), but also by filmic elements (the use of close-ups, the amount of screen time allotted to that person, etc.). In this respect we situate ourselves more in the lineage of writers such as Philip Slater and Nancy Chodorow, and less in that of writers like Diane Waldman in "There's More to a

Positive Image than Meets the Eye," *Jump-Cut*, No. 18 (August 1978); reprinted in the present volume, pp. 13–18. One of us is currently carrying out empirical research on positive identification and voyeurism in female film viewers which, we feel, supports our position.

3. See Julia Lesage, B. Ruby Rich, and Michelle Citron in *New German Critique*, No. 13 (Winter 1978), pp. 90–91.

4. Laura Mulvey, "Visual Pleasure and Narrative Cinema," *Screen* 16, No. 3 (Autumn 1975). Rpt. Bill Nichols, ed. *Movies and Methods*, Berkeley: University of California Press (1976), p. 415.

5. Phillip Slater, "Toward a Dualistic Theory of Identification," *Merrill-Palmer Quarterly of Behavior and Development* 7, No. 2 (1961), pp. 113–26.

6. Adrienne Rich, "Compulsory Heterosexuality and Lesbian Existence," *Signs* 5, No. 4 (Summer 1980), pp. 631–60.

7. Nancy Henley and Jo Freeman, "The Sexual Politics of Interpersonal Behavior," in Jo Freeman, *Women: A Feminist Perspective*, pp. 474–86, 2nd ed., Palo Alto: Mayfield (1979).

8. The Monroe character also adopts a "masculine" stride and stance, but far less consistently than the Russell character. More often, Monroe plays the "lady" to Russell's manly moves. For example, Russell open doors for Monroe; Monroe sinks into Russell's strong frame, allowing Russell to hold her protectively.

9. T. N. Willis, Jr., "Initial Speaking Distance as a Function of the Speakers's Relationship," *Psychonomic Science* 5 (1966), pp. 221–22.

10. Marjorie Rosen, *Popcorn Venus*, New York: Avon (1973).

11. Nancy Chodorow, *The Reproduction of Mothering*, Berkeley: University of California Press (1978).

THE CASE OF THE MISSING MOTHER

MATERNAL ISSUES IN VIDOR'S *STELLA DALLAS*

E. Ann Kaplan

For complex reasons, feminists have focused on the Mother largely from the daughter position.[1] When I first joined a consciousness-raising group in 1969, we dealt with Mothering only in terms of our own relationships to our mothers, and this despite the fact that a few of us in the group already had children. As a graduate student and mother of a one-year-old girl, I badly needed to talk about issues of career versus Motherhood, about how having the child affected my marriage, about the conflict between my needs and the baby's needs; but for some reason, I felt that these were unacceptable issues.

I think this was because at that time feminism was very much a movement of daughters. The very attractiveness of feminism was that it provided an arena for separation from oppressive closeness with the Mother; feminism was in part a reaction against our mothers, who had tried to inculcate the patriarchal "feminine" in us, much to our anger. This made it difficult for us to identify with Mothering and to look from the position of the Mother.

Unwittingly, then, we repeated the patriarchal omission of the Mother. From a psychoanalytic point of view, we remained locked in ambivalence toward the Mother, at once still deeply tied to her while striving for an apparently unattainable autonomy. Paradoxically, our complex oedipal struggles prevented us from seeing the Mother's oppression (although we had no such problems in other areas), and resulted in our assigning the Mother, in her heterosexual, familial setting, to an absence and silence analogous to the male relegation of her to the periphery.

Traditional psychoanalysis, as an extension of patriarchy, has omitted the Mother, except when she is considered from the child's point of view. Since patriarchy is constructed according to the male unconscious, feminists grew up in a society that repressed the Mother. Patriarchy chose, rather, to foreground woman's status as *castrated*, as lacking, since this construction benefits patriarchy. If the phallus defines everything, legitimacy is granted to the subordination of women. Feminists have been rebellious about this second construction of ourselves as *castrated*, but have only recently begun to react strongly against the construction of the Mother as marginal.

This reaction began in the mid-seventies with the ground-breaking books about motherhood by Adrienne Rich, Dorothy Dinnerstein, and Jane Lazarre.[2] Rich and Dinnerstein exposed the repression of the Mother, and analyzed the reasons for it, showing both psychoanalytic and socio-economic causes. Building on Melanie Klein's and Simone de Beauvoir's ideas, Dinnerstein described the early childhood experience as one of total dependency on a Mother who is not distinguished from the self (she is "good" when present, "bad" when absent). This, together with the Mother's assimilation to natural processes through her reproductive function, results in her split cultural designation and representation.

Rich shows in numerous ways how the Mother is either idealized, as in the myths of the nurturing, ever-present but self-abnegating figure, or disparaged, as in the corollary myth of the sadistic, neglectful Mother who puts her needs first. The Mother as a complex person in her own right, with multiple roles to fill and conflicting needs and desires, is absent from patriarchal representations. Silenced by patriarchal structures that have no room for her, the Mother-figure, despite her actual psychological importance, has been allotted to the symbolic margins, put in a position limited to that of spectator.

These constructions contributed to feminists' negative attitude toward mothering in the early days of the movement. We were afraid not only of becoming like our own mothers, but also of falling into one or the other of the mythic paradigms, should we have children. Put on the defensive, feminists rationalized their fears and anger, focusing on the destructiveness of the nuclear family as an institution, and seeing the Mother as an agent of the patriarchal establishment. We were unable then to see that the Mother was as much a victim of patriarchy as ourselves, constructed as she is by a whole series of discourses—psychoanalytic, political, and economic.

The Hollywood cinema is as responsible as anything for perpetuating the oppressive patriarchal myths. Relatively few Hollywood films make the Mother central, relegating her, rather, to the periphery of a narrative focused on a husband, son, or daughter. The dominant paradigms are similar to those found in literature and mythology throughout Western culture, and may be outlined quite simply:

1. The Good Mother, who is all-nurturing and self-abnegating—the "Angel in the House." Totally invested in husband and children, she lives only through them, and is marginal to the narrative.[3]

2. The Bad Mother or Witch—the underside to the first myth. Sadistic, hurtful, and jealous, she refuses the self-abnegating role, demanding her own life. Because of her "evil" behavior, this mother often takes control of the narrative, but she is punished for her violation of the desired patriarchal ideal, the Good Mother.[4]

3. The Heroic Mother, who suffers and endures for the sake of husband and children. A development of the first Mother, she shares her saintly qualities, but is more central to the action. Yet, unlike the second Mother, she acts not to satisfy herself but for the good of the family.[5]

4. The Silly, Weak, or Vain Mother. Found most often in comedies, she is ridiculed by husband and children alike, and generally scorned and disparaged.[6]

As these limited paradigms show, Hollywood has failed to address the complex issues that surround mothering in capitalism. Each paradigm is assigned a moral position in a hierarchy that facilitates the smooth functioning of the system. The desirable paradigm purposely presents the Mother from the position of child or husband, since to place the camera in the Mother's position would raise the possibility of her having needs and desires of her own. If the Mother reveals her desire, she is characterized as the Bad Mother (sadistic, monstrous), much as the single woman who expresses sexual desire is seen as destructive.

It is significant that Hollywood Mothers are rarely single and rarely combine mothering with work.[7] Stahl's and Sirk's versions of *Imitation of Life* are exceptions (although in other ways the Mother figures reflect the myths). Often, as in *Mildred Pierce*, the Mother is punished for trying to combine work and mothering. Narratives that do focus on the Mother usually take that focus because she resists her proper place. The work of the film is to reinscribe the Mother in the position patriarchy desires for her and, in so doing, teach the female audience the dangers of stepping out of the given position. *Stella Dallas* is a clear example: the film "teaches" Stella her "correct" position, bringing her from resistance to conformity with the dominant, desired myth.[8]

> How could she—oh how could she have become a part of the picture on the screen, while her mother was still in the audience, out there, in the dark, looking on?

This quotation is taken from the 1923 novel *Stella Dallas*, by Olive Higgins. It shows how the cinema had already, by 1923, become a metaphor for the oppositions of reality and illusion, poverty and wealth. Within the film *Stella Dallas*, we find the poor on the outside (Laurel's mother, Stella) and the rich on the inside (Laurel and the Morrisons). This mimics, as it were, the situation of the cinema spectator, who is increasingly subjected to a screen filled with rich people in luxurious studio sets.

But it is not simply that the 1937 version of *Stella Dallas* makes Stella the working-class spectator, looking in on the upper-class world of Stephen Dallas and the Morrison family. She is excluded not only as a working-class woman, but also as the Mother. Ben Brewster notes that the 1923 novel moves Laurel "decisively into the world of Helen Morrison, shifting its point of identification to Laurel's mother, Stella Dallas, who abolishes herself as visible to her daughter so as to be able to contemplate her in that world."[9] It is the process by which Stella Dallas makes herself literally Mother-as-spectator that interests me, for it symbolizes the position that the Mother is most often given in patriarchal culture, regardless of which paradigm is used.

Stella is actually a complex mixture of a number of the Mother paradigms. She tries to resist the position as Mother that patriarchal marriage, within the film, seeks to put her in—thus, for a moment, exposing that position. First, she literally objects to mothering because of the personal sacrifices involved; then, she protests by expressing herself freely in her eccentric style of dress. The film punishes her for both forms of resistance by turning her into a "spectacle" produced by the upper class's disapproving gaze, a gaze the audience is made to share through the camera work and editing.

The process by which Stella is brought from resistance to passive observer highlights the way the Mother is constructed as marginal or absent in patriarchy. As the film opens, we see Stella carefully preparing herself to be the object of Stephen Dallas's gaze; she self-consciously creates the image of the sweet, innocent but serious girl as she stands in the garden of her humble dwelling pretending to read a book. Despite all her efforts to be visible, her would-be lover fails to notice her. The cinema spectator, seeing that Stephen is as much someone *with* class as Stella is without it, realizes that Stella is overlooked because she is working class.

Stella's plan to escape from her background is understandable, given the place her mother occupies within the family. This gaunt and haggard figure slaves away at sink and stove in the rear of the frame, all but invisible on a first viewing. She only moves into the frame to berate Stella for refusing to give her brother the lunch he wants. "What do you want to upset him for? What would I do without him?" she asks, betraying her economic and psychological dependence on this young man, not yet ground down (as is her husband) by toil at the mill. As Stella narcissistically appraises her own fresh beauty in the kitchen's dismal mirror, she is inspired to take her brother his lunch after all, hoping to meet Stephen Dallas, whom she now knows is a runaway millionaire.

Stella's "performance" at the mill office, where Stephen has settled down to a lonely lunch, is again self-conscious. But this time her flawless acting wins her what she wants. Dressed as a virginal young lady, she gazes adoringly up at Stephen instead of following the directions he is giving her—an attention that surprises but flatters the heart-sick man.

Shortly after this, we find Stephen and Stella at the movies. A shot of upper-class men and women dancing on a screen, filmed from the perspective of the theater audience, is followed by a front shot of Stella and Stephen. He munches disinterestedly on popcorn while she snuggles up to him, intensely involved in the film. This scene confirms that Stella has been acting "as if in the movies," performing with Stephen according to codes learned through watching films. We see how films indeed do "teach" us about the life we should desire and about how to *respond* to movies. As the film ends, Stella is weeping; and as women watching Stella watching the screen, we are both offered a model of how *we* should respond to films and given insight into the mechanisms of cinematic voyeurism and identification. Stella, the working-class spectator, is outside the rich world on the screen, offered as spectacle for her emulation and envy. "I want to be like the women in the movies," Stella says to Stephen on their way home.

Meanwhile, Stella and Stephen themselves become objects of the envious, voyeuristic gaze of some passersby when they embrace outside the cinema. The women watching are now "on the outside," while Stella is beginning her brief sojourn "inside" the rich world she envied on screen. Thus, to the basic audience-screen situation of the *Stella Dallas* film itself, Vidor has added two levels: Stella and Stephen in the movie house, and Stella and Stephen as "spectacle" for the street "audience." Stella will herself create yet another spectator-screen experience (one that is indeed foreshadowed in the movie scene here), when she becomes "spectator" to the screen/scene of her daughter's luxurious wedding in the Morrison household at the end of the film. Stella has made her daughter into a "movie star" through whom she can live vicariously.

This is only possible through Motherhood as constructed in patriarchy, and thus Stella's own mothering is central to her trajectory. It is fitting that the movie scene cuts directly to Stella's haggard mother laboring in her kitchen the following morning. Her victimization is underscored by her total fear of Stella's father, who is yelling loudly. Both the mother and son are terrified that the father will discover that Stella has not come home. Indeed, the father angrily ejects his daughter from his house—until her smiling arrival, already wed to Stephen Dallas, mitigates all sins.

This is the last we see of Stella's family. For all intents and purposes the working-class family is eliminated on Stella's entrance into Stephen Dallas's upper-class world—it is made as invisible in filmic terms as it is culturally. What Stella has to contend with are her remaining working-class desires, attitudes, and behaviors, which the film sees ambiguously as either ineradicable (which would involve an uncharacteristic class determinism), or as deliberately retained by Stella. Women are socialized to be flexible precisely so that they can marry into a higher class, taking their family up a notch as they do so. We have seen that Stella is aware of how she *should* behave. ("I want to be with you," she tells Stephen after seeing the movie, "I want to be like you. I want to be like all the people you've been around.") But Stella resists this change once she has won her upper-class man, which makes her at once a more interesting and a more tragic heroine. Given the structures that bind her, she has more sense of self than is ultimately good for her.

It is both Stella's (brief) resistance to mothering and her resistance to adapting to upper-class mores that for a moment expose the construction of Mothering in patriarchy and at the same time necessitate her being *taught* her proper construction. Stella first violates patriarchal codes when, arriving home with her baby, she manifests not delight but impatience with her new role, demanding that she and Stephen go dancing that very night. Next, she violates the codes by wearing a garish dress and behaving independently at the club, leaving the table to dance with a stranger, Mr. Munn (who is from the wrong set), and going to sit at Munn's table.

This behavior is immediately "placed" for the spectator when the camera takes Stephen's point of view on the scene, although it could as easily have stuck with Stella's perspective and shown the stuffiness of the upper class. Staying with Stephen, who has now collected their coats and is waiting by the dance floor, the camera exposes Stella's vigorous dancing and loud behavior as "unseemly." At home, Stephen begs Stella to "see reason," in other words, to conform to his class. He does not take kindly to Stella's round reply ("How about you doing some adapting?"), and when he asks her to move to New York because of his business she refuses on account of "just beginning to get into the right things" (which the spectator already knows are the *wrong* things from Stephen's perspective).

The following scene shows even more clearly how the film wrenches Stella's point of view away from the audience, forcing us to look at Stella through Stephen's eyes. As a Mother, Stella is no longer permitted to control her actions, or to be the camera's eye (as she was in the scenes before her marriage and Motherhood). The scene with Laurel as a baby opens with the camera still in Stella's point of view. We see her with her maid, feeding the baby and delighting in her. Munn and his friends drop by, and a spontaneous little party develops. Everyone is having fun, Laurel included. Suddenly Stephen arrives, and the camera shifts to his perspective: The entire scene changes in an instant from a harmless gathering to a distasteful brawl, rendering Stella a neglectful Mother. The camera cuts to the stubbed-out cigarettes in Laurel's food bowl, to the half-empty liquor glasses, to the half-drunk, unshapely men; we get Stephen's eye moving around the room. Laurel begins to cry at her father's shouting, as the friends hurriedly and shamefacedly slip away. Stella has become the "object," and judged from Stephen's supposedly superior morality, is found to be lacking in Motherliness.

These scenes initiate a pattern through which Stella is made into a "spectacle" (in a negative sense) both within the film story and for the cinema spectator. It is the first step on the way to her learning her "correct" place as "spectator," as *absent* Mother (as she gradually realizes through the upper-class judgments of her that she is an embarrassment to her child). The second step is for both audience and Stella to validate the alternative model of the upper-class Morrison family, set up over and against Stella. The lower-class Stella and the cinema audience thus become the admiring spectators of the Morrison's perfect lifestyle. Other figures are brought in to provide further negative judgments of Stella as Mother. For example, Stella does not take Laurel to cultural events, so the schoolteacher has to do this; Stella then behaves loudly in public with an ill-mannered man, where she is seen by the teacher. Moreover, Laurel's peers indicate disapproval of Stella by refusing to attend Laurel's party, and later on her upper-class friends at a hotel laugh outright at Stella's appearance. By implicating us—the cinema spectator—in this process of rejection, we are made to accede to the "rightness" of Stella's renunciation of her daughter, and thus made to agree with Stella's position as absent Mother.

Once the lacks in Stella's Mothering have been established from the upper-class perspective (which is synonymous with patriarchy's construction of the ideal Mother), we are shown this "Ideal" in the concrete form of Helen Morrison. Refined, calm, and decorous, devoted to her home and children, she embodies the all-nurturing, self-effacing Mother. She is a saintly figure, worshipped by Laurel because she gives the child everything she needs and asks nothing in return (she is even tender toward Stella, for whom she shows "pity" without being condescending). Modern viewers may find these scenes embarrassingly crude in their idealization of upper-class life, but within the film's narrative this is obviously the desired world: the happy realm where all oedipal conflicts are effaced and family members exude perfect harmony. The contrast with Stella's world could not be more dramatic; it reveals her total lack of refinement.

But if unmannerliness were the sum of Stella's faults, patriarchy would not be as threatened by her as it evidently is, nor demand such a drastic restitution as the renunciation of her child. What is behind this demand for such an extreme sacrifice on Stella's part? What has she really done to violate patriarchy's conception of the Mother?

The clue to answering these questions lies in her initial *resistance* to Mothering, for "selfish" reasons, and her subsequent enthusiastic embracing of Motherhood. The refusal and then the avid assumption of the role are linked from a patriarchal point of view through the same "fault," namely that Stella is interested in *pleasing herself*. She refuses Mothering when she does not see anything in it for her, when it seems only to stand in the way of fun; but she takes it up avidly once she realizes that it can give her pleasure, and can add more to her life than the stuffy Stephen can! Shortly after Stephen has left, Stella says, "I thought people were crazy to have kids right away. But I'm crazy about her. Who wouldn't be?" And later on, talking on the train to Munn (who would clearly like a fully sexual relationship with her), Stella remarks, "Laurel uses up all the feelings I have; I don't have any for anyone else."

In getting so much pleasure for herself out of Laurel, Stella violates the patriarchal myth of the self-abnegating Mother, who is supposed to be completely devoted and nurturing but not satisfy any of her needs through the relationship with her child. She is somehow supposed to keep herself apart while giving everything to the child; she is certainly not supposed to prefer the child to the husband, since this kind of bonding threatens patriarchy.

That Laurel returns Stella's passion only compounds the problem: The film portrays Laurel as devoted to her mother to an unhealthy degree, as caring too much, or more than is good for her. In contrast to the worshipful stance that Laurel has to Mrs. Morrison, her love for her own mother is physical, tender, and selfless. For instance, on one occasion Stella's crassness offends the child deeply (she nearly puts face cream all over Laurel's lovely picture of Mrs. Morrison), but Laurel forgives her and tenderly brushes her hair. Most remarkable is the train sequence, where Laurel overhears her friends ridiculing her mother. Hurt for her mother (not for herself), she creeps down into Stella's bunk and kisses her tenderly, snuggling up to her under the covers. Finally, of course, Laurel is almost ready to give up her own chance for the pleasures of the Morrison family and upper-class life when she realizes why Stella wanted to let the Morrisons have her. It takes Stella's trick to make Laurel stay (and I'll come back to this "trick" in a moment).

The very mutuality of this mother-daughter relationship makes it even more threatening and in need of disruption than, for example, the one-sided dedication to the daughter in *Mildred Pierce*. That film highlights the dangerous narcissism of a love like Mildred's (where the investment in the child is tantamount to merging, to abandoning the boundaries altogether). This love must be punished not only because it excludes men (as does Stella's relationship to Laurel), but also because of the threat that deep female-to-female bonding poses in patriarchy. Veda's negative bonding (she is tied through hatred) offers a kind of protection for patriarchy; it ensures that Mildred's love will be destructive and self-defeating.

In contrast, *Stella Dallas* in the end provides an example of Mother love that is properly curtailed and subordinated to what patriarchy considers best for the child. In renouncing Laurel, Stella is only doing what the Good Mother should do, according to the film's ideology. By first making Stella into a "spectacle" (i.e., by applying an external standard to her actions and values), the film "educates" Stella into her "correct" position of Mother-as-spectator, Mother as absent.

Stella's entry into the Morrison household at once summarizes her prior "unfitness" and represents her readiness to succumb to the persistent demands that have been made on her throughout the film. In this amazing scene, shot from the butler's perspective, she is still a "spectacle" viewed from the upper-class position: She stands, more ridiculously clad than ever, on the threshold of the huge mansion, her figure eclipsed by the luxurious surroundings that overwhelm her with awe and admiration. It is the lower-class stance, as Stella gawks *from the outside* at the way the rich live.

Incongruous within the house, Stella must be literally pushed outside—but of her own volition. The decorous, idealized Morrison family could not be seen depriving Stella of her child (remember: Mrs. Morrison is represented as tender toward Stella), so Stella must do it herself. Paradoxically, the only method she can conceive of, once she realizes Laurel's unwavering commitment to her, is by pretending to step outside of her Mother role. "A woman wants to be something else besides a mother," she tells a crestfallen Laurel, who has left the Morrisons to be at home with her. Ironically, through these deceptive words, Stella is binding herself into the prescribed Mother role; her self-sacrificing "trick"—her pretense that she is weary of Mothering—is the only way she can achieve her required place as "spectator," relinquishing the central place she had illicitly occupied.

Structured as a "screen" within the screen, the final sequence of Laurel's wedding literalizes Stella's position as the Mother-spectator. We recall the previous movie scene (Stephen and Stella looking at the romantic upper-class couples on the screen) as Stella stands outside the window of the Morrison house, looking in on her daughter's wedding, unseen by Laurel. Stella stares from the outside at the upper-class "ideal" world inside. And as spectators in the cinema, identifying with the camera (and thus with Stella's gaze), we learn what it is to be a Mother in patriarchy—it is to renounce, to be on the outside, and to take pleasure in this positioning. Stella's triumphant look as she turns away from the window to the camera assures us she is satisfied to be reduced to spectator. Her desires for herself no longer count, merged as they are with those of her daughter. While the cinema spectator feels a certain sadness in Stella's position, she also identifies with Laurel and with her attainment of what we have all been socialized to desire—romantic marriage into the upper class. We thus accede to the necessity for Stella's sacrifice.

With *Stella Dallas*, we begin to see why the Mother has so rarely occupied the center of the narrative: For how can the *spectator* be subject, at least in the sense of controlling the action? The Mother can only be subject to the degree that she resists her culturally prescribed positioning, as Stella does at first. It is Stella's *resistance* that sets the narrative in motion, and provides the opportunity to teach her as well as the spectator the Mother's "correct" place.

Given the prevalence of the Mother-as spectator myth, it is not surprising that feminists have had trouble dealing with the Mother as subject. An analysis of the psychoanalytic barriers to "seeing" the Mother needs to be accompanied by an analysis of cultural myths that define the Good Mother as absent, and the Bad Mother as present but resisting. We have suppressed too long our anger at our mothers because of the apparently anti-woman stance this leads to. We need to work through our anger so that we can understand how the patriarchal construction of the Mother has made her position an untenable one.

Unfortunately, today's representations of the Mother are not much better than that in *Stella Dallas,* made in 1937. Ironically, the mass media response to the recent women's movement has led to numerous representations of the nurturing *Father,* as well as a split of the female image into old-style Mothers and new-style efficient career women. *Kramer Versus Kramer* established the basic model for the 80s: The wife leaves her husband to become a successful career woman, willingly abandoning her child to pursue her own needs. The husband steps into the gap she leaves and develops a close, loving relationship to his son, at some cost to his career—which he willingly shoulders. If the wife, like Stella, is reduced to a "spectator" (she returns to peek in on her child's doings), it is ultimately because she is also (albeit in a very different way) a Bad Mother. Meanwhile, the husband pals up with a solid, old-style earth Mother who lives in his apartment building, just so that we know how far his wife has strayed. Cold, angular career women, often sexually aggressive, have come to dominate the popular media while Fathers are becoming nurturing. (*The World According to Garp* is another recent example.) And there are also plenty of sadistic Mothers around (e.g., *Mommie Dearest*).

Thus, the entire structure of sex-role stereotyping remains intact. The only change is that men can now acquire previously forbidden "feminine" qualities. But career women immediately lose their warm qualities, so that even if they do combine mothering and career, they cannot be Good Mothers. It is depressing that the popular media have only been able to respond to the women's movement in terms of what it has opened up for *men.* It is up to feminists to redefine the position of the Mother as participant, initiator of action—as subject in her own right, capable of a life with many dimensions.

NOTES

1. Since writing this essay in 1983, my own work on motherhood has progressed and other people have also entered the fray. My own book, *Motherhood and Representation: The Maternal USA Melodrama 1830 to the Present* (Routledge, 1991) is currently in press. In that book, I develop some of the ideas here, sometimes altering my arguments from those presented in this article. The volume is part of a new crop of books on mothering by second-wave feminists (among whom I include myself): Cf., for example, Barbara Katz Rothman, *Recreating Motherhood: Ideology and Technology in a Patriarchal Society* (New York and London: Norton, 1989; or Sara Ruddick, *Maternal Thinking: Toward a Politics of Peace* (Boston: Beacon Press, 1989).

2. See Adrienne Rich, *Of Woman Born: Motherhood as Experience and Institution*, New York: Norton, (1976); Dorothy Dinnerstein, *The Mermaid and the Minotaur*, New York: Harper & Row (1977); Jane Lazarre, *The Mother-Knot*, New York: McGraw-Hill (1976).

3. Examples of films embodying this myth are: *A Fool There Was* (1914), *Meet Me in St. Louis* (1944), *Christopher Strong* (1933), *Our Daily Bread* (1937), *The River* (1950), *The Searchers* (1956).

4. Examples are: *Craig's Wife* (1936), *Little Foxes* (1941), *Now Voyager* (1942), *Marnie* (1966); most recently: *Mommie Dearest* (1981), *Frances* (1982).

5. Examples are: Griffith's films, *The Blot* (1921), *Imitation of Life* (1934, 1959: the black Mother in both versions), *Stella Dallas* (1937), *The Southerner* (1945), *Mildred Pierce* (1946), *The Best Years of Our Lives* (1946).

6. Examples are: *Alice Adams* (1935), *Pride and Prejudice* (1940), *Man Who Came to Dinner* (1941), *Rebel Without a Cause* (1955), *Splendour in the Grass* (1961).

7. For more information regarding representations of motherhood and work, cf. E. Ann Kaplan, "Sex, Work and Motherhood: The Impossible Triangle" (with reference to recent Hollywood films), in *Journal of Sex Research*, vol. 27, no. 3 (August 1990).

8. Shortly after I wrote this essay, Linda Williams published her essay, " 'Something Else besides a Mother': *Stella Dallas* and the Maternal Melodrama," in *Cinema Journal*, vol. 24, no. 1 (Fall 1984), where she challenges some points in my essay (Williams's essay is included in the present volume). There ensued a series of responses (some by me) that readers might want to follow up. They can be found in *Cinema Journal*, vol. 24, no. 2 (Winter 1985), pp. 22–43; *Cinema Journal*, vol. 25, no. 1 (Fall 1985), pp. 51–54; and *Cinema Journal*, vol. 25, no. 4 (Summer 1986), pp. 49–53.

9. Ben Brewster, "A Scene at the Movies," *Screen* 23, No. 2 (July–August 1982), p. 5.

"SOMETHING ELSE BESIDES A MOTHER"

STELLA DALLAS AND THE MATERNAL MELODRAMA

Linda Williams

> Oh, God! I'll never forget that last scene, when her daughter is being married inside the big house with the high iron fence around it and she's standing out there—I can't even remember who it was, I saw it when I was still a girl, and I may not even be remembering it right. But I am remembering it—it made a tremendous impression on me—anyway, maybe it was Barbara Stanwyck. She's standing there and it's cold and raining and she's wearing a thin little coat and shivering, and the rain is coming down on her poor head and streaming down her face with the tears, and she stands there watching the lights and hearing the music and then she just drifts away. How they got us to consent to our own eradication! I didn't just feel pity for her; I felt that shock of recognition—you know, when you see what you sense is your own destiny up there on the screen or on the stage. You might say I've spent my whole life trying to arrange a different destiny![1]

These words of warning, horror, and fascination are spoken by Val, a character who is a mother herself, in Marilyn French's 1977 novel *The Women's Room*. They are especially interesting for their insight into the response of a woman viewer to the image of her "eradication." The scene in question is from the end of *Stella Dallas*, King Vidor's 1937 remake of the 1925 film by Henry King. The scene depicts the resolution of the film: that moment when the good hearted, ambitious, working-class floozy, Stella, sacrifices her only connection to her daughter in order to propel her into an upper-class world of surrogate family unity. Such are the mixed messages—of joy in pain, of pleasure in sacrifice—that typically resolve the melodramatic conflicts of "the woman's film."

It is not surprising, then, that Marilyn French's mother character, in attempting to resist such a sacrificial model of motherhood, should have so selective a memory of the conflict of emotions that conclude the film. Val only remembers the tears, the cold, the mother's pathetic alienation from her daughter's triumph inside the "big house with the high iron fence," the abject loneliness of the woman who cannot belong to that place and so "just drifts away." Val's own history, her own choices, have caused her to forget the perverse triumph of the scene: Stella's lingering for a last look even when a policeman urges her to move on; her joy as the bride and groom kiss; the swelling music as Stella does not simply "drift away" but marches triumphantly toward the camera and into a close-up that reveals a fiercely proud and happy mother clenching a handkerchief between her teeth.

It is as if the task of the narrative has been to find a "happy" ending that will exalt an abstract ideal of motherhood even while stripping the actual mother of the human connection on which that ideal is based. Herein lies the "shock of recognition" of which French's mother-spectator speaks.

The device of devaluing and debasing the actual figure of the mother while sanctifying the institution of motherhood is typical of "the woman's film" in general and the sub-genre of the maternal melodrama in particular.[2] In these films it is quite remarkable how frequently the self-sacrificing mother must make her sacrifice that of the connection to her children—either for her or their own good.

With respect to the mother-daughter aspect of this relation, Simone de Beauvoir noted long ago that because of the patriarchal devaluation of women in general, a mother frequently attempts to use her daughter to compensate for her own supposed inferiority by making "a superior creature out of one whom she regards as her double."[3] Clearly, the unparalleled closeness and similarity of mother to daughter sets up a situation of significant mirroring that is most apparent in these films. One effect of this mirroring is that although the mother gains a kind of vicarious superiority by association with a superior daughter, she inevitably begins to feel inadequate to so superior a being and thus, in the end, to feel inferior. Embroiled in a relationship that is so close, mother and daughter nevertheless seem destined to lose one another through this very closeness.

Much recent writing on women's literature and psychology has focused on the problematic of the mother-daughter relationship as a paradigm of a woman's ambivalent relationship to herself.[4] In *Of Woman Born* Adrienne Rich writes, "The loss of the daughter to the mother, mother to the daughter, is the essential female tragedy. We acknowledge Lear (father-daughter split), Hamlet (son and mother), and Oedipus (son and mother) as great embodiments of the human tragedy, but there is no presently enduring recognition of mother-daughter passion and rapture." No tragic, high culture equivalent perhaps. But Rich is not entirely correct when she goes on to say that "this cathexes between mother and daughter—essential, distorted, misused—is the great unwritten story."[5]

If this *tragic* story remains unwritten, it is because tragedy has always been assumed to be universal; speaking for and to a supposedly universal "mankind," it has not been able to speak for and to womankind. But melodrama is a form that does not pretend to speak universally. It is clearly addressed to a particular bourgeois class and often—in works as diverse as *Pamela, Uncle Tom's Cabin,* or the "woman's film"—to the particular gender of woman.

In *The Melodramatic Imagination* Peter Brooks argues that late eighteenth and nineteenth century melodrama arose to fill the vacuum of a post-revolutionary world where traditional imperatives of truth and ethics had been violently questioned and yet in which there was still a need for truth and ethics. The aesthetic and cultural form of melodrama thus attempts to assert the ethical imperatives of a class that has lost the transcendent myth of a divinely ordained hierarchical community of common goals and values.[6]

Because the universe had lost its basic religious and moral order and its tragically divided but powerful ruler protagonists, the aesthetic form of melodrama took on the burden of rewarding the virtue and punishing the vice of undivided and comparatively powerless characters. The melodramatic mode thus took on an intense quality of wish-fulfillment, acting out the narrative resolution of conflicts derived from the economic, social, and political spheres in the private, emotionally primal sphere of home and family. Martha Vicinus notes, for example, that in much nineteenth century stage melodrama the home is the scene of this "reconciliation of the irreconcilable."[7] The domestic sphere where women and children predominate as protagonists whose only power derives from virtuous suffering thus emerges as an important source of specifically female wish-fulfillment. But if women audiences and readers have long identified with the virtuous sufferers of melodrama, the liberatory or oppressive meaning of such identification has not always been clear.

Much recent feminist film criticism has divided filmic narrative into male and female forms: "male" linear, action-packed narratives that encourage identification with predominantly male characters who "master" their environment; and "female" less linear narratives encouraging identification with passive, suffering heroines.[8] No doubt part of the enormous popularity of *Mildred Pierce* among feminist film critics lies with the fact that it illustrates the failure of the female subject (the film's misguided, long-suffering mother-hero who is overly infatuated with her daughter) to articulate her own point of view, even when her own voice-over introduces subjective flashbacks.[9] *Mildred Pierce* has been an important film for feminists precisely because its "male" film noir style offers such a blatant subversion of the mother's attempt to tell the story of her relationship to her daughter.

The failure of *Mildred Pierce* to offer either its female subject or its female viewer her own understanding of the film's narrative had made it a fascinating example of the way films can construct patriarchal subject-positions that subvert their ostensible subject matter. More to the point of the mother-daughter relation, however, is a film like *Stella Dallas*, which has recently begun to receive attention as a central work in the growing criticism of melodrama in general and maternal melodrama in particular.[10] Certainly the popularity of the original novel, of the 1925 (Henry King) and 1937 (King Vidor) film versions, and finally of the later long-running radio soap opera, suggests the special endurance of this mother-daughter love story across three decades of female audiences. But it is in its film versions in particular, especially the King Vidor version starring Barbara Stanwyck, that we encounter an interesting test case for many recent theories of the cinematic presentation of female subjectivity and the female spectator.

Since so much of what has come to be called the classical narrative cinema concerns male subjects whose vision defines and circumscribes female objects, the mere existence in *Stella Dallas* of a female "look" as a central feature of the narrative is worthy of special scrutiny. Just what is different about the visual economy of such a film? What happens when a mother and daughter, who are so closely identified that the usual distinctions between subject and object do not apply, take one another as their primary objects of desire? What happens, in other words, when the look of desire articulates a rather different visual economy of mother-daughter possession and dispossession? What happens, finally, when the significant viewer of such a drama is also a woman? To fully answer these questions we must make a detour through some recent psychoanalytic thought on female subject formation and its relation to feminist film theory. We will then be in a better position to unravel the mother-daughter knot of this particular film. So for the time being we will abandon *Stella Dallas* to her forlorn place in the rain, gazing at her daughter through the big picture window—the enigma of the female look at, and in, the movies.

Feminist Film Theory and Theories of Motherhood

Much recent feminist film theory and criticism has been devoted to the description and analysis of Oedipal scenarios in which, as Laura Mulvey has written, woman is a passive image and man the active bearer of the look.[11] The major impetus of these forms of feminist criticism has been less concerned with the existence of female stereotypes than with their ideological, psychological, and textual means of production. To Claire Johnston, the very fact of the iconic representation of the cinematic image guarantees that women will be reduced to objects of an erotic male gaze. Johnston concludes that "woman as woman" cannot be represented at all within the dominant representational economy.[12] A primary reason for this conclusion is the hypothesis that the visual encounter with the female body produces in the male spectator a constant need to be reassured of his own bodily unity.

It is as if the male image producer and consumer can never get past the disturbing fact of sexual difference and so constantly produces and consumes images of women designed to reassure himself of his threatened unity. In this and other ways, feminist film theory has appropriated some key concepts from Lacanian psychoanalysis in order to explain why subjectivity always seems to be the province of the male.

According to Lacan, through the recognition of the sexual difference of a female "other" who lacks the phallus that is the symbol of patriarchal privilege, the child gains entry into the symbolic order of human culture. This culture then produces narratives which repress the figure of lack that the mother—former figure of plenitude—has become. Given this situation, the question for woman becomes, as Christine Gledhill puts it: "*Can women speak, and can images of women speak for women?*"[13] Laura Mulvey's answer, and the answer of much feminist criticism, would seem to be negative:

> Woman's desire is subjected to her image as bearer of the bleeding wound, she can exist only in relation to castration and cannot transcend it. She turns her child into the signifier of her own desire to possess a penis (the condition, she imagines, of entry into the symbolic). Either she must gracefully give way to the word, the Name of the Father and the Law, or else struggle to keep her child down with her in the half-light of the imaginary. Woman then stands in patriarchal culture as signifier for the male other, bound by a symbolic order in which man can live out his fantasies and obsessions through linguistic command by imposing them on the silent image of woman still tied to her place as bearer of meaning, not maker of meaning.[14]

This description of the "visual pleasure of narrative cinema" delineates two avenues of escape which function to relieve the male viewer of the threat of the woman's image. Mulvey's now-familiar sketch of these two primary forms of mastery by which the male unconscious overcomes the threat of an encounter with the female body is aligned with two perverse pleasures associated with the male—the sadistic mastery of voyeurism and the more benign disavowal of fetishism. Both are ways of not-seeing, of either keeping a safe distance from, or misrecognizing what there is to see of, the woman's difference.

The purpose of Mulvey's analysis is to get "nearer to the roots" of women's oppression in order to break with those codes that cannot produce female subjectivity. Her ultimate goal is thus an avant-garde filmmaking practice that will break with the voyeurism and fetishism of the narrative cinema so as to "free the look of the camera into its materiality in space and time," and the "look of the audience into dialectics, passionate detachment."[15] To Mulvey, only the radical destruction of the major forms of narrative pleasure so bound up in looking at women as objects can offer hope for a cinema that will be able to represent not woman as difference but the differences of women.

It has often been remarked that what is missing from Mulvey's influential analysis of visual pleasure in cinematic narrative is any discussion of the position of the female viewing subject. Although many feminist works of film criticism have pointed to this absence, very few have ventured to fill it.[16] It is an understandably easier task to reject "dominant" or "institutional" modes of representation altogether than to discover within these existing modes glimpses of a more "authentic" (the term itself is indeed problematic) female subjectivity. And yet I believe that this latter is a more fruitful avenue of approach, not only as a means of identifying what pleasure there is for women spectators within the classical narrative cinema, but also as a means of developing new representational strategies that will more fully speak to women audiences. For such speech must begin in a language that, however circumscribed within patriarchal ideology, will be recognized and understood by women. In this way, new feminist films can learn to build upon the pleasures of recognition that exist within filmic modes already familiar to women.

Instead of destroying the cinematic codes that have placed women as objects of spectacle at their center, what is needed, and has already begun to occur, is a theoretical and practical recognition of the ways in which women actually do speak to one another within patriarchy. Christine Gledhill, for example, makes a convincing case against the tendency of much semiotic and psyochoanalytic feminist film criticism to blame realist representation for an ideological complicity with the suppression of semiotic difference. Such reasoning tends to believe that the simple rejection of the forms of realist representation will perform the revolutionary act of making the viewer aware of how images are produced. Gledhill argues that this awareness is not enough: the social construction of reality and of women cannot be defined in terms of signifying practice alone. "If a radical ideology such as feminism is to be defined as a means of providing a framework for political action, one must finally put one's finger on the scales, enter some kind of realist epistemology."[17]

But what kind? Any attempt to construct heroines as strong and powerful leaves us vulnerable, as Gledhill notes, to the charge of male identification:

> However we try to cast our potential feminine identifications, all available positions are already constructed from the place of the patriarchal other so as to repress our "real" difference. Thus the unspoken remains unknown, and the speakable reproduces what we know, patriarchal reality.[18]

One way out of the dilemma is "the location of those spaces in which women, out of their socially constructed differences as women, can and do resist."[19] These include discourses produced primarily for and (often, but not always) by women and which address the contradictions that women encounter under patriarchy: women's advice columns, magazine fiction, soap operas, and melodramatic "women's films." All are places where women speak to one another in languages that grow out of their specific social roles—as mothers, housekeepers, caretakers of all sorts.[20]

Gledhill's assertion that discourses about the social, economic, and emotional concerns of women are consumed by predominantly female audiences could be complemented by the further assertion that *some* of these discourses are also differently inscribed to necessitate a very different, female reading. This is what I hope to show with respect to *Stella Dallas*. My argument, then, is not only that some maternal melodramas have historically addressed female audiences about issues of primary concern to women, but that these melodramas also have reading positions structured into their texts that demand a female reading competence. This competence derives from the different way women take on their identities under patriarchy and is a direct result of the social fact of female mothering. It is thus with a view to applying the significance of the social construction of female identity to the female positions constructed by the maternal melodrama that I offer the following cursory summary of recent feminist theories of female identity and motherhood.

While Freud was forced, at least in his later writing, to abandon a theory of parallel male and female development and to acknowledge the greater importance of the girl's preoedipal connection to her mother, he could only view such a situation as a deviation from the path of "normal" (e.g., male heterosexual) separation and individuation.[21] The result was a theory that left women in an apparent state of regressive connection to their mothers.

What Freud viewed as a regrettable lack in a girl's self development, feminist theorists now view with less disparagement. However else they may differ over the consequences of female mothering, most agree that it allows women not only to remain in connection with their first love objects but to extend the model of this connectedness to all other relations with the world.[22]

In *The Reproduction of Mothering* the American sociologist Nancy Chodorow attempts to account for the fact that "women, as mothers, produce daughters with mothering capacities and the desire to mother."[23] She shows that neither biology nor intentional role training can explain the social organization of gender roles that consign women to the private sphere of home and family, and men to the public sphere that has permitted them dominance. The desire and ability to mother is produced, along with masculinity and femininity, within a division of labor that has already placed women in the position of primary caretakers. Superimposed on this division of labor are the two "oedipal asymmetries"[24] that

Freud acknowledged: that girls enter the triangular oedipal relation later than boys; that girls have a greater continuity of preoedipal symbiotic connection to the mother.

In other words, girls never entirely break with their original relationship to their mothers, because their sexual identities as women do not depend upon such a break. Boys, however, must break with their primary identification with their mothers in order to become male identified. This means that boys define themselves as males negatively, by differentiation from their primary caretaker who (in a culture that has traditionally valued women as mothers first, workers second) is female.

The boy separates from his mother to identify with his father and take on a masculine identity of greater autonomy. The girl, on the other hand, takes on her identity as a woman in a positive process of becoming like, not different than, her mother. Although she must ultimately transfer her primary object choice to her father first and then to men in general if she is to become a heterosexual woman, she still never breaks with the original bond to her mother in the same way the boy does. She merely *adds* her love for her father, and finally her love for a man (if she becomes heterosexual) to her original relation to her mother. This means that a boy develops his masculine gender identification in the *absence* of a continuous and ongoing relationship with his father, while a girl develops her feminine gender identity in the *presence* of an ongoing relationship with the specific person of her mother.

In other words, the masculine subject position is based on a rejection of a connection to the mother and the adoption of a gender role identified with a cultural stereotype, while the female subject position identifies with a specific mother. Women's relatedness and men's denial of relatedness are in turn appropriate to the social division of their roles in our culture: to the man's role as producer outside the home and the woman's role as reproducer inside it.[25]

Chodorow's analysis of the connectedness of the mother-daughter bond has pointed the way to a new value placed on the multiple and continuous female identity capable of fluidly shifting between the identity of mother and daughter.[26] Unlike Freud, she does not assume that the separation and autonomy of the male identification process is a norm from which women deviate. She assumes, rather, that the current social arrangement of exclusive female mothering has prepared men to participate in a world of often alienated work, with a limited ability to achieve intimacy.[27]

Thus Chodorow and others[28] have questioned the very standards of unity and autonomy by which human identity has typically been measured. And they have done so without recourse to a biologically determined essence of femaleness.[29]

Like Nancy Chodorow, the French feminist psychoanalyst Luce Irigaray turns to the problems of Freud's original attempt to sketch identical stages of development for both male and female. In *Speculum de l'autre femme*

Irigaray echoes Chodorow's concern with "oedipal asymmetries." But what Irigaray emphasizes is the *visual* nature of Freud's scenario—the fact that sexual difference is originally perceived as an absence of the male genitalia rather than the presence of female genitalia. In a chapter entitled "Blind Spot for an Old Dream of Symmetry," the "blind spot" consists of a male vision trapped in an "oedipal destiny" that cannot *see* woman's sex and can thus only represent it in terms of the masculine subject's own original complementary other: the mother.[30]

"Woman" is represented within this system as either the all-powerful (phallic) mother of the child's preoedipal imaginary or as the unempowered (castrated) mother of its postoedipal symbolic. What is left out of such a system of representation is the whole of woman's pleasure—a pleasure that cannot be measured in phallic terms.

But what Freud devalued and repressed in the female body, Irigaray and other French feminists engaged in "writing the female body" in an *écriture feminine*,[31] are determined to emphasize. In *Ce sexe qui n'en est pas un* (This sex which is not one) Irigaray celebrates the multiple and diffuse pleasures of a female body and a female sex that is not just one thing, but several. But when forced to enter into the "dominant scopic economy" of visual pleasure she is immediately relegated, as Mulvey has also pointed out with respect to film, to the passive position of "the beautiful object."[32]

Irigaray's admittedly utopian[33] solution to the problem of how women can come to represent themselves to themselves is nevertheless important. For if women cannot establish the connection between their bodies and language, they risk either having to forego all speaking of the body—in a familiar puritanical repression of an excessive female sexuality—or they risk an essentialist celebration of a purely biological determination. Irigaray thus proposes a community of women relating to and speaking to one another outside the constraints of a masculine language that reduces everything to its own need for unity and identity—a "female homosexuality" opposed to the reigning "male homosexuality" that currently governs the relations between both men and men, and men and women.[34]

A "female homosexual economy" would thus challenge the dominant order and make it possible for woman to represent herself to herself. This suggests an argument similar to that of Adrienne Rich in her article "Compulsory Heterosexuality and Lesbian Existence." Rich argues that lesbianism is an important alternative to the male economy of dominance. Whether or not a woman's sexual preferences are actually homosexual, the mere fact of "lesbian existence" proves that it is possible to resist the dominating values of the male colonizer with a more nurturing and empathic relationship similar to mothering.[35] The female body is as necessary to Rich as it is to Irigaray as the place to begin.

Adrienne Rich's critique of psychoanalysis is based on the notion that its fundamental patriarchal premises forclose the envisioning of relationships between women outside of patriarchy. Irigaray's recourse to the female body ironically echoes Rich's own but it is constructed from *within* psychoanalytic theory. The importance of both is not simply that they see lesbianism as a refuge from an oppressive phallic economy—although it certainly is that for many women—but that it is a theoretical way out of the bind of the unrepresented, and unrepresentable, female body.

The excitement generated when women get together, when they go to the market together "to profit from their own value, to talk to each other, to desire each other," is not to be underestimated.[36] For only by learning to recognize and then to represent a difference that is not different to other women, can women begin to see themselves. The trick, however, is not to stop there; woman's recognition of herself in the bodies of other women is only a necessary first step to an understanding of the interaction of body and psyche, and the distance that separates them.[37]

Perhaps the most valuable attempt to understand this interaction is Julia Kristeva's work on the maternal body and preoedipal sexuality. Like Irigaray, Kristeva attempts to speak the preoedipal relations of woman to woman. But unlike Irigaray, she does so with the knowledge that such speech is never entirely authentic, never entirely free of the phallic influence of symbolic language. In other words, she stresses the necessity of positing a place from which women can speak themselves, all the while recognizing that such places do not exist. That is, it cannot be conceived or represented outside of the symbolic language which defines women negatively.[38]

Thus, what Kristeva proposes is a self-conscious dialectic between two imperfect forms of language. The first is what she calls the "emiotic": a pre-verbal, maternal language of rhythm, tone, and color linked to the body contact with the mother before the child is differentiated by entrance into the symbolic. The second is the "symbolic" proper, characterized by logic, syntax, and a phallocratic abstraction.[39] According to Kristeva, all human subjects articulate themselves through the interaction of these two modes. The value of this conception is that we no longer find ourselves locked into an investigation of different sexual *identities*, but are freed rather into an investigation of *sexual differentiations*—subject positions that are associated with maternal or paternal functions.

Speaking from the mother's position, Kristeva shows that maternity is characterized by division. The mother is possessed of an internal heterogeneity beyond her control:

> Cells fuse, split and proliferate; volumes grow, tissues stretch, and body fluids change rhythm, speeding up or slowing down. Within the body, growing as a graft, indomitable, there is an other. And no one is present, within that simultaneously dual and alien space, to signify what is going on. "It happens, but I'm not here."[40]

But even as she speaks from this space of the mother, Kristeva notes that it is vacant, that there is no unified subject present there. Yet she speaks anyway, consciously recognizing the patriarchal illusion of the all-powerful and whole phallic mother. For Kristeva it is the dialectic of two inadequate and incomplete sexually *differentiated* subject positions that is important. The dialectic between a maternal body that is too diffuse, contradictory, and polymorphous to be represented and a paternal body that is channeled and repressed into a single representable significance makes it possible for woman to be represented at all.

So, as Jane Gallop notes, women are not so essentially and exclusively body that they must remain eternally unrepresentable.[41] But the dialectic between that which is pure body and therefore escapes representation and that which is a finished and fixed representation makes possible a different kind of representation that escapes the rigidity of fixed identity. With this notion of a dialectic between the maternal unrepresentable and the paternal already-represented we can begin to look for a way out of the theoretical bind of the representation of women in film and at the way female spectators are likely to read *Stella Dallas* and its ambivalent final scene.

"Something Else Besides a Mother"

Stella's story begins with her attempt to attract the attention of the upper-class Stephen Dallas (John Boles), who has buried himself in the small town of Milhampton after a scandal in his family ruined his plans for marriage. Like any ambitious working-class girl with looks as her only resource, she attempts to improve herself by pursuing an upper-class man. To distinguish herself in his eyes, she calculatingly brings her brother lunch at the mill where Stephen is the boss, insincerely playing the role of motherly caretaker. The refinement that she brings to this role distinguishes her from her own drab, overworked, slavish mother (played by Marjorie Main, without her usual comic touch).

During their brief courtship, Stella and Stephen go to the movies. On the screen they see couples dancing in an elegant milieu followed by a happy-ending embrace. Stella is absorbed in the story and weeps at the end. Outside the theater she tells Stephen of her desire to "be like all the people in the movies doing everything well-bred and refined." She imagines his whole world to be like this glamorous scene. Her story will become, in a sense, the unsuccessful attempt to place herself in the scene of the movie without losing that original spectatorial pleasure of looking on from afar.

Once married to Stephen, Stella seems about to realize this dream. In the small town that once ignored her she can now go the "River Club" and associate with the smart set. But motherhood intervenes, forcing her to cloister herself unhappily during the long months of pregnancy. Finally out of the hospital, she insists on a night at the country club with the smart set that has so far eluded her. (Actually many of them are a vulgar *nouveau-riche* lot of whom Stephen, upper-class snob that he is, heartily disapproves.) In her strenuous efforts to join in the fun of the wealthy, Stella makes a spectacle of herself in Stephen's eyes. He sees her for the first time as the working-class woman that she is and judges her harshly, reminding her that she once wanted to be something more than what she is. She, in turn, criticizes his stiffness and asks *him* to do some of the adapting for a change.

When Stephen asks Stella to come with him to New York City for a fresh start as the properly upper-class Mrs. Dallas, she refuses to leave the only world she knows. Part of her reason must be that to leave this world would also be to leave the only identity she has ever achieved, to become nobody all over again. In the little mill town where Stephen had come to forget himself, Stella can find herself by measuring the distance traveled between her working-class girlhood and upper-class wifehood. It is as if she needs to be able to measure this distance in order to possess her new self from the vantage point of the young girl she once was with Stephen at the movies. Without the memory of this former self that the town provides, she loses the already precarious possession of her own identity.

As Stephen drifts away from her, Stella plunges into another aspect of her identity: motherhood. After her initial resistance, it is a role she finds surprisingly compelling. But she never resigns herself to being *only* a mother. In Stephen's absence she continues to seek an innocent but lively pleasure—in particular with the raucous Ed Munn. As her daughter Laurel grows up, we observe a series of scenes that compromise Stella in the eyes of Stephen (during those rare moments he comes home) and the more straight-laced members of the community. In each case Stella is merely guilty of seeking a little fun—whether by playing music and drinking with Ed or playing a practical joke with itching powder on a train. Each time we are assured of Stella's primary commitment to motherhood and of her many good qualities as a mother. (She even says to Ed Munn, in response to his crude proposal: "I don't think there's a man livin' who could get me going anymore.") But each time the repercussions of the incident are the isolation of mother and daughter from the upper-class world to which they aspire to belong but into which only Laurel fits. A particularly poignant moment is Laurel's birthday party where mother and daughter receive, one by one, the regrets of the guests. Thus the innocent daughter suffers for the "sins" of taste and class of the mother. The end result, however, is a greater bond between the two as each sadly but nobly puts on a good face for the other and marches into the dining room to celebrate the birthday alone.

In each of the incidents of Stella's transgression of proper behavior, there is a moment when we first see Stella's innocent point of view and then the point of view of the community or estranged husband that judges her a bad mother.[42] Their judgment rests on the fact that Stella insists on making her motherhood a pleasurable experience by sharing center stage with her daughter. The one thing she will not do, at least until the end, is retire to the background.

One basic conflict of the film thus comes to revolve around the *excessive presence* of Stella's body and dress. She increasingly flaunts an exaggeratedly feminine presence that the offended community prefers not to see. (Barbara Stanwyck's own excessive performance contributes to this effect. I can think of no other film star of the period so willing to exceed both the bounds of good taste and sex appeal in a single performance.) But the more ruffles, feathers, furs, and clanking jewelry that Stella dons, the more she emphasizes her pathetic inadequacy.

Her strategy can only backfire in the eyes of an upper-class restraint that values a streamlined and sleek ideal of femininity. To these eyes Stella is a travesty, an overdone masquerade of what it means to be a woman. At the fancy hotel to which Stella and Laurel repair for their one fling at upper-class life together, a young college man exclaims at the sight of Stella, "That's not a woman, that's a Christmas tree!" Stella, however, could never understand such a backward economy, just as she cannot understand her upper-class husband's attempts to lessen the abrasive impact of her presence by correcting her English and toning down her dress. She counters his efforts with the defiant claim, "I've always been known to have stacks of style!"

"Style" is the war paint she applies more thickly with each new assault on her legitimacy as a woman and a mother. One particularly affecting scene shows her sitting before the mirror of her dressing table as Laurel tells her of the "natural" elegance and beauty of Helen Morrison, the woman who has replaced Stella in Stephen's affections. Stella's only response is to apply more cold cream. When she accidentally gets cold cream on Laurel's photo of the ideal Mrs. Morrison, Laurel becomes upset and runs off to clean it. What is most moving in the scene is the emotional complicity of Laurel, who soon realizes the extent to which her description has hurt her mother, and silently turns to the task of applying more peroxide to Stella's hair. The scene ends with mother and daughter before the mirror tacitly relating to one another through the medium of the feminine mask—each putting on a good face for the other, just as they did at the birthday party.

"Stacks of style," layers of make-up, clothes, and jewelry—these are, of course, the typical accoutrements of the fetishized woman. Yet such fetishization seems out of place in a "woman's film" addressed to a predominantly female audience. More typically, the woman's film's preoccupation with a victimized and suffering womanhood has tended, as Mary Ann Doane has shown, to repress and hystericize women's bodies in a medical discourse of the afflicted or in the paranoia of the uncanny.[43]

We might ask, then, what effect a fetishized female image has in the context of a film "addressed" and "possessed by" women? Certainly this is one situation in which the woman's body does not seem likely to pose the threat of castration—since the significant viewers of (and within) the film are all female. In psychoanalytic terms, the fetish is that which disavows or compensates for the woman's lack of a penis. As we have seen above, for the male viewer the successful fetish deflects attention away from what is "really" lacking by calling attention to (over-valuing) other aspects of woman's difference. But at the same time it also inscribes the woman in a "masquerade of femininity"[44] that forever revolves around her "lack." Thus, at the extreme, the entire female body becomes a fetish substitute for the phallus she doesn't possess. The beautiful (successfully fetishized) woman thus represents an eternal essence of biologically determined femininity constructed from the point of view, so to speak, of the phallus.

In *Stella Dallas,* however, the fetishization of Stanwyck's Stella is unsuccessful; the masquerade of femininity is all too obvious; and the significant point of view on all this is female. For example, at the fancy hotel where Stella makes a "Christmas Tree" spectacle of herself she is as oblivious as ever to the shocking effect of her appearance. But Laurel experiences the shame of her friends' scorn. The scene in which Laurel experiences this shame is a grotesque parody of Stella's fondest dream of being like all the glamorous people in the movies. Stella has put all of her energy and resources into becoming this glamorous image. But incapacitated by a cold, as she once was by pregnancy, she must remain offscene as Laurel makes a favorable impression. When she finally makes her grand entrance on the scene, Stella is spied by Laurel and her friends in a large mirror over a soda fountain. The mirror functions as the framed screen that reflects the parody of the image of glamour to which Stella once aspired. Unwilling to acknowledge their relation, Laurel runs out. Later, she insists that they leave. On the train home, Stella overhears Laurel's friends joking about the vulgar Mrs. Dallas. It is then that she decides to send Laurel to live with Stephen and Mrs. Morrison and to give Laurel up for her own good. What is significant, however, is that Stella overhears the conversation at the same time Laurel does—they are in upper and lower berths of the train, each hoping that the other is asleep, each pretending to be asleep to the other. So Stella does not just experience her own humiliation; she sees for the first time the travesty she has become by sharing in her daughter's humiliation.

By seeing herself through her daughter's eyes, Stella also sees something more. For the first time Stella sees the reality of her social situation from the vantage point of her daughter's understanding, but increasingly upperclass, system of values: that she is a struggling, uneducated woman doing the best she can with the resources at her disposal. And it is *this* vision, through her daughter's sympathetic, mothering eyes—eyes that perceive, understand, and forgive the social graces Stella lacks—that determines her to perform the masquerade that will alienate Laurel forever by proving to her what the patriarchy has claimed to know all along: that it is not possible to combine womanly desire with motherly duty.

It is at this point that Stella claims, falsely, to want to be "something else besides a mother." The irony is not only that by now there is really nothing else she wants to be, but also that in pretending this to Laurel she must act out a painful parody of her fetishized self. She thus resurrects the persona of the "good-times" woman she used to want to be (but never entirely was) only to convince Laurel that she is an unworthy mother. In other words, she proves her very worthiness to be a mother (her desire for her daughter's material and social welfare) by acting out a patently false scenario of narcissistic self-absorption—she pretends to ignore Laurel while lounging about in a negligee, smoking a cigarette, listening to jazz, and reading a magazine called "Love."

In this scene the conventional image of the fetishized woman is given a peculiar, even parodic, twist. For where the conventional masquerade of femininity can be read as an attempt to cover up supposedly biological "lacks" with a compensatory excess of connotatively feminine gestures, clothes, and accoutrements, here fetishization functions as a blatantly pathetic disavowal of much more pressing social lacks—of money, education, and power. The spectacle Stella stages for Laurel's eyes thus displaces the real social and economic causes of her presumed inadequacy as a mother onto a pretended desire for fulfillment as a woman—to be "something else besides a mother."

At the beginning of the film Stella pretended a maternal concern she did not really possess (in bringing lunch to her brother in order to flirt with Stephen) in order to find a better home. Now she pretends a lack of the same concern in order to send Laurel to a better home. Both roles are patently false. And though neither allows us to view the "authentic" woman beneath the mask, the succession of roles ending in the final transcendent self-effacement of the window scene—in which Stella forsakes all her masks in order to become the anonymous spectator of her daughter's role as bride—permits a glimpse at the social and economic realities that have produced such roles. Stella's real offense, in the eyes of the community that so ruthlessly ostracizes her, is to have attempted to play both roles at once.

Are we to conclude, then, that the film simply punishes her for these untimely resistances to her proper role? E. Ann Kaplan has argued that such is the case, and that throughout the film Stella's point of view is undercut by those of the upper-class community—Stephen, or the snooty townspeople—who disapprove of her behavior. Kaplan notes, for example, that a scene may begin from Stella's point of view but shift, as in the case of an impromptu party with Ed Munn, to the more judgmental point of view of Stephen halfway through.[45]

I would counter, however, that these multiple, often conflicting, points of view—including Laurel's failure to see through her mother's act—prevent such a monolithic view of the female subject. Kaplan argues, for example, that the film punishes Stella for her resistances to a properly patriarchal view of motherhood by turning her first into a spectacle for a disapproving upper-class gaze and then finally into a mere spectator, locked outside the action in the final window scene that ends the film.[46]

Certainly this final scene functions to efface Stella even as it glorifies her sacrificial act of motherly love. Self-exiled from the world into which her daughter is marrying, Stella loses both her daughter and her (formerly fetishized) self to become an abstract (and absent) ideal of motherly sacrifice. Significantly, Stella appears in this scene for the first time stripped of the exaggerated marks of femininity—the excessive make-up, furs, feathers, clanking jewelry, and ruffled dresses—that have been the weapons of her defiant assertions that a woman *can* be "something else besides a mother."

It would be possible to stop here and take this ending as Hollywood's last word on the mother, as evidence of her ultimate unrepresentability in any but patriarchal terms. Certainly if we only remember Stella as she appears here at the end of the film, as Val in French's *The Women's Room* remembers her, then we see her only at the moment when she becomes representable in terms of a "phallic economy" that idealizes the woman as mother and in so doing, as Irigaray argues, represses everything else about her. But although the final moment of the film "resolves" the contradiction of Stella's attempt to be a woman *and* a mother by eradicating both, the 108 minutes leading up to this moment present the heroic attempt to live out the contradiction.[47] It seems likely, then, that a female spectator would be inclined to view even this ending as she has the rest of the film: from a variety of different subject positions. In other words, the female spectator tends to identify with contradiction itself—with contradictions located at the heart of the socially constructed roles of daughter, wife, *and* mother—rather than with the single person of the mother.

In this connection the role of Helen Morrison, the upper-class widowed mother whom Stephen will be free to marry with Stella out of the way, takes on special importance. Helen is everything Stella is not: genteel, discreet, self-effacing, and sympathetic with everyone's problems—including Stella's. She is, for example, the only person in the film to see through Stella's ruse of alienating Laurel. And it is she who, knowing Stella's finer instincts, leaves open the drapes that permit Stella's vision of Laurel's marriage inside her elegant home.

In writing about the narrative form of daytime soap operas, Tania Modleski has noted that the predominantly female viewers of soaps do not identify with a main controlling figure the way viewers of more classic forms of narrative identify. The very form of soap opera encourages identification with multiple points of view. At one moment, female viewers identify with a woman united with her lover, at the next with the sufferings of her rival. While the effect of identifying with a single controlling protagonist is to make the spectator feel empowered, the effect of multiple identification in the diffused soap opera is to divest the spectator of power, but to increase empathy. "The subject/spectator of soaps, it could be said, is constituted as a sort of ideal mother: a person who possesses greater wisdom than all her children, whose sympathy is large enough to encompass the conflicting claims of her family (she identifies with them all), and who has no demands or claims of her own (she identifies with no character exclusively)."[48]

In *Stella Dallas* Helen is clearly the representative of this idealized, empathic but powerless mother. E. Ann Kaplan has argued that female spectators learn from Helen Morrison's example that such is the proper role of the mother; that Stella has up until now illicitly hogged the screen. By the time Stella has made her sacrifice and become the mere spectator of her daughter's apotheosis, her joy in her daughter's success assures us, in Kaplan's words, "of her satisfaction in being reduced to spectator. . . . While the cinema spectator feels a certain sadness in Stella's position, we also identify with Laurel and with her attainment of what we have all been socialized to desire; that is, romantic marriage into the upper class. We thus accede to the necessity for Stella's sacrifice."[49]

But do we? As Kaplan herself notes, the female spectator is identified with a variety of conflicting points of view as in the TV soap opera: Stella, Laurel, Helen, and Stephen cannot resolve their conflicts without someone getting hurt. Laurel loses her mother and visibly suffers from this loss; Stella loses her daughter and her identity; Helen wins Stephen but powerlessly suffers for everyone including herself (when Stella had refused to divorce Stephen). Only Stephen is entirely free from suffering at the end, but this is precisely because he is characteristically oblivious to the suffering of others. For the film's ending to be perceived as entirely without problem, we would have to identify with this least sensitive and, therefore, least sympathetic point of view.

Instead, we identify, like the ideal mother viewer of soaps, with *all* the conflicting points of view. Because Helen is herself such a mother, she becomes an important, but not an exclusive, focus of spectatorial identification. She becomes, for example, the significant witness of Stella's sacrifice. Her one action in the entire film is to leave open the curtains—an act that helps put Stella in the same passive and powerless position of spectating that Helen is in herself. But if this relegation to the position of spectator outside the action resolves the narrative, it is a resolution not satisfactory to any of its female protagonists.

Thus, where Kaplan sees the ending of *Stella Dallas* as satisfying patriarchal demands for the repression of the active and involved aspects of the mother's role, and as teaching female spectators to take their dubious pleasure from this empathic position outside the action, I would argue that the ending is too multiply identified, too dialectical in Julia Kristeva's sense of the struggle between maternal and paternal forms of language, to encourage such a response. Certainly the film has constructed concluding images of motherhood—first the high-toned Helen and finally a toned-down Stella—for the greater power and convenience of the father. But because the father's own spectatorial empathy is so lacking—Stephen is here much as he was with Stella at the movies, present but not identified himself—*we* cannot see it that way. We see instead the contradictions between what the patriarchal resolution of the film asks us to see—the mother "in her place" as spectator, abdicating her former position *in* the scene—and what we as empathic, identifying female spectators can't help but feel—the loss of mother to daughter and daughter to mother.

This double vision seems typical of the experience of most female spectators at the movies. One explanation for it, we might recall, is Nancy Chodorow's theory that female identity is formed through a process of double identification. The girl identifies with her primary love object—her mother—and then, without ever dropping the first identification, with her father. According to Chodorow, the woman's sense of self is based upon a continuity of relationship that ultimately prepares her for the empathic, identifying role of the mother. Unlike the male who must constantly differentiate himself from his original object of identification in order to take on a male identity, the woman's ability to identify with a variety of different subject positions makes her a very different kind of spectator.

Feminist film theorists have tended to view this multiple identificatory power of the female spectator with some misgiving. In an article on the female spectator, Mary Ann Doane has suggested that when the female spectator looks at the cinematic image of a woman, she if faced with two main possibilities: she can either over-identify (as in the masochistic dramas typical of the woman's film) with the woman on the screen and thus lose herself in the image by taking this woman as her own narcissistic object of desire; or she can temporarily identify with the position of the masculine voyeur and subject this same woman to a controlling gaze that insists on the distance and difference between them.[50] In this case she becomes, as Laura Mulvey notes, a temporary transvestite.[51] Either way, according to Doane, she loses herself.

Doane argues that the only way a female spectator can keep from losing herself in this over-identification is by negotiating a distance from the image of her like—by reading this image as a sign as opposed to an iconic image that requires no reading. When the woman spectator regards a female body enveloped in an exaggerated masquerade of femininity, she encounters a sign that requires such a reading. We have seen that throughout a good part of *Stella Dallas* this is what Stella does with respect to her own body. For Doane, then, one way out of the dilemma of female over-identification with the image on the screen is for this image to act out a masquerade of femininity that manufactures a distance between spectator and image, to "generate a problematic within which the image is manipulable, producible, and readable by women."[52]

In other words, Doane thinks that female spectators need to borrow some of the distance and separation from the image that male spectators experience. She suggests that numerous avant-garde practices of distanciation can produce this necessary distance. This puts us back to Mulvey's argument that narrative pleasure must be destroyed by avant-garde practices. I would argue instead that this manufacturing of distance, this female voyeurism-with-a-difference, is an aspect of *every* female spectator's gaze at the image of her like. For rather than adopting either the distance and mastery of the masculine voyeur or the over-identification of Doane's woman who loses herself in the image, the female spectator is in a constant state of juggling all positions at once.

B. Ruby Rich has written that women experience films much more dialectically than men. "Brecht once described the exile as the ultimate dialectician in that the exile lives the tension of two different cultures. That's precisely the sense in which the woman spectator is an equally inevitable dialectician."[53] The female spectator's look is thus a dialectic of two (in themselves) inadequate and incomplete (sexually and socially) differentiated subject positions. Just as Julia Kristeva has shown that it is the dialectic of a maternal body that is channeled and repressed into a single, univocal significance that makes it possible for women to be represented at all, so does a similar dialectic inform female spectatorship when a female point of view is genuinely inscribed in the text.

We have seen in *Stella Dallas* how the mediation of the mother and daughter's look at one another radically alters the representation of them both. We have also seen that the viewer cannot choose a single "main controlling" point of identification but must alternate between a number of conflicting points of view, none of which can be satisfactorily reconciled. But the window scene at the end of the film would certainly seem to be the moment when all the above contradictions collapse into a single patriarchal vision of the mother as pure spectator (divested of her excessive bodily presence) and the daughter as the (now properly fetishized) object of vision. Although it is true that this ending, by separating mother and daughter, places each within a visual economy that defines them from the perspective of patriarchy, the female spectator's own look at each of them does not acquiesce in such a phallic visual economy of voyeurism and fetishism.

For in looking at Stella's own look at her daughter through a window that strongly resembles a movie screen,[54] the female spectator does not see and believe the same way Stella does. In the final scene, Stella is no different than the naive spectator she was when, as a young woman, she went to the movies with Stephen. In order to justify her sacrifice, she must *believe* in the reality of the cinematic illusion she sees: bride and groom kneeling before the priest, proud father looking on. We, however, *know* the artifice and suffering behind it—Laurel's disappointment that her mother has not attended the wedding; Helen's manipulation of the scene that affords Stella her glimpse; Stella's own earlier manipulation of Laurel's view of her "bad" motherhood. So when we look at Stella looking at the glamorous and artificial "movie" of her daughter's life, we cannot, like Stella, naively believe in the reality of the happy ending, any more than we believe in the reality of the silent movements and hackneyed gestures of the glamorous movie Stella once saw.

Because the female spectator has seen the cost to both Laurel and Stella of the daughter's having entered the frame, of having become the properly fetishized image of womanhood, she cannot, like Stella, believe in happiness for either. She knows better because she has seen what each has had to give up to assume these final roles. But isn't it just such a balance of knowledge and belief (of the fetishist's contradictory phrase "I know very well but just the same . . . ")[55] that has characterized the sophisticated juggling act of the ideal cinematic spectator?

The psychoanalytic model of cinematic pleasure has been based on the phenomenon of fetishistic disavowal: the contradictory gesture of *believing* in an illusion (the cinematic image, the female penis) and yet *knowing* that it is an illusion, an imaginary signifier. This model sets up a situation in which the woman becomes a kind of failed fetishist: lacking a penis she lacks the biological foundation to engage in the sophisticated game of juggling presence and absence in cinematic representation; hence her presumed over-identification, her lack of the knowledge of illusion[56] and the resulting one, two, and three handkerchief movies. But the female spectator of *Stella Dallas* finds herself balancing a very different kind of knowledge and belief than the mere existence or non-existence of the female phallus. She *knows* that women can find no genuine form of representation under patriarchal structures of voyeuristic or fetishistic viewing, because she has seen Stella lose herself as a woman and as a mother. But at the same time she *believes* that women exist outside this phallic economy, because she has glimpsed moments of resistance in which two women have been able to represent themselves to themselves through the mediation of their own gazes.

This is a very different form of disavowal. It is both a *knowing* recognition of the limitation of women's representation in patriarchal language and a contrary *belief* in the illusion of a preoedipal space between women free of the mastery and control of the male look. The contradiction is as compelling for the woman as for the male fetishist, even more so because it is not based on the presence or absence of an anatomical organ, but on the dialectic of the woman's socially constructed position under patriarchy.

It is in a very different sense, then, that the psychoanalytic concepts of voyeurism and fetishism can inform a feminist theory of cinematic spectatorship—not as inscribing woman totally on the side of the passive object who is merely seen, as Mulvey and others have so influentially argued, but by examining the contradictions that animate women's very active and fragmented ways of seeing.

I would not go so far as to argue that these contradictions operate for the female viewer in every film about relations between women. But the point of focusing on a film that both addresses female audiences and contains important structures of viewing *between* women is to suggest that it does not take a radical and consciously feminist break with patriarchal ideology to represent the contradictory aspects of the woman's position under patriarchy. It does not even take the ironic distancing devices of, for example, the Sirkian melodrama to generate the kind of active, critical response that sees the work of ideology in the film. Laura Mulvey has written that the ironic endings of Sirkian melodrama are progressive in their defiance of unity and closure:

> It is as though the fact of having a female point of view dominating the narrative produces an excess which precludes satisfaction. If the melodrama offers a fantasy escape for the identifying women in the audience, the illusion is so strongly marked by recognizable, real and familiar traps that the escape is closer to a daydream than a fairy story. The few Hollywood films made with a female audience in mind evoke contradictions rather than reconciliation, with the alternative to mute surrender to society's overt pressures lying in defeat by its unconscious laws.[57]

Although Mulvey here speaks primarily of the ironic Sirkian melodrama, her description of the contradictions encountered by the female spectator apply in a slightly different way to the very un-ironic *Stella Dallas*. I would argue that *Stella Dallas* is a progressive film not because it defies both unity and closure, but because the definitive closure of its ending produces no parallel unity in its spectator. And because the film has constructed its spectator in a female subject position locked into a primary identification with another female subject, it is possible for this spectator, like Val—the mother spectator from *The Women's Room* whose reaction to the film is quoted at the head of this essay—to impose her own radical feminist reading on the film. Without such female subject positions inscribed within the text, the stereotypical self-sacrificing mother character would flatten into the mere maternal essences of so many motherly figures of melodrama.

Stella Dallas is a classic maternal melodrama played with a very straight face. Its ambivalences and contradictions are not cultivated with the intention of revealing the work of patriarchal ideology within it. But like any melodrama that offers a modicum of realism yet conforms to the "reconciliation of the irreconciliable" proper to the genre,[58] it must necessarily produce, when dealing with conflicts among women, what Val calls a "shock of recognition." This shock is not the pleasurable recognition of a verisimilitude that generates naive belief, but the shock of seeing, as Val explains, "how they got us to consent to our own eradication." Val and other female spectators typically do *not* consent to such eradicating resolutions. They, and we, resist the only way we can by struggling with the contradictions inherent in these images of ourselves and our situation. It is a terrible underestimation of the female viewer to presume that she is wholly seduced by a naive belief in these masochistic images, that she has allowed these images to put her in her place the way the films themselves put their women characters in their place.

It seems, then, that Adrienne Rich's eloquent plea for works that can embody the "essential female tragedy" of mother-daughter passion, rapture, and loss is misguided but only with respect to the mode of tragedy. I hope to have begun to show that this loss finds expression under patriarchy in the "distorted" and "misused" cathexes of the maternal melodrama. For unlike tragedy, melodrama does not reconcile its audience to an inevitable suffering. Rather than raging against a fate that the audience has learned to accept, the female hero often accepts a fate that the audience at least partially questions.

The divided female spectator identifies with the woman whose very triumph is often in her own victimization, but she also criticizes the price of a transcendent "eradication" which the victim-hero must pay. Thus, although melodrama's impulse towards the just "happy ending" usually places the woman hero in a final position of subordination, the "lesson" for female audiences is certainly not to become similarly eradicated themselves. For all its masochism, for all its frequent devaluation of the individual person of the mother (as opposed to the abstract ideal of motherhood), the maternal melodrama presents a recognizable picture of woman's ambivalent position under patriarchy that has been an important source of realistic reflections of women's lives. This may be why the most effective feminist films of recent years have been those works—like Sally Potter's *Thriller*, Michelle Citron's *Daughter Rite*, Chantal Akerman's *Jeanne Dielman . . .* , and even Jacques Rivette's *Celine and Julie Go Boating*—that work *within and against* the expectations of female self-sacrifice experienced in maternal melodrama.

NOTES

1. *The Women's Room*, New York: Summit Books (1977), p. 227.

2. An interesting and comprehensive introduction to this sub-genre can be found in Christian Viviani's "Who is Without Sin? The Maternal Melodrama in American Film, 1930–1939," *Wide Angle* 4, no. 2 (1980): 4–17. Viviani traces the history of maternal melodrama in American films back to the original French play *Madame X* about an adulterous woman who expiates her sin in lifelong separation from a son whose social rise would be jeopardized by the revelation of her relation

to him. Two successful twenties screen versions of *Madame X* set a pattern of imitators. Within them Viviani traces two different "veins" of this melodramatic sub-genre: those films with European settings in which the originally sinning mother descends to anonymity, and those films with American settings where the more "Rooseveltian" mother displays a greater energy and autonomy before descending to anonymity. Viviani suggests that King Vidor's *Stella Dallas* is the "archetype" of this more energetic, American vein of maternal melodrama. He also adds that although Stella is not actually guilty of anything, her unwillingness to overcome completely her working class origins functions as a kind of original sin that makes her seem guilty in her husband's and finally in her own eyes.

B. Ruby Rich and I have also briefly discussed the genre of these sacrificial maternal melodramas in our efforts to identify the context of Michelle Citron's avant-garde feminist film, *Daughter Rite*. Citron's film is in many ways the flip side to the maternal melodrama, articulating the daughter's confused anger and love at the mother's sacrificial stance. "The Right of Re-Vision: Michelle Citron's *Daughter Rite*," *Film Quarterly* 35, no. 1 (Fall 1981):17–22.

3. *The Second Sex*, trans. H. M. Parshley, New York: Bantam (1961), 488–89.

4. An excellent introduction to this rapidly growing area of study is Marianne Hirsch's review essay, "Mothers and Daughters," *Signs: Journal of Women in Culture and Society* 7, no. 1 (1981): 200–22. See also Judith Kegan Gardiner, "On Female Identity and Writing by Women," *Critical Inquiry* 8, no. 2 (Winter 1981): 347–61.

5. *Of Woman Born*, New York: Bantam (1977), 240, 226.

6. *The Melodramatic Imagination: Balzac, Henry James, Melodrama and the Mode of Excess*, New Haven: Yale University Press (1976).

7. Martha Vicinus, writing about the nineteenth century melodrama, suggests that melodrama's "appropriate" endings offer "a temporary reconciliation of the irreconcilable." The concern is typically not with what is possible or actual but what is desirable. "Helpless and Unfriended: Nineteenth Century Domestic Melodrama," *New Literary History* 13, no. 1 (Autumn 1981): 132. Peter Brooks emphasizes a similar quality of wish-fulfillment in melodrama, even arguing that psychoanalysis offers a systematic realization of the basic aesthetics of the genre: "If psychoanalysis has become the nearest modern equivalent of religion in that it is a vehicle for the cure of souls, melodrama is a way station toward this status, a first indication of how conflict, enactment, and cure must be conceived in a secularized world" (202).

8. Most prominent among these are Claire Johnston's "Women's Cinema as Counter-Cinema" in *Notes on Women's Cinema*, BFI Pamphlet (September 1972); and Laura Mulvey's "Visual Pleasure and Narrative Cinema," *Screen* 16, no. 3 (Autumn 1975): 6–18.

9. The list of feminist work on this film is impressive. It includes: Pam Cook, "Duplicity in Mildred Pierce," in *Women in Film Noir*, ed. E. Ann Kaplan, London: BFI (1978), 68–82; Molly Haskell, *From Reverence to Rape: The Treatment of Women in the Movies*, N.Y.: Holt, Rinehart and Winston (1973), 175–80; Annette Kuhn, *Women's Pictures: Feminism and Cinema*, London: Routledge and Kegan Paul (1982), 28–35; Joyce Nelson, "*Mildred Pierce* Reconsidered," *Film Reader* 2 (January 1977): 65–70; and Janet Walker, "Feminist Critical Practice: Female Discourse in *Mildred Pierce*," *Film Reader* 5 (1982): 164–71.

10. Molly Haskell only gave the film brief mention in her chapter on "The Woman's Film," *From Reverence to Rape: The Treatment of Women in the Movies*, New York: Holt, Rinehart and Winston (1973), 153–88. Since then the film has been discussed by Christian Viviani (see note 2); Charles Affron in *Cinema and Sentiment*, Chicago: University of Chicago Press (1983), 74–76; Ben Brewster, "A Scene at the Movies," *Screen* 23, no. 2 (July-August 1982): 4–5; and E. Ann

Kaplan, "Theories of Melodrama: A Feminist Perspective," *Women and Performance: A Journal of Feminist Theory* 1, no. 1 (Spring/Summer 1983): 40–48. Kaplan also has a longer article on the film, "The Case of the Missing Mother: Maternal Issues in Vidor's *Stella Dallas*," *Heresies* 16 (1983): 81–85. Laura Mulvey also mentions the film briefly in her "Afterthoughts on 'Visual Pleasure and Narrative Cinema' Inspired by 'Duel in the Sun' (King Vidor, 1946)," *Framework* 15/16/17 (Summer 1981): 12–15—but only in the context of Vidor's much more male-oriented western. Thus, although *Stella Dallas* keeps coming up in the context of discussions of melodrama, sentiment, motherhood, and female spectatorship, it has not been given the full scrutiny it deserves, except by Kaplan, many of whose arguments I challenge in the present work.

11. Mulvey, 11. See also most of the essays in *Re-Vision: Essays in Feminist Film Criticism*, eds. Mary Ann Doane, Patricia Mellencamp, and Linda Williams, Los Angeles: AFI Monograph Series (1983).

12. Claire Johnston, for example, writes, "Despite the enormous emphasis placed on women as spectacle in the cinema, woman as woman is largely absent." "Woman's Cinema as Counter-Cinema," *Notes on Woman's Cinema*, Screen Pamphlet 2, ed. Claire Johnston, 26.

13. Christine Gledhill, "Developments in Feminist Film Criticism," *Revision: Essays in Feminist Film Criticism*, eds. Mary Ann Doane, Patricia Mellencamp, and Linda Williams, Los Angeles: American Film Institute Monograph Series (1983), 31. Originally published in *Quarterly Review of Film Studies* 3, no. 4, (1978): 457–93.

14. Mulvey, 7.

15. Mulvey, 7, 18.

16. The few feminists who have begun this difficult but important work are: Mary Ann Doane, "Film and the Masquerade: Theorizing the Female Spectator," *Screen* 23, no. 3–4 (Sept.-Oct. 1982): 74–87; Gertrud Koch, "Why Women Go to the Movies," *Jump Cut* 27 (July 1982), trans. Marc Silberman: 51–53; Judith Mayne, "The Woman at the Keyhole: Women's Cinema and Feminist Criticism," *Re-Vision: Essays in Feminist Film Criticism*, 44–66; and Mulvey herself in "Afterthoughts on 'Visual Pleasure and Narrative Cinema' Inspired by 'Duel in the Sun' (King Vidor, 1946)," *Framework* 15/16/17 (Summer 1981): 12–15; B. Ruby Rich, in Michelle Citron et al., "Women and Film: A Discussion of Feminist Aesthetics," *New German Critique* 13 (1978): 77–107; and Tania Modleski, *Loving with a Vengence: Mass Produced Fantasies for Women*, Hamden, Conn.: Archon Books (1982). Since I wrote this article, two important new books on women and film have appeared. Both take considerable account of the processes by which the female spectator identifies with screen images. They are: E. Ann Kaplan's *Women and Film: Both Sides of the Camera*, New York: Metheun (1983); and Teresa de Lauretis, *Alice Doesn't: Feminism, Semiotics, Cinema*, Bloomington: Indiana University Press (1984).

17. Gledhill, 41.

18. Gledhill, 37.

19. Gledhill, 42.

20. Gledhill, 44–45.

21. Freud begins this shift in the 1925 essay, "Some Psychological Consequences of the Anatomical Distinction between the Sexes," *Standard Edition of the Complete Psychological Works*, Hogarth Press (1953–74), vol. XIX. He continues it in the 1931 essay "Female Sexuality," vol. XXI.

22. Marianne Hirsch's review essay, "Mothers and Daughters," *Signs: Journal of Women in Culture and Society* 7, no. 1, (Autumn 1981): 200–22, offers an excellent summary of the diverse strands of the continuing re-appraisal of the mother-daughter relation. Hirsch examines theories of this relation in Anglo-

American neo-Freudian object relations psychology (Chodorow, Miller, Dinnerstein), in Jungian myth criticism, and in the French feminist theories developing out of structuralism, post-structuralism, and Lacanian psychoanalysis. A recent study of how female connectedness affects female moral development is Carol Gilligan's *In a Different Voice*, Cambridge: Harvard University Press (1982).

23. Chodorow, *The Reproduction of Mothering: Psychoanalysis and the Sociology of Gender*, Berkeley: University of California Press (1978), 7.

24. "Oedipal asymmetries" is Chodorow's term, 7.

25. Chodorow, 178.

26. Marianne Hirsch surveys the importance of this point in her review essay "Mothers and Daughters," 209. So, too, does Judith Kegan Gardiner in "On Female Identity and Writing by Women," *Critical Inquiry: Writing and Sexual Difference* 8, no. 2 (Winter 1981): 347–61.

27. Chodorow, 188.

28. These others include: Dorothy Dinnerstein, *The Mermaid and the Minotaur: Sexual Arrangements and the Human Malaise*, New York: Harper and Row (1976); Jessie Bernard, *The Future of Motherhood*, New York: Dial Press (1974); and Jean Baker Miller, *Toward a New Psychology of Women*, Boston: Beacon Press (1976).

29. This is the real advance of Chodorow's theories over those of an earlier generation of feminist psychoanalysts. Karen Horney, for example, found it necessary, as both Juliet Mitchell and Jane Gallop point out, to resort to generalizing statements of women's essential, biologically determined nature, thus leaving no possibility for change. Horney, "On the Genesis of the Castration Complex in Women," *International Journal of Psycho-Analysis*, V, 1924: 50–65.

30. Paris: Editions de Minuit, 1974.

31. Other French feminists involved in this "feminine writing" are Hélène Cixous, Monique Wittig, Julia Kristeva, and Michele Montrelay. A critical introduction to these writers can be found in Ann Rosalind Jones, "Writing the Body: Toward an Understanding of L'Ecriture feminine," and Helene Vivienne Wenzel's "The Text as Body/Politics: An Appreciation of Monique Wittig's Writings in Context," both in *Feminist Studies* 7, no. 2 (Summer 1981): 247–87.

32. "Ce sex qui n'en est pas un," trans. Claudia Reeder, *New French Feminisms*, ed. Elaine Marks and Isabelle de Courtivron, Amherst: University of Massachusetts Press (1980), 100–1.

33. Anglo-American feminists have thus been critical of the new French feminists for two different reasons: American feminists have criticized an essentialism that would seem to preclude change (see, for example, the essay by Jones referred to in note 31); British feminists have criticized their apparent failure to account for the way the female body is mediated by language (see, for example, Beverly Brown and Parveen Adams, "The Feminine Body and Feminist Politics," *m/f*, no. 3, (1979): 35–50).

34. Irigaray, 106–7.

35. Rich, *Signs* 5, no. 4 (Summer 1980): 631–60.

36. Irigaray, 110.

37. Mary Ann Doane, "Woman's Stake: Filming the Female Body," *October* 17 (Summer 1981): 30.

38. Kristeva's work has been translated in two volumes: *Desire in Language: A Semiotic Approach to Literature and Art*, trans. Thomas Gora, Alice Jardine, Leon S. Roudiez, New York: Columbia University Press (1980); and *About Chinese Women*, trans. Anita Barrows, New York: Horizon Books, (1977).

39. Alice Jardine, "Theories of the Feminine: Kristeva" *enclitic* 4, no. 2 (Fall 1980): 13.

40. Kristeva, "Motherhood According to Giovanni Bellini," in *Desire in Language*, 237–70.

41. Jane Gallop, "The Phallic Mother: Freudian Analysis," in *The Daughter's Seduction: Feminism and Psychoanalysis,* Ithaca, New York: Cornell University Press (1982), 113–31.

42. Ann Kaplan emphasises this "wrenching" of the filmic point of view away from Stella and towards the upper-class values and perspectives of Stephen and the townspeople. "The Case of the Missing Mother," 83.

43. Doane, "The Woman's Film: Possession and Address," in *Re-Vision: Essays in Feminist Film Criticism,* 67–82.

44. The term—originally used by Joan Riviere—is employed in Mary Ann Doane, "Film and the Masquerade: Theorizing the Female Spectator," *Screen* 23, no. 34 (Sept/Oct. 1982): 74–87.

45. Ann Kaplan, "The Case of the Missing Mother," 83.

46. Ibid.

47. Molly Haskell notes this tendency of women audiences to come away with a memory of heroic revolt, rather than the defeat with which so many films end, in her pioneering study *From Reverence to Rape: The Treatment of Women in the Movies,* New York: Holt, Rinehart and Winston (1973), 31.

48. Modleski, "The Search for Tomorrow in Today's Soap Opera: Notes on a Feminine Narrative Form," *Film Quarterly* 33, no. 1, (Fall 1979): 14. A longer version of this article can be found in Modleski's book *Living with a Vengence: Mass Produced Fantasies for Women,* Hamden, Connecticut: Archon Books (1982): 85–109.

49. Kaplan, "Theories of Melodrama," 46.

50. Doane, "Film and the Masquerade," 87.

51. Mulvey, "Afterthoughts on 'Visual Pleasure and Narrative Cinema' Inspired by 'Duel in the Sun' (King Vidor, 1946)," 13.

52. Doane, 87.

53. B. Ruby Rich, in Michelle Citron et al., "Women and Film: A Discussion of Feminist Aesthetics," *New German Critique* 13 (1978): 87. Although Rich goes on to suggest that this dialectic is an either/or choice—"to identify either with Marilyn Monroe or with the man behind me hitting the back of my seat with his knees"—I think the more proper sense of the word would be to construe it as a continuous conflict and tension that informs female viewing and which in many cases does not allow the choice of one or the other.

54. Ben Brewster has cited the many cinematic references of the original novel as an indication of just how effective as an appeal to reality the cinematic illusion has become. "A Scene at the Movies," *Screen* 23, no. 2 (July-Aug. 1983): 4–5.

55. Freud's theory is that the little boy believes in the maternal phallus even after he knows better because he has seen evidence that it does not exist has been characterized by Octave Manoni as a contradictory statement that both asserts and denies the mother's castration. In this "Je sais bien mais quand mème" (I know very well but just the same), the "just the same" is the fetish disavowal. Manoni, *Clefs pour l'imaginaire,* Paris: Seuil (1969), 9–30. Christian Metz later applied this fetishistic structure of disavowal to the institution of the cinema as the creator of believable fictions of perceptually real human beings who are nevertheless absent from the scene. Thus the cinema aims all of its technical prowess at the disavowal of the lack on which its "imaginary signifier" is based. *The Imaginary Signifier: Psychoanalysis and the Cinema,* trans. Celia Britton, Annwyl Williams, Ben Brewster, and Alfred Guzzetti, Bloomington, Indiana: Indiana University Press (1982), 69–76.

56. Doane, "Film and the Masquerade," 80–81.

57. Mulvey, "Notes on Sirk and Melodrama," 1 *Movie* 25 (n.d.): 56.

58. Vicinus, 132.

SEDUCED AND ABANDONED

RECOLLECTION AND ROMANCE IN *LETTER FROM AN UNKNOWN WOMAN*

Lucy Fischer

> Man's love is of man's life a thing apart;
> 'Tis woman's whole existence.
>
> —Lord Byron[1]

> One gets an impression that a man's love and a woman's are a phase apart psychologically.
>
> —Sigmund Freud[2]

It is a truism of the commercial cinema that the subject of love is central to the standard plot mechanism. Whether the genre is western, musical, crime film, or comedy, the fulcrum of the drama typically rests on a heterosexual romance. In this respect, films partake of a broader feature of the storied world which (contemporary critical theory has shown) relentlessly enacts the erotic quest.[3] Roland Barthes writes: "At the origin of Narrative, desire."[4] And Teresa de Lauretis applies that notion to the cinema: "The very work of [film] narrativity is the engagement of the subject in certain positionalities of meaning and desire."[5]

In their portrayal of love, however, diegetic forms have not been neutral; they have plotted the romantic quest along the lines of sexual difference, for desire does not exist in the abstract but attaches to a subject, either male or female. Here it is important that the clichéd summary of a love story is the phrase "boy meets girl," revealing the male bias at its core. As de Lauretis points out, storytelling involves the "mapping . . . of sexual difference into each text."[6]

This essay will consider the portrayal of heterosexual romance in the cinema through an examination of Max Ophuls's *Letter from an Unknown Woman* (1948), a text from the Hollywood cinema that advances rather conventional attitudes toward the woman in love. In considering this film, attention will be paid to the notion of fiction as structured by desire, as "mapping" sexual difference into the text.

Kiss Me Deadly

> The service of women (as well as the military service of the State) demands that nothing relating to that service be subject to forgetting.
>
> —Sigmund Freud[7]

As critic Michael Walker has noted, the "woman's film" has always stressed "love as the most crucial determining factor in women's actions."[8] By this standard, *Letter from an Unknown Woman* emerges as an exemplary work. It recounts the story of the lifelong passion of Lisa Berndle (Joan Fontaine) for a renowned musician, Stefan Brand (Louis Jourdan), who has seduced and abandoned her as a young woman.[9] Given this emphasis, we will want to evaluate the film's stylistic and thematic assumptions, locating them as either endorsing or resisting traditional romantic views. We will be asking whether *Letter* conforms to the ideology of the dominant cinema or whether it invites a reading "against the grain."

Contemporary feminist Shulamith Firestone has written that "a book on radical feminism that did not deal with love would be a political failure."[10] One of the most profound and comprehensive discussions of this issue occurs in an early feminist classic—Simone de Beauvoir's *The Second Sex*, a treatise I will examine in some detail.

The author begins by making the crucial point that love has a different meaning for men and women—a phenomenon that explains the perennial misunderstandings between them.[11] She then enumerates these distinctions, starting with the discrepant emphasis placed on love by the two sexes:

> Men have found it possible to be passionate lovers at certain times in their lives, but . . . even on their knees before a mistress . . . they remain sovereign subjects; the beloved woman is only one value among others; . . . For woman, on the contrary, to love is to relinquish everything.[12]

Woman is willing to do so because she has very little to lose. Without a career or a respected cultural position, what else is there to structure her life but a *grand amour* that delivers her into the proper roles of wife and mother?

But de Beauvoir makes more subtle points. She notes that women devote themselves to men in order to *partake* of male power—a sphere from which they are otherwise excluded: "The adolescent girl wishes at first to identify herself with males; when she gives that up, she then seeks to share in their masculinity by having one of them in love with her."[13] In adoring a man, woman is allowed to live through him and to experience vicariously what it means to be a subject in the world. Through his admiration, she perceives herself valuable: "Love is the developer that brings out in clear, positive detail the dim negative, otherwise as useless as a blank exposure."[14]

In living through man, however, woman obliterates her own existence, "lets her . . . world collapse in contingence." She becomes "another incarnation of her loved one, his reflection, his double."[15] Thus she is likely to take on his interests: to read the same books, to admire the same artworks, to indulge in the same eccentricities. Given woman's deferential attitude to her lover, it is no wonder that de Beauvoir likens their relationship to master and slave. But de Beauvoir's real insight is to perceive how woman masks her servitude through overvaluation of her mate:

> Since [woman] is anyway doomed to dependence, she will prefer to serve a god, rather than obey tyrants. . . . She chooses to desire her enslavement so ardently that it will seem to her the expression of her liberty.[16]

De Beauvoir's use of the term "god" for the male lover is not gratuitous. She asserts that love is (for the traditional woman) "a religion," an infatuation comparable to a mystical frenzy[17]:

> The same words fall from the lips of the saint on her knees and the loving woman on her bed; the one offers her flesh to the thunderbolt of Christ, she stretches out her hands to receive the stigmata of the Cross, she calls for the burning presence of divine Love; the other, also, offers and awaits: Thunderbolt, dart, arrow, are incarnated in the male sexual organ.[18]

By transforming her master into a deity, woman obscures the nature of her servitude, but she also creates an illusion that is hard to maintain. De Beauvoir suggests that this "ideal" love can endure only at a distance that allows the fantasy to be sustained:

> [Woman's] worship sometimes finds better satisfaction in [her lover's] absence than his presence . . . there are women who devote themselves to dead or otherwise inaccessible heroes, so that they may never have to face them in person, for beings of flesh and blood would be fatally contrary to their dreams.[19]

Woman's overinvestment in romance places her in a precarious mental position. She "is one who waits," and her life hangs in the balance of her paramour's comings and goings.[20] She often succumbs to "self-mutilation" and "paranoia."[21]

De Beauvoir stresses the possessiveness that women feel toward the men who occupy such a disproportionate place in their world. Love "comes in the form of a gift," she writes, "when it is really a tyranny."[22] Jealousy soon emerges, for she who has all invested in love "feels in danger at every moment."[23] Finally, de Beauvoir speaks of the catastrophe of abandonment for women—a situation she suffers more profoundly than man: "A break can leave its mark on a man; but . . . he has his man's life to live. The abandoned woman no longer has anything."[24] Interestingly, Freud, in discussing the behavior of an hysterical patient, selects (as exemplary) her fantasy of desertion by a man:

> She told me that on one occasion she had burst into tears in the street, and that, thinking quickly what she had been crying about, she realized the existence of a phantasy in her mind that a pianist well known in the town (but not personally acquainted with her) had entered into an intimate relationship with her, that she had had a child by him (she was childless) and that he had deserted her and her child and left them in misery. It was at this point of her romance that she burst into tears.[25]

If love, for woman, can be an experience of mystical ecstasy, it can also be an occasion for monumental pain.

In characterizing the woman in love, de Beauvoir is not dealing with "the laws of nature." It is not female biology that places woman in this vulnerable position. "It is the difference in their *situations* that is reflected in the difference men and women show in their conceptions of love."[26]

Significantly, de Beauvoir's remarks on women in love—written in the 1940s and based on observation, diaries, letters, and novels—have recently been corroborated. In *Women Who Love Too Much*, Robin Norwood finds that an obsession with romance "is primarily a female phenomenon."[27] And in *Swept Away: Why Women Fear Their Own Sexuality*, psychologist Carol Cassell concludes (from her survey of hundreds of individuals) that women are "love junkies" who consistently place a higher value on amorous relationships than men do.[28] Cassell also advances a rather interesting new theory concerning female romanticism. Women allow themselves to be "swept off their feet" in order to *justify* their repressed sexual attraction to men—an impulse censored by traditional patriarchal society:

> Swept Away is a sexual strategy, a coping mechanism, which allows women to be sexual in a society that is, at best, still ambivalent about, and at worst, condemnatory of female sexuality.[29]

Although Cassell's theory goes beyond that of de Beauvoir, the two formulations converge. Both see the woman in love as propagating illusions—ones that represent her situation as more benign than it is. Cassell states:

> The romantic aura is false and confusing. We become deceived about the meaning of our experience. . . . We use this syndrome to inject the thrill of romance into our lives, lives still subject to the constraints imposed on us because we are women, the female gender.[30]

Letter from an Unknown Woman (based on a story by Stefan Zweig) literalizes and exemplifies the plight of the woman in love, as characterized by de Beauvoir, Norwood, and Cassell. To analyze the film, we will focus on the heroine, Lisa Berndle, and compare her fictional experiences with the theorists more abstract formulations.

V. F. Perkins has stated that "Lisa's offense is the 'excessive' enactment of those qualities which are held out as being woman's nature and woman's glory."[31] This is nowhere so true as in her embodiment of the woman in love. For de Beauvoir, the traditional woman views love as an all-encompassing experience, the structuring principle of life. This is surely our impression of Lisa's passion—an emotion that rules out all other possibilities for her future. As her letter to Stefan informs us (rendered in voice-over narration): "Everyone has two birthdays—the day of his physical birth and the beginning of his conscious life." For Lisa, reality begins (and ends) on the day Stefan moves into her apartment complex, and she is smitten with love.

In keeping with this view, the narrative focuses every moment on Lisa's relation to Stefan. Even if *she* thought her life began with his appearance, the diegesis might have presented her world independent of that fateful event—but its point of view is consonant with hers. From the moment she meets Stefan, her life (and the filmic story) is consecrated to him, and all subsequent events are subordinated to their encounters. This contrasts with Stefan's world, filled with friends, lovers, and career milestones. Significantly, most of the important events in Lisa's relationship with Stefan occur at railroad stations (their amusement-park ride, his leave-taking, the departure of their son). From the moment she meets him, she leads a decidedly "one-track" existence.

The film does offer some "explanation" for Lisa's monomania by indicating the lack of options in her life. If her energies were not dedicated to a *grand amour,* they would be assigned to a bourgeois marriage. The grim social horizon is invoked in the Linz sequence, in which Lisa dates a young lieutenant. All aspects of the scene (analyzed in detail by V. F. Perkins) attest to the constraints of this cultural world: the couple's dull conversation, the young man's military role, the deafening church bells, the marching-band music, the entrapping camera movements. Although the film's sympathy is obviously with Lisa's romantic, unconventional goal (her desire to have a great passion rather than a pedestrian love), it never questions the assumption that woman's main concern in life should be *love*. Rather, it seems only to inquire what *kind* of love it should be—traditional or otherwise.

If Stefan's creative possibilities include being a renowned concert pianist, Lisa's expressive outlet is limited to that of an "artist of love." As Firestone notes: "Men [have been involved with] thinking, writing and creating, because women were pouring their energy into those men; *women are not creating culture because they are preoccupied with love.*"[32]

De Beauvoir also makes the point that women find self-worth in their lovers' eyes. For Lisa Berndle, actualization comes through association with Stefan Brand. On the day he moves into her house, she watches his possessions carted in and wonders "about [her] neighbor who owned such beautiful things." The quest of her life is to become another such object that he might possess and cherish. As she remarks in her letter, she "prepared" herself for him by careful grooming. She "kept [her] clothes neater so [he] wouldn't be ashamed of [her]." Throughout the narrative, Lisa's wish to be prized by Stefan eludes her, but at the film's conclusion, her value is finally acknowledged. As though to literalize de Beauvoir's metaphor of love as a "developer," a series of images of Lisa crystallize before Stefan's eyes.

De Beauvoir notes how women live entirely *through* their men. For Lisa Berndle, this is true not only of her relationship with Stefan but also with her father. On the night of Stefan and Lisa's fairground date, they sit in a mock train car, watching false scenery pass outside the window; Lisa tells Stefan of her imaginary childhood travels with her dad. This image of Lisa—stationary (amidst the illusion of movement)—objectifies the way in which her false "travels" in life are predicated on men.

De Beauvoir postulates that woman's intense experience of romance comes from her desire to share in male power—a wish begun in adolescence. Significantly, Lisa is smitten at this precise moment—a period when a girl abruptly learns the constraints of her female role. Her status as Stefan's "double" comes out quite clearly in her statements and actions. She tells him: "Though I was not able to go to your concerts, I found ways of *sharing* in your success," and we see her steal a concert program from a man's pocket on a crowded trolley. Of course, the most profound way that she lives through Stefan occurs in adulthood, when she secretly bears his child and dedicates her life to father and son.

De Beauvoir sees this obsessive quality of female love as a misguided means of appropriating male power. But, as Tania Modleski has noted, in the woman's film "it is . . . not the virile, masculinized male . . . who elicits woman's desire . . . but the feminine man: the attractive, cosmopolitan type . . . or the well-bred, charming foreigner."[33] Stefan Brand stands among this fraternity. Modleski sees woman's attraction to this figure as a means to subvert masculine power, since "the man with 'feminine' attributes frequently functions as a figure upon whom feminine desires for freedom from patriarchal authority may be projected." However, given de Beauvoir's theory, we might read woman's choice of this type of man in an alternate manner. Rather than undermining patriarchy, he may secure it by making a woman's "doubling" of him that much easier, invoking what Mary Ann Doane calls "a thematics of narcissim."[34]

In *Letter*, Lisa fully accepts the fact that her entrée to power comes only through Stefan, and, in his absence, she bears him a child (as surrogate lover). She thereby enacts the Freudian scenario by which woman "adjusts" to her castrated status by converting her desire for a penis into the wish for a baby (a transformation made more "perfect" by the birth of a son). Echoing this sentiment, Lisa writes to Stefan: "My life was measured by the moments with you and our child."

Lisa's love for Stefan also embodies the master/slave dynamic. (At one point she even talks of wanting "to throw [herself] at [his] feet.") Like a vassal, she expects nothing from him. She is content to sit in her bed at night listening to his music, believing that he is "giving [her] some of the happiest hours of [her] life."

If Stefan offers her nothing, she makes of her life a gift to him. The night he first notices her and they enjoy a romantic interlude, she asks, "How could I help you?" And later, when she explains to him why she has never come for assistance, she says, "I wanted to be one woman whom you had known who asked you for nothing." Finally, when they reencounter each other at the opera, she says, "I'd come to offer you my whole life," and regrets that he cannot recognize "what was always [his]." Thus, in love, man is to be the consumer and woman the consumed.

Not only does Lisa make of her life a gift to Stefan but, as in all classical narratives, her love is "present"-ed to him at the conclusion of the story with the arrival of her confessional note. This pattern of "boy getting girl" is traditional in drama: one need only think of Northrop Frye's analysis of comic structure as a case in point.[35] This archetypal narrative pattern also conforms to the male oedipal scenario, whereby the young boy is "assured" the prize of a woman if he relinquishes his love for mother.[36]

Within traditional literature, woman's position and story is quite different from man's. Her narrative does not recount the achievement of *her* romantic goals but, rather, charts her role in the fulfillment of male desire. She functions as a character in somebody else's plot. As de Lauretis writes:

> The end of the girl's journey, if successful, will bring her to the place where the boy will find her, like Sleeping Beauty, awaiting him, Prince Charming. For the boy has been promised, by the social contract he has entered into at his Oedipal phase, that he will find a woman waiting at the end of *his* journey.[37]

In *Letter*, Stefan realizes the gift of Lisa's love before he faces his fatal duel. Lisa, however, never receives her reward: by the time Prince Charming bestows his kisses, Sleeping Beauty is already dead.

De Beauvoir's perception of woman's deification of the male lover resounds in *Letter*. Critics have noted the film's Catholic sense of fate, and some have even offhandedly characterized Lisa as a "Lady Madonna."[38] But none have surfaced the parallels between her stance and that of a religious novitiate. Her attitude toward Stefan is one of worship for a god, and she seems more like a nun than a schoolgirl. Most evocative is the scene in which she sneaks into Stefan's apartment, and walks through it in a religious thrall. His rooms have more the hallowed ambience of a church than the atmosphere of a bachelor apartment. Her worship of Stefan is apparent in her desire to "throw [herself] at [his] feet" and in her adoration of him playing the piano. As though aware of her pure transcendent quality, Stefan gives her a white (rather than a red) rose, a tribute to her bloodless holiness. Like the religious devotee, Lisa's god/lover is conveniently absent—someone to adore in the abstract, at a material and physical distance. Significantly, she gives birth to Stefan's child in a Catholic hospital, tended by sisters—and the letter telling Stefan of her death comes on stationery emblazoned with a cross. Both the epistolary format and the transcendent ending of the film are reminiscent not so much of other woman's pictures as of Robert Bresson's *Diary of a Country Priest* (1951). For Lisa, the struggle to maintain a self-negating love seems not so much the achievement of ideal romance as that of spiritual grace.

Stefan's removal from Lisa also insures that his presence will be in the form of an illusory mental image. She is with him for only one night, and during the rest of her life she sustains him as a fantasy. Rather than a real flesh-and-blood man, he is like a wax figure—a comparison she suggests on the night of their carriage ride when she predicts that his likeness will one day appear in a museum.

The sense of Stefan as a mere image on Lisa's mind screen suggests certain parallels between him and a male film star. For Stefan, love is an act: on the night of the couple's first encounter, they sit together in a restaurant booth, framed on two sides by curtains that make the site of their tête-à-tête into a kind of stage. Stefan is also, quite literally, a performer; in the same scene, he autographs a woman's concert program and eight-by-ten glossy photo. If Stefan is a matinee idol, Lisa is a loyal and adoring "fan." Like a classic female viewer, she watches the romantic lead from afar—as an unseen voyeur.

Perhaps, in some sense, all women in love share Lisa's predicament. For traditional heterosexual romance to work, they must assume the role of passive spectators of masculine power and transpose their lovers into distant, overblown images. De Lauretis finds parallels between the act of seduction and woman's film-viewing experience:

> If women spectators are to buy their tickets and their popcorn, the work of cinema . . . may be said to require woman's consent; and we may well suspect that narrative cinema in particular must be aimed, like desire, toward seducing women into femininity.[39]

The situation involves a complex and infinite regression: as Lisa is seduced by Stefan (an ersatz "movie" image), so the female spectator watching *Letter* is seduced by the image of Stefan seducing her.

Cassell's notion of women as Swept Away is also relevant to *Letter*, for the film obliquely suggests such repression of female desire. Modleski cites a particular moment in the film when Lisa reencounters Stefan at the opera house and looks at him with the erotic concentration usually reserved for men: "Here we find . . . the possibility of feminine desire being actively aimed at the passive, eroticized male." But this impulse is ultimately denied by Lisa's voice-over narration, which says: "Somewhere out there were your eyes and I knew I couldn't escape them." Thus, although the film depicts Lisa enraptured with desire for Stefan, she conceives of herself as being desired by *him*. Thus, as Doane notes, the patriarchal "flaw" of the traditional love story is "to posit the very possibility of female desire." But "for this reason, it often ends badly."[40]

De Beauvoir tells us that the woman in love is one who waits. On the evening of Lisa's departure for Linz, she bolts from the train station and returns to her vacant apartment. She runs to Stefan's door and, finding him out, decides to stay. Ultimately, he comes back with another woman, and Lisa retreats. But her vigil does not end on Stefan's doorstep. The rest of her life is lived in suspended animation, marking time with another man but anticipating Stefan.

In *The Desire to Desire*, Doane discusses Roland Barthes's insight that woman's conventional pose of waiting generates powers of fantasy. He writes: "It is Woman who gives shape to absence, elaborates its fiction, for she has the time to do so."[41] But Doane expands the point by noting that female desire itself can take on an imaginary quality, a fact that is evident in many 1940s love stories:

> The essentially fictive character of female desire is frequently demonstrated by the woman's demand for "all of nothing." . . . The ultimate consequence of this . . . attitude . . . is illustrated by those films in which a woman spends almost her entire life loving a man who, when he meets her again, does not recognize her.[42]

Letter stands among these works, and Lisa's desire for Stefan is so fanciful that it sustains an entire life without him.

Doane also makes the point that women's pictures reproduce scenarios of female masochism. In characterizing that syndrome (via Freud), she notes how women's masochistic fantasies are de-eroticized. For men, sexual reveries are utilized in conjunction with masturbation, whereas for women, the "fantasy . . . becomes an end in itself." Masochistic daydreams function not as vehicles for sexuality but *instead* of it.[43] It is this substitution of fantasy for eroticism that we find in the life of Lisa Berndle, who survives on imaginary images of Stefan in lieu of any carnal relation with him. Perhaps there is even a way that the camera work employed in *Letter* accentuates Lisa's fiction. The tracking shot is so omnipresent, so tied to her (in its anthropomorphic fluctuations), that we almost feel it her companion—a dream lover that stands in Stefan's place.

While much of *Letter* conforms to de Beauvoir's portrait of the woman in love, one aspect of her characterization is missing: the experience of malaise. (Robin Norwood will later equate woman's enactment of romance with the sensation of pain.)[44] Whereas de Beauvoir's female lover is possessive and jealous, Lisa Berndle is saintly and selfless. While de Beauvoir's woman veers toward madness, Lisa Berndle seems stoic and sane. On the one hand, this portrayal seems a positive view of woman, avoiding certain stereotypes of neurosis. On the other hand, the film's denial of woman's suffering only encourages martyrdom by imagining that such devotion can be practiced at no psychic cost.

In *Letter*, the difficult periods of Lisa's life have been excised from the text. The narrative cuts directly from Stefan's departure at the train station to Lisa's stay at the maternity hospital, eliminating the undoubtedly stressful period of her pregnancy. Likewise, her letter skips from the nine-year period of her single parenthood to her marriage to the affluent Johann Stauffer. We are allowed to see only the high points of her life when she is seemingly in control. Yet de Beauvoir has indicated how abandonment by a lover precipitates a major crisis for woman. Despite *Letter*'s excision of this trauma, the repressed returns in the form of the heroine's death. As Doane has noted, this conclusion is a staple of the genre and reveals its precarious ideological position: "The inability of a large proportion of love stories in the 40s to produce the classical happy ending . . . is a sign of the love story's vulnerability, the fragility of its project."[45]

In discussing the woman's film, many theorists have linked the configuration of melodrama to conversion hysteria and have likened its heroines to neurotic victims.[46] (Recall, too, the fantasy of Freud's hysterical patient, who imagines an unrequited love affair with a pianist—a virtual "script" for *Letter*.) Modleski, however, questions the applicability of this concept to Lisa Berndle. On the one hand, her struggle could be read as "the classic dilemma of . . . the hysterical woman," and her chronic muteness seen as a sign of this illness.[47] Although Modleski admits that Lisa's life is marked by nostalgia, she does not see her as suffering from reminiscence in the orthodox Freudian sense.[48] Rather, Modleski turns critical clichés on their head and points to *Stefan* as the true hysteric:

> Superficially it appears in the film woman's time is hysterical time. . . . Closer analysis, however, reveals Stefan is the hysteric. . . . For Stefan is the one who truly suffers from reminiscences. . . . Unable to remember the woman who alone gives his life significance, Stefan is doomed to an existence of meaningless repetition, especially in relation to women, who become virtually indistinguishable to him.[49]

In conceiving Stefan as an hysteric, and in positioning the *male* lover as potentially unbalanced, Modleski has pointed to a crucial issue—that heterosexual love, as contained in patriarchal culture, breeds pathology. If women in love hover on the brink of destruction, men will fare no better. Thus the film gives us a sense of the limitations of *both* characters—of the struggles enacted by both individuals in the dynamics of love. Perhaps this is even figured into one of its stylistic tropes, which connects (with a "blur-in"/"blur-out" motif) shots of Stefan reading and flashbacks of Lisa—a technical metaphor for the psychic murkiness of their relationship. Rather than simply reverse polarities, we might also consider whether the classic male pattern is a different one, whose distinctive features explain his perils in romantic engagement.

We might begin by configuring Stefan as a particular type of hysteric, specifically an *amnesiac*. If Lisa is haunted by an inability to *forget* (anyone but herself), Stefan is plagued by an inability to *remember*. In a way, Stefan even suffers a double amnesia by forgetting Lisa twice—as an adolescent and as a young woman. His memory lapse runs even deeper, however. It is the fact that he has forgotten his trip to Milan that leads him to break his date with Lisa after their first night of love. Although he vows to return in two weeks, he forgets that promise as well. Through it all, Stefan even forgets his recurrent amnesia: the night after rediscovering Lisa at the opera, he thoughtlessly tells her that he "couldn't get [her] out of [his] mind."

In its classic configuration, amnesia constitutes a "partial or total loss of memory" and is attributed to "shock, psychological disturbance, brain injury or illness."[50] But, as Freud tells us in *The Psychopathology of Everyday Life,* even quotidian forgetting has its tendentious causes. He refers to such mental lapses officially as "amnesia" and says that "in all cases" they "proved to be founded on a motive of displeasure"[51]: "One . . . finds abundant indications which show that even in healthy, not neurotic, persons resistances are found against the memory of disagreeable impressions and the idea of painful thoughts."[52] Thus Stefan's forgetting of Lisa can be seen as more than accidental. As Freud remarks: "Lack of attention does not in itself suffice to explain . . . the forgetting of intentions."[53] But what does?

To pursue this question, let us analyze the character of Stefan once more—this time looking to the psychic syndrome of *Don Juanism* for clues to his motivation. Stefan is an inveterate womanizer, an "obsessive seducer."[54] He is a selfish man for whom love is a game that he seeks to win at the least possible psychic cost. Hélène Cixous has commented on how the Lothario exemplifies the patriarchal stance to the world:

> Take Don Juan and you have the whole masculine economy getting together to "give women just what it takes to keep them in bed" then swiftly taking back the investment, then reinvesting etc., so that nothing ever gets given, everything gets taken back, while in the process the greatest possible dividend of pleasure is taken. Consumption without payment, of course.[55]

But what is the accepted psychological explanation for Don Juan's behavior? In *Beyond the Male Myth,* Anthony Pietropinto and Jacqueline Simenauer advance the theory of the womanizer as a sexually insecure man who is led "to seek new women in order to validate again and again that [he] can satisfy a woman."[56] Although this explanation works up to a point, they note that it does not account for why a man "would repeatedly risk failure and discount the approval of many women in the hope of adding one more to his growing list."[57] Rather, they see this quest for the confirmation of manhood as "only half the story."

The other part involves the idealization of women, the unconscious search for the perfect mother—a quest resulting in inevitable disillusionment and retreat. The Don Juan is a man who has not recovered from the oedipal shock of maternal separation—and the introduction of the paternal "third term." In his adult romantic relationships, he continues to look for a "doting mother," despite the fact that each successive woman will fail to meet his impossible expectations.[58]

In *Letter,* Stefan enacts an oedipal scenario. As Modleski has noted, for most of the film he refuses the Law of the Father; only at the end does he learn to "accept the values of duty and sacrifice espoused by his patriarchal society."[59] Furthermore, he flits from woman to woman in a hopeless and repetitious hunt for the mother. The teenaged Lisa observes Stefan kissing a woman on the stairs of his apartment building, and later she occupies the same position herself. In filming her with Stefan, the identical camera stance is adopted, implying that there will yet be others. Stefan's search for the ideal woman is clearly driven and relentless: at one point (when he reencounters Lisa after many years), he questions which of them is the pursuer and which the pursued. This dual sense attaches to Stefan himself, who, in seeking women, is also sought by the maternal imago.

Although Stefan is an adult, sophisticated "older man" who sweeps the pubescent Lisa off her feet, he displays childlike qualities. On the night of their fateful tryst, he says that Lisa "may be able to *help* [him] some day." And during the evening, she acts like a fussing parent, bundling him up on the carriage ride and putting a scarf at his neck. "It's a long time since anyone did that for me," he sighs, and we can guess what he means. Years later, when he meets Lisa at the opera, though he does not recognize her, he says she's the face he's been waiting for and asks quizzically: "Who *are* you?" Finally, when they rendezvous at his apartment, he tells her of a mystery goddess he has sought but never found—one who (like a mother) could makes his life "begin."

Lisa serves a double function in Stefan's world: she is both lover and maternal surrogate. She is familiar to him not only because he has really met her before but because all women embody for him (and recall) the archetypal mother. Because of this, she must be forgotten—for his attraction represents too great a threat.

Beyond the Don Juan's excessive love for the mother are feelings of a darker nature, perhaps shared by all men. Nancy Friday has commented on this male hostility toward women, ascribing it to the controlling position of the mother. She notes that "power in women produces an enormous rage in men but since their need for us is equally powerful, they bury their anger."[60] Hence, it is easy to see the Don Juan's sadistic treatment of his female lovers as a punitive, misogynistic act—one that misses its mark (the mother) and strikes other women instead. The classic Don Juan has two reasons to repress the mother figure: he loves her too much, and he hates her for claiming that affection. In *Letter,* even the mechanism of Stefan's "amnesia" (his forgetting Lisa instead of his mother) conforms to Freud's model, by which the mind "misses the target and causes something else to be forgotten—something less significant, but which has fallen into associative connection with the disagreeable material."[61]

This sense of Stefan's psychosexual repression of Lisa is particularly intriguing since any representation of the couple's lovemaking is excised from the screen by a fade (as it is from Stefan's mind). Stephen Heath rejects the notion that this absence is merely the result of 1940s censorship:

> As always . . . the centered image mirrors a structure that is in excess of its effect of containment, that bears the traces of the heterogeneity—the trouble—it is produced to contain: sexuality here is also the "more" that the look elides, that is eluded from, the look, and that returns.[62]

Hence the fade, and more crucially Stefan's forgetfulness, represents not only repression but oedipal blindness—an inability to see the psychic roots of his distress; and it seems no accident that his visual nonrecognition of Lisa is at the core of the story. Significantly, there are only two memorable shot/countershot sequences between the protagonists in *Letter* (which is reasonable, considering it is a film about Stefan *not* returning Lisa's look). But even these moments, which, on the surface, emphasize Stefan's apprehension of her, ultimately reveal his failed vision.

The first sequence occurs when he reencounters Lisa as a young woman, as she stalks the square where he resides. After a resonant exchange of glances (when we *hope* that he will recognize her), he says only that he has seen her there before—a few nights ago. The second time this dramatic shot/countershot structure is used occurs during the opera sequence. Stefan tells Lisa, "I have seen you somewhere," but adds that he "can't place [her.]" Only after reading Lisa's letter does he acknowledge his love for a woman, and only then can he "see" her. Significantly, the film ends with a series of Stefan's recollections of Lisa, whereby he finally re-vises their relationship. Ironically, at this moment of insight, Stefan covers his eyes in remorse, as thought to underscore his previous blindness. For Lisa, it has always been possible to see the invisible (to imagine Stefan in his absence). But, for Stefan it has been impossible to see what was there. His forgetfulness is made more poignant by the fact of the cinematic medium. If Stefan forgets, the film constantly "recalls" in its role as re-presentational. As de Lauretis has noted: "Film re-members (fragments and makes whole again) the object of vision for the spectator."[63]

For final confirmation of Stefan as a Don Juan, we might look to the manner in which he meets his death. After realizing his repression of Lisa (and ostensibly the oedipal desire at its base), he faces a duel with Lisa's husband—an act that Modleski has noted evokes castration.[64] Johann Stauffer is an older man and the legitimate possessor of the woman Stefan loves; hence, it is not a distortion to see him as a father figure.[65] At the moment of Stefan's comprehension of the *dual* nature of his attraction to women (lover as mother/mother as lover), he faces a *duel* (a challenge of phallic swords) with an elderly opponent worthy of his infantile hostility and fear.

Thus the film configures Lisa's sublime amorous posture not as some hysterical aberration but rather, as a "reproduction of mothering." We should recall that Freud, in his essay on femininity, stated that a heterosexual relationship "is not made secure until the wife has succeeded in making her husband her child as well as in acting as mother to him."[66] Like a good parent, Lisa offers Stefan unconditional love—and requires nothing in return. Like a good parent, she accepts the fact that he will abandon her and go off into the world. Lisa even literalizes her maternal/romantic role by bearing Stefan's child—a boy (named Stefan) who stands in his place. Obviously, this role for the woman in love can function only because it satisfies the traditional man, who seeks in his mate a mother substitute.

The sense of male/female relationships as being mired in the infantile past comes out on many levels in the film. Critics have remarked on its temporal complexity which involves (1) the time of Lisa's writing the letter (as represented by her off-screen narration); (2) the time to which the letter refers (as represented by flashbacks to her childhood, adolescence, and youth); (3) the time of Stefan's reading of the letter (the night before the duel); and (4) the time of Lisa's death and the delivery of the letter to Stefan (which we never see). Although this chronological intricacy has been acknowledged, its symbolization of psychic entrapment has not been underscored. Direct reference to stasis is made by Stefan on several occasions in the film. On the night he first notices Lisa in his neighborhood square, he comments that he "almost never get[s] to the place [he] start[s] out for." And later, on the fairground train ride, he jokes with Lisa about "reliving the scenes of their youth." Finally, on the night following their meeting at the opera, he talks of how "all clocks stopped" the moment he saw her. In truth, for Stefan, all clocks stopped even earlier—at the oedipal stage. This emphasis on stagnation is made still more poignant in the film by Ophuls's formal reliance on camera *movement*—a technical (and ironic) counterpoint to the narrative impasse.

It would be a mistake to think of the film as naive or sentimental in its depiction of love. Wood, for instance, states that "irony is as essential to the Ophuls tone as his romanticism."[67] What *Letter* shows us, after all, is a case of *amour fou*, one whose consummation comes in death—hardly a very sanguine circumstance. But what remains an open question is how to characterize the film's precise attitude.

Critics have struggled with this issue and arrived at divergent conclusions. Michael Walker, for example, sees the woman's film not merely as depicting the plight of the woman in love but as confronting the issue head-on:

> In the woman's film . . . what we so often see is how love serves to lead women into positions of oppression: to sacrifice themselves for their families/lovers, to submit "willingly" to suffering and endure wasted lives—in short, to embrace the role of "victim." And so the woman's film raises, very acutely, the *problem* of love.[68]

V. F. Perkins, on the other hand, reads the woman's film in a contrary manner, finding in it only "an indulgence of the stereotyped opposition of emotional woman . . . and rational man."[69]

This is clearly a very slippery issue. How do we know if the hyperbolic strategies of the text (its presentation of an extreme case of the woman in love) amount to an exaggeration of the situation or a critique? To pursue this, we must inquire how the film constructs its two protagonists. Despite *Letter*'s ironic presentation of Lisa's delusional love (its emphasis on her folly and self-destructiveness), melodramatic *heroism* still attaches to her actions. The film tacitly endorses her hopeless passion as a valiant spiritual goal. In this respect, it denies her the tragic position, which would characterize her life as ill spent on unrequited love. Rather, it reserves that stance for Stefan, and the film recounts *his* loss. The tragedy lies *not* in the fact that a woman has made of her life a hollow tribute to a callous male but in the fact that the man has not accepted the gift. Some critics have not only refused Lisa her own tragedy but have seen her responsible for Stefan's. Wood writes:

> The more times one sees the film, the more one has the sense . . . of the possibility of a film *against* Lisa: it would require only a shift of emphasis for this other film to emerge. It is not simply that Ophuls makes it possible for us to blame Lisa for destroying her eminently civilized marriage to a kind (if unpassionate) man, and the familial security he has given her and her son; it is also *almost* possible to blame Lisa and her refusal to compromise for Stefan's ruin.[70]

Lisa's status is also denied through the undermining of her point of view. Although the story seems to be offered from her perspective, her subjectivity is qualified. Wood speaks of how the film frequently violates the conventions of first-person cinematic narrative, "taking great liberties with such an assumption."[71] If we examine the structure of *Letter*, we find many episodes that validate this observation. During the Linz sequence, the camera leaves Lisa to focus on secret conversations with her parents, who discuss their hopes for her engagement. Later in the film, when she and Stefan go to a café, the camera focuses on Stefan secretly instructing the maître d' to give his excuses to another woman. These are both scenes that delineate actions unknown to Lisa and, hence, obviate her point of view.

Lisa's position is also subverted by the narrative structure of the film. It is true that the screen story issues from her letter, which determines the diegetic events. But her *writing* of the letter (and, hence, her female voice) is subsumed by the act of Stefan's *apprehension* of it. Once more, the presentation of woman's world is mediated by male consciousness; she is "read" by him. But the film is about reading in a broader sense than simply comprehending words on a page; it is about one person "reading" (or "misreading") another. As a teenager and young woman, Lisa "reads" Stefan as a passionate lover and a promising artist—an interpretation that turns out to be grossly distorted. Likewise, Stefan "misreads" Lisa as a shallow, infatuated young woman who will recover from his callow rebuff; furthermore, he mistakes her passion for a "crush." But the film argues for a larger sense of misprision in heterosexual relationships, whereby men and women misread their lovers by seeing them as mythic gods, children, or parents rather than as equal human beings. Ironically, when Stefan eventually "reads" Lisa correctly, on the night he scans her letter, the process kills him. Stefan's tendency to regard Lisa as a text may also explain his inveterate amnesia. As Roland Barthes claims: "It is precisely because [we] forget that [we] read."[72]

Finally, there seems a resonant truth in the film's emphasis on the issue of visibility and invisibility, on presence and absence. Stefan not only has trouble remembering Lisa, he has difficulty envisioning her at all! She is transparent to him as a teenager, and later, as a young woman, she must stalk his street repeatedly before he notices her. For Lisa, the problem is the opposite; Stefan burns such a potent visual impression on her mind that she continues to see him when he is not there—as a haunting "afterimage" on her emotional life. Within the terms of the film, we might say that woman is invisible and man is visible; he is seen and she is unseen.

Luce Irigaray comments that in Western culture, "the male sex [has become] *the* sex because it is very visible," while "[woman's] sexual organ represents *the horror of nothing to see*. A defect in this systematics of representation and desire. A 'hole' in its scopophilic lens."[73] She also implies that, within masculine society, what is visible is valued, while what is invisible is worthless; hence, discrepant attitudes arise toward male and female sexuality.

Irigaray also discusses the two sexes' opposing relation to the act of vision: "investment in the look is not privileged in women as in men." With control of the gaze comes male power, for "the eye objectifies and masters" and "sets at a distance."[74] The unseen female sex does not wield or value vision like the specular/spectacular male.

In *Letter*, man is superficially associated with the look—be it Stefan's seductive glance or that of the voyeuristic camera. As Irigaray implies, the look tends to objectify and master woman, establishing her as a figure of desire. In Stefan's case, it clearly "sets" Lisa "at a distance"—one that spans their entire lifetime. But if Stefan *looks* at Lisa, he never *sees* her; thus the master of the eye is blind to more profound in-sights. As Stefan is oblivious to Lisa, so is he to his own motives for spurning her. If she is invisible to him, so is the awesome maternal ghost that haunts him—the *real* "unknown woman" in his life.

In some oblique fashion, these issues circle back to the plight of the woman in love (much as the film circles back to its own beginning). Though conceived as a vision of pleasure, woman remains fundamentally *invisible* to man. If he sees her at all, he looks right through her to the background figure of the maternal imago. Perhaps all female lovers are "unknown women"—unrecognized by the men they love. (Geoffrey Nowell-Smith writes that in melodrama, "Femininity . . . is not only unknown but unknowable."[75]) But it is an even greater loss that these women are "unknown" to themselves. In "doubling" the male lover, in living "through" him, they negate their own existence. Women may be seduced and abandoned not only by their paramours but by their own acceptance of restrictive views on love.

NOTES

1. Lord Byron, quoted in Simone de Beauvoir, *The Second Sex*, trans. H. M. Parshley, New York: Vintage (1974), p. 712.

2. Sigmund Freud, "Femininity," in James Strachey, ed., *The Standard Edition of the Complete Psychological Works of Sigmund Freud*, London: Hogarth Press

(1955), vol. 22, p. 134. Quoted in Teresa de Lauretis, *Alice Doesn't: Feminism, Semiotics, Cinema*, Bloomington: Indiana University Press (1984), p. 133.

3. Roland Barthes, *S/Z*, trans. Richard Miller, New York: Hill and Wang (1974); Roland Barthes, *The Pleasures of the Texts*, trans. Richard Miller, New York: Hill and Wang (1975); René Girard, *Deceit, Desire and the Novel: Self and Other in Literary Structure*, trans. Yvonne Freccero, Baltimore: Johns Hopkins University Press (1966); Edward Branigan, *Point of View in the Cinema: A Theory of Narration and Subjectivity in Classical Film*, New York: Mouton (1984).

4. Barthes, *S/Z*, p. 88.

5. De Lauretis, p. 106.

6. Ibid., p. 121.

7. Freud, *The Psychopathology of Everyday Life*, trans. A. A. Brill, New York: New American Library (1960), p. 79.

8. Michael Walker, "Ophuls in Hollywood," *Movie*, nos. 29–30 (Summer 1982). The section on *Letter* is on pp. 43–48.

9. *Letter* is set in Vienna in about 1900. Pianist Stefan Brand returns to his apartment in the early hours of the morning, having been challenged to a duel; he intends to flee from that engagement. His servant hands him a letter, which he begins to read. It is from Lisa Berndle, a woman who has loved him since her childhood, whom he can barely remember. In flashbacks, narrated by Lisa's voice-over monologue, the events of the past are recalled for Stefan: the day he moved into the apartment house where the adolescent Lisa lived, her crush on him, her refusal to marry a young officer because of her desire for Stefan. In addition to informing Stefan of events in which he did not participate, Lisa's letter reminds him of their encounters. After Lisa's parents move to Linz, she returns to Vienna, working as a model and stalking the streets on which Stefan lives. One night he notices her, and they share a romantic evening. He dates her once again, then informs her that he must leave on tour; he promises to return in two weeks but never does. We learn that Lisa has become pregnant by Stefan and bears his child without ever contacting him. She later marries Johan Stauffer, a wealthy officer, and settles into a comfortable bourgeois existence with him and Stefan's son. One night (some ten years later) at the opera, she recognizes Stefan in the audience, and he senses they have met before. The next day, Lisa sends her son back to boarding school without realizing that he is seated in a train car contaminated by typhus. Hoping that Brand will finally recognize her devotion, Lisa goes to his apartment but finds that he does not recall their romantic history—that he treats her like one more casual conquest. Lisa's husband learns that she has seen Stefan and challenges him to a duel. Upon reading the final lines of Lisa's letter (which reveals that she has contracted typhus and is dying), Stefan goes downstairs to fight Stauffer. As he walks out the door where he first met Lisa, he finally has an accurate vision of her.

10. Shulamith Firestone, in Sheila Ruth, ed., *Issues in Feminism: A First Course in Women's Studies*, Boston: Houghton Miffin (1980), p. 271.

11. De Beauvoir, p. 712.

12. Ibid., p. 713.

13. Ibid., p. 714.

14. Ibid., p. 718.

15. Ibid., p. 725.

16. Ibid., pp. 713–14.

17. Ibid., p. 714.

18. Ibid., p. 720.

19. Ibid., p. 727.

20. Ibid., p. 736.

21. Ibid., pp. 722, 732.

22. Ibid., p. 728.
23. Ibid., p. 735.
24. Ibid., p. 739.
25. Freud in "Hysterical Phantasies . . . " in *Dora: An Analysis of a Case of Hysteria*, ed. Philip Rieff, New York: Collier (1963), p. 146.
26. De Beauvoir, p. 713.
27. Robin Norwood, *Women Who Love Too Much*, New York: Pocket Books, (1986), p. xv.
28. Carol Cassell, *Swept Away: Why Women Fear Their Own Sexuality*, New York: Simon & Schuster (1981), pp. 490, 51.
29. Ibid., p. 25.
30. Ibid., pp. 26–27.
31. V. F. Perkins, "*Letter from an Unknown Woman*," *Movie*, nos. 29–30 (Summer 1982): 71.
32. Firestone, p. 271.
33. Tania Modleski, "Time and Desire in the Woman's Film," *Cinema Journal* 23, no. 3 (Spring 1984): 26.
34. Ibid.; Mary Ann Doane, *The Desire to Desire: The Woman's Film of the 1940s*, Bloomington and Indianapolis: Indiana University Press (1987), p. 116.
35. See Northrop Frye, "The Mythos of Spring: Comedy," in *The Anatomy of Criticism*, Princeton: Princeton University Press (1957), pp. 163–86.
36. Raymond Bellour, quoted in Janet Bergstrom, "Alternation, Segmentation, Hypnosis: Interview with Raymond Bellour," *Camera Obscura*, no. 3–4 (Summer 1979): 90.
37. De Lauretis, p. 133.
38. Robin Wood, "Ewig hin der Liebe Gluck," *Personal Views: Explorations in Film*, London: Gordon Fraser (1976), pp. 131–32; V. F. Perkins, "*Letter from an Unknown Woman*," *Movie*, nos. 29–30 (Summer 1982): 72.
39. De Lauretis, pp. 136–37.
40. Modleski, pp. 25–26; Doane, p. 118.
41. Roland Barthes, quoted in Doane, p. 109. The original citation is from *A Lover's Discourse*, trans. Richard Howard, New York: Hill and Wang (1978), p. 41.
42. Doane, p. 169.
43. Ibid., pp. 23, 24.
44. Norwood, p. xiii.
45. Doane, p. 118.
46. See Geoffry Nowell-Smith, "Minnelli and Melodrama," *Screen* 18 (Summer 1977): 117.
47. Modleski, p. 20.
48. Ibid., p. 23.
49. Ibid., p. 24.
50. William Morris, ed., *American Heritage Dictionary of the English Language*, Boston: Houghton Mifflin (1978), p. 43.
51. Freud, *Psychopathology*, p. 68.
52. Ibid., p. 74.
53. Ibid., p. 78.
54. Wood, p. 130.
55. Hélène Cixous, "Castration or Decapitation?" trans. Annette Kuhn, *Signs* 7, no. 1 (Autumn 1981): 47.
56. Anthony Pietropinto and Jacqueline Simenauer, *Beyond the Male Myth*, New York: New York Times Book (1977), p. 295.
57. Ibid.
58. Ibid.
59. Modleski, p. 19.

60. Nancy Friday, quoted in Cassell, pp. 150–51.
61. Freud, Psychopathology, p. 75.
62. Stephen Heath, *Questions of Cinema*, Bloomington: Indiana University Press (1981), p. 146.
63. De Lauretis, p. 67.
64. Modleski, p. 20.
65. Ibid., p. 24.
66. Sigmund Freud, quoted in Luce Irigaray, *This Sex Which is Not One*, trans. Catherine Porter and Carolyn Burke, Ithaca, NY: Cornell University Press (1985), p. 64. From "New Introductory Lectures on Psychoanalysis," in Strachey, 22: 117–18.
67. Wood, p. 124.
68. Walker, p. 43.
69. Perkins, p. 71.
70. Wood, pp. 129–30.
71. Ibid., p. 127.
72. Barthes, S/Z, p. 11.
73. Irigaray, quoted in Heath, p. 161; and Irigaray, *This Sex*, pp. 25–26.
74. Irigaray, in Heath, p. 161.
75. Nowell-Smith, p. 116.

ILLICIT PLEASURES
FEMINIST SPECTATORS AND *PERSONAL BEST*

Elizabeth Ellsworth

Feminist film critics have become increasingly involved with questions of how feminist film audiences struggle to construct their own social subjectivities around and despite dominant films. *Personal Best* (1982) offers an opportunity to ask how and why feminist communities interpret popular films.[1] In this essay, I will discuss how feminist reviewers used their interpretations of *Personal Best* as attempts to build alignments and pleasurable identifications with particular feminist communities as oppositional groups.[2]

This question intersects with current work in cultural studies about how an audience's use, interpretation and pleasure of a specific film event is linked to that audience's social history and political position. Cultural studies has made significant contributions to investigating how groups collectively construct alternative interpretations of their lived experiences against those offered by dominant institutions and cultural representations.

But as Richard Johnson argues, a "major gap" remains in our understanding of the role that signifying practices like popular films play as specific cultural determinations.[3] In an attempt to begin to fill that gap, this essay offers the hypothesis that social groups use cultural forms in the process of defining themselves. Women involved in the feminist movement collectively construct self-identities to make sense of the privileges and limitations they experience in daily life as women. These identities form the basis and motivation for individual political action. A social group's interpretation of popular culture forms like films plays a significant role in this process.

Feminist reviewers writing in a variety of feminist publications appropriated *Personal Best* into oppositional spaces constructed by feminist political practice.[4] This interpretive activity is not only a rejection of dominant meanings attached to the film by the popular press. It is also one process by which social subjects constitute themselves collectively and politically, and is therefore itself one of the grounds for feminist political practice. In the case of *Personal Best,* conditions of lived experience and film reception made it possible for feminist viewers to produce illicitly pleasurable and politically oppositional interpretations. Feminist reviews of the film constitute moments of feminist communities' discursive self production that contradict or oppose the positions offered to them within hegemonic ideology.

Before offering arguments in support of these claims, I want to define what I mean by discursive self production and its relation to film interpretation. Systems of domination (economic, sexual, racial, representational) shared within particular groups (like feminists) generate specific patterns of hope, anxiety, and desire. Social actors may experience these patterns initially as private, idiosyncratic, even isolated responses to cultural forms like films. But through material practices like consciousness raising groups, women's studies courses, and feminist film reviewing, feminist communities collectively develop interpretive strategies for making sense of those structures of feelings, moving them into the sphere of public discourse by giving social, semantic form to anxieties and desires.[5]

Feminist communities, as interpretive communities, constantly construct, negotiate, and defend discursive boundaries between feminist and nonfeminist discourses, a process which shapes the variety of feminist identities assumed by women active in the women's movement in the United States. These discursive boundaries, as Teresa de Lauretis argues, are made up of terms, concepts, and rhetorical practices that distinguish feminist writing and speech. They also include particular shared assumptions and inferences drawn from references that are often unstated because they have become part of the discourse. These boundaries function not only negatively as constraints, but positively as horizons of meaning.[6]

To argue that feminist horizons of meaning are oppositional is to argue that interpretation with feminist communities has certain effects. Feminist interpretations become "meaning-full," they are "significant" to feminist communities in protest when they displace patriarchal discourses from their positions of "salience" to those communities. As a noun, "salient" is defined as "the area of battle line, trench, fortification or other military defense that projects closest to the enemy." Feminist communities found *Personal Best* to be "salient"—that is, "striking and conspicuous," because various aspects of its text, production, distribution, exhibition, and reception occupied what I will call discursive salients *against* contemporaneous feminist political, social, and representational initiatives.

For example, by 1982, a variety of dominant media had mounted an "area of battle line" and "defense" against feminist initiatives to eliminate oppressive definitions of "beauty" and the objectification of women's bodies within popular culture in the United States. In August 1982, a *Time* cover story entitled "Coming On Strong, The New Ideal of Beauty" featured photos of "athletic" women striking now familiar poses that one critic described as "trained seals flexing their muscles to male awe and approval." The cover story reads in part: "Spurred by feminism's promise of physical, domestic, and economic freedom, you have done what few generations of women have dared or chosen to do. You have made muscles—a body of them—and it shows. And you look great."[7] The article continues: "The new body is here and men may decide it is sexy for one basic reason: it can enhance sex . . . A woman who is more aware of her physicality probably will be more aware of her sexuality."[8] This discursive salient "projects closest to the enemy"—to feminists—by presuming to speak to women in an attempt to define women to themselves, from a position that attempts to repulse feminist initiatives in this area by sexualizing women's strength and "physicality" in the service of male pleasure.

Most feminist reviewers saw *Personal Best* as occupying a space within this discursive salient—sometimes contradictorily. For example, while it celebrated women athletes, its camera "voyeuristically" focused on legs, crotches and breasts with the "obsessive" eye of a "lascivious" man.[9] Feminist reviewers responded to the discursive salients of *Personal Best* by exposing their contradictory effects, i.e., in the process of resisting feminist initiatives *Personal Best* actually incorporated them into a dominant film event. Feminist reviewers also mobilized and constructed discursive frameworks and contexts based on a rejection of the film's salients. The oppositional effects of feminist interpretations are discussed below.

I use the concept of saliency, then, in order to help to explain why feminist reviewers chose some elements of the film's performance as requiring "interpretation" and not others. The aspects of the film's text, production, distribution, exhibition, or reception that feminist reviewers selected for interpretation were those that occupied positions of saliency in relation to feminist challenges to hegemonic power relations. They required interpretation precisely because they constituted sites of struggle over which "interpretations were to prevail and win credibility."[10]

The sites for struggle over interpretation are potentially infinite—but practically constrained by the type and availability of interpretive strategies developed to address the specific antagonisms played out by specific groups at specific historical moments. For example, some elements of the film's performance that feminist reviewers did not interpret were left as already "meaningful" in a "literal," recognizable, denotative sense. Elements such as certain character motivations, significance of certain aspects of the film's setting, decor and attitude of the narrator were unquestioned as constituting social reality. Others were left as temporarily conceded connotations not immediately salient to a specific feminist community. For example, some feminist reviewers made no mention of the film's representation of black women athletes, while others charged the film with racism for its portrayal of blacks and its exclusion of Latinas. Others writing in publications for lesbians chose to call attention to the film's racism only in passing and to focus interpretive activity instead on issues "more relevant" to white lesbians.

In the case of *Personal Best*, feminist reviewers generated contradictory, diverse, and competing interpretations of the film event. But they agreed widely that this dominant film event had mounted three discursive salients against feminist political struggles occurring outside of the film event, and that these required (re) interpretation. Reviewers defined these salients as issues of media representation of women's bodies, the status of women in sports, and lesbianism. The bulk of the reviewers' interpretive activities attempted to understand the way the film's style and narrative structure worked to undermine and/or celebrate feminist initiatives on each of these issues.

The conjuncture of feminist political practice, pressbook prereadings, reviews in the dominant media, and the feminist reviews around one of these issues—that of lesbianism, forms a discursive configuration riddled with tension and contradiction. I will offer a brief sketch of this reception context as a basis for arguing that interpretation became a political act when feminist reviewers negotiated those tensions in a way to make pleasurable lesbian/feminist spectatorship possible.

Feminist Political Practice

Feminist reviewers "met" *Personal Best* as issues of lesbianism, representation of women's bodies, and feminist sexualities were becoming increasingly controversial within and between various feminist communities. Lesbian feminists, academic feminists, liberal feminists, radical feminists, feminists of color, all formed competing interpretive strategies around these issues. Those communities' responses to cultural practices aside from cinematic representation informed the terms in which reviewers associated these issues with *Personal Best*.

The configuration of discourses that defined the stance of the U.S. women's movement toward pornography became the primary mechanism through which reviewers linked *Personal Best* to issues of lesbianism, representation of women's bodies, and feminist sexualities. After an initial euphoria of mass demonstrations against pornography in 1979 that reaffirmed solidarity reminiscent of the early seventies, alternative interpretations of pornography emerged and gained legitimacy within some communities (primarily academic communities). Lesley Stern distinguished five trajectories of dissent within feminists' criticism of the anti-pornography movement: its moralism, calls for censorship, focus on patriarchal imaging of women, exclusion of female erotica or pornography, and failure to theorize the codes and conventions of pornographic representations.[11]

The dissent around pornography contributed to a continuing controversy over feminist sexualities that added to the interpretive strategies available to feminist reviewers of *Personal Best*. Objections to some feminist discourses on lesbianism and proscriptions of certain sexual behaviors erupted in *Heresies* No. 12 and at the highly controversial conference at Barnard in April 1981. Entitled "The Scholar and the Feminist IX: Towards a Politics of Sexuality," that conference addressed "women's sexual pleasure, choice, and fantasy."[12] It raised the questions of "whether the intensity of the 'gay/straight' split (in the mid 1970s) caused feminists to back away from sex as an issue and why there's been a 'desexualization' of lesbianism—an emphasis on lesbianism as a political and social choice rather than a sexual, erotic one."[13] One of the legacies of this split is that feminist communities have placed themselves in the position of formulating strategies against pornography and homophobia without an adequate theory of sexuality.

Reports and debates on the conference (in *The Village Voice* and *Off Our Backs*), books on "politically incorrect sexuality"[14] and "workshops" on "incorrect" sexuality at gatherings of lesbians and feminist at events like music festivals have added to the repertoire of interpretive strategies available to feminist reviewers about the "issue" of lesbianism.

Feminist reviewers of course also met *Personal Best* on the terrain of the wider culture's ongoing negotiation of what counts as legitimate and illegitimate sexuality. The film appeared not long after an alleged lesbian lover named tennis player Billie Jean King in a "palimony suit." Reviews of the film appearing in dominant media referred to this incident as proof of realism in the film. Feminists discussed how and whether they should address inferences in the dominant press that lesbianism was common in women's sports.

The film also appeared in the context of a series of films from major American studios that tried to appeal to the gay market. It was the first to depict a lesbian relationship. This trend had as much to do with the attractiveness in 1982 of "the recession proof," "upscale" market of gay men with high earning power and low financial obligations as it did with shifts in public attitude about the social acceptability of homosexuality.

Personal Best thus became an event within feminist communities not solely because its "surface subject matter" apparently referred to real events that were relevant to the political positions of women in 1982. Feminist reviewers actively gave it the status of event by using it in ongoing debates *within* feminist communities themselves. It gave reviewers the chance to ask how well their own interpretive strategies met the task of assessing patriarchal salients in a variety of cultural "messages" (like the news, Olympic competition policies, soft core pornography and popular culture) not directly related to *Personal Best*. This particular film gave feminist communities the chance to apply their already constructed interpretive strategies to Hollywood mainstream films and a new instance of filmic representation of women and women's issues like lesbianism. In this way it became the occasion for feminist reviewers to process internal controversies by directly or implicitly referring to the shortcomings of competing feminist reviews and positions. At the same time, they negotiated positions from which to oppose interpretations by Hollywood's promotional campaign and by non-feminist or anti-feminist film reviewers in the dominant press.

Pressbook Prereadings of *Personal Best*

A pressbook is made up of feature articles about the film's text, actors, and production; glossy photos of scenes from the film, its production; and "glamour" portraits of the stars. It constitutes the industry's interpretation of the film event in light of its specific economic imperatives. It is a mechanism for meeting those imperatives that mobilizes dominant interpretive norms to attempt, but never achieve, a unified, univocal definition of the film event designed to attract and satisfy the target audience.

Hollywood's promotion of its own products suggests which interpretive strategies can be legitimately applied to the film, and by implication, which contexts of reception (made up of which audiences and which interpretive communities) can be legitimately inhabited.

In the seventies, the film industry responded to the increasingly fragmented nature of filmgoing audiences in the United States by targeting films to specific audiences. Some feminist audiences (primarily white, middle-class feminists) found themselves addressed by the film industry as the market audience for a number of "New Women's Films" produced and distributed throughout the seventies.[15] Promotion for films like *Julia* (1977), *Girlfriends* (1978), *It's My Turn* (1980), *An Unmarried Woman* (1977), *The Turning Point* (1977), *Rich and Famous* (1982), and *Alice Doesn't Live Here Anymore* (1975) authorized interpretive strategies that see their protagonists as "strong," "independent" women defining their lives in some ways against patriarchal norms, but not against capitalist values. This type of promotion privileged readings of the films through definitions of feminism current within the dominant media and within dominant culture.

Personal Best's intertextual relations with these new women's films and Hollywood's gay theme films open its reading to both feminist and lesbian feminist interpretive strategies. But the pressbook prereading of *Personal Best* set up discursive salients that refused to lend legitimacy to reception contexts that would interpret *Personal Best* as a "lesbian" film. Instead, the prereading mobilized dominant interpretive norms in an attempt to define the film as a sports movie starring beautiful, scantily clad women in (hetero) sexualized motion.

For example, the pressbook relied upon dominant notions of realism and authenticity to establish a discursive salient to support its claim that the film was primarily about sports and women athletes (not about a lesbian relationship). The pressbook gave most weight and description to the money and time spent on insuring the authenticity of the film's representation of women as athletes in track events. It celebrated facts like these: some scenes were shot on location during the 1980 Olympic trials, 19 world class athletes made up the cast, director Robert Towne consulted with athletes for technical accuracy throughout the planning and production of the film, Mariel Hemingway spent a year training for her role as an Olympic pentathlete, Towne chose Patrice Donnelly to co-star because of her athletic ability as much as for the likelihood that she could act.

The most detailed description and interpretation of their relationship appears in the pressbook's "production notes." That article defines their relationship with: "They met as strangers at the 1976 Olympic trials. They became friends, lovers, and ultimately competitors facing each other in the pentathlon at the Olympic trials in 1980." It goes on to interpret their relationship this way:

> Theirs is a relationship that suggests that the "war between the sexes" is not a battle over gender, but over sexuality. Male or female, how do you compete with a body you have already surrendered to your opponent?
>
> Wars and races inevitably come down to one moment, and whatever you call that moment, "going for it," or "laying your ass on the line," it calls for everything in you—total risk fueled by fierce discipline and even fiercer desire. It's the surest way to win a race, and the surest way to lose a lover.

These references to "gender" and "sexuality" are so ambiguous that they border on unintelligibility. What is clear is the attempt to explain the relationship between the two women from within the structures of heterosexual relationships. It is a heterosexual orientation that defined their relationship as a "war between the sexes." While that phrase could be read in the "traditional" sense, within the historical context of the film's release it constitutes a discursive salient against feminist interpretive strategies. It asserts that "male or female," sexuality is the same, since sports, sexuality and feminism are all characterized by a competitiveness that both men and women share. In the second paragraph, it asserts that fierce competition, discipline and desire (sexual/competitive?) is the "surest way to lose a lover"—i.e. that feminism makes heterosexual relationships impossible.

Unlike the production of *Making Love* (1982), for which scriptwriters consulted with gay men for matters of "authenticity," and then tried to attract gay male audiences by publicizing this fact, no members of the lesbian or feminist communities were hired as technical assistants to insure the authenticity of the portrayal of the lesbian relationship or the position of women/lesbians in Olympic sports. This is consistent with other instances in which media producers (like those for broadcast television's *Dynasty*) hire gay consultants to insure the "correct" representation of a gay male couple, but lesbians remain comparatively "invisible" within dominant culture.

The pressbook prereading further resisted feminist or lesbian feminist interpretive strategies by constructing a second discursive salient around the issue of the nature and significance of the relationship between Chris and Tory. Pressbook feature articles and photo captions marginalized their relationship by confining references to their becoming "lovers" to single sentences, like: "They become friends, lovers, and ultimately competitors at the 1976 Olympic Trials." The pressbook further marginalizes their relationship by undercutting whatever potentially radical critique of heterosexual relations it might imply. Pressbook features tried to "tame" the lesbian relationship by using heterosexual norms to explain it—describing it in terms like "the war between the sexes," as competitive, as "only sexual," as erotic spectacle, as romance—all norms that are the objects of vigorous critique by feminist communities. The feature article on Scott Glenn, the coach, describes him as "always trying to guess how his demands for excellence are best served—by their [Chris and Tory's] being in each other's bed or at each other's throat." Even this explicit reference to their sexual relationship subordinates it to competition and male control.

But of course, the radical potential of their relationship cannot be contained within these norms. The pressbook attempts to make the excess safe by trivializing lesbian sexuality as adolescent (describing the women as "awkward," "embarrassed," and "rambunctious" when together). Photographs and captions masculinize Tory and feminize Chris, thus perpetuating butch/femme stereotypes and protecting the star (Mariel Hemingway) from the stigma of lesbianism. The pressbook uses the word "love" to describe only one relationship in the film—the heterosexual Chris/Denny couple in a photo caption that reads: "Time for Love—Mariel Hemingway is comforted by her boyfriend Denny Stites, played by Kenny Moore, in a tender moment from *Personal Best*."

Dominant Media Reviews

Dominant media reviews of the film show how the institution of popular, liberal film criticism established a discursive space that challenges the attempted unity and univocality of the promotion's interpretations. As a result, dominant reviews draw the pressbook into alternative discursive formations competing within the hegemonic bloc. As such, the dominant reviews register the contradictions that the hegemonic bloc tolerates—in fact celebrates as pluralistic.

Reviews of the film appeared in the dominant media in the context of the feminist movement's ongoing production of increasingly numerous and visible oppositional interpretive strategies. This context required the dominant reviewer to ignore, argue against, adopt, or adapt feminist positions when interpreting the film. Reviewers recognized elements of *Personal Best* as "issues," or "interesting," or "significant" and worthy of comment because the antagonisms raised by alternative feminist interpretive strategies around these issues made simple application of dominant interpretive strategies problematic.

The ethic of journalistic "objectivity" and "fairness" and the dominant political ideology of pluralism made it difficult for dominant media reviewers to aggressively undercut the numerous, visible feminist interpretive strategies constructed by the women's movement. Unlike the pressbook, dominant reviewers typically resisted feminist interpretive strategies by acknowledging them, but deforming them in the service of a sexist and heterosexist hegemony.

For example, two central feminist interpretive strategies redefine the private as public and socially constructed; and redefine women as a social group united in struggle against common oppressors. Each of these is deformed by dominant reviewers who, against the pressbook, acknowledged that the women in *Personal Best* engaged in a significant sexual relationship and gave much space to interpreting that relationship. But they psychologized and individualized the lesbian relationship, describing it in terms of the problems and passages of individuals. In *Rolling Stone*, Sragow asserts that "Towne imbues the film with a carnality that's completely pure: the euphoria of an adolescent's struggle for self-creation . . . the movie itself is, in part, a panegyric to female youth."[16] This defines the relationship as a stage in each woman's individual development, not as an end in itself or as a mutual exploration of alternative social relations. Parfit's review in *The Runner* accepts director Towne's interpretation without question: " . . . it has nothing to do with lesbianism—it just has to do with people whose bodies are really a mode of knowledge. They learn their limitations and coincidentally, they struggle with the burden of their own sexuality, whatever it is."[17] This interprets the relationship not as a struggle existing within politics and sexuality, but as a natural, "innocent" consequence of circumstances. Dominant reviewers consistently gave the lesbian relationship the status of the film's plot device for drawing out more worthy, primary themes like competition, coming of age, goal seeking.

Feminist Reviews of *Personal Best*

Recently, cultural critics have begun to investigate the social production of the conditions for pleasure and the historically specific nature of formations of pleasure. Feminist communities' interpretations of *Personal Best* became illicitly pleasurable when oppositional viewing contexts and interpretive strategies allowed them to reject the terms for pleasure offered by the pressbook and dominant reviews—namely, that women spectators identify pleasurably with their own oppression and objectification. An analysis of the terms by which feminist communities appropriated *Personal Best* shows two very different types of interpretive activities and the illicit pleasures which they make possible.

First, reviewers writing in both liberal and socialist feminist publications seemed "satisfied" with strategizing for what Terry Lovell calls intellectual pleasures. Their activity validates film studies rhetoric of "audience as producer of meanings," which defines the work of meaning production as "intellectual labor of thinking."[18] For example, liberal feminist reviewers expressed pleasure in seeing satisfaction of that community's goals within a dominant media text, namely the undermining of stereotypes, the achievement of women in male-dominated fields, and the representation of women athletes as beautiful, graceful, and strong. Pleasure in viewing became a possibility as liberal feminists matched the "positive" and "negative" representations of women already existing in the liberal feminist communities' discourses about how media images affect women's social status to the representations in *Personal Best*. Socialist feminist reviewers reported finding pleasure in undermining the pressbook's prereading or the dominant reviewers' interpretations and the patriarchally defined pleasures they offered. Their pleasure lay in the intellectual activity of exposing the working of patriarchal discourses and constructing a discourse in opposition to it.

Liberal and socialist reviewers rejected dominant media interpretations of *Personal Best* without altering the conventional significance of what most popular and academic audiences consider to be fundamental formal and stylistic elements of narrative films. For example, liberal and socialist feminist reviewers assessed the ending within its "own terms." That is, they retained the conventionally agreed upon status and significance of the ending to the interpretation of the film's overall theme. They left "intact" dominant definitions of how length of time on screen defines major and minor characters, and what counts as causes and effects in the narrative chain of events.

But this does not describe the appropriation of *Personal Best* by the lesbian feminist reviewers. The position within feminist communities that is one of the most marginalized, silenced, and debased by the current hegemonic bloc launched the most radical rewriting of the film event of *Personal Best*. Lesbian feminist reviewers launched this rewriting in order to create discursive conditions supportive of what Terry Lovell calls social pleasures in addition to "intellectual" pleasures—pleasures of identification, of recognition, of validation.

Lesbian feminist reviewers strategized for those pleasures through a variety of interpretive moves. Some resisted the narrative's heterosexist closure and imagined what would happen to the characters in a lesbian future. For example, one reviewer offered a fantasized description of a romantically successful reunion of Chris and Tory at the next Olympics that would complete her rewritten version of the film in which the two women really were in love and committed to each other, despite what she recognized to be the film's attempt to trivialize their commitment.[19]

Most lesbian feminist reviewers ignored large sections of narrative material focusing on heterosexual romance, making no reference to their existence or conventionally obvious implications for the film's preferred heterosexist "meaning." Some redefined "main characters" and "supporting character" in order to elevate Patrice Donnelly as the film's star despite the publicity's promotion of Mariel Hemingway as star and the relative length of screen time each character occupied. Lesbian feminist reviewers consistently referred to Patrice Donnelly's performance as convincingly "lesbian" and pleasurable to identify with, reinterpreting Donnelly as the appropriate "object of desire" against the pressbook's and dominant media reviews contextualization of Mariel Hemingway as appropriate object of heterosexual desire.

In a move that points to possibilities of strategizing for pleasure that go beyond reading films "against the grain," some reviewers named and illicitly eroticized moments of the film's "inadvertent lesbian verisimilitude." The "otherness" of lesbian cultures' codes of body language, facial expression, use of voice, structuring and expression of desire, and assertions of strength in the face of male domination and prerogative, makes these codes unavailable and inaccessible to most dominant media producers and audiences, except as they enter dominant discourse in antiquated or stereotyped and clichéd forms. Those aspects of Donnelly's performance the *dominant* reviewers labeled "lesbian," i.e., her "bawdiness," "fierce combativeness," and "loyalty" (read: "clinging"), were interpreted by lesbian feminist reviewers as antiquated, stereotyped, or clichéd representations of lesbian behavior. They expressed pleasure in watching the dominant media "get it wrong," in watching it attempt, but fail, to colonize "real" lesbian space.

The otherness of lesbian culture thus raises the possibility for films like *Personal Best* to "get it right"—unintentionally. Lesbian feminists employing their own communities' interpretive strategies "recognized" moments of lesbian verisimilitude in Donnelly's performance, for example, as "definitely lesbian" within those communities' current practices. Lesbian reviewers referred to the verisimilitude of Donnelly's body language, facial expression, use of voice, expression of desire, and strength in the face of male heterosexual dominance. Reviewers celebrated these moments with references to the viewing behavior of other lesbians in theaters—clapping, laughter, and feelings of validation in a context otherwise reserved for the reproduction of heterosexist romance.

Lesbian feminist reviewers interpreted inadvertent verisimilitude as uncolonized by dominant discourse, that is, unrecognized as part of those private, personal spaces created by oppositional cultures and therefore unarticulated to dominant stereotypes and myths of lesbianism. Those moments became opportunities for pleasurable identification with Patrice Donnelly as lesbian, who could become the object of lesbian desire in terms that felt uncontrived, "real," unthreatening, unco-opted.

I am claiming that in addition to intellectual pleasures, lesbian feminist appropriations of *Personal Best* consciously engaged with discursive fields of what Terry Lovell calls intersubjectively constituted social pleasures:

> The pleasures of a text may be grounded in pleasures of an essentially public and social kind. For instance, pleasure of common experiences identified and celebrated in art, and through this celebration, given recognition and validation; pleasures of solidarity to which this sharing may give rise; pleasure in shared and socially defined aspirations and hopes, in a sense of identity and community. Thus, film viewing is turned into an oppositional act when lesbian feminist audiences are able to find pleasure and objects for illicit desire in that which is most threatening to dominant sexual politics.[20]

Collectively constructed social pleasures define, in part, the possibilities and limitations of feminist and lesbian feminist sexualities, including erotically pleasing identifications with aspects of the film image and narrative. The history of lesbian feminist communities is primarily one of struggles to carve out of dominant discourses space for their own sexualities, identities, and existence *as* communities. Lesbian feminist reviewers seem to have responded to the marginalization, silencing, and debasement that dominant discourses work on lesbian feminist discourses by moving the field of social pleasures described by Lovell to the center of their interpretive activities. Social pleasures like identification, recognition, and validation became, in the case of *Personal Best, the* articulating terms through which reviewers inflected dominant discourses with changes in meaning.

The terms of lesbian feminist social pleasures require a rejection and alteration of discourses and practices at the very center of the hegemonic bloc. These changes send reverberations throughout the social formation. Likewise, lesbian feminist viewing pleasures depend upon interpretive strategies capable of rejecting and altering the "meaning" of film practices considered central to filmic representation. This sends reverberations throughout the film's system of signification. For example, against dominant interpretations of Hollywood film practice, but consistent with the conditions for lesbian feminist social pleasure, lesbian feminists interpreted Donnelly as the main character in the narrative. The result: the significance of key narrative events is altered in a way that makes it possible to interpret the film's ending as a validation of lesbianism.

Contemporary ideological film criticism is capable of discussing how we can see *Personal Best* as a limit case that defines what is currently possible and acceptable within dominant discourses like Hollywood films for the representation of lesbian communities and sexualities. I am suggesting that we try to understand lesbian feminist reviews of *Personal Best* as limit cases of what is currently possible within that community's strategizings for pleasure. For example, lesbian feminist reviewers stopped short of rearranging the film's chronological order, severing or rearranging cause-effect relationships in the narrative and changing who does what in the narrative.

These limits in oppositional appropriation are set in the specific relations between this film event and this audience, and the antagonisms between this audience and other audiences. The terms of the antagonisms between groups generate constraints, pressures, possibilities and desires that inform the nature and priorities of their interpretive strategies.

Dominant mechanisms of promotion and criticism mounted discursive salients against feminist initiatives around the status of women in sports, the representation of women and lesbianism by co-opting, deforming, or ignoring those initiatives in the production and promotion of *Personal Best*. Liberal feminists adapted to these constraints, social feminists exposed them, and lesbian feminists found pleasure in moments of uncolonized verisimilitude of the "otherness" of their culture. An understanding of this process can help protesting groups use the public discourses their communities generate around film events as indicators of the constraints on their own oppositional interpretive strategies and as challenges to generate interpretive strategies and political action that meet current political imperatives.

NOTES

Another version of this article appears in *Becoming Feminine: The Politics of Popular Culture*, ed. Leslie G. Roman and Linda K. Christian-Smith (Philadelphia: Falmer Press, 1988).

1. *Personal Best* is a 1982 Warner Brothers release about two women athletes, Chris Cahill (Mariel Hemingway) and Tory Skinner (Patrice Donnelly), who meet at the 1976 Olympic Track Trials and become friends and lovers. They live together for three years, but after their male coach places them in direct competition with each other for a place on the Olympic Pentathlon team and hints that Tory is deliberately sabatoging Chris's training progress, they break up. Chris has an affair with a male Olympic swimmer, Denny. The two women meet again at the 1980 Olympic Track Trials. They reaffirm their friendship after Chris sacrifices her own

chance to place first in the trials by burning out the lead runner early in the race so that Tory can place in the 800 meter event. Both women win a place in the 1980 Olympic team.

2. When referring to feminist and lesbian feminist communities throughout this article, I use the plural to indicate the multiplicity of feminist positions and identities in the United States women's movement depending upon race, class, and sexual orientation.

3. Richard Johnson, "What is Cultural Studies Anyway?" Occasional Paper No. 75, Birmingham, England: Center for Contemporary Cultural Studies (1983), 44.

4. The liberal and socialist feminist reviews I used appeared in the following publications in 1982: *The Feminist Connection*, Madison, WI; *New Directions for Women*, Westwood, NJ; *Sojourner: The New England Women's Journal of News, Opinion, and the Arts*, Cambridge, MA; *The NOW Times*, Washington, DC; *Jump Cut*, Chicago, IL; *Amazon*, Milwaukee, WI; *Valley Women's Voice*, Northampton, MA. The lesbian feminist reviews appeared in *Gay Madison*, Madison, WI; *The Lesbian News*, Los Angeles, CA; *Off Our Backs*, Washington, DC; *TeleWoman*, Pleasant Hill, CA; *Lesbian Connections*. This article summarizes conclusions and implications drawn from my larger study entitled "The Power of Interpretive Communities: Feminist Appropriations of *Personal Best*," unpublished dissertation, University of Wisconsin-Madison, 1984.

5. The concepts of "interpretive conventions" and "interpretive communities" have been offered in contemporary literary criticism as a way of understanding how readers determine the reading experience. See Stanley Fish, *Is There a Text In This Class? The Authority of Interpretive Communities*, Cambridge: Harvard University Press (1980) and Steven Mailloux, *Interpretive Conventions: The Reader in the Study of American Fiction*, Ithaca: Cornell University Press (1982). For a critique of these concepts and a politicization of their use, see Ellsworth.

6. Teresa de Lauretis, *Alice Doesn't: Feminism, Semiotics, Cinema*, Bloomington: Indiana University Press (1984).

7. Richard Corliss, "Coming on Strong, The New Ideal of Beauty," *Time*, August 1982, 75–76.

8. Ibid., 76.

9. Camille Kittrell, "Better, Not Best," *Sojourner*, April 1982, 22.

10. Stuart Hall, "The Rediscovery of 'Ideology': Return of the Repressed in Media Studies," *Culture, Society, and the Media*, London: Methuen (1982), 78.

11. Lesley Stern, "Feminism and Cinema: Exchanges," *Screen* 20, Nos. 3/4 (1979–80), 89–105.

12. A collection of papers presented at this conference has been published in Ann Snitow, ed., *Powers of Desire: The Politics of Sexuality*, New York: Monthly Review (1983).

13. Lisa Orlando, "Bad Girls and 'Good' Politics," *The Village Voice Literary Supplement*, December 1982, 17.

14. See for example, Samois, *Coming to Power: Writings and graphics on Lesbian S/M*, 2nd ed., Boston: Alyson Publishing (1982).

15. Charlotte Brundson, "A Subject for the Seventies . . . " *Screen* 23, No. 3 (1982): 20–29.

16. Michael Sragow, "First-time Director Robert Towne Comes Upon Winner," *Rolling Stone*, 15 April 1982, 34.

17. Michael Parfit, "*Personal Best*," *The Runner*, February 1982, reprint, 2.

18. Terry Lovell, *Pictures of Reality: Aesthetics, Politics, Pleasure*, London: British Film Institute (1980), 94.

19. Anne J. D'Arcy, "*Personal Best*," *Telewoman*, May 1982, 5.

20. Ibid., 95.

WHITE PRIVILEGE AND LOOKING RELATIONS

RACE AND GENDER IN FEMINIST FILM THEORY

Jane Gaines

Born in Flames, a feminist science fiction film set ten years after a Social-Democratic "revolution" in the U.S., provides an abrupt reminder of the place of theory in the context of social change. Toward the end of the film, with the women's takeover of New York communications channels in progress, the voice of theory is heard over the image, insisting that women also need to take over the production of language. Although the film gives credence to the voice of theory (a white female British-accented voice), it is clear that the militant Women's Emergency Brigade and the martyred Black lesbian leader are carrying the revolutionary moment. What strikes me about the juxtaposition—images of women hot-wiring U-Haul trucks and the voice of theory urging women to take control of their own images—is that the voice sounds so crisply detached and arid.[1]

What I want to discuss is not so much the scene as the tenor of the female intellectual voice, which immediately recalls for me the tone of feminist film theory—firm in its insistence on attention to cinematic language and strict in its prohibition against making comparisons between "actuality" and the text. Let me be clear that this is something of a caricature of a stance which many of us who work on feminist film theory find less and less tenable.[2] Certainly, the intense concentration on cinema as language has helped to remedy a naiveté about form which characterized early feminist film criticism. However, as interest in the operations of the cinematic text increased, we witnessed the banishment of sociological reference points and historical detail from criticism. From this viewpoint it seems that one can only analyze the ideological through its encoding in the conventions of editing or the mechanics of the motion picture machine.[3]

For Marxists, this textual detachment, as I will call it, has special implications: concentration on the functioning of discourse creates the impression that developments in an ideological realm are unrelated to developments elsewhere in social life. As feminist film theory has emphasized the irresistible allure and captivating power of classical narrative cinema, it has located determination exclusively in the ideological realm. At the center of this difficulty has been the effort to understand the ideological work of mainstream cinema in terms of the psychoanalytic concept of sexual difference, which has largely meant casting formal structures such as narrative and point of view as masculine, and locating the feminine, the opposite term, in the repressed or excluded. Since this theory has focused on sexual difference, class and racial differences have remained outside its problematic, divorced from textual concerns by the very split in the social totality that the incompatibility of these discourses misrepresents. Adorno has remarked on this split, although in the context of an argument for the merger of sociology and psychology:

> The separation of sociology and psychology is both correct and false. False because it encourages the specialists to relinquish the attempt to know the totality which even the separation of the two demands; and correct insofar as it registers more intransigently the split that has actually taken place in reality than does the premature unification at the level of theory.[4]

In the interest of understanding the social totality, I am suggesting that our criticism should work to demystify this apparent separation by raising questions of race and class exactly where they have been theoretically disallowed.

Here I want to show how a theory of the text and its spectator, based on the psychoanalytic concept of sexual difference, is unequipped to deal with a film which is about racial difference and sexuality. Immediately, the Diana Ross star-vehicle, *Mahogany* (Berry Gordy, 1975), suggests a psychoanalytic approach because the narrative is organized around the connections between sadism, voyeurism, and photographic acts. Furthermore, it is a perfect specimen of classical narrative cinema which has been so fully theorized in Freudian terms. The psychoanalytic mode, however, works to block out considerations which take a different configuration. For instance, the Freudian scenario, based on the male/female distinction, is incongruous with the scenario of racial and sexual relations in Afro-American history. Where we use a psychoanalytic model to explain Black family relations, we force an erroneous universalization, and inadvertently reaffirm white middle-class norms.

Since it has taken gender as its starting point in the analysis of oppression, feminist theory has helped to reinforce white middle-class values, and to the extent that it works to keep women from seeing other structures of oppression, it functions ideologically. In this regard, Bell Hooks specifically criticizes a feminism which seems unable to imagine women's oppression in terms other than gender:

> Feminist analyses of woman's lot tend to focus exclusively on gender and do not provide a solid foundation on which to construct feminist theory. They reflect the dominant tendency in Western patriarchal minds to mystify women's reality by insisting that gender is the sole determinant of woman's fate.[5]

This gender analysis illuminates the condition of white middle-class women rather exclusively, Hooks explains, and its centrality in feminist theory suggests that the women who have contributed to the construction of this theory have been ignorant of the way women in different racial groups and social classes experience oppression. How should the white middle-class feminist who does not want to be racist in her work respond to this criticism? In her essay, "On Being White," one of the few considerations of this delicate dilemma, Marilyn Frye urges us not to do what middle-class feminists have historically done: to assume responsibility for everyone. To take it upon oneself to rewrite feminist theory so that it encompasses our differences is another exercise of racial privilege.[6] What one can, with conscience, do is to undertake the difficult study of our own "determined ignorance"; one can begin to learn about the people whose history cannot be imagined from a position of privilege.[7] In this context, my argument takes two directions. One juxtaposes Black feminist theory with those aspects of feminist theory which have a tendency to function as normative; the other transposes these issues, as Marxist theory would understand them, into the question of how we are to grasp the interaction of the various levels.

The feminist commitment to revealing the patriarchal assumptions behind familiar cinematic language dates from the mid-seventies with the appearance of Claire Johnston's "Women's Cinema as Counter-Cinema"[8] and Laura Mulvey's often reprinted "Visual Pleasure and Narrative Cinema."[9] The latter essay, coinciding as it did with the publication of Christian Metz's "The Imaginary Signifier," paired with a supporting theoretical statement from the editors of the British *Screen*, helped introduce psychoanalytic concepts into contemporary film theory where they quickly streamlined a Marxist problematic which dealt awkwardly with the social individual.[10] The terms of psychoanalysis, introduced through the permission of Althusserian Marxism, made it possible to investigate the sites outside the workplace where oppression is experienced. For Marxist feminists, this connection between Marxism and psychoanalysis immediately enriched the study of the construction of subjectivity in its prime location—the family.

Althusser's antidote to empiricism and economic reductionism has been welcomed by Marxists working in cultural studies, and the appeal is understandable. If materiality is no longer elsewhere, scholars are suddenly free to concentrate on textual matters without having to concern themselves simultaneously with economic specificity. Marxists in cultural studies outside *Screen*, however, believe that Althusser's understanding of ideology as having a materiality of its own contradicts basic Marxist tenets.[11] Within British cultural studies, then, psychoanalysis is held in check by the larger debates around Althusserian Marxism. This is not, however, the case in the U.S. where these traditions are often a distant point of reference. Thus the *Screen* film theory imported to the U.S. comes furnished with idealist assumptions that are mistaken for Marxist underpinnings. Because traditional Marxist terms do not support the critical context in film and television studies in the U.S. as they do in Britain, the challenge to psychoanalytic film theory here may have to come from other critical vantage points.

Lesbian feminists in the U.S. have already raised objections to the way in which contemporary film theory explains the operation of the classic realist text in terms of tensions between masculinity and femininity. Drawing on Freud and Lacan, this position (which is basically Mulvey's) defines the classic cinema as an expression of the patriarchal unconscious in the way it constructs points of view or "looking positions." At issue here is the way these viewing vantage points control the female body on the screen and privilege the visual position (the gaze) of the male character(s) within the film. The governing "look" of the male character in the film merges with the spectator's viewing position in such a way that the spectator sees as that character sees. This theory goes beyond the understanding of the text as producing its own ideal reader; the text is also able to specify the gender of the imputed subject, which in the classic cinema is male.

This understanding of the viewing pleasure in classical cinema as inherently male has drawn an especially sharp response from critics who have argued that this response cancels the lesbian spectator whose viewing pleasure would never be male pleasure. Positing a lesbian spectator would significantly change the trajectory of the gaze since the eroticized star body might be the visual objective of another female character in the film with whose "look" the viewer might identify. (Marilyn Monroe and Jane Russell in *Gentlemen Prefer Blondes*, according to this argument, are "only for each other's eyes.")[12] Following the direction of an early lesbian reading of *Gentlemen Prefer Blondes*, studies of *Personal Best* show lesbian readership as subverting dominant meanings and confounding textual structures.[13] Consistently, lesbians have charged that cultural theory posed in psychoanalytic terms is unable to conceive of desire or explain pleasure without reference to the binary oppositions male/female. This is, as Monique Wittig sees it, the function of the heterosexual assumption, or the "straight mind," that unacknowledged structure built not only into Lacanian psychoanalysis, but underlying the basic divisions of Western culture, organizing all knowledge, yet escaping any close examination:

> With its ineluctability as knowledge, as an obvious principle, as a given prior to any science, the straight mind develops a totalizing interpretation of history, social reality, culture, language. . . . I can only underline the oppressive character that the straight mind is clothed in its tendency to immediately generalize its production of concepts into general laws which claim to hold true for all societies, all epochs, all individuals . . . [14]

I want to suggest further that the male/female opposition, so seemingly fundamental to feminism, may actually lock us into modes of analysis which will continually misunderstand the position of many women.

Women of color, like lesbians, have been added to feminist analysis as an afterthought. Standard feminist anthologies consistently include articles on Black female and lesbian perspectives as illustration of the liberality and the inclusiveness of feminist work. However, the very concept of "different perspectives," while validating distinctness and maintaining a common denominator (woman), still places the categories of race and sexual preference in theoretical limbo. Our political etiquette is correct, but our theory is not so perfect. A familiar litany in our work is the broad-minded conclusion to a feminist argument: "Of course, the implications are somewhat different if race, class, and sexual preference are considered." In Marxist feminist analysis, the factors of race and sexual preference often remain loose ends because these categories of oppression do not fit easily into a model based on class relations in capitalist society. Some gay historians have been able to determine a relationship between the rise of capitalism and the creation of the social homosexual.[15] However, only with a very generous notion of sexual hierarchies, such as the one Gayle Rubin uses in her recent work on the politics of sexuality, can sexual oppression (as different from gender oppression) be *located in relation to* a framework based on class.[16] Race has folded more neatly than sexual preference into Marxist models, but the orthodox formulation which understands racial conflict as class struggle is unsatisfactory to Marxist feminists who want to know exactly how gender intersects with race. The oppression of *women* of color remains incompletely grasped by this paradigm.

Just as the classic Marxist model of social analysis based on class has obscured the function of gender, the feminist model based on the male/female division under patriarchy has obscured the function of race. The dominant feminist paradigm actually encourages us *not to think* in terms of any oppression other than male dominance and female subordination. Feminism seems, as Barbara Smith states, " . . . blinded to the implications of any womanhood that is not white womanhood."[17] Black feminists agree that for purposes of analysis, class is as significant as race; however, if these feminists hesitate to emphasize gender as a factor, it is in deference to the way Black women describe their experience.[18] Historically, Afro-American women have formulated political allegiance and identity in terms of race rather than gender or class.[19] Feminism, however, has not registered the statements of women of color who realize oppression first in relation to race rather than to gender: for them exploitation is personified by a white female.[20] Even more difficult for feminist theory to digest is Black female identification with the Black male. On this point, Black feminists diverge from white feminists as they repeatedly remind us that Black women do not necessarily see the Black male as patriarchal antagonist but feel instead that their racial oppression is "shared" with men.[21] In the most comprehensive analysis, Black lesbian feminists have described race, class, and gender oppression as "interlocking" in reference to the way these oppressions are synthesized in the lives of Black women.[22]

The point here is not to rank the structures of oppression in a way that implies the need for Black women to choose between solidarity with men or with women and between race or gender as the basis for a political strategy. At issue is the question of the fundamental antagonism relevant to any Marxist feminist theory.[23] Where we have foregrounded one antagonism in our analysis, we have misunderstood another, and this is most dramatically illustrated in the applications of the notion of patriarchy. Feminists have not been absolutely certain what they mean by patriarchy: alternately it has referred to either father right or to the domination of women;[24] but what is consistent about the use of the concept is the rigidity of the structure it describes. Patriarchy is incompatible with Marxism where it is used trans-historically without qualification and where it becomes the source to which all other oppressions are tributary, as in the radical feminist theory of patriarchal order which sees oppression in all forms and through all ages as derived from the male/female division.[25] Unfortunately, this deterministic model, which in Sheila Rowbotham's analysis almost functions like a "feminist base-superstructure," has the disadvantage of leaving us with no sense of movement, or no idea of how women have acted to change their condition, especially in comparison with the fluidity of the Marxist conception of class.[26] The radical feminist notion of absolute patriarchy has also one-sidedly portrayed the oppression of women through an analogy with slavery, and since this theory has identified woman as man's savage or repressed Other it competes with theories of racial difference which understand the Black as the "unassimilable Other."[27] Finally, the notion of patriarchy is most obtuse when it disregards the position white women occupy over Black men as well as Black women.[28] In order to rectify this tendency in feminism, Black feminists refer to "racial patriarchy," based on an analysis of the white patriarch/master in American history and his dominance over the Black male as well as the Black female.[29]

For Black feminists, history also seems to be the key to understanding Black female sexuality. "The construction of the sexual self of the Afro-American women," says Rennie Simson, "has its roots in the days of slavery."[30] Looking at this construction over time reveals a pattern of patriarchal phases and women's sexual adjustments that has no equivalent in the history of white women in the U.S. In the first phase, characterized by the dominance of the white master during the period of slavery, Black men and women were equal by default. To have allowed the Black male any power over the Black woman would have threatened the power balance of the slave system. Thus, as Angela Davis explains social control in the slave community, "The man slave could not be the unquestioned superior within the 'family' or community, for there was no such thing as the 'family provided' among the Slaves."[31] The legacy of this phase has involved both the rejection of the pedestal the white female has enjoyed and the heritage of retaliation against white male abuse. If the strategy for racial survival was resistance during the first phase, it was accommodation during the following phase. During Reconstruction, the Black family, modelled after the white bourgeois household, was constituted defensively in an effort to preserve the race.[32] Black women yielded to their men in deference to a tradition that promised respectability and safety. Reevaluating this history, Black feminists point out that during Reconstruction the Black male, following the example of the white patriarch, "learned" to dominate. The position consistently taken by Black feminists, that patriarchy was originally foreign to the Afro-American community and was introduced into it historically, then, represents a significant break with feminist theories which see patriarchal power invested in all men throughout history.[33]

Black history also adds another dimension to the concept of rape which has emerged as the favored metaphor for defining women's jeopardy in the second wave of feminism.[34] The charge of rape, conjuring up a historical connection with lynching, is always connected with the myth of the Black man as archetypal rapist. During slavery, this abuse provided an opportunity to strike a blow at Black manhood, but the increase in the sexual violation of Black women during Reconstruction reveals its political implications. After emancipation, the rape of Black women was a "message" to Black men which, as one historian describes the phenomenon, could be seen as "a reaction to the effort of the freedman to assume the role of patriarch, able to provide for and protect his family."[35] If, as feminists have argued, women's sexuality evokes an unconscious terror in men, then Black women's sexuality represents a special threat to white patriarchy; the possibility of its "eruption" stands for the aspirations of the Black race as a whole. The following analysis poses the questions raised when race complicates sexual prohibition. In the context of race relations in U.S. history, sexual looking carries with it the threat of actual rather than symbolic castration.

In *Mahogany*, the sequel to *Lady Sings the Blues*, Diana Ross plays an aspiring fashion designer who dreams of pulling herself up and out of her Chicago South Side neighborhood through a high-powered career. During the day, Tracy Chambers is assistant to the modelling supervisor for a large department store resembling Marshall Field & Company. At night she attends design school where the instructor reprimands her for sketching a cocktail dress instead of the assignment, the first suggestion of the exotic irrelevance of her fantasy career. Although she loses her job with the department store, the renowned fashion photographer Sean McEvoy (Tony Perkins) discovers her as a model and whisks her off to Rome. There Tracy finally realizes her ambition to become a designer when a wealthy Italian admirer gives her a business of her own. After the grand show, unveiling her first line of clothes, she decides to return to Chicago where she is reunited with community organizer Brian Walker (Billy Dee Williams) whose political career is organized as a kind of counterpoint to Tracy's.

With its long fashion photography montage sequences temporarily interrupting the narrative, *Mahogany* invites a reading based on the alternation between narrative and woman-as-spectacle as theorized in "Visual Pleasure and Narrative Cinema." To the allure of pure spectacle these sequences add the fascination of masquerade and transformation. Effected with wigs and make-up colors, the transformations are a play on and against "darkness"; Diana Ross is a high-tech Egyptian queen, a pale medieval princess, a turbaned Asiatic, and a body-painted blue nymph. As her body color is washed out in bright light or powdered over, and as her long-haired wigs blow around her face, she becomes suddenly "white."

Motion pictures seem never to exhaust the narrative possibilities associated with the metaphor of the camera-as-deadly-weapon; *Mahogany* adds to this the sadomasochistic connotations of high fashion photography with reference to the mid-seventies work of Guy Bourdin and Helmut Newton that is linked to the tradition of "attraction by shock."[36] The montage sequences chronicling Tracy's career, from perfume ads to high fashion magazine covers, equate the photographic act with humiliation and violation. Camera zoom and freeze frame effects translate directly into aggression, as in the sequence in which Sean pushes Tracy into a fountain: her dripping image solidifies into an Italian Revlon advertisement. Finally, the motif of stopping-the-action-as-aggression is equated with the supreme violation—the attempt to murder. Pressing his favorite model to her expressive limits, Sean drives her off an expressway ramp. Since this brutality escalates after the scene in which he fails with Tracy in bed, the film represents her punishment as a direct consequence of his impotence.[37]

With its classic castration threat scenario, its connection between voyeurism and sadism, and its reference to fetishization as seen in Sean's photographic shrine to the models he has abused, *Mahogany* is the perfect complement to a psychoanalytic analysis of classical Hollywood's "visual pleasure." The film feeds further into the latter by producing its own "proof" that there is only an incremental difference between voyeurism (fashion photography) and the supreme violation—murder. The black and white photographic blow-ups of Tracy salvaged from the death car seem undeniable evidence of the fine line between looking and killing, or, held at another angle, between advertising imagery and pornography. These, then, are the points that the analysis of cinema as patriarchal makes when it characterizes classical film form as ideologically insidious in its control of the female image, its assuagement of women's threat, and its denial of its own complicity in this signifying activity.

To explain the ideological function of this film in terms of the construction of male pleasure, however, is to "aid and abet" the film's other ideological project. Following this line of analysis, one is apt to step into an ideological signifying trap set up by the chain of meanings that lead away from seeing the film in terms of black and white conflict. Because there are so many connotative paths—photographer exploits model, madman assaults woman, voyeur attempts murder—we may not immediately see white man as the aggressor against Black woman. Other strategies encourage the viewer to forget or not notice racial issues. For instance, the narrative removes Tracy from racially polarized Chicago to Rome where the brown Afro-American woman with Caucasian features is collected by the photographer who names his subjects after inanimate objects. Losing her Black community identity, Tracy becomes *Mahogany*, a dark, rich, valuable substance; that is, her Blackness becomes commodified.

Mahogany functions ideologically for Black viewers in the traditional Marxist sense, that is, in the way the film obscures the class nature of social antagonisms. This has certain implications for working-class Black viewers who would benefit the most from seeing the relationship between race, gender, and class oppression. This film experiences the same problem in its placement of Black femaleness that the wider culture has had historically; a Black female is either all woman and tinted Black, or mostly Black and scarcely woman. These two expectations correspond roughly to the two worlds and two struggles the film contrasts: the struggle over the sexual objectification of Tracy's body, targeting commercial exploiters, and the class struggle of the Black-community, targeting slum landlords. The film identifies this antagonism as the hostility between fashion and politics, corresponding roughly with Tracy and Brian and organizing their conflict and reconciliation. Intensifying the conflict between the two characters, the film brings "politics" and "fashion" together in one daring homage to the aesthetic of "attraction by shock." Sean arranges his models symmetrically on the back stairwell of a run-down Chicago apartment building and plants the confused tenants and street people as props. Flamboyant excess, the residue of capital, is juxtaposed with a kind of dumbfounded poverty. For a moment, the scene figures the synthesis of gender, class, and race, but the political glimpse is fleeting. Forced together as a consequence of the avant-garde's socially irresponsible quest for new outrage, the political antagonisms are suspended—temporarily immobilized as the subjects pose.

The connection between gender, class, and race oppression is also denied as the ghetto photography session illustrates the analogy between commercial and race/class exploitation which registers on the screen as visual incongruity. Visual discrepancy, which is finally used for aesthetic effect, also makes it difficult to grasp the confluence of race, class, and gender oppression in the image of Tracy Chambers. Her class background magically becomes decor in the film; it neither radicalizes her nor drags her down—rather it sets her off. Diana Ross is alternately weighed down by the glamour iconography of commercial modelling and stripped to a Black body essence. But the *haute couture* iconography ultimately dominates the film. Since race is decorative and class does not reveal itself to the eye, she can only be seen as "exploited" in terms of her role as a model.

If the film plays down race, it does so not only to accommodate white audiences. While it worships the success of the Black cult star and treats aspiring young Blacks to Diana Ross's dream come true—a chance to design all the costumes in her own film, *Mahogany* also hawks the philosophy of Black enterprise. Here it does not matter where you come from, but you should ask yourself, in the words of the theme song, "Where are you going to, do you know?"[38] Race is like any other obstacle—to be transcended through diligent work and dedication to a goal. Supporting the film's self-help philosophy is the related story of Diana Ross's discovery as a skinny teenager singing in a Baptist Church in Detroit. With *Mahogany*, Motown president and founder Berry Gordy (who fired Tony Richardson to take over the film's direction himself) helps Diana Ross make something of herself again (on a larger scale) just as he helped so many aspiring recording artists by coaching them in money management and social decorum in his talent school.[39]

The phenomenon of Motown Industries comments less on the popularity of the self-help philosophy and more on the discrepancy between the opportunity formula and the social existence of Black Americans. Ironically, Black capitalism's one big success thrives on the impossibility of Black enterprise: soul entertainment as compensation and release sells because capitalism cannot deliver well-being to all.[40] Black music and performance, despite the homogenization of the original forms, represent a utopian aspiration for Black Americans as well as white suburbanites. Simon Frith describes the "need" supplied by rock fantasy:

> Black music had a radical, rebellious edge: it carried a sense of possibility denied in the labor market; it suggested a comradeship, a sensuality, a grace and joy and energy lacking in work . . . the power of rock fantasy rests, precisely on utopianism.[41]

Here I am drawing on a theory of culture which sees capitalism as erratically supplying subversive "needs" as well as "false" desires, often through the same commodities which produce the ideological effect. Given that popular culture can accommodate the possibility of both containment and resistance in what Stuart Hall calls its "double movement," I want to turn, then, to the ways *Mahogany* can be seen to move in the other direction.[42]

Racial conflict surfaces or recedes in this film rather like the perceptual trick in which, depending on the angle of view, one swirling pattern or the other pops out at the viewer. Some ambiguity, for instance, is built into the confrontation between Black and white, as in the scene where Sean lures Brian into a struggle over an unloaded weapon. The outcome, in which Sean, characterized as a harmless eccentric, manipulates Brian into pulling the trigger, could be read as confirming the racist conception that Blacks who possess street reflexes are murderous aggressors. *Ebony* magazine, however, features a promotional still of the scene (representing Brian holding a gun over Sean), with a caption describing how Brian is tricked but still wins the fight.[43] Viewers, who choose the winners of ambiguous conflicts, may also choose to inhabit "looking" structures. The studies of lesbian readership already cited show that subcultural groups can interpret popular forms to their advantage, even without "invitation" from the text. Certainly more work needs to be done with the positioning of the audience around the category of race, considering, for instance, the social prohibitions against the Black man's sexual glance, the interracial intermingling of male "looks," and other visual taboos related to sanctions against interracial sexuality, but these issues are beyond the scope of this essay.

What I do find is that one of the basic tenants of contemporary feminist film theory—that the (male) spectator possesses the female indirectly through the eyes of the male protagonist (his screen surrogate)—is problematized in a film in which racial difference structures a hierarchy of access to the female image. These racial positions relate to other scenarios which are unknown by psychoanalytic categories. Considering the racial categories which psychoanalysis does not recognize, we see that the white male photographer monopolizes the classic patriarchal look controlling the view of the female body, and that the Black male protagonist's look is either repudiated or frustrated. The sumptuous image of Diana Ross is made available to the spectator via the white male character (Sean) but *not* through the look of the Black male character (Brian). In the sequence in which Tracy and Brian first meet outside her apartment building, his "look" is renounced. In each of the three shots of Tracy from Brian's point of view, she turns from him, walking out of his sight and away from the sound of his voice as he shouts at her through a megaphone. The relationship between the male and female protagonists is negotiated around Brian's bullhorn, emblem of his charismatic Black leadership, through which he tries to reach both the Black woman and his constituents. Thus both visual and audio control is denied the Black male, and the failure of his voice is consistently associated with Tracy's publicity image. The discovery by Brian's aides of the Mahogany ad for Revlon in *Newsweek* coincides with the report that the Gallup polls show the Black candidate trailing in the election. Later, the film cuts from Mahogany on the *Harper's Bazaar* cover to Brian's limping campaign where the sound of his voice magnified through a microphone is intermittently drowned out by a passing train as he makes his futile pitch to white factory workers. The manifest goal of the film, the reconciliation of the Black heterosexual couple, is thwarted by the commercial appropriation of her image, but, in addition, her highly mediated form threatens the Black political struggle.

Quite simply, then, there are structures relevant to any interpretation of this film which override the patriarchal scenario feminists have theorized as formally determining. From Afro-American literature, for instance, we should consider the scenario of the talented and beautiful mulatta who "passes" in white culture, but decides to return to Black society.[44] From Afro-American history, we should recall the white male's appropriation of the Black woman's body which weakened the Black male and undermined the community. We need to develop a theory of Black female representation which takes account of "passing" as an eroticizing alternation and a peculiar play on difference, and the corresponding double consciousness it requires of those who can seem either Black or White. Further, we need to reconsider the woman's picture narrative convention—the career renounced in favor of the man—in the context of Black history. Tracy Chambers's choice recapitulates Black aspiration and the white middle-class model which equates stable family life with respectability, but Tracy's decision is complicated since it favors Black community cooperation over acceptance by white society. Finally, one of the most difficult questions raised by Afro-American history and literature has to do with interracial heterosexuality and sexual "looking." *Mahogany* suggests that, since a Black male character is not allowed the position of control occupied by a white male character, race could be a factor in the construction of cinema language. More work on looking and racial taboos might determine whether or not mainstream cinema can offer the spectator the pleasure of looking at a white female character via the gaze of a Black male character. Framing the question of male privilege and viewing pleasure as the "right to look" may help us to rethink film theory along more materialist lines, considering, for instance, how some groups have historically had the license to "look" openly while other groups have "looked" illicitly.[45] Or, does the psychoanalytic model allow us to consider also the prohibitions against homosexuality and miscegenation?

Feminists who use psychoanalytic theory are careful to point out that "looking" positions do not correlate with social groups, and that ideological positioning is placement in a representational system which has no one-to-one correspondence with social reality. This, of course, keeps the levels of the social totality hopelessly separate. While I would not want to argue that form is ideologically neutral, I would suggest that we have overemphasized the ideological function of "signifying practice" at the expense of considering other ideological implications of the conflicting meanings in the text. Or, as Terry Lovell puts it:

> . . . while interpretation depends on analysis of the work's signifying practice, assessment of its meanings from the point of view of its validity, or of its ideology, depends on comparison between those structures of meaning and their object of reference, through the mediation of another type of discourse.[46]

The impetus behind Marxist criticism, whether we want to admit it or not, is to make comparisons between social reality as we live it and ideology as it does not correspond to that reality.

Mahogany is finally about the mythical existence of some illusive and potent substance. We know it only through what white men do to secure it, and what Black men are without it. It is the ultimate substance to the photographer-connoisseur of women who dies trying to record its "trace" on film. It is known by degree—whatever is most wild and enigmatic, whatever cannot be conquered or subdued—the last frontier of female sexuality. Although it is undetectable to the advertising men who analyze physical attributes, it is immediately perceptable to a woman (Gavina herself, the owner of the Italian advertising agency), who uses it to promote the most inexplicable and subjective of commodities—perfume. In one of the fullest considerations of Black female sexuality to date, Hortense J. Spillers correlates the great silence on this subject with the unmarked territory that has not yet been designated as culture. Paradoxically, the Black female is thought to have " . . . so much sexual potential that she has none at all that anybody is ready and able to recognize *at the level of culture*."[47] Black women's sexuality remains unfathomed, Spillers goes on, because the opportunity to codify one's sexuality belongs only to those in power; even as feminists have theorized women's sexuality, they have universalized from the particular experience of white women, thus effecting a "deadly metonomy."[48]

While white feminists theorize the female image in terms of objectification, fetishization, and symbolic absence, their Black counterparts describe the body as the site of symbolic resistance and the "paradox of non-being."[49] What strikes me immediately in this comparison is the stubbornness of the terms of discourse analysis which cannot be made to deal, for instance, with both what it has historically meant to be designated as not-human and how Black women whose bodies were not legally their own fought against treatment based on this determination. Further, feminist analysis of culture as patriarchal cannot conceive of any connection between the female image and class or racial exploitation which includes the male. Historically, Black men and women, although equally endangered, have been simultaneously implicated in incidents of interracial brutality. During two different periods of Afro-American history, sexual assault, " . . . symbolic of the effort to conquer the resistance the black woman could unloose," was a warning to the entire Black community.[50] My frustration with the feminist voice that insists on change *at the level of language* is that this position can only deal with the historical situation described above by turning it into discourse, and even as I write this, acutely aware as I am of the theoretical prohibitions against mixing representational issues with real historical ones, I feel the pressure to transpose people's struggles into more discursively manageable terms.

A theory of ideology which separates the levels of the social formation in such a way that it is not only inappropriate but theoretically impossible to introduce the category of history cannot be justified with Marxism. This has been argued elsewhere by British Marxists, among them Stuart Hall, who finds the "universalist tendency" found in both Freud and Lacan responsible for this impossibility. The incompatability between Marxism and psychoanalytic theory is insurmountable at this time, he argues, because " . . . the concepts elaborated by Freud (and reworked by Lacan) cannot, *in their in-general and universalist form,* enter the theoretical space of historical materialism. . . . " What is needed is "further specification and elaboration—specification at the level at which the concepts of historical materialism operate (historically-specific modes of production, specific social formations, ideology as a determinate and over-determining instance, etc.)."[51] In discussions within feminist film theory, it often seems the other way around—that historical materialism cannot enter the space theorized by discourse analysis drawing on psychoanalytic concepts. Sealed off as it is (in theory), this analysis may not comprehend the category of the real historical subject, but its use will always have implications *for* that subject.

NOTES

A longer version of this essay is found in *Screen* 29, no. 4 (Autumn 1988).

1. Feminist discussions around Lizzie Borden's 1983 feature, such as the one in June, 1985, at the Society for Cinema Studies Conference at New York University, actually exemplify my argument. Holding ourselves to consideration of the film's representational system was a frustrating exercise since crucial issues of subcultural reception and feminist political strategy were also at stake.

2. For an overview, see my "Women and Representation: Can We Enjoy Alternative Pleasure?" in *Entertainment as Social Control,* ed. Donald Lazere, Berkeley: University of California Press, forthcoming.

3. In "Aesthetics and Politics," *New Left Review* 107 (1978): 23, Terry Eagleton describes his exasperation with *Screen,* the journal which introduced this analytical style into British criticism:

> And yet, perusing still another article in that journal on the complex mechanisms by which a shot/reverse shot reinstates the imaginary, or the devices by which a particular cinematic syntagm permits the interruption of symbolic heterogeneity into the positioned perceptual space of the subject, one is forced to query with certain vehemence why ideological codes have been so remorselessly collapsed back into the intestines of the cinematic machine.

4. T. W. Adorno, "Sociology and Psychology," *New Left Review* 46 (November-December 1967): 78.

5. *Feminist Theory: From Margin to Center*, Boston: South End Press (1984), 12.

6. *The Politics of Reality*, Trumansburg, New York: The Crossing Press (1984), 113.

7. Frye, 118.

8. *Notes on Women's Cinema*, ed. Claire Johnston, London: Society for Education in Film and Television (1973); rpt. *Sexual Strategems*, ed. Patricia Erens, New York: Horizon (1979), 133–143; *Movies and Methods*, ed. Bill Nichols, Berkeley and Los Angeles: University of California Press (1976), 208–17.

9. *Screen* 16, no. 3 (Autumn 1975): 6–18; rpt. *Women and Cinema*, eds. Karyn Kay and Gerald Peary, New York: E. P. Dutton (1977), 412–28; *Film Theory and Criticism*, eds. Gerald Mast and Marshall Cohen, 3rd ed., New York: Oxford (1985).

10. Trans. Ben Brewster, *Screen* 16, no. 2 (Summer 1975): 14–76.

11. Examples include Simon Clarke, Victor Jeleniewski Seidler, Kevin McDonnell, Kevin Robins, and Terry Lovell, *One-Dimensional Marxism*, London: Alison & Busby (1980); Kevin Robins, "Althusserian Marxism and Media Studies: The Case of *Screen*," *Media, Culture and Society* 1, no. 4 (October 1979): 355–70; Ed Buscombe, Christine Gledhill, Alan Lovell, Christopher Williams, "Statement: Psychoanalysis and Film," *Screen* 20, no. 1 (Spring 1979): 121–33; Christine Gledhill, "Recent Developments in Feminist Criticism," *Quarterly Review of Film Studies* 3, no. 4 (Fall 1978): 457–93; rpt. *Re-Vision*, eds. Mary Ann Doane, Patricia Mellencamp, and Linda Williams, Frederick, Maryland: University Publications of America (1984), 18–48.

12. Lucie Arbuthnot and Gail Seneca, "Pre-Text and Text in *Gentlemen Prefer Blondes*," *Film Reader* 5 (Winter 1981): 13–23.

13. Chris Straayer, "*Personal Best*: Lesbian/Feminist Audience," *Jump Cut* 29 (February 1984): 40–44; Elizabeth Ellsworth, "The Power of Interpretive Communities: Feminist Appropriations of *Personal Best*," paper delivered at Society for Cinema Studies Conference, University of Wisconsin-Madison, March, 1984.

14. "The Straight Mind," *Feminist Issues* (Summer 1980): 107–111.

15. See, for instance, John D'Emilio's *Sexual Politics, Sexual Communities*, Chicago: University of Chicago Press (1984).

16. In "Thinking Sex: Notes for a Radical Theory of the Politics of Sexuality," in *Pleasure and Danger*, ed. Carol Vance, Boston and London: Routledge & Kegan Paul (1984), 307, Rubin stresses the need to make this distinction because feminism does not immediately apply to both oppressions. As she clarifies this:

> Feminism is the theory of gender oppression. To automatically assume that this makes it the theory of sexual oppression is to fail to distinguish between gender, on the one hand, and erotic desire, on the other.

17. *Towards a Black Feminist Criticism*, Trumansburg, New York: Out and Out Books (1977), 1.

18. Bonnie Thornton Dill, "Race, Class, and Gender: Prospects for an All-In-

clusive Sisterhood," *Feminist Studies* 9, no. 1 (Spring 1983): 134; for a slightly different version of this essay, see " 'On the Hem of Life': Race, Class, and the Prospects for Sisterhood," in *Class, Race, and Sex: The Dynamics of Control*, eds. Amy Swerdlow and Hanna Lessinger, Boston: G. K. Hall (1983).

19. Margaret Simons, "Racism and Feminism: A Schism in the Sisterhood," *Feminist Studies* 5, no. 2 (Summer 1979): 392.

20. Adrienne Rich, in *On Lies, Secrets, and Silence*, New York: W. W. Norton (1979), 302–303, notes that while Blacks link their experience of racism with the white woman, this is still patriarchal racism working through her. It is possible, she says, that "a black first grader, or that child's mother, or a black patient in a hospital, or a family on welfare, may experience racism most directly in the person of a white woman, who stands for those service professions through which white male supremacist society controls the mother, the child, the family, and all of us. It is *her* racism, yes, but a racism learned in the same patriarchal school which taught her that women are unimportant or unequal, not to be trusted with power; where she learned to mistrust and hear her own impulses for rebellion; to become an instrument."

21. Gloria Joseph, "The Incompatible Menage à Trois: Marxism, Feminism, and Racism," in *Women and Revolution*, ed. Lydia Sargent, Boston: South End Press (1981), 96; The Combahee River Collective in "Combahee River Collective Statement," in *Home Girls*, ed. Barbara Smith, New York: Kitchen Table Press (1983), 275, compares their alliance with Black men with the negative identification white women have with white men:

> Our situation as Black people necessitates that we have solidarity around the fact of race, which white women of course do not need to have with white men, unless it is their negative solidarity as racial oppressors. We struggle together with Black men against racism, while we also struggle with Black men about sexism.

22. "Combahee River Collective Statement," 272.

23. E. Ann Kaplan, in *Women and Film*, New York and London: Methuen (1983), 140, says the danger for Marxists in employing the connection between Althusser and Lacan is that "the theories do not accommodate the categories of either class or race: economic language as the primary shaping force replaces socioeconomic relations and institutions as the dominant influence. Sexual difference becomes the driving force of history in place of the Marxist one of class contradictions."

24. Michèle Barrett, *Women's Oppression Today*, London: Verso (1980), 15.

25. For a comparison between radical feminism, liberal feminism, Marxism and socialist feminism, see Alison Jaggar, *Feminist Politics and Human Nature*, Sussex: The Harvester Press (1983).

26. "The Trouble with Patriarchy," in *People's History and Socialist Theory*, ed. Raphael Samuel, London and Boston: Routledge & Kegan Paul (1981), 365.

27. Franz Fanon, *Black Skin, White Masks*, trans. Charles Lam Markmann, Paris, 1952; rpt. New York: Grove Press (1967), 161.

28. Simons, 387.

29. Barbara Omolade, "Hearts of Darkness," in *Powers of Desire*, eds. Ann Snitow, Christine Stansell, and Sharon Thompson, New York: Monthly Review Press (1983), 352.

30. The Afro-American Female: The Historical Context of the Construction of Sexual Identity," in *Powers of Desire*, 230. The "days of slavery" is a recurring reference point in the writings of Black feminists. Although I am arguing that studying the Black condition *in history* is the antithesis of theorizing subjectivity ahistorically, I can also see how the "days of slavery" might function as an ideo-

logical construct. We do the evolving work of Black feminists a disservice if we do not subject it to the same critique we would apply to white middle class feminism. How, for instance, can equal subjugation during slavery have anything to do with ideals of male/female equality? I am indebted to Brackette Williams for calling this to my attention.

31. "The Black Woman's Role in the Community of Slaves," *The Black Scholar* (December 1971): 5–6.

32. Omolade, 352.

33. Joseph, 99; Audre Lorde, in *Sister Outsider*, Trumansburg, New York: The Crossing Press (1984), 119, sees sexism in Black communities as not original to them, but as a plague that has struck. She argues:

> Because of the continuous battle against racial erasure that Black women and Black men share, some Black women still refuse to recognize that we are also oppressed as women, and that sexual hostility against Black women is practiced not only by the white racist society, but implemented within our Black communities as well. It is a disease striking the heart of Black nationhood, and silence will not make it disappear.

34. Linda Gordon and Ellen DuBois, in "Seeking Ecstasy on the Battlefield: Danger and Pleasure in Nineteenth Century Feminist Sexual Thought," *Feminist Review* 13 (Spring 1983): 43, note that in its two stages the feminist movement has developed two major themes which have expressed women's sexual danger. Whereas prostitution articulated women's fears in the nineteenth century, rape summarizes the contemporary terror.

35. Jacquelyn Dowd Hall, " 'The Mind That Burns in Each Body': Women, Rape, and Racial Violence," in *Powers of Desire*, 332.

36. Nancy Hall-Duncan, *The History of Fashion Photography*, New York: Alpine Books (1979), 196.

37. White reviewer Jay Cocks, in "Black and Tan Fantasy," *Time*, 27 October, 1975, 71, interprets the scene in which Tony Perkins is represented as severely devastated after his failure in bed with Diana Ross as a "romantic interlude," and the "one pearl" in the entire film.

38. Simon Frith, in "Mood Music," *Screen* 25, no. 3 (May-June 1984): 78, says that theme songs are more significant than critics have realized. It is the last of the motion picture experience to touch us as we leave the theatre, and it works to "rearrange our feelings."

39. Stephen Birmingham, *Certain People*, Boston & Toronto: Little, Brown, and Co. (1977), 262–63.

40. Manning Marable, in *How Capitalism Underdeveloped Black America*, Boston: South End Press (1983), 157, lists Motown Industries as the largest grossing Black-owned corporation in the U.S., which did $64.8 million in business in 1979.

41. *Sound Effects*, New York: Pantheon (1981), 264.

42. "Notes on Deconstructing 'The Popular'," in *People's History and Socialist Theory*, 228.

43. "Spectacular New Film for Diana Ross: *Mahogany*," *Ebony*, October 1975, 146.

44. See, for instance, Jessie Fauset's *There is Confusion*, New York: Boni and Liveright (1924), and *Plum Bun*, New York: 1928; rpt. New York and London: Routledge and Kegan Paul (1985); Nella Larsen's *Quicksand*, New York: 1928; and *Passing*, New York: 1929; rpt. New Bunswick, N.J.: Rutgers University Press, 1986.

45. Fredric Jameson, in "Pleasure: A Political Issue," *Formations of Pleasure*, Boston and London: Routledge & Kegan Paul (1983), 7, interprets Mulvey's connection between viewing pleasure and male power as the conferral of a "right to

look." He does not take this further, but I find the term suggestive and at the same time potentially volatile. I refer to the current division in the women's movement over the need for anti-pornography legislation. Feminist supporters of the legislation argue that male pornographic reading and "looking" should be illegal because it is an infringement of women's civil rights. For an overview of the debates around pornography as they relate to film theory see Chuck Kleinhans and Julia Lesage, "The Politics of Sexual Representation," in *Jump Cut* 30 (March, 1985): 24–26. In the same issue, two articles argue the political significance of sexual looking for the gay male subculture (Richard Dyer's "Coming to Terms," 28–29, and Tom Waugh's "Men's Pornography: Gay vs. Straight," 30–33.) For one of the most provocative analyses of the feminist position on pornography, see Joanna Russ, *Magic Mommas, Trembling Sisters, Puritans, and Perverts*, Trumansburg, New York: The Crossing Press (1985).

46. *Pictures of Reality*, London: British Film Institute (1980), 90.

47. "Interstices: A Small Drama of Words," in *Pleasure and Danger*, 85.

48. Spillers, 78. It is very tempting to contrast the colonized (the body or other cultural terrain) with a notion of the "authentic," as though something has escaped or eluded colonization. We often argue for the integrity of people's indigenous culture or alternative experience by characterizing it as "pure"; we hope that the colonizer will find the alien culture incomprehensible or "unfathomable." Feminists have recently slipped into this position as they have created a new mystique based on women's "unrealized" sexuality—a wild place as yet uncharted by the dominant culture. The problem is that even this space is filled out with well worn notions of pleasure and fulfillment. Given the opportunity to symbolize, to codify sexuality, the sexual subordinate can never represent or experience in complete cultural isolation. In borrowing Spillers's argument, I have made a case for Black women's sexuality that I would never have made for female sexuality as a whole. Brackette Williams has corrected me here again.

49. Spillers, 77.

50. Davis, 11.

51. "Debate: Psychology, Ideology and the Human Subject," *Ideology and Consciousness* 2 (October 1977): 118–119.

III.

Critical Methodology Feminist Filmmaking

Beginning in the early seventies, feminist documentaries formed a strong element in women's cinema. The first films addressed subjects such as health care, abortion, rape and other types of violence against women, day care, divorce, jobs, wages, sexual harassment, and aging. Later films dealt with outstanding individuals and the involvement of women in historical events (an involvement previously ignored). And even in the fictional narratives created by women, the documentary impulse was strong, manifesting itself in the use of documentary and reconstructed documentary footage.

The first essay in section three, "The Political Aesthetics of the Feminist Documentary" (1978) by Julia Lesage, describes the emergence of the feminist documentary as a genre, especially its aesthetics and relationship to the women's movement from which it sprang. Using a traditional "realist" documentary approach, these first films often presented women who spoke directly to the camera as they told of their efforts to deal with "the public world of work and power." By defining or redefining women's experience, the filmmakers and their subjects challenged previously accepted ideas about male superiority and women's "natural" roles. These explorations established a structure for social and psychological change and thus constituted a political attack on patriarchy.

Lesage discusses *Self Health*, a film made by the San Francisco Women's Health Collective (1974), as an exemplary work. For Lesage, the film opposes both the artistic and the medical tradition of viewing women's nude bodies. In its place the filmmakers present women collectivity, enhanced by a sense of warmth, intimacy, and friendliness. According to Lesage, "Reclaiming 'the lost territory' of women's bodies and health care is a personal act that has a strong effect on women's identity, emotional life, and sense of control."[1]

Lesage discusses the adoption by women in the late 1960s of *cinéma vérité* documentary techniques and describes how feminist filmmakers used these techniques in new and different ways, often identifying personally with their subjects or working collaboratively, so that subject and filmmaker shared in the political goals of the project. She explains how such relationships were analogous to the mutual, nonhierarchical structure of women's consciousness-raising groups.

Lesage addresses the criticism of some scholars that feminist documentaries assume a naive sense of realism or appear dull due to the preponderance of "talking heads." In response, Lesage states that what is of prime importance are the stories the women tell: "The sound track, usually told in the subjects' own words, serves the function of rephrasing, criticizing, or articulating for the first time the rules of the game as they have been and as they should be for women."[2] Furthermore, feminist filmmakers, by using an accessible form, encourage a politicized "conversation" among women. Lesage ends with a brief mention of the experimental feminist documentary, which will be taken up in more detail in the essay by Annette Kuhn.

Despite Lesage's defense of the feminist documentary as a means of asserting sexual difference and achieving political ends, other critics voiced certain reservations. Among them is Sonya Michel, whose essay "Feminism, Film, and Public History" (1981) raises questions about the presentation of history. Michel first praises three films about U.S. working women—*Union Maids* (Julia Reichert, Jim Klein, and Miles Mogulescu, 1977), *With Banners and Babies* (Lorraine Gray, 1978), and *The Life and Times of Rosie the Riveter* (Connie Field, 1980)—for their value as correctives to mainstream history. She discusses the difficulty of producing accessible films which can reach a wide audience, while simultaneously fostering a critical sense of awareness. In particular, she concentrates on the difficulties of turning history into cinema.

Michel focuses on the use of "talking heads," which appear in all three works. She notes how this technique establishes the women as subjects within the film, in their own lives, and in history. But she adds, "From a historian's point of view . . . these privileged subjects can become problematic if a film limits its perspective by relying on them as the sole or even primary informants. While oral history subjects are frequently both engaging and uniquely informative, their accounts of historical events of periods can be partial, fragmentary, idiosyncratic and sometimes—deliberately or unintentionally—misleading."[3] A second problem arises from the fact that the filmmakers have not always selected subjects who are truly representative of the events depicted. Finally, Michel finds that often the lack of a critical context leaves viewers with the impression that the women's experiences occurred in something of a political vacuum. She reviews how each of the three films handled these issues, giving special praise to *The Life and Times of Rosie the Riveter* for being the most sensitive to these problems and the most sophisticated in working out creative solutions. She further commends *Rosie* for its presentation of older women, who are allowed a sexuality often denied them in mainstream cinema, and for the film's ability to integrate women's work experience with their personal lives.

Along with the production and criticism of realist documentaries, feminist film critics began to think about a new cinema, a cinema not only directed by women and presenting new images, but also a cinema that was appreciably different in *form* as well as in content. In "Textual Politics," Annette Kuhn takes up Claire Johnston's call for a deconstructive cinema. Johnston had urged women filmmakers to reject an illusionistic realism by rupturing narrative flow and interrogating the processes of the film's production in the hopes of creating a more critical audience and exposing areas of women's oppression that had previously been unrepresented. This cinematic practice she called "counter-cinema."

Focusing on works that use such strategies, Kuhn discusses Sara Gomez's *One Way or Another* (Cuba, 1974) and *Whose Choice?* (1976), produced by the London Women's Film Group. In analyzing the Gomez film, Kuhn shows how documentary sequences are interspersed with fictional ones, creating alternations that prevent viewers from becoming totally absorbed in the narrative fiction. In many ways a model for counter-cinema, *One Way or Another* forces audiences to come to terms with the political implications of its subject matter. Similarly, in *Whose Choice?*, a film about abortion, the three discourses—information, interviews, and narrative—separately and in combination serve to transform the ways in which audiences relate to the film. "If *One Way Or Another* deconstructs the conventions of Hollywood and socialist realist narrative and traditional documentary, *Whose Choice?* offers a challenge to the kinds of documentary address commonly associated with the agitational/political film"[4]

Kuhn next discusses four experimental works—*Thriller* (Sally Potter, Britain, 1979), *Lives of Performers* (Yvonne Rainer, USA, 1972), *Daughter Rite* (Michelle Citron, USA, 1978), and *Jeanne Dielman, 23 Quai du Commerce, 1080 Bruxelles* (Chantal Akerman, Belgium, 1975)—each of which collapses the usual distinction between documentary and fiction. She highlights the strategies found in several of these works. Most prominent are the following: ellipses which allow the viewer to piece together story fragments, long single takes which allow time to contemplate an image, open narratives which allow for multiple interpretations, lack of certain manipulative shots (close-ups, cut ins, and point-of-view shots) which leave the viewer free to build up her or his own narrative expectations, and asynchronous sound (not tied to on-screen speakers) which allows for indiviudal responses regarding sound and image relationships. According to Kuhn, these stratagems, with their emphasis on heterogeneity and the multiplicity of meanings, set up "the possibility of sexual difference in spectator-text relations by privileging a 'feminine voice' " and thus offer new forms of pleasure for female viewers.

The next essay, "In the Name of Feminist Film Criticism" (1980)[5] by B. Ruby Rich, is also concerned with strategies used by feminist filmmakers. But first Rich focuses on critical responses to several works by women. As two examples, Rich cites *Maedchen in Uniform* (Leontine Sagan, Germany, 1931) and *Jeanne Dielman*, where most of the laudatory reviews ignored the works' feminist underpinnings—in the former, by discussing the anti-Fascist elements while ignoring the lesbianism, and in the latter, by praising the work as hyper-realist or ethnographic, without discussing its feminist sensibility.

Similarly, much writing on filmmaker Yvonne Rainer highlights her use of distancing devices and post-modern structures, while Rich believes "Rainer's films deal with the relations between the sexes . . . explicitly with woman as victim" and with "the burden of patriarchal mythology," leading ultimately to "reworking melodrama for women today."[6] Such disregard for feminist elements, or misnamings, as Rich terms it, results in a failure to recognize the strengths of individual works or to acknowledge women's oppression.

Rich next covers the two views of feminist film criticism, the British concern for the production of meaning and the U.S. interest in social change. Rich sees women's film-going experience as one characterized by an active engagement with the film text, which produces dialectical readings, and thus finds British theory, which emphasizes women's passivity, as too limiting. She argues, "It is crucial to emphasize here the possibility for texts to be transformed at the level of reception and not to fall into a trap of condescension toward our own developed powers as active producers of meaning."[7]

Rich airs her concern that the process of misnaming is reducing "feminist cinema" to works that explicitly and exclusively treat feminism as their subject matter. She calls for a broader definition and suggests several provisional categories for feminist works. Rich's categories can be seen as an attempt to map out an aesthetics of feminist filmmaking. They include: validative, correspondence, reconstructive, medusan, corrective realism, and projectile, all of which are explained in the body of the essay.

Teresa de Lauretis's "Rethinking Women's Cinema: Aesthetics and Feminist Theory" (1987)[8] begins with a discussion of Sylvia Bovenschen's essay, "Is There a Feminist Aesthetic?" (1976). De Lauretis observes that it is now time to alter the terms of the question. "The emphasis must be shifted away from the artist behind the camera, the gaze, or the text as origin and determination of meaning, toward the wider public sphere of cinema as a social technology. . . . The effort and challenge now are how to effect another vision."[9]

Using Chantal Akerman's *Jeanne Dielman*, de Lauretis claims that the film is not just a picture of a female experience, but rather a work that addresses a spectator as female. "In saying that a film whose visual and symbolic space is organzied in this manner *addresses its spectator as a woman*, regardless of the gender of the viewers, I mean that the film defines all points of identification (with character, image, camera) as female, feminine, or feminist."[10] This cinema is not only *by* women, but *for* women.

De Lauretis also calls for more attention to be paid to the differences both "among and within women." She views Lizzie Borden's 1983 film, *Born in Flames*, as a project of great originality which portrays "differences which are not purely sexual or merely racial, economic, or (sub)cultural, but all of these together and often enough in conflict with one another."[11]

De Lauretis closes by offering a new theory of women's cinema, one in which "the spectator is the film's primary concern—primary in the sense that it is there from the beginning, inscribed in the filmmaker's project and even in the very marking of the film."[12]

"Dis-Embodying the Female Voice," by Kaja Silverman, unlike the previous pieces, is more concerned about voice than image. As Silverman points out, despite women's access to language in the real world, in film male characters have linguistic as well as specular authority, which is enhanced by their function as off-screen narrators, granting them additional control as the possessors of superior knowledge.

Silverman points out that not surprisingly a good deal of feminist filmmaking has focused attention on the female voice, especially the dis-embodied, off-screen voice. She analyzes six works in which filmmakers have dislocated the sound from the image track, citing individual techniques such as the alignment of the female voice with a male body (Marjorie Keller's *Misconception*); the delineation of more than one female body to which story and speech can be pinned (Yvonne Rainer's *Film About a Woman Who*); the disassociation of female characters from the words they utter (*Sigmund Freud's Dora* by Weinstock, Pajaczkowska, Tyndall, and McCall); the separation of voice (the daughter's) and words (the mother's) (Chantal Akerman's *News From Home*); the 'traveling' voice which, like the Rainer film, can be projected onto a diversity of female bodies (Bette Gordon's *Empty Suitcases*); and finally Yvonne Rainer's *Journeys From Berlin/71*, which she calls "the most remarkable deployment of female voices within the feminist avant-garde."[13] She sees *Journeys From Berlin/71* as an exposé, not only of the female voice, but also of the voice's relationship to psychic, symbolic, and political forces.

The debates over what constitutes a feminist film practice continue, enhanced by the production of new works by women. Some of these films will be discussed in detail in the next section.

NOTES

1. Julia Lesage, "The Political Aesthetics of the Feminist Documentary Film," *Quarterly Review of Film Studies* 3, no. 4 (Fall 1978), p. 514.
2. Ibid., p. 519.
3. Sonya Michel, "Feminism, Film and Public History," *Radical History Review*, no. 25 (1981), p. 51. This essay also appears in the present volume.
4. Annette Kuhn, "Textual Politics," *Women's Pictures: Feminism and Cinema*, London: Routledge & Kegan (1982), p. 166.
5. This article originally appeared in *Jump Cut*, no. 19 (1978).
6. B. Ruby Rich, "In the Name of Feminist Film Criticism," *Heresies* 3, no. 1, issue 9 (1980). Reprinted in *Movies and Methods*, Vol. II, ed. Bill Nichols, Berkeley: University of California Press (1985), p. 347.
7. Ibid., p. 350.

8. This article originally appeared under the title "Aesthetic and Feminist Theory: Rethinking Women's Cinema," in *New German Critique*, no. 34 (Winter 1985).

9. Teresa de Lauretis. *Technologies of Gender: Essays on Theory, Film, and Fiction*, Bloomington: Indiana University Press (1987), p. 131.

10. Ibid., p. 133.

11. Ibid., p. 139.

12. Ibid., p. 141.

13. Kaja Silverman, "Dis-Embodying the Female Voice," *Re-Vision: Essays in Feminist Film Criticism*, Los Angeles: American Film Institute (1984), p. 143.

THE POLITICAL AESTHETICS OF THE FEMINIST DOCUMENTARY FILM

Julia Lesage

Feminist documentary filmmaking is a cinematic genre congruent with a political movement, the contemporary women's movement.[1] One of that movement's key forms of organization is the affinity group. In the late 1960s and early 1970s in the United States, women's consciousness-raising groups, reading groups, and task-oriented groups were emerging from and often superseded the organizations of the antiwar New Left. Women who had learned filmmaking in the antiwar movement and previously "uncommitted" women filmmakers began to make self-consciously feminist films, and other women began to learn filmmaking specifically to contribute to the movement.[2] The films these people made came out of the same ethos as the consciousness-raising groups and had the same goals.

Clearly the cinematic sophistication and quality of political analysis vary from film to film, but aside from an in-depth discussion of *Self Health*, which I value both cinematically and politically, to explore such differences would be beyond the scope of this essay. Here I shall describe the emergence of the feminist documentary as a genre, the aesthetics, use, and importance of this genre, and its relation to the movement from which it sprang—a discussion important to any consideration of the aesthetics of political films.

Many of the first feminist documentaries used a simple format to present to audiences (presumably composed primarily of women) a picture of the ordinary details of women's lives, their thoughts—told directly by the protagonists to the camera—and their frustrated but sometimes successful attempts to enter and deal with the public world of work and power. Among these films, which now have a wide circulation in libraries and schools, are *Growing Up Female* by Julia Reichert and Jim Klein, *Janie's*

Janie by Geri Ashur, and *The Woman's Film* by the women of San Francisco Newsreel. Other films dealing with women talking about their lives include Kate Millet's *Three Lives,* Joyce Chopra's *Joyce at 34,* Donna Deitch's *Woman to Woman,* and Deborah Schaffer and Bonnie Friedman's *Chris and Bernie.* Some films deal with pride in the acquisition of skills, such as Bonnie Friedman's films about a girl's track team, *The Flashettes,* or Michelle Citron's study of her sister learning the concert violin from a woman teacher, *Parthenogenesis.* Others have more political analysis and are often collective productions that provide a feminist analysis of women's experience with the following: (a) prison (*Like a Rose* by Tomato Productions, *We're Alive* by California Institute for Women Video and UCLA Women's Film Workshop); (b) the health care system (*Self Health* by San Francisco Women's Health Collective, *Taking Our Bodies Back* by Margaret Lazarus, Renner Wunderlich, and Joan Fink, *The Chicago Maternity Center Story* by Kartemquin Films, and *Healthcaring* by Denise Bostrom and Jane Warrenbrand); and (c) rape (*Rape* by JoAnn Elam).

It is no coincidence that films about working-class women show their subjects as the most confident and militant about their rights in the public sector, and their willingness to fight for those rights. Yet even these films, from Madeline Anderson's *I am Somebody* to Barbara Kopple's *Harlan County, USA,* focus on problems of identity in the private sphere—how one strikeleader's husbands views her union organizing unenthusiastically, or how miners' wives reach a new solidarity only by overcoming sexual suspicions and jealousies. As feminist films explicitly demand that a new space be opened up for women in women's terms, the collective and social act of feminist filmmaking has often led to entirely new demands in the areas of health care, welfare, poverty programs, work, and law (especially rape), and in the cultural sphere proper in the areas of art, education, and the mass media.

And if the feminist filmmakers deliberately used a traditional "realist" documentary structure, it is because they saw making these films as an urgent public act and wished to enter the 16mm circuit of educational films especially through libraries, schools, churches, unions, and YWCAs to bring feminist analysis to many women it might otherwise never reach.

Biography, simplicity, trust between woman filmmaker and woman subject, a linear narrative structure, little self-consciousness about the flexibility of the cinematic medium—these are what characterize the feminist documentaries of the 1970s. The films' form and their widespread use raise certain questions. Why are they patterned in so similar a way? Why are these films the first ones thought of whenever a group of women decide they want to "start learning something about women" and set up showings in churches, public libraries, high schools, Girl Scout meetings, union caucuses, or rallies for the ERA? Why do activists in the women's movement use the same films over and over again? What is the films' appeal?

These films often show women in the private sphere getting together to define/redefine their experiences and to elaborate a strategy for making inroads on the public sphere. Either the filmmaker senses that it is socially necessary to name women's experience, or women together within the film do so, or a "strong" woman is filmed who shares her stance with the filmmaker and, by extension, with the women who see the film. Conversations in these films are not merely examples of female introspection; the filmmakers choose not to explore the corners of women's psyches (as in Romantic art). Rather, the women's very redefining of experience is intended to challenge all the previously accepted indices of "male superiority" and of women's supposedly "natural" roles. Women's personal explorations establish a structure for social and psychological change and are filmed specifically to combat patriarchy. The filmmaker's and her subjects' intent is political. Yet the films' very strength, the emphasis on the experiential, can sometimes be a political limitation, especially when the film limits itself to the individual and offers little or no analysis or sense of collective process leading to social change.[4]

Self Health

Among feminist documentaries, *Self Health* is an exemplary film in terms of its cinematic style, the knowledge it conveys, and the self-confidence and understanding it gives women about themselves. The film presents women in a group situation, collectively learning to do vaginal self-exams with a speculum, breast exams, and vaginal bimanual exams. Such groups have been conducted over the past five or six years by women who are part of an informal "self-help" or "self-health" movement in the United States; sometimes their work is connected with the home-birth movement and sometimes with pregnancy testing and abortion referral services. As the health care industry grows like a mushroom under capitalism, the general North American public has become more and more aware of the poor quality of the expensive services offered to them. The women in the self-health movement form part of a large, often informally constituted radical movement to improve health care delivery for the masses of people instead of for an elite.

The place where such a self-health session takes place is usually someone's home or a women's center, rather than a medical clinic. In the film *Self Health*, the locale is a sunny apartment or informal women's meeting place. Although we see two women giving most of the explanations and demonstrations, no one is distinguished as nurse or doctor. As important to the film as the conveying of anatomical information is the fact that all the women discuss together their feelings about and experiences with their bodies and their sexuality, and that they very naturally look at and feel each others' bodies. To gain knowledge by looking at and feeling each other is acknowledged perhaps for the first time as woman's right.

Such a film attacks both the artistic and medical tradition of viewing women's bodies. These traditions, as well as the mass media's use of women's image to sell consumer goods, have robbed most women of a real knowledge of both their own and other women's bodies. Furthermore, many women have little personal sense of rightfully possessing their own bodies, little sense of what's "normal" for themselves physically, and little sense of what sexuality on their terms or on women's terms in general might mean.

Toward the end of the film, one of the women puts on a rubber glove to demonstrate how to do a bimanual vaginal exam. The subject is a woman lying on a table in a sunny room with a flowered pillow under head and a green fern near her. The "teacher" inserts two lubricated fingers into the vagina and pushes up underneath the cervix. First she shows the woman being examined and then the other women gathered around the table, how to press down hard on the abdomen to ascertain the size and location of the uterus and then the ovaries. "Why does it always hurt when the doctor does it?" they ask. They also express surprise about the size and location of the uterus ("about the size of a walnut") and the ovaries ("feels like a Mexican jumping bean").

Women watching the film usually find this information about the uterus completely new. Medical textbook drawings have traditionally shown the uterus as big and near the navel, with large fallopian tubes winding around prominent ovaries. The clitoris, until Masters and Johnson's studies, was not "taught" in medical school as women's organ of sexual sensation. Although I was raised in a doctor's family, I faced similar ignorance, for I learned only three years ago—after having a vaginal cyst cauterized without any local anesthesia—what was to me a startling fact, that the vagina has relatively little sensation because there are few nerve endings there. Why, women are asking, has such ignorance about women's sexuality been promoted in our society—especially since both pornography and modern medicine pretend to be so liberal about sex?

Doctors, male lovers, photographers, artists, and filmmakers have taken woman's nude body as their "turf," especially as an *object* of study. John Berger, in his film series and book, *Ways of Seeing*, has described the tradition of female nudity in oil painting and the presentation of women's bodies in advertising. He understands how the fact that women are "an object of vision, a sight," has affected women's view of themselves: women constantly "survey" themselves to judge how they appear, to try to gain some kind of control over how they might be treated in a circumscribed, patriarchal world.

> In the art-form of the European nude, the painters and spectator-owners were usually men, the persons treated as objects, women. . . . The essential

> way of seeing women, the essential use to which their images are put, has not changed.[5]

In the film *Self Health,* one of the instructors relates how she attacked the depersonalization a woman feels when her body is an "object," especially as she experienced it during a gynecological exam:

> This summer I went to have the regular pap smear and pelvic exam. As soon as I got into the stirrups, the whole feeling came back. I really remembered it and felt completely vulnerable and terrified. There was like this miner's cap sticking up, and finally I said, "OK. I have to deal with this some way," and I just took the curtain and tore it off and threw it into the garbage can. It really blew his mind. He said, "You know, I never thought how ominous it is to see the head of this person, and this part of you divided, not yours."

That so much of the basic physical information conveyed by the film is very new for women viewers (e.g., the film lets us see the cervix and the os, or the normal sebaceous secretion from the nipple) indicates just how colonized a space women's bodies still are. *Self Health* goes a long way toward reconquering that space.

Cinematically, the film is characterized by its presentation of women in a collective situation sharing new knowledge about their physical sexuality. About fifteen young women are gathered in a friendly, mundane environment rather than in a clinical white office where the woman patient is completely isolated from her ordinary social context. As the group does breast self-examinations together, they sit around in a circle in what might be a living room; hanging on the wall we see a Toulouse-Lautrec reproduction of a woman. Warm brown-red and pink tones predominate. As the women remove their tops, we notice them as individuals—some with rings and other jewels, some with glasses, many with different hairstyles. The group is young, they look like students or young working women in flowered peasant blouses and dresses, shirts and jeans. In sum, the colors and the mise-en-scène create a sense of warmth, intimacy, and friendliness.

Even more important to the mise-en-scène is the women's collectivity. Women look at and touch each other; they all see their own sexual organs and those of others, probably for the first time. They learn the variety of physical types and the range or "normality" in sexual organs in look, color, texture, and feel. The fact that almost any woman would feel shy and embarrassed about doing such an overt exploration is mitigated by these women's doing it in a group where everyone feels the same way. The women realize that their fears and doubts about their bodies do not originate from their individual situation as much as from women's physical and psychological "colonization" under patriarchy. Too often, women have experienced as degrading getting contraception information, having a gynecological exam, and having a baby. Certainly at those moments, women's ignorance about their bodies was rarely dispelled. But this collective process gives them the self-confidence to demand answers from doctors face to face and to demand a different kind of health care overall. That such a film does not provide an institutional analysis of the health-care industry, as does *The Chicago Maternity Center Story*, limits how much this one film can achieve in directly promoting a different kind of health care for women; yet, because of the wide range of discussion and kinds of challenges to the established order it encourages women to formulate, it is useful in a wide range of women's struggles.

Visually and in terms of its overall structure, the film moves as far away as you can get from pornography, yet the cinematography also captures that kind of nervous tension and excitement of discovery which the women themselves undoubtedly felt. The film opens on a close up of naked skin, the surface moving to the rhythm of a woman's breathing; there is a pan to a breast and a shot of either pubic or axillary hair in close up. As it starts out, the film could be porn. For most women audience members, the initial sequence provides a moment of tension—"Do we dare to or want to look at this?" The voice over assures us of what we want to hear: "We're learning from our bodies, teaching ourselves and each other how each of us is unique . . . and the same . . . We see it as reclaiming lost territory that belonged to our doctors, our husbands, everyone but us." As the title comes on, we hear the excited voices of women speaking all at once, a device also used at the end of the film over the credits. The voices of discovery, talking in a simultaneous outburst or sharing observations, needs and experiences—these are the tension-breaking devices, the part of the film that an audience unfamiliar with such a situation first identifies with. And these voices imply an outburst of discussion that cannot be contained, that begs to be continued after the film is seen.

In an early sequence, a woman lying on a table is surrounded by other women as she talks about and demonstrates the external genitalia, using her own body as a model. Various women talk here about their sense of being at a distance from their own sexual parts, of feeling squeamish about them. Alternating shots show close ups of the demonstration and of faces looking intently at what they are being shown. When the woman on the table demonstrates the use of the speculum and inserts it into her vagina, one woman's voice exclaims, "Oh, God!" which elicits nervous laughter in the audience and expresses the group's tension. As the woman inserts the speculum and shines the light inside it, the camera cuts to another angle and zooms in to show her cervix and its opening, the os, that which the doctor always "examines" but which we never see. Laughter and sounds of excitement are heard as the onlooking women comment and ask questions about what they see.

After this sequence, a high-angle long shot shows three women lying on the floor against pillows and sleeping bags propped up against the wall. Their legs are spread apart and they are all doing vaginal self-exams with speculum, flashlight, and mirror. A pan shot shows the whole group of women on the floor, lined up along the wall, doing the same thing with some women looking at or helping each other. A mixture of voices exclaim and comment on what they see, especially on the variety and uniqueness of the genitalia. The sequence is a first in narrative cinema. It decolonizes women's sexuality. Women occupy the whole space of the frame as subjects in a collective act of mutual, tangible self-exploration. As one of my students said of this sequence, "It has none of the 'Wow!' of *Candid Camera* and none of the distance of medical or so-called sex education films." Particularly in this one section of *Self Health*, women filmmakers have found a way to show and define women's sexuality on their terms—not with the thrill of possession and not with objectification, but with the excitement of coming to knowledge.

Later, as the film shows the women doing breast self-exams together, they and we notice and let ourselves deliberately look at the variety of women's breasts. The women themselves feel each others' breasts to learn what normal breast tissue is like. Although the Cancer Society promotes breast self-examination, women's breast tissue is fibrous and also varies with the menstrual cycle and the individual. As a result, women often do not know what is normal or what a "lump" might be. A doctor can spot such phenomena from having had the opportunity to feel many women's breasts. Why should such knowledge not be made available to, or seized by, women themselves?

The anatomy lesson, the sharing of feelings, and the learning about others are all part of the self-health experience and all have equal importance in the film. Close ups demonstrate specific examination techniques or show individuals talking and listening; long shots convey the sense of a communal experience in the self-health group. No woman is filmed as an object; everyone is a subject who combines and presents physical, emotional, intellectual, and political selves. The women filmed have an amazing spontaneity and lack of self-consciousness about the camera, particularly given the close range at which the filming was done.

Self-health groups and this film itself both function in an explicitly political way. Reclaiming "the lost territory" of women's bodies and health care is a personal act that has a strong effect on women's identity, emotional life, and sense of control. This film also directly attacks the medical establishment. Women who see the film immediately want to talk about two things—sex education and health care—mainly in terms of what patriarchal society lacks.

In one sense, the film is utopian. It shows a new, collective form of women learning together. It would be an ideal film, for example, to show in high schools. But when I showed the film on the university level to women's studies classes and to film students, both sets of students agreed that the idea of such a collective form of learning about sexuality would have been viewed as "pornography" in their high schools by the teachers, the school boards, and many of the parents. In cinematic terms, the film's vision of women's sexuality, of their being total subjects to one another and to the audience, is also utopian. Women's very physical presence is defined here in women's terms, collectively. And some might ask, in referring to documentary film alone, why haven't these images and these concepts of women's united physical and intellectual selves been presented by filmmakers before?

Feminist Documentaries and the Consciousness-Raising Group

Cinéma vérité documentary filmmaking had features that made it an attractive and useful mode of artistic and political expression for women learning filmmaking in the late 1960s. It not only demanded less mastery of the medium than Hollywood or experimental film, but also offered the very documentary recording of women's real environments. Their stories immediately established and valorized a new order of cinematic iconography, connotations, and range of subject matter in the portrayal of women's lives. Furthermore, contemporary feminist filmmakers, often making biographical or autobiographical films, have used cinéma vérité in a new and different way. They often identify personally with their subjects. Their relation to that subject while filming often is collaborative, with both subject and filmmaker sharing the political goals of the project. The feminist documentarist uses the film medium to convey a new and heightened sense of what *woman* means or can mean in our society—this new sense of female identity being expressed both through the subject's story and through the tangible details of the subject's milieu.

Yet why do so many feminist filmmakers choose to film the same thing? Film after film shows a woman telling her story to the camera. It is usually a woman struggling to deal with the public world. It seems that these feminist documentarists just plug in different speakers and show a certain variation in milieu—especially in class terms—from the aristocratic home of *Nana, Mom, and Me* by Amalie Rothschild to the union organizers' photos of their younger days in *Union Maids* by Julia Reichert and Jim Klein. In fact, the feminist documentaries have as a narrative structure a pattern that is as satisfying for activists in the contemporary women's movement to watch as it is for women just wanting to learn more about women. That is, these films evince a consistent organization of narrative materials that functions much like a deep structure, the details of the individual women's lives providing the surface structure of these films.[6]

Such an organization serves a specific social and psychological function at this juncture in history. It is the artistic analogue of the structure and function of the consciousness-raising group. Furthermore, it indicates to the filmmaker a certain reason to be making the film, a certain relation to her subject matter and to the medium, and a certain sense of the function of the film once released. The narrative deep structure sets the filmmaker in a mutual, nonhierarchical relation with her subject (such filming is not seen as the male artist's act of "seizing" the subject and then presenting one's "creation") and indicates what she hopes her relation to her audience will be.[7]

The major political tool of the contemporary women's movement has been the consciousness-raising group. Self-consciously, a group of about a dozen women would reevaluate any and all areas of their past experiences in terms of how that experience defined or illuminated what it meant to be a woman in our culture. It was an act of naming previously unarticulated knowledge, of seeing that knowledge as political (i.e., as a way of beginning to change power relations), and of understanding that the power of this knowledge was that is was arrived at collectively. This collective process served to break down a sense of guilt for one's own problems and provided a sense of mutual support and of the collective's united strength and potential for action. It was and is a political act carried out in the private sphere.

Initially, there is a healing in the very act of naming and understanding women's general oppression, in collectively creating this new knowledge and identity. Then, the group usually elaborates specific strategies to make inroads on, help its individual members enter, and change power relations in the public sphere. They may, for example, discuss tactics for helping one of their members say no to making coffee at work or demand that the department hire a woman in an executive position. They may strive to get gynecological services at a school clinic. They may help a member of the group insist at work that no more clerical staff be hired and that all women be upgraded, which would mean that everyone in the office do both writing and typing. But consciousness-raising groups cannot be idealized as revolutionary structures. Their problems have been well analyzed by women who have used them and learned how much more organization and economic power is needed to make major changes in the public sphere.[8]

In many ways—for feminists and all the rest of the women in the United States—the private sector of society is uniquely women's space. In that private space, the home, women of my mother's generation were systematically robbed of their sense of being the possessors of their own bodies. Throughout patriarchy, women have been men's possession and the reflection of men's desires in the sexual act, especially in marriage. Mothers are the childbearers and self-sacrificers, which is the constant theme of soap operas and domestic melodramas in film. The sense of self for women under capitalism has traditionally had to come from their children, their house, their jewelry, and their clothes. All the physical, peripheral extensions of themselves that they've been allowed to "possess" have been a mock analog of the real patriarchal possession of themselves, their families, and the sources of economic power that they and their families have had to depend on.[9]

In testimony to the psychological condition of living out one's life in a state of mental colonization and in a sphere where one's labor is not valorized socially by either a salary or public power, many women's narratives are about identity, madness, and the fluidity or fragmentation of woman's ego. Yet the very act of writing a diary, of writing poems, or of consulting a neighbor woman about how to get along when times are hard—all these are testimonies to the struggle women wage to create a language, to formulate a stable sense of self, and to survive economic dependency on men. Just as women's domestic labor and way of relating to each other are disdained, so too their forms of resistance in that sphere tend to go unnoticed and unvalorized in a world where the hegemonic male culture, the public culture, has established the socially acknowledged "rules," appropriated women's bodies, and institutionalized the modes of discourse, especially through the Church, education, literature, the medical profession, the law, and the state.

Because women's identity is shaped and sustained in a sphere where men are largely absent, and because girls grow up in an emotional continuum with their mothers and the other women in their intimate environment (unlike a boy's Oedipal development), their emotional ties are deep to other women.[10] Women have traditionally constantly consulted with each other about domestic matters. One of the functions of the consciousness-raising group of the contemporary women's movement is to use an older form of subcultural resistance, women's conversation, in a new way. There is a knowledge that is already there about domestic life, but it has not necessarily been spoken in uncolonized, women-identified terms. Women's art, especially the feminist documentary films, like consciousness-raising groups, strive to find a new way of speaking about what we have collectively known to be really there in the domestic sphere and to wrest back our identity there in women's terms.

A Shift in Iconography

Much has been lost in women's iconography as it has been purveyed in films, advertising, and television. We have, in fact, maintained a rich photographic history of women over the last hundred years, yet this source is not tapped in its richness and variety in patriarchal narrative film. For example, the women that Dorothea Lange photographed do not "speak" to us either visually or verbally in mainstream cinema. In the United States in the early 1900s, many strikes were led by working women dressed in their best clothes and striding down city streets arm in arm. Why did that iconography get lost?

In the cinematic portrayal of contemporary life, we must question how the details of childrearing, women's crafts, and women's intellectual endeavors are or are not presented in films, news, or ads. We rarely see media images that match the variety of clothes that women wear in daily life, women's varieties of weight and age and tone of voice or accent, and women's varieties of gesture according to their mood and the specific moment in their lives. The patriarchal visual iconography of female figures in film includes the following: mother, child, virago, granny (variant, old maid), ingenue, good wife, and siren. Good wives are blonde, sirens dark-haired; erotically eligible figures of both sexes are slender and not yet old. An occasional comic figure escapes the classification by body type. Women's gestures in cinema are rigidly codified, and women's mise-en-scène predetermined by the connotative requirements of a previously established narrative scheme.

There are both psychological and economic reasons why the domestic world is devalued in our culture.[11] It is rarely seen or interpreted by hegemonic patriarchal culture for what it is and contains, and its elements are named and defined primarily within the context of a seemingly powerless women's subculture. The domestic sphere, except in melodrama, is rarely depicted in film as an interesting place or the locus of socially significant, multiple, interpersonal relationships. Rather, the domestic sphere is the place where a woman is possessed and a man possesses a woman, a man's castle, a place that the woman clings to. Feature films often judge the woman in the home as narrow, as having a stance morally inferior to the male protagonist's commitment to public duty; or home may become the projection backward to the security and presumed moral strength of the mother, regained through an alliance with a good wife. The home is out of history; cinematic heroes go out into the public sphere to do whatever it is that makes them the hero.

Connotative elements in cinema—here the connotative aspects of film's portrayal of the domestic sphere—are shaped both according to a film's narrative and to what people already know and have seen and experiences.[12] What the elements of the domestic sphere suggest is already conventionalized, already thought about before it gets in a film. But traditional filmmaking has drawn very narrowly even from the pool of conventional knowledge about domestic life.

One of the self-appointed tasks of contemporary feminist art is to articulate, expand, and comment on women's own subcultural codification of the connotations of those visual elements and icons familiar to them in their private sphere. Thus, painter Judy Chicago paints "cunt" flowers, and other artists, notably sculptors, have elaborated sculptures or artifacts of paper crafts, sewing, quilting, feathers, enclosed spaces and cubicles, and family photos, such materials being used for the suggestive value they bear from the domestic sphere.

For feminist writers and filmmakers, autobiography and biography provide an essential took for looking in a self-conscious way at women's subculture, their role in or exclusion from the public sphere, their fantasy life, their sense of "embeddedness" in a certain object world. In other words, they become the way both back and forward toward naming and describing what woman really is, in that political and artistic act that Adrienne Rich calls "diving into the wreck."

Feminist films look at familiar women's elements to define them in a new, uncolonized way. Among the connotative elements to which feminist documentaries draw our attention and give an added complexity are the visual cues that define womanliness in film. The women characters' gestures, clothes, age, weight, sexual preference, race, class, embeddedness in a specific social milieu elicit our reflection on both the specificity of the subjects' and our own lives, and on the difference between these cinematic representations and those of dominant cinema. As a result of these films, a much broader range of and more forceful and complex women characters now engage our interest as cinematic subjects, and they are shown doing a wider range of activities in greater detail than ever before in narrative cinema. The biographical documentary serves as a critique of and antidote to past cinematic depictions of women's lives and women's space.

In the film *Self Health*, two whole areas of visual imagery are challenged: the portrayal of women's sexuality and nudity, and health care. Domestic space in this film becomes the locus for a collective coming to knowledge about women's bodies and simultaneously the locus for a new kind of health care delivery. *The Chicago Maternity Center Story*, contrasting home delivery with hospital care, valorizes the same iconic contrasts: health care at home is more "human."

Talking Heads/New Rules of the Game

The visual portrayal of the women in feminist documentaries is often criticized for its transparency (film's capturing reality) or for the visual dullness of talking heads. Yet the stories that the filmed women tell are not just "slices of experience." These stories serve a function aesthetically in reorganizing women viewers' expectations derived from patriarchal narratives and in initiating a critique of those narratives. The female figures talking to us on the screen in *Janie's Janie*, *Joyce at 34*, *Union Maids*, *Three Lives*, *The Woman's Film*, and *We're Alive* are not just characters whom we encounter as real-life individuals. Rather, the filmmakers have clearly valorized their subjects' words and edited their discourse. In all the feminist documentaries, the sound track, usually told in the subjects' own words, serves the function of rephrasing, criticizing, or articulating for the first time the rules of the game as they have been and as they should be for women.

The sound track of the feminist documentary film often consists almost entirely of women's self-conscious, heightened, intellectual discussion of role and sexual politics. The film gives voice to that which had in the media been spoken for women by patriarchy. Received notions about women give way to an outpouring of real desires, contradictions, decisions, and social analyses. After I showed Kate Millet's *Three Lives* to an introductory film class in 1972, a woman student came up to me gratefully after class and commented, "I'll bet that's the first time a lot of those guys have had to sit and listen uninterruptedly to women talking for ninety minutes. I wonder what it means to them to listen to women without having the chance to butt in and have their say."

More than what it means for men to listen to women's self-consciously told "stories," what has it meant for us women in the course of the contemporary women's movement—what have we learned? We have learned what our sexuality is, how mothers can hate and need and love their children, how we can tell a boss or a lover or a friend or a sexist fool off, how "it's not our fault," and where our personal struggles are located in and contribute to and are supported by the larger forces that define our historical period. These films both depict and encourage a politicized "conversation" among women; and in these films, the self-conscious act of telling one's story as a woman in a politicized yet personal way gives the older tool of women's subcultural resistance, conversation, a new social force as a tool for liberation.

Contribution to Public Struggle

The feminist documentaries speak to working women, encourage them in their public struggles, and broaden their horizons to make demands in other spheres as well. To define structures of patriarchy is as important to women workers as to define structures of capitalism. An existential or gut-level militancy becomes refined by a political movement that offers an analysis of and provides a way for seeing both the parameters and details of the struggle as a whole. Yet because of male competitiveness, aggressiveness and bluff are not skills women learn as children (and many women do not necessarily want to learn these tactics as adults either); the women's movement seeks to create new structures to facilitate women's entry into the public sphere of work and power, and to make that public sphere one they would want to inhabit.

Clearly, the powerless will want power, especially once they specifically define the ways they have systematically been robbed of it. But women also want to imagine what that power would be if executed in a form commensurate with feminist goals. Although it is seemingly filmed in domestic space, *Self Health* is a powerful public document in the model for sex education and the vision of collective, community control that it presents. And its sense of women together, coming to (creating, seizing) knowledge is subversive. As one of my women students said, in a single-sex discussion we had after the film and which become an outpouring of women's concerns, "My mother is a liberal and thinks children and adolescents should have sex education. But where she'd accept a film showing a nurse or doctor examining a woman, she'd be horrified to see this one where women are doing it in a group."

JoAnn Elam's *Rape* represents perhaps a new trend in feminist documentaries.[13] Coming out of an experimental film tradition, Elam uses both Brechtian intertitles and a symbolic iconography intercut with a video transfer of a conversation she taped with rape victims one night in one of the women's apartment. The women's conversation forms the sound track of the film, and Elam both heightens and comments wittily on their points by repeating some of their lines in the intertitles. The film is an angry one that elaborates a whole new film style adequate to treating the subject of rape with neither titillation nor pathos. The women filmed are impassioned and intellectual. They are discussing their experiences with the group's support and within the security of domestic space; most of them are political activists in organizations against rape, and all saw the making of this film as an explicitly public act. The feminist documentary films articulate a vision, in part being realized now, of what the shift in relations in the public sphere would be and how power would be enacted if women were to gain and use power in a feminist way.

The feminist documentaries represent a use of, yet a shift in, the aesthetics of *cinéma vérité* due to the filmmakers' close identification with their subjects, participation in the women's movement, and sense of the films' intended effect. The structure of the consciousness-raising group becomes the deep structure repeated over and over in these films. Within such a narrative structure, either a single woman tells her story to the filmmaker or a group of women are filmed sharing experiences in a politicized way. They are filmed in domestic space, and their words serve to redefine that space in a new, "women-identified" way. Either the stance of the people filmed or the stance of the film as a whole reflects a commitment to changing the public sphere as well; and for this reason, these filmmakers have used an accessible documentary form. In the "surface structure" of the films, a new iconography of women's bodies and women's space emerges that implicitly challenges the general visual depiction of women in capitalist society, perhaps in many socialist ones, too. The sound tracks have women's voices speaking continuously; and the films' appeal lies not only in having strong women tell about their lives but even more in our hearing and having demonstrated that some women have deliberately altered the rules of the game of sexual politics. All *cinéma vérité* is not the same, and much of the current discussion of and attack on cinematic realism dismisses the kind of documentary film style that most people are used to. If one looks closely at the relation of this politicized genre to the movement it is most intimately related to, we can see how both the exigencies and forms of organization of an ongoing political movement can affect the aesthetics of documentary film.

NOTES

1. This essay is part of a book-length project on the presentation of women's bodies and women's space in contemporary documentary film.

2. Many of the feminist documentaries (I have given only a representative list of them) are described briefly in Linda Artel's and Susan Wengraf's *Positive Images: Non-Sexist Films for Young People*, San Francisco: Booklegger Press (1976). Interviews with feminist filmmakers often appear alongside review of their films in *Jump Cut*.

3. Experimental filmmaking techniques or an innovative "stretching" of the cinéma vérité form are particularly well used in JoAnn Elam's *Rape*, Michelle Citron's *Parthenogenesis*, and the collectively produced *We're Alive*.

4. An activist in health care struggles criticizes the political analyses offered in feminist health care films in Marcia Rothenberg's "Good Vibes *vs.* Preventive Medicine: Healthcaring From our End of the Speculum," *Jump Cut*, No. 17 (April, 1978), p. 3.

5. John Berger, *Ways of Seeing*, New York: The Viking Press (1973), pp. 63–64.

6. Such an idea loosely derives from the work of Claude Lévi-Strauss in *Structural Anthropology*, trans. C. Jacobson and B. G. Schoepf, Garden City, N.Y.: Doubleday Anchor (1967).

7. Cinéma vérité films in the United States made by male filmmakers are characterized precisely by the film's ironic distance from the subject and the filmmaker's presentation of his vision of the subject as his "creation." Films by Frederick Wiseman, Richard Leacock, David Pennebaker, Tom Palazzolo, and the Maysles brothers fall in this category.

8. For an extended discussion of consciousness-raising groups, see Jo Freeman, *The Politics of Women's Liberation*, New York: David McKay (1975).

9. For a consideration of these issues—women's "dispossession," their loss of a sense of self, and their role in the domestic sphere—see the following: Susan Brownmiller, *Against Our Will: Men, Women, and Rape*, New York: Bantam (1975); Ti-Grace Atkinson, "The Institution of Sexual Intercourse," *Amazon Odyssey*, New York: Links Books (1971); Charles Kleinhans, "Notes on Melodrama and the Family under Capitalism" (contains useful bibliography), *Film Reader*, No. 3 (1978); Laura Mulvey, "Douglas Sirk and Melodrama," and Geoffrey Nowell-Smith, "Minelli and Melodrama," *The Australian Journal of Film Theory*, No. 3 (1977).

10. Nancy Chodorow, "Mothering, Object-Relations and the Female Oedipal Configuration," *Feminist Studies* 4, No. 1, (February 1978); "Family Structure and Feminine Personality," *Woman, Culture and Society*, Michelle Rosaldo and Lois

Lamphere, eds., Stanford: Stanford University Press (1974); "Oedipal Assymetries and Heterosexual Knots," *Social Problems* 23, No. 4 (April 1976).

11. Sheila Rowbotham, *Woman's Consciousness, Man's World*, Baltimore: Penguin (1973); Eli Zaretsky, *Capitalism, the Family, and Personal Life*, New York: Harper (1976); Juliet Mitchell, *Woman's Estate*, New York: Pantheon (1971).

12. Lesage, "S/Z and *Rules of the Game*," *Jump Cut*, No. 12/13 (1976).

13. An expanded version of this essay, including an in-depth analysis of *Rape* as a feminist experimental documentary, appears in *"Show Us Life": Toward a History and Aesthetics of the Committed Documentary*, ed. Thomas Waugh, Metuchen, N.J.: Scarecrow Press (1984).

FEMINISM, FILM, AND PUBLIC HISTORY

Sonya Michel

The public history of American working women has been greatly enriched in the past few years by the release of three important films: Julia Reichert and Miles Mogulescu's *Union Maids* (1976); Lyn Goldfarb and Lorraine Gray's *With Babies and Banners* (1978); and, most recently, Connie Field's *The Life and Times of Rosie the Riveter* (1980). The two earlier films have already proven to be classroom favorites, but all three have also reached the non-academic public through community showings, theatrical distribution, and television airings. Their broad and continuous distribution is significant because these films are effective vehicles for multiple radical messages: class struggle, labor militancy, and feminism. Precisely because they have won such a strong following, it is appropriate to look at the issues raised by the use of film in public history generally—and by these films particularly.

Film has the advantages of flexibility and accessibility for feminists and other radical filmmakers bent on providing a corrective to mainstream history and on reaching a wide audience. Feminists have naturally used film because it can help to fill the still-gigantic gaps in public awareness of women's past. But the use of film poses a number of challenges. There are the problems intrinsic to all documentary filmmaking: fundraising, distribution, the translation of factual material into visual form which is both informative and entertaining.[1] More important for leftists are the intellectual and political issues raised by recent radical and feminist historiography and film criticism. Although film critics and filmmakers are more concerned with questions of form and historians with those of content, the difference is one of degree rather than kind. Radicals in both groups share a common commitment to demystifying the past and fostering a critical consciousness in the public.

However, these two goals can put them at cross-purposes, for experimental film techniques often go down badly with popular audiences. With this in mind, the makers of radical public history documentaries have tended to be less formally experimental than other radical filmmakers, focusing primarily on content and apparently assuming that a suitable film style would arise more or less naturally from the subject matter itself. But this approach often lapses into an updated form of socialist realism, with all of its attendant problems. To the extent that they move beyond this, the three films under review here succeed in transforming the conventional left documentary film into a vehicle for a new kind of public history. Before evaluating their strengths and weaknesses, let us first look more closely at the challenge posed by a radical cultural critique.

In response to the thrust of Marxist cultural criticism, radical filmmakers and critics have long been concerned with the problem of ideology. Briefly, they have been critical of the ways in which mass culture reinforces hegemony, but they have also understood that false consciousness cannot be dissolved in the mode of socialist realism, by simple assertions of "the truth." Rather, they have attempted to understand how the medium of film serves to reproduce ideology—how it works on its audience, so that they may then devise ways to offset this effect; they have sought to learn how an audience comes to question what is presented to it, so that they can create films which foster not certainty but a critical consciousness.[2] In this sense, the problem of radical filmmakers is not dissimilar to that faced by radical historians and teachers who come to believe that they have their own insights to communicate, but also want their students to learn to reach independent conclusions through a critical process.

The filmmaker's project is both easier and more difficult. Easier insofar as film is a "lazier" medium than books, essays, or lectures: viewers needn't read or take notes; they can just sit back and let it all happen to them.[3] But more difficult because filmmaker must then compensate for the propensity of film to generate a sense of reality (and hence credibility) through its immediacy, sensuousness, and naturalizing tendencies. While producers of mass culture exploit this propensity, certain radical filmmakers and critics have attempted to counteract it. In documentary films, this effort has taken the form of montage, *cinéma vérité,* and, most recently, the self-reflexive techniques inspired by Brecht and first worked out cinematically by Jean-Luc Godard.[4]

Self-reflexive films continually interrogate themselves and undermine the grounds of their own credibility. By exposing the conditions of production, such films demystify their origins and point to the filmmakers' role in the production of meaning. They use a variety of techniques such as multiple discourses, disrupted sequences, slowed or speeded-up pace, non-matching sound tracks and visuals, unanticipated shot angles and the like to jar the perceptions of the spectator and denaturalize what occurs on the screen. The spectator is forced to play an active role not only in interpreting the film but in constructing its very meaning by piecing together disparate, incomplete, incongruous, or contradictory images and sounds.[5] Although the filmmaker controls the selection and arrangement of audio-visual elements, the spectator is finally responsible for creating cinematic meaning.

One of the chief objections raised against this film style—by radicals as often as anyone else—is that it often surpasses the ability, not to say the willingness, of the audience to do its part. Instead of raising critical consciousness, it can foster anything from cacaphony to derision. Feminist film critics have been particularly responsive to this objection, for they are faced with a dilemma. On the one hand, feminist politics call for democratic, anti-elitist practice in art as in anything else. On the other, feminist film theory at its most radical rejects conventional discourse as "phallocentric" and calls for the construction of an entirely new cinematic language—a project which, like any form of avant-garde art, tends to exclude to the extent that it succeeds.[6] A solution to this dilemma proposed by one student of feminist films is to construct an audience along with the new language.[7] This can be done through extra-cinematic materials such as reviews, critical essays, and panel discussions of film theory, but this presupposes a self-conscious, highly-motivated—probably academic—audience. More practical, and more to the point for public history filmmakers, would be a process of immanent education through the use of increasingly sophisticated techniques in films which, intentionally or not, form a series and thus create their own public.[8]

The three films under review here may be said to comprise such a series, not because they were actually designed to do so but because they attract a common audience through shared subject matter. While all three contribute to the same branch of public history, each has a distinct focus. *Union Maids* treats the history of women in the trade union movement, primarily in the 1930s; *Babies and Banners* recreates the role women played in the UAW sit-down strike of 1937; *Rosie the Riveter* illuminates the experience of women in the industrial work force during World War II. The three films share form as well as content: they all employ a technique which has been labelled, somewhat disparagingly, as "talking heads"—that is, women speaking into the camera—but do so in a way that film critic Julia Lesage has identified as particularly feminist.[9] Lorraine Gray has said that she sought an "in the kitchen atmosphere" in *Babies and Banners* where "women talk to each other over a cup of coffee and get down to the real nitty-gritty of what their feelings are. . . . "[10] This technique becomes progressively complex in the three films, so that viewers who have seen all of them will not only learn a great deal of history, but will also become more critical watchers of films. Nevertheless, there are problems in all three which illustrate some of the difficulties inherent in turning history into cinema, and into feminist cinema.

The "talking head" technique links these films to two separate epistemological codes or sources—that of oral history and that of the consciousness-raising group. Lesage, in an essay on feminist documentaries, notes that "the structure of the consciousness-raising group becomes the deep structure repeated over and over." This effect is the result of the fact that the filmmakers identify closely with their subjects, participate (sometimes with their subjects) in the women's movement, and make films with political, feminist intentions. In each of the three films discussed here, the presence of the filmmakers is seen or heard at some point. This acknowledgment of the filmmakers serves several purposes: it deconstructs the question of "authorship" of the film—and thus of any illusion that the subjects are simply speaking spontaneously; and, according to Lesage, it creates or recreates the sense of mutual discourse, of having one's experience validated by telling it to someone else who is interested in hearing it—a phenomenon central to feminism and a frequent by-product of oral history.[11] At the same time, the dialogue between filmmaker and subject valorizes the subject as an expert on, at least, her own experience.

Lesage contends that the effect of women telling their stories goes beyond mere "talking heads" in another important sense: the strength of a sound track full of women's voices

> lies not only in having strong women tell about their lives but even more in our hearing and having demonstrated that some women have deliberately altered the rules of the game of sexual politics.[12]

Thus they constitute themselves not only as subjects—as actors in their own lives—but simultaneously as actors in history and in feminist politics, *and* as subject/actors in cinema.

Once women are so constituted, their discourse becomes privileged in the film; that is, we are led to believe what they have to say and to credit it above any other. Of the three films, *Rosie* makes the most sophisticated use of this hierarchy of discourse. In several sequences, Field intercuts clips from *March of Time* propaganda films depicting women's wartime industrial work as safe, pleasant, and harmonious with testimony from her subjects detailing workplace hazards, discrimination (both racial and sexual), childcare problems and the like. Even without the critical commentary of the subjects, alert viewers might be predisposed to take a critical stance toward these excerpts, for their saccharine tone belies a euphemistic intent; the hierarchy of discourse in the film makes this position unavoidable.

From a historian's point of view, however, these privileged subjects can become problematic if a film limits its perspective by relying on them as the sole or even primary informants. While oral history subjects are frequently both engaging and uniquely informative, their accounts of historical events or periods can be partial, fragmentary, idiosyncratic, and sometimes—deliberately or unintentionally—misleading. Precisely because of their position within the situations they are describing, participants seldom regard events with the dispassion required for historical synthesis or interpretation.[13]

The writer can overcome this difficulty more gracefully than the filmmaker. Writing, a historian can incorporate material from oral history interviews in an interpretive article or provide a synthetic introduction to an unbroken oral history narrative, thus granting oral history its due while situating it within a range of historical discourses. But it is clumsy, not to say condescending, for a filmmaker to cut from the "talking head" of a historical actor to that of an "expert."[14] Rather, the documentarist must devise cinematic techniques for locating informants' testimony both critically and circumstantially within a larger historical context.

These three films illustrate some of the ways this can be done. All use montages of contemporary footage (and, in the case of *Rosie*, mass media graphics as well) to depict both the general mood of the country and the specific events or phenomena being discussed by the subjects. Such sequences provide a sense of the texture of the period—the look of the material culture—as well as the atmosphere of working-class life: plant interiors, machinery, assembly lines; picket lines; the faces of bosses and policemen. Yet all of these are external, surface. When the subjects speak of their experience, describing their responses and feelings, they not only add a dimension of intimacy to the account, but they implicitly set up an interrogation of the public by the private—often of the male perspective by the female.

Because these juxtapositions offer a compelling view of the history of personal life, it seems legitimate to ask how representative are the subjects chosen. The codes of journalistic interviewing ordinarily lead an audience to conclude that, unless some specific identification is made, people being questioned about a particular event are typical of the population involved. Filmmakers must come to terms with this phenomenon of implicit typicality in selecting their subjects, especially when making public history films. This task raised different issues in each of the documentaries here.

The women in *Babies and Banners* were apparently chosen at random from those who had belonged to the Women's Emergency Brigade in the 1937 sit-down strike, supposedly representing the age, race, and marital status of Brigade members. Yet Lillian Hatcher, the only Black woman in the film, was married to a man who actually worked at Chrysler, not GM. The film is dominated by Genora Dollinger, who was clearly a leader in 1937 and continues to play a principal role as she leads a confrontation with the UAW on behalf of women's issues in 1977. She seems well-known to the other women being interviewed, suggesting that perhaps they were part of an inner leadership group. If this were the case, their account of the Brigade would take on a certain caste—legitimate enough, if it were made clear. But since Gray and Goldfarb never clarify their principles of selection, the status of their subjects' accounts remains in question.[15]

There is a better match between selection and intention in *Union Maids*.

Two of the three women who relate their experiences in some detail were among those interviewed first by Staughton and Alice Lynd for their book, *Rank and File.*[16] Their self-described commitment and life-long activism lend these women a certain celebrity, an implicit a-typicality—an impression which is reinforced by their near-total silence on certain issues like work/family tensions and sex-role conflicts which usually crop up in working women's accounts. But since they never claim to describe the general experience of women in the 1930s or even that of most female labor activists, they do not create a false sense that their lives *were* typical. Accepting this qualification means, however, that the filmmakers must also accept a certain limitation in the scope of their project and its potential for inspiring identification by vast numbers of women with similar experiences.

Rosie seemingly seeks the opposite effect, presenting women who, although few in number, vary in many ways. Its filmmakers interviewed some 700 women and then chose five to be filmed, ostensibly because they represented the whole population of working women (or at least the sample interviewed). But the results are somewhat misleading. Of the five, three are Black, one Jewish, one white Protestant; three worked in California, one in the Midwest, and one in New York. While there was a substantial amount of war industry all over the country (the South is the one area notably missing here), the disproportionate geographic distribution is not as far off as the racial (im)balance: although Black women were disproportionately represented in the work force both before and during the war, they still comprised only about 11% of the total female work force at its peak in 1944.[17] All five women apparently were or had been married (one was a widow), four had children and all were working-class. While it is true that wartime employment drew more married women into the work force than ever before, there was still a sizeable percentage of single women whose experience is not represented here, except in clips from propaganda films. Likewise, Field interviewed no middle-class "Rosies." It is necessary to understand their responses—especially those who had never held jobs before the war—for their experience was an important part of the feminism which finally emerged in the 1960s.

By concentrating on married, working-class women, Field apparently intended to dispel the myth that the wartime work force consisted primarily of middle-class women who didn't really need jobs and were more than willing to give them up when the war was over. She shows how this impression was created at the time by using clips from a *March of Time* film in which several women attest that it is not only their patriotic duty but their heartfelt desire to yield their jobs to deserving vets as soon as the war ended. (At a recent screening of *Rosie,* Lola Weixel wryly commented that since many of the jobs only came into being with the growth of defense industries, they hadn't belonged to men before the war—and wouldn't exist after.) Although a 1944 Women's Bureau survey contradicts the notion that these sentiments were predominant (75% of the women interviewed wanted to continue working after the war), a significant number of women *did* want to go home, and their consciousness should have been explored as well.[18]

The lack of a critical context becomes even more problematic with regard to the three films' elucidation of the political dimension of working women's experience. Providing only the testimony of their subjects, all three leave the impression that much of women's activism occurred in something of a political vacuum. In *Babies and Banners*, for example, all the women are wearing—significantly—red berets, but while several mention receiving training and organizing assistance from both the Communist and Socialist Parties, they neither affirm nor deny membership in either. Given the long history of sectarian tensions in the UAW, one is left wondering how this played itself out with regard to the Brigade.[19] Similarly, the political affiliations of the three subjects in *Union Maids* are never fully clarified, although Kate Hyndman brings out 1950s newspaper clippings of articles redbaiting her. In *Rosie*, two of the subjects delimit the political topography of the 1940s: Lola Weixel frequently refers to herself as a "working person" with "progressive ideas"; not surprisingly, she led efforts to organize her welding shop for the United Electrical Workers. Her euphemisms contrast markedly with an anecdote related by Lyn Childs: when her shipyard boss accuses her of being a "commie," she unhesitatingly affirms that if sticking up for a fellow worker meant being a commie, then by golly, she was!

Such references to anti-communism suggest that many of the people interviewed in these films may have been reluctant to discuss openly their political pasts. Yet at least one "union maid," Stella Nowicki, had already related her activities as a member of the Young Communist League and the Communist Party in *Rank and File*. This indicates that it may have been the choice of the filmmakers, not the subjects, to omit information about the left. Whatever the reasons, all three films leave a rather confused impression of the links between the left and the labor movement, a connection which is a central concern of twentieth-century labor historians. The dilemma for radical filmmakers who rely on oral history subjects for the content of their work is to avoid reproducing political mystification while respecting and safeguarding the integrity of their subjects.

The three films raise another set of questions about the politics of film: the presentation of women on the screen. According to one school of thought, any cinematic representation of women within patriarchal culture inevitably constitutes them as objects of desire.[20] Lesage disagrees with this position, arguing that it is possible to "decolonize women's sexuality," to overcome objectification, through the presentation of female subjectivity, especially with regard to their own sexuality and physicality.[21] The three films considered here shed some light on this debate.

The subjects of all three are women in their late 50s or older; according to the dominant patriarchal code governing female sexuality, these women are almost automatically de-sexualized on the basis of age alone.[22] But by discussing issues of sexuality in their pasts, they re-sexualize themselves, this time in a particularly feminist way which simultaneously calls attention to the narrowness of the patriarchal code and evokes their sexuality from a subjective perspective. This process is paralleled on the visual level, reaching a high degree of complexity in *Rosie.* Field sets up a tripartite interrogation of women's visual representation: the mass-culture iconography of the 1940s, illustrated by propaganda film clips and magazine graphics; candid photographs of both the subjects themselves and other women taken during the period; and images of the subjects today. The subjects first appear in the present, commenting on their wartime experience; they are established as individuals—as historical actors—before we see them as young women. Timed otherwise, these images might have the effect of validating the patriarchal code of female beauty (only attractive young women are worth attending to—and even then, not to be taken seriously), but as assembled here, they serve to interrogate the code by making viewers aware of changes in individual physical appearance which inevitably occur over time.

The film also draws attention to the relationship between women and mass culture. The wartime photos indicate that each woman in her own way followed fashion and maintained a conventionally "feminine" appearance (at least off the job) while working in defense plants. Such behavior is ordinarily regarded as evidence of the hegemony of mass culture—women under the influence of advertising and marketing. Feminine style, moreover, is usually associated with fragility and vulnerability. Yet the recollections of these women affirm their actual strength and independence during this period. The duality between appearance and reality suggests that women followed fashion out of their own choice. Wanita Allen comments that while some people saved as much as they could (memories of the Depression still vivid), she spent money on anything she could find; her voice is heard over a photo of herself sitting in a night club, a fur stole draped proudly over one shoulder and a sparkling smile on her lips. For Allen, spending money on expensive clothing and jewelry was an outward sign of her new-found economic independence. She was not a "conspicuous consumer" in Veblen's sense, for she was not parading her husband's wealth, but rather enjoying the fruits of her own labor.

In providing this sort of insight into the meaning of women's wartime jobs, *Rosie* marks another point in the progression of films about women and work, a broadening of their scope. *Union Maids* began by following the contours of conventional labor history, fitting women into previously established categories. Yet even while it was doing so, the film implicitly challenged and transformed those categories. Its three subjects established beyond question that women were crucial in day-to-day shopfloor struggles in the 1930s. For workers, management and the labor movement alike, it was not immaterial that these militant actions were undertaken *by women*. However, the subjects tell us little about what difference work and politics made in their personal lives. Except for brief references to their childhoods, they give the impression of having spent their entire lives at work or in union activities. Moreover they maintain an almost Victorian silence on the question of sexuality and the labor struggle. While it is important to affirm women's identity as workers and as activists, it would seem to be a capitulation to a patriarchal form of economism to assume that women in these roles have the same experience as men. By focusing only on discrimination against women by management, *Union Maids* cannot account for the ways in which family life and patriarchal ideology and culture also situate women within the work force.

Babies and Banners takes the analysis one step further, although because its scope is limited to a single event, the film does not fully explore the relationship between union activism and the rest of women's experience and gives only scant attention to women as workers in their own right. Its chief contribution is in exposing the union's role in perpetuating male domination, showing how, as a bastion of male culture, it encouraged social as well as occupational divisions between the sexes. Flint, as one Brigade woman acerbically describes it, was a town of churches and bars—churches to console the women while their men lined the bars. A double standard was clearly at work: women who dared enter union halls risked their reputations, yet the union was not above using women as buffers between all-male picket lines and the police, relying on the latter's deference to the "fair sex." (Ironically, as the film shows, the women were not as innocent as they appeared; they were all armed with blackjacks fastened by garters under their sleeves!) Once the UAW strike had been won, however, patriarchy reasserted itself, and the Women's Emergency Brigade was dispersed and sent home.

The film attempts to show that the Brigade had unintended consequences—that, once organized, its members developed a new sense of themselves and felt more important. As one woman put it, the red beret they all wore became "the symbol of a new woman who was ready to make sacrifices and could be counted on"; another felt that the actions of the Brigade gave men a "different outlook on the ordinary housewife." But it is unclear that this new consciousness produced major changes in these women's lives at home, at work, or in the UAW. Bringing the struggle up to date, the film concludes with Genora Dollinger's impassioned speech at the reunion commemorating the 40th anniversary of the strike in 1977. She recalls the courage of the Women's Emergency Brigade and then calls upon the union to support the ERA and encourage and allow women greater representation within its ranks. While dramatic, her speech has the ring of "automatic feminism," for the film leaves a large gap between the 30s and the present which rhetoric alone cannot fill.

Rosie expands the framework of working women's history in several directions. It explores labor market segregation by sex and race, showing that women were generally given inferior job assignments in defense industries, and black women relegated to the most menial sweeping and cleaning jobs which had been held by black men before the war. The film makes no direct comment on unions' policies toward women either during the war or in the postwar demobilization of labor. However, the job segregation of these women in defense industries and their subsequent job histories (all five returned to lower-paid, unskilled or semi-skilled work, mainly in the pink-collar sector) stands as mute testimony to trade union failures to defend them in a job market structured by capitalist patriarchy.[23]

Both the subjects and creators of *Rosie* seem to have understood that working women's experience is not constituted by the worker-management-union triangle alone, but that personal and social issues also intervene and must be explored simultaneously. More than its predecessors, this film attempts to provide a fuller view of women's work in its personal context. Lola Weixel's account of the housework she did after a full day of welding, while her brother-in-law lay on the couch listening to jazz records, is a vivid example of the "double day" put in by most female war workers. Margaret Wright provides another version, telling how she returned home after finishing the night shift in time to wake her children, bathe and feed them, do the laundry, and fix a meal for her husband, who worked days. There is visible emotion in Lyn Child's face as she describes leaving her small daughter with her mother when she came to Oakland to work in the shipyard because a lack of housing and child care facilities made it impossible for her to keep the child with her. Wanita Allen is also critical of the lack of child care services, concluding that they were probably available only to middle-class women, and inconveniently located (especially given gas and tire rationing) at that. A frequent theme in wartime articles about female employment is the opposition some women had to face from their husbands. The four married women in *Rosie*, because they had all worked before the war, recall no tension between themselves and their men; defense jobs were not only taken for granted but actually celebrated, since they brought in much higher wages. What all the women do note, however, is their regret over losing jobs that were satisfying as well as lucrative. And finally, both the narratives and images from contemporary footage and graphics testify to the increasing importance of female camaraderie and homosexuality during the war, phenomena that developed as women's isolation in the home (either as housewives or domestic workers) was broken down through their concentration in industry. The overall effect of war time work on women's personal lives was, then, ambiguous: on the other hand, it produced greater strains on them and their families; on the other, it fostered individual self-confidence and self-consciousness as a social group. Both tendencies were, of course, to play themselves out in the postwar decades.

All three films leave many questions unanswered. They tend to lack specificity: dates, names, and places are either absent or hard to determine; connections between events are unclear. In some cases, omissions or misrepresentations were, apparently, deliberate. Lyn Goldfarb has been quoted as saying, "there was always a tension between what was historically accurate and what was visually best. We felt obligated to set the record straight, but we also wanted to be appealing."[24] Daniel Leab, reviewing *Babies and Banners* in *Labor History*, criticizes the film for numerous inaccuracies, concluding it is "bad history," but then *defends* it as "splendid 'agit-prop', an excellent look at the past from a feminist perspective, a consciousness-raising document of the first order. The film well deserves all the accolades it has received . . . as a film."[25] Leab's distinction between historical documentary and "agit-prop" (especially used in the neutral sense he does) is dangerous. Such cynicism legitimizes films which simply replace one ideology with another, "correctness" being determined by politics instead of historical accuracy. Only viewers with prior knowledge will be the wiser.

The effect of such films is quite different from those in which contradictions and gaps are immanent, those which, by themselves, stimulate critical consciousness and provoke viewers to consider the issues raised and seek further. Of the three films considered here, *Rosie* comes closest to fulfilling this function with its use of contemporary footage in conjunction with oral history and its sophisticated interrogation of female imagery. Incorporating the feminist interview techniques which made *Union Maids* and *Babies and Banners* so appealing, it takes the feminist documentary film one step further, pointing to new, important directions for cinematic public history.

NOTES

I would like to thank Andrea Walsh, Anson Rabinbach and the issue editors, particularly Sue Benson, Steve Brier and Roy Rosenzweig, for comments which helped me clarify a number of points in this review.

1. See Connie Field's comments on the need for high technical standards in radical films, "Institutional Obstacles to Creativity in Media," a Round Table with Media Workers, *Tabloid* 1 (Spring-Summer 1980), 48.

2. For an excellent summary of Marxist discussions of ideology, see Stuart Hall, "Culture, the Media, and the 'Ideological Effect,' " in James Curran, et. al., eds., *Mass Communication and Society*, London, (1977), 315–48.

3. Roland Barthes, "Rhetoric of the Image," in *Image-Music-Text*, trans. Stephen Heath, New York, (1977), 41.

4. Reviews and theoretical discussions of these issues appear in *Screen, Jump Cut, Cineaste* and other film journals beginning in the late 1960s. For these and other discussions, see Jack Ellis, "Documentary Film Bibliography," *Jump Cut* 23 (November 1980), 30–31.

5. Hall, "Culture, the Media," 326–27; Peter Gidal, "Theory and Definition of Structural/Materialist Film", in Gidal, ed., *Structural Film Anthology*, London, (1976), 1–21.

6. For overviews see "Feminism and Film: Critical Approaches," editorial in *Camera Obscura* 1 (Fall 1976), 3–10; Christine Gledhill, "Recent Developments in Feminist Film Criticism," *Quarterly Review of Film Studies* 3 (Fall 1978), 457–93. A key article is Laura Mulvey, "Visual Pleasure and Narrative Cinema," *Screen* 16 (Autumn 1975), 6–18. Lesley Stern discusses the conflicts between feminist film theory and politics in "Feminism and Cinema—Exchanges." *Screen* 20 (Winter 1979), 89–105.

7. Stern, "Feminism and Cinema," 92.

8. Producers of mass media consciously form series when they use a formula derived from one hit film or television program to clone others; but series can also be used for progressive purposes, with educational effects.

9. Julia Lesage, "The Political Aesthetics of the Feminist Documentary Film," *Quarterly Review of Film Studies* 3 (Fall 1978), 507–23.

10. Quoted in Jayne Loader, "Flint Sit-down Veterans Speak," *Seven Days*, October 13, 1978, 32.

11. Lesage, "Political Aesthetics," 521.

12. Lesage, "Political Aesthetics," 521.

13. Lesage notes that "the emphasis on the experiential . . . can sometimes be a political limitation, especially when the film limits itself to the individual and offers little or no analysis or sense of collective process leading to social change," "Political Aesthetics," 509. On the relationship between historical actors and historical knowledge, see E. P. Thompson, "The Poverty of Theory or An Orrery of Errors," in *The Poverty of Theory and Other Essays*, New York, (1978), 19.

14. A rather ludicrous example of such an effort may be seen in Lee Grant's *Willmar Eight*, when a bespectacled young man with a rather pompous manner (identified as a sociologist) is consulted on the effects of a strike by eight female bank employees. His remarks were barely audible over the audience laughter when I saw the film.

15. Daniel Leab, "Writing History on Film: Two Views of the 1937 Strike against General Motors by the UAW," *Labor History* 21 (Winter 1979–80), 110–11. See also Susan Reverby, review of " 'With Babies and Banners,' " *Radical America* 13 (September-October 1979), 63–69.

16. Staughton and Alice Lynd, *Rank and File*, Boston (1973).

17. Chester Gregory, *Women in Defense Work During World War II*, New York, (1974), 4, 144.

18. William Chafe, *The American Woman* (New York, 1972), 181.

19. Reverby, " 'With Babies,' " 64.

20. Gledhill, "Recent Developments," 458–61.

21. Lesage, "Political Aesthetics," 513.

22. Simone de Beauvoir, *The Second Sex*, New York, (1961), 541–60.

23. Ruth Milkman, "Organizing the Sexual Division of Labor: Historical Perspectives on 'Women's Work' and the American Labor Movement," *Socialist Review* 49 (January-February 1980), 94–150.

24. Quoted in Reverby, " 'With Babies,' " 66.

25. Leab, "Writing History," 112.

TEXTUAL POLITICS

Annette Kuhn

In previous writings I have discussed film practices as examples of realism: as representations, that is, which present an appearance of transparency by effacing the processes of meaning production in their own textual operations. Realism is a feature of dominant cinema, but non-dominant film practices like socialist realism and feminist documentary draw on this transparency both in order to appeal to as wide an audience as possible, and also with the assumption that a politically oppositional message will come across the more clearly to the extent that it is not complicated by "noise" from foregrounded textual operations. Such a cultural politics is grounded in an assumption that meanings—even politically oppositional meanings—exist already in society, that human subjects are already formed for such meanings, and that representations can operate as neutral vehicles for conveying those meanings from source to recipient.

Other approaches to cultural politics may, however, take different positions as to the nature of meaning. The construction of meanings may, for example, be regarded as an ongoing process of texts and reader-text relations which may work in some respects independently of the operations of other social formations. Such a stance on signification suggests that in the moment of reading, recipients of texts are themselves involved in producing meanings, even if—as in the case of realism—they are not aware of the fact. To the extent that the signification process is effaced in realist representations, it is argued, realism perpetuates illusionism, the notion that, in the case of cinema, what is on the screen is an uncoded reflection of the "real world." Illusionism may then be regarded as an ideological operation, on at least two grounds: first that the concealment of processes of signification through codes of transparency mystifies both the spectator and the signification process by setting up a view of the world as monolithically preconstructed "out there," and secondly that spectator-text relations characteristic of realist representations—identification and closure, for example—position their reading subjects as unitary and non-contradictory, and thus as neither active, nor as capable of intervention, in the signification process. These critiques of illusionism may underpin a cultural politics which takes textual signifiers to be a legitimate area of intervention. If illusionism is a feature of certain textual practices, then it may be challenged on the level of the text by means of nonrealist or antirealist strategies and modes of address.

The present essay is devoted to a consideration of what might be termed "anti-illusionism" in cinema, and to anti-illusionist film practices as they touch on feminism. From this point of view, then, I will address the question of feminist counter-cinema. Counter-cinema may be defined as film practice which works against and challenges dominant cinema, usually at the levels of both signifiers and signifieds. Although it may challenge the institutional practices of dominant cinema too, my concern here is primarily with the text.

As textual practice, counter-cinemas attempt to challenge and subvert the operations of dominant cinema. Before proceeding to an examination of some approaches to and examples of counter-cinema, therefore, I will briefly look at features of dominant cinema which counter-cinemas (feminist or otherwise), may set out to challenge. I have already touched on the argument—and the reasoning behind it—that the effacement of processes of signification in dominant cinema is an ideological operation. The question of how this ideological operation works in cinema may be dealt with by considering how codes in dominant cinema work to construct certain kinds of spectator-text relations. For example, classic narrative codes structure relations of spectator identification with fictional characters and also with the progress of the narrative itself. By means of these identifications, the spectator is drawn into the film, so that when the questions posed by the narrative are resolved by its closure, the spectator is also "closed," completed or satisfied: in cinema, this partly operates through the "binding-in" process of suture. In documentary forms of film realism, closure, completion, and unity are brought about through identification with the coded self-presentation of the "truthfulness" of the representation, as well as through identification with, or recognition of, real-life protagonists on the screen.

But what kind of relationship might there be between the practices of counter-cinema and those of feminism? It could be argued, for example, that there is nothing specifically feminist about challenging the modes of identification and subjectivity set up by dominant cinema. If this is the case, where does feminism enter into counter-cinema? In answer to this question, I will point to two interrelated arguments on behalf of feminist counter-cinema. The first is premised on the notion that all forms of illusionism are ideologically implicated, while the second focuses more specifically on the forms of pleasure generated in the relations of specularity set up by dominant cinema, classic Hollywood narrative in particular.

In her 1973 pamphlet *Notes on Women's Cinema*, Claire Johnston argues that "It has been at the level of the image that the violence of sexism and capitalism has been experienced."[1] In other words, the image constructs a specific set of signifiers (as distinct from those, say, of the written word) for constructing the worldviews of a society which is both patriarchal and bourgeois. The ideological discourse of dominant cinema, certainly at the level of the film image, is therefore seen as sexist as well as capitalist. The specificity of the "patriarchal" nature of the film image is at this point analysed in terms of Lévi-Strauss's anthropological argument about woman's status as "sign" in relations of exchange between males,[2] while the bourgeois character of dominant cinema is associated with the mystification involved in the naturalization of operations of signification by the surface appearance of transparency of meaning. The task of constructing a feminist counter-cinema, according to this argument, involves first of all "an analysis of the functioning of signs within the discourse"[3] and then a subversion of this discourse by means of antirealist or anti-illusionist textual strategies. What is at stake here, then, is a deconstructive counter-cinema whose project is to analyze and break down dominant forms as they are embedded in bourgeois and patriarchal ideology.

Following the early work of Johnston and Cook, feminist film theory began to turn its attention away from a concern with the film text as an autonomous set of formal operations and towards the question of spectator-text relations in cinema. Here, particular regard was given to relations of looking and their psychic inscription. Laura Mulvey's work on the look and cinematic representations of women was an important development in this area, and in it Mulvey also argues for the creation of new forms of pleasure in cinema. Given her argument that the codes of dominant cinema "and their relationship to formative external structures must be broken down before mainstream film and the pleasure it provides can be challenged,"[4] Mulvey is clearly also advocating a deconstructive counter-cinema. Her suggestion is that in such a counter-cinema the "voyeuristic-scopophilic look" can be broken down in certain ways. However, although Mulvey's analysis appears to arrive at a prescription for film practice rather similar to Johnston's—deconstruction—her concern with the psychic structures of subjectivity opens up possible new areas of work for feminist counter-cinema. As well as shifting the debate from a consideration of the film text as an autonomous set of formal strategies, towards a notion of interaction between spectator and text, Mulvey's analysis also raises the questions of specularity and gendered subjectivity. Although the consequences of this for feminist film practice are not explicitly addressed in her article, crucial questions are implicitly raised, in that the issue of gendered subjectivity poses in turn that of a specifically feminine film language and its potential for feminist counter-cinema.

The discussion which follows is structured around the argument that oppositional textual practices in cinema which may be regarded as of relevance to feminism fall roughly into two categories. The premises grounding each correspond more or less with those underlying the respective analyses of Johnston/Cook and Mulvey. I say more or less, because the film practices I shall be examining have not for the most part arisen in any immediate or determined sense from the theories with which I associate them. Although I would maintain that certain types of theorizing have been important in shaping feminist film practice, the influence is rarely either one way or direct. In any case, any identifiable influences emerge as much from the ways in which films may be read as from the intentions of their makers. Thus although in this case theory and practice are in important respects interrelated, it is neither possible nor desirable to map the one immediately and unproblematically onto the other. The two areas of textual practice discussed here, then, are constituted on the one hand by a counter-cinema grounded in the deconstruction of dominant cinema, and on the other by a form of cinema marked as more "other" to dominant cinema, as "feminine writing." Although it will be clear that these two areas of practice do have certain things in common, I believe their differences permit a consideration of some crucial developments and prospects for feminist counter-cinema. I shall therefore deal with them separately.

Deconstruction

As the term suggests, deconstructive cinema works by a process of breaking down. On one level, the object of the deconstruction process is the textual operations and modes of address characteristic of dominant cinema, the aim being to provoke spectators into awareness of the actual existence and effectivity of dominant codes, and consequently to engender a critical attitude toward these codes. Provocation, awareness, and a critical attitude suggest in turn a transformation in spectator-text relations from the passive receptivity or unthinking suspension of disbelief fostered by dominant modes of address to a more active and questioning position. Deconstructive cinema aims therefore to unsettle the spectator. But there is more at stake in deconstructive cinema than simply a challenge to the textual operations of dominant cinema. After all, many forms of avant-garde and experimental cinema may be read as doing just this, without—except in the very broadest sense—being defined as deconstructive. The distinguishing mark of deconstructive cinema, as against other non-dominant or anti-dominant forms, is its recruitment of the spectator's active relation to the signification process for certain signifieds, or areas of substantive concern. The distinction between form and content may help clarify this point: deconstructive cinema, it can be argued, is not definable simply by its formal strategies. Departure from the formal conventions of dominant cinema may be a necessary condition of deconstructive cinema, but it is certainly not a sufficient one. Deconstructive cinema departs from dominant cinema in its content as well as in its form: it speaks from politically oppositional positions or concerns itself with subject matters commonly ignored or repressed in dominant cinema. But although oppositional content is necessary, it is not a sufficient condition of deconstructive cinema, either. Deconstructive cinema then may be defined by its articulation of oppositional forms with oppositional contents. If deconstructive cinema thus defines itself in relation to dominant cinema, it is not a static entity, because its character at any moment is always shaped, in an inverse manner, by dominant cinema. Deconstructive cinema is always, so to speak, casting a sideways look at dominant cinema. The term "counter-cinema"—which is in fact often understood to be synonymous with deconstruction—conveys this sense of conscious opposition very well.

It can be helpful to compare the operations and political objectives of deconstructive cinema with those of the "epic" theater associated with Berthold Brecht. Epic theater departs from more conventional theatrical forms in that, for example, narratives may be fragmented and subject to interruptions, characters may not be presented as psychologically rounded, narrative time may not be linear, and so on. The effect of these epic devices is to render impossible the kinds of spectator identification typically set up by "realist" theater. The analogy between epic theater and deconstructive cinema is grounded, in fact, in the anti-illusionist stance and strategies of distanciation common to both. As Walter Benjamin says of epic theater, it

> advances by fits and starts, like the images on a film strip. Its basic form is that of the forceful impact on one another of separate, distinct situations in the play. The songs, the captions included in the stage decor, the gestural conventions of the actors, serve to separate each situation. Thus distances are created everywhere which are, on the whole, detrimental to illusion among the audience. These distances are meant to make the audience adopt a critical attitude.[5]

It is clear from this that the effect of this epic form derives from the spectator-text relations it constructs. Formal devices are justified only to the extent that they evoke distanciation rather than involvement, a critical attitude rather than passive receptivity.

Therefore although both epic theater and deconstructive cinema are often discussed in terms of their formal strategies—sometimes, in fact, to the extent that forms are fetishized—these strategies are important only in relation to their consequences for the address of the representation—the film or play—as a whole. The impact of epic or deconstructive representations thus arises in direct relation to the challenge they offer the operations of dominant strategies. The importance of the contextual specificity of deconstructive strategies is emphasized here mainly because my discussions of particular films will focus on their formal attributes, which seems a regrettable, but perhaps unavoidable, consequence of singling out individual texts for attention. It is important to stress, therefore, that the films I discuss as examples of deconstructive cinema acquire their deconstructive force in the final instance only from their context: only in their relation, that is, to the contemporary state of dominant cinema and to their place in the history and institutions of non-dominant cinematic forms. The films I shall look at here are *One Way Or Another* (*De Cierta Manera*) (Gomez, ICAIC, 1974) and *Whose Choice?* (London Women's Film Group, BFI, 1976). Both of them deal with fairly well-defined and circumscribed topics, and draw upon and articulate, while at the same time also challenging, certain conventions of narrative and documentary realism.

One Way Or Another deals with the problem of "marginalism" in post-revolution Cuba. Marginalism is the culture of poverty associated with the urban slums and shanty towns of pre-revolution days, areas marked by high levels of unemployment and delinquency, poor educational provision, violence, and economic poverty. The integration of "marginal" populations into the wider society is regarded as a priority and a problem for the revolution. The film investigates the contradictions—both personal and social—involved in the integration process by examining some of the effects of, and causal links between, certain cultural features of marginalism. It is because of its concern with tracing the relationship between the personal and familial and other social structures that *One Way or Another* may be regarded as a film which prioritizes feminist issues and political perspectives: although it does this, of course, within the terms of a broader concern with the effects of a socialist revolution. The problem of contradictions between marginal culture and the revolution present the film not only with its analytical project, but also with the problem of accessible cinematic forms for that project. The project and the problem are dealt with by the film's mobilization of two discourses: a story which has many of the qualities of a socialist realist narrative, and a documentary with voice-over.

The narrative discourse is focused primarily on the progress of a loving relationship between Mario, a worker living in a marginal district, and Yolanda, a teacher of middle-class origins drafted into a school in the area. In the socialist realist manner, the narrative discourse "traces how the internal dynamics of a single personality, family, or love affair are related to the larger social processes of the revolution."[6] But at the same time, it does not construct the kinds of identification typical of socialist realist modes of address, primarily because the narrative is articulated with another, and very different, discourse, that of documentary realism.

Throughout the film, there are sequences of documentary with voice-over commentary, which address the problem of marginalism from the point-of-view of a distanced, if sympathetic, social observer. Thus for instance, following immediately on the pre-credit and credit sequences is a documentary sequence showing the demolition of some city slums and the reconstruction of the area, with a voice-over which explains that elimination of the slum conditions has not resulted in the disappearance of certain features of marginal culture. In this way, the notion of contradictory relations between social formations and an analytical approach to such contradictions are established within both the signifiers and the signifieds of the text. The film takes up two different conventions of cinematic realism, but in combining them in certain ways undercuts the spectator-text relations which would be set up by each one on its own. This type of deconstruction works by means of its direct reference to dominant cinematic codes, setting up, through familiarity with such codes, certain expectations in the spectator. These expectations are then cut off because the film offers no single internally consistent discourse.

Examples of distanciation in the discourses of *One Way Or Another* may be cited with reference to some of the formal strategies associated with epic theater. For example, the interaction of narrative and documentary discourses in the film works in a similar way to the separations and "fits and starts" of epic theater. During a sequence in which Mario and Yolanda exchange confidences about their past lives Mario confesses that he once seriously considered becoming a *ñañigo*, a member of a male secret society. At this point, the narrative is cut off by an intertitle: "Abacua society—documentary analysis"—followed by an account, with documentary footage and voice-over, of the history of these secret societies and their roots in and connections with marginalism. The first concern at this point is with a description and analysis of one of the ways in which marginal culture still persists after the revolution. At the same time, however, this documentary interlude is marked as functioning analogously to a flashback (Mario's), for afterwards the narrative discourse resumes where it left off, with Yolanda telling Mario the story of her own background—her marriage, divorce, and current independence.

Epic theater is characterized also by an undercutting of identification with fictional characters, in that psychologically rounded representations are refused. While epic interruptions will in themselves function to cut off spectator identification with characters, there is another Brechtian device associated specifically with this form of distanciation—"acting as quotation." Instead of inhabiting and "becoming" their characters, actors will, as it were, stand in for them in the distanced mode of "quoting" characters' words. Although in *One Way Or Another* much of the acting is in fact quite naturalistic, it does take on some of the features of "quotation" but usually through cinematic, rather than dramatic, means. The first documentary sequence, for example, which ends with a reference to education in the marginal areas, is immediately followed by a close-up of a woman talking directly to the camera in lip-synch, *cinéma vérité* style, about her work as a teacher. It subsequently transpires that the woman is Yolanda, who actually belongs to the fictional part of the film, but at this point her discourse is marked as "documentary" by its codes and context. This has the effect of cutting off identification and relativizing the acting in later sequences.

How do these distanciation devices serve the analytical project of *One Way Or Another*? In the first place, the distanciation itself tends to force the spectator into an active relation with the text, opening up the potential for questioning and analysis. The different discourses, moreover, are put together in such a way as to integrate analysis at the levels of signifier and signified. Halting Mario's talk about being a *ñañigo* with a descriptive "aside" about Abacua society serves both to complete the reference and also to unpack the wealth of social, cultural, and historical meaning encapsulated by it. The interaction of narrative and documentary codes, then, underscores the substantive sociological analysis. The enunciating discourse of the film as a whole thereby privileges an analytical approach to its signifieds.

Whose Choice? constructs similar modes of address in its treatment of the issues of contraception and abortion. The film operates in a relatively complex manner, by presenting its material as three discourses—information, interviews, and narrative. In the interviews, two women detail the current situation in Britain as regards abortion and present a number of arguments in favor of "a woman's right to choose." The film also includes documentary footage of the June 1975 National Abortion Campaign demonstration in London. Added to—and transformed by—the documentary/informational aspects of these two discourses is a fictional narrative about a young woman's attempt to obtain an abortion. This third discourse is marked also by some of the distanciation devices characteristic of epic theater, in particular lack of characterization and narrative interruptions. The address of the film is constructed not only severally by its three discourses, but also as a whole by the ways in which the discourses are articulated together. There is little rigid separation in terms of the overall organization of the film between elements of narration, information, and interview, for example. Throughout, one discourse leads into, or is interrupted by, another—once more in the Brechtian manner.

Like *One Way Or Another*, *Whose Choice?* takes up familiar realist forms, and then deconstructs them by means of fragmentation and interruption, thereby transforming the spectator-text relations which would be privileged by each discourse on its own. This transformation marks a move away from identification, involvement, and suspension of disbelief and toward a more active and questioning attitude to the processes of signification of the film and to its areas of concern. If *One Way Or Another* deconstructs the conventions of Hollywood and socialist realist narrative and traditional documentary, *Whose Choice?* offers a challenge to the kinds of documentary address commonly associated with the agitational/

political film. The intended consequence of these deconstructive strategies is to open up space for active intervention on the part of spectators in the meaning production process, to subvert the completion and closure of meaning proposed by dominant cinema, and thus to offer spectators the opportunity to consider their positions on the issues at hand through their own processes of active reading, questioning, and discussion. The oppositional character of the forms of expression of deconstructive cinema thus ideally works in conjunction with its matters of expression. *One Way Or Another* presents itself as oppositional on a fairly general level—as an example of Third World cinema and as dealing with problems arising in a developing and revolutionary society. Its treatment of the personal and the familial underscores this oppositionality, for these concerns have frequently been repressed even in revolutionary cinema. *Whose Choice?* deals with a topic which is either repressed in dominant discourses or, if not actually repressed, treated from different political perspectives: the film may be regarded as oppositional by virtue of its treatment of contraception and abortion from a feminist standpoint.

Feminine Voices

A concern shared by feminist representations of many kinds and across all media is an intent to challenge dominant modes of representation. This concern is premised on the notion that in a sexist society, women have no language of their own and are therefore alienated from culturally dominant forms of expression. This permits a feminist politics of intervention at the levels of language and meaning, which may be regarded as equally applicable to the "language" of cinema as it is to the written and spoken word. A politics of this kind can have two aspects: it may on the one hand challenge the dominance of certain forms of signification, and on the other move toward the construction of new, non-dominant, forms. The latter, of course, includes the former, but also goes further by posing the possibility of a specifically feminist or feminine language. Deconstructive cinema, in taking up and breaking down dominant forms and matters of expression, operates predominantly as a challenge to dominant cinema. I want now to look at some signifying practices which may be regarded as moving beyond the modes of expression privileged within patriarchal ideology. The distinction between the deconstruction of existing forms of representation and the creation of new ones is to some extent one of degree rather than of kind. In the first place, deconstruction may be regarded as an important—and perhaps even a necessary—step toward more radical forms of rupture. And in any case, in a situation where certain forms of representation are culturally dominant, alternative forms—however radical and regardless of their actual textual operations and modes of address—will always tend to be construed as a challenge to dominant forms. It should be emphasized, then, that the films discussed in this context may also be read (and indeed most of them have been read) as examples of deconstructive cinema.

The issue of a non-patriarchal language immediately raises the question of the relationship between such a language and feminism. Although it is clear that the question of women and language could not be raised in the ways it has been without the impetus of feminist politics, the nature and provenance of such a language remains rather more problematic. Posing the question of a women's language may be a feminist act, but are we talking here about a feminist language or a feminine language? If the question is of a feminine language, where does such a language come from? I have discussed elsewhere certain theories of femininity and language which are being developed by feminist writers and theorists and will not repeat the arguments here, save to reiterate that they are grounded in theories of female subjectivity as constructed in and by language. To this extent, then, the concern is with feminine language rather than feminist language. And although the possibility of feminine language could not even begin to be raised were it not for the existence of feminist politics, the converse is not necessarily true. This point has to be borne in mind in any consideration of the possibility of "authentic" forms of expression for women, and it is certainly at issue in "feminine writing" in the cinema.

Arguments on the question of feminine writing suggest first of all that certain texts privilege relations of subjectivity which are radically "other" to the fixity of subject relations set up by dominant forms of signification, and secondly, that the "otherness" of such texts is related to, or emerges from, their articulation of feminine relations of subjectivity. This is perhaps the crucial point of distinction between deconstructive texts and feminine texts. Whereas the former tend to break down and challenge the forms of pleasure privileged by dominant texts, the latter set up radically "other" forms of pleasure (in Roland Barthes's term, *jouissance*, or bliss). The possibility of such "other" forms of pleasure in cinematic representations is raised in Laura Mulvey's theoretical work (as well as in her film practice, as co-director of *Riddles of the Sphinx* in particular). If the pleasure of dominant cinema draws on narcissistic and fetishistic scopophilia, Mulvey argues, any alternative approach needs to construct forms of pleasure based in different psychic relations.[7] A suggestion by Claire Johnston that a feminist film practice should aim at "putting . . . the subject in process by textual practice"[8] indicates moreover that what is at stake here is a feminine cinematic writing, a cinema of *jouissance*.

Certain recent film practices may in fact be read as developments in this direction, and in this context, I shall look at four specific examples: *Thriller* (Potter, Arts Council of Great Britain, 1979), *Lives of Performers* (Rainer, 1972), *Daughter Rite* (Citron, 1978) and *Jeanne Dielman, 23 Quai du Commerce, 1080 Bruxelles* (Akerman, Paradise Films/Unité Trois, 1975). My argument is that these films share a discourse which sets up the possibility of sexual difference in spectator-text relations by privileging a "feminine voice." They pose the possibility of a feminine writing which would construct new forms of pleasure in cinema. The areas through which the "feminine voice" speaks in these films include relations of looking, narrativity and narrative discourse, subjectivity and autobiography, fiction as against non-fiction, and openness as against closure.

Thriller is structured around a rearrangement of narrative discourse in dominant cinema by the instatement of a woman's questioning voice as the film's organizing principle. The film is a reworking of the opera *La Bohème*, which is about a doomed love affair between a poet and a young seamstress: the woman finally dies of consumption. *Thriller* is told from the narrative point-of-view of Mimi, the tragic heroine, whose interrogatory voice-over pervades the film. The enigma set up by the film's narrative is the question of how and why Mimi died, the investigator ("I") being Mimi herself. By its recruitment of investigatory narrative structure and first-person voice-over, *Thriller* at once draws upon, parodies, challenges, and transforms the narrative and cinematic codes of the Hollywood film noir. The female victim adds a twist to the reconstruction of her own death not only by telling the story herself, but also by considering causes for the unhappy romance and death of a young French working woman of a kind—social and historical conditions, for instance—that could not possibly enter the universe either of operatic tragedy or of the private investigator of film noir.

Lives of Performers is also, on one level, a reworking of the conventions of popular narrative genres. The film is subtitled "a melodrama," and the narrative conventions it draws on are those of the "backstage romance." In thirteen long sequences, it tells the story of the relationships between a man and two women, a triangle. The characters, however, are "playing" themselves—they are real-life performers in the group of dancers working with the filmmaker, Yvonne Rainer. The film departs quite radically from dominant conventions of film narrative in its ordering and structure, and in the freedom with which it articulates elements of fiction and non-fiction. The plot, for instance, proceeds by leaps and bounds punctuated by runnings on the spot—by ellipsis and accretion, in other words. Rainer says of her films: "For me the story is an empty frame on which to hang images and thoughts which need support. I feel no obligation to flesh out this armature with credible details of location and time."[9] The story of *Lives of Performers* is told with so many asides that we never quite get to the end or the bottom of it. There is no resolution. The "asides" are the accretions, and the accretions are so many that they seem to call forth gaps elsewhere in the story, as if to make up for lost time. The first sequence shows the performers, whose lives the melodrama is about, in rehearsal for what turns out to be a real-life Rainer performance. An intertitle: "all at once our tension vanished" leads into the next sequence, in which the three star performers "recall," as voice-over, their first meeting, with still photographs of Rainer's dance piece "Grand Union Dreams" on the image track. These recollections are punctuated at points by the filmmaker's explanations of what is going on in the photographs. Where does the "real" end and the "fiction" begin? The subsequent cinematic rendering of the romance is interrupted wherever "other concerns" seem more important—by a disquisition on acting, for example ("The face of this character is a fixed mask"), or a direct question to the spectator about the problem of character identification ("Which woman is the director most sympathetic to?" asks one of the women in the triangle, looking directly into camera). The narrative of *Lives of Performers* has its own logic, then, but it is not that of the enigma-resolution structure of classic narrative. Nor does it construct a closed and internally coherent fictional world: on the contrary, it opens itself up at numerous points to intrusions from the "real world."

What does this heterogeneous narrative voice imply for spectator-text relations? It is clear that none of the subject relations posed by classic narrative is at work here: identification with characters is impossible, and there is no narrative closure. The narrative processes of ellipsis and accretion offer, on the contrary, the possibility of pleasures other than those of completion. Firstly, in moments of accretion (for example, during a long single-take sequence with virtually static camera, in which one of the performers dances a solo), the spectator has the option of pleasurable and open-ended contemplation of an image which constructs no particularly privileged viewpoint. The ellipses offer the possibility of a rather different pleasure, that of piecing together fragments of the story—the active pleasure, that is, of working on a puzzle. The interpenetration of fictional and non-fictional worlds and the lack of narrative closure set up a radical heterogeneity in spectator-text relations, and finally refuse any space of unitary subjectivity for the spectator. The textual practice of *Lives of Performers* may then be regarded as a "putting in process of the viewing subject."

As part of its articulation of fiction and non-fiction, *Lives of Performers* includes, at times, discourses readable as autobiographical. The second sequence of the film, mentioned above, exemplifies this, and the autobiographical concern becomes more apparent in Rainer's next film, *Film About A Woman Who . . .* (1974). *Daughter Rite*, Michelle Citron's film about mother-daughter and sister-sister relations, is even more pervasively autobiographical, but whereas in Rainer's films, the would-be autobiographical material is somewhat distanced—it may be told in the third person, "she" instead of "I," or characters may be substituted for one another—the discourse of *Daughter Rite* seems more immediate and intimate: the autobiographical voice of the film, for example, is always the same and always speaks in the first person. Splitting in the film's discourse arises elsewhere, however, in the relationships between sound and image and in the juxtaposition of the film's different sequences. The film as a whole proceeds by alternations between sequences of "journal discourse" in which a woman (the filmmaker?) talks about her relationship with her mother, and sequences—marked cinematically as "direct" documentary—in which two sisters act out their relationships with one other and with their absent mother. In the "journal discourse," the image is composed of 8mm home movies, presumably of the speaker's childhood, optically printed on 16mm, and slowed down, looped, and replayed.

Previously, I discussed the autobiographical structure which is common to many feminist documentary films, and argued that the combination of autobiographical material with documentary codes permitted identification on the part of female spectators with the women in the films. *Daughter Rite* may be read as both drawing on and critiquing the autobiographical structures of these earlier examples of feminist filmmaking.[10] The directness and universality of the experience remains, particularly in the daughter's voice-over. But the film nevertheless adopts a quite complex and critical stance on the question of the "truthfulness" of autobiographical and documentary discourses. This is evident first of all in the sound/image relationship of the "journal" sequences. The daughter talks about her relationship with her mother by referring to events in the daughter's childhood. At the same time, the home movie footage, in depicting childhood scenes, may be read as "illustrating" the voice-over. The magnification and graininess of the image and its slow movement and repetitiousness suggest also a close scrutiny of the past for clues about the present. The irony is that however hard the image is examined for clues, it cannot in the end deliver the goods. The assumption that sound and image support one another is a trap. The spectator has to draw her own conclusions about, for instance, the laughing and smiling mother of the family world of the home movies—a world where the sun constantly shines and whose inhabitants are always on holiday—and the pitiful mother talked about on the soundtrack who "works so hard to fill her empty hours." The film's critical position in relation to autobiography, too, works in the articulation, the one interrupting the other, of the "journal" with the "sisters" sequences. The latter scenes, despite their "documentary" appearance, actually tread a borderline between fiction and non-fiction, as becomes apparent in the increasing unlikeliness of some of the situations acted out in them. The uncertainty evoked by this play of fiction and non-fiction may remain until the end of the film, when it is revealed in the credits that the "sisters" are in fact actresses.

Although at one level the articulation of the different discourses of *Daughter Rite* works to produce distance in the relation between spectator and text, the film is difficult to read purely as an example of deconstructive cinema. The distanciation, if such it is, is not that of the critical spectator of the Brechtian film. The subject matter and the intimacy of the address of *Daughter Rite* draw the spectator closely into the representation, in effect replicating the pain and ambivalence of our hostile and loving feelings towards those to whom we are closest, our mothers in particular. At the same time, its discourses open up space for an involved but critical approach to those feelings, a kind of detached passion. Moreover, if only by virtue of the kinds of issues it deals with, the film constructs an address which acknowledges sexual difference as crucial in the signification process. Male and female spectators will surely read this film differently. At the same time, the representation clearly constructs no unitary subjectivity for spectators of either gender. *Daughter Rite* appears to offer a relationship of spectator and text in which distanciation does not necessarily ensue from gaps between discourses, although an actively critical perspective might.

Jeanne Dielman . . . also invites a distanced involvement, but of a rather different kind. This 3½-hour long narrative film is a document of three days in the life of a Belgian petit-bourgeois widow, housewife and mother. Her movements around her flat, her performance of everyday chores, are documented with great precision: many of her tasks are filmed in real time. Jeanne's rigid routine includes a daily visit from a man—a different one each day—whose fees for her sexual services help maintain her and her son. The man's visit is slotted neatly between Jeanne's preparations for dinner and her son's arrival home. Every shot in the film is photographed at medium distance from its subject, with static camera mounted at about five feet from the ground. Many shots also work as autonomous sequences—a whole scene unfolds in a single take. There is thus none of the cutting back and forth characteristic of classic narrative. There are no reverse shots, match cuts, or cut-ins, for example, and camera point-of-view maintains a relentless distance from the action. These cinematic elements of *Jeanne Dielman . . .* function to establish the rhythm and order of Jeanne's repetitive household routines, the woman's means of maintaining control over her life. By the afternoon of the second day, the narrative has set up a series of clear expectations as to what Jeanne will do and when. At this point something (an orgasm with her second client?) provokes disorder in Jeanne's highly-structured world, and a series of parapraxes ensues. Jeanne forgets to comb her hair when the client leaves, she burns the potatoes, she leaves the lid off the tureen where she keeps her earnings. Erupting into Jeanne's ordered routine, and disrupting the expectations set up for the spectator by the cinematic representation of that routine, these tiny slips assume enormous and distressing proportions. *Jeanne Dielman . . .* can in some respects be read as a structural/minimalist film (like Michael Snow's *Wavelength*, for example), in that the nature and duration of the representation call on the spectator to work out the structures governing the film's organization, and thus eventually to predict what will happen next. Any disruption of these expectations can then seem quite violent. It is established, for instance, that Jeanne "always" gets up in the morning before her son, puts on a blue robe, and buttons it meticulously from top to bottom. On the third day, however, she misses a button, a slip which is immediately noticeable and assumes great significance—but the enunciation of the film nevertheless ensures that it is no more nor less significant than Jeanne's final "slip," the murder of her third client.

Jeanne Dielman . . . may be regarded as important in several ways for the question of feminine writing in cinema. Of particular significance are the qualities of the cinematic image and the relations of looking which it sets up. In the first place, the very fact that the film shows a woman doing housework sets *Jeanne Dielman . . .* apart from virtually all other fiction films. Domestic labor has probably never been documented in such painstaking detail in a fiction film: for example, one sequence-shot about five minutes in length shows Jeanne preparing a meat loaf for dinner on the third day. The positioning of the camera in relation to the profilmic event at the same time constructs the representations of the woman's routine work as "a discourse of women's looks, through a woman's viewpoint."[11] Chantal Akerman, the film's director, has said that the relatively low mounting of the camera corresponds with her own height and thus constructs a "woman's-eye-view" on the action. More important, perhaps, is the refusal to set up privileged points-of-view on the action by close-ups, cut-ins, and point-of-view shots. The relentless distance of the camera's (and the spectator's) look and the duration involved in representations of Jeanne's activities mean that "the fact of prostitution, the visualization of the murder, in some respects evens out into equal significance with the many conventionally less important images: Jeanne peeling potatoes; Jeanne kneading raw hamburger into a meat loaf."[12] Finally, the refusal of reverse shots in the film entails a denial of the "binding-in" effect of the suture of classic cinema: the spectator is forced to maintain a distance in relation to both narrative and image, constructing the story and building up narrative expectations for herself. The familiarity of Jeanne's tasks and the precision with which they are represented, combined with the refusal of suture, serve to free the look of the spectator while also, perhaps, shifting it toward the attitude of "passionate detachment" that Laura Mulvey speaks of.

These four films—*Thriller, Lives of Performers, Daughter Rite,* and *Jeanne Dielman . . .*—hold out the possibility of a "feminine language" for cinema, by offering unaccustomed forms of pleasure constructed around discourses governed either—quite literally—by a woman's voice, or by a feminine discourse that works through other cinematic signifiers. What I am suggesting is that although part of the project of feminine writing in cinema is obviously to offer a challenge to dominant modes of cinematic representation, its procedures for doing so go beyond deconstruction, in that their references to dominant cinema are oblique rather than direct. There are other differences, too, between deconstructive cinema and feminine cinematic writing. First, if it is accepted that feminine writing privileges heterogeneity and multiplicity of meanings in its modes of address, then it will have a tendency towards openness. The deconstructive text seems to work rather differently, however, in that although it too refuses the fixed subjectivity characteristic of classic spectator-text relations, meanings are limited by the fact that the various discourses of the text tend to work in concert with one another to "anchor" meaning. Thus although the spectator may be unsettled or distanced by epic interruptions, "acting as quotation," and so on, each of the fragmented discourses will tend to work in a common direction—in terms, certainly, of their matters of expression. It is perhaps no coincidence that both the examples of deconstructive cinema discussed here have highly circumscribed and predefined subject matters. The different discourses of the text may address these topics in different ways, but in the end there is a degree of overdetermination in the signification process. The space for active participation in the viewing process is opened up by the different modes of address of the discourses structuring the text, as well as by the ways in which they are articulated together. If, for example, *Whose Choice?* presents different discourses around its central concerns, those discourses when taken together constitute the film's subject matter in a particular way, so that the act of reading tends to be directed at differences of position and point of view on contraception and abortion between, say, the medical profession, the ordinary woman who requires an abortion, and feminists. It may therefore be concluded that deconstructive cinema can be tendentious, while at the same time allowing the spectator the space to negotiate her or his own position, but always in relation to a specific set of issues. If this is indeed the case, then a feminist deconstructive cinema is possible: feminist, that is, in its textual operations and matters of expression, and also feminist in intent.

I would argue, on the other hand, that tendentiousness and feminine cinematic writing do not necessarily go together. If the "femininity" of a film emerges in the moment of reading, then clearly the intentions of its producers are not necessarily either here or there. This is well illustrated in the case of *Lives of Performers*: although there is some uncertainty as to whether or not Rainer is actually a feminist,[13] it does seem clear that when she made *Lives of Performers* she did not consciously intend any specifically feminist input, either as "form" or as "content." And yet the film has been widely taken up by feminists. This suggest two things: first, that a text may be feminist, or of interest to feminists, without being tendentious, and second, that non-tendentious texts may be seized as feminist in the moment of reading. Rainer's films were made in the milieu of the New York *avant-garde* art scene, whose practices at the time generally had little connection with feminist politics. Rainer's films have, however, subsequently been taken up within other cultural milieux, notably among feminists, and read as being of feminist interest. The context within which such films are received is therefore obviously crucial for the meanings they can generate.

But this is not the whole story. It would surely be wrong to suggest that signifiers, even in "feminine" film texts, are completely free-floating: there are limitations to openness. Certain feminine film texts are not regarded as feminist simply because, by pure chance, they have been interpreted as such by certain audiences. Each of the films discussed here draws on certain matters of expression which, although not necessarily speaking feminist issues directly, may be regarded as doing so tangentially. Again, Yvonne Rainer's films usefully illustrate the point, precisely because Rainer's stance on feminism might problematize her films for those who want to claim them as feminist in intent. B. Ruby Rich, for example, argues that Rainer's work is central to feminism, not because of any intentionality on the part of the filmmaker, but because of the narrative conventions they take up and the modes of address they construct.[14] The "backstage romance" of *Lives of Performers* refers to a film genre that, in classic cinema, has been both attractive to and manipulative of women—the melodrama. The film offers both a pleasurable reworking and an ironic undercutting of this genre. The other three films I have discussed here similarly draw on, criticize, and transform the conventions of cultural expressions traditionally associated with women: *Thriller*, the melodramatic story of doomed love, *Daughter Rite*, autobiography and the "family romance," and *Jeanne Dielman . . .* , the family melodrama.

If deconstructive cinema sets up the possibility of an active spectator-text relation around a specific set of signifieds, and if feminine cinematic writing offers an openness of address in combination with matters of expression in relation to which spectators may situate themselves as women and/or as feminists, then clearly a feminist counter-cinema is not simply a matter of texts or "form plus content." In different ways and in varying degrees, the moment and conditions of reception of films are also crucial. The question of feminist counter-cinema is by no means exhausted by a discussion of feminist or feminine film texts: it has, in the final instance, to be considered also in terms of its institutional conditions of production and reception.

NOTES

1. Claire Johnston, "Introduction," in *Notes on Women's Cinema*, ed. Claire Johnston, London: Society for Education in Film and Television (1973), p. 2.

2. Pam Cook and Claire Johnston, "The Place of Women in the Cinema of Raoul Walsh," in *Raoul Walsh*, ed. Phil Hardy, Edinburgh: Edinburgh Film Festival (1974).

3. Johnston, "Introduction," p. 3.

4. Laura Mulvey, "Visual Pleasure and Narrative Cinema," *Screen* 16, no. 3 (1975), p. 17.

5. Walter Benjamin, *Understanding Brecht*, London: New Left Books (1973), p. 21.

6. Julia Lesage, "*One Way Or Another*: Dialectical, Revolutionary, Feminist," *Jump Cut*, no. 20 (1979), p. 21.

7. Mulvey.

8. Claire Johnston, "Towards a Feminist Film Practice: Some Theses," *Edinburgh Magazine*, no. 1 (1976), p. 58.

9. *Camera Obscura*, "Yvonne Rainer: An Introduction," *Camera Obscura*, no. 1 (1976), p. 89.

10. Jane Feuer, "*Daughter Rite*: Living with Our Pain and Love," *Jump Cut*, no. 23 (1980).

11. Janet Bergstrom, "*Jeanne Dielman, 23 Quai du Commerce, 1080 Bruxelles* by Chantal Akerman," *Camera Obscura*, no. 2 (1977), p. 118.

12. Ibid., p. 116.

13. Lucy Lippard, "Yvonne Rainer on Feminism and Her Film," in *From the Center: Feminist Essays on Women's Art*, New York: Dutton (1976); B. Ruby Rich, "The Films of Yvonne Rainer," *Chrysalis*, no. 2 (1977).

14. Ibid.

IN THE NAME OF FEMINIST FILM CRITICISM

B. Ruby Rich

> Whatever is unnamed, undepicted in images, whatever is omitted from biography, censored in collections of letters, whatever is misnamed as something else, made difficult-to-come-by, whatever is buried in the memory by the collapse of meaning under an inadequate or lying language—this will become, not merely unspoken, but unspeakable.
>
> —Adrienne Rich[1]

The situation for women working in filmmaking and film criticism today is precarious. While our work is no longer invisible, and not yet unspeakable, it still goes dangerously unnamed. There is even uncertainty over what name might characterize that intersection of cinema and the women's movement within which we labor, variously called "films by women," "feminist film," "images of women in film," or "women's films." All are vague and problematic. I see the lack of proper name here as symptomatic of a crisis in the ability of feminist film criticism thus far to come to terms with the work at hand, to apply a truly feminist criticism to the body of work already produced by women filmmakers. This crisis points to a real difference between the name "feminist" and the other names that have traditionally been applied to film (i.e., "structuralist" for certain avant-garde films or "melodrama" for certain Hollywood films).[2] "Feminist" is a name which may have only a marginal relation to the film text, describing more persuasively the context of social and political activity from which the work sprang. Such a difference is due, on the one hand, to a feminist recognition of the links tying a film's aesthetics to its modes of production and reception; and, on the other hand, to the particular history of the cinematic field which "feminist" came to designate—a field in which filmmaking-exhibition-criticism-distribution-audience have always been considered inextricably connected.

The History

The great contribution of feminism, as a body of thought, to culture in our time has been that it has something fairly direct to say, a quality all too rare today. And its equally crucial contribution, as a process and style, has been women's insistence on conducting the analysis, making the statements, in unsullied terms, in forms not already associated with the media's oppressiveness toward women. It is this freshness of discourse and distrust of traditional modes of articulation that placed feminist cinema in a singular position vis-à-vis both the dominant cinema and the avant-garde in the early 70s. By the "dominant," I mean Hollywood and all its corresponding manifestations in other cultures; but this could also be termed the Cinema of the Fathers. By the "avant-garde," I mean the experimental/personal cinema, which is positioned, by self-inclusion, within the art world; but this could also be termed the Cinema of the Sons. Being a business, the Cinema of the Fathers seeks to do only that which has been done before and proved successful. Being an art, the Cinema of the Sons seeks to do only that which has not been done before and so prove itself successful.

Into such a situation, at the start of the 70s, entered a feminist cinema. In place of the Fathers' bankruptcy of both form and content, there was a new and different energy; a cinema of immediacy and positive force now opposed the retreat into violence and the revival of a dead past which had become the dominant cinema's mainstays. In place of the Sons' increasing alienation and isolation, there was an entirely new sense of identification—with other women—and a corresponding commitment to communicate with this now-identifiable audience, a commitment which replaced, for feminist filmmakers, the elusive public ignored and frequently scorned by the male formalist filmmakers. Thus, from the start, its link to an evolving political movement gave feminist cinema a power and direction entirely unprecedented in independent filmmaking, bringing issues of theory/practice, aesthetics/meaning, process/representation into sharp focus.

Since the origin and development of feminist film work are largely unexamined, the following chronology sketches some of the major events of the 70s in North America and Great Britain. Three sorts of information are omitted as beyond the scope of this survey: (1) European festivals and publications, although some have been extremely significant; (2) beyond the first entry, the hundreds of films made by women during the decade; and (3) the publication in 1969–70 of key feminist writings such as *Sexual Politics*, *The Dialectic of Sex*, and *Sisterhood Is Powerful*, which must be remembered as the backdrop and theoretical impetus for these film activities.

1971: Release of *Growing Up Female*, *Janie's Janie*, *Three Lives*, and *The Woman's Film*: first generation of feminist documentaries.

1972: First New York International Festival of Women's Films and the Women's Event at Edinburgh Film Festival. First issue of *Women & Film* magazine; special issues on women and film in *Take One*, *Film Library Quarterly*, and *The Velvet Light Trap*; filmography of women directors in *Film Comment*.

1973: Toronto Women and Film Festival, Washington Women's Film Festival, season of women's cinema at National Film Theatre in London, and Buffalo women's film conference. Marjorie Rosen's *Popcorn Venus* (first book on women in film) and *Notes on Women's Cinema*, edited by Claire Johnston for British Film Institute (first anthology of feminist film theory).

1974: Chicago Films by Women Festival. First issue of *Jump Cut* (quarterly on contemporary film emphasizing feminist perspective); two books on images of women in film: Molly Haskell's *From Reverence to Rape* and Joan Mellen's *Women and Their Sexuality in the New Film*.

1975: Conference of Feminists in the Media, New York and Los Angeles. *Women & Film* ceases publication; *The Work of Dorothy Arzner* (BFI monograph edited by Johnston) and Sharon Smith's *Women Who Make Movies* (guide to women filmmakers).

1976: Second New York International Festival of Women's Films (smaller, noncollective, less successful than first) and Womanscene, a section of women's films in Toronto's Festival of Festivals (smaller, noncollective, but comparable in choices to 1973).

1977: First issue of *Camera Obscura* (journal of film theory founded largely by former *Women & Film* members, initially in opposition to it); Karyn Kay and Gerald Peary's *Women and the Cinema* (first anthology of criticism on women and film).

1978: *Women in Film Noir* (BFI anthology edited by E. Ann Kaplan); special feminist issues of *Quarterly Review of Film Studies* and *New German Critique*; Brandon French's *On the Verge of Revolt: Women in American Films of the Fifties* (study on images of women).

1979: Alternative Cinema Conference, bringing together over 100 feminists in the media for screenings, caucuses, and strategizing within the left; Feminism and Cinema Event at Edinburgh Film Festival, assessing the decade's filmmaking and theory and debating what might come next. Patricia Erens's *Sexual Stratagems: The World of Women in Film* (anthology on women and cinema).

It is immediately apparent from this chronology that the 1972–73 period marked a cultural watershed that has not since been equaled and that the unity, discovery, energy, and brave, we're-here-to-stay spirit of the early days underwent a definite shift in 1975, mid-decade. Since then, the field of vision has altered. There is increased specialization, both in the direction of genre studies (like film noir) and film theory (particularly semiotic and psychoanalytic); the start of sectarianism, with women partitioned off into enclaves defined by which conferences are attended or journals subscribed to; increased institutionalization, both of women's studies and cinema studies departments—twin creations of the 70s; a backlash emphasis on "human" liberation, which by making communication with men a priority can leave woman-to-woman feminism looking déclassé. Overall, there is a growing acceptance of feminist film as an area of study rather than as a sphere of action. And this may pull feminist film work away from its early political commitment, encompassing a wide social setting; away from issues of life that go beyond form; away from the combative (as an analysis of and weapon against patriarchal capitalism) into the merely representational.

The chronology also shows the initial cross-fertilization between the women's movement and cinema, which took place in the area of practice rather than in written criticism. The films came first. In fact, we find two different currents feeding into film work: one made up of women who were feminists and thereby led to film, the other made up of women already working in film and led therein to feminism. It was largely the first group of women who began making the films which were naturally named "feminist,"[3] and largely the second group of women, often in university film studies departments, who began holding the film festivals, just as naturally named "women and/in film." Spadework has continued in both directions, creating a new women's cinema and rediscovering the antecedents, with the two currents feeding our film criticism.

The past eight years have reduced some of the perils of which Adrienne Rich speaks. No longer are women "undepicted in images": even four years ago, Bonnie Dawson's *Women's Films in Print* could list over 800 available films by U.S. women alone, most depicting women. No longer are women omitted from all biography, nor are letters always censored. (In this respect, note the ongoing work of the four-woman collective engaged in "The Legend of Maya Deren Project" to document and demystify the life and work of a major, underacknowledged figure in American independent cinema.) No longer are women's films so hard to come by: the establishment of New Day Films (1972), the Serious Business Company (c. 1973–1983) and the Iris Films collective (1975) ensures the continuing distribution of films by or about women, although the chances of seeing any independently made features by women in a regular movie theatre are still predictably slim (with Jill Godmilow's *Antonia* and Claudia Weill's *Girlfriends* the only U.S. films to succeed so far). Returning to Rich's original warning, however, we reach the end of history's comforts and arrive at our present danger: "whatever is unnamed . . . buried in the memory by the collapse of meaning under an inadequate or lying language—this will become, not merely unspoken, but unspeakable." Herein lies the crisis facing feminist film criticism today; for after a decade of film practice and theory, we still lack our proper names. The impact of this lack on the films themselves is of immediate concern.

The Films

One classic film rediscovered through women's film festivals indicates the sort of misnaming prevalent in film history. Leontine Sagan's *Maedchen in Uniform*, a 1931 German film, details the relationship between a student and her teacher in a repressive girls' boarding school.[4] The act of naming is itself a pivotal moment in the narrative. Toward the end of the film, the schoolgirls gather at a drunken party after the annual school play. Manuela has just starred as a passionate youth and, drunk with punch, still in boy's clothing, she stands to proclaim her happiness and love—naming her teacher Fraulein von Bernburg as the woman she loves. Before this episode, the lesbian substructure of the school and the clearly shared knowledge of that substructure have been emphasized; the school laundress even points to the prevalence of the Fraulein's initials embroidered on the girls' regulation chemises as evidence of the adulation of her adolescent admirers. This eroticism was *not* in the closet. But only when Manuela stands and names that passion is she punished, locked up in solitary—for her speech, not for her actions.

Such is the power of a name and the valor of naming. It is ironic that the inscription of the power of naming within the film has not forestalled its own continuous misnaming within film history, which has championed its antifascism while masking the lesbian origins of that resistance. The problem is even more acute in dealing with contemporary films, where the lack of an adequate language has contributed to the invisibility of key aspects of our film culture—an invisibility advantageous to the existing film tradition.

> The women say, unhappy one, men have expelled you from the world of symbols and yet they have given you names . . . their authority to accord names . . . goes back so far that the origin of language itself may be considered an act of authority emanating from those who dominate . . . they have attached a particular word to an object or a fact and thereby consider themselves to have appropriated it. . . . The women say, the language you

> speak poisons your glottis tongue palate lips. They say, the language you speak is made up of words that are killing you . . . the language you speak is made up of signs that rightly speaking designate what men have appropriated. Whatever they have not laid hands on . . . does not appear in the language. This is apparent precisely in the intervals that your masters have not been able to fill with their words . . . this can be found in the gaps, in all that which is not a continuation of their discourse, in the zero. . . . (Monique Wittig)[5]

The act of misnaming functions not as an error, but as a strategy of the patriarchy. The lack of proper names facilitates derogatory name-calling; the failure to assign meaningful names to contemporary feminist films eases the acquisition of misnomers. Two key films of the 70s reveal this process and the disenfranchisement we suffer as a result.

Chantal Akerman's *Jeanne Dielman* (1975) is a chronicle of three days in the life of a Brussels housewife, a widow and mother who is also a prostitute. It is the first film to scrutinize housework in a language appropriate to the activity itself, showing a woman's activities in the home in real time to communicate the alienation of woman in the nuclear family under European post-war economic conditions. More than three hours in length and nearly devoid of dialogue, the film charts Jeanne Dielman's breakdown via a minute observation of her performance of household routines, at first methodical and unvarying, later increasingly disarranged, until by film's end she permanently disrupts the patriarchal order by murdering her third client. The film was scripted, directed, photographed, and edited by women with a consciously feminist sensibility.

The aesthetic repercussions of such a sensibility are evident throughout the film. For example, the choice of camera angle is unusually low. In interviews, Akerman explained that the camera was positioned at her own height; since she is quite short, the entire perspective of the film is different from what we are used to seeing, as shot by male cinematographers. The perspective of every frame thus reveals a female ordering of that space, prompting a reconsideration of point-of-view that I had felt before only in a few works shot by children (which expose the power of tall adults in every shot) and in the films by the Japanese director Yasujiro Ozu (where the low angle has been much discussed by Western critics as an entry into the "oriental" detachment of someone seated on a tatami mat, observing). Akerman's decision to employ only medium and long shots also stems from a feminist critique: the decision to free her character from the exploitation of a zoom lens and to grant her an integrity of private space usually denied in close-ups, thereby also freeing the audience from the insensitivity of a camera barreling in to magnify a woman's emotional crisis. Similarly, the activities of shopping, cooking, and cleaning the house are presented without ellipses, making visible the extent of time previously omitted from cinematic depictions. Thus, the film is a profoundly feminist work in theme, style, and representation; yet it has been critically received in language devoted to sanctifying aesthetics stripped of political consequence.

Shortly after *Jeanne Dielman's* premiere at the Cannes film festival, European critics extolled the film as "hyper-realist" in homage both to the realist film (and literary) tradition and to the super-realist movement in painting. Two problems arise with such a name: first, the tradition of cinematic realism has never included women in its alleged veracity; second, the comparison with super-realist painters obscures the contradiction between their illusionism and Akerman's anti-illusionism. Another name applied to *Jeanne Dielman* was "ethnographic," in keeping with the film's insistence on real-time presentation and non-elliptical editing. Again, the name negates a basic aspect by referring to a cinema of clinical observation, aimed at "objectivity" and noninvolvement, detached rather than engaged. The film's warm texture and Akerman's committed sympathies (the woman's gestures were borrowed from her own mother and aunt) make the name inappropriate.

The critical reception of the film in the *Soho Weekly News* by three different reviewers points up the confusion engendered by linguistic inadequacy.[6] Jonas Mekas questioned, "Why did she have to ruin the film by making the woman a prostitute and introduce a murder at the end, why did she commercialize it?" Later, praising most of the film as a successor to *Greed*, he contended that the heroine's silence was more "revolutionary" than the murder, making a case for the film's artistic merit as separate from its social context and moving the work into the area of existentialism at the expense of its feminism. Amy Taubin considered the film "theatrical" and, while commending the subjectivity of the camera-work and editing, she attacked the character of Jeanne: "Are we to generalize from Jeanne to the oppression of many women through their subjugation to activity which offers them no range of creative choice? If so, Jeanne Dielman's pathology mitigates against our willingness to generalize." By holding a reformist position (i.e., she should vary her menu, change her wardrobe) in relation to a revolutionary character (i.e., a murderer), Taubin was forced into a reading of the film limited by notions of realism that she, as an avant-garde film critic, would have ordinarily tried to avoid: her review split the film along the lines of form/content, annexing the aesthetics as "the real importance" and rejecting the character of Jeanne as a pathological woman. Again we find a notion of pure art set up in opposition to a feminism seemingly restricted to positive role models. Finally, Annette Michelson wrote a protest to Mekas which defended the film for "the sense of renewal it has brought both to a narrative mode and the inscription *within it* of feminist energies" (my italics). Yes, but at what cost? Here the effect of inadequate naming is precisely spelled out: the feminist energies are being spent to create work quickly absorbed into mainstream modes of art that renew themselves at our expense. Already, the renaissance of the "new narrative" is under way in film circles with nary a glance back at filmmakers like Akerman or Yvonne Rainer, who first incurred the wrath of the academy by reintroducing characters, emotions, and narratives into their films.

The critical response to Rainer's recent films, especially *Film about a Woman Who*, adds instances of naming malpractice.[7] Much of the criticism has been in the area of formal textual analysis, concentrating on the "post-modernist" structures, "Brechtian" distancing or cinematic deconstruction of the works. Continuing the tactic of detoxifying films via a divide-and-conquer criticism, critic Brian Henderson analyzed the central section in *Film about a Woman Who* according to a semiological model, detailing the five channels of communication used to present textual information.[8] The analysis was exhaustive on the level of technique but completely ignored the actual meaning of the information (Rainer's "emotional accretions")—the words themselves and the visualization (a man and woman on a stark bed/table). At the opposite extreme, a *Feminist Art Journal* editorial condemned Rainer as a modernist, "the epitome of the alienated artist," and discounted her film work as regressive for feminists, evidently because of its formal strategies.[9]

Rainer's films deal with the relations between the sexes and the interaction of life and art within a framework combining autobiography and fiction. Whatever the intent of Rainer's filmmaking in political terms, the work stands as a clear product of a feminist cultural milieu. The films deal explicitly with woman as victim and the burden of patriarchal mythology; they offer a critique of emotion, reworking melodrama for women today, and even (*Kristina Talking Pictures*) provide an elegy to the lost innocence of defined male/female roles. The structure of the themes gives priority to the issues over easy identification with the "characters" and involves the audience in an active analysis of emotional process. Yet little of the criticism has managed to reconcile an appreciation for the formal elements with an understanding of the feminist effect. Carol Wikarska, in a short review for *Women & Film*, could only paraphrase Rainer's own descriptions in a stab at *Film about a Woman Who* seen in purely art-world terms.[10] More critically, the feminist-defined film journal *Camera Obscura* concentrated its first issue on Rainer but fell into a similar quandary. While an interview with Rainer was included, the editors felt obliged to critique the films in the existing semiological vocabulary, taking its feminist value for granted without confronting the points of contradiction within that methodology. The lack of vocabulary once again frustrates a complete consideration of the work.

Lest the similarity of these misnamings merely suggest critical blindness rather than a more deliberate tactic, an ironic reversal is posed by the response to Anne Severson's *Near the Big Chakra*. Silent and in color, the film shows a series of 36 women's cunts photographed in unblinking close-up, some still and some moving, with no explanations or gratuitous presentation. Formally the film fits into the category of "structuralist" cinema: a straightforward listing of parts, no narrative, requisite attention to a predetermined and simplified structure, and fixed camera position (as defined by the namer—P. Adams Sitney). Yet Severson's image is so powerfully uncooptable that her film has never been called "structuralist" to my knowledge, nor—with retrospective revisionism—have her earlier films been so named. Evidently any subject matter that could make a man vomit (as happened at a London screening in 1973) is too much for the critical category, even though it was founded on the "irrelevance" of the visual images. Thus a name can be withheld by the critical establishment if its application alone won't make the film fit the category.

"Whatever they have not laid hands on . . . does not appear in the language you speak," wrote Monique Wittig. Here is the problem: not so much that certain names are used, but that other names are not—and therefore the qualities they describe are lost. Where patriarchal language holds sway, the silences, the characteristics that are unnamed, frequently hold the greatest potential strength. In Chantal Akerman's work, what is most valuable for us is her decoding of oppressive cinematic conventions and her invention of new codes of non-voyeuristic vision; yet these contributions go unnamed. In Yvonne Rainer's work, the issue is not one of this or that role model for feminists, not whether her women characters are too weak or too victimized or too individualistic. Rather, we can value precisely her refusal to pander (visually and emotionally), her frustration of audience expectation of spectacle (physical or psychic), and her complete reworking of traditional forms of melodrama and elegy to include modern feminist culture. Yet these elements, of greatest value to us, are not accorded critical priority.

The effect of not naming is censorship, whether caused by the imperialism of the patriarchal language or the underdevelopment of a feminist language. We need to begin analyzing our own films, but first it is necessary to learn to speak in our own name. The recent history of feminist film criticism indicates the urgency of that need.

"Feminist Film Criticism: In Two Voices"

There have been two types of feminist film criticism,[11] motivated by different geographical and ideological contexts, each speaking in a very different voice.

> History of philosophy has an obvious, repressive function in philosophy; it is philosophy's very own Oedipus. "All the same, you won't dare speak your own name as long as you have not read this and that, and that on this, and this on that. . . . To say something in one's own name is very strange." (Gilles Deleuze)[12]

Speaking in one's own name versus speaking in the name of history is a familiar problem to anyone who has ever pursued a course of study, become involved in an established discipline, and then tried to speak out of personal experience or nonprofessional/nonacademic knowledge without suddenly feeling quite schizophrenic. Obviously it is a schizophrenia especially familiar to feminists. The distinction between one's own voice and the voice of history is a handy one by which to distinguish the two types of feminist film criticism. At least initially, these two types could be characterized as either American or British: the one, American, seen as sociological or subjective, often a speaking out in one's own voice; the other, British, seen as methodological or more objective, often speaking in the voice of history. (The work of the past few years has blurred the original nationalist base of the categories: for example, the Parisian perspective of the California-based *Camera Obscura*.)

The originally American, so-called sociological, approach is exemplified by early *Women & Film* articles and much of the catalogue writing from festivals of that same period. The emphasis on legitimizing women's own reactions and making women's contributions visible resulted in a tendency toward reviews, getting information out, a tendency to offer testimony as theory. Fruitful in this terrain, the weakness of the approach became the limits of its introspection, the boundaries established by the lack of a coherent methodology for moving out beyond the self. An example of this approach would be Barbara Halpern Martineau's very eccentric, subjective, and illuminating analyses of Nelly Kaplan and Agnes Varda films.[13] A dismaying example of the decadent strain of this approach was Joan Mellen's mid-70s book *Big Bad Wolves*, which offered personal interpretations of male characters and actors in a move to shift attention to the reformist arena of "human liberation."

The originally British, so-called theoretical, approach is exemplified by the British Film Institute monograph on women and film (see above), by articles in *Screen*, and by the initial issues of *Camera Obscura* (which, like the British writing, defers to the French authorities). Committed to using some of the most advanced tools of critical analysis, like semiology and psychoanalysis, this approach has tried to come to terms with *how* films mean—to move beyond regarding the image to analyzing the structure, codes, the general subtext of the works. Fruitful for its findings regarding signification, the weakness of the approach has been its suppression of the personal and a seeming belief in the neutrality of the analytic tools, so that the critic's feminist voice has often been muted by this methodocracy. Two of the most important products of this approach are pieces by Laura Mulvey and Claire Johnston.[14] Johnston has critiqued the image of woman in male cinema and finds her to be a signifier, not of woman, but of the absent phallus, a signifier of an absence rather than any presence. Similarly, Mulvey has analyzed the nature of the cinematic spectator and finds evidence—in cinematic voyeurism and in the nature of the camera look—of the exclusively male spectator as a production assumption.

Another way of characterizing these two approaches would be to identify the American (sociological, or in one's own voice) as fundamentally phenomenological, and the British (theoretical, or the voice of history) as fundamentally analytical. Johnston and Mulvey's texts taken together, for example, pose a monumental absence that is unduly pessimistic. The misplaced pessimism stems from their overvaluation of the production aspect of cinema, a misassumption that cinematic values are irrevocably embedded at the level of production and, once there, remain pernicious and inviolable. Woman is absent on the screen and she is absent in the audience, their analysis argues. And yet here a bit of phenomenology would be helpful, a moment of speaking in one's own voice and wondering at the source in such a landscape of absence. As a woman sitting in the dark, watching that film made by and for men with drag queens on the screen, what is my experience? Don't I in fact interact with that text and that context, with a conspicuous absence of passivity? For a woman's experiencing of culture under patriarchy is dialectical in a way that a man's can never be: our experience is like that of the exile, whom Brecht once singled out as the ultimate dialectician for that daily working out of cultural oppositions within a single body. It is crucial to emphasize here the possibility for texts to be transformed at the level of reception and not to fall into a trap of condescension toward our own developed powers as active producers of meaning.

The differences implicit in these two attitudes lead to quite different positions and strategies, as the following selection of quotations helps to point up.[15] When interviewed regarding the reason for choosing her specific critical tools (auteurist, structuralist, psychoanalytic), Claire Johnston replied: "As far as I'm concerned, it's a question of what is theoretically correct; these new theoretical developments cannot be ignored, just as feminists cannot ignore Marx or Freud, because they represent crucial scientific developments." In contrast to this vision of science as ideologically neutral would be the reiteration by such theoreticians as Adrienne Rich and Mary Daly that "you have to be constantly critiquing even the tools you use to explore and define what it is to be female." In the same interview as Johnston, Pam Cook elaborated their aim as: "Women are fixed in ideology in a particular way, which is definable in terms of the patriarchal system. I think we see our first need as primarily to define that place—the place that women are fixed in." In marked contrast to such a sphere of activity, the Womanifesto of the 1975 New York Conference of Feminists in the Media stated: "We do not accept the existing power structure and we are committed to changing it by the content and structure of our images and by the ways we relate to each other in our work and with our audience." In her own article, Laura Mulvey identified the advantage of psychoanalytic critiques as their ability to "advance our understanding of the status quo," a limited and modest claim; yet she herself went beyond such a goal in making (with Peter Wollen) *The Riddles of the Sphinx*, a film which in its refusal of patriarchal codes and feminist concerns represented in fact a Part Two of her original theory.

I have termed the British approach pessimistic, a quality which may be perceived by supporters as realistic or by detractors as colonized. I have termed the American approach optimistic, a quality which may be viewed by supporters as radical or by detractors as unrealistic, utopian. It is not surprising, however, that such a dualism of critical approach has evolved. In *Woman's Consciousness, Man's World*, Sheila Rowbotham points out:

> There is a long inchoate period during which the struggle between the language of experience and the language of theory becomes a kind of agony.[16]

It is a problem common to an oppressed people at the point of formulating a new language with which to name that oppression, for the history of oppression has prevented the development of any unified language among its subjects. It is crucial for those of us working in the area of feminist film criticism to mend this rift, confront the agony, and begin developing a synthesis of maximally effective critical practice. Without names, our work remains anonymous, insecure, our continued visibility questionable.

Anticlimax: The Names

Without new names, we run the danger of losing title to films that we sorely need. By stretching the name "feminist" beyond all reasonable elasticity, we contribute to its ultimate impoverishment. At the same time, so many films have been partitioned off to established traditions, with the implication that these other names contradict or forestall any application of the name "feminist" to the works so annexed, that the domain of "feminist" cinema is fast becoming limited to that work concerned only with feminism as explicit subject matter. "Feminist," if it is to make a comeback from the loss of meaning caused by its all-encompassing overuse, requires new legions of names to preserve for us the inner strengths, the not-yet-visible qualities of these films still lacking in definition.

Because this need is so very urgent, I here offer an experimental glossary of names as an aid to initiating a new stage of feminist criticism. These names are not likely to be an immediate hit. First of all, it's all well and good to call for new names to appear in the night sky like so many constellations, but it's quite another thing to invent them and commit them to paper. Second, there's the inevitable contradiction of complaining about names and then committing more naming acts. Third, there's the danger that, however unwieldy, these new names might be taken as formulas to be applied willy-nilly to every hapless film that comes our way. The point, after all, is not to set up new power institutions (feminist banks, feminist popes, feminist names) but rather to open the mind to new descriptive possibilities. Not to require alternate glossaries of Talmudic herstory, but to suggest the revolutionary possibilities of non-patriarchal, non-capitalist imaginings.

Validative

One of feminist filmmaking's greatest contributions is the body of films about women's lives, political struggles, organizing, etc. These films have been vaguely classified under the *cinéma vérité* banner, where they reside in decidedly mixed company. Since they function as a validation and legitimation of women's culture and individual lives, the name "validative" would be a better choice. It has the added advantage of aligning the work with products of oppressed peoples (with the filmmaker as insider), whereas the *cinéma vérité* label represents the oppressors, who make films as superior outsiders documenting alien, implicitly inferior cultures, often from a position of condescension. The feminist films of the early 70s were validative, and validative films continue to be an important component of feminist filmmaking. They may be ethnographic, documenting the evolution of women's lives and issues (as in *We're Alive*, a portrait and analysis of women in prison) or archaeological, uncovering women's hidden past (as in *Union Maids*, with its recovery of women's role in the labor movement, or Sylvia Morales's *Chicana*, the first film history of the Mexican-American woman's struggle). The form is well established, yet the constantly evolving issues require new films, such as *We Will Not Be Beaten*, a film on domestic violence culled from videotaped interviews with women. By employing the name "validative" in place of *cinéma vérité*, we can combat the patriarchal annexation of the woman filmmaker as one of the boys, i.e., as a professional who is not *of* the culture being filmed. It is a unifying name aimed at conserving strength.

Correspondence

A different name is necessary for more avant-garde films, like those of Yvonne Rainer, Chantal Akerman, Helke Sander, or Laura Mulvey/Peter Wollen. Looking to literary history, we find a concern with the role played by letters ("personal" discourse) as a sustaining mode for women's writing during times of literary repression. The publication of historical letters by famous and ordinary women has been a major component of the feminist publishing renaissance, just as the long-standing denigration of the genre as not "real" writing (i.e., not certified by either a publishing house or monetary exchange) has been an additional goad for the creation of feminist alternatives to the literary establishment. A cinema of "correspondence" is a fitting homage to this tradition of introspective missives sent out into the world. Equally relevant is the other definition of "correspondence" as "mutual response, the answering of things to each other," or, to take Swedenborg's literal Doctrine of Correspondence as an example, the tenet that "every natural object symbolizes or corresponds to some spiritual fact or principle which is, as it were, its archetype."[17] Films of correspondence, then, would be those investigating correspondences, i.e., between emotion and objectivity, narrative and deconstruction, art and ideology. Thus *Jeanne Dielman* is a film of correspondence in its exploration of the bonds between housework and madness, prostitution and heterosexuality, epic and dramatic temporality.

What distinguishes such films of correspondence from formally similar films by male avant-garde filmmakers is their inclusion of the author within the text. *Film about a Woman Who* corresponds to very clear experiences and emotional concerns in Rainer's life and *Jeanne Dielman* draws on the gestures of the women in Akerman's family, whereas Michael Snow's *Rameau's Nephew* uses the form to suppress the author's presence. (Of course, there is a tradition of "diary" movies by men as well as women, but, significantly, the presence of Jonas Mekas in most of his diary films—like that of Godard in *Numéro deux*—is of the filmmaker rather than the "man" outside that professional role.) Similarly, Helke Sander in *The All Around Reduced Personality* revises the ironic, distanced narration of modernist German cinema to include the filmmaker in a same first-person-plural with her characters, unlike her compatriot Alexander Kluge, who always remains external and superior to his characters. It is this resolute correspondence between form and content, to put it bluntly, that distinguishes the films of correspondence. Such films are essential to the development of new structures and forms for the creation and communication of feminist works and values; more experimental than validative, they are laying the groundwork of a feminist cinematic vocabulary.

Reconstructive

Several recent films suggest another name, located midway between the two described above, and dealing directly with issues of form posed by the political and emotional concerns of the work. One such film is Sally Potter's *Thriller*, a feminist murder mystery related as a first-person inquiry by the victim: Mimi, the seamstress of Puccini's *La Bohème*, investigates the cause of her death and the manner of her life, uncovering in the process the contradictions hidden by the bourgeois male artist. Michelle Citron's *Daughter Rite* probes relations between women in the family, using dramatic sequences to critique *cinéma vérité* and optical printing to reexamine home movies, that U.S. index to domestic history. Both *Thriller* and *Daughter Rite* are reconstructive in their rebuilding of other forms, whether grand opera or soap opera, according to feminist specifications. At the same time both Potter and Citron reconstruct some basic cinematic styles (psychodrama, documentary) to create new feminist forms, in harmony with the desires of the audience as well as the theoretical concerns of the filmmakers. By reconstructing forms in a constructive manner, these films build bridges between the needs of women and the goals of art.

Medusan

Humor should not be overlooked as a weapon of great power. Comedy requires further cultivation for its revolutionary potential as a deflator of the patriarchal order and an extraordinary leveler and reinventor of dramatic structure. An acknowledgment of the subversive power of humor, the name "Medusan" is taken from Hélène Cixous's "The Laugh of the Medusa," in which she celebrates the potential of feminist texts "to blow up the law, to break up the 'truth' with laughter."[18] Cixous's contention that when women confront the figure of Medusa she will be laughing is a rejoinder to Freud's posing the "Medusa's head" as an incarnation of male castration fears. For Cixous, women are having the last laugh. And, to be sure, all the films in this camp deal with combinations of humor and sexuality. Vera Chytilova's *Daisies* was one of the first films by a woman to move in the direction of anarchic sexuality, though its disruptive humor was received largely as slapstick at the time. Nelly Kaplan's two films, *A Very Curious Girl* and *Nea*, also offer an explosive humor coupled with sexuality to discomfort patriarchal society (even though her fondness for "happy" endings that restore order has discomfited many feminist critics). Jan Oxenberg's *A Comedy in Six Unnatural Acts* is an excellent recent example of a Medusan film, attacking not just men or sexism but the heterosexually defined stereotypes of lesbianism; its success has been demonstrated by its raucous cult reception and, more pointedly, by its tendency to polarize a mixed audience along the lines not of class but of sexual preference. It is disruptive of homophobic complacency with a force never approached by analytical films defending lesbianism. Another highly Medusan film is Jacques Rivette's *Celine and Julie Go Boating* (which may be curious, as it is directed by a man, but production credits indicate a total collaboration with the four actresses and co-scenarists). Celine and Julie enter each other's lives by magic and books, joined in a unity of farce; once they are together, each proceeds to demolish the other's ties to men (an employer, a childhood lover) by using humor, laughing in the face of male fantasies and expectations and thus "spoiling" the relationships with a fungus of parody. The film has been criticized as silly, for Juliet Berto and Dominique Labourier do laugh constantly—at the other characters, themselves, the audience, acting itself—yet their laughter ultimately proves their finest arsenal, enabling them to rescue the plot's girlchild from a darkly imminent Henry Jamesian destruction simply through a laughing refusal to obey its allegedly binding rules. Again, *Celine and Julie* has consistently divided its audience according to whom it threatens: it has become a cult feminist movie even as the male critical establishment (except for Rivette fan Jonathan Rosenbaum) has denounced the film as silly, belabored, too obvious, etc.

Corrective Realism

As mentioned earlier, the tradition of realism in the cinema has never done well by women. Indeed, extolling realism to women is rather like praising the criminal to the victim, so thoroughly have women been falsified under its banner. A feminist feature cinema, generally representational, is now developing with a regular cast of actresses, a story line, aimed at a wide audience and generally accepting of many cinematic conventions. The women making these films, however, are so thoroughly transforming the characterizations and the narrative workings of traditional realism that they have created a new feminist cinema of "corrective realism." Thus, in Margarethe von Trotta's *The Second Awakening of Christa Klages*, it is the women's actions that advance the narrative; bonding between women functions to save, not to paralyze or trap, the characters; running away brings Christa freedom, while holding his ground brings her male lover only death. The film has outrageously inventive character details, an attention to the minutiae of daily life, an endorsement of emotion and intuitive ties, and an infectious humor. Marta Meszaros's *Women* presents a profound reworking of socialist realism in its depiction of the friendship between two women in a Hungarian work hostel. The alternating close-ups and medium shots become a means of social critique, while the more traditional portrayal of the growing intimacy between the two women insistently places emotional concerns at the center of the film. Both films successfully adapt an existing cinematic tradition to feminist purposes, going far beyond a simple "positive role model" in their establishment of a feminist cinematic environment within which to envision their female protagonists and their activities.

These, then, are a few of the naming possibilities. However, it is not only the feminist films that demand new names, but also (for clarity) the films being made by men about women.

Projectile

One name resurrected from the 50s by 70s criticism was Molly Haskell's recoining of the "woman's film," the matinee melodramas which, cleared of pejorative connotations, were refitted for relevance to women's cinematic concerns today. Wishful thinking. The name was Hollywood's and there it stays, demonstrated by the new "woman's films" that are pushing actual women's films off the screen, out into the dark. These are male fantasies of women—men's projections of themselves and their fears onto female characters. The name "projectile" identifies these films' true nature and gives an added awareness of the destructive impact of male illusions on the female audience. It is time the bluff was called on the touted authenticity of these works, which pose as objective while remaining entirely subjective in their conception and execution. The clearest justification for this name can be found in director Paul Mazursky's description of his *An Unmarried Woman*: "I don't know if this is a woman's movie or not. I don't know what that means anymore. . . . I wanted to get inside a woman's head. I've felt that all the pictures I've done, I've done with men. I put myself inside a man's head, using myself a lot. I wanted this time to think like a woman. That's one of the reasons there was so much rewriting. . . . There were many things the women I cast in the film . . . wouldn't say. They'd tell me why, and I'd say, 'Well, what would you say?' and I'd let them say that. I used a real therapist; I wanted a woman, and I had to change what she said based on what she is. In other words, the only thing I could have done was to get a woman to help me write it. I thought about that for a while, but in the end I think it worked out."[19] Films such as this one (and *The Turning Point*, *Pretty Baby*, *Luna*, and so on ad infinitum) are aimed fatally at us; they deserve to be named "projectile."

Certainly the names offered here do not cover all possibilities, nor can every film be fitted neatly into one category. But I hope their relative usefulness or failings will prompt a continuation of the process by others. The urgency of the naming task cannot be overstated.

Warning Signs: A Postscript

We are now in a period of normalization, a time that can offer feminists complacency as a mask for co-option. Scanning the horizon for signs of backlash and propaganda, we see the storm clouds within feminist film criticism are gathering most clearly over issues of form.

It has become a truism to call for new forms. Over and over, we have heard the sacred vows: you can't put new revolutionary subjects/messages into reactionary forms; new forms, a new anti-patriarchal film language for feminist cinema, must be developed. While certainly true to an extent, form remains only one element of the work. And the valorization of form above and independent of other criteria has begun to create its own problems.

There is the misconception that form, unlike subject matter, is inviolate and can somehow encase the meaning in protective armor. But form is as co-optable as other elements. A recent analysis by critic Julianne Burton of the *cinema novo* movement in Brazil raised this exact point by demonstrating how the Brazilian state film apparatus took over the forms and styles of *cinema novo* and stripped them of their ideological significance as one means of disarming the movement.[20] If we fetishize the long take, the unmediated shot, etc., as feminist per se, then we will shortly be at a loss over how to evaluate the facsimiles proliferating in the wake of such a definition. Furthermore, the reliance on form as the ultimate gauge of a film's worth sets up an inevitable hierarchy that places reconstructive films or films of correspondence at the top of a pyramid, leaving corrective realist or validative approaches among the baser elements. This itself is a complex problem. First, such a view reproduces the notion of history as "progress" and supposes that forms, like technology, grow cumulatively better and better; some believe in that sort of linear quality, but I don't. Second, recent criticism by Christine Gledhill (of film) and Myra Love (of literature) has questioned the naturalness of the Brechtian, post-modernist, deconstructive model as a feminist strategy, pointing out the real drawbacks of its endemic authoritarianism and ambiguity.[21] Third, our very reasons for supporting such work must at least be examined honestly. Carolyn Heilbrun's point should be well taken: "critics, and particularly academics, are understandably prone to admire and overvalue the carefully construed, almost puzzlelike novel [read: film], not only for its profundities, but because it provides them, in explication, with their livelihood."[22] Just as a generosity of criticism can provide the strongest support for feminist filmmakers, so acceptance of a variety of filmic strategies can provide the vigor needed by the feminist audience.

For we must look to the filmmaker and viewer for a way out of this aesthetic cul-de-sac. Aesthetics are not eternally embedded in a work like a penny in a cube of Lucite. They are dependent on and subject to the work's reception. The formal values of a film cannot be considered in isolation, cut off from the thematic correspondents within the text and from the social determinants without. Reception by viewers as well as by critics is key to any film's meaning. As my chronology indicates, feminist cinema arose out of a need not only on the part of the filmmakers and writers, but on the part of the women they knew to be their audience. Today we must constantly check feminist film work to gauge how alive this thread of connection still is, how communicable its feminist values are. We are in a time of transition now, when we still have the luxury of enjoying feminist work on its makers' own terms, without having to sift the sands paranoically for impostors. But this transitional period is running out: as the cultural lag catches up, the dominant and avant-garde cinema may begin to incorporate feminist success before we recognize what we've lost. The emphasis on form makes that incorporation easier. Burton ended her article with a call for the inscription of modes of production within the body of Third World film criticism. Therein lies a clue. Feminism has always emphasized process; now it's time that this process of production and reception be inscribed within the critical text. How was the film made? With what intention? With what kind of crew? With what relationship to the subject? How was it produced? Who is distributing it? Where is it being shown? For what audience is it constructed? How is it available? How is it being received? There is no need to establish a tyranny of the productive sphere over a film's definition, nor to authorize only immediately popular films, but it will prove helpful in the difficult times ahead of us to keep this bottom line of method and context in mind, to avoid painting ourselves into a corner.

Formal devices are progressive only if they are employed with a goal beyond aesthetics alone. Here, finally, is the end of the line. Feminist film criticism cannot solve problems still undefined in the sphere of feminist thought and activity at large. We all are continually borrowing from and adding to each other's ideas, energies, insights, across disciplines. We also need to develop lines of communication across the boundaries of race, class, and sexuality. Last year in Cuba, I heard a presentation by Alfredo Guevara, founder and director of the Cuban Film Institute. He explained its efforts to educate the Cuban audience to the tricks of cinema, to demystify the technology, to give the viewers the means with which to defend themselves against cinematic hypnosis, to challenge the dominant ideology of world cinema, to create a new liberated generation of film viewers. I will never forget his next words: "We do not claim to have created this audience already, nor do we think it is a task only of cinema." The crisis of naming requires more than an etymologist to solve it.

NOTES

Many of the ideas in the section on "The Names" originated in the context of a germinative discussion published as "Women and Film: A Discussion of Feminist Aesthetics," *New German Critique*, no. 13 (1978), pp. 83–107. I am grateful to the other participants in that discussion, including Michelle Citron, Julia Lesage, Judith Mayne, Anna Marie Taylor, and the three *New German Critique* editors, for their support. This piece has been strengthened by the opportunity to test my new ideas in a winter program at the Walker Art Center, Minneapolis, and at the 1979 Edinburgh Film Festival's Feminism and Cinema Event, where the last section on "Warning Signs" comprised a portion of my talk.

1. Adrienne Rich, "It is the Lesbian in Us," *Sinister Wisdom*, no. 3 (1977) and "The Transformation of Silence into Language and Action," *Sinister Wisdom*, no. 6 (1978). See also Mary Daly, *Beyond God the Father*, Boston: Beacon Press (1973) for her pioneering analysis of naming as power.

2. "Melodrama" and "structuralist" cinema were the two names analyzed in papers presented by my co-panelists, William Horrigan and Bruce Jenkins, at the 1978 Purdue Conference on Film, where the ideas in this paper were first presented.

3. Women artists working in film continued, as before, to make avant-garde films, but those without feminist material lie outside my present concerns.

4. For a fuller discussion of the film, see my "*Maedchen in Uniform*: From Repressive Tolerance to Erotic Liberation," *Jump Cut*, nos. 24–25 (1981).

5. Monique Wittig, *Les Guérillères*, New York: Avon (1973), pp. 112–14.

6. See *Soho Weekly News*, November 18 (p. 36), November 25 (p. 31), and December 9 (p. 35), all 1976.

7. See also my article, "The Films of Yvonne Rainer," *Chrysalis*, no. 2 (1977).

8. Presented at the International Symposium of Film Theory and Practical Criticism, Center for 20th-Century Studies, University of Wisconsin-Milwaukee, in 1975.

9. Cindy Nemser, "Editorial: Rainer and Rothschild, an Overview," *Feminist Art Journal* 4, no. 2 (1975): 4. The same issue contained Lucy Lippard's "Yvonne Rainer on Feminism and Her Film." Lippard, however, is the exception in her ability to handle both the formal value and feminist strengths of Rainer's work.

10. *Women & Film*. no. 7, p. 86; also *Camera Obscura*, no. 1 (1977).

11. Here I am considering only English-language feminist film criticism; there are other complex issues in French and German criticism, for example.

12. Gilles Deleuze, "I Have Nothing To Admit," *Semiotexte*, no. 6 (1977), p. 112.

13. See Barbara Halpern Martineau, "Nelly Kaplan" and "Subjecting Her Objectification, or Communism Is Not Enough" in *Notes On Women's Cinema*, ed. Claire Johnston, London: Society for Education in Film and Television (1973).

14. See Claire Johnston, "Women's Cinema as Counter-Cinema" in *Notes on Women's Cinema* and Laura Mulvey, "Visual Pleasure and Narrative Cinema" in *Women and the Cinema*, ed. Karyn Kay and Gerald Peary, New York: Dutton (1977), pp. 412–28, and reprinted in this volume.

15. Quotations are taken from: E. Ann Kaplan, "Interview with British Cine-Feminists" in *Women and the Cinema*, pp. 400–401; Barbara Charlesworth Gelpi and Albert Gelpi, *Adrienne Rich's Poetry*, New York: Norton (1975), p. 115; Barbara Halpern Martineau, "Paris/Chicago" in *Women & Film*, no. 7, p. 11; Laura Mulvey, "Visual Pleasure and Narrative Cinema" (op. cit.), p. 414, as well as personal communications. See also E. Ann Kaplan, "Aspects of British Feminist Film Theory" in *Jump Cut*, nos. 12–13, for an in-depth examination of the British theories and their implications.

16. Sheila Rowbotham, *Woman's Consciousness, Man's World*, London: Penguin (1973), p. 33. See also her statement (p. 32) that language always is "carefully guarded by the superior people because it is one of the means through which they conserve their supremacy."

17. *The Compact Edition of the Oxford English Dictionary*.

18. Hélène Cixous, "The Laugh of the Medusa," *Signs* 1, no. 4 (1976): 888.

19. "Paul Mazursky Interviewed by Terry Curtis Fox," *Film Comment* 14, no. 2 (1978): 30–31.

20. These remarks by Burton are taken from memory of her talk at the 1979 Purdue Conference on Film. As stated, they are a simplification of complexities that she was at pains to elucidate without distortion.

21. Christine Gledhill, "Recent Developments in Feminist Criticism," *Quarterly Review of Film Studies* 3, no. 4 (1979); and Myra Love, "Christa Wolf and Feminism: Breaking the Patriarchal Connection," *New German Critique*, no. 17 (1979).

22. Carolyn G. Heilbrun, Introduction to May Sarton, *Mrs. Steven Hears the Mermaids Singing*, New York: Norton (1974), p. xii.

RETHINKING WOMEN'S CINEMA
AESTHETICS AND FEMINIST THEORY

Teresa de Lauretis

When Silvia Bovenschen in 1976 posed the question "Is there a feminine aesthetic?" the only answer she could give was, yes and no: "Certainly there is, if one is talking about aesthetic awareness and modes of sensory perception. Certainly not, if one is talking about an unusual variant of artistic production or about a painstakingly constructed theory of art."[1] If this contradiction seems familiar to anyone even vaguely acquainted with the development of feminist thought over the past fifteen years, it is because it echoes a contradiction specific to, and perhaps even constitutive of, the women's movement itself: a twofold pressure, a simultaneous pull in opposite directions, a tension toward the positivity of politics, or affirmative action in behalf of women as social subjects, on one front, and the negativity inherent in the radical critique of patriarchal, bourgeois culture, on the other. It is also the contradiction of women in language, as we attempt to speak as subjects of discourses which negate or objectify us through their representations. As Bovenschen put it, "We are in a terrible bind. How do we speak? In what categories do we think? Is even logic a bit of virile trickery? . . . Are our desires and notions of happiness so far removed from cultural traditions and models?" (p. 119).

Not surprisingly, therefore, a similar contradiction was also central to the debate on women's cinema, its politics and its language, as it was articulated within Anglo-American film theory in the early 1970s in relation to feminist politics and the women's movement, on the one hand, and to artistic avant-garde practices and women's filmmaking, on the other. There, too, the accounts of feminist film culture produced in the mid- to late seventies tended to emphasize a dichotomy between two concerns of the women's movement and two types of film work that seemed to be at odds with each other: one called for immediate documentation for purposes of political activism, consciousness raising, self-expression, or the search for "positive images" of woman; the other insisted on rigorous, formal work on the medium—or, better, the cinematic apparatus, understood as a social technology—in order to analyze and disengage the ideological codes embedded in representation.

Thus, as Bovenschen deplores the "opposition between feminist demands and artistic production" (p. 131), the tug of war in which women artists were caught between the movement's demands that women's art portray women's activities, document demonstrations, etc., and the formal demands of "artistic activity and its concrete work with material and media"; so does Laura Mulvey set out two successive moments of feminist film culture. First, she states, there was a period marked by the effort to change the *content* of cinematic representation (to present realistic images of women, to record women talking about their real-life experiences), a period "characterized by a mixture of consciousness-raising and propaganda."[2] It was followed by a second moment, in which the concern with the language of representation as such became predominant, and the "fascination with the cinematic process" led filmmakers and critics to the "use of and interest in the aesthetic principles and terms of reference provided by the avant-garde tradition" (p. 7).

In this latter period, the common interest of both avant-garde cinema and feminism in the politics of images, or the political dimension of aesthetic expression, made them turn to the theoretical debates on language and imaging that were going on outside of cinema, in semiotics, psychoanalysis, critical theory, and the theory of ideology. Thus, it was argued that, in order to counter the aesthetic of realism, which was hopelessly compromised with bourgeois ideology, as well as Hollywood cinema, avant-garde and feminist filmmakers must take an oppositional stance against narrative "illusionism" and in favor of formalism. The assumption was that "foregrounding the process itself, privileging the signifier, necessarily disrupts aesthetic unity and forces the spectator's attention on the means of production of meaning" (p. 7).

While Bovenschen and Mulvey would not relinquish the political commitment of the movement and the need to construct other representations of woman, the way in which they posed the question of expression (a "feminine aesthetic," a "new language of desire") was couched in the terms of a traditional notion of art, specifically the one propounded by modernist aesthetics. Bovenschen's insight that what is being expressed in the decoration of the household and the body, or in letters and other private forms of writing, is in fact women's aesthetic needs and impulses, is a crucial one. But the importance of that insight is undercut by the very terms that define it: the "*pre*-aesthetic realms." After quoting a passage from Sylvia Plath's *The Bell Jar*, Bovenschen comments:

> Here the ambivalence one again: on the one hand we see aesthetic activity deformed, atrophied, but on the other we find, even within this restricted scope, socially creative impulses which, however, have no outlet for aes-

> thetic development, no opportunities for growth. . . . [These activities] remained bound to everyday life, feeble attempts to make this sphere more aesthetically pleasing. But the price for this was narrowmindedness. The object could never leave the realm in which it came into being, it remained tied to the household, it could never break loose and initiate communication. (pp. 132–33)

Just as Plath laments that Mrs. Willard's beautiful home-braided rug is not hung on the wall but put to the use for which it was made, and thus quickly spoiled of its beauty, so would Bovenschen have "the object" of artistic creation leave its context of production and use value in order to enter the "artistic realm" and so to "initiate communication"; that is to say, to enter the museum, the art gallery, the market. In other words, art is what is enjoyed publicly rather than privately, has an exchange value rather than a use value, and that value is conferred by socially established aesthetic canons.

Mulvey, too, in proposing the destruction of narrative and visual pleasure as the foremost objective of women's cinema, hails an established tradition, albeit a radical one: the historic left avant-garde tradition that goes back to Eisenstein and Vertov (if not Méliès) and through Brecht reaches its peak of influence in Godard, and on the other side of the Atlantic, the tradition of American avant-garde cinema.

> The first blow against the monolithic accumulation of traditional film conventions (already undertaken by radical filmmakers) is to free the look of the camera into its materiality in time and space and the look of the audience into dialectics, passionate detachment.[3]

But much as Mulvey and other avant-garde filmmakers insisted that women's cinema ought to avoid a politics of emotions and seek to problematize the female spectator's identification with the on-screen image of woman, the response to her theoretical writings, like the reception of her films (co-directed with Peter Wollen), showed no consensus. Feminist critics, spectators, and filmmakers remained doubtful. For example, B. Ruby Rich:

> According to Mulvey, the woman is not visible in the audience which is perceived as male; according to Johnston, the woman is not visible on the screen. . . . How does one formulate an understanding of a structure that insists on our absence even in the face of our presence? What is there in a film with which a woman viewer identifies? How can the contradictions be used as a critique? And how do all these factors influence what one makes as a woman filmmaker, or specifically as a feminist filmmaker?[4]

The questions of identification, self-definition, the modes or the very possibility of envisaging oneself as subject—which the male avant-garde artists and theorists have also been asking, on their part, for almost one hundred years, even as they work to subvert the dominant representations or to challenge their hegemony—are fundamental questions for feminism. If identification is "not simply one psychical mechanism among others, but the operation itself whereby the human subject is constituted," as Laplanche and Pontalis describe it, then it must be all the more important, theoretically and politically, for women who have never before represented ourselves as subjects, and whose images and subjectivities—until very recently, if at all—have not been ours to shape, to portray, or to create.[5]

There is indeed reason to question the theoretical paradigm of a subject-object dialectic, whether Hegelian or Lacanian, that subtends both the aesthetic and the scientific discourses of Western culture; for what that paradigm contains, what those discourses rest on, is the unacknowledged assumption of sexual difference: that the human subject, Man, is the male. As in the originary distinction of classical myth reaching us through the Platonic tradition, human creation and all that is human—mind, spirit, history, language, art, or symbolic capacity—is defined in contradistinction to formless chaos, *phusis* or nature, to something that is female, matrix and matter; and on this primary binary opposition, all the others are modelled. As Lea Melandri states,

> Idealism, the oppositions of mind to body, of rationality to matter, originate in a twofold concealment: of the woman's body and of labor power. Chronologically, however, even prior to the commodity and the labor power that has produced it, the matter which was negated in its concreteness and particularity, in its "relative plural form," is the woman's body. Woman enters history having already lost concreteness and singularity: she is the economic machine that reproduces the human species, and she is the Mother, an equivalent more universal than money, the most abstract measure ever invented by patriarchal ideology.[6]

That this proposition remains true when tested on the aesthetic of modernism or the major trends in avant-garde cinema from visionary to structural-materialist film, on the films of Stan Brakhage, Michael Snow, or Jean-Luc Godard, but is not true of the films of Yvonne Rainer, Valie Export, Chantal Akerman, or Marguerite Duras, for example; that it remains valid for the films of Fassbinder but not those of Ottinger, the films of Pasolini and Bertolucci but not Cavani's, and so on, suggests to me that it is perhaps time to shift the terms of the question altogether.

To ask of these women's films: What formal, stylistic, or thematic markers point to a female presence behind the camera? and hence to generalize and universalize, to say: This is the look and sound of women's cinema, this is its language—finally only means complying, accepting a certain definition of art, cinema, and culture, and obligingly showing how women can and do "contribute," pay their tribute, to "society." Put another way, to ask whether there is a feminine or female aesthetic, or a specific language of women's cinema, is to remain caught in the master's house and there, as Audre Lorde's suggestive metaphor warns us, to legitimate the hidden agendas of a culture we badly need to change. Cosmetic changes, she is telling us, won't be enough for the majority of women—women of color, black women, and white women as well; or, in her own words, "assimilation within a solely western-european herstory is not acceptable."[7]

It is time we listened. Which is not to say that we should dispense with rigorous analysis and experimentation on the formal processes of meaning production, including the production of narrative, visual pleasure, and subject positions, but rather that feminist theory should now engage precisely in the redefinition of aesthetic and formal knowledges, much as women's cinema has been engaged in the transformation of vision.

Take Akerman's *Jeanne Dielman* (1975), a film about the routine daily activities of a Belgian middle-class and middle-aged housewife, and a film where the pre-aesthetic is already fully aesthetic. That is not so, however, because of the beauty of its images, the balanced composition of its frames, the absence of the reverse shot, or the perfectly calculated editing of its still-camera shots into a continuous, logical, and obsessive narrative space; it is so because it is a woman's actions, gestures, body, and look that define the space of our vision, the temporality and rhythms of perception, the horizon of meaning available to the spectator. So that narrative suspense is not built on the expectation of a "significant event," a socially momentous act (which actually occurs, though unexpectedly and almost incidentally, one feels, toward the end of the film), but is produced by the tiny slips in Jeanne's routine, the small forgettings, the hesitations between real-time gestures as common and "insignificant" as peeling potatoes, washing dishes, or making coffee—and then not drinking it. What the film constructs—formally and artfully, to be sure—is a picture of female experience, of duration, perception, events, relationships, and silences, which feels immediately and unquestionably true. And in this sense the "pre-aesthetic" is *aesthetic* rather than *aestheticized*, as it is in films such as Godard's *Two or Three Things I Know about Her*, Polanski's *Repulsion*, or Antonioni's *Eclipse*. To say the same thing in another way, Akerman's film addresses the spectator as female.

The effort, on the part of the filmmaker, to render a presence in the feeling of a gesture, to convey the sense of an experience that is subjective yet socially coded (and therefore recognizable), and to do so formally, working through her conceptual (one could say, theoretical) knowledge of film form, is averred by Chantal Akerman in an interview on the making of *Jeanne Dielman*:

> I *do* think it's a feminist film because I give space to things which were never, almost never, shown in that way, like the daily gestures of a woman.

> They are the lowest in the hierarchy of film images. . . . But more than the content, it's because of the style. If you choose to show a woman's gestures so precisely, it's because you love them. In some way you recognize those gestures that have always been denied and ignored. I think that the real problem with women's films usually has nothing to do with the content. It's that hardly any women really have confidence enough to carry through on their feelings. Instead the content is the most simple and obvious thing. They deal with that and forget to look for formal ways to express what they are and what they want, their own rhythms, their own way of looking at things. A lot of women have unconscious contempt for their feelings. But I don't think I do. I have enough confidence in myself. So that's the other reason why I think it's a feminist film—not just what it says but *what* is shown and *how* it's shown.[8]

This lucid statement of poetics resonates with my own response as a viewer and gives me something of an explanation as to why I recognize in those unusual film images, in those movements, those silences, and those looks, the ways of an experience all but unrepresented, previously unseen in film, though lucidly and unmistakably apprehended here. And so the statement cannot be dismissed with commonplaces such as authorial intention or intentional fallacy. As another critic and spectator points out, there are "two logics" at work in this film, "two modes of the feminine": character and director, image and camera, remain distinct yet interacting and mutually interdependent positions. Call them femininity and feminism; the one is made representable by the critical work of the other; the one is kept at a distance, constructed, "framed," to be sure, and yet "respected," "loved," "given space" by the other.[9] The two "logics" remain separate:

> The camera look can't be construed as the view of any character. Its interest extends beyond the fiction. The camera presents itself, in its evenness and predictability, as equal to Jeanne's precision. Yet the camera continues its logic throughout; Jeanne's order is disrupted, and with the murder the text comes to its logical end since Jeanne then stops altogether. If Jeanne has, symbolically, destroyed the phallus, its order still remains visible all around her.[10]

Finally, then, the space constructed by the film is not only a textual or filmic space of vision, in frame and off—for an off-screen space is still inscribed in the images, although not sutured narratively by the reverse shot but effectively reaching toward the historical and social determinants which define Jeanne's life and place her in her frame. But beyond that, the film's space is also a critical space of analysis, a horizon of possible meanings which includes or extends to the spectator ("extends beyond the fiction") insofar as the spectator is led to occupy at once the two positions, to follow the two "logics," and to perceive them as equally and concurrently true.

In saying that a film whose visual and symbolic space is organized in this manner *addresses its spectator as a woman*, regardless of the gender of the viewers, I mean that the film defines all points of identification (with character, image, camera) as female, feminine, or feminist. However, this is not as simple or self-evident a notion as the established film-theoretical view of cinematic identification, namely, that identification with the look is masculine, and identification with the image is feminine. It is not self-evident precisely because such a view—which indeed correctly explains the working of dominant cinema—is now accepted: that the camera (technology), the look (voyeurism), and the scopic drive itself partake of the phallic and thus somehow are entities or figures of a masculine nature.

How difficult it is to "prove" that a film addresses its spectator as female is brought home time and again in conversations or discussions between audiences and filmmakers. After a screening of *Redupers* in Milwaukee (in January 1985), Helke Sander answered a question about the function of the Berlin wall in her film and concluded by saying, if I may paraphrase: "but of course the wall also represents another division that is specific to women." She did not elaborate, but again, I felt that what she meant was clear and unmistakable. And so does at least one other critic and spectator, Kaja Silverman, who sees the wall as a division other in kind from what the wall would divide—and can't, for things do "flow through the Berlin wall (TV and radio waves, germs, the writings of Christa Wolf)," and Edda's photographs show the two Berlins in "their quotidian similarities rather than their ideological divergences."

> All three projects are motivated by the desire to tear down the wall, or at least to prevent it from functioning as the dividing line between two irreducible opposites. . . . *Redupers* makes the wall a signifier for psychic as well as ideological, political, and geographical boundaries. It functions there as a metaphor for sexual difference, for the subjective limits articulated by the existing symbolic order both in East and West. The wall thus designates the discursive boundaries which separate residents not only of the same country and language, but of the same partitioned space.[11]

Those of us who share Silverman's perception must wonder whether in fact the sense of that other, specific division represented by the wall in *Redupers* (sexual difference, a discursive boundary, a subjective limit) is in the film or in our viewers' eyes. Is it actually there on screen, in the film, inscribed in its slow montage of long takes and in the stillness of the images in their silent frames; or is it, rather, in our perception, our insight, as—precisely—a subjective limit and discursive boundary (gender), a horizon of meaning (feminism) which is projected into the images, onto the screen, around the text?

I think it is this other kind of division that is acknowledged in Christa Wolf's figure of "the divided heaven," for example, or in Virginia Woolf's "room of one's own": the feeling of an internal distance, a contradiction, a space of silence, which is there alongside the imaginary pull of cultural and ideological representations without denying or obliterating them. Women artists, filmmakers, and writers acknowledge this division or difference by attempting to express it in their works. Spectators and readers think we find it in those texts. Nevertheless, even today, most of us would still agree with Silvia Bovenschen.

"For the time being," writes Gertrud Koch, "the issue remains whether films by women actually succeed in subverting this basic model of the camera's construction of the gaze, whether the female look through the camera at the world, at men, women, and objects will be an essentially different one."[12] Posed in these terms, however, the issue will remain fundamentally a rhetorical question. I have suggested that the emphasis must be shifted away from the artist behind the camera, the gaze, or the text as origin and determination of meaning, toward the wider public sphere of cinema as a social technology: we must develop our understanding of cinema's implication in other modes of cultural representation, and its possibilities of both production and counterproduction of social vision. I further suggest that, even as filmmakers are confronting the problems of transforming vision by engaging all of the codes of cinema, specific and nonspecific, against the dominance of that "basic model," our task as theorists is to articulate the conditions and forms of vision for another social subject, and so to venture into the highly risky business of redefining aesthetic and formal knowledge.

Such a project evidently entails reconsidering and reassessing the early feminist formulations or, as Sheila Rowbotham summed it up, "look[ing] back at ourselves through our own cultural creations, our actions, our ideas, our pamphlets, our organization, our history, our theory."[13] And if we now can add "our films," perhaps the time has come to re-think women's cinema as the production of a feminist social vision. As a form of political critique or critical politics, and through the specific consciousness that women have developed to analyze the subject's relation to sociohistorical reality, feminism not only has invented new strategies or created new texts, but, more important, it has conceived a new social subject, women: as speakers, writers, readers, spectators, users, and makers of cultural forms, shapers of cultural processes. The project of women's cinema, therefore, is no longer that of destroying or disrupting man-centered vision by representing its blind spots, its gaps, or its repressed. The effort and challenge now are how to effect another vision: to construct other objects and subjects of vision, and to formulate the conditions of representability of another social subject. For the time being, then, feminist work in film seems necessarily focused on those subjective limits and discursive boundaries that mark women's division as gender-specific, a division more elusive, complex, and contradictory than can be conveyed in the notion of sexual difference as it is currently used.

The idea that *a film may address the spectator as female*, rather than portray women positively or negatively, seems very important to me in the critical endeavor to characterize women's cinema as a cinema for, not only by, women. It is an idea not found in the critical writings I mentioned earlier, which are focused on the film, the object, the text. But rereading those essays today, one can see, and it is important to stress it, that the question of a filmic language or a feminine aesthetic has been articulated from the beginning in relation to the women's movement: "the new grows only out of the work of confrontation" (Mulvey, p. 4); women's "imagination constitutes the movement itself" (Bovenschen, p. 136); and in Claire Johnston's nonformalist view of women's cinema as counter-cinema, a feminist political strategy should reclaim, rather than shun, the use of film as a form of mass culture: "In order to counter our objectification in the cinema, our collective fantasies must be released: women's cinema must embody the working through of desire: such an objective demands the use of the entertainment film."[14]

Since the first women's film festivals in 1972 (New York, Edinburgh) and the first journal of feminist film criticism (*Women and Film*, published in Berkeley from 1972 to 1975), the question of women's expression has been one of both self-expression and communication with other women, a question at once of the creation/invention of new images and of the creation/imaging of new forms of community. If we rethink the problem of a specificity of women's cinema and aesthetic forms in this manner, in terms of address—who is making films for whom, who is looking and speaking, how, where, and to whom—then what has been seen as a rift, a division, an ideological split within feminist film culture between theory and practice, or between formalism and activism, may appear to be the very strength, the drive and productive heterogeneity of feminism. In their introduction to the recent collection *Re-vision: Essays in Feminist Film Criticism*, Mary Ann Doane, Patricia Mellencamp, and Linda Williams point out:

> If feminist work on film has grown increasingly theoretical, less oriented towards political action, this does not necessarily mean that theory itself is counter-productive to the cause of feminism, nor that the institutional form of the debates within feminism have simply reproduced a male model of academic competition. . . . Feminists sharing similar concerns collaborate in joint authorship and editorships, cooperative filmmaking and distribution arrangements. Thus, many of the political aspirations of the

> women's movement form an integral part of the very structure of feminist work in and on film.[15]

The "re-vision" of their title, borrowed from Adrienne Rich ("Re-vision—the act of looking back, of seeing with fresh eyes," writes Rich, is for women "an act of survival"), refers to the project of reclaiming vision, of "seeing difference differently," of displacing the critical emphasis from "images of" women "to the axis of vision itself—to the modes of organizing vision and hearing which result in the production of that 'image'."[16]

I agree with the *Re-vision* editors when they say that over the past decade, feminist theory has moved "from an analysis of difference as oppressive to a delineation and specification of difference as liberating, as offering the only possibility of radical change" (p. 12). But I believe that radical change requires that such specification not be limited to "sexual difference," that is to say, a difference of women from men, female from male, or Woman from Man. Radical change requires a delineation and a better understanding of the difference of women from Woman, and that is to say as well, *the differences among women*. For there are, after all, different histories of women. There are women who masquerade and women who wear the veil; women invisible to men, in their society, but also women who are invisible to other women, in our society.[17]

The invisibility of black women in white women's films, for instance, or of lesbianism in mainstream feminist criticism, is what Lizzie Borden's *Born in Flames* (1983) most forcefully represents, while at the same time constructing the terms of their visibility as subjects and objects of vision. Set in a hypothetical near-future time and in a place very much like lower Manhattan, with the look of a documentary (after Chris Marker) and the feel of contemporary science-fiction writing (the post-new-wave s-f of Samuel Delany, Joanna Russ, Alice Sheldon, or Thomas Disch), *Born in Flames* shows how a "successful" social democratic cultural revolution, now into its tenth year, slowly but surely reverts to the old patterns of male dominance, politics as usual, and the traditional Left disregard for "women's issues." It is around this specific gender oppression, in its various forms, that several groups of women (black women, Latinas, lesbians, single mothers, intellectuals, political activists, spiritual and punk performers, and a Women's Army) succeed in mobilizing and joining together not by ignoring but, paradoxically, by acknowledging their differences.

Like *Redupers* and *Jeanne Dielman*, Borden's film addresses the spectator as female, but it does not do so by portraying an experience which feels immediately one's own. On the contrary, its barely coherent narrative, its quick-paced shots and sound montage, the counterpoint of image and word, the diversity of voices and languages, and the self-conscious science-fictional frame of the story hold the spectator across a distance, projecting toward her its fiction like a bridge of difference. In short, what

Born in Flames does for me, woman spectator, is exactly to allow me "to see difference differently," to look at women with eyes I've never had before and yet my own; for, as it remarks the emphasis (the words are Audre Lorde's) on the "interdependency of different strengths" in feminism, the film also inscribes the differences among women as *differences within women.*

Born in Flames addresses me as a woman and a feminist living in a particular moment of women's history, the United States today. The film's events and images take place in what science fiction calls a parallel universe, a time and a place elsewhere that look and feel like here and now, yet are not, just as I (and all women) live in a culture that is and is not our own. In that unlikely, but not impossible, universe of the film's fiction, the women come together in the very struggle that divides and differentiates them. Thus, what it portrays for me, what elicits my identification with the film and gives me, spectator, a place in it, is the contradiction of my own history and the personal/political difference that is also within myself.

"The relationship between history and so-called subjective processes," says Helen Fehervary in a recent discussion of women's film in Germany, "is not a matter of grasping the truth in history as some objective entity, but in finding the truth of the experience. Evidently, this kind of experiential immediacy has to do with women's own history and self-consciousness."[18] That, how, and why our histories and our consciousness are different, divided, even conflicting, is what women's cinema can analyze, articulate, reformulate. And, in so doing, it can help us create something else to be, as Toni Morrison says of her two heroines:

> Because each had discovered years before that they were neither white nor male, and that all freedom and triumph was forbidden to them, they had set about creating something else to be.[19]

In the following pages I will refer often to *Born in Flames*, discussing some of the issues it has raised, but it will not be with the aim of a textual analysis. Rather, I will take it as the starting point, as indeed it was for me, of a series of reflections on the topic of this essay.

Again it is a film, and a filmmaker's project, that bring home to me with greater clarity the question of difference, this time in relation to factors other than gender, notably race and class—a question endlessly debated within Marxist feminism and recently rearticulated by women of color in feminist presses and publications. That this question should reemerge urgently and irrevocably now is not surprising, at a time when severe social regression and economic pressures (the so-called "feminization of poverty") belie the self-complacency of a liberal feminism enjoying its-modest allotment of institutional legitimation. A sign of the times, the recent crop of commercial, man-made "woman's films" (*Lianna, Personal Best, Silkwood, Frances, Places of the Heart*, etc.) is undoubtedly "authorized," and made financially viable, by that legitimation. But the success, however modest, of this liberal feminism has been bought at the price of reducing the contradictory complexity—and the theoretical productivity—of concepts such as sexual difference, the personal is political, and feminism itself to simpler and more acceptable ideas already existing in the dominant culture. Thus, to many today, "sexual difference" is hardly more than sex (biology) or gender (in the simplest sense of female socialization) or the basis for certain private "life styles" (homosexual and other nonorthodox relationships); "the personal is political" all too often translates into "the personal instead of the political"; and "feminism" is unhesitantly appropriated, by the academy as well as the media, as a discourse—a variety of social criticism, a method of aesthetic or literary analysis among others, and more or less worth attention according to the degree of its market appeal to students, readers, or viewers. And, yes, a discourse perfectly accessible to all men of good will. In this context, issues of race or class must continue to be thought of as mainly sociological or economic, and hence parallel to but not dependent on gender, implicated with but not determining of subjectivity, and of little relevance to this "feminist discourse" which, as such, would have no competence in the matter but only, and at best, a humane or "progressive" concern with the disadvantaged.

The relevance of feminism (without quotation marks) to race and class, however, is very explicitly stated by those women of color, black, and white who are not the recipients but rather the "targets" of equal opportunity, who are outside or not fooled by liberal "feminism," or who understand that feminism is nothing if it is not at once political and personal, with all the contradictions and difficulties that entails. To such feminists it is clear that the social construction of gender, subjectivity, and the relations of representation to experience do occur within race and class as much as they occur in language and culture, often indeed across languages, cultures, and sociocultural apparati. Thus, not only is it the case that the notion of gender, or "sexual difference," cannot be simply accommodated into the preexisting, ungendered (or male-gendered) categories by which the official discourses on race and class have been elaborated; but it is equally the case that the issues of race and class cannot be simply subsumed under some larger category labeled femaleness, femininity, womanhood, or, in the final instance, Woman. What is becoming more and more clear, instead, is that all the categories of our social science stand to be reformulated *starting from* the notion of gendered social subjects. And something of this process of reformulation—re-vision, rewriting, rereading, rethinking, "looking back at *ourselves*"—is what I see inscribed in the texts of women's cinema but not yet sufficiently focused on in feminist film theory or feminist critical practice in general. This point, like the relation of feminist writing to the women's movement, demands a much lengthier discussion than can be undertaken here. I can do no more than sketch the problem as it strikes me with unusual intensity in the reception of Lizzie Borden's film and my own response to it.

What *Born in Flames* succeeds in representing is this feminist understanding: that the female subject is en-gendered, constructed and defined in gender across multiple representations of class, race, language, and social relations; and that, therefore, differences among women are differences *within* women, which is why feminism can exist despite those differences and, as we are just beginning to understand, cannot continue to exist without them. The originality of this film's project is its representation of woman as a social subject and a site of differences; differences which are not purely sexual or merely racial, economic, or (sub)cultural, but all of these together and often enough in conflict with one another. What one takes away after seeing this film is the image of a heterogeneity in the female social subject, the sense of a distance from dominant cultural models and of an internal division within women that remain, not in spite of but concurrently with the provisional unity of any concerted political action. Just as the film's narrative remains unresolved, fragmented, and difficult to follow, heterogeneity and difference within women remain in our memory as the film's narrative image, its work of representing, which cannot be collapsed into a fixed identity, a sameness of all women as Woman, or a representation of Feminism as a coherent and available image.

Other films, in addition to the ones already mentioned, have effectively represented that internal division or distance from language, culture, and self that I see recur, figuratively and thematically, in recent women's cinema (it is also represented, for example, in Gabriella Rosaleva's *Processo a Caterina Ross* and in Lynne Tillman and Sheila McLaughlin's *Committed*). But *Born in Flames* projects that division on a larger social and cultural scale, taking up nearly all of the issues and putting them all at stake. As we read on the side of the (stolen) U-Haul trucks which carry the free women's new mobile radio transmitter, reborn as Phoenix-Regazza (girl phoenix) from the flames that destroyed the two separate stations, the film is "an adventure in moving." As one reviewer saw it,

> An action pic, a sci-fi fantasy, a political thriller, a collage film, a snatch of the underground: *Born in Flames* is all and none of these. . . . Edited in 15-second bursts and spiked with yards of flickering video transfers . . . *Born in Flames* stands head and shoulders above such Hollywood reflections on the media as *Absence of Malice, Network,* or *Under Fire.* This is less a matter of its substance (the plot centers on the suspicious prison "suicide," à la Ulrike Meinhoff, of Women's Army leader Adelaide Norris) than of its form, seizing on a dozen facets of our daily media surroundings.[20]

The words of the last sentence, echoing Akerman's emphasis on form rather than content, are in turn echoed by Borden in several printed statements. She, too, is keenly concerned with her own relation as filmmaker to filmic representation ("Two things I was committed to with the film were questioning the nature of narrative . . . and creating a process whereby I could release myself from my own bondage in terms of class and race").[21] And she, too, like Akerman, is confident that vision can be transformed because hers has been: "Whatever discomfort I might have felt as a white filmmaker working with black women has been over for so long. It was exorcized by the process of making the film." Thus, in response to the interviewer's (Anne Friedberg) suggestion that the film is "progressive" precisely because it "demands a certain discomfort for the audience, and forces the viewer to confront his or her own political position(s) (or lack of political position)," Borden flatly rejects the interviewer's implicit assumption.

> I don't think the audience is solely a white middle-class audience. What was important for me was creating a film in which that was *not* the only audience. The problem with much of the critical material on the film is that it assumes a white middle-class reading public for articles written about a film that they assume has only a white middle-class audience. I'm very confused about the discomfort that reviewers feel. What I was trying to do (and using humor as a way to try to do it) was to have various positions in which everyone had a place on some level. Every woman—with men it is a whole different question—would have some level of identification with a position within the film. Some reviewers over-identified with something as a privileged position. Basically, none of the positioning of black characters was *against* any of the white viewers but more of an invitation: come and work with us. Instead of telling the viewer that he or she could *not* belong, the viewer was supposed to be a repository for all these different points of view and all these different styles of rhetoric. Hopefully, one would be able to identify with one position but be able to evaluate all of the various positions presented in the film. Basically, I feel this discomfort only from people who are deeply resistant to it.[22]

This response is one that, to my mind, sharply outlines a shift in women's cinema from a modernist or avant-garde aesthetic of subversion to an emerging set of questions about filmic representation to which the term *aesthetic* may or may not apply, depending on one's definition of art, one's definition of cinema, and the relationship between the two. Similarly, whether or not the terms *post-modern* or *post-modernist aesthetic* would be preferable or more applicable in this context, as Craig Owens has suggested of the work of other women artists, is too large a topic to be discussed here.[23]

At any rate, as I see it, there has been a shift in women's cinema from an aesthetic centered on the text and *its* effects on the viewing or reading subject—whose certain, if imaginary, self-coherence is to be fractured by the text's own disruption of linguistic, visual, and/or narrative coherence—to what may be called an aesthetic of reception, where the spectator is the film's primary concern—primary in the sense that it is there from the beginning, inscribed in the filmmaker's project and even in the very making of the film.[24] An explicit concern with the audience is of course not new either in art or in cinema, since Pirandello and Brecht in the former, and it is always conspicuously present in Hollywood and TV. What is new here, however, is the particular conception of the audience, which now is envisaged in its heterogeneity and otherness from the text.

That the audience is conceived as a heterogeneous community is made apparent, in Borden's film, by its unusual handling of the function of address. The use of music and beat in conjunction with spoken language, from rap singing to a variety of subcultural lingos and nonstandard speech, serves less the purposes of documentation or *cinéma vérité* than those of what in another context might be called characterization: they are there to provide a means of identification of and with the characters, though not the kind of psychological identification usually accorded to main characters or privileged "protagonists." "I wanted to make a film that different audiences could relate to on different levels—if they wanted to ignore the language they could," Borden told another interviewer, "but not to make a film that was anti-language."[25] The importance of "language" and its constitutive presence in both the public and the private spheres is underscored by the multiplicity of discourses and communication technologies—visual, verbal, and aural—foregrounded in the form as well as the content of the film. If the wall of official speech, the omnipresent systems of public address, and the very strategy of the women's takeover of a television station assert the fundamental link of communication and power, the film also insists on representing the other, unofficial social discourses, their heterogeneity, and *their* constitutive effects vis-à-vis the social subject.

In this respect, I would argue, both the characters and the spectators of Borden's film are positioned in relation to social discourses and representations (of class, race, and gender) within particular "subjective limits and discursive boundaries" that are analogous, in their own historical specificity, to those which Silverman saw symbolized by the Berlin wall in *Redupers*. For the spectators, too, are limited in their vision and understanding, bound by their own social and sexual positioning, as their "discomfort" or diverse responses suggest. Borden's avowed intent to make the spectator a locus ("a repository") of different points of view and discursive configurations ("these different styles of rhetoric") suggests to me that the concept of a heterogeneity of the audience also entails a heterogeneity of, or in, the individual spectator.

If, as claimed by recent theories of textuality, the Reader or the Spectator is implied in the text as an effect of its strategy—either as the figure of a unity or coherence of meaning which is constructed by the text (the "text of pleasure"), or as the figure of the division, dissemination, incoherence inscribed in the "text of *jouissance*"—then the spectator of *Born in Flames* is somewhere else, resistant to the text and other from it. This film's spectator is not only *not* sutured into the "classic" text by narrative and psychological identification; nor is it bound in the time of repetition, "at the limit of any fixed subjectivity, materially inconstant, dispersed in process," as Stephen Heath aptly describes the spectator intended by avant-garde (structural-materialist) film.[26] What happens is, this film's spectator is finally not liable to capture by the text.

And yet one is engaged by the powerful erotic charge of the film; one responds to the erotic investment that its female characters have in each other, and the filmmaker in them, with something that is neither pleasure nor *jouissance*, oedipal nor pre-oedipal, as they have been defined for us; but with something that is again (as in *Jeanne Dielman*) a recognition, unmistakable and unprecedented. Again the textual space extends to the spectator, in its erotic and critical dimensions, addressing, speaking-to, making room, but not (how very unusual and remarkable) cajoling, soliciting, seducing. These films do not put me in the place of the female spectator, do not assign me a role, a self-image, a positionality in language or desire. Instead, they make a place for what I will call me, knowing that I don't know it, and give "me" space to try to know, to see, to understand. Put another way, by addressing me as *a* woman, they do not bind me or appoint me as Woman.

The "discomfort" of Borden's reviewers might be located exactly in this dis-appointment of spectator and text: the disappointment of not finding oneself, not finding oneself "interpellated" or solicited by the film, whose images and discourses project back to the viewer a space of heterogeneity, differences and fragmented coherences that just do not add up to one individual viewer or one spectator-subject, bourgeois or otherwise. There is no one-to-one match between the film's discursive heterogeneity and the discursive boundaries of any one spectator. We are both invited in and held at a distance, addressed intermittently and only insofar as we are able to occupy the position of addressee; for example, when Honey, the Phoenix Radio disc jockey, addresses to the audience the words: "Black women, be ready. White women, get ready. Red women, stay ready, for this is our time and all must realize it."[27] Which individual member of the audience, male or female, can feel singly interpellated as spectator-subject or, in other words, unequivocally addressed?

There is a famous moment in film history, something of a parallel to this one, which not coincidentally has been "discovered" by feminist film critics in a woman-made film about women, Dorothy Arzner's *Dance, Girl, Dance*: it is the moment when Judy interrupts her stage performance and, facing the vaudeville audience, steps out of her role and speaks to them as a woman to a group of people. The novelty of this direct address, feminist critics have noted, is not only that it breaks the codes of theatrical illusion and voyeuristic pleasure, but also that it demonstrates that no complicity, no shared discourse, can be established between the woman performer (positioned as image, representation, object) and the male audience (positioned as the controlling gaze); no complicity, that is, outside the codes and rules of the performance. By breaking the codes, Arzner revealed the rules and the relations of power that constitute them and are in turn sustained by them. And sure enough, the vaudeville audience in her film showed great discomfort with Judy's speech.

I am suggesting that the discomfort with Honey's speech has also to do with codes of representation (of race and class as well as gender) and the rules and power relations that sustain them—rules which also prevent the establishing of a shared discourse, and hence the "dream" of a common language. How else could viewers see in this playful, exuberant, science-fictional film a blueprint for political action which, they claim, wouldn't work anyway? ("We've all been through this before. As a man I'm not threatened by this because we know that this doesn't work. This is infantile politics, these women are being macho like men used to be macho. . . . ")[28] Why else would they see the film, in Friedberg's phrase, "as a *prescription* through fantasy"? Borden's opinion is that "people have not really been upset about class and race. . . . People are really upset that the women are gay. They feel it is separatist."[29] My own opinion is that people are upset with all three, class, race, and gender—lesbianism being precisely the demonstration that the concept of gender is founded across race and class on the structure which Adrienne Rich and Monique Wittig have called, respectively, "compulsory heterosexuality" and "the heterosexual contract."[30]

The film-theoretical notion of spectatorship has been developed largely in the attempt to answer the question posed insistently by feminist theorists and well summed up in the words of B. Ruby Rich already cited above: "How does one formulate an understanding of a structure that insists on our absence even in the face of our presence?" In keeping with the early divergence of feminists over the politics of images, the notion of spectatorship was developed along two axes: one starting from the psychoanalytic theory of the subject and employing concepts such as primary and secondary, conscious and unconscious, imaginary and symbolic processes; the other starting from sexual difference and asking questions such as, How does the female spectator see? With what does she identify? Where/How/In what film genres is female desire represented? and so on. Arzner's infraction of the code in *Dance, Girl, Dance* was one of the first answers in this second line of questioning, which now appears to have been the most fruitful by far for women's cinema. *Born in Flames* seems to me to work out the most interesting answer to date.

For one thing, the film assumes that the female spectator may be black, white, "red," middle-class or not middle-class, and wants her to have a place within the film, some measure of identification—"identification with a position," Borden specifies. "With men [spectators] it is a whole different question," she adds, obviously without much interest in exploring it (though later suggesting that black male spectators responded to the film "because they don't see it as just about women. They see it as empowerment").[31] In sum, the spectator is addressed as female in gender and multiple or heterogeneous in race and class; which is to say, here too all points of identification are female or feminist, but rather than the "two logics" of character and filmmaker, like *Jeanne Dielman, Born in Flames* foregrounds their different discourses.

Second, as Friedberg puts it in one of her questions, the images of women in *Born in Flames* are "unaesthetícized": "you never fetishize the body through masquerade. In fact the film seems consciously de-aestheticized, which is what gives it its documentary quality."[32] Nevertheless, to some, those images of women appear to be extraordinarily beautiful. If such were to be the case for most of the film's female spectators, however socially positioned, we would be facing what amounts to a film-theoretical paradox, for in film theory the female body is construed precisely as fetish or masquerade.[33] Perhaps not unexpectedly, the filmmaker's response is amazingly consonant with Chantal Akerman's, though their films are visually quite different, and the latter's is in fact received as an "aesthetic" work.

> Borden: "The important thing is to shoot female bodies in a way that they have never been shot before. . . . I chose women for the stance I liked. The stance is almost like the gestalt of a person."[34]
>
> And Akerman (cited above): "I give space to things which were never, almost never, shown in that way. . . . If you choose to show a woman's gestures so precisely, it's because you love them."

The point of this cross-referencing of two films that have little else in common beside the feminism of their makers is to remark the persistence of certain themes and formal questions about representation and difference which I *would* call aesthetic, and which are the historical product of feminism and the expression of feminist critical-theoretical thought.

Like the works of the feminist filmmakers I have referred to, and many others too numerous to mention here, *Jeanne Dielman* and *Born in Flames* are engaged in the project of transforming vision by inventing the forms and processes of representation of a social subject, women, that until now has been all but unrepresentable; a project already set out (looking back, one is tempted to say, programmatically) in the title of Yvonne Rainer's *Film about a Woman Who . . .* (1974), which in a sense all of these films continue to reelaborate. The gender-specific division of women in language, the distance from official culture, the urge to imagine new forms of community as well as to create new images ("creating something else to be"), and the consciousness of a "subjective factor" at the core of all kinds of work—domestic, industrial, artistic, critical, or political work—are some of the themes articulating the particular relation of subjectivity, meaning, and experience which en-genders the social subject as female. These themes, encapsulated in the phrase "the personal is political," have been formally explored in women's cinema in several ways: through the disjunction of image and voice, the reworking of narrative space, the elaboration of strategies of address that alter the forms and balances of traditional representation. From the inscription of subjective space and duration inside the frame (a space of repetitions, silences, and discontinuities in *Jeanne Dielman*) to the construction of other discursive social spaces (the discontinuous but intersecting spaces of the women's "networks" in *Born in Flames*), women's cinema has undertaken a redefinition of both private and public space that may well answer the call for "a new language of desire" and actually have met the demand for the "destruction of visual pleasure," if by that one alludes to the traditional, classical and modernist, canons of aesthetic representation.

So, once again, the contradiction of women in language and culture is manifested in a paradox: most of the terms by which we speak of the construction of the female social subject in cinematic representation bear in their visual form the prefix *de-* to signal the deconstruction or the destructuring, if not destruction, of the very thing to be represented. We speak of the deaestheticization of the female body, the desexualization of violence, the deoedipalization of narrative, and so forth. Rethinking women's cinema in this way, we may provisionally answer Bovenschen's question thus: There is a certain configuration of issues and formal problems that have been consistently articulated in what we call women's cinema. The way in which they have been expressed and developed, both artistically and critically, seems to point less to a "feminine aesthetic" than to a feminist *deaesthetic*. And if the word sounds awkward or inelegant . . .

NOTES

I am very grateful to Cheryl Kader for generously sharing with me her knowledge and insight from the conception through the writing of this essay, and to Mary Russo for her thoughtful critical suggestions.

1. Silvia Bovenschen, "Is There a Feminine Aesthetic?" trans. Beth Weckmueller, *New German Critique*, no. 10 (Winter 1977): 136. [Originally published in *Aesthetik und Kommunikation* 25 (September 1976).]

2. Laura Mulvey, "Feminism, Film, and the Avant-Garde," *Framework*, no. 10 (Spring 1979): 6. See also Christine Gledhill's account "Recent Developments in Feminist Film Criticism," *Quarterty Review of Film Studies* 3, no. 4 (1978).

3. Laura Mulvey, "Visual Pleasure and Narrative Cinema," *Screen* 16, no. 3 (Autumn 1975): 18.

4. B. Ruby Rich, in "Women and Film: A Discussion of Feminist Aesthetics," *New German Critique*, no. 13 (Winter 1978): 87.

5. J. Laplanche and J.-B. Pontalis, *The Language of Psycho-analysis*, trans. D. Nicholson-Smith, New York: Norton (1973), p. 206.

6. Lea Melandri, *L'infamia originaria*, Milano: Edizioni L'Erba Voglio (1977), p. 27; my translation. For a more fully developed discussion of semiotic theories of film and narrative, see Teresa de Lauretis, *Alice Doesn't: Feminism, Semiotics, Cinema*, Bloomington: Indiana University Press (1984).

7. See Audre Lorde, "The Master's Tools Will Never Dismantle the Master's House," and "An Open Letter to Mary Daly," in *This Bridge Called My Back: Writings by Radical Women of Color*, ed. Chérrie Moraga and Gloria Anzaldúa, New York: Kitchen Table Press (1983), p. 96. Both essays are reprinted in Audre Lorde, *Sister Outsider: Essays and Speeches*, Trumansburg, N.Y.: Crossing Press (1984).

8. "Chantal Akerman on *Jeanne Dielman*," *Camera Obscura*, no. 2 (1977): 118–19.

9. In the same interview, Akerman said: "I didn't have any doubts about any of the shots. I was very sure of where to put the camera and when and why. . . . I *let* her [the character] live her life in the middle of the frame. I didn't go in too close, but I was not *very* far away. I let her be in her space. It's not uncontrolled. But the camera was not voyeuristic in the commercial way because you always knew where I was. . . . It was the only way to shoot that film—to avoid cutting the woman into a hundred pieces, to avoid cutting the action in a hundred places, to look carefully and to be respectful. The framing was meant to respect the space, her, and her gestures within it" (ibid., p. 119).

10. Janet Bergstrom, "*Jeanne Dielman, 23 Quai du Commerce, 1080 Bruxelles* by Chantal Akerman," *Camera Obscura*, no. 2 (1977): 117. On the rigorous formal consistency of the film, see also Mary Jo Lakeland, "The Color of Jeanne Dielman," *Camera Obscura*, nos. 3–4 (1979): 216–18.

11. Kaja Silverman, "Helke Sander and the Will to Change," *Discourse*, no. 6 (Fall 1983): 10.

12. Gertrud Koch, "Ex-changing the Gaze: Re-visioning Feminist Film Theory," *New German Critique*, no. 34 (Winter 1985): 144.

13. Sheila Rowbotham, *Woman's Consciousness, Man's World*, Harmondsworth: Penguin Books (1973), p. 28.

14. Claire Johnston, "Women's Cinema as Counter-Cinema," in *Notes on Women's Cinema*, ed. Claire Johnston, London: SEFT (1974), p. 31. See also Gertrud Koch, "Was ist und wozu brauchen wir eine feministische Filmkritik," *frauen und film*, no. 11 (1977).

15. Mary Ann Doane, Patricia Mellencamp, and Linda Williams, eds., *Re-vision: Essays in Feminist Film Criticism*, Frederick, Md.: University Publications of America and the American Film Institute (1984), p. 4.

16. Ibid., p. 6. The quotation from Adrienne Rich is in her *On Lies, Secrets, and Silence*, New York: Norton (1979), p. 35.

17. See Barbara Smith, "Toward a Black Feminist Criticism," in *All the Women Are White, All the Blacks Are Men, but Some of Us Are Brave: Black Women's Studies*, ed. Gloria T. Hull, Patricia Bell Scott, and Barbara Smith, Old Westbury, N.Y.: Feminist Press (1982).

18. Helen Fehervary, Claudia Lenssen, and Judith Mayne, "From Hitler to Hepburn: A Discussion of Women's Film Production and Reception," *New German Critique*, nos. 24–25 (Fall/Winter 1981–82): 176.

19. Toni Morrison, *Sula*, New York: Bantam Books (1975), p. 44.

20. Kathleen Hulser, "Les Guérillères," *Afterimage* 11, no. 6 (January 1984): 14.

21. Anne Friedberg, "An Interview with Filmmaker Lizzie Borden," *Women and Performance* 1, no. 2 (Winter 1984): 43. On the effort to understand one's relation as a feminist to racial and cultural differences, see Elly Bulkin, Minnie Bruce Pratt, and Barbara Smith, *Yours in Struggle: Three Feminist Perspectives on Anti-Semitism and Racism*, Brooklyn, N.Y.: Long Haul Press (1984).

22. Interview in *Women and Performance*, p. 38.

23. Craig Owens, "The Discourse of Others: Feminists and Postmodernism," in *The Anti-Aesthetic: Essays in Postmodern Culture*, ed. Hal Foster, Port Townsend, Wash.: Bay Press (1983), pp. 57–82. See also Andreas Huyssen, "Mapping the Postmodern," *New German Critique*, no. 33 (Fall 1984): 5–52, now reprinted in Huyssen, *After the Great Divide: Modernism, Mass Culture, Postmodernism*, Bloomington: Indiana University Press (1986).

24. Borden's nonprofessional actors, as well as her characters, are very much part of the film's intended audience: "I didn't want the film caught in the white film ghetto. I did mailings. We got women's lists, black women's lists, gay lists, lists that would bring different people to the Film Forum . . . " (Interview in *Women and Performance*, p. 43).

25. Betsy Sussler, "Interview," *Bomb*, no. 7 (1983): 29.

26. Stephen Heath, *Questions of Cinema*, Bloomington: Indiana University Press (1981), p. 167.

27. The script of *Born in Flames* is published in *Heresies*, no. 16 (1983): 12–16. Borden discusses how the script was developed in conjunction with the actors and according to their particular abilities and backgrounds in the interview in *Bomb*.

28. Interview in *Bomb*, p. 29.

29. Interview in *Women and Performance*, p. 39.

30. Adrienne Rich, "Compulsory Heterosexuality and Lesbian Existence," *Signs* 5, no. 4 (Summer 1980): 631–60; Monique Wittig, "The Straight Mind," *Feminist Issues* (Summer 1980): 110.

31. Interview in *Women and Performance*, p. 38.

32. Ibid., p. 44.

33. See Mary Ann Doane, "Film and the Masquerade: Theorising the Female Spectator," *Screen* 23, nos. 3–4 (September/October 1982): 74–87.

34. Interview in *Women and Performance*, pp. 44–45.

DIS-EMBODYING THE FEMALE VOICE

Kaja Silverman

It is by now axiomatic that the female subject is the object rather than the subject of the gaze in mainstream narrative cinema. She is excluded from authoritative vision not only at the level of the enunciation, but at that of the fiction. At the same time she functions as an organizing spectacle, as the lack which structures the symbolic order and sustains the relay of male glances.[1]

It is equally axiomatic that the female subject as she has been constructed by Hollywood cinema is denied any active role in discourse. The mechanisms of that exclusion are much more complex than those which deny her access to authoritative vision, though, and they warrant a very careful formulation.

Like the male subject, the female subject emerges only within discourse; she knows herself from the place of language, and once inside the symbolic order she has no more access to her biological real than does her masculine counterpart. Both are spoken by discourses and desires which exceed them. However, whereas the male subject has privileges conferred upon him by his relationship to discourse, the female subject is defined as insufficient through hers.

A corollary of this very important difference (and it is at this level that sexual difference must be conceptualized) is that the male subject is granted access to what Foucault calls "discursive fellowships," is permitted to participate in the unfolding of discourse.[2] In other words, he is allowed to occupy the position of the speaking subject—in fiction, and even to some degree in fact. Within dominant narrative cinema the male subject enjoys not only specular but linguistic authority.

The female subject, on the contrary, is associated with unreliable, thwarted, or acquiescent speech. She talks a great deal; it would be a serious mistake to characterize her as silent, since it is in large part through her prattle, her bitchiness, her sweet murmurings, her maternal admonitions, and her verbal cunning that we know her. But her linguistic status is analogous to that of a recorded tape, which endlessly plays back what was spoken in some anterior moment, and from a radically external vantage. The participation of the male subject in the production of discourse may be limited, and contingent upon his "willingness" to identify with the existing cultural order, but the participation of the female subject in the production of discourse is nonexistent.[3]

Classical cinema projects these differences at the formal as well as the thematic level. Not only does the male subject occupy positions of authority within the diegesis, but occasionally he also speaks extra-diegetically, from the privileged place of the Other. The female subject, on the contrary, is excluded from positions of discursive authority both inside and outside the diegesis; she is confined not only to safe places *within* the story (to positions, that is, which come within the eventual range of male vision or audition), but to the safe place *of* the story.[4] Synchronization provides the means of that confinement.

> Prisoner of a sensible appearance, doubly mastered by the camera lens and the gaze of the spectator, the [female] voice is subject to the most rapid of critiques, that of the eye.
>
> —Pascal Bonitzer[5]

Synchronization functions as a virtual imperative within fiction film. Although the male voice is occasionally permitted to transcend that imperative altogether, and the female voice is from time to time allowed a qualified respite from its rigors, it organizes all sound/image relationships. It is the norm to which those relationships either adhere, or from which they deviate. Since within dominant cinema the image track is cut to the measure of the human form, and the sound track to the measure of the human voice, the rule of synchronization must be understood as referring above all to the smooth alignment of the human form with the human voice—i.e., to the representation of a homogeneous thinking subject whose exteriority is congruent with its interiority. The "marriage" of sound and image is thus performed in the name of homo-centricity, and under Cartesian auspices.

However, the union is less harmonious than it seems. It is based not so much on mutual respect as on mutual antagonism: body and voice are played off against each other in a way calculated narrowly to circumscribe their signifying potential. Both Heath and Bettetini speak of the voice as a device for mastering the body ("Everything that the image shows of its own accord becomes specifically indicated by the words that accompany it and restrict its sense to one or more meanings"),[6] while Bonitzer describes the body as a mechanism for restraining the voice—for diminishing "its resonance, its amplitude, its tendency to stray, its power and its restlessness."[7] Synchronization plays a major part in the production not only of a homo-centric but an ideologically consistent cinema; by insisting that the body be read through the voice, and the voice through the body, it drastically curtails the capacity of each for introducing into the narrative something heterogeneous or disruptive (it minimizes, that is, the number and kinds of connotations which can be activated).

Like the shot/reverse shot and other elements within the system of suture, synchronization helps to stitch together the fabric of the fiction over the apparatus.[8] It asserts the primacy of the diegetic over the extra-diegetic, creating the illusion that speech arises spontaneously from bodies, and that narrative proceeds from the desires and movements of self-present actants. The promptness with which sounds follow images—their seeming simultaneity—makes the former seem immanent within the latter, rather than the product of a complex enunciation. Script, dialogue coach, the voices of the actors, sound engineer, recording and mixing equipment all fade into oblivion before the impression of "direct" speech.

By deepening the diegesis and concealing the apparatus, synchronization also maintains the viewing/listening subject in a protective darkness and silence. Metz has discussed at length the connections between voyeurism and film viewing ("the obscurity surrounding the onlooker, the aperture of the screen with its inevitable keyhole effect . . . the spectator's solitude . . . the segregation of spaces").[9] However, not only does the moviegoer see without being seen; he or she listens without being heard. As Mary Ann Doane observes, "in the fiction film, the use of synchronous dialogue and the voice-off presuppose a spectator who overhears and, overhearing, is unheard and unseen himself."[10] (The synchronic instance is here, as elsewhere, to be distinguished from the voice-over, which not only assumes a listener, but addresses the listener directly, over the "heads" of the characters.)

What has not yet been remarked is that the rule of synchronization is imposed much more strictly on the female than on the male voice within dominant cinema. Although the latter, like the former, is largely limited to diegetic appearances (i.e., to speaking parts which remain "inside" the narrative, even when they are "outside" the frame), and although most of these appearances take the form of synchronous dialogue, it does on occasion manifest itself in both dis-embodied and extra-diegetic ways. In other words, from time to time the male voice speaks from an anonymous and transcendental vantage, "over" the narrative.

Apart from the documentary, where it is almost an institution, the disembodied male voice-over occurs most frequently in police thrillers and prison dramas of the "B" variety. The foregrounding of criminality in these films, as well as their rather low production values, would seem to necessitate a kind of "voice on high," whose superior knowledge and diegetic detachment promise eventual justice, despite the vitality of the robbers, the impotence of the cops, and the sleaziness of the mise-en-scène. As Bonitzer observes, this voice is a pure distillate of the law; not only does it "forbid questions about its enunciation, its place and its time," but it speaks with an unqualified authority:

> . . . the voice-over represents a power, that of disposing of the image and of that which it reflects from a place which is absolutely other. Absolutely other and absolutely indeterminable. In this sense, transcendent. . . . In so far as it arises from the field of the Other, the voice-off is assumed to know: such is the essence of its power.[11]

The capacity of the male subject to be cinematically represented in this disembodied form aligns him with transcendence, authoritative knowledge, potency, and the law—in short, with the symbolic father. Since these are the qualities to which he most aspires at the narrative level, but which he never altogether approximates, we could say that the male subject finds his most ideal realization when he is heard but not seen; when the body (what Lacan would call the "pound of flesh" which must be mortgaged in man's relationship to the signifier)[12] drops away, leaving the phallus in unchallenged possession of the scene. Thus, despite its rather rare occurrence in the fiction film, the dis-embodied voice-over can be seen as "exemplary" for male subjectivity, attesting to an achieved invisibility, omniscience, and discursive power.

It would be schematically gratifying to say that the female subject finds *her* most ideal representation when she is seen but not heard. However, as I indicated above, the female voice plays an important part in classical cinema, serving as the means by which she is established as occupying the positions of mother, siren, patient, innocent, etc. Mark Rutland, for instance, does not attempt to silence Marnie in the film of the same title; on the contrary, he extorts speech from her, using it first as a tool of diagnosis, and then as a device for inserting her into a more orthodox subject-position. The female voice serves a similar function in *The Snake Pit* and *A Woman's Face*. The first of these films, which dramatizes the rehabilitation of a female inmate in a mental institution, contains the memorable line: "Oh, you've talked—you're going to get well now, I know you will." The second, which is structured around a courtroom scene in which a woman is on trial for murder, concludes happily when that woman speaks the desires which she has previously escaped ("I've always wanted to get married . . . I want a home and children, to go to the market and cheat the butcher . . . I want to belong to the human race").

Lola Montes, most writerly of "woman's films," suggests that it would be more correct to say that ideally the female subject is both *over-seen* and *over-heard*, and that as a consequence of this system of double surveillance she is spoken even when she seems to be in control of her own speech. Lola pays for her notorious past, in which she exercised power rather than submitting to it, by playing not only to the eye but to the ear of an all-male circus audience. The story which she tells "in her own inimitable words" belongs to Mammoth Circus, "copyright reserved"; when she forgets her lines the ringmaster prompts her, bending her voice to the contours of the confession he has scripted for her. He even determines which of the audience's questions she is to answer. Lola is the prototype of the female subject within dominant narrative film, an extension both of male vision and male discourse.

Both constituents of the surveillance system—visual and auditory—must be in effect in order for it to be successful. To permit the female subject to be seen without being heard would be to activate the hermeneutic and cultural codes which define woman as a "dark continent," inaccessible to definitive male interpretation. To allow her to be heard without being seen would be even more dangerous, since it would disrupt the specular regime upon which mainstream cinema relies; it would put her beyond the control of the male gaze, and release her voice from the signifying obligations which that gaze sustains. It would be to open the possibility of woman participating in a phallic discourse, and so escaping the interrogation about her place, her time and her desires which constantly re-secures her. Indeed, to dis-embody the female subject in this way would be to challenge every conception by means of which we have previously known her, since it is precisely *as body* that she is constructed.

If, as I proposed a moment ago, male subjectivity is most fully realized when it is most invisible—when it approaches a kind of theological threshold—female subjectivity is most fully achieved when it is most visible. Through a kind of paradox, the male subject, with his "strikingly visible" organ, is defined primarily in terms of abstract and immaterial qualities (potency, power, knowledge, etc.) whereas the female subject, whose organ does not appeal to the gaze, becomes almost synonymous with the corporeal and the specular.

It is of course precisely what is invisible to a symbolic order which is organized around the phallus—that which the symbolic order can only perceive as an absence or lack—which threatens to escape its structuration, and to return as heterogeneity or a foreclosed real. Hence the fascination with the female body, the concern to construct it in ways which are accessible to the gaze and to hear it attest in a familiar language to dominant values.

Thus (with the exception of music) there are no instances within mainstream cinema where the female voice is not matched up in some way, even if only retrospectively, with the female body. For the most part woman's speech is synchronized with her image, and even when it is transmitted as a voice-off the divorce is only temporary; the body connected to the female voice is understood to be in the next room, just out of frame, at the other end of a telephone line. In short, it is always fully recoverable.

The female voice almost never functions as a voice-over, and when it does it enjoys a comparable status to the male voice-over in film noir—i.e., it is autobiographical, evoking in a reminiscent fashion the diegesis which constitutes the film's "present," a diegesis within which the speaker figures centrally. Lisa's narration in *Letter From an Unknown Woman*, which provides one of the most extended voice-overs in classical cinema, is a case in point. Not only is it at every point anchored to a specific female body, but the temporal interval which separates it from that body constantly diminishes as the film unfolds. Moreover, Lisa speaks to a male auditor (Stephan) whose willingness to read her letter activates its discourse. In a sense what we *hear* is what he *overhears*; her voice is his mental construction. (In the same way, what we see is what he imagines, as the final, montage flashback makes clear.) Lisa's narration is obedient to Stephan's desires, to his ear.

Not surprisingly, feminist cinema has focused an enormous amount of attention on the female voice. Three examples from New German Cinema suggest that this is true not only of experimental work, but also of documentary and even more conventionally narrative films. Helga Reidemeister's documentary, *Apropos of Fate*, is in large part the deployment of cinema by the female members of a family for the express purpose of talking through their relationships to each other, men, work, and the social order. The director participates in this conversation, but her dis-embodied status—the fact that she remains "pure" voice—indicates the irreducible distance which separates her, both as an effect of the apparatus and as someone external to the family, from the pro-filmic event. Helke Sander's *All-Round Reduced Personality* utilizes an anonymous female voice-over to situate the work and personal problems of a woman photographer (Etta) within the context of West Berlin politics and culture, a device which emphasizes the general fragmentation to which the central character is subjected (since that voice remains so close to Etta, we are encouraged to think of it as something of her own from which she has become alienated).

Jutta Bruckner introduces *Hunger Years* with an autobiographical voice-over which enjoys an unusual relationship with the image track: the film's narrative concludes with the apparent suicide of its female protagonist, a suicide prompted by her inability either to tolerate or to break with the maternal legacy—with the legacy, that is, of classical female subjectivity forcibly bequeathed to her by her mother. However, both the profound pessimism of the larger text and the finality of the act of self-destruction with which it concludes, are qualified by the introductory voice-over, which speaks about survival, transformation, escape. That voice converts the images of a highly ritualized suicide into metaphors of rupture and change—in short, it de-literalizes them.

It is in feminist avant-garde practice, though, that the female voice has been most exhaustively interrogated and most innovatively deployed. A statement by Laura Mulvey in an interview about *Riddles of the Sphinx* can be taken as an epigraph to this practice:

> . . . there is an important theme: the difficulties of women being articulate and putting emotion or thought into words. In *Riddles*, I think, I felt the time had come not to deal with that kind of silence which so many in the women's movement had felt and talked about, a kind of cultural silence essentially. Having taken that as a fact, one had to go ahead and try to fill in the gaps and think of what ways one would give voice to female desires.[13]

However, whereas *Riddles of the Sphinx* attempts to exhume a female voice which has been repressed by patriarchy, but which has nevertheless remained intact for thousands of years at some unconscious level, the films about which I would like to talk for the remainder of this essay function more as a series of responses to cultural "givens" about female subjectivity. In other words, rather than searching for a pre-symbolic female language, they confine themselves to an examination of the place of the female voice within the existing discursive field.

In each case that examination involves the dislocation of the sound from the image track. Indeed, all of these films—*Misconception, Film About a Woman Who, Dora, News From Home, Empty Suitcases*, and *Journeys From Berlin/71*—resort in one way or another to the principle of non-synchronization, devising various strategies for divorcing the female voice from the female body. *Journeys From Berlin/71* makes clearer than any of the other films precisely what is at stake in this disassociation of sound and image: the freeing-up of the female voice from its obsessive and indeed exclusive reference to the female body, a reference which turns woman—in representation and in fact—back upon herself, in a negative and finally self-consuming narcissism.

Perhaps the simplest strategy for challenging the imperative of synchronization, especially insofar as it provides the support for sexual difference, is the alignment of the female voice with a male body, or that of a male voice with a female body. This is the strategy employed by Marjorie Keller at a key moment of *Misconception*, a film which is devoted to the exploration of the three-way relationship between the male voice, the female voice, and the female body.

Misconception, which records the birth of the filmmaker's niece, uses heavily edited documentary footage to dispell the myth that childbirth is not only painless but a kind of *jouissance*. Shots from the delivery room are intercut with both interior and exterior shots of the wife, the husband, and their son taken at an earlier moment in the pregnancy. The sounds from one context are often connected with the images from the other, but no extra-diegetic information is introduced.

The film's complex ironies are produced primarily through the juxtaposition of the mother's voice and image with the voices of the husband and doctor. Indeed, the pregnant woman's voice is edited more at the level of the documentary "fiction" than at that of the enunciation, by the verbal pressure of those two men. She is encouraged to emit only those sounds—linguistic and pre-linguistic—which belong to the sanctioned discourse of motherhood. The cries of childbirth enjoy a particularly prominent place here, as does a telephone conversation immediately after delivery in which the mother expresses her pleasure that "it's a girl." Contradictory statements are usually interrupted or corrected. When she confesses, for instance, that if she had it to do over again, she wouldn't have become a mother, her husband firmly responds that she is forgetting the "joys" of her position.

The chief expositor of these joys is the doctor, who, after the successful delivery of the second child, speaks almost orphically about the agents of childbirth:

> Those who feel they've done perfectly, they'll feel godlike. They might feel actual ecstasy and look back on it as having transcended. If they are critical the worst that happens is that they recognize they are human beings, that they feel pain, may react other than perfectly, in their own eyes that is, to pain.

But the image track belies this mystical interpretation of childbirth, showing us blood, tissue, the umbilical cord, the afterbirth: signifiers of suffering and toil. It also dramatizes the failure of the spectatorial paradigm by means of which the doctor defines motherhood—a paradigm which demands of the female subject that she "look" at her body and its response to labor in order to determine whether or not she is "perfect."

The failure of that paradigm is anticipated earlier in the film, when the voice of the pregnant woman takes exception to an article in *Esquire* addressed to the topic of childbirth: "I think there is a lot of difference between men's view of having a baby and a woman's. . . . A woman's view is that I just want to make it as easy as possible . . . and a man's view is that it shouldn't hurt to begin with." Non-synchronization thus occurs within the diegetic as well as the extra-diegetic discourse; not only do the images in the delivery room not correspond to the doctor's voice-off, but the female subject refuses to look at herself from the place which is prescribed for her, insisting instead on the disequivalence between her own self-image and that projected for her by the discourse of motherhood.

In an interview with the *Camera Obscura* Collective, Yvonne Rainer suggests that one of the central projects of *Film About a Woman Who* is the establishment of a dialectical relationship between sound and image, the replacement of synchronization with counterpoint:

> . . . I was . . . concerned with interweaving psychological and formal content, i.e., with images being "filled up" or "emptied" by readings or their absence, with text and speech being "illustrated" to varying degrees by images. This made for a situation where the story came and went, sometimes disappearing altogether as in the extreme prolongation of certain soundless images. . . . I was trying to make a silent film—with occasional sound.[14]

These remarks are indicative not so much of an impulse to privilege image over sound as the desire to interrupt their conventional and mutually impoverishing marriage, to establish different lines of communication between them. The female subject is seen as having a particular stake in the reconceptualization of the relationship between cinema's two tracks.

Film About a Woman Who resorts to a number of devices for dislodging the female voice from the female image. One of these devices, which is taken even further in *Kristina Talking Pictures*, is the delineation of more than one female body to which story and speech can be "pinned." The automatic signifying transfer from a particular female voice to a particular female image is thus frustrated; the semic code is rendered inoperative by the absence of a proper name, a stable visual representation, and a predictable cluster of attributes.

The film's reliance upon voice-over and intertitles further denaturalizes the female voice, also contributing to the jamming of the semic code. The episode entitled "Emotional Accretion in 48 Steps" utilizes both of these strategies, as well as periods of complete silence. It also makes startlingly evident what is at issue for woman in the avoidance of synchronized sound.

In this episode a man and a woman lie in bed together, sometimes turning towards each other and sometimes away. Each movement or gesture is separated by a number introducing a new "step," some of which include intertitles and others of which do not. The intertitles narrate rather than offering direct dialogue, substituting the pronouns "he" and "she" for "you" and "I."

The intrusion of a fragmented but nonetheless intensely psychological narrative into a cinematic system which provides none of the usual supports for viewer identification results in a good deal of free-floating anxiety. The woman who tosses and turns on the bed, and who is described as first wanting to tell the man to go and then deciding to demand his attention, seems to be constrained by a discourse (the discourse of the "affair") within which she is not entirely comfortable, and to which moreover she does not entirely accede. The use of the pronoun "she," and of an indirect rather than a direct construction, indicates her unwillingness fully to activate her own subjectivity within that discourse, an event which, as Benveniste tells us, requires the articulation of the first-person pronoun.[15]

The climactic moment in this episode involves precisely such an articulation. In the only use of synchronized sound in any of the 48 steps, the woman asks: "Would you hold me?" The contradiction between the discourse to which she here accedes and her own desires is indicated in steps 43 through 48, where we read:

> She arrives home. She is very angry. She knows the crucial moment was when she said "hold me." Somehow she had betrayed herself. She hadn't wanted to be held. (Do you think she could figure her way out of a paper bag?) She had wanted to bash his fucking face in.[16]

The convergence of synchronization and the first-person pronoun ("me") is highly significant, emphasizing the part played by the former in the production of a coherent, stable, and "manageable" subject. *Film About a Woman Who* shows the alignment of image and sound to be an agency of entrapment, one of the means by which the female subject emerges within a discourse contrary to her desires, submits at least temporarily to a fixed identity.

Weinstock, Pajaczkowska, Tyndall, and McCall's film, *Sigmund Freud's Dora*, does not at any juncture actually disengage the female voice from the female image. Indeed, it employs synchronized sound throughout. However, by overtly and literally appropriating the text of Freud's case study, and by introducing footage from "adult" movies and television advertisements, it creates a space between its female voices and the words they speak, a space which shows those words to proceed from a source external to them. In short, the film foregrounds a number of discourses by means of which female subjectivity is presently constituted.

It also suggests—and this may be its most important contribution—that the female voice plays a vital (albeit passive) role in at least two of these discourses: psychoanalysis and advertising. It indicates, that is, that these two discourses require a female subject who speaks about herself in rigorously codified ways, who implicates her body at every turn of phrase. *Sigmund Freud's Dora* thus demonstrates that for psychoanalysis and advertising, as for cinema, the ideal female subject is one who permits herself to be heard as well as seen, who participates in the discursive alignment of her body with male desire (that of the father, Herr K, Freud), commodities (liquid Tylenol, F.D.S. deodorant), and the scopic drive, always testifying to the excellence of the "fit."

The concluding section of the film adds a voice which has been conspicuously absent from its earlier sections, as from Freud's case study—

that of the mother. Once again the female voice is oddly disassociated from the words it utters; in fact, this sequence indicates more clearly than any of the others that the female voice is, within the existing social order, a reading voice, one which repeats what has always already been written or spoken elsewhere. However, a series of disruptions at the discursive level effectively frees the female voice from any signifying relationship to the words she articulates. The mother, whose image remains stable but whose identity is put into extreme flux towards the end of the film (she could be the psychotic housewife, the grandmother, the woman both Herr K and Dora's father "got nothing out of," the image of the madonna, the mother Dora sought in her brother, the real or the symbolic mother), reads aloud from a group of postcards written by a daughter whose own identity remains equally indeterminate. Although that daughter is also called Dora, she is not always—as Jane Weinstock observes—a resident of the same century:

> . . . the postcards could not have the same return address. The early letters seem to be sent by a 19th century daughter, very much like Freud's Dora, and the later ones by a 1970s feminist, also named Dora. Moreover, the 19th century Dora's postcards of twentieth century pornography set up a literal contradiction. The spectator, already uprooted by a shifting address, is now split between centuries. . . . [17]

The proper name thus no longer serves as the locus for a relatively stable cluster of attributes, but is itself the site of an extreme temporal and discursive division.

Chantal Akerman uses the letter-reading device as a means for introducing an even more radically split subjectivity into one of her films. She inscribes both a mother and a daughter into *News From Home* through a voice which at no juncture meshes with the images we see, images of New York City. That voice reads aloud letters sent to New York from a mother who remains in Belgium, and it is defined only as the receiving point for this maternal address.

Its formal status is also extremely ambiguous. Because it is dis-embodied it is technically a voice-over of the transcendental variety, but it has none of the authority or appeal to superior knowledge which are the usual attributes of that device. In fact, it is often drowned out by the noises of the city, and because of the monotony of its message we only periodically attend to it. Moreover, it at no point connects with the image track, either as diegetic complement or metalanguage. Whereas the former depicts a sultry Manhattan, the latter dwells persistently on the domestic situation back "home," in Belgium.

Finally, we are asked to distinguish between the voice itself and the words it utters, a distinction which the classic text would work hard to erase. To begin with, this voice has a very definite flavor or grain, in contrast to the carefully standardized voice used in documentaries and police thrillers. To its qualities of youthfulness and softness the English version of *News From Home* adds foreignness, for it speaks with a strong Belgian accent. Disembodied though it is, Barthes would say that this voice engages the flesh ("The 'grain' is that: the materiality of the body speaking its mother tongue").[18]

Secondly, the words "belong" to the mother, and the voice to the daughter, which is another way of saying that they represent very diverse points of view. In her own gloss on the largely autobiographical *News From Home* Akerman emphasizes that diversity; she describes her mother, source of the film's words, as an uneducated woman who has never been to America, and whose entire existence revolves around her tightly integrated family. Each detail underscores the daughter's distance from the home front:

> My mother wrote me love-letters, and that was marvelous. With her own words. . . . My mother didn't learn to write, she quit school at 11, and then there was the war. She writes as she can, she formulates her feelings in an unsophisticated way, they really reflect her. If she were more sophisticated, she wouldn't have dared to ask me all the time 'When are you coming back? You know very well that we love you, you know that we miss you.' She wouldn't have dared, she would have said it by a thousand 'detours.' But she's not sophisticated, she used the words she had, so she had a more direct relationship.[19]

The film indicates the same thing through its non-continuous sound and image tracks: the claustral and repetitive quality of the mother's phrases contrasts markedly with the detachment and open-endedness of the cinematography and editing, which are here signifiers of the daughter's "outlook" on the world.

There is never, however, any implied hierarchy between these two points of view. Nor is there any implied hierarchy between the New York we see, and the Belgium we hear. Fundamentally, the letters which the daughter reads and the city which she visits belong to two different discourses, neither of which is capable of "containing" her. We hear her voice reading one, and we participate in her vision of the other, but she remains on the edges of each. Significantly, all of the film's shots, with the exception of those inside the subway system, are exterior, and the final one leaves us stranded in the New York harbor, neither "here" nor "there."

The dis-embodied voice of *News From Home* anticipates what might be called the "traveling" voice of *Empty Suitcases*. This film, like *Kristina Talking Pictures* and *Film About a Woman Who*, frustrates the spectator's attempts to connect the sound and image tracks by projecting a diversity of female bodies, any one of which could be the "heroine." However, the real mobility of the film—not just the shift from one female representation to another, but the movement from one city to another, and one discourse to another—is an effect of the sound track.

Near the beginning of *Empty Suitcases* we journey back and forth from New York to Chicago dozens of times in the space of five minutes, as a female voice reads aloud from a stack of postcards, some of which are addressed from one of those cities, and some from the other. Even more spectacular are the transits from one melodramatic mode to another—from the subject-position of the suffering artist to that of the rejected professor, the angry mistress, the terrorist, the teller of oedipal dreams. Filmmaker Bette Gordon negotiates these constant relocations through a multiplicity of female voices and discursive strategies, including not only the voice-over but the voice-off, synchronized dialogue and monologue, and musical lyrics.

It is through the last of these aural modes that *Empty Suitcases* makes both its wittiest and perhaps its most important statement about the female voice. In the episode in question a woman lies on a bed lip-synching the words to the Billie Holiday song, "All of me." Although there is a perfect match of the movements of the woman's lips with the lyrics we hear, it is belied by the complete disequivalence between her facial expression and the affect of the music; she remains completely impassive as Holiday's voice reaches ever new crescendos of masochistic ardor. The song is ostensibly about a woman's complete surrender of herself to her lover, but it takes the form of a series of auto-references. Holiday's voice offers up her body piece by piece, in an elaborate dismemberment ("Take my lips . . . take my arms . . . you took my heart, so why not take all of me?").

This sequence points to the intimate connection between the synchronization of the female voice with the female image in classical cinema, and the semiotics of self-reference which it habitually promotes in its women viewers and listeners. That semiotics, which obliges the female voice to signify the female body, and the female body to signify lack, isolates the female subject from effective political action, prevents her from making investments in a new social order, and guarantees that she will remain in the same place.

These issues are treated at much greater length in what is unquestionably the most remarkable deployment of female voices within the feminist avant-garde, if not within the whole of experimental cinema: Yvonne Rainer's *Journeys From Berlin/71*. Two of its many voices—those of the "patient," also called Annette, and that belonging to Rainer herself—are synchronized with the image track, while a third—that of the female analyst—connects up with a woman's back. Two other female voices remain completely dis-embodied, although the persona represented by each is evoked with extraordinary vividness. These voices "belong" to an adolescent girl, and to an adult woman who is engaged simultaneously in a conversation about political violence and the preparations for a meal.

One other voice must be included in this list, although it derives from a man. This last voice could best be characterized as a dirty phone-caller, but during his longest and most persistent intrusion he delivers one of the film's most important female monologues:

> My daddy called me Cookie. I'm really a good girl. I'll go along with anything as long as you'll like me a little. I'll even promise not to bring up all that business about being such a low element, such primeval slime, such an amoeba, such an edible *thing*. I'm not one for fussing. Not like those movie women: Katy Hepburn facing the dawn in her posh pad with stiff upper chin. Merle Oberon facing the Nazi night with hair billowing in the electric breeze. Roz Russell sockin' the words 'n' the whiskey to the best of them. Rita Hayworth getting shot in the mirror and getting her man. Jane Wyman smiling through tears. I never faced the music, much less the dawn; I stayed in bed. I never socked anything to anybody; why rock the boat? I never set out to get my man, even in the mirror; they all got me. I never smiled through my tears; I choked down my terror. I never had to face the Nazis, much less their night. Not for me that succumbing in the great task because it must be done; not for me the heart beating in incomprehensible joy; not for me the vicissitudes of class struggle; not for me the uncertainties of political thought. . . . [20]

The dirty phone-caller speaks from the position of the traditional female viewer; "her" voice registers the subjectivity conferred upon women by classical cinema—a subjectivity which is the effect of a masochistic misrecognition. Rita Hayworth, Katharine Hepburn, Merle Oberon, Rosalind Russell and Jane Wyman (both as stars and as characters) provide some of the ideal representations by means of which that misrecognition occurs, propelling the female viewer into a negative narcissism.[21]

Images of the kind cited above both structure and exceed the female viewer; indeed, they structure largely through excess, through the elaboration of hyperbolic spectacle. The felt inadequacy of the female subject in the face of these ideal images induces in her an intense self-loathing. At the same time it is impossible for her simply to turn away from them, to retreat into herself, since she has only a relational identity, knows herself only through representation. Her inability either to approximate or transcend the mirror in which she sees herself as the dim reflection of a luminous original locks her into a deadly narcissism, one more conducive of self-hatred than self-love. It must further be noted that each of the movie citations enumerated by the dirty phone-caller constitues a masochistic inscription. Each glamorizes pain, renunciation, death. Classical cinema thus overdetermines the production of a docile and suffering female subject.

Journeys From Berlin/71 explores the relationship of subjectivity to the existing symbolic order not only through the voice of the dirty phone-caller but through those of the adolescent girl, the patient, the cooking woman, and the director herself. Each is located within a context in which women have traditionally been encouraged to talk, contexts which structure and circumscribe their subjectivity. Thus the adolescent girl addresses her diary, the patient her analyst, the cooking woman the man with whom she presumably lives, and Rainer her mother. Each of these discourses is characterized by a high degree of reflexivity; although they all probe the relationship between the personal and the social, the accent falls increasingly on the first of those terms. Toward the end of the film the four voices converge more and more, until they finally seem to be participating in the same narcissistic speech.

The diary entries read aloud by the voice of the adolescent girl range across a wide variety of topics. However, the self is a constant point of reference. The first entry describes a number of events whose common denominator is that they induce in the writer what she calls the "chills" or the "shivers." Subsequent entries return obsessively to the feelings evoked in the adolescent girl by other people and things. The one dated Friday, September 28 is symptomatic:

> The tears are here again. Brush them away. Something just happened. Mama just finished listening to one of those one-hour dramas, a real tragedy. She said, "I shouldn't listen to those stories, they really move me too much. But I don't know what else to do with my time." And the tears came. Sometimes I feel an overwhelming tenderness for her. I don't know if it's love. Right now I am being strangely moved by my feeling for her.

The object is virtually eclipsed in this libidinal economy, whose extensions are all circular.[22]

Events in the external world function as signifiers of the self in much the same way in the patient's discourse. Vietnam provides material for masturbatory fantasies, Samuel Beckett finds his way into a story about shopping in Bloomingdale's and the defeat of the patient's hard-won independence, and statistics about political prisoners lead to the seemingly unconnected observation that "rejection and disappointment are the two things that I've always found impossible to take." The most breathtaking assimilation of the public into the private is effected during a reverie about the body:

> Some people don't seem to notice their own body changes. . . . I can predict exactly where new pressures of clothing will occur the next day—buttocks, thighs, belly, breasts—what new topography will appear on my face: creases and barrows as conspicuous as the scars slashed by two world wars into the soil of Europe.

Here all of twentieth-century history and a large portion of the world's geography yield metaphoric precedence to a woman's face and figure, and to the self-loathing of which they are the distillate. The patient's voice is synchronized to her image in more ways than one.

The voice associated with kitchen noises speaks about virtually nothing but women anarchists and revolutionaries, reading at length from their letters. However, when asked whether she has read the political writings of Emma Goldman, she responds: "No, I have a collection of her essays, but all I've read is her autobiography." Moreover, towards the end of the film this voice talks a good deal about the difficulty she has always experienced in empathizing with oppressed groups. Instead, she gravitates toward radical "stars," ideal representations which frustrate rather than assist her desire to transcend traditional female subjectivity. Like classical cinema's exemplary woman viewer, she both identifies with the suffering of these ideal representations, and defines herself as lacking through them (thus whereas the figures she most admires all heroically subordinate the personal to the political, she herself despairs of even achieving "correct social behavior"). *Journeys From Berlin/71* draws attention to the similarities between these two sets of images when it shows the female analyst looking through a stack of photographs in which Jane Wyman and Rita Hayworth coexist with Vera Figner, Ulrike Meinhof, and Vera Zasulich.

Finally, there is the voice—and the image—of Yvonne Rainer, speaking from Europe to her mother about a movie she has just seen, a movie filmed in Berlin before the war. Rainer talks about how affected she and the other viewers were by the shots of a city which no longer exists. Again the emphasis falls on the feelings evoked in the female subject by external occurrences, on sentiment rather than history or the social order. The autoreferentiality of all these voices is periodically accentuated by the appearance against a black background of rolling white titles providing facts and figures about West German postwar politics, i.e., by a discourse traditionally associated with values of "objectivity" and "neutrality," as well as by the interpolation at the level of the sound track of other, more strident political statements and accounts (here excerpts from a letter written by Ulrike Meinhof to Hannah Krabbe about the necessity of resisting prison psychiatrification).

In the general conversation about narcissism to which all of the female voices contribute during the last third of the film, a conversation which often occurs simultaneously on several registers, the adolescent girl confesses:

> Everything I've written has been put down for the benefit of some potential reader. It is a titanic task to be frank with myself. I fear my own censure. Even my thoughts sometimes appear to my consciousness in a certain form for the benefit of an imaginary mind-reader. And strangely enough, *I* am that reader of these pages; *I* am that reader of this mind. I have very strong

> impressions of my childhood "acting." Up to a few years ago, whenever I was alone I would "perform." I didn't think I did anything unusual or dramatic at these times, but the things I did do I did with the thought in mind that I was being watched. Now this reaction is becoming more and more unconscious, having been transmitted to my actions, speech, writing, and my thoughts. This last is the most unfortunate of all.

What this female voice records is the internalization of the specular and auditory regime upon which classical cinema relies, and which it helps to perpetuate within the larger cultural order. The notion of performance is of course an important one in all of Rainer's films, but in *Journeys From Berlin/71* it gains new resonance.[23] It becomes a metaphor for female subjectivity, for the interiorization of discursive demands which must be met at every moment of psychic existence, and which carry out the functions of overseeing and over-hearing the ego even in the most solitary of situations. The rigors of that performance are so severe that they leave the female subject with no capacity for struggle on any other front, and result in extreme cases in suicide.

Journeys From Berlin/71 engages in a relentless exposé not only of the female voice, but of the psychic mechanisms which operate it, and the symbolic field of which they are an extension. It suggests that by taking into herself the power-relations which organize the existing cultural order the female subject can never be anything but smoothly aligned with it—that her speech and her image will always be perfectly synchronized not only with each other, but with those discourses which are dominant at any given moment. The invocation by the woman analyst of Freud's *Mourning and Melancholia* is not coincidental, since it is there that we find the most chilling account of a condition which may be pathological for the male subject, but represents the norm for the female subject—that condition of negative narcissism which blights her relations both with herself and her culture:

> The patient represents [her] ego to us as worthless, incapable of any achievement and morally despicable; [she] reproaches [herself], vilifies [herself] and expects to be cast out and punished. [She] abases [herself] before everyone and commiserates [her] own relatives for being connected with anyone so unworthy . . . [she] declares that [she] was never any better.[24]

Journeys From Berlin/71 does more than deconstruct this closed theater of female subjectivity; it also points beyond. Not only does it detach voice from body, interrupting in the process the coherence upon which the performance relies, and revealing the degree to which the former has been obliged to talk about and regulate the latter, but in its final moments it involves its female speakers in a choric repudiation of ideal images and self-hatred. It also broaches, in a tentative and fragmentary manner, the possibility of moving beyond masochism toward externally directed action—the possibility, that is, of political struggle: "one might conceivably take greater risks . . . in using one's power . . . for the benefit of others . . . resisting inequities close at hand."

NOTES

1. See in particular Laura Mulvey, "Visual Pleasure and Narrative Cinema," *Screen* 16, no. 3 (Autumn 1975), pp. 6–18; Linda Williams, "Film Body: An Implantation of Perversions," *Ciné-Tracts* 3, no. 4 (Winter 1981), pp. 19–34, and "When the Woman Looks"; Teresa de Lauretis, "Through the Looking Glass," in *The Cinematic Apparatus*, ed. Teresa de Lauretis and Stephen Heath, New York: St. Martin's Press (1980), pp. 187–202; and Sandy Flitterman, "Woman, Desire and the Look: Feminism and the Enunciative Apparatus in Cinema," *Ciné-Tracts* 2, no. 1 (Spring 1978), pp. 63–68.

2. In *The Archaeology of Knowledge and the Discourse on Language*, trans. A. M. Sheridan-Smith, London: Tavistock (1972), Foucault speaks of " 'fellowships' of discourse, whose function is to preserve or to reproduce discourse, but in order that it should circulate within a closed community, according to strict regulation, without those in possession being dispossessed by this very distribution." (p. 225).

3. For a more extended discussion of the connections between sexual difference and discourse, see my "*Histoire d'O*: The Story of a Disciplined and Punished Body," *Enclitic* 7, no. 2 (1983).

4. Stephen Heath describes the insertion of the voice into the diegesis as its preservation within a "safe place," and adds that this place is carefully maintained in the fiction film (see "Narrative Space," *Screen* 17, no. 3 [Autumn 1976], p. 100).

5. Pascal Bonitzer, *Le Regard et la voix*, Paris: Union Générale d'Editions (1976), p. 30.

6. In "Body, Voice," (in *Questions of Cinema*, Bloomington: Indiana University Press [1981]) Stephen Heath writes "the sound cinema is the development of a powerful standard of the body and of the voice as hold of the body in image, the voice literally ordered and delimited as speech for an intelligibility of the body . . . " (p. 191); Gianfranco Bettetini, *The Language and Technique of the Film*, ed. Thomas A. Sebeok, The Hague: Mouton (1973), p. 161.

7. Bonitzer, p. 30.

8. "Suture" designates any cinematic element which encourages the viewer/listener's identification with fictional characters and narrative progression. The shot/reverse shot formation has been seen by many theoreticians as virtually synonymous with the system of suture, functioning as it often does to align a character who looks with the supposed object of that character's gaze. Such an alignment organizes the spectator's point of view around character, and inspires in him or her the desire for the next shot, i.e., for more narrative. For a fuller treatment of the system of suture, see Chapter 5 of my *The Subject of Semiotics*, New York: Oxford University Press (1983).

9. Christian Metz, "The Imaginary Signifier," trans. Ben Brewster, *Screen* 16, no. 2 (Summer 1975), p. 64.

10. Mary Ann Doane, "The Voice in Cinema: The Articulation of Body and

Space," *Yale French Studies*, no. 60 (1980), p. 43. See also "Ideology and the Practice of Sound Editing and Mixing," in *The Cinematic Apparatus*, pp. 47–56.

11. Bonitzer, p. 33.

12. Jacques Lacan, "Desire and the Interpretation of Desire in *Hamlet*," trans. James Hulbert, *Yale French Studies*, no. 55/56 (1977), p. 28.

13. "An Interview with Laura Mulvey and Peter Wollen on *Riddles of the Sphinx*," *Millennium Film Journal*, no. 4/5 (1979), p. 24.

14. "Yvonne Rainer: Interview," *Camera Obscura* 1, no. 1 (Fall 1976), p. 89.

15. In *Problems in General Linguistics*, trans. Mary Meek, Coral Gables, FL: University of Miami Press (1971) Emile Benveniste writes that "Language is . . . the possibility of subjectivity because it always contains the linguistic forms appropriate to the expression of subjectivity and discourse provokes the emergence of subjectivity because it consists of discrete instances. In some way language puts forth 'empty' forms which each speaker, in the exercise of discourse, appropriates to his 'person,' at the same time defining himself as *I* and a partner as *you*. The instance of discourse is thus constitutive of all coordinates that define the subject, and of which we have briefly pointed out only the most obvious (i.e., pronouns, verb forms, etc.)." (p. 227)

16. See *October* 2 (1976), pp. 36–67 for the script of *Film About a Woman Who*.

17. Jane Weinstock, "Sigmund Freud's Dora?" *Screen*, vol. 22, no. 2 (1981), p. 73.

18. Roland Barthes, "The Grain of the Voice," in *Image—Music—Text*, trans. Stephen Heath (New York: Hill and Wang, 1977), p. 182.

19. Christina Creveling, "Chantal Akerman," *Camera Obscura*, vol. 2, no. 2 (1977), p. 137.

20. All quotations from *Journeys From Berlin/71* are taken from the complete, unpublished script.

21. For a fuller and somewhat different discussion of this condition, see my "*Hamlet* and the Common Theme of Fathers," *Enclitic*, vol. 3, no. 2 (1979), pp. 106–121.

22. A passage quoted in *Journeys From Berlin/71* from Sigmund Freud's "Mourning and Melancholia" suggests that melancholia (or negative narcissism, as I prefer to call it) always involves the loss of any external object: "The analysis of melancholia now shows that the ego can kill itself only if, owing to the return of the object-cathexis, it can treat itself as an object—if it is able to direct against itself the hostility which relates to an object and which represents the ego's original reaction to objects in the external world. . . . In the two opposed situations of being most intensely in love and of suicide the ego is overwhelmed by the object, though in totally different ways." (In *The Standard Edition of the Complete Psychological Works of Sigmund Freud*, trans. James Strachey [London: Hogarth Press, 1953], Vol. XIV, p. 252.)

23. B. Ruby Rich treats this metaphor at some length in *Yvonne Rainer* (Minneapolis, MN: Walker Art Center, 1981).

24. Freud, p. 246.

IV.

Assessing Films Directed by Women

The films discussed in this section are predominantly works directed by women, mainly feminist filmmakers, who are more than familiar with film theory and who have worked out their own strategies for a feminist film practice. Two essays address Hollywood production; the rest focus on works by filmmakers who have specifically chosen to work outside of the mainstream, both here and abroad. In addition to representing a diverse body of work, this section attempts to apply a variety of methodologies.

A comment on the selection process is needed, perhaps. I favored films that had been widely seen in commercial or alternative venues or that had been frequently discussed among those concerned with feminist filmmaking. Priority was given to works that raised questions about feminist theory and/or practice and articles that addressed the issues previously discussed in this book.

Several directors have now produced a sizeable body of work. Among the most active Europeans working in narrative fiction are: Marta Meszaros of Hungary; Vera Chytilova of Czechoslovakia; Doris Dorrie, Ulrike Ottinger, Helke Sander, Helma Sanders-Brahams, and Margarethe von Trotta of West Germany; Diane Kurys and Agnes Varda of France; Liliana Cavani and Lina Wertmuller of Italy; and Chantal Akerman of Belgium, as well as Gillian Armstrong of Australia. In the U.S., Martha Coolidge, Elaine May, Susan Seidelman, and Joan Micklin Silver each have directed several works. All of these women are still active and all of their feature films have demonstrated both creativity and, in most cases, a concern for women's issues. For an overview of their contributions, see Barbara Quart's *Women Directors: The Emergence of a New Cinema.*

In addition, there is a large group of independent women filmmakers in the United States, Canada, Australia, and elsewhere, such as Yvonne Rainer, Lizzie Borden, Michelle Citron, and Bette Gordon in the U.S. and Laura Mulvey (with Peter Wollen) and Sally Potter in the U.K., who have expanded the boundaries of filmmaking practice. All of these filmmakers are treated in brief in the essays in Section Three. Further information on women's independent filmmaking is provided in the Bibliography.

In "Images and Women" (1986), Robin Wood asserts that for feminism to be admitted to the Hollywood cinema, it had to undergo a drastic change, namely the repression of politics. To demonstrate how this operates, he provides a structural analysis of the two films most associated with feminism during the 1970s—Paul Mazursky's *An Unmarried Woman* and Martin Scorsese's *Alice Doesn't Live Here Anymore*—exposing how the structures define the limits of what is ideologically acceptable and how these films defuse feminism, making it "safe and unthreatening." In the end, what is conveyed is "a huge communal sigh of relief; the women don't have to be independent after all; there are strong, protective males to look after them."[1]

Wood then takes a close look at four commercial films of the 1980s (three independent productions and one mainstream Hollywood movie) which attempt to walk a thin line between making a statement and vying for commercial success. These include Claudia Weill's *Girlfriends* (1978), Lee Grant's *Tell Me a Riddle* (1980), Joan Micklin Silver's *Chilly Scenes of Winter* (1979), and Amy Heckerling's *Fast Times at Ridgemont High* (1982). He discusses these works within the larger question of "What possibilities exist for a female (not necessarily feminist) discourse to be articulated within a patriarchal industry through narrative conventions and genres developed by and for a male-dominate culture?"[2] He is especially intrigued by *Fast Times at Ridgemont High* because of its ability to satisfy all of the genre requirements of the high school cycle and at the same time to construct a position for the female spectator that is neither masochistic nor merely compliant. Further, the film allows for both the expression of women's desire and their critique of male assumptions, although it stops short of exploring any issues which would be threatening to male viewers.

"Unspoken and Unsolved: *Tell Me a Riddle*" (1985), by Florence Jacobowitz and Lori Spring, takes up the issue of Hollywood-style realism, a denigrated tradition since the days of Claire Johnston's writings about counter-cinema. Like Robin Wood, the authors are interested in the degree to which such works can serve as a source for political and/or social change. Jacobowitz and Spring review the objections of some feminists to the realist tradition—specifically, its potential for disguising the ways in which woman's image has been appropriated for the pleasure of the male spectator. However, they note that films like *Tell Me a Riddle* "reformulate, expand, and evolve generic possibilities by offering different kinds of images than those long perpetuated in mainstream culture."[3] Concomitantly, the film's treatment of gender, class, and ethnic issues expresses social criticism and paves the way for change in the concrete world by affecting the viewer's consciousness.

The authors discuss *Tell Me a Riddle*, focusing on how Eva, a poor, elderly, Jewish-Russian immigrant, seeks to resist the constraints of her life by carving out a place of dignity within her limited world. They see Eva's withdrawal into the past and her attachment to her home as forms of resistance that provide solace, but also isolation. They demonstrate how the film foregrounds issues of gender and economic oppression through Eva's relationship with her husband, her granddaughter, and Mrs. Mays, a recent widow. Through the growing support of the two women, Eva is able to emerge from her alienation. This is marked narratively by her ability to vocalize her feelings and is visualized by images of space and air. Memories of her past imprisonment in Russia and ceaseless economic struggles in America give way to cries of "freiheit" ("freedom"). In the end Eva finds the means to bridge the gap, brought about by years of resentment, between herself and her husband. Jacobowitz and Spring credit Grant, though, for not imposing a false happy ending. Instead we are left with a legacy of spirit and principle. The authors conclude that "by exposing images, voices, and narratives long suppressed and silenced" the film "attests to the possibility of producing art which is both popular and politically significant."[4]

Using two films which focus on one woman's obsession with another, Jackie Stacey in "Desperately Seeking Difference" (1987), raises questions concerning the representation of women's desire and identification and how these produce pleasure for the female spectator, questions which are absent in Mulvey's article on visual pleasure. Before addressing the male-directed *All About Eve* and the female-directed *Desperately Seeking Susan*, Stacey lays out three possibilities for female spectatorship: masculinization (Laura Mulvey), masochism (Raymond Bellour), and marginality (Mary Ann Doane). Finding all of these unsatisfying for most female viewers, she argues for "a more complex model of cinematic spectatorship," one that separates "gender identification from sexuality."[5]

In selecting *All About Eve* and *Desperately Seeking Susan*, Stacey claims that both works have "female protagonists whose desires and identifications move the narratives forward."[6] Further, *All About Eve* is of particular interest because "it is precisely about the pleasures and dangers of spectatorship for women. One of its central themes is the construction and reproduction of feminine identities, and the activity of looking is highlighted as an important part of these processes."[7]

Stacey compares *All About Eve* with *Desperately Seeking Susan*, another film about a woman's obsession, but one that does not result in punishment of the heroine. Like the character of the aspiring actress Eve (Anne Baxter) in the previous work, who wants to be another star like Margot (Bette Davis), Roberta (Rosanna Arquette), a suburban housewife, desires to become Susan. But despite the fact that Susan (Madonna) serves in the traditional function of "woman as spectacle," Stacey feels that the crucial difference in this film is not sexual difference, but the difference between two women. Stacey points out how both films "tempt the woman spectator with the fictional fulfillment of becoming an ideal feminine other, while denying complete transformation by insisting upon differences between women."[8]

The next essay, Judith Mayne's "Female Narration, Women's Cinema: Helke Sander's *The All-Round Reduced Personality/Redupers*" (1981–82), picks up on some of the issues raised by Kaja Silverman in her essay on the dis-embodied female voice (Section Three). Here Mayne analyzes Sander's attempt to define Edda, the film's heroine, as the active, looking subject rather than as the object of the male gaze. She sees this attempt as connected with Edda's work as a photographer and with the voice of the female narrator. As Edda and her coworkers set up a curtain on a platform at the Berlin Wall to look into East Berlin, they affect certain conditions of perception, not just what objects are seen, but how the viewer sees them. Mayne explains how Sander thus offers viewers the possibility of identifying with a woman who controls "the look" and with a female voice who controls our access to knowledge.

Mayne points out the various uses of the female voice in *Redupers*: (a) it personalizes the opening tracking shots of the city and describes the history of the women's group; (b) it serves as a third-person narrator by introducing and summarizing scenes; (c) it creates a first-person voice by expressing fantasies and desires; (d) it becomes a quoting voice, referring to literary and cinematic sources; and (e) "perhaps most important, the narrator becomes, at the same time, a reader: the female voice performs two functions at once, thus taking the consolidation of 'first person' and 'third person' to another level, condensing the narrator within the text with the reader outside it."[9]

Like Sander, Marleen Gorris of Holland is committed to a feminist film practice. Her 1982 film *A Question of Silence* stimulated animated controversy during its initial screenings, eliciting accusations of didacticism and prompting much provocative writing, among which is Mary C. Gentile's "Feminist or Tendentious?: Marleen Gorris's *A Question of Silence*" (1985). The film depicts the brutal murder of a male shopkeeper by four women, previously unknown to one another, who seemingly lack a motive.

Gentile notes that Gorris, like many feminist filmmakers, had an obvious investment in generating certain political interpretations for *A Question of Silence*. This contradicts Gentile's belief that "feminism exists in the film reading, not the film text, and that a feminist film reading is one which seeks to hold contradictory perspectives in tension."[10] Her essay uses *A Question of Silence* to explore these two ways of responding to the film, especially how the work leaves a space for individual viewer response.

For Gentile, *A Question of Silence* functions as an oppositional film, meaning that it reacts against the status quo, in terms of both film content and film technique. She explains how this oppositional stance elicits a multiplicity of viewer responses, which works in tandem with the director's intended meanings.

Gentile then offers an analysis of the film's stratagems for promoting this diversity. These include: (a) the extremity of the narrative situation which raises questions about the filmmaker's intent; (b) the narrative structure wherein each segment closes with several unanswered questions; (c) the denial of the shot/reverse shot paradigm which prevents viewers from identifying with certain characters; (d) the tendency to present the women in isolation, disconnected from one another, which pulls viewers in and out of the film; (e) the rejection of rationality, especially in the murder and courtroom scenes, which serves to expose patriarchal assumptions; (f) the stylized murder sequence which leaves viewers free to draw their own conclusions; and finally (g) the subversive laughter of the women which encourages viewers to reflect. In sum, Gentile feels Gorris achieves an uneasy balance, gaining our attention and involvement in the narrative, while at the same time, allowing us the freedom to make our own intellectual judgments. It is this dual consciousness and the tensions it produces (what she terms "Critical Subjectivity") that constitutes a feminist film viewing.

The last two essays in this section deal with issues related to pornography and female sexuality, topics which have come to be hotly debated both within and outside of film studies, and have stimulated a good deal of writing.[11] Perhaps it was inevitable that after image studies and an interest in female spectatorship, feminist scholars would turn their attention to pornography. Clearly, if critics had noted the exploitation of women's image in mainstream and most alternative cinema and had theorized on the alienation of women as spectators, then pornography represented the extreme of both conditions.

"Anti-Porn: Soft Issue, Hard World" (1983), by B. Ruby Rich, turns its attention to Bonnie Klein's *Not A Love Story*, the first documentary to address the subject of pornography from a woman's perspective. The film is influenced by the work of "Women Against Pornography" and the writings of Kathleen Barry, Susan Griffin, and Robin Morgan,[12] all of whom appear in the film.

For Rich, the documentary poses several problems. Rich views *Not a Love Story* as "a secret form of voyeurism disguised as outrage." She finds it hardly surprising that the mass media, which thrives on explicit and latent sexual imagery, would accommodate this work, one she feels ultimately poses very little threat to male prerogative. Furthermore, Rich objects to the ways in which Klein has shot and edited the footage, placing the camera in the place of the male customer and thus doubly objectifying the film's central figure, stripper Tracy Lee. As Rich points out, we are never privy to Lee's point of view.

In the second part of the article, following her analysis of *Not a Love Story* as a latter day "religious parable" (or what she calls "conversion cinema"), Rich addresses the broader questions stimulated by the anti-porn debates, questions dealing with sex and violence, power relations between men and women, issues of class and race, the relationship between porn and advertising, and finally, women's sexual expression—issues not dealt with in the documentary. She ends with a sense of dismay at the degree to which pornography has absorbed women's attention and a plea that women now turn to the necessary and ground-breaking work of creating "alternative sexual discourses."

The final selection, by filmmaker Bette Gordon, takes up the possibility of women controlling the gaze. In this respect, "*Variety*: The Pleasure in

Looking" (1984) and her film of the same name can be seen as a direct response to Mulvey's essay in Section One. Beginning with the assumption that "film plays on voyeuristic fantasy," Gordon sets herself the task of exploring female fantasy and pleasure. In *Variety* she has reversed the rules of the game so that it is the woman who is positioned as voyeur and the man who becomes the object of "the look."

Throughout the film, Christine, the film's heroine who works as a ticket taker at a Times Square porn house, observes men and male activities. Like the articulation of her sexual fantasies which makes her boyfriend uncomfortable, her observation of men "looking" challenges a social taboo and thus constitutes a radial activity within the film.

Unlike *Not a Love Story*, there is no graphic depiction of sex in *Variety*. The purpose of *Variety* was to raise questions and explore issues such as the active and passive components of voyeurism, the relationship between fantasy and pleasure, and in particular how sexuality, along with fantasy and pleasure, are constructed in culture and therefore in cinema. For Gordon, pornography is just an extreme example of Hollywood cinema which exploits women by creating them as objects of male fantasy. In the end, it is the effect of pornography on Christine and Gordon's efforts to make us "see" in a new way that form the major developments of the film.

As the final selection in this collection, Gordon's essay, like all that precede it, encourages us to recognize the relationship between *all* representations of women and the socio-political structures in which women live. It speaks to the need for women to take up the means of production, to expose the sexual stratagems operative in contemporary society, and to recreate the world in their own image.

NOTES

1. Robin Wood, *Hollywood from Vietnam to Reagan*, New York: Columbia University Press (1986), p. 204.
2. Ibid., p. 211.
3. Florence Jacobowitz and Lori Spring, "Unspoken and Unsolved: *Tell Me a Riddle*," *CineAction!*, no. 1 (Spring 1985), p. 15.
4. Ibid., p. 20.
5. Jackie Stacey, "Desperately Seeking Difference," *Screen* 28, no. 1 (Winter 1987), p. 53.
6. Ibid., p. 54.
7. Ibid., p. 54.
8. Ibid., p. 61.
9. Judith Mayne, "Female Narration, Women's Cinema," *New German Critique*, nos. 24–25 (Fall/Winter 1981–2), p. 166.
10. Mary C. Gentile, "Feminist or Tendentious? Marleen Gorris's *A Question of Silence*," in *Film Feminisms: Theory and Practice*, Wesport, CT: Greenwood (1985), p. 153.

11. The split between those women who actively campaigned against pornography and those women on the other side was reflected in two important conferences and the anthologies which resulted from these conferences. The first conference, organized by Women Against Pornography in the Media, was held in San Francisco in November, 1978, and was entitled "Feminist Perspectives on Pornography." This resulted in the founding of the New York group, Women Against Pornography, the following year and the publication of *Take Back the Night: Women on Pornography*, ed. Laura Lederer, New York: William Morrow (1980). The second conference was held at Barnard College in May, 1982, and was called "Towards a Politics of Sexuality." This was followed by the publication of *Pleasure and Danger: Exploring Female Sexuality*, ed. Carole S. Vance, Boston: Routledge & Kegan Paul (1984).

12. Among the important works that take and anti-porn stance, see Kathleen Barry's *Female Sexual Slavery*, New York: New York University Press (1985); Andrea Dworkin's *Pornography: Men Possessing Women*, New York: Perigee (1981); and Susan Griffin's *Pornography and Silence: Culture's Revenge Against Nature*, New York: Harper and Row (1981). For books with a different perspective on pornography, see Angela Carter, *Sadeian Woman And the Ideology of Pornogrpahy*, New York: Pantheon (1978); *Powers of Desire: The Politics of Sexuality*, ed. Ann Snitow, Christine Stansell, and Sharon Thompson, New York: Monthly Review Press (1983); *Caught Looking: Feminism, Pornography and Censorship*, ed. Caught Looking, Inc., 1986. Dist. Seattle, WA: Real Comet Press; *For Adult Users Only*, ed. Susan Gubar and Joan Hoff, Bloomington: Indiana University Press (1989); and Linda Williams, *Hardcore: Power, Pleasure and the 'Frenzy' of the Visible*, Berkeley: University of California Press (1989).

IMAGES AND WOMEN

Robin Wood

Hollywood Feminism: The 70s

In order to be admitted to the Hollywood cinema at all, feminism had to undergo various drastic changes, the fundamental one, from which all the rest follow, being the repression of politics. In Hollywood films—even the most determinedly progressive—there is no "Women's Movement"; there are only individual women who feel personally constrained.

Hollywood's intermittent concern with social problems has, in fact, almost never produced radically subversive movies (and if so, then incidentally and inadvertently). A social problem, explicitly stated, must always be one that can be resolved within the existing system, i.e., patriarchal capitalism; the *real* problems, which can't, can only be dramatized obliquely, and very likely unconsciously, within the entertainment movie. Just as *Cruising* can tell us far more about the relationship between patriarchy and homophobia than *Making Love*, so *Looking for Mr. Goodbar* can tell us far more about the oppression of women and the tensions inherent in contemporary heterosexual relations than *An Unmarried Woman*.

The two films generally singled out to represent Hollywood feminism are Paul Mazursky's *An Unmarried Woman* and Martin Scorsese's *Alice Doesn't Live Here Anymore*. It seems superfluous at this point to rehearse yet again their limitations. What seems not to have been noticed is that they share a common structure, in which those limitations are embodied. The significance of this—given that there are no tangible connections between the two films, in the form of common writers, producers, directors, stars, studios—should be obvious: the structure defines the limits of the ideologically acceptable, the limits that render feminism safe. It is with structure rather than texture that I shall be concerned here, so I shall preface the account by saying that Scorsese's film seems to me not just the more immediately engaging (by virtue of that surface aliveness that is due, especially, to Scorsese's work with actors), but the richer and more complex work, despite the fact that superficially it appears the more compromised, the heroine's capitulation being more complete. Partly, this is bound up with its working-class milieu: it is simply too easy to make a film about the liberation of an upper-class career woman with a lucrative position in the fashionable art world. Scorsese's film cannot resolve its problems satisfactorily, but at least it doesn't so glibly evade them.

The common structure can be broken down into its main components (for the sake of brevity, I shall indicate variations on the pattern by the directors' initials):

1. At the outset, the heroine is married (in M. apparently happily, in S. unhappily).

2. She has a child, signified as on the verge of or just into adolescence (M.: a daughter; S.: a son). Despite the gender difference, the resemblance is remarkable, the dominant characteristic being precocity. In both films the child is young enough to be still dependent; mature enough to be a semi-confidant, engaging with the mother in arguments and intimate exchanges; independent enough to demand his/her own rights. Hence, the child functions in both films as a problem, and simultaneously provides reassurance that the marriage breakdown isn't *irremediably* damaging.

3. The marriage ends (M.: the husband leaves the heroine for another woman; S.: the husband is killed in an accident), and the woman has to make a new life for herself and the child.

4. The heroine is already (M.) or becomes (S.) involved in a group of women who provide emotional support (M.: Erica's friends; S.: the other waitresses). The development of Alice's mutually supportive relationship with Flo is among the most positive and touching things in Scorsese's film.

5. The heroine has an unsuccessful and transitory relationship with an unsatisfactory lover (M.: because he is promiscuous and rejects commitment; S.: because he is psychotic and already married). Harvey Keitel, in a generally atypical film, is in the direct line of descent of Scorsese's male protagonists, complete with Scorpio pendant.

6. The heroine meanwhile pursues, or attempts to pursue, a career that satisfies her need for self-respect (M.: successfully, as a receptionist in an art gallery; S.: unsuccessfully, as a singer).

7. In the course of her work, she meets a non-oppressive male to whom she can relate on equal terms and with whom she develops a satisfying, if troubled, relationship.

This last development—felt in both cases as the film's necessary culmination—is obviously crucial. It occurs roughly two-thirds of the way through, and represents the end of the heroine's trajectory; both men (M.: Alan Bates; S.: Kris Kristofferson), despite the fact that one is an artist and the other a rancher, are strikingly similar in type: burly, bearded, emphatically masculine, physically strong, and emotionally stable: reassuring, not only for the woman in the film, but for women in the audience and—perhaps most important of all—for *men* in the audience. The films share a certain deviousness. On the explicit level, both preserve a determined ambiguity, refusing to guarantee the permanence of the happy ending. Yet the final effect is of a huge communal sigh of relief: the women don't *have* to be independent after all; there are strong, protective males to look after them. Their demand for independence is accordingly reduced to a token gesture, becoming little more than an irrational "feminine" whim. The "nonoppressiveness" and the "equality," though heavily signaled, are also extremely problematic, existing purely on the personal level in terms of sympathetic individual men and never clearly examined in terms of social positions. *Alice Doesn't Live Here Anymore*, with its richer generic background, develops a particular irony here, although it is never brought to a sharp focus: the Western traditionally offered women two options, the rancher's wife or the saloon entertainer; they remain, in a consciously feminist film of 1974, precisely the options open to Alice.

In a brilliant article in the 1983 *Socialist Register* ("Masculine Dominance and the State"), Varda Burstyn distinguishes between women's *liberation* and women's *equality*:

> The notion of equality for women rather than the notion of women's liberation denies a transformative dynamic to women's struggles. . . . It implicitly but firmly sets the lifeways and goals of masculine existence as the standards to which women should aspire and against which official estimates of their "progress" will be made. It poses the problem as one of the women's "catching up to men," rather than as a problem for women and men to solve together by changing the conditions and relations of their shared lives—from their intimate to their large-scale social interaction.

What *Alice Doesn't Live Here Anymore* and *An Unmarried Woman* offer is, at best, equality, not liberation, and even the equality is precarious and compromised.

Hollywood Antifeminism: The 80s

The precariousness of what was achieved in the 70s can be gauged from the ease with which it has been overthrown in the 80s. The pervasiveness of antifeminism in current Hollywood cinema (it is seldom of course explicitly presented as such, and often embodied merely in the reinstatement of traditional role models, as if nothing had happened) has been noted elsewhere. Here I want to focus simply on two pairs of parallel examples, one from the beginning of the period and one representing the subsequent, more brazen development of the implications. The examples are offered as representative: if they stand out, it is only by virtue of their clarity.

Urban Cowboy and *Bronco Billy* were released almost simultaneously in 1980. The dramatic tension in both is centered on the efforts of an active, even aggressive woman to assert herself within a strongly male-dominated environment, in activities associated with masculinity: Debra Winger proves that she can ride the mechanical bull at least as well as John Travolta; Sondra Locke proves herself at least as good a sharp-shooter as Clint Eastwood. The narrative then moves to the point where the woman comes to understand that she isn't happy with this "equality": Debra Winger realizes that what she's really wanted all along is to wash her husband's socks; Sondra Locke ends up spread-eagled on a revolving wheel, as Bronco Billy's target in his traveling Wild West show. Both films, though contemporary in setting, explicitly locate themselves in the tradition of the Western, and use this as a means of putting assertive women back where they belong—respectively, as wife and object-of-the-gaze; both narratives teach the woman to be fully complicit in her own oppression. One must also note the uncomprehending vacuity of the underlying premise: the principles of feminism reduced to the demand to participate in the violent rites of masculinity.

Two of the ugliest moments in recent Hollywood films occur in *An Officer and a Gentleman* and in *Terms of Endearment*. In the first, Debra Winger turns on her friend and denounces her for having pretended to be pregnant in order to trap a man into marriage ("God help you"). In the second, Debra Winger turns on a group of her New York acquaintances and denounces them for their divorces, abortions, etc. Both narratives are careful to justify the outburst dramatically: in the former, the feigned pregnancy has precipitated the lover's suicide; in the latter, the New York friends are presented, stereotypically, as superficial, trendy, and blasé. Yet again, the alibi of realism masks ideology: the insidious purpose of each film is to suggest that the only alternative for a woman to being a "good" wife/mother is to be duplicitous or fashionably desensitized.

The two moments have a good deal in common. Each occurs at roughly the same point in the narrative (about two-thirds through the film, around the point where the development of the relationship with the acceptable male occurred in the 70s movies), and marks a decisive step in its progression. Each uses a woman to denounce other women, the woman in both cases having come fully to accept her correct traditional role, even though both she and the film know that role to be fairly ignominious (affirmation in the 80s is never free of cynicism). In *An Officer and a Gentleman* this movement is used to support the film's glorification of militarism, the ultimate embodiment of masculinity. Just what it supports in *Terms of Endearment* is less easy to define, though central to it is a mystique of motherhood—hence the emphasis on abortion—that has given the film an unfortunate credibility for many women (in combination with its maddening "great acting," which amounts to no more than a relentless parade of knowing mannerisms). There is also, of course, the presence in both films of Debra Winger. One might say that Winger, having learned to oppress herself in *Urban Cowboy*, has gone on to dedicate her career to the oppression of other women. But that is perhaps putting it too personally. What is at issue is not Winger's acting ability or even her presence as a personality (both could be inflected in various ways), but the star image that has been constructed around her: Winger-as-star has become the indispensable 80s woman, a major focus for the return to the good old values of patriarchal capitalism and the restoration of women to their rightful place.

It is a profoundly depressing and alienating experience to sit in a packed auditorium watching these films with an audience who actually cheer their grossest moments. Doubtless, at the end of the world, bourgeois society will sit dying among the ruins still congratulating itself on the rightness of its good old values: a spectacle literally enacted in Lynne Littman's *Testament.*

Directing Women

The first great wave of feminism, around the turn of the century, coincided roughly with the invention of cinema; the second, through the 60s and 70s, produced an impressive body of critical/theoretial work and some distinguished avant-garde, "alternative" filmmaking. Neither, so far, has managed radically to affect the structures of mainstream film production (either the economic and power structures of an overwhelmingly patriarchal industry or the aesthetic and thematic structures of the films it turns out). It would be wrong, however, to assume that feminism has had no effect on Hollywood whatever. On the level of content it has provoked, negatively, a massive retaliation (ranging from the shameless grossness of the mad slasher movie to the far more insidious reinstatement of compliant women to their safe, traditional roles enacted in films like *An Officer and a Gentleman* and *Terms of Endearment*) that testifies at least to the magnitude of the threat; less negatively, if not entirely positively, feminism has aroused a pervasive sense of disturbance and unease. On the professional level, the grudging recognition that women can do the work of men (a superficial but not unimportant response to feminism) has made it somewhat less difficult, if by no means easy, for women to work as directors. During the past ten years or so we have seen more or less distinguished films by Elaine May (*The Heartbreak Kid*), Claudia Weill (*Girlfriends*), Joan Micklin Silver (*Chilly Scenes of Winter*), Jane Wagner (*Moment by Moment*), Lee Grant (*Tell Me a Riddle*), Amy Heckerling (*Fast Times at Ridgemont High*), Lynne Littman (*Testament*), and Barbra Streisand (*Yentl*), together with entirely negligible ones by Joan Rivers (*Rabbit Test*), Joan Darling (*First Love*), Nancy Walker (*Can't Stop the Music*), Barbara Peeters (*Humanoids from the Deep*) and Martha Coolidge (*Joy of Sex*). I have not seen Anne Bancroft's *Fatso.* In terms of numbers, the tally is unprecedented in any previous period, though of course still enormously outweighed by the films made by men.

The continuing inequality between the sexes can be measured not only in numbers but in terms of the conditions under which women are permitted to make films (and that word "permitted," deliberately chosen, speaks volumes). Ten of the fourteen in the above list have made, at time of writing, only one commercial theatrical movie, though Heckerling is currently working on a second;[1] six of the fourteen established themselves as performers first (a route proportionately uncommon for men); none has so far managed to establish a stable, continuous career (May, with three films, has not directed since 1974; Silver, also with three, not since 1979; Weill, with two, not since 1980). One may ask why no woman (Streisand the partial exception) has ever made a really big-grossing box office hit. Treating the possible sexist response with the contempt it deserves, one may suggest that one reason is that no woman (Streisand again excepted) has been entrusted with the kind of material from which box office hits are made: the projects that women directors have been able to set up are, typically, modest, low-budget affairs on unassuming subjects, usually without major stars. During the Classical Hollywood period, Dorothy Arzner (20s to 40s) working intermittently with major female stars (Hepburn, Crawford) was able to build an impressively solid body of films, but always on projects regarded by the studios as minor and feminine, which came to the same thing. Ida Lupino (again an established star before becoming a director) made half-a-dozen films in the 50s, all B movies on restricted budgets. Stephanie Rothman, courageously plunging into the exploitation field of beach parties, horror, violence and sex, practiced some remarkable, though not widely celebrated, strategies of subversion in the 60s and early 70s, and has been unable to set up a film since, though still eager and certainly able.

So much for statistics. The problems they indicate go far beyond what might seem the simple, obvious explanation that men continue to resent women in positions of power—which is not to deny that that explanation carries a lot of weight. The male aversion seems to be primarily a practical one: less objection exists to women's power behind the scenes, as screenwriters or producers; the aversion is to women's power made visible and concrete. An obvious parallel: there are very few female orchestral conductors, and no very famous ones. A woman can be a pianist or violinist of international status (and presumably Cécile Ousset and Kyung-Wha Chung, when they play concertos, determine the tempi and overall conception), but she cannot stand up in front of an orchestra composed mainly of males and be seen to direct and dominate them. I have heard wonderful broadcast concerts by the Milwaukee Symphony under Margaret Hawkins, but Ms. Hawkins, as far as I know, never leaves Milwaukee for the international tours taken for granted by her male, and often inferior, jet-setting counterparts.

The deeper problem can be suggested through a series of questions: What films might women of integrity *want* to make? If no woman has made an overwhelming box office smash, may this be because no woman in her senses would *want* to make *Raiders of the Lost Ark, An Officer and a Gentleman*, or *Return of the Jedi*? Entrusted with such projects, what could a woman director decently do but struggle to subvert them? Their commercial success is intimately bound up with their flattering of patriarchy. What possibilities exist for a female (not necessarily feminist) discourse to be articulated within a patriarchal industry through narrative conventions and genres developed by and for a male-dominated culture? The closure of classical narrative (of which the Hollywood happy ending is a typical form) enacts the restoration of patriarchal order; the transgressing woman is either forgiven and subordinated to that order, or punished, usually by death. The seminal writings of Claire Johnston and Pam Cook on Dorothy Arzner suggest that Arzner's intervention in patriarchal projects could do little to alter the course of such narrative conventions; what it *could* do was to create disturbances and imbalances, rendering the happy ending problematic or unsatisfying. In effect, the films are being praised for their incoherence, their unresolved contradictions, their tendency to leave audiences dissatisfied—scarcely a recommendation within a commercially motivated industry (try going to a producer with "I've got this great idea for a really incoherent movie").

I shall consider here some of the genuinely distinguished achievements of women directors in the past decade (especially Grant, Weill, Silver, and Heckerling). First, however, it seems fitting to focus briefly on *Yentl*, because it provides apparent answers to some of the problems. It is a big-budget production obviously intended to have wide popular appeal, directed, co-produced, and co-written by a woman as her own cherished project, on an explicitly feminist theme (a woman's rebellion against patriarchal constraints), quite free of any of the obvious symptoms of incoherence (awkwardness, tentativeness, strain, imbalance, working against the grain). Yet—while a generally agreeable entertainment with a few wonderful moments—*Yentl* is really the answer to nothing. It is scarcely a breakthrough for women directors, as its existence is entirely dependent on Streisand's status as Superstar. Its precise nature seems determined by her desire to give her audiences what they expect of her: there was a neat, sharp little ninety-minute movie there somewhere, but it has become almost submerged in lush production values (*Sound of Music* meets *Fiddler on the Roof*) and an inordinate number of songs as undistinguished as they are superfluous. Apart perhaps from some interesting if equivocal play with gender roles and sexual ambiguity, the film offers no challenge to anyone: its feminist theme is placed in the context of a culture so remote from our own that we can view it with a complacent sense of "how things used to be," a sense confirmed by the ending, where Yentl emigrates to America and emancipation. As for the film's coherence, it is precisely that of classical narrative, left completely undisturbed: the exceptional individual (Young Mr. Lincoln, Shane, Yentl) leaves a society too narrow to contain her/him, but only after ensuring the continuance of the patriarchal order through the reconstitution of the family or the couple. The general sense the film communicates of unearned self-congratulation calls to mind the slogan on the notorious advertisement for Virginia Slims: "You've come a long way, baby." For truly progressive work by women in mainstream cinema we must look elsewhere.

Four Films

It will be clear from the works I discuss (Claudia Weill's *Girlfriends*, Lee Grant's *Tell Me a Riddle*, Joan Micklin Silver's *Chilly Scenes of Winter*, and Amy Heckerling's *Fast Times at Ridgemont High*) that I am using the term "mainstream" somewhat loosely. Of the four, the first two were produced independently on the margins of the industry, and would never have been made but for the pertinacity of the filmmakers; only the last belongs squarely within the contemporary development of Hollywood genres and cycles. I use the term solely to distinguish fictional feature films intended to reach general audiences from experimental or avant-garde work produced without expectation of widespread distribution and standing resolutely apart from anything that could reasonably be called "entertainment." Many feminist critics have argued persuasively that the language (what one might call the organization of the look, both within the film and of the spectator) of mainstream cinema was developed by patriarchy for patriarchy and must be rigorously rejected; certain feminist filmmakers have put that argument into practice (the Laura Mulvey/Peter Wollen *Riddles of the Sphinx* is among the most impressive examples). Yet it seems to me desirable that all avenues be kept open, that the widest range of strategies and practices be attempted; it remains unproven that the patriarchal language of mainstream narrative film cannot be transformed and redeemed, that a woman's discourse cannot speak through it. The four films on which I here offer brief notes (each deserves detailed attention) provide some evidence to the contrary.

It is significant that only the two independent movies embody overtly feminist projects, and even they never manage to acknowledge the existence of a political women's movement: the obligatory conditions for a woman working for a major studio would appear to be discretion, subterfuge, deviousness, and compromise. *Girlfriends* is the only American commercial movie I can think of that explicitly calls marriage as an institution into question, as opposed to admitting that there are unsuccessful marriages, though a number of mainstream Hollywood movies (von Sternberg's *Blonde Venus*, Sirk's *There's Always Tomorrow*, Cukor's *Rich and Famous*—which owes a lot to *Girlfriends*) can be read as suggesting this implicitly, under cover of being "just entertainment." *Tell Me a Riddle* is the only commercial American movie I can think of that explicitly parallels feminism and socialist revolution (though somewhat tactfully). Why should major studios, which are patriarchal capitalist structures from top to bottom, be expected to finance films that call into question their very premises? It is surprising enough that they agreed to distribute them. A culture committed to freedom of speech but built on money and private enterprise has a very simple means of repressing the former by using the latter, with no inconvenient or disturbing sense of hypocrisy. *Girlfriends* presents marriage as patriarchy's means of containing and separating women: the friendship of the title is effectively destroyed by the marriage of one of the women, whose priorities then *necessarily* become her house, her husband, her child. The view of marriage in *Tell Me a Riddle*, though less negative, is not entirely dissimilar. Here, the husband feels threatened, not by a female friendship, but by the woman's intellectual interests and revolutionary sympathies—in both cases, but in different ways, by the possibility of her autonomy. What is unique, and deeply moving, about Grant's film is its generosity in allowing the husband to recognize, though much too late, the destruction his attitude has caused: the scene of marital reconciliation is among the great moments in modern American cinema, not least because it triumphantly breaks another taboo by permitting old people erotic contact.

The independence of these two films is as much a matter of narrative/thematic content as of production setup. Neither fits comfortably into traditional generic expectations. *Girlfriends*, predominantly comic in tone but taking up the themes (marriage vs. career, etc.) of the "woman's melodrama," ends on a note of regret at the formation of the heterosexual couple rather than the traditional glow of relief and satisfaction; *Tell Me a Riddle* continues beyond the reconciliation scene to the old woman's death, the husband's remorse at lost opportunities, the younger woman's confirmed independence. The latter film, especially, is an extremely unorthodox project even aside from its feminist thrust: one of a very small handful of commercial films from *any* country on the highly uncommercial subject of old age.[2]

The achievement of *Chilly Scenes of Winter* and *Fast Times at Ridgemont High*, by contrast, can really only be appreciated in relation to the generic expectations and formulae they at once part fulfill, part undermine. *Chilly Scenes* is one of the very few woman-directed films centered on a male consciousness (men have never hesitated to make films centered on women, whereas women are always assigned or permitted feminine projects): an interesting strategy for the indirect expression of a woman's discourse.

The relationship of the film to Ann Beattie's novel is complex, balancing fidelity with subtle transformation. Silver, who wrote the screenplay as well as directing the film, retains Beattie's premise, plot, and characters (realized with wonderful delicacy and precision by the actors), adding inventions of her own (some of the flashbacks, Charles's construction of the model of Laura's house, his visit with Sam to the actual house, hence the entire scene with Laura and her husband) that are perfectly compatible with the original but give Beattie's somewhat tenuous narrative, with its frequent recourse to internal monologues, a more concrete dramatization. Much of the dialogue is taken from the book, the film preserving the quality of its oblique, offbeat humor. However, the spirit of the book is subtly transformed. The transformation is due partly to the fact that the film owes as much to Hollywood—to a specific Hollywood tradition—as to its literary source. Its essence can be made clear by comparing Beattie's and Silver's endings. To put it succinctly, where Beattie gives us an unhappy happy ending, Silver substitutes a happy unhappy ending. (I am discounting here the ending that was tacked on to the film for its initial release, when its title was also changed to *Head Over Heels*.) At the end of the novel, the lovers get back together, yet it is clear that Laura has merely given up the struggle and is now wearily acquiescing to the insistence of Charles's romantic (and thoroughly possessive) passion for her: nothing has changed, neither has learned anything. The book's highly idiosyncratic and engaging humor becomes complicit in its defeatism: as people are incapable of growth or change, there is really nothing to do but laugh sadly and ironically at their predicament. Silver's film ends with the lovers separated and with Charles at last finding himself able to accept the separation: each has learned to recognize, slowly and painfully, the oppressiveness of romantic possession/dependence. It is perhaps the first Hollywood film where the happy ending consists, not in the lovers' union, but in their relinquishing its possibility.

The genre to which *Chilly Scenes* relates is not exactly topical: essentially, it belongs to the type of light comedy that flourished in the 30s and now seems virtually a lost art. The closeness of the fit can be suggested by the simple expedient of recasting it. The male protagonist trying to regain the woman he loves would have been Cary Grant, with Irene Dunne opposite him once again; the alternative but impossible lovers—"dumb blonde" secretary, dull businessman—would have been Lucille Ball and (of course!) Ralph Bellamy, with Billie Burke as the hero's comic-eccentric, scatterbrained mother. Once one has grasped the pattern, Silver's subtle inflections of it become quite fascinating. Crucial to the operation is her refusal to take romantic love for granted as an unquestionable value, or to assume the happy ending as the hero's inalienable right. Our classical prototype would have been what Stanley Cavell calls a "comedy of remarriage": the final reunion of the estranged couple would have been guaranteed from the outset by the fact that they were husband and wife. But in *Chilly Scenes* the male protagonist is the other man, the *husband* the dull businessman, and the woman ultimately rejects them both. Silver's handling of the comic female stereotypes (secretary, mother) is also idiosyncratic: if still comic, they are also disturbingly vulnerable, so that our laughter is made uneasy.

If I devote more space to *Fast Times at Ridgemont High*, it is not because I consider it a better film, but because it was made right in the mainstream of contemporary Hollywood production and because it belongs to a cycle one would never have expected a woman of intelligence and integrity to be able, or indeed want, to infiltrate. If *Eyes of a Stranger* proves that the terms of even the most apparently intractable generic formulae can be partially subverted (on the condition of meeting the demand that they also be partially fulfilled), the same can be argued for Amy Heckerling's disarming and exhilarating movie.

The terms of the 80s high school cycle (the obvious touchstones are *American Graffiti* and *Porky's*, respectively its pre-80s initiation and its most fully representative 80s manifestation) can be set forth quite succinctly:

1. *Sex*. Even though school is the setting, the films at no point show the slightest interest in education (unless negatively, as a nuisance). The need to graduate may occasionally be an issue, but chiefly because it interferes with the real one. The cynicism (typical in general of our civilization, but especially a feature of the 80s) is total, and totally taken for granted; to the extent that reviewers never comment on it, one assumes they share it. There is never any hint of serious or reasoned rebellion against the educational system: education is a nuisance and a farce, yet somehow mysteriously necessary: one must study in order to graduate, and one must graduate in order to take one's place within the adult society one despises. The only film I have seen (marginal to the cycle, as its leading characters are preadolescent) that allows its characters to express overt antagonism to the educational system is Ronald Maxwell's *Kidco*: the objection is that school fails to teach children how to make money. Generally, the assumption is that teenagers could not possibly be interested in anything except sex, and it would be rather absurd to expect it (serious students are by definition "nerds"—though nerds need not be serious students). The films are at once a significant product and reinforcement of the commodification of sex in contemporary capitalist culture, most of the consumer products of which must be advertised and sold on their sexual appeal, blatant or subtle.

2. *The Suppression of Parents*. Given that the teenagers of the films still live at home, the almost total absence of parents is rather remarkable. Peewee's mother (in *Porky's*) appears in one brief scene; Stacey's mother (in *Fast Times*) appears in one shot; fathers are either absent altogether or, in the case of the violent macho father of *Porky's*, so obviously monstrous as to be easily repudiated. Like education, parents are a mysteriously necessary evil, to be avoided whenever possible. Of course, what the films dare not suggest (they would instantly lose all their appeal) is that these teenagers will grow up—inevitably, given their total lack of political

awareness—to be replicas of their parents. Like education, parents interfere actually or potentially with the pursuit of sex: the less they are present in the films, the better. They are, in fact, reduced to the ignominious role of supplying occasional suspense (can the son/daughter get away in time for the next sexual encounter?).

3. *Multicharacter Movies.* The aim is to reach and satisfy as wide a youth audience as possible; there must, therefore, be a range of identification figures, and no minority group (with one significant exception) must be entirely neglected (though arranged within a careful hierarchy).

4. *Hunter/Hunted.* Two male figures recur, with variations, often in close juxtaposition—the one (there are likely to be several) who "knows all about it" and the one who doesn't. A central plot thread concerns the male virgin who has to "get laid." With both figures, the innocent and the experienced, the basic pattern is the same: male as hunter, female as hunted, male as looker, female as looked-at. The initiation of the male virgin is clearly crucial: the emphasis is less on his desire to achieve a pleasure already experienced by his fellows than on his need to prove himself, to become a "real man": Getting laid is the guarantee of masculinity/heterosexuality, the denial of a possibility that the films cannot even mention.

5. *The Repression of Homosexuality.* There are no gay teenagers in America: such, at least, is the films' implicit message.[3] No surprise, of course. What is marginally more surprising is that the films never acknowledge the possibility of teenage homosexual *behavior*, despite the fact that this is widely recognized as a normal phase in the progress toward true normality ("normally abnormal" might put the attitude more precisely). The phenomenon is common enough to demand explanation, various of which have been given: adolescent boys need sexual outlets, and girls are not always (or are not perceived to be) readily available, so they take "second best"; adolescents need to experiment in order to reject the inferior form of sexuality for the superior; the onset of adult sexuality can be experienced as frightening, and many boys are intimidated by the implicit demands on their potency. All these explanations are variously homophobic in asserting the superiority of heterosexuality over homosexuality. The most logical explanation—which is not homophobic—is consistently repressed: that the phenomenon represents the final struggle of our innate bisexuality to find recognition, before it capitulates to the demands of normality, the nuclear family, and the patriarchal order. The films' often quite hysterical and obsessive emphasis on "getting laid" can be seen as an unconscious acknowledgment of the reality of the threat: though the adult world is treated with contempt, no *serious* challenge to normality can be countenanced.

By this point it will be clear that the syndrome I have described is shared by another, exactly contemporary and equally popular, cycle discussed previously: the teenie-kill pic. The parallel development is intriguing, especially as the overall import of the two cycles is (superficially at least) quite opposite: in the high school movies promiscuity is generally indulged, in the teenie-kill pics it is ruthlessly punished. The opposition may be less total than it first appears (see, for example, the obsessive emphasis on castration in *Porky's*). The cycles seem premised on a common assumption: that, despite all the lip service to female equality, it is still the male who decides what movie young heterosexual couples will go to. Audiences for both cycles have been (in my experience) predominantly male, with all-male groups quite common. Any satisfaction the films offer the female spectator seems at once marginal and perverse: she is invited to contemplate, as something at once funny and desperately important, male initiation rites; or she is invited to contemplate reiterated punishment for sexual pleasure, with a special emphasis on female pleasure. One can see well enough why young males conditioned by the ideological assumptions of our culture in its current phase should want to drag their compliant girlfriends along to participate in what are essentially male rituals of desire and guilt, part of the films' function being the reinforcement of that compliance.

The relation of *Fast Times at Ridgemont High* to this syndrome is extremely complex. Clearly, there are certain bottom-line generic conditions that must be satisfied for such a film to get made at all (just as *Eyes of a Stranger* could not exist if it did not contain sequences in which women are terrorized and brutally murdered): here, heterosexism and the commodification of sex. In fact, the film's treatment of adolescent sexuality is consistently enlightened and intelligent, but it is compelled to subscribe to the myth that sex is all teenagers ever think about, with all its consequent ramifications. "Packaging"—a term that encompasses all the purely commercial interests involved from conception to publicity—is crucial here: it is interesting that the last line of dialogue ("Awesome—totally awesome"), which in the film has nothing whatever to do with sexual activity, was lifted out of context and used as an advertising slogan.

Where *Fast Times* succeeds, against all reasonable expectations, is in constructing a position for the female spectator that is neither masochistic nor merely compliant. One may begin at the end where Heckerling, in a single simple gesture, quietly rectifies the sexism of *American Graffiti*. Lucas ended his film with captions succinctly synopsizing the destinies of his four *male* characters; the implication was that the females were either of no consequence or so dependent on the men as to *have* no destinies of their own. Heckerling repeats the device, but allows the women full equality. Nor is this a mere afterthought; rather, it concludes the logic of the entire film. Heckerling's six main characters include four males and two females. Yet, if there is a character who takes precedence over the others, it is clearly Stacey (Jennifer Jason Leigh). Where the cycle as a whole is obsessed with male sexual desire and anxieties (the girls in *Porky's* have no problems, and exist purely in relation to the boys, whose "needs" they either satisfy or frustrate), *Fast Times* allows its young women both desire and disturbance: see, for example, the delightful scene in which Linda (Phoebe Cates), with the aid of a carrot, instructs an anxious Stacey in the techniques of the "blow job." And, as the women cease to be objects of the male gaze, their autonomous desire is used to express, not merely an appreciation of male beauty ("Did you see his cute little butt?"), but a critique of male presumption. When Stacey responds to her date's "You look beautiful" with an enthusiastic "So do *you*," the film immediately registers his discomfiture, and the reaction prepares us for his behavior in the ensuing scene of intercourse: he shows no concern for Stacey's sexual pleasure and no awareness of her pain (she was a virgin). During it, Heckerling cuts in a shot from Stacey's point-of-view: a graffito, "Surf Nazis," scrawled on the wall above her.

Similar strategies characterize the treatment of Stacey's brief relationship with Mike (Robert Romanus), the school lady-killer. It is she who takes the initiative, and the film suggests that this is what undermines him: he is accustomed to being the hunter. His sexual insecurity surfaces in the changing-cabin by Stacey's family's pool when Stacey asks, "You want to take off your clothes, Mike?" and his automatic response ("You first") is answered by her "Both of us at the same time"; he then "comes too soon." Subsequently (*before* he learns that she is pregnant), he is too embarrassed to confront her, evading her friendly overtures: the film is clear that what is being "put down" is not sexual failure in itself, but the male vanity that makes so much of it.

The principle of rectifying the cycle's sexist imbalance is not restricted to the development of the narrative; it determines the details of shooting and editing. This is established right at the outset, during the brilliantly precise and economical credits sequence: the second shot—Mike eyeing a girl—is answered instantly by the third, in which two girls eye Brad (Judge Reinhold). A little later, a traveling shot along a row of asses in tight jeans bent over pinball machines looks like a typical sexist cliché until one realizes that the asses are not identifiable as female. Two sequences are built upon the visual objectification of women; both are defined as male fantasies and are clearly placed by the context within which they occur. In one, Spicoli (Sean Penn) fantasizes his victory as surfing champion, a beautiful bikini-clad girl on each arm (the film elsewhere gives him no contact with real females whatever, defining his existence in terms of permanently doped amiability). The other is treated even more pointedly. Brad (Stacey's brother), arriving home in the Captain Hook uniform of the fish restaurant where he works, finds Linda beside the pool and is embarrassed at being seen in a costume; he watches her from the washroom, fantasizes that she is offering herself to him, and begins to masturbate; entering the washroom without knocking, she catches him in the act.

The film takes up many of the cycle's recurrent schemata but always uses them creatively. The economy of the various plot expositions depends upon the instant recognizability of the characters, but in every case the stereotype is resourcefully extended, varied, or subverted. Especially interesting is the treatment of the male virgin, Mark (Brian Backer): the whole progression of his relationship with Stacey is built, not upon his desire to "get laid"—to become a "real man"—but on his continuing sexual reticence and diffidence, maintained beyond the ending of the film, where we are informed that he and Stacey are having a passionate love affair but still haven't "gone all the way." On the other hand the film, while firmly implying that the best relationships are based upon mutual respect and concern, is strikingly nonjudgmental in its treatment of promiscuity and experimentation. It is also firmly "pro-choice": abortion is certainly not presented as a pleasant experience, but neither is it treated as in the least shocking. The abortion episode is also used to establish what is otherwise conspicuously absent from the cycle, the positive potential of certain family ties, in Brad's gentle, understanding, and nonpaternalist acceptance of his sister.

The film's unobtrusive critique of male positions exists within the context of Heckerling's generosity to all her characters, male and female alike. The film manages the extremely difficult feat of constructing a tenable position for the female spectator without threatening the male: this defines, one might say, both its success and its limitations. It is clearly impossible, in the current phase of social evolution, for a film that rigorously and radically explores the oppression of women to be nonthreatening. *Fast Times* must be seen as a reflection of current attitudes rather than a radical challenge to them; what it proves—a very rare phenomenon in contemporary Hollywood cinema—is that it is still possible to reflect (hence reinforce) the progressive tendencies in one's culture, not merely the reactionary ones. Flawlessly played by a uniformly wonderful cast (Heckerling is obviously marvelous with actors), it restores a certain credibility to the concept of "entertainment." Of the four films discussed *Fast Times* is predictably enough the only one that has had an appreciable box office success. It pays a price for this, of course. The other three women whose films I have considered are paying a different price: none is currently working on a theatrical feature film.

—1985

NOTES

1. *Johnny Dangerously* has appeared just in time for a footnote which, alas, it barely deserves: Heckerling has allowed herself to be absorbed (temporarily, one hopes) into a comic mode that derives from TV (*Saturday Night Live* is the most obvious influence) in which a woman's discourse is quite obliterated, and the film

proves no more than that women can make movies that are just as bad as most of those made by men.

2. For a detailed analysis of *Tell Me a Riddle*, see the article by Florence Jacobowitz and Lori Spring in *CineAction!*, no. 1 (also in Section Four of this book).

3. Since this was written the curious and confused *Revenge of the Nerds* has supplied a gay college student. The film carefully compounds his otherness by making him black as well as gay and, in one disarming but not exactly uncompromised moment, equips him with a "limp-wristed javelin" with which to win a sporting event.

UNSPOKEN AND UNSOLVED
TELL ME A RIDDLE

Florence Jacobowitz and Lori Spring

Many socialist theorists and critics in the 20s and 30s recognized the political potential of Hollywood movies: here was a mass medium of the industrial age that could both express social dissatisfaction and entertain notions of a better world. Brecht and Benjamin, amongst others, insisted that politically effective art should be popular, accessible, and pleasurable. Today "materialist" film theorists and critics, ostensibly committed to social change, are still debating the viability of these hopes, and have produced a number of widely differing positions.

The most extreme or "purist" of these positions, championed in particular by a number of feminists, rejects the Hollywood style of Realism and the industry's still largely studio conglomerate control of distribution and exhibition; instead, they look to the "avant-garde" and other alternative forms of film production, distribution, and exhibition. Realism is rejected as a mystificatory style which seamlessly conceals its formal devices in order to invisibly direct viewer response along an ideologically-safe projectile. This position maintains that Hollywood has perpetuated images of women that cater to masculine pleasure. As a result, women have been alternately objectified, fetishized, worshiped, or destroyed, according to the desires/needs of the male spectator. These feminists suggest that women must find new stylistic modes to accommodate feminist images of women. Whether or not one disagrees with the above, one undeniable consequence of the total rejection of Hollywood Realism is the accompanying loss of a large audience—in terms of political effect, a major loss.

Other theorists/critics are more willing to recognize the progressive potential of Realist art, however ultimately constrained it may be by the interests in power. This group claims that within certain Realist filmic genres spectator response is not entirely contained and determined. The audience can be distanced from the narrative world through a heightening of formal/aesthetic elements of style beyond what is necessary to maintain an illusion of reality, in such a manner that thematic elements are foregrounded and parallels between the fictional world and the world outside of the movie theater are strongly suggested. The extreme lighting of film noir or the emotional crescendos of the melodrama and the visual iconography suggesting entrapment are examples (and one can think of numerous others from the musical, the western, the horror film) of this manner of subversion. The melodrama is of particular interest to feminist critics as it was directed to female spectatorship. Films within these genres can be distinguished from those within others which may also employ stylistic extremes in the form of fantastic locales (for example, certain science fiction films, like *Star Wars*, or adventure films, like *Raiders of the Lost Ark*) but fail to suggest that these alternate worlds are in any way related to social reality.[1]

Another area of attention has been the "incoherent" text—a term used to describe films which, while outwardly satisfying the strictures and demands of the political system within which they are produced, remain riddled with contradictions which often work to subvert the films' overt, ideologically-acceptable project. It is often unclear by what mechanisms these subversive impulses manage to erupt within a system which works to contain them: it has generally been more acceptable in the milieu of radical criticism to claim that they surface unintentionally, as censored impulses do in dreams, to the surprise of the dreamer/creator; it is less appropriate to suggest that these messages may also have been intentionally articulated in part or whole, in the films of such male "bourgeois" directors as Ophuls, Sternberg, or Scorsese.

There is a group of films within mainstream narrative art yet to be accounted for. How does one rationalize or explain works which are within the Hollywood aesthetic but which appear to be making no attempt to satisfy any externally-imposed social/aesthetic strictures, which are not particularly noteworthy in terms of stylistic "excess" (in the sense of employing conventions and elements of style as distancing devices), and which seem entirely *too* conscious and consistent in their raising of political issues to be labelled incoherent?

Aptly named, *Tell Me a Riddle* is one of these films which crop up within a patriarchal/bourgeois film industry. The film is not entirely anomalous, nor is it divorced form the venerable stylistic and generic traditions of Hollywood—but it does signal change and raises issues generally ignored in popular representational art. We would like to suggest that films like *Tell Me a Riddle* reformulate, expand, and evolve generic possibilities by offering different kinds of images than those long perpetuated in mainstream culture. By operating within these parameters, the film neither relinquishes the communicative modes of popular narrative Realist film nor compromises its intentions to communicate fundamental issues of gender/class/ethnicity to a large audience often deprived of significant images which mirror their experiences. The film attests to the possibility that Hollywood Realist film can both express social criticism and articulate the desire for change, and in so doing, pave the way for such change in the concrete world by affecting consciousness.

The fact that the film was directed by a woman does not entirely account for its elements of difference. We will not elaborate upon Lee Grant's and the production company's difficulties in seeing the project come to fruition. There have been a number of articles on women directors in Hollywood describing their struggles within a very masculine industry and within a society which generally will not risk large sums of money on women (and certainly never on projects as unbankable as this one in terms of subject matter). Clearly the woman's discourse can in part be attributed to Lee Grant's efforts, to Tillie Olsen's novella *Tell Me a Riddle*, and to the input of the feminist collective of Godmother Productions. However just as often, women directors and writers, like women spectators, produce and consume patriarchal discourses without disturbance, having largely come to internalize an image of themselves dictated by a male dominant society. Films about female experience are too often tossed aside by spectators and critics unfamiliar with (or uninterested in) the "Other" side of difference—both in terms of gender experience and class experience. Feminist/socialist critics have place a high priority on filling in the gaps of experience either suppressed or ignored in our culture, having become aware that the inability to conceptualize change, and to articulate the experiences of Other-ness, has been a major factor in ensuring the maintenance of the status quo.

Tell Me a Riddle touches on the kinds of issues, associations, memories, and stories which receive little, if any, attention on the Hollywood screen. The film tells the story of an elderly couple and their struggle to assert differing concepts of their future together. David/Melvin Douglas, the husband, feels overwhelmed by the maintenance needs of their familial home, and by their continual struggle to make ends meet. He wants to spend his remaining years with his friends and co-workers in a retirement home in Florida, called "Union Haven." Eva/Lila Kedrova, the wife, wishes to remain in her house: the familiarity of what was for so many years a place of domestic confinement has ultimately become a source of solace for her, a place of solitude and retreat. As the narrative progresses, it is revealed to all except Eva (ironically, an additional exclusion from the social world) that she is dying of cancer. As a result, David sells their house without Eva's knowledge or consent in order to finance their final journey together so that Eva may see, and unwittingly say farewell to, their various children and grandchildren. The journey assumes a metaphoric resonance as well, as Eva and David confront their walls of resentment and move towards an understanding based on the equal consideration of their mutual needs.

One can already note the differences in the issues the film investigates from those otherwise treated in popular mainstream culture. Not since the 1937 McCarey film, *Make Way for Tomorrow*, has Hollywood released a serious dramatic film concerning the needs and desires of the elderly coupled with the reality of borderline poverty.[2] In neither film are the hero and heroine typical figures of identification, being neither young nor particularly sexually attractive in the conventional sense. Yet *Tell Me a Riddle* does not stop there. In it, both Eva and David reminisce about their youthful ideals in the Socialist movement in both Russia and America. Although the film's allusions to their Socialist allegiances are quite subtle, there are enough clear references made to establish their ideological history. Not only are these central protagonists elderly, poor, and vaguely socialist, they are also Russian Jewish immigrants, an additional element of "Otherness." Although the film is about both Eva and David, the central character investigated in the narrative, the more problematic protagonist, is Eva; and part of this problematic, aside from the issue of her illness (which is never exploited as it is in other Hollywood movies dealing with fatal illnesses[3]), is her exclusion from active participation in the masculine world of intellectual activity and social politics, and her entrapment in the confined sphere of what society deems the feminine.

This theme of exclusion, along with that of entrapment, links the concerns of *Tell Me a Riddle* with those of the melodrama (referring here to both the literary and cinematic traditions). The problematic of the melodrama includes the expression of women's resistance to their confined and subordinated positions in a male-dominated world. This "expression of resistance," whether conscious or unconscious, takes many forms. One of the most celebrated in the melodrama is that of rebellion through adultery (whether consummated or wished for) as in quintessential melodramas such as *Anna Karenina* and *Madame Bovary*. Another manifestation of resistance to the inequalities inherent in the gender-determined division of labor is the heroine's withdrawal: "For them, inwardness alone provides transcendence, and their world within has heroic dimensions."[4] In order to protest their exclusion, these heroines often withdraw into a world which, ironically, increases their isolation and oppression.

In *Tell Me a Riddle*, Eva protests her exclusion by moving inward—not into an interior world of romantic obsession in the more conventional sense of the genre, but into an "adulterous" relationship with her memories, her "friends" (her books and photographs), the remnants of the world she has lost access to. The film avoids equating the male protagonist with patriarchy: as in many of the most significant melodramas, her husband David is a victim of the same social system which oppresses Eva. In the words of Tillie Olsen's novella, " . . . he remembered she had not always been isolated, had not always wanted to live alone . . . But again he could reconstruct, image, nothing of what had been before, or when, or how, it had changed."[5]

The battle the film describes is not easily reduced to male versus female, husband versus wife, but elaborates itself against the larger social background of the gender-determined division of labor, and economic inequality. As suggested in the novella's opening (" . . . How deep back the stubborn, gnarled roots of the quarrel reached, no one could say"), the quarrel is rooted in the fundaments of gender and class.

As much as the film encourages one to identify and empathize with Eva (we see *her* memories, *her* associations and no one else's), she is simultaneously portrayed as a victim of her own oppression.[6] Although one hasn't yet met Eva, the opening images of the film—photographs from her past—align one with her sphere. As one sees these photographs—some of a man with a young girl (likely Eva), images of Eva as a young woman with her comrades—one hears the sounds of a child humming, some instrumental Russian folk music, and a voice calling "Eva!" These images are followed by pictures of immigrants coming to America (to the sound of boat whistles) and a photo of Eva as a young mother. This collage from the past ends with an abrupt cut to the present: elderly feet moving along a porch, followed by images of a woman's domestic labor—laundry, vacuuming. A man is seen walking across a railway yard, slowly negotiating the steep front stairs of a large house. David's voice asks, "What do we need all this for? Seven rooms . . . ", while Eva puts on her scratchy Russian records at a high volume (to both hear and close out) and proceeds to examine her photo album—images of Gorky, Hugo, Voltaire, Chekhov—and is visibly content. The image cuts to David trying to climb a ladder; a low-angle shot from David's point of view makes the ladder seem endless. He knocks on the window of the porch where Eva is sitting, enclosed within the panes of glass (a common visual motif of entrapment within the melodrama, of which Max Ophuls, for example, makes use). "I'm too old for this," he proclaims. "It's a sinking ship." Eva's response is to close the door, to further enclose herself within her own space. "My books are my friends," she tells herself, and the scene cuts to the film's actual flashbacks: images of Eva and another young woman reading in the woods. Eva's reverie is interrupted by David's "Where is my TV guide? . . .anyway, I'm selling the house." Eva moves towards the TV, blocking the screen, as she proclaims, "You cannot sell this house." (Throughout the scene one hears bits of the soundtrack of the TV documentary David has been watching: in reference to "female rhinos and their young cubs," the announcer comments, "Roger is eager to see how they adapt to their temporary captivity.") The oppositions in the struggle are laid out: Eva's insistence on remaining in a house in which, although she is visualized as being "captive," she can choose to withdraw to the privacy of her inward world; and David's wish to sell a house which he can no longer maintain and in which he feels isolated from both his wife and the outside world.

Eva's insistence hinges on her need to remain in the space familiar to her, however imprisoning. Her memories indicate that she resents her imprisonment. Later, on the night described above, David's request to turn out the light is linked to a cut to Eva's memory of a young man (presumably

David) gently touching Eva, as a young woman, as she reads in bed. His soft words ("Don't read, not now") pull her away from her books to the opposing world of children—sexual relations, without birth control, almost inevitably result in babies and therefore further exclusion, and endless circularity which isolates Eva from her own needs relating to the outside world as represented in her books. Eva resents the steady consumption of *her* time, her need to relax, and insists on using the present to indulge in the past she has lost. David resents Eva's introversion ("Are you on or off?" he continually asks, in reference to the hearing aid which she frequently turns off, shutting him out), just as Eva has always resented his connections to the world outside—his card games, his leisure to joke and entertain. Eva never has experienced the leisure afforded men; as she tells her grandchildren, she knows no riddles—it seems she has never had the time for anything beyond immediate and pressing domestic demands.

During a family dinner, Eva defends her wish to remain in the house by telling her family, "I can't live with people anymore." "But Mama," her daughter protests, "you've lived your whole life for people." "Not *with* . . . many different things now." "Then live alone!" David retorts. This is a constant battle reiterated throughout. In Olsen's words, "She would not exchange her solitude for anything. Never again to be forced to move to the rhythms of others. For in this solitude she had won to a reconciled peace."

When visiting her youngest daughter Vivi, Eva turns away from holding her newborn grandchild. "I can't," she protests. The moment is followed by memories of herself as a young mother lying in bed, her husband's arms holding out a baby while she turns her face away, resentful, refusing. The following shot is of Eva nursing, but instead of offering the archetypical image of joyous sustenance, the feeling is one of being drained, of having demands imposed which are resented. Again, in Olsen's words, "A new baby. How many warm, seductive babies . . . warm flesh like this that had claims and nuzzled away all else and with lovely mouths devoured. . . . " Eva cannot listen to her children reminiscing of her duties as a mother—the food she cooked, the dresses she sewed: "Too much past, Vivi. I just don't remember." She doesn't want to remember.

Painful memories are evoked for Eva as she watches her grandson playing atop a "jungle gym": we see flashback images of Cossack guards outside of the jail cell in which she and another woman are being held. The sequence continues, intercutting between Eva lying in bed remembering and the flashbacks which culminate in the image of her friend, Lisa, hanging. Eva wakes up in a sweat and David soothes: "No prison, Omaha." Still in Omaha, Eva again relives her prison experience in a sequence which ends with her granddaughter discovering her huddled in a closet: "Are you hiding here too, Grandma?" Eva's memories of her imprisonment in the "old country" as a result of political oppression (due either to her socialist activities or her status as a Jew or perhaps both) constantly interrupt her feeling of oppression and entrapment in the "new world" resulting from her role as mother combined with her battle to feed and clothe her children. Eva never stops reliving her prison experience as long as she still feels imprisoned, isolated, and ghettoized by the demands of domestic and reproductive labor. In describing the divisions of working class along gender lines in the Soviet Union, Varda Burstyn comments: "imploding discontent and alienation prevents the full demonstration of resistance."[7] This concept can be applied to women's feelings of alienation in any society. *Implosion* prevents resistance and leads to internal breakdown. In Andrew Britton's article on Ophuls's melodrama, *Madame De . . .*, he discusses the illness of the central protagonist, Louise. Patronizingly indulged at first, "her illness becomes a metaphor for the systematic impoverishment and curtailment of emotional resources and allegiances produced by Louise's oppression."[8] One can similarly read Eva's degenerative illness as a manifestation of her body succumbing to stress and physical exploitation. Following Eva's initial visit to the doctor, before the results revealing the gravity of Eva's illness have come in, her daughter-in-law reprovingly reports to David that Eva was told to "start living like a human being." Her family cannot understand that Eva has never been afforded that luxury.

The "gnarled roots of the quarrel" between David and Eva originate in the sexual division of labor and economic/class divisions, the interconnectedness of which the film insists upon throughout. Both Eva and David were Jewish socialists, active in the Russian revolution, or at least in the task of raising political consciousness against oppression in Russia. The film goes on to suggest that these ideals followed them to America. David talks of organizing the Union Haven retirement home and later comments that Eva has him "organizing again"—advocating rent controls in their friend, Mrs. Mays's, apartment building. Eva's contemporary experience of racial/class oppression in San Francisco is evident in scenes in which she walks past Chilean murals commemorating freedom and independence. These murals recall her memories of past oppression. David and Eva's economic struggles are stressed throughout: Eva's fight to feed and clothe their family during the depression; the humiliation of having to scrounge for day-old bread and soup bones; their recent struggles to keep up their house and finally now, the pressures of meeting medical expenses and the cost of the visits to their children.

Perhaps the clearest indication of gender and economic oppression, coupled with the oppression of the elderly in a youth-oriented society, is embodied in the plight of Mrs. Mays/Lili Valenty, the old friend Eva rediscovers in San Francisco. Her husband has passed away, her family has grown up and she is no longer socially relevant. The first shot of Mrs. Mays—rifling through trash bins in the background of the image—arouses middle-class sentiments of pity mixed with indifference and perhaps mild disgust. Lee Grant brilliantly foregrounds the prejudices informing this response by immediately transforming the anonymous "bag lady" into an important character in the remaining narrative. The sequence in which Mrs. Mays invites David and Eva home for tea is startling in its explicit critique of the exploitation of the elderly. She describes her apartment as being near "where they show the porno movies." As Eva and David approach Mrs. Mays's apartment, she apologizes for the elevator being out of order. As they breathlessly "rest and climb" to the top, she admits that it is always out of order. She mentions the rent hikes due to minor "renovations" and goes on to explain that the cans she collects earn her 21¢ a pound, "nothing to sniff at." As her fridge has broken down, she explains that she treats herself to 65¢ meals at the "Center," although "the food's not good." As she excuses herself to go to the washroom down the hall, Eva nearly collapses, unable to breathe, sputtering, " . . . a lifetime of rooms . . . now only one room . . . no room . . . can't talk . . . eight children and now only one room."

Images of old age, poverty, and neglect connected to an elderly female are the realization of all of Eva's fears: after years of devoted domestic labor (eight children) and isolation from the social world of production (Mrs. Mays's husband died of a heart attack; hence she is no longer connected to that world), women are neglected, shut away in apartments like these, collecting reusable refuse. The entire Mrs. Mays sequence is one which underlines the film's thematic of constriction, confinement, airlessness. One might describe the film as being structured around the movement from the vocal, active past through the airless, repressed present towards the future—marked by the moments in which Eva rediscovers her "voice" and can reciprocate again in her relationships with David, with Jeannie, her granddaughter, and with her friend, Mrs. Mays. The motif of airlessness and suffocation is linked with spatial confinement throughout. Near the beginning of the film, when Eva and David are still in their own home, David wakes up in the middle of the night and finds Eva outside during a rainstorm, ecstatically singing an old Russian love song. "David, I can breathe now, my lungs are filled with air." Mrs. Mays's room, which reminds Eva of a coffin, re-evokes her fear of being unable to breathe, of imprisonment.

The sequences in San Francisco mark a significant turning point in Eva's life. She develops two important relationships (primarily one with Jeannie/Brooke Adams, but also with Mrs. Mays), and she begins to emerge from her inner space into the outside world. The transition is marked by her increasing ability to vocalize her sentiments and to confront and share elements of her past which she has secretly guarded. This transition is visualized by a use of space which is open and unrestrictive: Jeannie's airy loft, walks along the Pacific, and picnics by the sea. One day, while walking with David, Eva rushes through an arched passageway (the walls of which are sprayed with the graffitti message: "Smash Racism"), kicks off her shoes, and frolics in the wide open Pacific. In another scene, Eva,

Mrs. Mays, and Jeannie are having a picnic in the sunshine by the sea. Jeannie is rollerskating, an activity which subtly underlines her mobility, her freedom, her positive outlook. It is the first time that Eva is heard openly and willingly describing her past: "So I said to my father, why can't I go to school? My brothers go to school . . . I lived with my father, a man of God. He said, 'A woman is a footstool for a man.' So I run to Lisa and she teaches me how to read." Jeannie proceeds to share the news of her break-up with the man she has been living with and ends up proclaiming, "I'm gonna live! Here I am! I survived!" The sequence beautifully illustrates the growing support these women offer one another. In later sequences Jeannie and Mrs. Mays are seen massaging and comforting Eva through her illness. On another occasion at the seashore with Jeannie, Eva says, "To think what is beyond . . . Korea, China . . . Geography, I could just eat it up." These moments are significant in the way they reflect Eva's renewed interest in the world outside of the domestic realm.

One can discern two clearly-related narratives in the film, the turning point of each beginning when David regretfully confesses he has sold their house. One narrative line entails the conflict over the sale of the house marked by Eva's desire to return to her home and her inability to do so; the more profound narrative line involves Eva's emergence from confinement into relative freedom prior to her death. Ironically, what seems a loss in the more overt narrative (that of the sale of the house) turns out to be an important victory in the more general struggle. Eva learns that her home is not equivalent to her domestic/familial house, and that the moments of satisfaction she previously enjoyed inwardly can now be shared with and passed on to others.

The sequence following David's revelation of having sold the house is one of attempted reconciliation. On the eve of Mrs. Mays's birthday party, David offers Eva a flower which she outwardly rejects, then sniffs appreciatively. Eva asserts her desire to attend the party even though she is feverish. The party reawakens images of her past. The master of ceremonies/accordionist dedicates some songs to the Jewish-Russian immigrants, victims of "pogroms" (anti-Semitic attacks). He begins to dance with Eva, wheeling her in her chair. The familiar music transports her back to Olshana, her hometown, where she sees herself (in intercut flashbacks) as a child, dancing to these same tunes. As the politically-evocative music continues, Eva suddenly stops, attempts to get up, and cries out, "Freiheit! Freiheit!" The scene cuts to Eva's memory of herself, clasping her friend/comrade's hands, delivering a rousing speech ending with these cries for freedom, but in her present, older voice. The moment in which Eva shouts "freedom" signifies an important change—the world remembered finally breaks through to the present. Eva's assertions of freedom overwhelm her earlier memories of imprisonment. She no longer represses her demands to be politically/socially active and her voice rings out in strength. It is not suggested as an "embarrassing incident" for either Eva or David. The scene following, in Jeannie's apartment, continues their mutual outpouring of much which has been withheld for so long. As Eva and David share a cup of tea, their reconciliation continues. David offers to have Eva's books sent and Eva replies, "I don't need them . . . it's all here" (pointing to her head). She continues by suggesting that David should go to Union Haven: "You have a right to your own life," and David counters, "What about me? Alone without you, you always leave me." "How do I leave you?" "You shut off your hearing. You go inside you. Back to Olshana. To your books. Books, books, always your books. I don't know how I'd bear it without my comrade. My enemy. My girl. You're the only one who knew me when I was a boy. . . . " At this point, Eva, murmuring his name, approaches David. The scene cuts back to the recurring images of Eva's memory of herself as a young woman reading in bed, approached by her husband who whispers "Not now" as he closes her book. It is a flashback the audience has seen a number of times by this point; however, the earlier references all suggested Eva's resentment, in the sense of her lack of time to read, and the inevitable babies that compounded this lack. This time, though, the flashback continues, intercut with the older Eva as initiator, approaching David, comforting, touching and embracing him. They continue their caress during a long take. The image cuts back and forth between the older couple and their youthful counterparts caressing, bridging over time with an embrace.

This sequence, laden with resonances rarely captured on the Hollywood screen, is one of extraordinary beauty. The completion of the embrace has an enormous impact on a number of levels simultaneously: it separates Eva's sexual pleasure from the earlier scenes indicating her resentment of the difficulties of caring for the babies that followed; it visualizes Eva's emergence from behind the walls within which she has enclosed herself; it indicates David's needs—his feelings of loss and abandonment by, not the wife/mother, but rather his comrade; and it severs social taboos against depicting the elderly as sensual beings (instead of the more usual association of sexuality with age in the form of lewd satire of such "abnormal" behavior).

The film never suggests that Eva is cured, either spiritually or physically, or that husband and wife can now continue together without any obstacles and that some permanent order can be imposed. Besides the fact that the "roots" run deep, the film has continuously laid the framework of the conflict against the larger complex of social systems that oppress people, often without their realization or consciousness. Eva's fears and anxieties are still threatening to her and continue to erupt: fears of the "goy gasse" ("street of gentiles"—probable sites for pogroms)—"No streets like that," David comforts. "No ghetto?" "No ghetto"; flashback images seen during the delirium of the final stages of Eva's illness, of Eva pregnant with their son Arnie (who was killed in Korea), hanging laundry, begging for a quarter to buy day-old bread; fears of being pursued; fleeing and losing her ability to run.

The final movement of the film is towards Eva's inevitable death; however, the narrative does not equate death with defeat. In fact, one might argue that the film not only confronts but celebrates death (transgressing another taboo in a society scrupulously devoted to denying age and death) through Jeannie's inheritance of the principles her grandmother has lived for and perhaps died for.[9] Part of the significance of *Tell Me a Riddle* resides in its reminder that women's struggles for liberation were not invented in the 70s or even in the Suffragettes' fight for the vote in the early part of this century in the liberal democracies of Britain or America. The film links Eva's struggles in the Socialist movement to concerns that the relatively emancipated Jeannie must still confront. Eva empathizes with Jeannie in her anguish over having had an abortion (a narrative element the film inserts which is absent from the novella): "How could I have another baby I couldn't feed? I know about abortion." Leafing through her book of photographs with Jeannie, Eva introduces Jeannie to her comrade, Lisa, "the one who taught me how to read and how to fight," and to various individuals, mainly writers, telling her, "These people will sustain you," thereby effectively passing on to her granddaughter these sources of sustenance. Jeannie helps Eva regain access to the world around her, through Tai Chi, through the Rosita doll which emblemizes the memory of a child's life, and above all through her companionship (as Jeannie rightly advised Eva upon their first meeting, "I'm a big strong girl. Lean on me, Grandma.").

As in all Realist art, the final images work towards "closure"—the narrative elements are tied together in an attempt to answer and reconcile the problematic set out at the beginning. However, *Tell Me a Riddle* offers these pleasures of the narrative without restoring the order that was. Eva does not get her house back but then, she has learned to live beyond its walls. As David examines a sketch Jeannie has made of him and Eva curled up, asleep together in her bed, he offers his eulogy of the woman he loved and respected: "You don't know . . . how she was . . . so eloquent . . . a beautiful young girl surrounded by all those people in the woods . . . all those years, she kept those speeches inside. . . . " Unlike so many of the melodramas which end with the heroine's death, Eva's does not leave one paralyzed, immobile, in despair. The film is committed to rekindling those speeches: "She wants to pass it on," Jeannie explains, as does the film, in a most eloquent, communicable manner, and in this way redefines the limits of the genre of the melodrama.

Tell Me a Riddle utilizes the accessible, pleasurable modes of popular narrative art to articulate the most fundamental experiences of sex, gender, and class. By representing a woman's dreams, fears, and memories, the film begins to fill a huge vacuum in mainstream representation. As feminists have theorized, these seemingly small personal experiences are profoundly political. By exposing images, voices, and narratives long suppressed and silenced, the film reformulates and stretches the possibilities of expression within a language familiar to the viewing audience, attesting to the possibility of producing art which is both popular and politically significant.

NOTES

1. See Andrew Britton's article in *Movie* 31/32, "Blissing Out: The Politics of Reaganite Entertainment," and Robin Wood's article " '80s Hollywood: Dominant Tendencies" in *Cine-Action!* 1, Spring 1985, pp. 2–6 for an elaboration of these ideas.
2. *Harry and Tonto* (1974) and *Going in Style* (1979) do address some of these issues, although more within the conventions of comedy.
3. Compare, for instance, *Terms of Endearment* (1983).
4. Andrew Britton quotes from James Walton's "Caleb Williams and the Novel Form" (*Salzburg Studies in English Literature* No. 47, Institut for Englische Sprache und Literatur, 1975) in "Mimesis and Metaphor in *Madame de*", *Movie* 29/30, p. 104.
5. Olsen, Tillie, *Tell Me a Riddle* (London: Faber and Faber), p. 21.
6. In Britton's article cited in footnote 4, he makes the same argument in reference to Louise, the protagonist in Ophuls's melodrama, *Madame de*. He discusses the spectator's inability to condone her "morbid withdrawal into romantic despair" (p. 107).
7. Burstyn, Varda, "Masculine Dominance and the State" (*The Socialist Register*, 1983, pp. 45–89), p. 71.
8. Britton, Andrew, op. cit., p. 107.
9. It is interesting to note that the film greatly elaborates on the character of Jeannie as she is depicted in the novella, in order to stress this continuance.

DESPERATELY SEEKING DIFFERENCE

Jackie Stacey

During the last decade, feminist critics have developed an analysis of the constructions of sexual difference in dominant narrative cinema, drawing on psychoanalytic and post-structuralist theory. One of the main indictments of Hollywood film has been its passive positioning of the woman as sexual spectacle, as there "to be looked at," and the active positioning of the male protagonist as bearer of the look. This pleasure has been identified as one of the central structures of dominant cinema, constructed in accordance with masculine desire. The question which has then arisen is that of the pleasure of the woman spectator. While this issue has hardly been addressed, the specifically homosexual pleasures of female spectatorship have been ignored completely. This article will attempt to suggest some of the theoretical reasons for this neglect.

Theories of Feminine Spectatorship: Masculinization, Masochism, or Marginality

Laura Mulvey's "Visual Pleasure and Narrative Cinema"[1] has been the springboard for much feminist film criticism during the last decade. Using psychoanalytic theory, Mulvey argued that the visual pleasures of Hollywood cinema are based on voyeuristic and fetishistic forms of looking. Because of the ways these looks are structured, the spectator necessarily identifies with the male protagonist in the narrative, and thus with his objectification of the female figure via the male gaze. The construction of woman as spectacle is built into the apparatus of dominant cinema, and the spectator position which is produced by the film narrative is necessarily a masculine one.

Mulvey maintained that visual pleasure in narrative film is built around two contradictory processes: the first involves objectification of the image and the second identification with it. The first process depends upon "direct scopophilic contact with the female form displayed for [the spectator's] enjoyment"[2] and the spectator's look here is active and feels powerful. This form of pleasure requires the separation of the "erotic identity of the subject from the object on the screen."[3] This "distance" between spectator and screen contributes to the voyeuristic pleasure of looking in on a private world. The second form of pleasure depends upon the opposite process, an identification with the image on the screen "developed through narcissism and the constitution of the ego."[4] The process of identification in the cinema, Mulvey argued, like the process of objectification, is structured by the narrative. It offers the spectator the pleasurable identification with the main male protagonist, and through him the power to indirectly possess the female character displayed as sexual object for his pleasure. The look of the male character moves the narrative forward and identification with it thus implies a sense of sharing in the power of his active look.

Two absences in Mulvey's argument have subsequently been addressed in film criticism. The first raises the question of the male figure as erotic object,[5] the second that of the feminine subject in the narrative, and, more specifically in relation to this essay, women's active desire and the sexual aims of women in the audience in relationship to the female protagonist on the screen. As David Rodowick points out:

> her discussion of the female figure is restricted only to its function as masculine object-choice. In this manner, the place of the masculine is discussed as both the subject and object of the gaze: and the feminine is discussed only as an object which structures the masculine look according to its active (voyeuristic) and passive (fetishistic) forms. So where is the place of the feminine subject in this scenario?[6]

There are several possible ways of filling this theoretical gap. One would use a detailed textual analysis to demonstrate that different gendered spectator positions are produced by the film text, contradicting the unified masculine model of spectatorship. This would at least provide some space for an account of the feminine subject in the film text and in the cinema audience. The relationship of spectators to these feminine and masculine positions would then need to be explored further: do women necessarily take up a feminine and men a masculine spectator position?

Alternatively, we could accept a theory of the masculinization of the spectator at a textual level, but argue that spectators bring different subjectivities to the film according to sexual difference,[7] and therefore respond differently to the visual pleasures offered in the text. I want to elaborate these two possibilities briefly, before moving on to discuss a third which offers a more flexible or mobile model of spectatorship and cinematic pleasure.

The first possibility is, then, arguing that the film text can be read and enjoyed from different gendered positions. This problematizes the monolithic model of Hollywood cinema as an "anthropomorphic male machine"[8] producing unified and masculinized spectators. It offers an explanation of women's pleasure in narrative cinema based on different processes of spectatorship, according to sexual difference. What this "difference" signifies, however, in terms of cinematic pleasure, is highly contestable.

Raymond Bellour has explored the way the look is organized to create filmic discourse through detailed analyses of the system of enunciation in Hitchcock's work.[9] The mechanisms for eliminating the threat of sexual difference represented by the figure of the woman, he argues, are built into the apparatus of the cinema. Woman's desire only appears on the screen to be punished and controlled by assimilation to the desire of the male character. Bellour insists upon the masochistic nature of the woman spectator's pleasure in Hollywood film.

> I think that a woman can love, accept, and give positive value to these films only from her own masochism, and from a certain sadism that she can exercise in return on the masculine subject, within a system loaded with traps.[10]

Bellour, then, provides an account of the feminine subject and women's spectatorship which offers a different position from the masculine one set up by Mulvey. However, he fixes these positions within a rigid dichotomy which assumes a biologically determined equivalence between male/female and the masculine/feminine, sadistic/masochistic positions he believes to be set up by the cinematic apparatus. The apparatus here is seen as determining, controlling the meaning produced by a film text unproblematically.

> . . . the resulting picture of the classical cinema is even more totalistic and deterministic than Mulvey's. Bellour sees it as a logically consistent, complete and closed system.[11]

The problem here is that Bellour's analysis, like those of many structural functionalists, leaves no room for subjectivity. The spectator is presumed to be an already fully constituted subject and is fixed by the text to a predetermined gender identification. There is no space for subjectivity to be seen as a process in which identification and object choice may be shifting, contradictory, or precarious.

A second challenge to the model of the masculinized spectator set up by Mulvey's 1975 essay comes from the work of Mary Ann Doane. She draws on Freud's account of asymmetry in the development of masculinity and femininity to argue that women's pleasures are not motivated by fetishistic and voyeuristic drives.

> For the female spectator there is a certain over-presence of the image—she is the image. Given the closeness of this relationship, the female spectator's desire can be described only in terms of a kind of narcissism—the female look demands a becoming. It thus appears to negate the very distance or gap specified . . . as the essential precondition for voyeurism.[12]

Feminist critics have frequently challenged the assumption that fetishism functions for women in the same way that it is supposed to for men. Doane argues that the girl's understanding of the meaning of sexual difference occurs simultaneously with seeing the boy's genitals; the split between seeing and knowing, which enables the boy to disown the difference which is necessary for fetishism, does not occur in girls.

> It is in the distance between the look and the threat that the boy's relation to the knowledge of sexual difference is formulated. The boy, unlike the girl in Freud's description, is capable of a re-vision. . . . This gap between the visible and the knowable, the very possibility of disowning what is seen, prepares the ground for fetishism.[13]

This argument is useful in challenging the hegemony of the cinema apparatus and in offering an account of visual pleasure which is neither based on a phallic model, nor on the determinacy of the text. It allows for an account of women's potential resistance to the dominant masculine spectator position. However, it also sets women outside the problematic pleasures of looking in the cinema, as if women do not have to negotiate within patriarchal regimes. As Doane herself has pointed out:

> The feminist theorist is thus confronted with something of a double bind: she can continue to analyze and interpret various instances of the repression of woman, of her radical absence in the discourses of men—a pose which necessitates remaining within that very problematic herself, repeating its terms; or she can attempt to delineate a feminine specificity, always risking a recapitulation of patriarchal constructions and a naturalization of "woman."[14]

In fact, this is a very familiar problem in feminist theory: how to argue for a feminine specificity without falling into the trap of biological essentialism. If we do argue that women differ from men in their relation to visual constructions of femininity, then further questions are generated for feminist film theory: do all women have the same relationship to images of themselves? Is there only one feminine spectator position? How do we account for diversity, contradiction, or resistance within this category of feminine spectatorship?

The problem here is one which arises in relation to all cultural systems in which women have been defined as "other" within patriarchal discourses: how can we express the extent of women's oppression without denying femininity any room to maneuver (Mulvey, 1975), defining women as complete victims of patriarchy (Bellour, 1979), or as totally other to it (Doane, 1982)? Within the theories discussed so far, the female spectator is offered only the three rather frustrating options of masculinization, masochism, or marginality.

Towards a More Contradictory Model of Spectatorship

A different avenue of exploration would require a more complex and contradictory model of the relay of looks on the screen and between the audience and the diegetic characters.

> It might be better, as Barthes suggests, neither to destroy difference nor to valorize it, but to multiply and disperse differences, to move towards a world where differences would not be synonymous with exclusion.[15]

In her 1981 "Afterthoughts" on visual pleasure, Mulvey addresses many of the problems raised so far. In an attempt to develop a more "mobile" position for the female spectator in the cinema, she turns to Freud's theories of the difficulties of attaining heterosexual femininity.[16] Required, unlike men, to relinquish the phallic activity and female object of infancy, women are argued to oscillate between masculine and feminine identifications. To demonstrate this oscillation between positions, Mulvey cites Pearl Chavez's ambivalence in *Duel in the Sun*, the splitting of her desire (to be Jesse's "lady" or Lewt's tomboy lover), a splitting which also extends to the female spectator. Mulvey's revision is important for two reasons: it displaces the notions of the fixity of spectator positions produced by the text, and it focuses on the gaps and contradictions within patriarchal signification, thus opening up crucial questions of resistance and diversity. However, Mulvey maintains that fantasies of action "can only find expression . . . through the metaphor of masculinity." In order to identify with active desire, the female spectator must assume an (uncomfortably) masculine position:

> . . . the female spectator's fantasy of masculinization is always to some extent at cross purposes with itself, restless in its transvestite clothes.[17]

Oppressive Dichotomies

Psychoanalytic accounts which theorize identification and object choice within a framework of linked binary oppositions (masculinity/femininity:

activity/passivity) necessarily masculinize female homosexuality. Mary Ann Doane's reading of the first scene in the film *Caught* demonstrates the limitations of this psychoanalytic binarism perfectly.

> The woman's sexuality, as spectator, must undergo a constant process of transformation. She must look, as if she were a man with the phallic power of the gaze, at a woman who would attract that gaze, in order to be that woman. . . . The convolutions involved here are analogous to those described by Julia Kristeva as "the double or triple twists of what we commonly call female homosexuality": "I am looking, as a man would, for a woman"; or else, "I submit myself, as if I were a man who thought he was a woman, to a woman who thinks she is a man."[18]

Convolutions indeed. This insistence upon a gendered dualism of sexual desire maps homosexuality onto an assumed antithesis of masculinity and femininity. Such an asumption precludes a description of homosexual positionality without resorting to the maneuvers cited by Doane. In arguing for a more complex model of cinematic spectatorship, I am suggesting that we need to separate gender identification from sexuality, too often conflated in the name of sexual difference.

In films where the woman is represented as sexual spectacle for the masculine gaze of the diegetic and the cinematic spectator, an identification with a masculine heterosexual desire is invited. The spectator's response can vary across a wide spectrum between outright acceptance and refusal. It has proved crucial for feminist film theorists to explore these variations. How might a woman's look at another woman, both within the diegesis and between spectator and character, compare with that of the male spectator?

This essay considers the pleasures of two narrative films which develop around one woman's obsession with another woman, *All about Eve* (directed by Joseph Mankiewicz, 1950) and *Desperately Seeking Susan* (directed by Susan Seidelman, 1984). I shall argue that these films offer particular pleasures to the women in the audience which cannot simply be reduced to a masculine heterosexual equivalent. In so doing I am not claiming these films as "lesbian films,"[19] but rather using them to examine certain possibilities of pleasure.

I want to explore the representation of forms of desire and identification in these films in order to consider their implications for the pleasures of female spectatorship. My focus is on the relations between women on the screen, and between these representations and the women in the audience. Interestingly, the fascinations which structure both narratives are precisely about difference—forms of otherness between women characters which are not merely reducible to sexual difference, so often seen as the sole producer of desire itself.

The Inscription of Active Feminine Desire

In *Alice Doesn't*, Teresa de Lauretis explores the function of the classic masculine oedipal trajectory in dominant narrative. The subjects which motivate the narrative along the logic of the "Oedipus," she argues, are necessarily masculine.

> However varied the conditions of the presence of the narrative form in fictional genres, rituals or social discourses, its movement seems to be that of a passage, a transformation predicated on the figure of the hero, a mythical subject . . . the *single* figure of the hero who crosses the boundary and penetrates the other space. In so doing, the hero, the mythical subject, is constructed as a human being and as male; he is the active principle of culture, the establisher of distinction, the creator of differences. Female is what is not susceptible to transformation, to life or death;[20]

De Lauretis then proceeds to outline the significance of this division between masculine and feminine within the textual narrative in terms of spectatorship.

> Therefore, to say that narrative is the production of Oedipus is to say that each reader—male or female—is constrained and defined within the two positions of a sexual difference thus conceived: male-hero-human, on the side of the subject; the female-obstacle-boundary-space, on the other.[21]

As de Lauretis herself acknowledges later in the essay, this analysis leaves little space for either the question of the feminine subject in the narrative, or the pleasures of desire and identification of the women in the audience. In order to explore these questions more concretely, I want to discuss two texts—one a Hollywood production of 1950, the other a recent U.S. "independent"—whose central narrative concern is that of female desire. Both *All About Eve* and *Desperately Seeking Susan* have female protagonists whose desires and identifications move the narratives forward. In de Lauretis's terms, these texts construct not only a feminine object of desire in the narrative, but also a feminine subject of that desire.

All About Eve is particularly well suited to an analysis of these questions, as it is precisely about the pleasures and dangers of spectatorship for women. One of its central themes is the construction and reproduction of feminine identities, and the activity of looking is highlighted as an important part of these processes. The narrative concerns two women, a Broadway star and her most adoring spectator, Eve. In its course, we witness the transformation of Eve Butler (Anne Baxter) from spectator to star herself. The pleasures of spectatorship are emphasized by Eve's loyal attendance at every one of Margot Channing's (Bette Davis) performances. Its dangers are also made explicit as an intense rivalry develops between them. Eve emerges as a greedy and ambitious competitor, and Margot steps down from stardom into marriage, finally enabling her protegée to replace her as "actress of the year" in a part written originally for Margot.

Eve's journey to stardom could be seen as the feminine equivalent to the masculine oedipal trajectory described by de Lauretis above. Freud's later descriptions of the feminine oedipal journey[22] contradict his previous symmetrical model wherein the girl's first love object is her father, as the boy's is his mother. In his later arguments, Freud also posited the mother as the girl's first love object. Her path to heterosexuality is therefore difficult and complex, since it requires her not only to relinquish her first object, like the boy, but to transform both its gender (female to male) and the aim (active to passive) directed at it. Up to this point, active desire towards another woman is an experience of all women, and its re-enactment in *All About Eve* may constitute one of the pleasures of spectatorship for the female viewer.

Eve is constantly referred to as innocent and childlike in the first half of the film and her transformation involves a process of maturation, of becoming a more confident adult. First she is passionately attached to Margot, but then she shifts her affection to Margot's lover Bill, attempting unsuccessfully to seduce him. Twice in the film she is shown interrupting their intimacy: during their farewell at the airport and then during their fierce argument about Margot's jealousy, shortly before Bill's welcome-home party. Eve's third object of desire, whom she actively pursues, is the married playwright, Lloyd Richards, husband to Margot's best friend. In both cases the stability of the older heterosexual couples, Margot and Bill, Karen and Lloyd, are threatened by the presence of the younger woman who completes the oedipal triangle. Eve is finally punished for her desires by the patriarchal power of the aptly named Addison de Wit, who proves to be one step ahead of her manipulations.

The binary opposition between masculinity and femininity offers a limited framework for the discussion of Eve's fascination with Margot, which is articulated actively through an interplay of desire and identification during the film. In many ways, Margot is Eve's idealized object of desire. She follows Margot from city to city, never missing any of her performances. Her devotion to her favourite Broadway star is stressed at the very start of the film.

Karen	But there are hundreds of plays on Broadway. . . .
Eve	Not with Margot Channing in them!

Margot is moved by Eve's representation of her "tragic" past, and flattered by her adoration, so she decides to "adopt" her.

Margot (voice-over)	We moved Eve's few pitiful possessions into my apartment. . . . Eve became my sister, mother, lawyer, friend, psychiatrist and cop. The honeymoon was on!

Eve acts upon her desire to become more like her ideal. She begins to wear Margot's cast-off clothes, appearing in Margot's bedroom one morning in her old black suit. Birdie, Margot's personal assistant, responds suspiciously to Eve's behaviour.

Margot	She thinks only of me.
Birdie	She thinks only *about* you—like she's studying you—like you was a book, or a play, or a set of blueprints—how you walk, talk, eat, think, sleep.
Margot	I'm sure that's very flattering, Birdie, and I'm sure there's nothing wrong with it.

The construction of Bette Davis as the desirable feminine ideal in this narrative has a double significance here. As well as being a "great star" for Eve, she is clearly the same for the cinema audience. The film offers the fictional fulfilment of the spectator's dreams as well as Eve's, to be a star like Bette Davis, like Margot. Thus the identifications and desires of Eve, to some extent, narrativize a traditional pleasure of female spectatorship.

Margot is not only a star, she is also an extremely powerful woman who intimidates most of the male characters in the film. Her quick wit and disdain for conventional politeness, together with her flare for drama offstage as much as on, make her an attractive figure for Eve, an "idealistic dreamy-eyed kid," as Bill describes her. It is this *difference* between the two women which motivates Eve, but which Eve also threatens. In trying to "become as much like her ideal as possible," Eve almost replaces Margot in both her public and her private lives. She places a call to Bill on Margot's behalf, and captures his attention when he is on his way upstairs to see Margot before his coming home party. Margot begins to feel dispensible.

Margot	I could die right now and nobody would be confused. My inventory is all in shape and the merchandise all put away.

Yet even dressed in Margot's costume, having taken her role in the evening's performance, Eve cannot supplant her in the eyes of Bill, who rejects her attempt at seduction. The difference between the two women is repeatedly stressed and complete identification proves impossible.

All About Eve offers some unusual pleasures for a Hollywood film, since the active desire of a female character is articulated through looking at the female star. It is by watching Margot perform on the stage that Eve becomes intoxicated with her idol. The significance of active looking in the articulation of feminine desire is foregrounded at various points in the narrative. In one scene, we see Eve's devoted spectatorship in progress during one of Margot's performances. Eve watches Margot from the wings of the stage, and Margot bows to the applause of her audience. In the next scene the roles are reversed, and Margot discovers Eve on the empty stage bowing to an imaginary audience. Eve is holding up Margot's costume to sample the pleasures of stardom for herself. This process is then echoed in the closing scene of the film with Eve, now a Broadway star herself, and the newly introduced Phoebe, an adoring schoolgirl fan. The final shot shows Phoebe, having covertly donned Eve's bejewelled evening cloak, holding Eve's award and gazing at her reflection in the mirror. The reflected image, infinitely multiplied in the triptych of the glass, creates a spectacle of stardom that is the film's final shot, suggesting a perpetual regeneration of intra-feminine fascinations through the pleasure of looking.

The Desire to Be Desperate

Like *All About Eve, Desperately Seeking Susan* concerns a woman's obsession with another woman. But instead of being punished for acting upon her desires, like Eve, Roberta (Rosanna Arquette) acts upon her desires, if in a rather more haphazard way, and eventually her initiatives are rewarded with the realization of her desires. Despite her classic feminine behavior, forgetful, clumsy, unpunctual, and indecisive, she succeeds in her quest to find Susan (Madonna).

Even at the very beginning of the film, when suburban housewife Roberta is represented at her most dependent and childlike, her actions propel the narrative movement. Having developed her own fantasy narrative about Susan by reading the personal advertisements, Roberta acts upon her desire to be "desperate" and becomes entangled in Susan's life. She anonymously attends the romantic reunion of Susan and Jim, and then pursues Susan through the streets of Manhattan. When she loses sight of her quarry in a second-hand shop, she purchases the jacket which Susan has just exchanged. The key found in its pocket provides an excuse for direct contact, and Roberta uses the personals to initiate another meeting.

Not only is the narrative propelled structurally by Roberta's desire, but almost all the spectator sees of Susan at the beginning of the film is revealed through Roberta's fantasy. The narrativization of her desires positions her as the central figure for spectator identification: through her desire we seek, and see, Susan. Thus, in the opening scenes, Susan is introduced by name when Roberta reads the personals aloud from under the dryer in the beauty salon. Immediately following Roberta's declaration "I wish I was desperate," there is a cut to the first shot of Susan.

The cuts from the Glass' party to Susan's arrival in New York City work to the same effect. Repelled by her husband's TV commercial for his bathroom wares, Roberta leaves her guests and moves towards the window, as the ad's voice-over promises "At Gary's Oasis, all your fantasies can come true." Confronted with her own image in the reflection, she pushes it away by opening the window and looking out longingly onto Manhattan's skyline. The ensuing series of cuts between Roberta and the bridge across the river to the city link her desiring gaze to Susan's arrival there via the same bridge.

At certain points within *Desperately Seeking Susan*, Roberta explicitly becomes the bearer of the look. The best illustration of this transgression of traditional gender positionalities occurs in the scene in which she first catches sight of Susan. The shot sequence begins with Jim seeing Susan and is immediately followed with Roberta seeing her. It is, however, Roberta's point of view which is offered for the spectator's identification. Her look is specified by the use of the pay-slot telescope through which Roberta, and the spectator, see Susan.

In accordance with classic narrative cinema, the object of fascination in *Desperately Seeking Susan* is a woman—typically, a woman coded as a sexual spectacle. As a star Madonna's image is saturated in sexuality. In many ways she represents the 80s "assertive style" of heterosexual spectacle, inviting masculine consumption. This is certainly emphasized by shots of Susan which reference classic pornographic poses and camera angles; for example, the shot of Susan lying on Roberta's bed reading her diary, which shows Susan lying on her back, wearing only a vest and a pair of shorts over her suspenders and lacy tights. (Although one could argue that the very next shot, from Susan's point of view, showing Gary upside down, subverts the conventional pornographic codes.) My aim is not to deny these meanings in *Desperately Seeking Susan*, in order to claim it as a "progressive text," but to point to cinematic pleasures which may be available to the spectator *in addition* to those previously analyzed by feminist film theory. Indeed, I believe such a project can only attempt to work within the highly contradictory constructions of femininity in mainstream films.

Susan is represented as puzzling and enigmatic to the protagonist, and to the spectator. The desire propelling the narrative is partly a desire to become more like her, but also a desire to know her, and to solve the riddle of her femininity. The protagonist begins to fulfill this desire by following the stranger, gathering clues about her identity and her life, such as her jacket, which, in turn, produces three other clues, a key, a photograph, and a telephone number. The construction of her femininity as a riddle is emphasized by the series of intrigues and misunderstandings surrounding Susan's identity. The film partly relies on typical devices drawn from the mystery genre in constructing the protagonist's, and thus the spectator's, knowledge of Susan through a series of clues and coincidences. Thus, in some ways, Susan is positioned as the classic feminine enigma; she is, however, investigated by another woman.

One line of analysis might simply see Roberta as taking up the position of the masculine protagonist in expressing a desire to be "desperate," which, after all, can be seen as identifying with Jim's position in relation to Susan, that of active desiring masculinity. Further legitimation for this reading could be seen in Jim's response to Roberta's advertisement to Susan in the personals. He automatically assumes it has been placed there by another man, perhaps a rival. How can we understand the construction of the female protagonist as the agent and articulator of desire for another woman in the narrative within existing psychoanalytic theories of sexual difference? The limitations of a dichotomy which offers only two significant categories for understanding the complex interplay of gender, sexual aim, and object choice, is clearly demonstrated here.

Difference and Desire between Women

The difference which produces the narrative desire in *Desperately Seeking Susan* is not sexual difference, but the difference between two women in the film. It is the difference between suburban marriage and street credibility. Two sequences contrast the characters using smoking as a signifier of difference. The first occurs in Battery Park, where Roberta behaves awkwardly in the unfamiliar territory of public space. She is shown sitting on a park bench, knees tightly clenched, looking around nervously for Susan. Jim asks her for a light, to which she timidly replies that she does not smoke. The ensuing cut shows Susan, signaled by Jim's shout of recognition. Susan is sitting on the boat rail, striking a match on the bottom of her raised boot to light a cigarette.

Smoking is used again to emphasize difference in a subsequent sequence. This time, Roberta, having by now lost her memory and believing she may be Susan, lights a cigarette from Susan's box. Predictably, she chokes on the smoke, with the unfamiliarity of an adolescent novice. The next cut shows us Susan, in prison for attempting to skip her cab fare, taking a light from the prison matron and blowing the smoke defiantly straight back into her face. The contrast in their smoking ability is only one signifier of the characters' very different femininities. Roberta is represented as young, inexperienced, and asexual, while Susan's behavior and appearance are coded as sexually confident and provocative. Rhyming sequences are used to emphasize their differences even after Roberta has taken on her new identity as Susan. She ends up in the same prison cell, but her childlike acquiescence to authority contrasts with Susan's defiance of the law.

Susan transgresses conventional forms of feminine behavior by appropriating public space for herself. She turns the public lavatory into her own private bathroom, drying her armpits with the hand blower, and changing her clothes in front of the mirror above the washbasins as if in her own bedroom. In the streets, Susan challenges the patronizing offer of a free newspaper from a passerby by dropping the whole pile at his feet and taking only the top copy for herself. In contrast to Susan's supreme public confidence, Roberta is only capable in her own middle-class privacy. Arriving home after her day of city adventures, she manages to synchronize with a televised cooking show, catching up on its dinner preparations with confident dexterity in her familiar domestic environment.

As soon as Roberta becomes entangled in Susan's world, her respectable sexuality is thrown into question. First she is assumed to be having an affair, then she is arrested for suspected prostitution, and finally Gary asks her if she is a lesbian. When the two photographs of Roberta, one as a bride and one as a suspected prostitute, are laid down side by side at the police station, her apparent transformation from virgin to whore shocks her husband. The ironic effect of these largely misplaced accusations about Roberta's sexuality works partly in relation to Susan, who is represented as the epitome of opposition to acceptable bourgeois feminine sexuality. She avoids commitment, dependency, or permanence in her relationships with men, and happily takes their money, while maintaining an intimate friendship with the woman who works at the Magic Box.

Roberta's desire is finally rewarded when she meets Susan in an almost farcical chase scene at that club during the chaotic film finale. Gary finds Roberta, Des finds "Susan" (Roberta), Jim finds Susan, the villain finds the jewels (the earrings which Susan innocently pocketed earlier in the film), Susan and Roberta catch the villain, and Susan and Roberta find each other. . . . The last shot of the film is a front-page photograph of the two women hand in hand, triumphantly waving their reward check in return for the recovery of the priceless Nefertiti earrings. In the end, both women find what they were searching for throughout the narrative: Roberta has found Susan, and Susan has found enough money to finance many future escapades.

Roberta's desire to become more like her ideal—a more pleasingly coordinated, complete, and attractive feminine image[23]—is offered temporary narrative fulfilment. However, the pleasures of this feminine desire cannot be collapsed into simple identification, since difference and otherness are continuously played upon, even when Roberta "becomes" her idealized object. Both *Desperately Seeking Susan* and *All About Eve* tempt the woman spectator with the fictional fulfilment of becoming an ideal feminine other, while denying complete transformation by insisting upon differences between women. The rigid distinction between *either* desire *or* identification, so characteristic of psychoanalytic film theory, fails to address the construction of desires which involve a specific interplay of both processes.

I would like to thank Sarah Franklin, Richard Dyer, Alison Light, Chris Healey, and the Women Thesis Writers Group in Birmingham for their inspiration, support, and helpful comments during the writing of this essay.

NOTES

1. Laura Mulvey, "Visual Pleasure and Narrative Cinema," *Screen* 16, no. 3 (Autumn 1975), pp. 6–18.
2. Ibid., p. 13.
3. Ibid., p. 10.
4. Ibid.
5. There have been several attempts to fill this theoretical gap and provide analyses of masculinity as sexual spectacle: see Richard Dyer, "Don't Look Now—The Male Pin-Up," *Screen* 23, nos. 3–4 (September-October 1982); Steve Neale, "Masculinity as Spectacle," *Screen* 24, no. 6 (November-December 1983); and Andy Medhurst, "Can Chaps Be Pin-Ups?" *Ten* 8, no. 17 (1985).
6. David Rodowick, "The Difficulty of Difference," *Wide Angle* 5, no. 1 (1982), p. 8.
7. Mary Ann Doane, "Film and the Masquerade: Theorizing the Female Spectator," *Screen* 23, nos. 3–4 (September-October 1982), pp. 74–87.
8. Constance Penley, "Feminism, Film Theory and the Bachelor Machines," *m/f*, no. 10 (1985), pp. 39–56.
9. *Enunciator*: "the term . . . marks both the person who possesses the right to speak within the film, and the source (instance) towards which the series of representations is logically channelled back," Raymond Bellour, "Hitchcock the Enunciator," *Camera Obscura*, no. 2 (1977), p. 94.
10. Raymond Bellour, "Psychosis, Neurosis, Perversion," *Camera Obscura*, nos. 3/4 (1979), p. 97.
11. Janet Bergstrom, "Enunciation and Sexual Difference," *Camera Obscura*, nos. 3/4 (1979), p. 57. See also Janet Bergstrom, "Alternation, Segmentation, Hypnosis: An Interview with Raymond Bellour," *Camera Obscura*, nos. 3/4 (1979).
12. Mary Ann Doane, "Film and the Masquerade," op. cit., p. 78.
13. Ibid., p. 80.
14. Mary Ann Doane, Patricia Mellencamp, and Linda Williams, "Feminist Film Criticism: An Introduction," in Mary Ann Doane, Patricia Mellencamp, and Linda Williams, eds., *Re-Vision*, Frederick, MD: American Film Institute (1984), p. 9.
15. Ibid., p. 14.
16. Laura Mulvey, "Afterthoughts on "Visual Pleasure and Narrative Cine-

ma" . . . Inspired by 'Duel in the Sun,' " *Framework*, nos. 15/16/17 (1981), pp. 12–15.

17. Ibid., p. 15.

18. Mary Ann Doane citing Julie Kristeva, *About Chinese Women*, in "Caught and Rebecca: The Inscription of Femininity as Absence," *Enclitic* 5, No. 2/6, no. 1 (Fall 1981/Spring 1982), p. 77.

19. For a discussion of films which might be included under this category, see Caroline Sheldon, "Lesbians and Film; Some Thoughts," in Richard Dyer, ed., *Gays and Film*, New York: Zoetrope, rev. ed. (1984).

20. Teresa de Lauretis, *Alice Doesn't: Feminism, Semiotics and the Cinema*, London: Macmillan (1984), pp. 113, 119.

21. Ibid., p. 121.

22. See, for example, Sigmund Freud, "Some Psychical Consequences of the Anatomical Distinction Between the Sexes" (1925), in *On Sexuality*, Pelican Freud Library, vol. 7, Harmondsworth (1977), pp. 331–43.

23. See Jacques Lacan, "The Mirror Stage as Formative of the Function of the I as Revealed in Psychoanalytic Experience," *Ecrits*, trans. Alan Sheridan, London: Tavistock (1977), pp. 1–7.

FEMALE NARRATION, WOMEN'S CINEMA

HELKE SANDER'S *THE ALL-ROUND REDUCED PERSONALITY/REDUPERS*

Judith Mayne

Christa Wolf, in *The Quest for Christa T.*, evokes the cinema as a form of illusory presence, as fantasy control of the past. Here is how the female narrator of *The Quest for Christa T.* describes not only her search for Christa, but for the very possibility of memory: " . . . I even name her name, and now I'm quite certain of her. But all the time I know that it's a film of shadows being run off the reel, a film that was once projected in the real light of cities, landscapes, living rooms."[1] Film is memory, to be sure, but reified memory. Film suggests, then, a past that has been categorized, hierarchized, and neatly tucked away.[2] The narrator of *The Quest for Christa T.* searches for the connections between female identity and language, and film is a form of memory to be resisted. The issue is one of female narration: of a female narrator engaged, in Christa Wolf's words, in a search for " . . . the secret of the third person, who is there without being tangible and who, when circumstances favor her, can bring down more reality upon herself than the first person: I."[3] The cinema concretizes what Wolf calls: "The difficulty of saying 'I.' "[4]

For Christa Wolf, film and writing correspond to two different relations between the narrator and the past. In her essay, "The Reader and the Writer," she says:

> We seem to need the help and approval of the imagination in our lives; it means playing with the possibilities open to us. But something else goes on inside us at the same time, daily, hourly, a furtive process hard to avoid, a hardening, petrifying, habituating, that attacks the memory in particular."[5]

Wolf speaks of "miniatures," the easily-summoned bits and pieces of past experience which we have arranged in our minds as if on shelves, and film belongs to the realm of miniatures.[6] Writing, however, is a "strenuous movement" requiring an active engagement with the past rather than simple observation of the miniatures.[7] Wolf writes:

> Prose should try to be unfilmable. It should give up the dangerous work of circulating miniatures and putting finished pieces together. It should be incorruptible in its insistence on the one and only experience and not violate the experiences of others; but it should give them the courage of their own experiences.[8]

But even though cinema is indicted by Wolf, one can also see in this formulation a vital encounter between the spectacle of cinema and the narration of a female protagonist.[9] This is not necessarily to say that film, and miniatures, are therefore "male." Wolf's indictment of the cinema does echo, if from a different perspective, recent feminist analyses of the cinema. These analyses have shown us, for example, that the codes of institutional narrative cinema establish the spectator as a passive consumer of the film spectacle; or that narrative flow is governed by a male-defined system of gazes; and that woman exists in the cinema as the projection of male fears and fantasies.[10]

But women *do* make movies. If I refer, via Wolf, to equations of cinema with domination and control, it is not to suggest that cinema is a hopelessly monolithic patriarchal institution. It is to suggest, rather, that the encounter of cinema and a female narrator has a corollary in the way in which women filmmakers have examined the juncture of spectacle and narrative within film itself. And then one might add: if cinema is indeed this reified form of domination, then explorations into the possibilities of female cinematic narration have a kind of strategic importance.

Some of the difficulties of such an encounter are evidenced by the fact that, with only some exceptions, we hesitate to use "feminist" to describe any but the most explicit films, and those are usually documentaries. As B. Ruby Rich points out, this reflects " . . . a crisis in the ability of feminist film criticism thus far to come to terms with the work at hand, to apply a truly feminist criticism to the body of work already produced by women filmmakers."[11] But perhaps our hesitation about what constitutes feminist cinema has more to do with the nature of film—that is, those qualities underscored by writers like Wolf—than with the connections between feminism and aesthetics in general. Super-8 cameras and home movies notwithstanding, film represents a formidable domain of technological expertise. And unlike the novel which preceded it as emblematic art form of capitalist society, there are virtually none of those "pre-aesthetic" (to use Silvia Bovenschen's words) realms, like diaries and letter-writing, to allow women access to film production.[12]

Yet the institution of cinema is narrative cinema. And in the writings of Christa Wolf, cinematic metaphors emerge in a specifically narrative context—that is, as part of the journey of a first-person female narrator attempting to distill and clarify experience. There are films which immediately come to mind as analogues to these literary examples: Michelle Citron's *Daughter Rite* (1978), for instance, in which a female narrator speaks, over home movies shown in slow motion, about dreams and fantasies; or Sally Potter's *Thriller* (1979), in which the Mimi of *La Bohème* conducts an investigation, of sorts, to discover who was responsible for her death. While such cross-media comparisons are always tenuous, the female voices articulated in these films play a role quite similar to that of the first-person narrator in *The Quest for Christa T.*, for they resist the "miniatures" offered through moving pictures.

Helke Sander's 1977 film *The All-Round Reduced Personality (Redupers)*[13] is concerned with these questions of female narration and film form, a concern evidenced, at least in a preliminary way, by several references to Christa Wolf. Sander's film raises narrative issues that are best considered in the context of women's cinema, but in no way should this category be construed in essentialist terms. Rather, I would argue that consideration of *Redupers* as a "women's film" permits a most active engagement with the different themes and contexts which the film evokes. It is tempting, of course, to immediately situate *Redupers* within the New German Cinema. Indeed, many aspects of the film echo works by better-known filmmakers like Kluge and Fassbinder. A distinctive feature of *Redupers* is its blend of documentary and fiction technique, recalling the narrative style of Alexander Kluge's films *Yesterday's Girls* (1966) or *The Artists under the Big Top; Perplexed* (1968). The city of Berlin figures prominently in Sander's film, echoing Kluge again, for his portrayals of Frankfurt, or Fassbinder, for his characterizations of Munich (in *Ali: Fear Eats the Soul*, or *Fox and his Friends*). Indeed, explorations of narrative cityscapes have been a pervasive feature of recent German cinema, explorations which lead in their turn, as in Sander's film, to inquiries into everyday life. This film surely is unique in its exploration of the particularities of the divided city of Berlin. Indeed, it is safe to say that *Redupers* is a first, of sorts, for its examination of the narrative ramifications of the Berlin cityscape (of West German films, only Johannes Schaaf's 1967 film *Tatooing* problematizes the city of Berlin in any way similar to *Redupers*).

Documentary and fiction, everyday life, and the city: it is tempting to assume rather simply that *Redupers* presents a "female perspective" on these characteristic preoccupations of the New German Cinema. While New German filmmakers have not been particularly renowned for their feminism, Sander's film cannot be so simply categorized as the "feminization'' of New German Cinema. As a women's film, *Redupers* is also part of a context, defined by a growing number of autobiographical films by women, on the one hand, and by a critical tradition of feminist film criticism centered around the journal *frauen und film*, of which Helke Sander is an editor.

Sander's film is constructed around the strain between Christa Wolf's polarities of ''writing'' and ''miniatures,'' and the film examines the cinematic ramifications of what Wolf calls the ''secret of the third person.'' *Redupers* tells the story of Edda Chiemnajewski (portrayed by Sander), a resident of West Berlin, mother of a young daughter, free-lance photographer, and member of a women's photography group. As a free-lance photographer, Edda is expected to produce photo-journalism, that is, ''objective'' images. Early in the film we see Edda as she photographs a state-sponsored party for elderly citizens. She stands on a stage, and photographs a speaker who mouths platitudes about ''one, big, happy family,'' while spectators look on. So much for the kind of photographs Edda is paid to produce. Within her professional work, Edda looks for other possibilities. And so, in the next shot, we see Edda talking to the elderly women, conversing with them about the social rituals of parties. In her official capacity, Edda conveys official trivia, performing a rote gesture that matches passive audience response. But in the space which she manages to open up a bit, Edda comes down off the stage to have a chat with the women.

Edda's group got money for a photographic project, a female narrator's voice explains, because there was pressure on the government to prove its interest in women's issues, but also—and primarily—because this group applied for less money than any other. The women's group executes two major projects in the film. They take a huge mounted photograph of the Berlin wall to a variety of places in the city, including the site photographed (creating a bizarre *mise-en-abyme* effect). The women also set up a curtain on one of the platforms from which West Berliners can gaze onto the East. The opening of the curtain enhances the act of seeing, as if the sight of East Berlin were indeed a spectacle to be eagerly consumed by the West. The women want, eventually, to execute a billboard project on a much larger scale. We are shown the various channels through which they must pass: encounters with businessmen who tell the women they'll ''be in touch''; a visit to a gallery opening in order to make contacts. The women's project does not correspond to what its supporters and funders perceive as a worthy women's project. For Edda and her group are concerned with images of the city, images of the fragmentation and possible connections between East and West Berlin. Edda imagines the ''all-round developed socialist personality'' who watches Western television, and so the ''all-round reduced personality'' is that self divided between East and West. For these women, a ''woman's perspective'' means a way of seeing, and not just the objects seen, and so their project evolves from their perception of the links between East and West, from their perception of "chinks" in the Berlin wall.

Feminist theorists have always stressed that the division of life between the realms of private and public existence is a false dichotomy.[14] Traditionally and historically, women's sphere has been the private, the realm of family, home, and personal relations. And men's sphere has been the public sphere of official work and production. But women have always worked, and men have always had a private sphere, and "private" and "public" are the ideological divisions which mask profound links. Once we understand that the private and public spheres are not so easily separated, there remains a difference in how the relations of the two realms are perceived. Links: these are the symptoms, the eruptions which lay bare the falseness of the division of experience into two opposing realms. And then there are *integrations*: the conscious work of *producing* connections, of examining those links in relation to one another. The women in *Redupers* perceive the links between East and West Berlin, links that are like those between private and public life. Indeed, the city of Berlin is emblematic in this sense. And for these women, photography is a means of creating integrations.

Redupers begins with a lengthy tracking shot of the city of Berlin, showing us the wall, buildings, and passers-by. The movement slows down at some points, and rounds a corner, making clear that we are observing the city like tourists inside a moving car. We hear a variety of urban noises, like airplanes and cars, and we hear bits and pieces of radio programs in a variety of languages. This, then, is the public sphere of Berlin: detached voices speaking in different tongues, a wall that is as naturalized a part of the urban environment as office buildings and graffiti, and the constantly-moving perspective of a car in motion. For the moment, we are being transported by the camera; there is virtually no depth, only lateral and continuous movement. Similar tracking shots of the city reappear throughout the film like punctuation marks, removing us from the space of "fiction" and returning us to the anonymous public sphere. And this public sphere is also heard throughout the film via the radios which are a constant element of the sound track.

At a meeting of the women's group, Edda shows a series of photographs that illustrate the similarities between East and West Berlin: an owner's pride in his car, a subway, graffiti. As we look at these pairs of images, there is, indeed, nothing to distinguish the capitalist from the socialist public sphere. Although the question is asked in the film (somewhat ironically), whether the workers' state changes much in the status of women, it would be mistaken to see *Redupers* as a film that seeks to underscore hopeless similarities between capitalism and socialism. The point, rather, is that the Berlin wall creates a false dichotomy between two entities united by their urban common denominator. Edda understands the wall as an *ideological* phenomenon—that is, as symptomatic of a mode of consciousness in which slashes and divisions are impenetrable, marking absolute and hierarchical differences. "Where does the wall have openings?" Edda asks, and she holds up a photograph of two apartment buildings on either side of the wall between which "full eye-contact is still possible." Hence photography is, for Edda, a mode of discovery of the hidden connections between East and West Berlin.

The definition of the female photographer in *Redupers* might be understood as an attempt to define woman as subject of the cinema; that is, to identify woman as the active, looking subject rather than as the object of the male gaze. But the creation of such a female subject is not such a self-evident aim. For the cinematic "subject" is hardly a vacant spot ready to be occupied by women simply by the force of good will. We are familiar with the problems of a female positive hero, after all. Gertrud Koch points out that for too long, feminist criticism has ignored the question: why do women like movies? Feminist film critics, says Koch, "have analyzed female film myths, likewise the relations of these myths to male fantasies, as well as the male producers and consumers of these myths. There have been however very few methodical attempts to explain how female spectators might deal with these myths."[15] Koch calls for an understanding of female subjectivity rooted in the female aesthetic experience, shaped by "women's work"—the production and reproduction of the rhythms of everyday existence. "Such an orientation in female labor leads to an aestheticization of women's everyday existence."[16]

If woman is subject in *Redupers*, then it is in terms of what Koch calls the "aestheticization of the everyday." But this aestheticization is more appropriately understood as female narration. For the city of Berlin becomes, for the women, a huge apartment just waiting to be tastefully decorated. Billboards become picture frames containing the city's equivalent of family photographs. Curtains transform the gaping space of a platform into a window, so that looking from west to east imitates the conditions of looking from inside to outside. The curtain project is another form of integration, in which conditions of perception of the private sphere are transported to the public sphere. There is a moment in the film where Edda pulls back the curtains in her apartment to look outside, a gesture that matches the pulling back of the curtains on the platform to reveal East Berlin. Thus, by producing certain conditions of perception, the women become storytellers.

Some of the implications, as well as the problems, of such female narration can be gauged by considering *Redupers* in relationship to another text that is concerned, in different ways, with women and the city, with the links of private and public, with image and subjectivity. This is Jean-Luc Godard's 1967 film *2 or 3 Things I Know About Her*. The most striking point of connection between these two films is not, however, their overall thematic and formal concerns, but rather the posters which "advertise" the films, as it were; or, better, which condense them.

In the image of Godard's film, Marina Vlady's face stares at me semi-passively, a very slight smile beginning to turn up the corners of her mouth. Her face is framed by a collage of words and images: three different types of Ajax cleanser, women's legs from an ad for one product or another; a brassière, panties, and so on. The image of woman, Vlady, is flattened out and equated with the products of consumer society. All of these objects "summarize" the film in that their arrangement imitates the collage-like structure characteristic of Godard's film. And these objects recall, as well, a specific scene in *2 or 3 Things . . .* , the final image of the film in which a group of boxes and packages, all of consumer products, form a miniature city set against the grass. We also see in the poster images drawn directly from the film: Juliette Janson with her child, a woman emerging from her bath, and finally, the American man who films Juliette and another prostitute in his hotel room. This is the only man depicted in the poster. He bears a remarkable resemblance to Jean-Luc Godard, the director, whose voice whispers commentary throughout the film. The man also looks at me, his eyes partially concealed by dark glasses, and his look thus a return of the look of Marina Vlady.

Sander's face is portrayed in close-up in the *Redupers* poster, and it too looks at me. But even though her head is at virtually the same angle as Marina Vlady's, this look has a wry expression, as if Sander were about to shrug her shoulders. To the left of Sander's face is the Berlin wall, on it written in graffiti-like script the same words which are the opening title of the film: "Berlin im März 1977." Running the entire length of the wall is a curtain, like that of the women's project. And on the right of Sander's face is a building, perhaps one of those buildings from which eye contact with the East is possible. A small triangle of sky is visible, and the wall and the building meet at an invisible vanishing point obscured by Sander's head.

Because of the striking resemblance between these two posters, the differences between them make it seem as though a positive image is being held up to a negative film strip. Marina Vlady, in the *2 or 3 Things . . .* poster, is nothing but image, flattened out to the same surface as Ajax boxes and brassière ads. But this is nonetheless an image that looks; that has a gaze. All of the faces surrounding Vlady draw attention, by virtue of their own eyeline direction, to her look. All the faces but one, that is: the lone man. This "bearer of the look" (to use Laura Mulvey's phrase) suggests that if the image of woman looks, it looks through the mediation of the male.[17]

What then to make of the absence of any such return of the look in the *Redupers* poster? We surely cannot be so naive as to assume that the male gaze has simply vanished from this film (and even if such a utopian state of affairs were possible, we would still have to account for how films are received according to certain conventions). Nor can we permit ourselves the even more naive assumption that this is "woman as woman" and not "woman as image."

Both posters signify an urban environment, *2 or 3 Things . . .* by a proliferation of signifiers, *Redupers* by a sparseness of them; *2 or 3 Things . . .* by the products of consumer society, *Redupers* by the space of the city. I know that Sander is not "really" standing in front of that vanishing point, just as I know that there is no curtain on top of the Berlin wall. But the "screen" against which this image of Sander is projected has depth. I look into this image, and Sander's look returns my look to me. Whereas in the *2 or 3 Things . . .* poster, there is no looking *into*; there is only the return of the look. If Godard's Juliette bathes in a consumer society from which the only critical perspective possible is the return of the (male) look, Sander offers us another possibility: the identification of the female look as mediation between viewer and imaginary space of the screen; the identification of woman as narrator. No wonder that the officials in *Redupers* are perplexed that these women photographers do not produce photographs of other women, but rather of the cityscape. For what is at stake is the disengagement of the female look from simplistic and deterministic definitions of woman as object of the male gaze. And no wonder, too, perhaps, that when I first saw the *Redupers* poster I unthinkingly assumed that this was an image of a young man.

Hence this poster for *Redupers* suggests, in skeletal form, the possibilities of female narration. At the beginning of *Redupers*, with the tracking shot that moves us through the city, the movement of the camera assumes the function of narrator. This is a kind of anonymous narration, a tourist's view. But in the course of the film, with the repetitions of tracking shots to signify the public sphere of the city, this narrative function is redefined. For the tracking shots are, most often, accompanied by the voice of the female narrator. The female narrator is a voice as unanchored in time and space as the numerous radio voices we hear throughout the film. Radio voices insinuate themselves into the spaces and cracks between everyday activities; radios allow you to go about your business and still be an informed citizen. The voice of the female narrator also insinuates itself into the cracks of everyday life. But radio voices are reducible to a single institutional voice; not so of the female narrator.

The female voice has several functions in *Redupers*. It personalizes the tracking shots of the city, describing the history of the women's group and the strategies the women have to use to get their project funded. The voice also functions as a narrator in the strictest sense of the word, when it introduces and summarizes scenes: at an anti-rape demonstration, for example, the voice explains that Edda does not think that enough of her socially-conscious photographs are purchased. In this sense, the female voice is a third-person narrator, an authority that perceives events from without.

Yet one can hardly resist perceiving the female voice as a first person narrator as well, even though it is somewhat beside the point to ask whether this voice is inside or outside of Edda. For this is a voice which narrates from both inside and outside; a voice which is simultaneously "we" and "they." In the same vein, the female voice gives "objective" information, but also slides off into other registers. Over a series of still photographs of a conference that Edda is photographing, for instance, the voice says: "For years Edda had been struck by the following: that the aesthetic imagination was the passion for things alien. The sorrows and fortunes of others, the fate of a leather ball. Passion for that without meaning. One should at least be able to choose freely those things alien." Here the voice articulates fantasies and desires repressed within the single image. And the voice also articulates another kind of repressed: in the same sequence, it describes in detail Edda's monthly income and expenses.

The female voice is also a quoting voice, referring to literary and cinematic sources. Surely the most striking quotation in *Redupers* occurs when three small screens appear, one after the other, over the image of a newspaper. In each screen we see a segment from a woman's film: a close-up of a woman from Ursula Reuter-Christiansen's *The Executioner* (Denmark, 1972); the beach scene from Yvonne Rainer's *Film About a Woman Who . . .* (U.S.A., 1974), in which man, woman, and child rearrange themselves as if for a series of snapshots; and a kitchen scene from Valie Export's *Invisible Adversaries* (West Germany, 1976) in which a woman cuts up a fish and insects and opens a refrigerator to reveal a baby inside. These are films concerned, like *Redupers*, with the juncture between narrative and the everyday. The only sound heard during the segment is the female voice which announces: "Obsessed by daily life as other women see it." The voice continues and quotes a "letter" from "Aunt Kate Chiemnajewski," a letter which contains the kind of fragmented logic typical of such forms of correspondence, as well as of, one might say, dreams:

> Dear Edda, Please don't stop showing women and the problems they have with their tyrant men! Tyrants are even worse in old age! They drive everyone meshugge! Your father sent Hatschi a good book written by a doctor from Berlin. We are both reading it. And Karlemann sent us one of his poems. He wrote it during the war, in Russia. He was thinking of your mother, Erika. The sun is shining into my room, but it rains a lot. Makes me sad, somehow. You can always call us, also at night. Please write soon, or phone. Love and kisses. Yours, Aunt Katherine.

This sequence functions as a formalized analogue of sorts to the previous sequence, in which Edda works on photographs and listens to the radio. Here there is a similar juxtaposition of image and official news. The newspaper becomes an object read virtually between the lines. And the miniature movie screens recall the billboards which the women want to cover with their photographs of the city. The function of the narrator is both to *name* the link between the three film sequences, and to make a further connection between these images and the activity of letter-writing—a connection which again brings to mind letter-writing as a pre-aesthetic realm that gave women entries into literary production.[18] Image-making and letter-writing: both activities are defined as the forms of reading central to female experience, forms of integration. And perhaps most important, the narrator becomes, at the same time, a reader: the female voice performs two functions at once, thus taking the consolidation of "first person" and "third person" to another level, condensing the narrator within the text with the reader outside of it.

Voice-over narration is quite common in the cinema, and is in particular associated with documentary film. But the female voice in *Redupers* is no authoritative commentator, aiding the image-track in the revelation of truth. Rather, the voice emphasizes the plurality of truths, the proliferation of perspectives that are possible. The female voice in *Redupers* exists as an ungrounded presence, emanating from a number of sources, none of them privileged as the center of the film.

So too is the overall narrative structure of *Redupers* characterized by a proliferation of possible centers, rather than by a hierarchy of concerns. The seeming open-ended nature of Sander's narrative suggests connections with her compatriots of the New German Cinema. But can Sander really be adequately situated by evaluating the project of *Redupers* as an "application" of the lessons of the New German Cinema to "women's issues"? Such an approach reads something like those analyses of social class which, in order to pay lip service to the women's movement, add: and all of this applies, of course, to women, too.

Rather, the "open-ended," fragmented narrative structure of *Redupers* follows from the position of the female voice. And the relevant context here is women's writing. We might turn again to Christa Wolf. The final words spoken in the film, over an image of Edda walking into the distance, are from an essay by Wolf on diaries:

> I don't want to go any further. Anyone who asks about a person's diary must accept the fact more is concealed than said. It was not possible to speak about plans, clearly set forth in the diary, that have arisen, been changed, dropped again, come to nothing, or were carried out, unexpectedly suddenly there, complete. And it wasn't possible to bring into focus through strenuous thought the stuff of life that was very near in time. Or the mistakes made in trying to do this. And, of course, no mention of the names that appear once or more often in the diary.[19]

For Wolf and for Sander, the diary form is hesitant. It is informed by the asking of questions (rather than by "exclamation marks," says Wolf). As a narrative structure, the diary-form collects hypotheses and creates fragments—paragraphs or scenes—in which ideas are tested. For Wolf, the diary is "training, a means to remain active, to resist the temptation to drift into mere consumption."[20] This is not quite the diary form of some avant-garde filmmakers, in which the *authority* of the narrator is assumed.[21] Within the context of women's filmmaking, the appropriation of the diary-form is a way of slowing down cinematic perception, a way of resisting the momentum of film as a panorama of "miniatures." And through the diary-form, fundamental questions concerning women's relation to aesthetic experience are formulated. Women's cinema is inscribed within a tradition defined by letters and diaries. Indeed, B. Ruby Rich, in her analysis of the categories of women's cinema, places *Redupers* in the category of a "cinema of correspondence": "Looking to literary history, we find a concern with the role played by letters ('personal' discourse) as a sustaining mode for women's writing during times of literary repression. . . . A cinema of 'correspondence' is a fitting homage to this tradition of introspective missives sent out into the world."[22] *Redupers* can be seen as a kind of notebook of work in progress. Wolf's comments on the diary as a form of collection are relevant here: "The diary collects material, anecdotes, stories, conversations, observations of people, towns and landscapes, extracts from books, new commentaries, new words and expressions, names. But it is not obliged, on the contrary it takes care to avoid, coming to hasty conclusions."[23]

If the narrative structure of *Redupers* imitates the diary-form, suggested as well is the importance of a narrative form close to the rituals of everyday life. Because diaries are "personal," they might seem to have closer links to the everyday lives of women than other narrative forms. But the very term "everyday life" is no more self-evident than the term "subject." And one of the projects of *Redupers* is, precisely, an examination of the *narrative* implications of the gestures and rituals of the everyday.

Particularly interesting in this respect is Edda's visit to the aikido studio. The narrator says in voice-over that "at age 34, Edda decided to do something for her body. She is taken by the beauty of the movements and decides to learn aikido." Edda seems a passive observer in the studio. First she watches an advanced student, and then other beginning students. The narrator explains: "But in three months she was able to participate only five times. Tonight she decides to give it up." Edda's lack of participation in her aikido class has less to do with those stereotypically-female responses of intimidation and passivity, than with a resistance to any form of physical activity which does not somehow connect with other threads in the fabric of everyday life. The movements of aikido are indeed beautiful, but they represent an aesthetics radically other than Edda's own creative framework (and the narrator emphasizes that aikido is a fad brought to West Berlin via the USA). Shortly after this scene, Edda performs a different kind of physical activity. Having returned home from a

GLOSSARY

The following definitions explain terms frequently used by feminist film critics and are intended to aid in reading the introductions and the essays. Though widely used, many of these terms are remarkably hard to pin down. Furthermore, many of the words have multiple meanings, some specific to one author only. However, I have tried to offer a succinct explanation of each term without going into a detailed history of its origin and development. Though individual essays will differ in their use of some terms, the definitions provided here should suffice for beginning students.

cinema apparatus = the process of film production and exhibition which takes into account economic and social forces
cinéma vérité = a style of filmmaking typified by a hand-held camera, natural lighting, synchronous sound, and the elimination of a narrator either on- or off-screen
closure = the ending or point in the narrative when all major conflicts are resolved
codes = rules or sets of identifiable elements which allow individuals to interpret a film (e.g., image code, music code, lighting code, etc.)
deconstructive cinema = a filmmaking practice devoted to breaking down the illusionistic aspect of cinema by interrupting the narrative flow and by calling attention to its own artificial construction
diegesis = the artificial world of the film, including the narration
discourse = a form of utterance which implies a speaker and a receiver; also a specialized utterance, such as a medical discourse, a feminist discourse, etc.
distancing devices = techniques which encourage an intellectual response from viewers, among which are ruptures of the narrative, direct address to the audience, and other techniques which create a distance between spectators and the screen
dominant cinema = used here as synonymous with Hollywood cinema; in our culture the most widely accepted form of cinema, which is Hollywood-style cinema, uses invisible editing and creates an illusionary world that hides the means of its own production
dominant meaning = the generally accepted meaning of a text
feminine = the socially-constructed ideas attached to the female sex
feminist film criticism = analyses of individual films or the mechanisms of film production and consumption from a feminist perspective
fetishization = 1. in Freudian terms, an unconscious disavowal of the threat of castration by idealizing the source of the threat—the sight of women and their lack of a penis; 2. in Marxist terms, a commodity of exchange
film text = the film plus the interpretation of the viewer
genre = a type of film (e.g., western, musical, melodrama, etc.)
ideology = a system of beliefs, including visual representations, universally accepted by a society to the degree that its tenets become invisible
Marxist ideology = a system of beliefs which sees economic and class struggle and the control of representation as primary historical and social forces
masochism (as applied in film studies) = a reference to the passive pleasures of film viewing or identification with the character being acted upon, which replicates the preoedipal phase of infant/mother bonding
the narrative = the story plus its cinematic presentation

negotiated reading = the meaning produced by a viewer which takes into account the generally accepted meaning of a film text together with one's individual interpretation, the latter deriving from one's social position within a culture
object of desire = the object of a viewer's erotic interest
patriarchy = a political and/or social system in which men control the major means of power
post-modernism = an aesthetic which emphasizes the fragmentary nature of images, the appropriation of images from previously created images and their resistance to a single unity logic or subject position
progressive film = one which encourages the possibilities of change in the status quo
psychoanalysis (as applied in film studies) = theories derived from Sigmund Freud and his followers, primarily Jacques Lacan, and especially those devoted to the development of identity, the Oedipus complex, and the process of identification
reading = a viewer's interpretation of the film text
realist documentary = non-fiction films which do not call attention to themselves as artificial constructs; based on the assumption of film's capacity to capture reality
sadistic scopophilia = a process whereby the instinctual pleasure in looking (scopophilia) is put into the service of castration fears so that pleasure derives from the sight of women's punishment, degradation, or fetishization
semiotics = the study of signification or meaning, especially in verbal language but also in non-linguistic cultural languages such as film
shot/reverse shot = a series of complementary images typically used to depict conversations between two or more individuals on the screen
signifier = in semiotics, the word or image which refers back to the concrete object or abstract idea (e.g., the word "rain" or the picture of drops which refer back to the actual water or to the concept of rain)
spectacle = object of display to be viewed
subversive reading = an interpretation based on contradictions within the film text in which a viewer recognizes the non-dominant, as well as the dominant meanings; also known as "reading against the grain"
"talking heads" = head shots of individuals speaking directly to the camera
the viewing subject = 1. the implied viewer of a film, an abstract concept structured into the work; 2. the actual viewer in the audience; the social subject
woman's cinema = films directed by women, not exclusively feminist women
women's desire = unconscious sexual impulses
women's pleasure = pleasures related to viewing an erotic object of desire or satisfactions related to cinema viewing in general

SELECTED BIBLIOGRAPHY

The following selection of books and articles represents feminist film criticism and material on women directors published between the years 1978–1988. In order to avoid duplication and undue length, I have not included individual citations to articles which appeared in special journal issues, which have been anthologized in *Issues in Feminist Film Criticism* or in the books listed below, or which were later incorporated into books by their authors. Thus, many well-known articles may not appear as separate entries in the following bibliography.

Special Journal Issues

"Alternative Feminist Cinema." *CineAction!*, no. 5 (Spring, 1986).

"Body/Masquerade." *Discourse* 11, no. 1 (Fall/Winter 1988–89).

"Cinema Histories/Cinema Practices II." *Wide Angle* 7, nos. 1–2 (1985).

"Deconstructing 'Difference'." *Screen* 28, no. 1 (Winter 1987).

"Female Representation and Consumer Culture." *Quarterly Review of Film and Video* 11, no. 4 (1989). Includes bibliography.

"Feminism." *Millenium Film Journal*, no. 12 (Fall/Winter 1982–83).

"Feminism and Film." *Millenium Film Journal*, no. 6 (1980).

"Feminism and Film." *Wide Angle* 6, no. 3 (1984).

"Feminism and Representation." *Screen* 21, no. 2 (Summer 1980).

"Feminist Film Criticism." *Film Reader*, no. 5 (1982).

"Feminist and Ideological Criticism." *Quarterly Review of Film Studies* 3, no. 4 (Fall 1978) and 4, no. 2 (Spring 1979).

"Feminist Retrospective." *Cinema Canada*, no. 106 (April 1984).

"German Film Women." *Jump Cut*, no. 29 (February 1984) and no. 30 (March 1985).

"Hollywood Reconsidered." *Jump Cut*, no. 32 (April 1986).

"Indian and European Melodrama." *Screen* 30, no. 3 (Summer 1989).

"Interviews with Women Filmmakers." *Cineaste* 15, no. 1 (1986) and 15, no. 4 (1987).

"Interviews with Women Filmmakers." *Millenium Film Journal*, nos. 7–9 (Fall/Winter 1980–81).

"Lesbians and Film." *Jump Cut*, no. 24/25 (March 1981).

"Melodrama and Transgression." *Screen* 29, no. 3 (Summer 1988).

"New German Women's Cinema." *Jump Cut*, no. 27 (July 1982).

"Radical Feminist Film." *Cine-Tracts* 3, no. 3 (Fall 1980).

"Sex." *CineAction!*, no. 10 (Fall 1987).

"Sex and Spectatorship." *Screen* 23, nos. 3/4 (September/October 1982).

"Sexual Difference." *Wide Angle* 5, no. 1 (1982).

"Sexual Difference." *Journal of Film and Video* 37, no. 2 (Spring 1985).

"Sexual Representation." *Jump Cut*, no. 30 (March 1985) and no. 32 (April 1986).

"Spectatorship, Narrativity and Feminist Revision." *Journal of Film and Video* 39, no. 4 (Fall 1987).

"Women and Representation." *Jump Cut*, no. 29 (February 1984).

"Women in Contemporary Hollywood." *CineAction!*, no. 2 (Fall 1982).

"Women's Cinema." *Screen* 28, no. 4 (Autumn 1987).

All issues of *Camera Obscura* (1977-present) and all issues of *Jump Cut* (1974-present). *Camera Obscura* is devoted to feminism and film theory, while *Jump Cut* regularly includes articles related to women and film. For a complete bibliography of feminist film criticism in *Jump Cut* from 1974–1980, see *Jump Cut* no. 24–25 (March 1981).

Books

Bell-Metereau, Rebecca. *Hollywood Androgyny*. New York: Columbia University Press, 1986.

Blache, Roberta, and Simone Blache, trans. *Memoirs of Alice Guy Blache*. Metuchen, NJ: Scarecrow Press, 1986.

Blonski, Annette, Barbara Creed, and Freda Freilberg. *Don't Shoot Darling!: Women's Independent Filmmaking in Australia*. Richmond, Australia: Greenhouse, 1987.

Bruno, Guiliana, and Maria Nadotti, eds. *Off Screen: Women and Film in Italy*. New York: Routledge, 1988.

Brunsdon, Charlotte, ed. *Films for Women*. London: British Film Institute, 1986.

Burchill, Julie. *Girls on Film*. New York: Pantheon, 1986.

Clark, VeVe A., Millicent Modson, and Catrina Neiman. *The Legend of Maya Deren*. Vol. 1, pts. 1 and 2. New York: Anthology Film Archives, 1984 and 1988.

De Lauretis, Teresa. *Alice Doesn't: Feminism, Semiotics, Cinema*. Bloomington: Indiana University Press, 1984.

———. *Technologies of Gender: Essays on Theory, Film, and Fiction*. Bloomington: Indiana University Press, 1987.

Doane, Mary Ann. *The Desire to Desire: The Woman's Film of the 1940s*. Bloomington: Indiana University Press, 1987.

Doane, Mary Ann, Patricia Mellencamp, and Linda Williams. *Re-Vision: Essays in Feminist Film Criticism*. Los Angeles: American Film Institute, 1984.

Dyer, Richard. *Heavenly Bodies: Film Stars and Society*. New York: St. Martin's Press, 1986.

———. *Stars*. London: British Film Institute, 1979.

Ecker, Gisela, ed. *Feminist Aesthetics*. trans. Harriet Anderson. Boston: Beacon Press, 1986.

Erens, Patricia. *Sexual Stratagems: The World of Women in Film*. New York: Horizon Press, 1979.

Fischer, Lucy. *Shot/Countershot: Film Tradition and Women's Cinema*. Princeton: Princeton University Press, 1989.

Flitterman-Lewis, Sandy. *To Desire Differently: Feminism and the French Cinema*. Urbana: University of Illinois Press, 1990.

French, Brandon. *On the Verge of Revolt: Women in American Films of the Fifties*. New York: Ungar, 1978.

Gaines, Jane M., and Charlotte Herzog. *Fabrications: Costume and the Female Body*. New York: Routledge, 1990.

Gamman, Lorraine, and Margaret Marshment, eds. *The Female Gaze*. Seattle, WA: Real Comet Press, 1989.

Gentile, Mary C. *Film Feminisms: Theory and Practice*. Westport, CT: Greenwood Press, 1985.

Gledhill, Christine. *Home Is Where the Heart Is: Studies in Melodrama and the Woman's Film*. London: British Film Institute, 1987.

Haskell, Molly. *From Reverence to Rape: The Treatment of Women in Movies*. 2d ed. Chicago: University of Chicago Press, 1987.

Heck-Rabi, Louise. *Women Filmmakers: A Critical Reception*. Metuchen, NJ: Scarecrow Press, 1984.

Kaplan, E. Ann. *Motherhood and Reproduction: The Maternal Melodrama in Literature and Film 1930–Present*. New York: Routledge, 1991.

———. *Psychoanalysis and Cinema*. New York: Routledge, 1989.

———. *Women and Film: Both Sides of the Camera*. New York: Methuen, 1983.

———. ed. *Women in Film Noir*. London: British Film Institute, 1978.

Kuhn, Annette. *The Power of the Image: Essays on Representation and Sexuality*. London: Routledge and Kegan Paul, 1985.

———. *Women's Pictures: Feminism and Cinema*. London: Routledge and Kegan Paul, 1982.

Lederer, Laura, ed. *Take Back the Night: Women on Pornography*. New York: William Morrow, 1980.

Lehman, Peter, ed. *Close Viewings: An Anthology of New Film Criticism*. Tallahassee: Florida State University Press, 1990.

MacDonald, Scott. *A Critical Cinema: Interviews with Independent Filmmakers*. Berkeley: University of California Press, 1988.

Maio, Kathi. *Feminist in the Dark: Reviewing the Movies*. Freedom, CA: Crossing Press, 1988.

Mayne, Judith. *Kino and the Woman Question: Feminism and Soviet Silent Film*. Columbus: Ohio State University Press, 1989.

———. *The Woman at the Keyhole: Feminism and Women's Cinema*. Bloomington: Indiana University Press, 1990.

McCreadie, Marsha. *Women on Film: The Critical Eye*. New York: Praeger, 1983.

Mellencamp, Patricia. *Avant-Garde Film, Video, and Feminism*. Bloomington: Indiana University Press, 1990.

Miller, Lynn Fieldman. *The Hand That Holds the Camera: Interviews with Women Film and Video Directors*. New York: Garland, 1988.

Modleski, Tania. *Loving with a Vengeance: Mass Produced Fantasies for Women*. Hamden, CT: Shoe String Press, 1982. Reprinted by Methuen, 1984.

———. *The Women Who Knew Too Much: Hitchcock and Feminist Theory*. New York: Methuen, 1988.

Mulvey, Laura. *Visual and Other Pleasures*. Bloomington: Indiana University Press, 1989.

Nichols, Bill, ed. *Movies and Methods*. Vol. 2. Berkeley: University of California Press, 1985.

Oshana, Maryann. *Women of Color: A Filmography of Minority and Third World Women*. New York: Garland, 1984.

Penley, Constance. *Feminism and Film Theory*. New York: Routledge, 1988.

Petro, Patrice. *Joyless Streets: Women and Melodramatic Representation in Weimar Germany*. Princeton: Princeton University Press, 1989.

Pribram, E. Deidre, ed. *Female Spectators: Looking at Film and Television*. London: Verso, 1988.

Quart, Barbara Koenig. *Women Directors: The Emergence of a New Cinema*. New York: Praeger, 1988.

Rabinowitz, Lauren. *Sex, Power and Politics in New York Avant-Garde Cinema*. Urbana: University of Illinois Press (forthcoming).

Rainer, Yvonne. *Profile* 4, no. 5. Chicago: Video Data Bank, 1984.

Renov, Michael. *Hollywood's Wartime Woman: Representation and Ideology*. Ann Arbor, MI: UMI, 1988.

Rich, B. Ruby. *Yvonne Rainer*. Minneapolis: The Walker Art Center, 1981.

Rodowick, David. *The Difficulty of Difference: Psychoanalysis, Sexual Difference and Film Theory*. New York: Routledge, 1990.

Rosenburg, Jan. *Women's Reflections: The Feminist Film Movement*. Ann Arbor, MI: UMI, 1983.
Russo, Vito. *The Celluloid Closet: Homosexuality in the Movies*. New York: Harper and Row, 1981.
Shipman, Nell. *The Silent Screen and My Talking Heart: An Autobiography*. Boise, ID: Boise State University Press, 1987.
Silverman, Kaja. *The Acoustic Mirror: The Female Voice in Pschoanalysis and Cinema*. Bloomington: Indiana University Press, 1988.
———. *The Subject of Semiotics*. New York: Oxford University Press, 1983.
Snitow, Ann, Christine Stansell, and Sharon Thompson. *Powers of Desire: The Politics of Sexuality*. New York: Monthly Review Press, 1983.
Studlar, Gaylyn. *In the Realm of Pleasure: Von Sternberg, Dietrich, and the Masochistic Aesthetic*. Urbana: University of Illinois Press, 1988.
Todd, Janet, ed. *Women and Film*. New York: Holmes and Meier, 1988.
Vance, Carole S., ed. *Pleasure and Danger: Exploring Female Sexuality*. New York: Routledge and Kegan Paul, 1984.
Walsh, Andrea. *Women's Film and Female Experience 1940–1950*. New York: Praeger, 1984.
Williams, Linda. *Hardcore: Power, Pleasure and the "Frenzy of the Visible."* Berkeley: University of California Press, 1989.

Articles

Acker, R. "The Major Directions of German Feminist Cinema." *Literature/Film Quarterly* 13, no. 4 (1985): 245–49.
Agostinis, V. "An Interview with Sally Potter." *Framework* 14, no. 47 (Spring 1981).
Alexandrova, T. "Women Film-Directors." *Soviet Film*, no. 250 (1978): 3–9.
Allen, J. T. "*Tell Me a Riddle*: Form Follows Function." *Journal of Film and Video* 38, no. 1 (Winter 1986): 66–72+.
———. "The Representation of Violence to Women: Hitchcock's *Frenzy*." *Film Quarterly* 38, no. 3 (1985): 30–38.
Alysen, B. "Australian Women Filmmakers: Part 4: Jeni Thornley and Martha Ansara." *Cinema Papers*, no. 23 (September/October 1979): 497–99.
Aspler-Burnett, M. "*Not a Love Story*: Notes on the Film." *Cine-Tracts*, no. 4 (1982): 1–3.
Bammer, A. "Through a Daughter's Eyes: Helma Sanders—Brahms' *Germany Pale Mother*." *New German Critique*, no. 36 (Fall 1985): 91–109.
Banes, S. "Imagination and Play: The Films of Ericka Beckman." *Millenium Film Journal*, no. 13 (Fall/Winter 1983–84): 98–112.
Banning, K. "Surfacing: Canadian Women's Cinema." *Cinema Canada*, no. 167 (October 1989): 12–16.
Barrowclough, S. "*Not a Love Story*." *Screen* 23, no. 5 (November/December 1982): 26–36.
Beard, W. "Interview with *Loyalties*' Director Anne Wheeler." *Cinema Canada*, no. 134 (October 1986): 24–28.
Beauvais, Y. "Barbara Hammer." *Spiral*, no. 6 (January 1986): 33–38.
Bergstrom, J. "Enunciation and Sexual Difference." *Camera Obscura*, nos. 3–4 (Summer 1979): 33–65.
———. "Sexuality at a Loss: The Films of F. W. Murnau." *Poetics Today* 6, nos. 1–2 (1985): 185–203.
Bovenschen, S. "Is There a Feminist Aesthetic?" Beth Weckmueller, trans. *New German Critique*, no. 10 (Winter 1977): 111–37.

Brown, B. "A Feminist Interest in Pornography: Some Modest Proposals." *m/f*, nos. 5–6 (1981): 5–18.

Brown, L. "*The Two Worlds of Marrakech.*" *Screen* 19, no. 2 (1978): 85–118.

Burdick, D. M. "Danger of Death: The Hawksian Woman as Agent of Destruction." *Post Script* 1, no. 1 (1981): 36–40.

Burstyn, V. "*Cries and Whispers* Reconsidered." *CineAction!*, no. 3–4 (Winter 1986): 32–45.

Burton, J. "Seeing, Being Seen: *Portrait of Teresa*: or Contradictions of Sexual Politics in Contemporary Cuba." *Social Text*, no. 4 (1981): 79–95.

———. "Sing the Beloved Country: An Interview with Tisuka Tamasaki on Patriamada." *Film Quarterly* 41, no. 1 (Fall 1987): 2–8.

Carter, E., and others. "Interview with Ulrike Ottinger." *Screen Education*, no. 41 (Winter/Spring 1982): 34–42.

Cartwright, L., and O. Swanson. "On Representation and Sexual Division: An Interview with Christine Delphy." *Undercut*, nos. 14–15 (Summer 1985): 15–22.

Chase, D. "The Director Who Came in from the Cold." *Millimeter*, no. 12 (September 1984): 173–77.

Christensen, F. "Sexual Callousness Re-examined." *Journal of Communication*, no. 36 (Winter 1986): 174–84.

Clover, C. J. "Her Body, Himself: Gender in the Slasher Film." *Representation*, no. 20 (Fall 1987): 187–228.

Coburn, M. F. "Ten Tough Broads." *American Film* 8, no. 8 (July/August 1983): 66–67.

Collins, F. "Reading Against the Grain: Independent Feminist Filmmaking and the Black Hole." *Filmnews* 8, nos. 11–12 (November/December 1983): 12–13.

Considine, D. M. "The Decline and Possible Rise of the Movie Mother." *Journal of Popular Film and Television* 13, no. 1 (Spring 1985): 4–15.

Cook, P. "Breaking Down the Myths: Feminist Film Distribution Today." *Monthly Film Bulletin* 53 (January 1986): 4–5.

———. "Femininity and the Masquerade: *Anne of the Indies.*" *Jacques Tourneur*, ed. Claire Johnston and Paul Willamen. Edinburgh: Edinburgh Film Festival, 1975.

———. "Star Signs." *Screen* 20, nos. 3–4 (1979–1980): 80–88.

———. "*The Gold Diggers*: An Interview with Sally Potter." *Framework*, no. 24 (Spring 1984): 12–30.

———. "Women in Jeopardy" *Monthly Film Bulletin* 52 (February 1985): 36–39.

Cowie, E. "Fantasy, Psychoanalysis and Feminism in Relation to *Now, Voyager* and *The Reckless Moment.*" *m/f*, no. 9 (1984).

Creed, B. "From Here to Modernity—Feminism and Postmodernism." *Screen* 28, no. 2 (Spring 1987): 47–67.

———. "Pornography and Pleasure: The Female Spectator." *Australian Journal of Screen Theory*, nos. 15–16 (1983): 27–31.

Davidson, D. "From Virgin to Dynamo: The 'Amoral Woman' in European Cinema." *Cinema Journal* 21, no. 1 (1981): 31–58.

Dawson, J. "Review of Yvonne Rainer's *Journeys from Berlin.*" *Sight and Sound* 49, no. 3 (1980): 196–97.

"Dialogue on Film: Karen Arthur." *American Film* 13, no. 1 (October 1987): 10–13.

"Dialogue on Film: Martha Collidge." *American Film* 9, no. 8 (June 1984): 15–18.

Dieckmann, K. "She Shot Him Dead and Good: Film Femmes Get Fatal." *Village Voice* (December 2 1986): 81+.

Dissanayake, W. "Questions of Female Subjectivity, Patriarchy, and Family: Perceptions of Three Indian Film Directors." *East-West Film Journal* 3, no. 2 (June 1989): 74–90.

Dittmar, L. "Beyond Gender, and Within It: The Social Construction of Female Desire." *Wide Angle* 8, nos. 3–4 (1986): 79–88.

Doane, M. A. "Misrecognition and Identity." *Cine-Tracts* 3, no. 3 (Fall 1980): 25–32.

———. "The Abstraction of a Lady: *La Signora di tutti.*" *Cinema Journal* 28, no. 1 (Fall 1988): 65–84.

———. "Woman's Stake: Filming the Female Body." *October*, no. 17 (Summer 1981): 22–36.

Donougho, M. "Margarethe von Trotta: Gynemagoguery and the Dilemmas of a Filmmaker." *Literature/Film Quarterly* 17, no. 3 (July 1989): 149–60.

Dowd, J. T. "Images of American Women Films: A Method of Analysis." *Women and Performance* 1, no. 1 (1983): 49–57.

Draper, E. "Zombie Women When the Gaze is Male." *Wide Angle* 10, no. 3 (1988): 52–62.

Eisen, K. "The Young Misogynists of American Cinema." *Cineaste* 13, no. 1 (1983): 30–35.

Ellis, J. "On Pornography." *Screen* 21, no. 1 (1980): 81–108.

Elsaesser, T. " 'It Started with These Images'—Some Notes on Political Film—Making After Brecht in Germany: Helke Sander and Harun Farocki." *Discourse*, no. 7 (Spring 1985): 95–120.

Erens, P. "*Penthesilea.*" *Wide Angle* 2, no. 3 (1978): 30–36.

———. "Women's Documentaries as Social History." *Film Library Quarterly* 14, nos. 1–2 (1981): 4–9.

Fedkiw, P. "Marguerite Duras: Feminine Field of Hysteria." *Enclitic* 6, no. 2 (1982): 78–86.

Fehervary, H., and others. "From Hitler to Hepburn: A Discussion of Women's Film Production and Reception." *New German Critique*, nos. 24–25 (Fall/Winter 1981–82): 172–85.

Fernley, A., and P. Maloof. "*Yentl.*" *Film Quarterly* 38, no. 3 (Spring 1985): 38–45.

Fischer, L. "The Lady Vanishes: Women, Magic and the Movies." *Film Quarterly* 33, no. 1 (1979): 30–40.

Fishbein, L. "The Demise of the Cult of True Womanhood in Early American Film, 1900–1930." *Journal of Popular Film and Television* 12, no. 2 (1984): 66–72.

———. "*The Snake Pit* (1948): The Sexist Nature of Sanity." *American Quarterly* 31, no. 5 (1979): 641–65.

Fitzgerald, T. "Now About These Women." *Sight and Sound* 58, no. 3 (Summer 1989): 191–94.

Flinn, C. "Sound, Woman and the Bomb: Dismembering the 'Great Whatsit' in *Kiss Me Deadly.*" *Wide Angle* 8, nos. 3–4 (1986): 115–27.

———. "The 'Problem' of Femininity in the Theories of Film Music." *Screen* 27, no. 6 (November/December 1986): 56–72.

Flitterman, S. "From Deesse to Idee: Agnes Varda's *Cleo from Five to Seven.*" *Enclitic* 7, no. 2 (Fall 1983): 82–90.

———. "Montage/Discourse: Germaine Dulac's *The Smiling Madame Beudet.*" *Wide Angle* 4, no. 3 (1981): 54–59.

———. "Woman, Desire and the Look: Feminism and the Enunciative Apparatus in Cinema." *Cine-Tracts* 2, no. 1 (1978): 63–68.

Flitterman, S., and J. Suter. "Textual Riddles: Woman as Enigma or Site of Social Meanings?: An Interview with Laura Mulvey." *Discourse*, no. 1 (Fall 1979): 86–127.

Foote, C. J. "Changing Images of Women in the Western Film." *Journal of the West*, no. 22 (October 1983): 64–71.
Forbes, J. "Agnes Varda: The Gaze of the Medusa?" *Sight and Sound* 58, no. 2 (Spring 1989): 122–24.
Friedberg, A. "Misconception = the 'Division of Labor' In the Childbirth Film." *Millenium Film Journal*, nos. 4–5 (Summer/Fall 1979): 64–70.
Friedman, L. "An Interview with Peter Wollen and Laura Mulvey on *Riddles of the Sphinx*." *Millenium Film Journal*, nos. 4–5 (Summer/Fall 1979): 14–32.
Fudakowska, A. "The Mirror of Feminism in Film." *Cinema Canada*, no. 108 (June 1984): 8–19.
Fussell, B. "The Films of Mabel Norman." *Film History* 2, no. 4 (1988): 373–91.
Gaines, J. "The Showgirl and the Wolf." *Cinema Journal* 20, no. 1 (1980): 53–67.
Georgakas, D. and W. A. Starr. " 'The Primal Fear': An Interview with Anne-Claire Poirer." *Cineaste* 10, no. 3 (1980): 20–21+.
Gever, M. "Girl Crazy: Lesbian Narratives in *She Must Be Seeing Things* and *Damned If You Don't*." *The Independent* 11, no. 6 (July 1988): 14–18.
Glassman, D. "The Feminine Subject as History Writer in *Hiroshima Mon Amor*." *Enclitic* 5, no. 1 (1981): 43–53.
Gledhill, C. and E. A. Kaplan. "Dialogue on *Stella Dallas* and Feminist Film." *Cinema Journal* 25, no. 4 (1986): 44–53.
Glicksman, M. "Women in Film (Just Barely): Ms Treatment." *Film Comment* 21, no. 6 (November/December 1985): 20–25.
Godwin, G. "The Mermaid as the Subject." *Cinema Canada*, no. 152 (May 1988): 23–25.
Goldman, D. "Woman with a Movie Camera." *The Independent* 8 (July/August 1985): 4–5.
Gubar, S. "Representing Pornography: Feminism, Criticism, and Depictions of Female Violation." *Critical Inquiry* 13, no. 4 (Summer 1987): 712–41.
Gustafson, J. "The Whore with the Heart of Gold: A Second Look at *Klute* and *McCabe and Mrs. Miller*." *Cineaste* 11, no. 2 (1981): 14–17.
Hansen, M. "Pleasure, Ambivalence, Identification: Valentino and Female Spectatorship." *Cinema Journal* 25, no. 1 (Summer 1986): 6–32.
———. "Visual Pleasure and the Problem of Feminine/Feminist Discourse: Ulrike Ottinger's *Ticket of No Return*." *New German Critique*, no. 31 (1984): 95–108.
Harbord, P. "Interview with Jutta Brueckner." *Screen Education*, no. 40 (Autumn/Winter 1981–82): 48–57.
Hark, I. R. "That Obscure Subject of Desire: Gender, Sexuality, and Subjugation in the Lewton/Tourneur *Cat People*." *New Orleans Review* 14, no. 2 (Summer 1987): 47–54.
Harrison, S. "The Representation of Women." In *Britain and the Cinema in the Second World War*, ed. by Phillip M. Taylor. New York: St. Martin's Press, 1988.
Hartog, S., and J. C. Rodrigues. "Anna Carolina Teixeira Soares: Conversation 2." *Framework*, no. 28 (1985): 64–69.
Harvey, S. "An Introduction to *Song of the Shirt*." *Undercut*, no. 1 (1981).
———. "A Passion for Her Work." (Bembeg) *Village Voice* (March 6, 1985): 52.
———. "*Doll's Eye*: An Interview with Jan Worth and Annie Brown." *Framework*, no. 21 (Summer 1983): 50–54.
Haskell, M. "Good Girls, Earth Mothers, and Sluts in Film." *Ms* 12 (February 1984): 35–37.
———. "Ideological Criticism: The Uses and Abuses of a Feminist Approach to Film." *Florida State Conference on Film and Literature*, no. 4 (1979): 119–31.

———. "Women in the Movies Grow Up." *Psychology Today* 17 (January 1983): 18–24+.

Heath, S. "Difference." *Screen* 19, no. 3 (1978): 51–112.

Heininger, J. E. "Not So Liberated Ladies: Images of Women in Films of the 1930's." *Film Library Quarterly* 14, nos. 1–2 (1981): 29–39.

Herman, J. "Just Like At Home." *Film Quarterly* 34, no. 1 (Fall 1980): 56–59.

Heung, M. "What's the Matter with Sara Jane?": Daughters and Mothers in Douglas Sirk's *Imitation of Life*." *Cinema Journal* 26, no. 3 (Spring 1987): 21–43.

Holmlund, C. "Sexuality and Power in Male Doppelganger Cinema: The Case of Clint Eastwood's *Tightrope*." *Cinema Journal* 26, no. 1 (1986): 31–42.

———. "Visible Difference and Flex Appeal: The Body, Sex, Sexuality, and Race in the *Pumping Iron* Films." *Cinema Journal* 28, no. 4 (Summer 1989): 38–51.

Hyams, B. "Is the Apolitical Woman at Peace?: A Reading of the Fairy Tale in *Germany, Pale Mother*. *Wide Angle* 10, no. 3 (1988): 40–51.

Ibbetson, P. "See You in My Dreams." *Film Journal* 1, no. 2 (Summer 1976): 76–89.

Insdorf, A. "From France: A Women's Wave." *American Film*, no. 5 (January/February 1980): 50–55.

Isaak, J. "Women: The Ruin of Representation." *Afterimage* 12 (April 1985): 6–8.

Jachne, K. "*Boat People*: And Interview with Ann Hui." *Cineaste* 13, no. 2 (1984): 16–19.

Jackson, L. "Labor Relations: An Interview with Lizzie Borden." *Cineaste* 15, no. 3 (1987): 4–9.

Jackson, L., and K. Jaehne. "Eavesdropping on Female Voices: A Who's Who of Contemporary Women Filmmakers." *Cineaste* 16, nos. 1–2 (1987–1988): 38–43.

Jackson, R. "British Cinema: Women Questioning Men." *Framework*, no. 21 (Summer 1983): 47–49.

———. "An Unsuitable Job For a Man?" *Framework*, no. 21, (1983): 47–49.

Jacobowitz, F. "Feminist Film Theory and Social Reality." *CineAction!*, no. 3–4 (Winter 1986): 21–31.

———. "Joan Bennett: Images of Femininity in Conflict." *CineAction!*, no. 7 (Winter 1986–1987): 22–34.

———. "Power and the Masquerade: *The Devil Is a Woman*." *CineAction!*, no. 8 (Spring 1987): 32–41.

Jacobowitz, F., and R. Lippe. "Obsessions in the Melodrama: Amy Jones' *Love Letters*." *CineAction!*, no. 2 (Fall 1985): 15–21.

Jacobs, L. "The Censorship of *Blonde Venus*: Textual Analysis and Historical Methods. *Cinema Journal* 27, no. 3 (Spring 1988): 21–31.

Jaehne, K. "Hooker: Two or Three Things We Know About Her." *Film Comment* 23, no. 3 (May/June 1987): 25–32.

———. "*I've Heard the Mermaids Singing*. An Interview with Patricia Rozema." *Cineaste* 16, no. 3 (1988): 22–23.

Jaehne, K., and L. Rubenstein. "A Great Woman Theory of History: An Interview with Margarethe von Trotta." *Cineaste* 15, no. 4 (1987): 24–28.

Jayamanne, L. "Modes of Performing Bodies and Texts (Some Thoughts on Female Performances)." *Australian Journal of Screen Theory*, nos. 9–10 (1981): 123–39.

———. "Modes of Performance in Chantal Akerman's *Jeanne Dielman, 23 Quai de Commerce, 1080 Bruxelles*." *Australian Journal of Screen Theory*, no. 8 (1981): 97–111.

Jeffords, S. "Friendly Civilians: Images of Women and the Feminization of the Audience in Vietnam Films." *Wide Angle* 7, no. 4 (1985): 13–22.

Jhirad, S. "Hitchcock's Women." *Cineaste* 13, no. 4 (1984): 30–33.
Judge, M., and L. Spring. "An Interview with Lizzie Borden." *CineAction!*, no. 8 (March 1987): 69–76.
Kaplan, E. A. "Feminist Film Criticism: Current Issues and Problems." *Studies in the Literary Imagination* 19, no. 1 (1986): 7–20.
———. "Integrating Marxist and Psychoanalytic Approaches in Feminist Film Criticism." *Millenium Film Journal*, no. 6 (Spring 1980): 8–17.
———. "Lina Wertmuller's Sexual Politics." *Marxist Perspective* 1, no. 2 (1978): 94–104.
———. "Movies and the Women's Movement: Sexuality in Recent European and American Films." *Socialist Review*, no. 66 (1982): 79–90.
———. "Patterns of Violence to Women in Fritz Lang's *While the City Sleeps*." *Wide Angle* 3, no. 3 (1980): 55–60.
———. "Pornography And/As Representation." *Enclitic* 9, nos. 1–2 (1987): 8–18.
———. "Problematizing Cross-Cultural Analysis: The Case of Women in the Recent Chinese Cinema." *Wide Angle* 11, no. 2 (1989): 40–50.
Kenny, L. "An Interview with Julia Lesage." *Afterimage* 13, no. 3 (October 1985): 6–9.
Kinder, M. "Ideological Parody in the New German Cinema: Reading The State of Things, *Veronika Voss* and *Germany, Pale Mother* as Postmodernist Rewritings of *The Searchers, Sunset Boulevard* and *Blonde Venus*." *Quarterly Review of Film and Video* (forthcoming).
King, N. "Recent 'Political' Documentary: Notes on *Union Maids* and *Harlan County, USA*." *Screen* 22, no. 2 (1981): 7–18.
Kirby, L. "From Marinetti to Vertov: Woman on the Track of Avant-Garde Representation." *Quarterly Review of Film Studies* 10, no. 4 (April 1989): 309–23.
Klonaris, M., and K. Thomadaki. "Cinema of the Body." *Undercut*, no. 2 (August 1981): 23–26.
Koch, G. "Ex-Changing the Gaze: Re-Visioning Feminist Film Theory." *New German Critique*, no. 34 (Winter 1985): 139–53.
Kolbenschlag, M. C. "The Female Grotesque: Gargoyles in the Cathedrals of Cinema." *Journal of Popular Film and Television* 6, no. 4 (1978): 328–41.
Kolker, R. P. " 'Your Brains Don't Show a Bit': Double Readings of *The Accused*." *Film Criticism* 9, no. 2 (1984–1985): 28–40.
Kotz, L. "Unofficial Stories: Documentaries by Latinas and Latin American Women." *The Independent* 12, no. 4 (May 1989): 21–27.
Kuhn, A. "The Camera I: Observations on Documentary." *Screen* 19, no. 2 (1978): 71–83.
Lamche, P. "Committed Women: Interview with Sheila McLaughlin and Lynne Tillman." *Framework*, nos. 26–27 (1985): 36–45.
———. "Interview with Merata Mita." *Framework*, no. 25 (1984): 2–25.
Lawson, S. "*Serious Under-Takings*—Deconstructions, Demolitions (plus script)." *Framework*, no. 24 (Spring 1984): 122–44.
Leibman, N. C. "Leave Mother Out: The Fifties Family in American Film and Television." *Wide Angle* 10, no. 4 (1988): 24–41.
Linville, S., and K. Casper. "The Ambiguity of Margarethe von Trotta's *Sheer Madness*." *Film Criticism* 12, no. 1 (Fall 1987): 1–10.
Lippe, R. "Kim Novak: Resistance to Definition." *CineAction!*, no. 7 (Winter 1986–1987): 4–21.
Longfellow, B. "Mirelle Dansereau: A Phase Apart." *Cinema Canada*, no. 146 (November 1987): 10–11.
Lurie, S. "The Construction of the 'Castrated Woman' in Psychoanalysis and Cinema." *Discourse*, no. 4 (Winter 1981–1982): 52–74.

MacDonald, S. "Confession of a Feminist Porn Watcher." *Film Quarterly* 36, no. 3 (1983): 10–17.
———. "*Damned If You Don't*: An Interview with Su Friedrich." *Afterimage* 15, no. 10 (May 1988): 6–10.
———. "Interview with Vivienne Dick." *October*, no. 20 (Spring 1982): 82–101.
———. "Yoko Ono: Ideas on Film (Interview/Scripts)." *Film Quarterly* 43, no. 1 (Fall 1989): 2–23.
Mael, P. "Course File: Images of Women in American Film, Part II." *AFI Educational Newsletter*, no. 6 (September/October 1982): 4–7+.
"Manifesto for a Non-Sexist Cinema." *Cineaste* 8, no. 4 (1978): 51.
Marchetti, G. "An Annotated Working Bibliography: Readings on Women and Pornography." *Jump Cut*, no. 26 (December 1981): 56–60.
———. " 'Four Hundred Years in a Convent, Fifty in Hollywood': Sexual Identity and Dissent in Contemporary Philippine Cinema." *East-West Film Journal* 2, no. 2 (June 1988): 24–48.
———. "The Threat of Captivity: Hollywood and the Sexualization of Race Relations in *The Girls of the White Orchid* and *The Bitter Tea of General Yen*." *Journal of Communication Inquiry* 11, no. 1 (Winter 1987): 29–42.
Marchetti, G., and K. Tishkeu. "An Interview with Scott B. and Beth B." *Film Journal*, nos. 10–11 (Fall/Winter 1981–1982): 158–67.
Martin, D. "Through the Directorial Gender Gap: The Uncompromising Daniele Suissa." *Cinema Canada*, no. 104 (February 1984): 8–9.
"Martin Kelly and Laura Mulvey in Conversation." *Afterimage* 13, no. 8 (March 1986): 6–8.
Martineau, B. H. "Leading Ladies Behind the Camera." *Cinema Canada*, no. 71 (January/February 1981): 17–32.
———. "Notes for a Study of Women's History in the Media." *Cinema Canada*, no. 51 (November/December 1978): 30–34.
———. "The Films of Marta Meszaros or, the Importance of Being Banal." *Film Quarterly* 34, no. 1 (1980): 21–27.
Mass, R. "The Mirror Cracked: The Career Woman in a Trio of Lansing Films." *Film Criticism* 12, no. 2 (Winter 1987–1988): 23–36.
Mayne, J. "Feminist Film Theory and Criticism." *Signs* 11, no. 1 (1985): 81–100.
———. "The Feminist Analogy." *Discourse*, no. 7 (Fall 1985): 31–41.
McCormick, R. "*One Sings, the Other Doesn't*: An Interview with Agnes Varda." *Cineaste* 8, no. 3 (1977–1978): 28–31.
McCormick, R., and B. Thompson. "Feminism in the Japanese Cinema: An Interview with Sachiko Hidari." *Cineaste* 9, no. 3 (1979): 26–29.
McCreadie, M. "Summing up the Seventies: Women: The Images." *American Film* 5 (December 1979): 31+.
McGarry, E. "Documentary, Realism and Women's Cinema." *Women and Film* 2, no. 7 (1975): 50–59.
McGilligan, P. "Faith Hubley: An Interview." *Film Quarterly* 42, no. 2 (Winter 1988–1989): 2–18.
McGreal, J. "*Not a Love Story*: Feminism and Pornography." *Undercut*, no. 6 (Winter 1982–1983): 1–5.
Mellencamp, P. "Film History and Sexual Economics." *Enclitic* 7, no. 2 (Fall 1983): 91–105.
———. "Images of Language and Indiscreet Dialogue—*The Man Who Envied Women*." *Screen* 28, no. 2 (Spring 1987): 87–101.
———. "Made in the Fade." *Cine-Tracts* 3, no. 4 (1981): 1–17.
———. "Oedipus and the Robot in *Metropolis*." *Enclitic* 5, no. 1 (Spring 1981): 20–42.

"Midsection: Sex and Censorship." *Film Comment* 20, no. 6 (November/December 1984): 29–49.

Modleski, T. "A Father Is Being Beaten: Male Feminism and the War Film." *Discourse* 10, no. 2 (Spring/Summer 1988): 62–77.

———. "Film Theory's *Detour.*" *Screen* 23, no. 5 (1982): 72–79.

Moeller, H. B. "West German Women's Cinema: The Case of Margarethe von Trotta." *Film Criticism* 9, no. 2 (1984–1985): 51–66.

Mordue, M. "Homeward Bound: Mark Mordue Talks to Australian Director Gillian Armstrong." *Sight and Sound* 58, no. 4 (Autumn 1989): 270–72.

Morrison, S. "The Ideological Consequences of Gender on Genre." *CineAction!*, nos. 12–13 (August 1988): 40–45.

Morton, J. "Women in Prison Films." *Re/search*, no. 10 (1986): 151–52.

Mueller, R. "Interview with Ulrike Ottinger." *Discourse*, no. 4 (Winter 1981–1982): 108–26.

———. "The Mirror and the Vamp." *New German Critique*, no. 34 (Winter 1985): 176–93.

Mulvey, L. "Afterthoughts on 'Visual Pleasure and Narrative Cinema' Inspired by *Duel in the Sun.*" *Framework*, no. 10 (Spring 1979): 3–10.

———. "Changes." *Discourse*, no. 7 (Fall 1985): 11–30.

———. "Feminism, Film and the Avante-garde." *Framework*, no. 10 (Spring 1979): 3–10.

Nelson, J. "Meditations on Media, Technology and the Repressed Feminine." *Cinema Canada*, no. 112 (November 1984): 10–13.

———. "Through Her Eyes: The Time of Sweet, Sweet Change: Changes in Feminist Film Practice." *Cinema Canada*, no. 116 (March 1985): 20–23.

Norden, M. F. " 'A Good Travesty Upon the Suffragette Movement': Women's Suffrage Films as Genre." *Journal of Popular Film and Television* 13, no. 4 (Winter 1986): 171–77.

O'Brien, K. P. "The Southern Heroine in the Films of the 1930's." *Journal of Popular Film and Television* 14, no. 1 (Spring 1986): 23–32.

Oppe, F. "Exhibiting *Dora.*" *Screen* 22, no. 2 (1981): 80–85.

Pajaczkowska, C. "The Heterosexual Presumption: A Contribution to the Debate on Pornography." *Screen* 22, no. 1 (1981): 79–94.

Pally, M. "Choice Parts." *Film Comment* 21, no. 5 (September/October 1985): 13–17.

———. "Object of the Game." *Film Comment* 21, no. 3 (May/June 1985): 68–73.

———. "Ordinary People." *Film Comment* 19, no. 6 (November/December 1983): 11–15.

———. "When the Gaze is Gay: Women in Love." *Film Comment* 22, no. 2 (March/April 1986): 35–39.

———. "Women and Porn." *Playboy* (November 1987): 41–44+.

———. "World of Our . . . Mothers." *Film Comment* 20, no. 2 (March/April 1984): 11–17.

Palmer, R. B. "The Successful Failure of Therapy in *Now Voyager*: The Woman's Picture as Unresponsive Symptom." *Wide Angle* 8, no. 1 (1986): 29–38.

Perkins, T. E. "Remembering Doris Day: Some Comments on the Season and the Subject." *Screen Education*, no. 39 (Summer 1981): 25–34.

Perlmutter, R. "Visible Narrative, Visible Woman." *Millenium Film Journal*, no. 6 (Spring 1980): 18–30.

Portuges, C. "Interview with Jackie Raynal." *Massachusetts Review* 24, no. 1 (1983): 218–28.

Quart, B. "A Conversation with Agnes Varda." *Film Quarterly* 40, no. 2 (Winter 1986): 3–10.

Rainer, Y. "Looking Myself in the Mouth." *October*, no. 17 (Summer 1981): 65–76.

Rapping, E. "Hollywood's New 'Feminist' Heroines." *Cineaste* 14, no. 4 (1986): 4–9.

Rayns, T. "The Position of Women in New Chinese Cinema." *East-West Film Journal* 1, no. 2 (June 1987): 32–44.

Rich, B. R. "Feminism and Sexuality inn the 1980's." *Feminist Studies* 12, no. 3 (Fall 1986): 525–61.

———. "She Says, He Says: The Power of the Narrator in Modernist Film Politics." *Discourse*, no. 6 (Fall 1983): 31–47.

Rickey, C. "Where the Girls Are." *American Film* 9, no. 1 (January/February 1984): 48–53+.

Riley, B. "A Woman's Turn: Claudia Weill Interviewed." *Film Comment* 16, no. 6 (November/December 1980): 34–37.

Rimoldi, O. A. "Dorothy Arzner: The First Woman Director to Achieve Success!" *Hollywood Studio* 17, no. 10 (1984): 18–21.

Rose, J. "*Dora*: Fragment of an Analysis." *Monthly Film Bulletin*, no. 2 (1978): 5–21.

Rovner, B. "A Special Day." *Film Journal* (May 28, 1989): 25–26.

Rudman, L. "Marriage—The Ideal and the Reel: or, The Marriage Manual (in Films of Lois Weber). *Film History* 1, no. 4 (1987): 327–39.

Sang, H. "The Ascendancy of China's Women Directors." *China Screen*, no. 1 (1986): 9.

Scheib, R. "Ida Lupino: Auteuress." *Film Comment* 16, no. 1 (January-February 1980): 54–64.

Schiff, S. "Gun-totin' Women." *Film Comment* 18, no. 1 (January/February 1982): 23–24+.

———. "Movie Women: Tough But Weak." *Film Comment* 18, no. 1 (January/February 1982): 25.

Schwichtenburg, C. "*Near the Big Chakra*: Vulvar Conspiracy and Protean Film/Text." *Enclitic* 4, no. 2 (1980): 78–90.

Seiter, E. "Men, Sex and Money in Recent Family Melodrama." *Journal of the University of Video Association* 35, no. 1 (Winter 1983): 17–27.

———. "The Role of the Woman Reader: Eco's Narrative Theory and Soap Opera." *Tabloid* 6 (1981): 36–43.

———. "Stereotypes and the Media: A Re-evaluation." *Journal of Communications* 36, no. 2 (Spring 1986): 569–81.

———. "Women's History, Women's Melodrama: *Deutschland, bleiche Mutter*." *The German Quarterly* 59, no. 4 (Fall 1986): 569–81.

Shirley, G. "A Woman's Place." *Cinema Papers*, no. 52 (July 1985): 36–38.

Silverman, K. "Helke Sander and the Will to Change." *Discourse*, no. 6 (Fall 1983): 10–30.

———. "*Histoire d'O*: The Story of a Disciplined and Punished Body." *Enclitic* 7, no. 2 (1983): 63–81.

———. "Masochism and Subjectivity." *Framework*, no. 12 (1981): 2–9.

Silverman, M. "Cine-Feminists in West Berlin." *Quarterly Review of Film Studies* 5, no. 2 (1980): 217–32.

Slade, J. W. "Violence in the Hard Core Pornographic Film: A Historical Survey." *Journal of Communications* 34, no. 3 (1984): 148–63.

Sloane, K. "Three Hitchcock Heroines: The Domestication of Violence." *New Orleans Review* 12, no. 4 (1985): 91–95.

Smith, G. "Post-Mod Squad: Mary Lambert on *Siesta* Set." *Film Comment* 23, no. 6 (November/December 1987): 24–29.

"Some of China's Women Directors." *China Screen*, no. 1 (1986): 10–11.

Starr, C. "Invisible Women." *Sight and Sound* 49, no. 4 (1980): 245–47.

Stefanoni, L. "Claudia Weill: *Girlfriends*." *Forum*, no. 190 (December 1979): 774–83.

Stein, S. "On *Pictures on Pink Paper* by Lis Rhodes." *Undercut*, nos. 14–15 (Summer 1985): 62–68.

Stephenson, R. "Interview with Trinh T. Minh-ha." *Millenium Film Journal*, no. 19 (1989): 122–29.

Stern, L. "Feminism and Cinema-exchange." *Screen* 20, nos. 3–4 (1979–1980): 89–105.

———. "Fiction/Film/Femininity—Paper One." *Australian Journal of Screen Theory*, nos. 9–10 (1981): 37–48.

———. "Image Forum: An Interview with Katsue Tomiyama." *Framework*, nos. 22–23 (Autumn 1983): 71–73.

———. "Independent Feminist Film-Making in Australia." *Australian Journal of Screen Theory*, nos. 5–6 (1979): 105–21.

———. "Point of View: The Blind Spot." *Film Reader* 4 (1979): 214–36.

———. "The Body as Evidence." *Screen* 23, no. 5 (1982): 38–60.

Studlar, G. "Masochism and the Perverse Pleasures of Cinema." *Quarterly Review of Film Studies* 9, no. 4 (Fall 1984): 267–82.

Tadros, C. "The Individualistic Drive of Daniele Suissa." *Cinema Canada*, no. 134 (October 1986): 30–33.

Taubin, A. "Daughters of Chaos: Feminist and Avant-Garde Filmmakers." *Village Voice* (November 30 1982): 80–81+.

Taylor, J. R. "Funny Girls and Funny Ladies." *Films and Filming*, no. 347 (August 1983): 17–19.

Tey, J. "Silent Screen Heroines: Idealizations on Film." *American Classic Screen* 5 (November/December 1980): 6–8.

Tibbetts, J. C. "A Matter of Definition: Out of Bounds in *The Girl Friends*." *Literature/Film Quarterly* 7, no. 4 (1979): 270–76.

Toolin, C. "Attitudes Toward Pornography: What Have the Feminist Missed?" *Journal of Popular Culture* 17, no. 2 (1983): 167–74.

Trinh, T. M. "Difference: 'A Special Third World Women Issue." *Discourse*, no. 8 (Fall/Winter 1986–1987): 11–38.

———. "Questions of Images and Politics." *The Independent* 10 (May 1987): 21–23.

Tuer, D. "Pleasure in the Dark: Sexual Difference and Erotic Deviance in the Articulation of Female Desire." *CineAction!*, no. 10 (October 1987): 55–59.

———. "Visions of the Heroic: An Interview with Kay Armatage." *Cinema Canada*, no. 145 (October 1987): 30–32.

Vincendeau, G. "Women As Auteures: Notes form Creteil." *Screen* 27, nos. 3–4 (1986): 156–62.

Waldman, D. " 'At Last I Can Tell It To Someone!': Feminine Point of View and Subjectivity in the Gothic Romance Film of the 1940s." *Cinema Journal* 23, no. 2 (1984): 29–40.

Ward, L. E. "Forgotten Women's Pictures." *American Classic Screen*, no. 131 (May 1986): 37–38.

Warrick, S. "*High Tide*." *Film Quarterly* 42, no. 4 (Summer 1989): 21–26.

Watney, S. "Katherine Hepburn and the Cinema of Chastisement." *Screen* 26, no. 5 (September/October 1985): 52–62.

Weinstock, J. "*Sigmund Freud's Dora*?" *Screen* 22, no. 2 (1981): 73–79.

Welsch, J. R. "College Course File: Feminist Film Theory/Criticism in the United States." *Journal of Film and Video* 39, no. 2 (Spring 1987): 66–82.

Welsch, J., and Tibbetts, J. "Visions of Dracula." *American Classic Screen*, no. 5 (November/December 1980): 12–16.

West, A. "A Textual Analysis of *Lady from Shanghai.*" *Enclitic* 5–6, nos. 1–2 (1981–1982): 90–97.

White, B. "Dealing with the Incommensureable: A Reading of Yvonne Rainer's *The Man Who Envied Women.*" *New Orleans Review* 15, no. 3 (Fall 1988): 30–37.

White, M. "Exploring *What We Take for Granted.*" *Afterimage* 12, no. 5 (December 1984): 7–11.

———. "Rehearsing Feminism: Women/History in *The Life and Times of Rosie the Riveter* and *Swing Shift.*" *Wide Angle* 7, no. 3 (1985): 34–43.

———. "Representing Romance: Reading/Writing/Fantasy and the 'Liberated' Heroine of Recent Hollywood Films." *Cinema Journal* 28, no. 3 (Spring 1989): 41–56.

Williams, L. "Film Body: An Implantation of Perversions." *Cine-Tracts* 3, no. 4 (1981): 19–35.

Williams, L., and B. R. Rich. "The Right of Re-Vision: Michelle Citron's *Daughter Rite.*" *Film Quarterly* 35, no. 1 (1981): 17–22.

Williams, T. "Feminism, Fantasy and Violence: An Interview with Stephanie Rothman." *Journal of Popular Film and Television* 9, no. 2 (1981): 84–90.

Williamson, J. "Images of 'Woman.' " *Screen* 24, no. 6 (1983): 102–16.

Wood, R. "Beauty Bests the Beast." *American Film* 8, no. 10 (September 1983): 62–65.

Yakir, D. "Celine and Julie Golightly: Side-by-side-by-Seidelman." *Film Comment* 21, no. 3 (May/June 1985): 16–21.

Yau, E. C. M. "Cultural and Economic Dislocations: Filmic Phantasies of Chinese Women in the 1980s." *Wide Angle* 11, no. 2 (1989): 6–21.

INDEX

A page number in italics indicates a photograph.

PATRICIA ERENS, Professor of Film Studies at Rosary College in River Forest, Illinois, is author of several books including *The Jew in American Cinema* and is editor of *Sexual Stratagems: The World of Women in Film*. She is a frequent contributor to film books and journals.